FOREIGN SOUNDS

A as in French **a•mi** (A mē′) [a vowel intermediate in quality between the **a** of *cat* and the **ä** of *calm*, but closer to the former]

KH as in German **ach** (äKH) or **ich** (iKH); Scottish **loch** (lôKH) [a consonant made by bringing the tongue into the position for **k** as in *key*, *coo*, while pronouncing a strong, rasping **h**]

N as in French **bon** (bôN) [used to indicate that the preceding vowel is nasalized. Four such vowels are found in French: **un bon vin blanc** (ŒN bôN vaN bläN)]

Œ as in French **feu** (fŒ); German **schön** (shŒn) [a vowel made with the lips rounded in the position for **o** as in *over*, while trying to say **a** as in *able*]

R as in French **rouge** (Rōōzh), German **rot** (Rōt), Italian **ma•re** (mä′Re), Spanish **pe•ro** (pe′Rô) [a symbol for any non-English **r**, including a trill or flap in Italian and Spanish and a sound in French and German similar to KH but pronounced with voice]

Y as in French **tu** (tY); German **ü•ber** (Y′bər) [a vowel made with the lips rounded in position for **ōō** as in *ooze*, while trying to say **ē** as in *east*]

ə as in French **Bas•togne** (bA-stôn′yə) [a faint prolongation of the preceding voiced consonant or glide]

A DICTIONARY of READING

and Related Terms

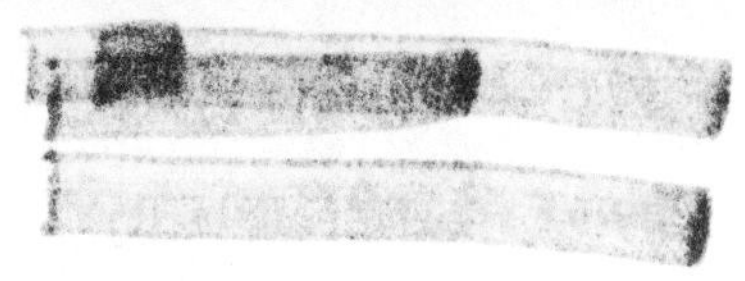

A DICTIONARY of READING and Related Terms

Theodore L. Harris and Richard E. Hodges, *Coeditors*

Richard S. Alm, Rebecca Barr, Marguerite Bougere, Johanna DeStefano, Frank Greene, Bob W. Jerrolds, *Associate Editors*

International Reading Association
Newark, Delaware

Library of Congress Cataloging in Publication Data
Main entry under title:

A Dictionary of reading and related terms.

Bibliography: p.
1. Reading—Dictionaries. I. Harris, Theodore Lester, 1910- II. Hodges, Richard E. III. International Reading Association.
LB1049.98.D53 428.4'03 81-12392
ISBN 0-87207-944-9 AACR2

Contents

v Foreword

vi Consultant Staff

vi Editorial Staff

viii Introduction

xii Special Features

xiii Guide to the Dictionary

xv Special Acknowledgements

1 Dictionary of Reading and Related Terms

362 Appendix A Word Meaning Equivalents for Selected Dictionary Entries in French, Spanish, German, Danish, and Swedish

376 Appendix B Bibliography

Foreword

Few persons who have occasion to talk or write about the reading process and how it is taught have not at some time suspected that they were not communicating clearly with an audience or, even, that they were being misunderstood. The vocabulary of reading instruction and its allied fields is not only very large; it also has often lacked preciseness of usage.

The preparation of a dictionary designed to bring clarity to meanings of terms and to serve as a reference when questions arise is certainly one of the most important publication projects ever undertaken by the International Reading Association. The thoroughness with which the project was designed and implemented underscores its importance and its potential for service to the profession.

As the introduction clearly indicates, many persons were involved in the task of preparing the dictionary. It was a long and arduous task as the contributors checked hundreds of sources to establish the list of terms to be defined and then to determine the definition(s) most widely accepted by the best writers and speakers in the field.

The task has been completed. It is a tribute to the skill, the persistence, the scholarship of many persons but particularly to the unremitting energies of Theodore L. Harris and Richard E. Hodges, coeditors. These scholars have given a large part of four years to directing the production of the dictionary, a contribution perhaps unparalleled in IRA publication history.

Because the language of every field is a living thing, growing and shifting constantly, the dictionary may need revision from time to time, but the big job is done. We can use these definitions with confidence that they represent the best scholarship available.

1981 may well be remembered by the Association as "the year of the dictionary."

Olive S. Niles, President
International Reading Association
1980-1981

Consultant Staff

Lexicographical Consultants: Jess Stein, Random House Dictionaries; Richard Venezky, University of Delaware.

Consultants on English Usage and Spellings: John Elkins, *Australia*; Warwick Elley, *New Zealand*; Jean E. Robertson, *Canada*; Desmond Swan, *Ireland*; Magdalen Vernon, *United Kingdom.*

Consultants on English Meaning Equivalents: Mogens Jansen, *Danish*; Eve Malmquist, *Swedish*; María Louisa Freyre, Adela Artola Stewart, *Spanish*; François Ters, Magdelhayne F. Buteau, Christine W. Lucas, *French*; Renate Valtin, *German.*

Editorial Staff

Introduction

Anyone who has examined the extensive literature concerning theoretical and practical aspects of reading is well aware of—and sometimes confused by—the varied meanings given to the terminology used in the reading field. This situation is brought about by at least three causes: 1) a proliferation of the fields of knowledge that contribute to reading; 2) an expansion of the conceptual dimensions of reading; and 3) the absence of an adequate, comprehensive guide to reading terms and their uses.

The major purpose of this dictionary is, therefore, to define in one volume salient terms in reading and in the related disciplines and supporting fields of study from which the vocabulary of reading is drawn. A further purpose of this dictionary is to attempt to clarify the meanings of these terms through the preparation of definitions and illustrative examples that, while technically correct, are expressed insofar as possible in easily comprehensible language rather than in the jargon of the specialist. Our goal has been to create a dictionary that will serve the widest spectrum of possible users—from college students to their instructors, from classroom teachers to reading specialists, from interested parents to scholars with interests in the reading field.

The Scope of the Dictionary. The dictionary contains a comprehensive sampling of 4,780 main entries and approximately 620 subentries totaling approximately 5,400 terms drawn from the initial body of some 10,000 terms that were identified in the reading literature. Each term was selected on the basis of its presumed relevance in this literature, especially the critical, clinical, and research literature concerning the processes of reading and its pedagogy, and in the literature of related disciplines and supporting fields. These terms were assigned by the coeditors and associate editors to 54 different categories (see Table 1) and then were assessed for their relevance by an Advisory Board comprised of experts in these categories. (A listing of Advisory Board members is presented on pages vi and vii).

In actuality, the number of definitions—nearly 7,500—contained in this dictionary considerably exceeds the number of entries since a substantial number of entries have several definitions both within a particulary category (e.g., the term *reading*) and in different categories (e.g., the term *assimilation*).

The parameters of the special fields were determined by the combined judgments of an Advisory Board member, the editor most competent to prepare the preliminary definitions in the special cateogory, and, in many cases, the editors as a group. In the process of selecting entries, each editor rated each term for exclusion or inclusion according to criteria the editorial team had agreed upon. Final judgments were the responsibility of the coeditors.

The Language of Reading. The vocabulary of reading revealed in this dictionary is affected by its purpose, intended audience(s), and the breadth and depth of coverage desired. Given the purpose of this dictionary to bring together key terms in reading pedagogy and in the disciplines that contribute to and support reading theory and practice, the vocabulary of reading is indeed extensive. Given the additional purpose of meeting the needs of the novice student of reading, as well as those of the reading specialist, the vocabulary of reading is also catholic, including definitions for such commonplace terms as *book* and *paper*, as well as such technical terms as *cortical localization* and *ostensive definition.* As users of this dictionary will readily determine, the language of reading is enhanced by the diversity of its sources and uses.

One way of viewing the language of reading is to examine the specific categories used to classify the 4,780 main entries in making this dictionary, as shown in the accompanying table.* In this table, the more conventional categories of reading are shown on the left, the categories relating to language on the right, and those of five supporting fields at the bottom.

The table also shows the approximate distribution of terms in Reading, Language, and Supporting Fields. Over 65 percent of the terms in this dictionary are contained in the general area of Reading with the relative contributions of four broad categories of Reading as follows: Sociology, 2 percent; Psychology, 17 percent; Physiology, 23 percent; and Pedagogy, 23 percent. Language and the Supporting Fields each contribute about 17 percent to the total. The proportional weight of these contributions by areas to the final entry list is not surprising, with the possible exception of the Physiology of Reading. For many years, reviews of reading research have carried very few articles under this heading. However, reading clinicians and others who deal with the technical language represented in this category need a clear, comprehensive understanding of it. Since medical dictionaries are the source of many terms in this area, and are written by medical doctors in technical medical terminology, the definitions of terms in the Physiology of Reading was a special challenge to the editors.

* The classifications were designed to be functional rather than strictly logical. The large number of classifications permitted the selection of a correspondingly large Advisory Board and aided in identifying multiple definitions of terms across classifications.

The two specific categories having the greatest number of entries are Literary Analysis and Speech and Hearing, with approximately 350 terms each. Determining the parameters of Literary Analysis was particularly difficult. The category includes terms related to such aspects as literary forms, interpretation, criticism, periods, styles, and figures of speech. In addition, many of the more common terms in this category are also used metaphorically and idiomatically, as are *read* and *style*.

Eight categories had from 200 to 300 entries: Cognition; General Linguistics; Grammar; Optometry and Ophthalmology; Neurology; Tests and Measurement; and Library Science. Eight other categories had from 100 to 200 entries: Learning; Clinical and Developmental Psychology; Perception; Medicine; Orthography; Statistics; Teacher Education; and Clincial Methods and Materials (Corrective and Remedial). The remaining 33 categories had from six to 98 entries each; and of these 33 categories, 16 were in the Pedagogy of Reading. It thus seems clear that this analysis upholds the frequently-made observation that the language of reading is to a great extent a borrowed one.

The language of reading is a meld of terms taken from many disciplines. This combination is both a fortunate and appropriate circumstance—fortunate because it allows the cross-fertilization of ideas from other special fields, appropriate because reading is a tool subject that is as much an art as it is a science. Reading remains, as Huey wrote shortly after the turn of the century, one of the most complex, magnificent, and awesome achievements of the human mind. "*...to completely analyze what we do when we read would almost be the acme of a psychologist's achievements, for it would be to describe very many of the most intricate workings of the human mind, as well as to unravel the tangled story of the most remarkable specific performance that civilization has learned in all its history.*"

Table 1

		Reading (3105)		**Language** (855)
Sociology (100)	Psychology (800)	Physiology (1105)	Pedagogy (1100)	
General Literacy Bilingualism Cultural Differences Content Analysis Readership Preferences and Effects	Models Clinical and Developmental Psychology Perception Cognition Piaget Readability Legibility	Medicine Neurology Learning Disabilities Optometry and Ophthalmology Speech and Hearing Atypical, General Atypical, Blind	History Status Comparative Teacher Education Teacher Effectiveness Readiness and Early Reading Elementary High School College Adult Word Identification Vocabulary Comprehension Interests, Tastes, and Attitudes Literary Analysis Children's Literature Literature for Adolescents Content Fields Clinical Methods and Materials: Corrective and Remedial	General Linguistics Psycholinguistics Grammar Semantics Sociolinguistics Orthography
			Supporting Fields (820)	
Media and Technology	Library Science	Statistics	Tests and Measurement Evaluation	

Note: Figures rounded to the nearest number divisible by 5.

Special Features

Accessibility of Terms. This dictionary brings together for the first time a wide range of terms related to reading that previously have been available only in specialized dictionaries and glossaries or in scholarly and technical journals.

Special Fields. The scope of the dictionary is unusual in its inclusion of a number of special fields related to but often not included in a lexicon of reading. A group of some 60 Piagetian terms is one example. Other fields of more than usual interest that are represented by a very substantial number of entries are Grammar, Orthography, Sociolinguistics, Literary Analysis, and Library Science.

Word Meaning Equivalents. With the cooperation of the Consultants on English Meaning Equivalents (see list on page vi), the English entries for approximately 150 "demons"—English terms whose meanings are either ambiguous, controversial, or otherwise difficult—are shown with their corresponding meanings in French, Spanish, German, Danish, and Swedish in Appendix A. This table enables one to locate entries quickly and easily in the languages given.

Illustrative Contexts. Many illustrative phrases and sentences are used in this dictionary to clarify definitions and to indicate typical usage. Such illustrative contexts are especially helpful for those terms which must be defined somewhat technically in order to be accurate.

Citations. An extensive citation file accumulated over a three-year period was drawn upon in preparing definitions and, where appropriate, these citations appear in the dictionary to authenticate a definition, or to extend or comment upon a definition.

Notes. Frequent use is made of notes indicated in italics as *Note:*. These notes serve to extend and clarify the meaning of a term. (See, for example, the entries *sentence pattern* and *reading tastes*.) The editors have attempted to refrain, though perhaps not entirely successfully, from editorializing.

Introductory Essays. A brief introductory essay or statement introduces some multiple definition entries. The essay places the numerous definitions for a particular entry in context. (See, for example, essays accompanying *dyslexia, language, reading*, and *word*.)

Historical vs. Current Entries. This dictionary includes a few terms that are taken from the extensive historical literature on reading as well as terms that are representative of the cutting edge of current theory and practice. About 50 terms relating to the historical development of reading are included.

The most recent additions to the reading vocabulary are taken from the recommendations of the Advisory Board members who were asked to aid the editors in identifying relatively new terms which give promise of continued use in the field of reading.

Principal Exclusions. Primarily because of problems in selection and in datedness, two types of terms are omitted as entries in this dictionary: personal names and reading tests, other than certain clinical instruments. Persons, however, are frequently mentioned in citations and notes. With respect to such types of terms as readability formulas or drugs, the editors adopted a selective policy of including only the better-known, more established terms. Terms in the content fields of the social sciences and of the natural sciences were excluded, as were mathematical terms not directly related to tests and measurement or to statistics.

Prefixes and Combining Forms. The dictionary lists over 140 prefixes and combining forms, with their appropriate variations, definitions, and illustrative examples. Only those prefixes and combining forms to be found in one or more entries in this dictionary were included. The editors made this decision in order to reasonably delimit the number of such terms, and in the interest of immediate aid to the dictionary user.

Regionalisms. By placing notices in International Reading Association journals, an attempt was made to include interesting regional terms sent in by volunteer helpers, but this request met with little success. A few such regionalisms (for example, *pickin' up corn*) are contained in the dictionary.

Sources. In the preparation of this dictionary, the editors used a great variety of professional books and journals, as well as general and specialized dictionaries, to aid in the entry selection and definition process. An illustrative but not exhaustive list of such sources is given in the bibliography in Appendix B.

Guide to the Dictionary

Entries. Main entry headings are given in large boldface. Undefined sub-entry headings are given in small boldface, typically at the end of the entry.

Variant Spellings. As a general rule, spellings found in the Random House Dictionaries are followed, except when other specialized sources have indicated otherwise. British spellings, as *behaviour, centre, programme*, etc., are not used, but a sizable number of British terms and definitions are included in this dictionary.

Pronunciation. The pronunciation of single word entries and closed and hyphenated compound forms is given immediately following the main entry heading. Pronunciations are ordinarily not given for other compounds and phrase terms except when a pronunciation guide for one or more words in the compound or phrase would be beneficial, as in medical terminology. For convenience, the pronunciation key has been placed on the front end paper of the dictionary. The pronunciation key, entry pronunciations, selected definitions, the International Phonetic Alphabet table, the proofreading chart, and the majuscule and minuscule letters are reprinted by permission of the publisher from the *Random House College Dictionary*, Revised Edition, Copyright © 1980, 1975 by Random House, Inc., and the *Random House Dictionary of the English Language*, The Unabridged Edition, Copyright © 1979, 1966 by Random House, Inc. *Note:* In this dictionary, *primary stress* is shown by a single accent mark (′), as in rē′ding, and *secondary stress* is shown by a double accent mark (″), as in rē′dər ship″.

Parts of Speech. The parts of speech for each definition and sub-entry heading of single words and hyphenated two-word compounds are given immediately before each definition or sub-entry, as noun (*n.*), verb (*v.*), adjective (*adj.*), and adverb (*adv.*).

Definition Order. In entries with multiple definitions, the most common or most pertinent meaning with respect to reading is usually given first. In some instances, a generic or historical meaning is given first to clarify following definitions.

Idioms and Definied Sub-Entries. Such entries are placed in small boldface and given definitions.

Special Type Signals. Italicized type is used to indicate citations, illustrative phrases and sentences, foreign word entries, and occasionally to emphasize a point, as in a note. It is also used in definitions to refer to a letter or letter cluster, as *a* in *hat*. (By contrast, the sound represented by such a letter(s) is indicated by virgules, as /a/ in *hat.*)

Cross References. For ease of identification, the definition of terms which are cited as cross references is given in most cases under the usual word order rather than inverted word order; **reading, rate of**. See **rate of reading**. *This is a reversal of usual dictionary practice.* Cross references are indicated either by *See* or *See also*. In addition to the standard symbols of *synonym* (*Syn.*) and *antonym* (*Ant.*), this dictionary also uses *Cp.* (compare) and *Ct.* (contrast) when such cross references serve to clarify or extend the meaning of the particular terms.

Restrictions. A minimal number of restrictions are used in this dictionary, chiefly *Cap.* (capitalized), *Informal, Brit.* (British), *An old use, pl.* (plural), *sing.* (singular).

Special Acknowledgements

Since this dictionary is the work of many persons over a five-year period, the specific contributions of such persons deserve recognition. The editors are especially grateful to the Board of Directors of the International Reading Association, to the Executive Director, and to the Director of Publications for their encouragement and support, with particular recognition of the indispensible technical assistance of Faye Branca, Professional Publications Editor, and her staff. The editors also wish to acknowledge the roles of two former presidents of the International Reading Association who were instrumental in initiating this project: Constance McCullough, who appointed the first committee on a Dictionary of Reading Terms, and Walter MacGinitie, who recommended to the Board of Directors that the dictionary be given project status, and who appointed a dictionary task force that became the nucleus of the present group of editors.

The Consultants deserve special thanks for their contributions. Jess Stein was most helpful in setting up an operational routine for building the dictionary, for recommending permission to use the pronunciation key and selected definitions from the Random House, Inc. Dictionaries, and for his strong moral support of the project. Richard Venezky was especially helpful during the early stages of the dictionary in identifying lexicon sources and in projecting editorial loads and a production schedule. The Consultants on English Usage and Spelling provided valuable assistance, calling attention to those English terms and usages in their respective countries which might be included in the dictionary. The Consultants on English Meaning Equivalents cooperated admirably in supplying the meanings of selected English terms in their languages. Franz Biglmaier, Clara Inez de Mira, Claude Langevin, and Tove Krogh also provided valuable assistance to these Consultants in German, Spanish, French, and Danish, respectively. Alida Cutts was instrumental in coordinating and editing the English Meaning Equivalents.

The work of the Advisory Board was invaluable in entry selection and definition, as their critical editorial comments revealed in their review of terms and definitions submitted by the editors. The dictionary has been greatly improved by the expertise they generously volunteered.

During the first three years of the dictionary project, several thousands of citations were gathered from the reading literature for use as definition sources. Many of these citations were identified by classroom teachers, graduate students, and university professors who acted as volunteer citation gatherers. (For example, graduate students at the University of Georgia screened, under the direction of their professors, all issues of the *Reading Research Quarterly* for appropriate citations.) The editors specifically acknowledge the assistance of: Ira Aaron, Georgia; Irwin Bergman, New York; Rosanna Blass, Ohio; Eva Bortman, Nevada; Mary Boswick, Illinois; John Boyd, Pennsylvania; Stella Bregman, Maryland; Eileen Burke, New Jersey; Julie Chan, California; Joan Chopchinski, Ohio; Hazel Craker, Colorado; Nancy Cuddeback, Michigan; Robert Emans, Virginia; Eldonna Evertts, Illinois; Ramons S. Frasher, Georgia; Estelle Fryburg, New York; Ronald Fyfe, Aberdeen, Scotland; June Gilstad, Alabama; Ulrich Hardt, Oregon; Mae C. Johnson, Virginia; Frances MacCannell, Edmonton, Alberta, Canada; George Mason, Georgia; Cynthia McCarthy, Michigan; Marie McNeff, Minnesota; Jeannete Miccinati, New York; Marie Morgello, New York; Mary Olson, Texas; Gordon Peterson, Michigan; Richard A. Powell, Bermuda; Patricia Pratt, Georgia; Billie Jo Rieck, West Virginia; Edward J. Rogers, Florida; Frances R. Ryan, Ohio; Carol Sager, Massachusetts; Barbara Sample, Arkansas; Mary Ann Stanko, Illinois; Jean Tracy, Florida; Bonnie Woelfel, California; Eleanore Woods, Mexico.

A number of other persons have provided welcome assistance to the dictionary project. M.H. Scargill of the University of Victoria proved to be a knowledgeable advisor on dictionary-making. Louise Matteoni and her colleagues in the City University of New York provided the dictionary task force at an early point with a lexicon of terms which they felt their students in graduate courses in reading needed to know. Graduate assistants Rosalie Bianco of the University of Georgia and Tobie Sanders of The Ohio State University aided the associate editors at these institutions in definition preparation. Irene Athey of Rutgers University provided helpful sources and citations for the definition of Piagetian terms. Suzanne Rose, a doctoral candidate in linguistics at the University of Victoria, served admirably as a special assistant in the definition of linguistic terms and as a *pro tem* member of the editorial group in 1979-1980. Ralph Staiger made a number of valuable suggestions of terms used internationally.

Colleagues of the coeditors at the University of Puget Sound likewise proved most cooperative. Wilbur Baisinger, LaVerne Goman, Philip Hager, Stephen Kerr, Edith Richards, and Esther Wagner in particular provided constructive aid on problem entries. The university library staff, especially Director Desmond Taylor, Reference Librarian Bradley Millard, and Technical Services Librarian Raimund Matthis were indispensible in providing access to needed library sources. The administration of the University of Puget Sound deserves special thanks for housing this long-term project.

Particularly competent technical help was required in the project headquarters. Assistant Editor Elodie Vandevert beautifully orchestrated the complex problems of getting the dictionary project started and maintaining its momentum. During the final year, Assistant Editor Joan Barnowe ably assumed the task of preparing the final manuscript of the dictionary. During the second and third years of the project, Grace Percival organized the flood of incoming entries with finesse and accuracy. Ginene Kennedy and Evelyn Montes were responsible for typing most of the citation cards, while Lynette Day and Becky Paulus helped in the final stages of manuscript preparation.

The splendid efforts of the associate editors remain to be acknowledged. In a project which required much sharing of responsibility, tough intellectual decisions, and untold hours of concentrated effort, the group worked together with unflagging good humor and sound judgment. Each brought different but complementary kinds of expertise and experience to the task. It has been a personal and professional privilege to work with such a fine group on this truly cooperative project.

Theodore L. Harris
Richard E. Hodges
Coeditors

Tacoma, Washington, 1981

A

DEVELOPMENT OF MAJUSCULE								
NORTH SEMITIC	GREEK		ETR.	LATIN		MODERN		
						GOTHIC	ITALIC	ROMAN
K	Δ	A	A	A	A	𝔄	*A*	A

DEVELOPMENT OF MINUSCULE					
ROMAN CURSIVE	ROMAN UNCIAL	CAROL. MIN.	MODERN		
			GOTHIC	ITALIC	ROMAN
λ	ɑ	ɑ	𝔞	*a*	a

The first letter of the English alphabet developed from North Semitic *aleph* and Greek *alpha* (*α*, A) through Etruscan and Latin. The capital (A) goes back to North Semitic *aleph,* which acquired its modern form in Greek and was retained in the Latin monumental script. The minuscule (a) derives from Latin cursive *a,* a variant form of A, through Anglo-Irish, Carolingian, and Florentine influence to yield both italic and roman forms.

a-, an- a prefix indicating *not, without, lacking*; as **agnosia, anacusia.**

ab-, abs- a prefix indicating *from, away, off;* as **abnormal, abstract.**

abasia (ə bā′zhə, -zhē a, -zē ə) *n.* an inability to walk resulting from a defect in coordination.

abbreviation (ə brē″vē ā′shən) 1. *n.* a shortened spelling or pronunciation or phrase used to minimize effort or conserve space, as *bot.* for *botany, bldg.* for *building*, or *cab* for *cabriolet. Note:* A written phrase may be shortened by using only the first letter of the key words, as in the acronym *NATO* for North Atlantic Treaty Organization, or by combining parts of different words, as in *you'd* for *you would* or *etc.* for *et cetera.* 2. *n.* a short form representing a word either by one symbol, as *$* for *dollar*, or by a sequence of letters or symbols which are not all part of the word being represented, as *lb.* for *pound* or *Xmas* for *Christmas.* 3. *n.* the process by which a word is shortened, either in pronunciation or spellings. *Cp.* **contraction** (def. 3); **clipping; acronym** (def. 1). *v.* **abbreviate.**

ABC *or* **ABC book** 1. See **alphabet book**. 2. a book used in the British Isles, from at least the 15th century, for combined reading and religious instruction. *Note:* The ABC originally included the alphabet, syllabarium, Pater Noster, Hail Mary, and Creed. *. . . next after their A.B.C. now by vs also set furth (1546).* Also spelled *ABC-book, abcee-book, absey-book.* See also **hornbook**; **battledore.**

ABC method See **alphabet method.**

ABC's *or* **ABCs** 1. the letters of the English alphabet. 2. the rudiments of a school subject, especially of reading, writing, and spelling.

abduction (ab duk′shən) 1. *n.* movement away from the center line of the body, as of an arm or leg. 2. *n.* movement of the eyeball toward the temple. 3. *n.* the position resulting from such movement. *Ct.* **adduction.** *adj.* **abductive.**

ABE adult basic education.

abecedarian (ā″bē sē dâr′ē ən) 1. *n.* one who is learning the fundamentals of anything. 2. *adj.* alphabetic. 3. *n.* (17th to 19th century) a beginning reader. 4. *n.* (17th to 19th century) one who teaches beginning reading.

abecedarium (ā″bē sē dâr′ē əm) *n.* a type of book used from about the 9th into the 18th century for combined reading and religious instruction, which contained the alphabet, columns of syllables such as *ab, eb, ib, ob, ub,* creeds, and prayers; ABC book; abecedary. See also **hornbook.**

abecedary (ā″bē sē′də rē) See **abecedarium.**

aberration (ab″ə rā′shən) 1. *n.* any

departure or deviation from a normal, proper, or expected path or behavior. *Note:* When applied to a deviation in mental processes, aberration indicates a minor mental lapse, as *an aberration of memory.* 2. **spherical aberration**, the spreading out of light waves of one color as they pass through a lens without forming a sharp focus or a clear image. 3. **chromatic aberration**, the blending of light waves in different ways as they pass through a lens so that rings of color surround an image, or so that light becomes a spectrum of color. *adj.* **aberrant**.

abilities, analytic See **analytic abilities**.

abilities, crystallized See **crystallized abilities.**

abilities, fluid See **analytic abilities.**

ability (ə bil′i tē) 1. *n.* the power to perform, without further training, a mental or physical activity, as *high mental ability.* 2. *n.* acquired skill or proficiency in an activity; competence; as *ability to ski.* 3. *n.* natural or acquired aptitude; talent; as *promising musical ability.* See also **capacity** (defs. 1, 2); **capability**. *Note:* Special types of ability, as *reading ability*, are given under the describing term.

ability grouping the division of students into groups according to similar levels of intelligence and/or achievement in some skill or subject, either within or among classes, or between schools. *Syn.* **homogeneous grouping.** *Ant.* **heterogeneous grouping**. See also **streaming** (*Brit.*).

abnormal (ab nôr′məl) 1. *adj.* not average, typical, or usual; deviating from normal. 2. *adj.* referring to statistical deviation in either direction from the mean interval of a distribution of scores. 3. *adj.* departing in a harmful, negative, or pathological way from a usual behavior or condition, as *abnormal blood pressure, abnormal fears, abnormal growth of body tissue. Note:* Defs. 1 and 2 refer to deviations above and below the norm, a common interpretation in education and psychology. Def. 3 is prominently used in medicine and in the biological sciences, and is also a favorite popular interpretation; i.e., the public usually perceives the mentally retarded as abnormal, but the gifted as normal. *n.* **abnormality.**

abnormal psychology the branch of psychology devoted to the investigation of disordered behaviors, deficiencies in behavior capacities, and the persons exhibiting such characteristics.

abreaction (ab″rē ak′s̱hən) *n.* the result of reducing anxiety by reliving, usually under psychotherapy, a traumatic experience. *Cp.* **catharsis** (def. 2).

abridged dictionary a shortened, selective dictionary containing fewer entries and definitions than the dictionary upon which it is based. The Random House College Dictionary *is an abridged dictionary. Ct.* **unabridged dictionary**.

abridged edition a condensed form of a book that omits some detail but retains the basic contents and aspects of the original work, including much of the author's original language. *Several minor characters do not appear in an abridged edition of Dickens's* Pickwick Papers. *Ct.* **unabridged edition.**

abscissa (ab sis′ə) *pl.* **-scissas, -scissae** (-sis′ē). 1. *n.* the horizontal axis of a graph or chart; base line; x axis. 2. *n.* the distance from a point in a two-dimensional graph along a line which is orthogonal, or perpendicular, to the vertical axis. *Cp.* **ordinate**.

abstract (*adj.* ab′strakt, ab strakt′; *n.* ab′ strakt; *v.* ab strakt′, ab′strakt) 1. *adj.*

expressed without reference to a specific object or instance, as *an abstract idea or meaning. Ant.* **concrete**. 2. *n.* a quality or characteristic so expressed, as *stated in the abstract.* 3. *v.* to consider such a quality or characteristic. 4. *adj.* theoretical rather than applied, as *the abstract nature of philosophy.* 5. *adj.* hard to understand. *Theoretical physics is an abstract subject for many people.* 6. *v.* to draw out; extract; summarize. 7. *n.* a brief summary of the most significant elements of a much longer work; précis; as *an abstract of a doctoral dissertation.*

abstraction (ab strak′shən) 1. *n.* the process of making a generalization from the members of a group or class. 2. *n.* the process of identifying a quality or characteristic of a concrete example. 3. *n.* a generalization, quality, or characteristic so identified. 4. *n.* the state of being preoccupied or lost in thought.

abstract noun a noun with a nonmaterial, general (but not abstract) referent, as *joy, bravery. Note:* This type of noun is often derived from a verb or adjective, as *movement* from *move, hardness* from *hard. Ct.* **concrete noun**.

abstract reasoning *or* **thinking** the use of symbolic thought processes involving abstraction and generalization. *Abstract thinking is characteristic of the higher mental processes.*

abstract word 1. a word that has many meanings or referents. *'Read' is an abstract word.* 2. a word that refers to a quality which cannot be experienced directly through the senses, as cleanliness, goodness, etc. *Ct.* **concrete word.**

abulia (ə byōō′lē ə) *n.* diminished ability to will effectively or to make up one's mind.

academic counseling advising that is concerned with the student's educational program and progress, especially that offered by school and college staff members.

academic *or* **scholastic ability** the power, or probability, based on abilities developed to date, of performing well in school tasks.

acalculia (ā″kal kyōō′lē ə) *n.* a variant form of aphasia involving the inability to recognize or use arithmetic or mathematical symbols. *Note:* A child with acalculia may read and write as well as his peers, but be unable to perform mathematical calculations.

acataphasia (a kat″ə fā′zhə) *n.* a sensory aphasia characterized by loss of power to use the phrasing and sentence structure of common speech.

accelerated reading (*Brit.*) See **speed reading.**

acceleration (ak sel″ə rā′shən) 1. *n.* a process by which the educational progress of a student is speeded up. *Skipping a grade, taking advanced subjects, or passing advanced tests are forms of acceleration.* 2. *n.* a rate of development greater than normal. *adj.* **accelerated.** *v.* **accelerate.**

accelerator, reading See **pacer.**

accent (*n.* ak′sent; *v.* ak sent′, ak′sent) 1. *n.* prominence given to a word or syllable during speech. *Accent may be made by voice stress, change of pitch, increased duration, or some combination of these. Note:* Stress is the main accent in English, *accent* and *stress* often being used as synonyms in reference to voice. 2. *n.* any marks used in print or writing to show the nature and placement of spoken accent; specifically: a. an orthographic symbol (′) placed above a vowel grapheme or adjacent to a syllable to indicate that the vowel or syllable is stressed, as in *a'bout,* or *a bout'*. *Cp.* **primary accent** (def. 2). b. an orthographic symbol placed above a vowel or adjacent to a syllable to indicate either primary or secondary stress. *Cp.* **primary accent** (def. 2); **secondary accent** (def. 2). c. an orthographic symbol placed above a vowel grapheme to indicate that the vowel quality is not identical with that of the non-accented vowel, as French *lèver, élève, être. Cp.* **acute accent; grave accent; circumflex**. d. an orthographic symbol placed above or below Hebrew consonants to indicate vowel quality or tone. e. in the metrical analysis of verse, an orthographic symbol placed above a syllable to indicate that the syllable is strongly-stressed (¯) or weakly-stressed (˘), as Hōw dŏ Ī lōve thĕe? See **diacritic** *or* **diacritic(-al) mark**. 3. *v.* to utter or mark with accent; accentuate. 4. *n.* the characteristic manner of speech which is particular to an individual, a region, or a social group, as *a foreign accent, a Southern accent.* 5. *n.* the manner in which anything is said, particularly to emphasize emotions; tone of voice. 6. *n.* hint; embellishment; detail; adornment; trimming. *The small touch of red was an accent in the flower arrangement.* 7. *n.* rhythm or meter of verse in poetry. *Accent forms the more or less regular intervals or beats in a poem.* See also **prosody**.

accent, primary See **primary accent.**

accent, secondary See **secondary accent.**

accessibility (ak ses″sə bil′i tē) *n.* ease of being able to get reading materials, as in libraries, the home, bookstores, supermarkets, etc.; availability. *Our reading is...determined by accessibility, readability, and subject interests in that order* — Waples and others (1940). *adj.* **accessible.**

accession (ak sesh′ən) 1. *n.* a book or other material acquired by a library to add to its collection. 2. *v.* to record such material in the order of its acquisition.

accession number the number given to a volume or other material that indicates the order of its addition to the library. *Each volume in the set has its own accession number.*

accidence (ak′si dəns) *n.* the study and system of inflection as a grammatical device.

accidental phonics a parody of 'incidental phonics,' but which makes the serious point that some children arrive at phonic generalizations without specific instruction or intent.

accommodation (ə kom″ə dā′ shən) 1. *n.* the changes made by an organism or in some body organ to fit a situation. *In social accommodation, changes are made to adjust to conflicting information and/or ideas.* 2. *n.* (J. Piaget) cognitive activity that involves the modification of mental structures. 3. *n.* the normal focusing adjustments of the eye, especially of the crystalline lens, for clear vision at near point distances. *v.* **accommodate.** *adj.* **accommodational.**

accommodative convergence a reflex change in the accommodative power of the eyes which accompanies changes in convergence, as the change in the focusing power of the lenses of the eyes when turned in to look at near point targets.

accountability (ə koun″tə bil′i tē) *n.* the obligation to justify something; specifically, the justification of educational programs, practices, and personnel, in terms of learner progress and cost effectiveness. See also **cost effectiveness.**

acculturation (ə kul″chə rā′shən) 1. *n.* the processes and results of learning to adapt to the culture of a group. 2. *n.* occasionally, the process of becoming accustomed to social norms or rules, including those involved in language.

accusative case in English, the case of the direct object of a transitive verb or a preposition, as *ball* and *him* in *I hit the ball toward him. Note:* In English, the accusative case is shown by word order, except for pronouns, which change form from the nominative case, as *she*, to the accusative case, as *her*.

achievement (ə chēv′mənt) 1. *n.* adequate performance or accomplishment, especially through effort and ability; proficiency; as *athletic achievement.* 2. *n.* school learning progress. *Ct.* **aptitude.**

achievement battery a group of selected educational tests, usually standardized on the same population, which yield separate scores for different aspects of achievement.

achievement drive *or* **motivation** the use of mental and physical energy to accomplish and produce; desire to do well, to be competent.

achievement quotient (AQ) a ratio, formerly used, of achievement age to mental age: (AA ÷ MA) 100.

achievement test a test of knowledge of or proficiency in something learned or taught; especially, a test of the effects of specific instruction or training. *Achievement tests measure the effects of learning that occurred under partially known and controlled conditions.* — Anastasi (1976). *Ct.* **aptitude test.**

achromatic (ak″rə mat′ik) 1. *adj.* without hue, as black, gray, or white. 2. *adj.* having to do with a lens made to minimize chromatic aberration. *Eyeglasses need achromatic lenses.* 3. *adj.* with no color sensitivity; colorblind; as *achromatic vision. n.* **achromate.**

acous- a combining form indicating *hearing,* as **acoustics.**

acoustic feature See **distinctive feature.**

acoustic feedback the familiar squeal and squawk heard when output from a loudspeaker is allowed to return to the microphone and reenter the amplification system.

acoustic impedance audiometry See **impedance audiometry.**

acoustic nerve See **auditory nerve.**

acoustic phonetics the experimental study of the physical structure of speech sounds; specifically, the study of the pitch, loudness, quality, and duration of speech sounds. *Cp.* **articulatory phonetics.**

acoustic reflex an involuntary response to sound. *The acoustic reflex may be as complex and gross as a startle response, or as minute and precise as changes in tonus of the tiny muscles in the middle ear.*

acoustics (ə ko͞o′stiks) 1. *n.* (*with pl. v.*) the characteristics of a room which affect sound loudness and distortion. 2. *n.* (*with sing. v.*) the study of sound; specifically, the transmission, reception, and modification of sound waves.

acoustic spectrum the visible analysis of a sound into its frequencies and duration as shown in a sound spectrograph.

acquired alexia the complete loss of the ability to read because of disease of or injury to the brain. *Cp.* **acquired dyslexia.**

acquired dyslexia the partial loss of existing reading skills because of disease of or injury to the brain. *Cp.* **acquired alexia.** See also **dyslexia.**

acquired word blindness See **alexia** (def. 2).

acquisition (ak″wi zish′ən) 1. *n.* the gaining of something, as *the acquisition of a new book.* See also **reading acquisition; language acquisition.** 2. *n.* an increase in response strength following reward. 3. *n.* See **accession** (def. 1). *v.* **acquire**.

acronym (ak′rə nim) 1. *n.* a word usually formed from the initial letters of words in a phrase. *SCUBA is an acronym for Self-Contained Underwater Breathing Apparatus.* 2. *n.* See **acrostic** (def. 1).

acrophobia (ak″rə fō′bē ə) *n.* the pathological fear of being in high places.

acrostic (ə krô′stik, ə kros′tik) 1. *n.* a kind of puzzle in which lines of verse or prose are arranged so that words, phrases, or sentences are spelled when letters are used in a certain sequence, as all first letters or all last letters of each line. 2. **acronym** (def. 1). 3. See **word square.**

act (akt) 1. *n.* something done; deed; as *an act of mercy.* 2. *n.* the process of doing, as *the act of reading.* 3. *n.* a unit of behavior considered as a psychological whole, as *the act of comprehension.* 4. *n.* a major division of a play, musical comedy, or opera. 5. *n.* a short performance, usually within a longer, varied program, as *a circus act.* 6. *n.* the performers in such a performance, as *a clown act.* 7. *n.* an insincere or pretended manner. *No one was fooled by his act.* 8. *v.* to perform one or more roles in a play, musical comedy, or opera. 9. *v.* to be performable. *Ibsen's plays act well.* 10. *v.* to behave as. *He acted the fool.*

action (ak′shən) 1. *n.* the story in a literary work or in the mass media. 2. *n.* the happenings or events that make up the plot of a story. *In drama, rising action leads to the climax; falling action follows it.* See also **climax** (def. 1); **plot** (def. 1). 3. *n.* the state of acting or performing. 4. *n.* what is performed.

action research field research or study designed for direct application to behavior or to a situation, as school learning programs. *Action research is one response to concern for needed changes in curriculum and instruction in the schools. Cp.* **applied research.** *Ct.* **basic research.**

active vocabulary the number of different words a person uses in speaking and writing. *Ant.* **passive vocabulary.**

active voice See **voice** (def. 7).

activity approach *or* **method** an informal way of teaching reading; natural method. *This method consists of supplying the children with an interesting reading environment and allowing them to learn by themselves whenever they are ready to learn* — S. Kirk (1970).

acuity (ə kyo͞o′i tē) 1. *n.* clarity or keenness of reception of sensory stimuli. 2. *n.* the extent to which the senses can detect the duration, intensity, position, and other properties of a target stimulus or array. *Ct.* **discrimination** (def. 1). *Note:* Special types of acuity, as *auditory acuity,* are given under the describing term.

acuity, visual. See **visual acuity.**

acute (ə kyo͞ot′) 1. *adj.* severe in effect, as *acute stuttering.* 2. *adj.* brief; reaching a crisis quickly. *Ct.* **chronic.** 3. *adj.* highly sensitive, as *acute hearing.*

acute accent an orthographic symbol (′) placed directly above a vowel grapheme to indicate that the vowel is rising in pitch (Greek), closed or tense (French), stressed (Spanish), or represents a speech sound (English, as in *café*). *Cp.* **primary accent** (def. 2); **grave accent** (def. 1). See also **diacritic** *or* **diacritic(-al) mark.**

-acy a suffix indicating *act, state, quality, condition;* as **literacy.**

ad- a prefix indicating *to, (motion) toward;* as **adduction.**

adage (ad′ij) *n.* a traditional saying that expresses an experience familiar to most people; proverb (def. 1): *a stitch in time saves nine; the early bird catches the worm. Cp.* **aphorism; maxim.**

adaptation (ad″əp tā′shən) 1. *n.* behavioral change that meets environmental demands. *Note:* In *biological adaptation*, changes in structure enable an organism to survive. In *social adaptation*, behavioral changes permit personal-social adjustment within a culture. See also **adaptive behavior; adjustment** (def. 1). 2. *n.* the rewriting or alteration of an original work. Toad of Town Hall *is an adaptation of portions of Kenneth Graham's* Wind in the Willows. *Note:* The change of a novel into a motion picture script is a common form of adaptation. 3. *n.* the regulation by the pupil of the amount of light entering the eye. *v.* **adapt.** *adj.* **adaptive.**

adapted classic a rewritten version of a classic in which the vocabulary and sentence structure of the original are simplified and some characters and sub-plots are omitted. *Note:* Adapted classics range from artfully rewritten stories to thin shadows of the original, retaining only the title and outline of the main plot.

adaptive behavior adjustment to the environment that is usually purposeful, flexible, and adequate for one's needs; coping behavior. See also **adjustment** (def. 1); **accommodation** (def. 1).

added entry any entry in addition to the main entry in a library catalog or any other bibliographic tool. *In cataloging, the name of the translator of a work is usually an added entry. Cp.* **main entry.**

addendum (ə den′dəm) *pl.* **-da**. *n.* a section of pertinent information following the main text of a book as part of the end matter. *Cp.* **supplement.**

address (*n.* ə dres′, ad′res; *v.* ə dres′) 1. *n.* a speech given before an audience. 2. *v.* to speak, call, or direct a communication to, as *address a person or audience.* 3. *n.* the form or forms of language used to refer to people. *'Herr,' 'Monsieur,' and 'Mr.' are formal types of address.* 4. *v.* to direct the speech or energy of, as *address oneself to the question, task, etc.* 5. *n.* a specific business or personal location. 6. *v.* to put such a location on, as *address an envelope.*

adduction (ə duk′shən) 1. *n.* movement toward the center line of the body, as of an arm or leg. 2. *n.* movement of the eyeball toward the nose. 3. *n.* the position resulting from such movement. *Ct.* **abduction.** *adj.* **adductive.**

adenoid (ad′ᵊnoid″) 1. *n.* (*usually pl.*) glandular tissue at the back of the nose, above the throat. *Enlarged adenoids make breathing through the nose difficult.* 2. *adj.* resembling a gland.

adenoidal (ad″ᵊnoi′dəl) 1. *adj.* having to do with the adenoid(s) 2. **adenoidal breathing**, breathing through the mouth because the nose is blocked by enlarged adenoids. 3. **adenoidal voice**, a speaking voice which lacks normal nasal speech sounds because enlarged adenoids are blocking the nasal cavities; or, more rarely, a very nasal speaking voice caused by forcing air into the nasal cavities after enlarged adenoids have been removed.

adiadochokinesia (ad″ē ad″ə kō ki nē′zhə, -zhē ə, -zē ə; -kī nē′-) 1. *n.* difficulty in making opposing or alternating motor movements, as flexing and extending the arm or the jaw. 2.

n. the inability to make rapid, repetitive movements of the articulators, as by quickly repeating /p/ /t/ /k/, in order several times. *Ant.* **diadochokinesia.**

adjectival (aj″ik tī′vəl) 1. *adj.* referring to an adjective. 2. *n.* a grammatical structure which modifies a noun, as *left behind* in *The six people left behind finally caught up with us. Cp.* **adverbial.**

adjective (aj′ik tiv) *n.* a word or word group that modifies a noun, as *good* in *a good book. Note:* Some grammarians limit the meaning of adjective to single words; others extend its meaning to a phrase that serves the same function as an adjective. See **adjectival** (def. 2).

adjustment (ə just′mənt) 1. *n.* the ability to achieve balance and satisfaction in one's personal-social needs and in the environment. See also **accommodation** (def. 1); **adaptive behavior; social adjustment** (def. 1). *Ct.* **maladjustment.** 2. *n.* the process of achieving such a condition. 3. *n.* change in function, parts, or sequence in response to varying needs, as *adjustment of reading speed, carburetor adjustment, rank-order adjustment. v.* **adjust.** *adj.* **adjustive.**

adjustment inventory a series of self-report items referring to emotional reactions.

adolescent literature See **literature for adolescents.**

ADP automatic data processing.

adrenal gland one of a pair of endocrine glands lying on top of the kidneys. *Note:* The central portion of the adrenal gland produces hormones which stimulate vigorous reaction to stress; the outer layers produce hormones related to metabolism and to sexual functioning.

adult basic education (ABE) the instruction of adults in fundamental literacy and arithmetic skills, sometimes with additional instruction in social survival and coping skills.

adultomorphic (ə dult″ə môr′fik) *adj.* referring to the interpretation of the behavior of children as if it were that of adults, as *an adultomorphic analysis of a beginning reader's behaviors. n.* **adultomorphism.**

advanced reading (*Brit.*) See **speed reading.**

advance organizer a learning strategy developed by D. Ausubel in which a passage is written to enhance the learning of other material and is presented prior to the other material. *Note:* The advance organizer may be written to draw parallels between something the reader already knows about and the new material; or, it may restate the new material at a different and often higher level of abstraction, generalizability, and inclusiveness.

adventure story a narrative which features the unknown, the uncharted, the unexpected, with elements of danger, excitement, and risk-taking.

adverb (ad′vûrb) *n.* a word, usually ending in *-ly*, that modifies a verb, as *steadily* in *run steadily*; an adjective, as *very* in *a very beautiful dress*; or an adverb, as *rather* in *go rather quickly. Note:* Some grammarians limit the meaning of adverb to single words; others extend its meaning to a phrase that serves the same function as an adverb. See **adverbial** (def. 2).

adverbial (ad vûr′bē əl) 1. *adj.* referring to an adverb. 2. *n.* a word or phrase that functions as an adverb. *Cp.* **adjectival.**

-aesthesia, -aesthesis See **-ethesia, -esthesis.**

aesthetic effect an effect of reading noted by D. Waples and others (1940); specifically, one which has to do with the appreciation of the beauty of the writer's ideas and style of expression, as in writing of high literary quality. *Cp.* **effects of reading.**

aesthetic reading a type of reading in which the reader *focuses attention upon what is being lived through during the reading, what is being stirred up in him, the rhythm of the words and the past experiences these words call up* — L. Rosenblatt (1978). *Cp.* **aesthetic effect; efferent reading.**

aetiology See **etiology.**

affect (*n.* af′ekt, ə fekt′; *v.* ə fekt′) 1. *n.* feeling or emotion, either general or particular; 2. *v.* to produce an effect; influence; modify. 3. *v.* to pretend, as *affect another's manners.*

affective disorder a severely disabling disorder of mood or feeling with a corresponding disturbance of thought and behavior.

affective domain the psychological field of emotional activity. *Ct.* **cognitive domain; psychomotor domain.**

affective fallacy a term in literary criticism introduced by W.K. Wimsatt, Jr. and M.C. Beardsley to describe the error of judging a literary work primarily by its emotional appeal. *Cp.* **pathetic fallacy; intentional fallacy**.

affective meaning that part of meaning which is composed of *emotional 'associations' or 'connotations'* — J. Lyons (1979); emotive meaning. *Note:* Affective meaning includes both the intentional and emotional force of words used by a speaker or writer and those meanings which evoke an emotional association in the listener or reader. *Ct.* **cognitive meaning.**

afferent (af′ər ənt) *adj.* toward the center of the body, as of a body part. *An afferent nerve carries impulses toward the central nervous system. Ct.* **efferent.**

affirmation (af″ər mā′shən) *n.* the act stating or otherwise positively indicating that something is so; confirmation.

affix (*n.* af′iks; *v.* ə fiks′) 1. *n.* any morpheme which is not an independent word; specifically, a normally meaningful speech element which is grammatical only if occurring as part of a word, as *im-* and *-er* in *importer. Note:* An affix may be inflectional or derivational depending on its grammatical function. See **prefix; suffix.** 2. *n.* in some languages, a morpheme which is not an independent word and is without content meaning, but does have grammatical meaning, as *o* in Greek *thermos. Ct.* **combining form.**

affixing language a language which uses affixes rather than words to express grammatical information such as tense or number.

affricate *or* **affricative** (af′rə kit; ə frik′ə tiv, af′rə kā″-) *n.* a speech sound which starts as a stop but ends as a fricative, as the /ch/ in *watch.*

a fortiori (ä fōʀ″ti ō′ ʀē; *Eng.* ā for″zhe ōr′i, ā fôr″she ôr′ī) 1. more compelling. *The critic presented an a fortiori conclusion.* 2. with more certainty. *The second view was stated a fortiori.* (*Latin.*)

Afro-American literature See **Black literature.**

after-glide See **off-glide.**

afterimage (af′tər im″ij, äf′-) *n.* a visual impression that continues after visual stimulation.

age (āj) 1. *n.* the number of years one has lived; chronological age. 2. *n.* an equivalent age, used metaphorically, as *mental age, emotional age. Note:* Special types of age, as *anatomical age,* are given under the describing term.

age equivalent an outmoded type of derived score based upon the age in the test standardization population at which the average person earns a given score. *Note:* The comparison of the performance of an individual of one age with the performance of individuals of another age is often misleading, especially in educational and intelligence testing. *Cp.* **grade equivalent**. See also **age norm.**

age norm for any test, the distribution of scores of persons of a certain age in a defined population, tabulated age by age, as *a table of age norms.*

agent (ā'jənt) 1. *n.* the person or thing doing, or responsible for the doing of, an action expressed by a verb. *Note:* In passive sentences, the agent is shown in the noun phrase which follows the preposition *by*, as *a young child* in *The story was written by a young child.* 2. *n.* a person who represents someone in the sale of material, as *a writer's agent.*

agentive case in case grammar, the case of an animate noun that is responsible for or initiates an action.

aggression (ə gresh'ən) 1. *n.* hostile behavior, either by destructive action or obstructive inaction, that is usually the result of frustration. *Aggression may be literal or symbolic.* 2. *n.* a presumed psychological drive necessary for survival. 3. *n.* a self-asserting act that is offensive to a person or group.

agitographia (aj''i tō graf'ē ə) *n.* a writing disability involving the omission or distortion of words or letters, and characterized by extremely rapid motor movements.

agnosia (ag nō'zhə, -zhē ə, -zē ə) *n.* the loss of the ability to recognize sensory information because of disease of or injury to the brain. *Cp.* **aphasia.** *Note:* The sense modality involved in agnosia is usually indicated, as *auditory agnosia, visual agnosia*, etc. *Finger agnosia*, the loss of the ability to name properly one's own fingers or to tell which finger is being touched, is occasionally seen in some forms of learning disabilities. Agnosia refers to higher order cognitive loss; blind persons would not be said to have a visual agnosia.

agrammatism (ā gram'ə tiz''əm) *n.* a form of expressive aphasia involving the loss of the ability to use words in correct syntactic sequence.

agraphia (ā graf'ē ə) *n.* the loss of the ability to produce handwriting because of disease of or injury to the brain; specifically, the loss of the motor and kinesthetic skills involved in writing.

agreement (ə grē'mənt) *n.* the grammatical correspondence of syntactically-related words; concord; as the noun plural ending *-s* and the plural verb *are* in *The trees are in bloom. Note:* In some languages adjectives must agree with the nouns and pronouns they modify with respect to gender, case, and person as well as number.

ahistorical method the study of the present, rather than the past behavior of a person in order to gain psychological understanding. *Ct.* **developmental method; historical method.**

AI artificial intelligence.

aide, teaching See **teaching aide.**

aided recall the act, or result, of recall helped by prompting.

air conduction the transmission of sound from the outer ear to the inner ear by way of the middle ear. *Ct.* **bone conduction**.

-al a suffix indicating *a connection with*; as **mental, nasal.**

alalia (ə lā'lē ə, ə lāl' yə) *n.* the complete inability to talk because of articulatory problems. See also **dyslalia.**

alexia (ə lek'sē ə) 1. *n.* the complete inability to read; specifically, a form of aphasia in which the visual modality is disabled, yet reasonable vision, intelligence, and language functions, other than reading, are intact; congenital or developmental alexia. 2. *n.* the loss, because of damage to or disease of the brain, of reading ability acquired earlier; acquired alexia. *Syn.* **word blindness.** *Ct.* **aphasia; agnosia; dyslexia.**

aliteracy (ā lit′ər ə sē) *n.* lack of the reading habit; especially, such a lack in capable readers who choose not to read. *Aliteracy...may guarantee continued, lifelong functional illiteracy* — L. Mikulecky (1979). *adj.* **aliterate.**

allegory (al′ə gōr″ē, -gôr″ē) *n.* an extended metaphor; specifically, a symbolic narrative in prose or verse in which the characters and often parts of the narrative usually represent moral and spiritual values, as in Bunyan's *Pilgrim's Progress. Cp.* **fable** (def. 1); **parable** (def. 1). *adj.* **allegorical.**

alliteration (ə lit″ə rā′shən) *n.* the repetition of the initial sounds in words or stressed syllables, spoken or written closely together: *The shepherd's swains shall dance and sing* — C. Marlowe. *v.* **alliterate.** *adj.* **alliterative.**

allograph (al′ə graf″, -gräf″) 1. *n.* one of the variant shapes of a grapheme, as *B, b. Cp.* **grapheme; graph** (defs. 1, 2). 2. *n.* a piece of writing, especially a signature, made by someone for another person. *adj.* **allographic.**

allomorph (al′ə môrf″) 1. *n.* one of a class of morphs having the same meaning and syntactic function, as the English allomorphs *-s, -en,* of *dogs, oxen.* 2. *n.* a morph which is in free variation with, and has the same meaning, as another morph. See **morph.**

allophone (al′ə fōn″) *n.* any of a class of speech sounds constituting a phoneme; phonetic variant. *Allophones in one language may be phonemes in another: /r/ and /l/ are allophones in Chinese and phonemes in English.*

ALM audiolingual method.

allusion (ə lo͞o′zhən) *n.* an indirect reference to something, presumably something assumed to be familiar. *Note:* The English language, especially in its literature, is rich in allusions. Myths gain much of their appeal by frequent allusion to the familiar. The use of formal classically-oriented allusions from the Renaissance on, as Christopher Marlowe's allusion to Helen of Troy, *Was this the face that launched a thousand ships, / And burnt the topless towers of Ilium?*, has been paralleled in writing and in speech by informal allusions, often witty, to contemporary persons and events. *v.* **allude.** *adj.* **allusive.**

almanac (ôl′mə nak″) *n.* a reference book, usually published annually, containing lists, charts, calendars, and miscellaneous information. See also **yearbook.**

alogia (ə lō′jə, -jē ə) 1. *n.* the complete inability to speak due to brain damage or dysfunction; aphasia. *Cp.* **dyslogia** (def. 1). 2. *n.* speechlessness because of mental retardation or extreme mental confusion; mutism.

alphabet (al′fə bet″) 1. *n.* the set of letters or other graphic symbols used in writing a language or in phonetic transcription to represent one or more speech sounds. See table on the front flyleaf of this dictionary. 2. *n.* a writing system in which graphic symbols represent speech sounds, or phonemes. 3. *n.* the particular sequential arrangement of the letters used to write a language. See also **letter** (def. 1); **writing system.** *n.* **alphabetization.** *adj.* **alphabetic; alphabetical.** *v.* **alphabetize.**

alphabet book a picture book which presents in sequence the letters of the alphabet, A to Z.

alphabetic (-al) order the conventional sequence of all letters in a language; specifically, the order or arrangement of cards in a library card catalog, based on the usual sequence of letters of a given language and with certain filing conventions, most of which are arbitrary. *In a Spanish dictionary, words beginning with 'll' are listed in alphabetical order after words beginning with 'l'.*

alphabetic principle the assumption underlying writing systems using alphabet letters or characters that each phoneme or speech sound of oral language should have its own distinctive graphic representation.

alphabetic writing a writing system in which one or several letters represents one speech sound or phoneme, but not a syllable, morpheme, or word. See also **writing system; alphabetic principle.**

alphabet method 1. a synthetic method of teaching reading and spelling in use from ancient times until the early part of the 19th century, and which was still the most widely used method in the United States up to the 1870's. *Note:* In this method, students first identified letters by their names; next spelled out syllables (see **syllabarium**); then words containing from one to eight syllables (see **cumulative spelling**); next, short sentences; and finally stories. When students met an unfamiliar word, they would spell it out in order to decode it. Also called *alphabetic, alphabetical, alphabet-spelling, ABC, a-b-c spelling,* or simply *spelling method.* 2. the technique of naming the letters of a word in sequence and then pronouncing the word for the learner.

alphabet verses 1. short poems constructed around twenty-six words which illustrate the letters of the alphabet. 2. religious or moral verses, usually couplets, designed to teach the alphabet; as 'In Adam's Fall,/We sinned all.' 'Thy Life to mend,/This Book attend.' (The New England Primer).

alphameric *or* **alphanumeric** (al″fə mer′ik; al″fə no͞o mer′ik, -nyo͞o-) *adj.* referring to a code of computer characters containing both letters and numbers.

alpha rhythm *or* **wave** a brain wave pattern of relatively low frequencies, between 8 to 13 cps, and relatively high voltage. *Alpha waves are associated with alert but relaxed wakefulness and are midway between the patterns of attention and sleep in frequency.* See also **electroencephalogram.**

alpha risk the possibility of making an error of decision whereby something that is true or acceptable is rejected as false or unacceptable; the chance of making a type I error. *If, for example, it were important that no one who might pass be rejected from a special program, the alpha risk will be made small by using a loose acceptance level: you will let in many who will fail, but you will not keep out many who might have passed.* See also **type I error.** *Ct.* **beta risk.**

alternate-form reliability the consistency of scores obtained by a group of individuals when reexamined with a different set of comparable items. *Note:* The correlation between the scores obtained on the two forms represents one type of reliability coefficient of the test.

alternating squint *or* **strabismus** the fixation of an image by either eye independently, and often alternately, but not simultaneously as in binocular fixation, with resultant alternating deviation of the non-fixating eye.

alternation (ôl″tər nā′shən, al″-) *n.* systematic linguistic variations: a. in related derived forms, as the alternanation of the present tense *think* with the past tense *thought*. b. in distinctive speech sounds, as the /k/ and /s/ sounds in *critic/criticize*. *v.* **alternate.**

alternative school *or* **education** a program or school that offers nontraditional education, as a storefront school or a school without walls.

alveolar (al vē′ə lər) 1. *n.* a consonant speech sound made when the tongue and the alveolar ridge stop or constrict the air flow, as /t/, /s/. 2. *adj.* having to do with such a sound.

alveolar ridge the ridge of the upper and lower jaw that is covered by the gums and contains the tooth sockets, or alveoli.

ambi- a prefix indicating *both*; as **ambidextrous.**

ambidextrous (am″bi dek′strəs) *adj.* being equally skillful with both hands or both sides of the body, as *ambidextrous penmanship. Note:* Literally, ambidextrous means having two right hands; thus the sense of superior quality often associated with the term is consistent with a bias against lefthandedness. *Cp.* **sinister; gauche; dexterity** (def. 1). *n.* **ambidexterity**.

ambiguity (am″bə gyo͞o′i tē) 1. *n.* a language expression which permits more than one interpretation: *angry steer maddens farmer with ax. Cp.* **equivocation** (def. 1). 2. *n.* the intentional use of language in literature to allow more than one level of interpretation, as in much of the writing of T.S. Eliot and James Joyce.

ambiguous (am big′yo͞o əs) 1. *adj.* having more than one possible meaning or interpretation. *In the sentence 'He designs locks,' the word 'locks' is ambiguous.* 2. *adj.* difficult to comprehend, distinguish, or classify, as *an ambiguous response to a questionnaire.* 3. *adj.* vague, as in the expression *I'm not sure.*

ambivalence (am biv′ə ləns) 1. *n.* the desire for mutually exclusive things at the same time, as *adolescent ambivalence between feelings of independence and dependence.* See also **cognitive dissonance**. 2. *n.* the rapid shifting to and from one emotion or intellectual position to a contradictory one. 3. *n.* a psychological state that pulls one in opposite directions. *adj.* **ambivalent.**

amblyopia (am″blē ō′pē ə) *n.* dimness of sight; specifically, reduced visual acuity, not correctable by refractive lenses, and not due to injury or defects in the structure of the eye. *Note:* Amblyopia is a descriptive term that does not indicate its cause nor whether the condition will change. Amblyopia is seen most commonly in school-aged children as a lazy eye in which vision is suppressed when strabismus is present. See **alternating squint**. *n.* **amblyope.** *adj.* **amblyopic.**

American Book Awards, The (TABA) a series of awards for distinguished writing by an American and published in the United States, including one for the most distinguished children's book, given by The Association of American Publishers. *Note:* The awards were formerly called the National Book Awards.

American Sign Language (Ameslan) See **sign** (def. 3).

Ameslan (am′slan) *n.* American sign language.

ametropia (am″i trō′pē ə) *n.* a refractive condition in the eye which causes an unclear image because light rays do not focus exactly on the retina, as in far-sightedness, nearsightedness, and astigmatism. See also **refraction** (def. 2). *adj.* **ametropic.**

amnesia (am nē′zhə) 1. *n.* the loss of

memory in whole or part. 2. *n.* a missing part of memory. *adj.* **amnesia**; **amnesic**. *n.* **amnesiac**.

amphetamine (am fet'ə mēn″, -min) *n.* a drug used as a stimulant or as a diet pill. *Amphetamine reduces hyperactivity in some children.*

amplitude (am'pli to͞od″, -tyo͞od″) 1. *n.* the intensity of sound as measured by taking half the distance between the highest and lowest points of a sound wave at a given frequency. See also **intensity** (def. 1). 2. *n.* the height of a sound or light wave as measured by taking the distance between its highest and lowest points. 3. *n.* the force with which the vocal cords vibrate in speech.

amplitude of accommodation the difference between the farthest and nearest point for clear vision, usually expressed in diopters, and for which there are several tests, especially for near-point reading distances.

anachronism (ə nak'rə niz″əm) *n.* in literature, a wrong time reference; specifically, the use of an incident, object, person, expression, etc., out of its proper historical time. *Sir Boss in Mark Twain's* A Connecticut Yankee in King Arthur's Court *is an anachronism. adj.* **anachronistic**.

anacusis *or* **anakusis** (an″ə ko͞o'sis) *n.* total deafness.

anagram (an'ə gram″) 1. *n.* a word or phrase whose letters also form one or more words or phrases when they are assembled in a different order, as *repair* from *rapier*. 2. *n.* a redistribution of the letters in a word or phrase which results in a different word or phrase. 3. *n.* a game in which letters of words or phrases are transposed to form one or more new words, as *dearer* from *reader*. *Cp.* **palindrome**.

analogue *or* **analog** (an'ᵊlôg″, -ᵊlog') 1. *n.* something similar in form, function, etc. to something else. *The German word 'gymnasium' is the analogue of the English word 'high school.'* 2. **analog computer**, a computer which uses some physical changes to represent directly the numbers being manipulated, as changes in voltage that vary with the size of the number.

analogy (ə nal'ə jē) 1. *n.* a likeness in some characteristics of two things which are not alike in others; similarity; as *the analogy of the computer to the brain*. 2. *n.* a comparison which suggests that since X and Y are alike in some respects, they are probably alike in other respects as well. *adj.* **analogous.**

analysis (ə nal'i sis) *pl.* **-ses** (sēz). 1. *n.* the process, or result, of identifying the parts of a whole and their logical relationships. *Ant.* **synthesis** (def. 1). 2. *n.* the use of this process as a method of study, as *word analysis*. 3. *n.* psychoanalysis. *Note:* Special types of analysis, as *content analysis*, are given under the describing term. *adj.* **analytic; analytical.** *v.* **analyze.**

analysis-by synthesis a theory of how infants learn to process speech; specifically, a theory which proposes that as speech sounds are produced, feedback from the sounds themselves, from the muscles that do the work, and from the neural mechanisms that control them, establishes a neural link between the speech sound and the production mechanism, so that upon hearing a sound, a child 'recognizes' the neural link rather than the muscular association.

analysis of covariance (ANCOVA) a form of analysis of variance for partialing out the effect of correlated variables so that dependent variables can be considered one at a time. *Analysis of covariance is sometimes* *used in an attempt to equate experimental groups by adjusting posttest scores for initial group differences.* See also **analysis of variance.**

analysis of variance (ANOVA) a statistical procedure for testing the significance of the difference between the means of two or more groups. See also **analysis of covariance.**

analytic abilities the abilities used in noting relationships and in making judgments; fluid abilities. *Complex reasoning tasks require analytic abilities. Ct.* **crystallized abilities.**

analytic approach *or* **method** a way of teaching beginning reading which starts with whole units of language, as words, phrases, or sentences, and later breaks these down into their parts; global method. See **word method.** *Ct.* **synthetic approach** *or* **method.**

analytic *or* **analytical entry** an entry in a library catalog or other bibliographic tool for a specific topic or publication to be found in a larger topic or publication.

analytic phonics a whole-to-part phonics approach to reading instruction in which the student learns a number of key sight words, is taught the relevant phonic generalizations, and applies these generalizations to particular examples in learning symbol-sound correspondences; deductive phonics. *Ct.* **synthetic phonics.** See also **whole word phonics.**

anapest (an′ə pest″) *n.* a metrical foot in verse which has three syllables, the first two unaccented, the third, accented: *Whăt thĕy méant bў thĕir síghĭng, ănd kíssĭng sŏ clóse* — J. Dryden. *adj.* **anapestic.**

anaphora (ə naf′ər ə) 1. *n.* a literary device of repeating initial sounds or words or phrases to achieve a certain effect: *Always Florida's green peninsula — always the priceless delta of Louisiana — always the cottonfields of Alabama and Texas* — Walt Whitman. 2. *n.* the use of a word as a substitute for a preceding word or group of words; backward reference, as *it* in *I know it and he does, too. Cp.* **cataphora.** *adj.* **anaphoric.**

anarthria (an är′thrē ə) *n.* the inability to form speech sounds as a result of damage to the nervous system. See also **dysarthria.**

anastrophe (ə nas′trə fē) *n.* a deliberate inversion of the usual order of the parts of a sentence to create some literary effect such as rhyme: *But trailing clouds of glory do we come / From God, who is our home* — W. Wordsworth.

anatomical age any age-equivalent measure of skeletal development based upon bone growth. See also **carpal age; metacarpal age.**

ANCOVA analysis of covariance.

anecdotal record a description of behavior, or a reporting of behavioral incidents, exactly as observed, keeping interpretation and fact separate.

anecdote (an′ik dōt) *n.* a brief narrative describing an interesting or amusing event.

angular gyrus a small area of the parietal lobe where it joins the upper back portion of the temporal lobe; Brodmann's area 41. *Note:* This area is involved in the comprehension of sounds and language. Damage to the angular gyrus leads to receptive aphasia. See illustration under **Brodmann's areas.**

animation (an″ə mā′shən) 1. *n.* the process, or product, of a motion picture film or cartoon using single-frame or stop-motion techniques to produce an illusion of movement. 2. *n.* the quality of liveliness in a person's expression and gestures. *The cheerleader glowed with animation.* *v.* **animate.** *adj.* **animated.**

animism (an′ə miz″əm) *n.* (J. Piaget) the tendency to conceive of objects as living, purposeful organisms.

anis- a prefix indicating *unequal*; as **aniseikonia.**

aniseikonia (an″ī sī kō′nē ə) *n.* a visual defect in which the size, and sometimes the shape, of retinal images from the two eyes are unequal. *Note:* Aniseikonia, while uncommon, may contribute to difficulties in reading by interfering with binocular vision, thus leading to discomfort and fatigue. Aniseikonia is correctable with special lenses. *adj.* **aniseikonic.**

anisometropia (an ī″sə mə trō′pē ə) *n.* a differing refractive condition in the two eyes; differential ametropia. *Note:* Anisometropia may refer to different degrees of the same refractive condition, or to different types of conditions, as one far-sighted eye and one near-sighted eye.

annals (an′ᵊlz) 1. *n.* a recorded history, reporting events, year by year, in chronological order. 2. *n.* any informal record of events: *The short and simple annals of the poor* — T. Gray. 3. *n.* the history of an organization.

annotated bibliography a list of books, periodicals, articles, etc. on a particular subject, with brief explanatory or evaluative comments on each entry.

annotation (an″ō tā′shən) *n.* a critical or explanatory comment or note. *The editor's annotations provided important historical background.*

anomaly (ə nom′ə lē) *n.* anything that differs considerably from the expected or common rule, form, or norm, but which is not defective or incorrect; oddity; pecularity; incongruity. *adj.* **anomalous.**

anomia (ə nō′mē ə) *n.* a form of aphasia involving the loss of ability to recall the names of objects.

ANOVA analysis of variance.

anoxia (an ok′sē ə, ə nok′-) *n.* a lack of oxygen; specifically, the lack or reduction of oxygen to the body or to specific tissues sufficient to cause damage or to reduce effectiveness. *Note:* The brain is particularly sensitive to anoxia; only a few minutes of deprivation of oxygen will cause brain damage. Anoxia at the time of birth is thought to contribute to various learning and reading problems.

ant-, anti- a prefix indicating *opposite, against, the reverse of*, as **antithesis, antonym;** or, *preventing, counteracting,* as **antibody.**

antagonist (an tag′ə nist) *n.* the character who opposes the protagonist; villain. *Ct.* **protagonist.**

ante- a prefix indicating *before* (in time or position); as **antecedent.**

antecedent (an″ti sēd′nt) *n.* a word, phrase, or clause to which a pronoun refers, as *Mary* in *Mary tried but she could not find her purse. Cp.* **anaphora** (def. 2).

anterior (an tēr′ē ər) 1. *adj.* toward the front. *The eyes are in the anterior part of the head.* See also **ventral** (def. 2). *Ant.* **posterior** (def. 1). 2. *adj.* going before in time or space; prior; as *an anterior argument in logic, the anterior part of the stage.* 3. *adj.* in phonology, sounds produced in the part of the oral tract nearest the lips, as the sound /p/.

anterior chamber the space inside the eyeball forward of the lens from the iris to the cornea, filled with aqueous humor. See illustration under **eye.** *Cp.* **posterior chamber.**

anthology (an thol′ə jē) *n.* a collection of complete works or extracts of works by various authors, either of the same literary form, as verse or short stories, or of a variety of forms dealing with a specific subject, as *an anthology of Elizabethan sonnets, an anthology of writings about war.*

anthropo- a combining form indicating *man, human;* as **anthropology.**

anthropomorphism (an″thrə pə môr′ fiz əm) *n.* the attribution of human characteristics to animals, plants, or objects, as in a beast tale.

anticipation (an tis″ə pā′shən) *n.* the act of expecting what is to come; specifically, in reading, the expectation of meaning or of subsequent units of language as one reads a word, phrase, sentence, or longer passage.

anticlimax (an″ti klī′maks) 1. *n.* in literature, a drop from a high or climactic point to one much lower than expected, especially in the action of a story or play. *The ending of Tennessee Williams'* The Glass Menagerie *is an anticlimax.* 2. *n.* the effect of such a drop on the reader or listener. *Note:* Anticlimax may be deliberately used for humorous effect, as in many jokes. It may also create disinterest if the writing or speaking is poor, as in many melodramas with predictable endings. 3. *n.* a shift in a discussion from expressing great and noble ideas to making commonplace remarks. *Cp.* **bathos** (def. 1). *adj.* **anticlimactic.**

anti-hero (an′tə hēr″ō, anti′-) *n.* the central figure of a modern novel or play who lacks such qualities as courage and nobility of mind and spirit that are found in the traditional hero. *Willie Loman is the anti-hero of Arthur Miller's* Death of a Salesman.

antithesis (an tith′i sis) *pl.* **-ses** (sēz). *n.* opposition; contrast; specifically, a figure of speech in which there is a strong contrast between ideas stated in balanced words, phrases, or sentences: *What dire offence from amorous causes springs!/ What mighty contests rise from trivial things!* — A. Pope. *adj.* **antithetical.**

antitropic (an″ti trō′pik) *adj.* being alike but reversed, as a mirror image. *The kidneys are antitropic. Some letters of the Roman alphabet are antitropic, as b and d. n.* **antitropism; antitrope.**

antonym (an′tə nim) *n.* a word opposite in meaning to another word. *'Up' is an antonym for 'down'. Ct.* **synonym** (def. 1). *adj.* **antonymous.**

anxiety (ang zī′i tē) *n.* an emotional state with physiological symptoms and usually characterized by worry or vague fears. *Note:* Anxiety may be nebulous or associated with a particular situation or object. Low levels of anxiety sometimes stimulate creativity and learning, but high levels are almost always debilitating. See also **anxiety hysteria.** *adj.* **anxious.**

anxiety hysteria an emotional disorder characterized by excessive overt expression of anxiety, often with symptoms of phobias and irritability. See also **hysteria.**

anxiety neurosis a neurosis characterized by anxiety, or dread, without apparent object or cause.

anxiety scale a series of items used to aid in judging the degree of an individual's fears of specific objects or occasions, or of generalized nonspecific worries about one's self.

aphasia (ə fā′zhə) *n.* a general term for any receptive and/or expressive disorder in the use of language because of disease of or injury to the brain, particularly in Brodmann's areas 22, 39, 40, 41, or 44. See illustration under

Brodmann's areas. *Note:* Alexia, dyslexia, and other symbolic manipulation disorders for which brain damage is presumed are considered variant forms of aphasia. Aphasia often follows a major stroke or head injury. There are many types and combinations of aphasia, depending on the amount and location of brain damage. *Cp.* **agnosia.** *Note:* Specific types of aphasia, as *auditory aphasia*, are found under the describing term. *adj.* **aphasic.**

aphesis (af'i sis) *n.* the loss of a short unstressed vowel at the beginning of a word, as *mid* for *amid. adj.* **aphetic.** *Ct.* **apocope.**

aphonia (ā fō'nē ə) *n.* loss of voice, usually completely. *Cp.* **dysphonia.**

aphorism (af'ə riz"əm) *n.* a brief statement of a principle, command, or truth, as *haste makes waste. Cp.* **adage; maxim.**

apocope (ə pok'ə pē) *n.* the loss of one or more sounds and/or letters at the end of a word, as the once-pronounced 'silent e' of *name. Ct.* **aphesis.**

apocrypha (ə pok'rə fə) *n.* (*often used as sing.*) writings of doubtful authorship or authenticity. *Note:* The current usage stems from the fourteen books at the end of the oldest Greek versions of the Old Testament. These do not appear in Jewish or Protestant versions of the Old Testament because they were not accepted as inspired writing. *adj.* **apocryphal.**

apoplexy (ap'ə plek"sē) 1. *n.* a stroke; specifically, a sudden stoppage or hemorrhage of the blood flow in the brain which usually causes some paralysis. 2. *n.* a hemorrhage in any body organ. *adj.* **apoplectic.**

a posteriori (ā"po stēr"ē ōr'ī, -ōr'i, -ōr'ē, -ôr'ē) 1. reasoning that derives generalizations from the observation of facts. 2. proved by induction from facts gathered from experience or experiment. *This principle was developed, a posteriori, from examining three studies.* (*Latin*) *Ct.* **a priori** (def. 2).

apostrophe (ə pos'trə fē) 1. *n.* a figure of speech in which an object is personified or a person not present is addressed: *O wild West Wind, thou breath of Autumn's being* — P.B. Shelley; *Milton! Thou should'st be living at this hour...* — W. Wordsworth. 2. the orthographic symbol (') used to show possession, as *Henry's hat*; omission, as *doesn't*; or stress in pronunciation, as *read'ing.*

appellation (ap"ə lā'shən) 1. *n.* a proper name or title, as Queen Mary. 2. *n.* a sentence or phrase with a naming function, as *I'm called Joe.* 3. *n.* the relation between a term and its referent. *Cp.* **signification** (def. 1). *adj.* **appellative.**

appendix (ə pen'diks) *pl.* **-dixes, -dices** (-di sēz). *n.* supplementary material that is related to the text, usually added at the end of a book, as chronological tables, genealogical charts, etc.

apperception (ap"ər sep'shən) *n.* the process, or result, of conscious perception; specifically, the arousal of understanding following attention to a presented display. *adj.* **apperceptive.**

application (ap"lə kā'shən) 1. *n.* the use to which an idea or object is put. *What application does the story theme have in your experience?* 2. *n.* putting an idea or object to use, as *application of vocabulary knowledge.* 3. *n.* careful, persistent effort, as *application in study.* 4. *n.* a request, written or spoken, or form for such a request.

applied reading 1. the use of basic reading skills in the content fields, *Note:* This use of the term refers to presumed differences between the more general purposes and content of primary reading and the more specific ones of later grades; i.e., 'learning to read,' vs. 'reading to learn.' 2. the use of reading skills in practical situations, as reading how-to-do texts, advertisements, income tax forms, etc.; functional reading.

applied research research or study primarily designed to produce practical applications rather than theoretical knowledge. *Action research is a form of applied research. Ct.* **basic research**. See also **action research.**

appositive (ə poz'i tiv) *n.* a word or phrase which restates or modifies an immediately preceding nominal, as *Chad* in *My son Chad is twelve years old,* or as *my favorite flowers* in *Violets, my favorite flowers, grew wild in the valley. n.* **apposition.**

appraisal (ə prā'zəl) 1. *n.* a judgment about performance, sometimes detailing specifics, as an appraisal of oral reading errors. *Cp.* **evaluation** (def. 1). 2. *n.* an informed opinion, as *a critic's appraisal of a novel.* 3. *n.* an estimate of a situation, condition, need, etc. *v.* **appraise.**

appreciation (ə prē″shē ā'shən) 1. *n.* a sensitive awareness of and reaction to aesthetic qualities, as *music appreciation. Note:* Appreciation is one of the major objectives in the teaching of literature. 2. *n.* a critical judgment, usually favorable, of another's work, performance, or achievement, as *an appreciation of Shakespeare.* 3. *n.* gratitude, as *a gift in appreciation. v.* **appreciate**.

apprehension (ap″ri hen'shən) 1. *n.* the direct, immediate awareness of something, as *apprehension of danger. Cp.* **perception**; **comprehension** (def. 5). 2. *n.* fear of future developments; foreboding. *v.* **apprehend.** *adj.* **apprehensive** (def. 2).

approach (ə prōch') *n.* a general instruction procedure for reaching an educational objective. *Note:* Special types of approach, as *experience approach,* are given under the describing term. See also **method.**

apraxia (ə prak'sē ə, ā prak'-) *n.* the loss of the ability to make voluntary movements because of disease of or injury to the brain. *Apraxia does not include paralysis but is a disorder of the production and sequencing of purposeful movements. adj.* **apraxic**; **apractic.**

a priori (ā″prī ōr'ī, -ôr'ī; ā″prē ōr'ē, -ôr'ē; ä″prē ōr'ē, -ôr'ē) 1. logical or reasonable, as a deduction. 2. existing in the mind prior to or independent of experience. 3. not based on empirical test or observation. *We know, a priori, that reading includes the visual perception of words.* (*Latin*) *Ct.* **a posteriori** (def. 2).

aptitude (ap'ti tōōd″, -tyōōd″) 1. *n.* the power, or probability, of performing well in a given situation. 2. *n.* a combination of native and/or acquired characteristics that indicates one's ability to learn. 3. *n.* talent. *Ct.* **achievement**.

aptitude test a test used to predict future performance in a given activity. *An aptitude test...is used to forecast... success in some future course or assignment* — L. Cronbach (1970). *Aptitude tests measure the effects of learning under relatively uncontrolled and unknown conditions* — A. Anastasi (1976). *Ct.* **achievement test**.

aptitude-treatment interaction an effect noted in comparing some methods of instruction; specifically, when some persons high on a given aptitude scale achieve better under one method of instruction, whereas those lower in aptitude achieve better under another instructional method: ...*if the tests are used to choose instructional treatments rather than merely for selection, there must be evidence that the aptitude interacts with the alternative treatments* — L. Cronbach (1970).

AQ achievement quotient.

aqueous humor the clear, watery fluid which fills the anterior chamber of the eyeball between the lens and the cornea. *Cp.* **vitreous humor.**

archaism (är′kē iz″əm, -kā′-) *n.* a linguistic construction used in an earlier period of a given language, now seldom used, as *methinks, forsooth*, etc. *Note:* Archaisms may still be in current use by the regionally isolated, as in parts of Appalachia, by the elderly, and by others for effect. *adj.* **archaic.**

archetypal criticism a critical study of the symbolic meaning in literature of those images, plots, and characters believed to be experienced by all. *Classical Greek tragedies are appropriate materials for archetypal criticism.*

archetype (är′ki tīp″) 1. *n.* the original form, pattern, or model from which other ones are taken; prototype. *Othello is the archetype of jealousy.* 2. *n.* the images, plots, characters, etc., that are thought to be common to everyone's experience, although not consciously so. *Note:* This definition is derived from Jung's concept of the 'collective unconscious' of the human race, which he believed to be shared by all people. *adj.* **archetypal; archetypical.**

archives (är′kīvz) *n. pl.* an organized collection of records relating to the activities of a family, a governmental body, or an organization.

argot (är′gō, -gət) 1. *n.* cant (def. 1). *Cp.* **slang** (def. 2); **jargon**. 2. *n.* the specialized vocabulary of the underworld, used primarily to conceal meaning from outsiders, as *thieves' argot.*

argument (är′gyə mənt) 1. *n.* a reasoning process. *The argument was hard to follow.* 2. *n.* reasons given to support a statement of position, as *a logical argument.* 3. *n.* theme or topic. *The talk had two major arguments.* 4. *n.* a summary or abstract of a literary work. 5. *n.* a talk or text intended to persuade. 6. *n.* a quarrel or disagreement, often loud and emotional.

argumentation (är″gyə men tā′shən) 1. *n.* the act or process of developing an argument. 2. *n.* discussion or debate; one of the four traditional forms of composition in speech or writing. *Cp.* **description** (def. 1); **exposition** (def. 1); **narration** (def. 1). 3. *n.* a set of reasons and the conclusions based on them, presented orally or in writing. 4. *n.* the giving of such reasons and conclusions. 5. *n.* argument (def. 1). *adj.* **argumentative.**

arithmetic average *or* **mean (M)** See **mean** (def. 3).

arteriosclerosis (är tēr″ē ō sklə rō′sis) *n.* the thickening and hardening of the walls of small and terminal arteries. *If arteriosclerosis seriously affects the blood supply to the brain, it may lead to serious and progressive language difficulties. Cp.* **atherosclerosis.**

arthr (o)- a combining form indicating *joint*; as **arthritis.**

article (är′ti kəl) 1. *n.* an essay or prose composition of nonfiction material, as news stories in a newspaper or factual pieces in a magazine. 2. *n.* a grammatical marker of a noun, as *the definite article 'the' and the indefinite articles 'a' and 'an'.* See also **determiner.** 3. *n.* a section or item, often numbered, in a creed or formal document, as *articles of incorporation.*

articulate (*v.* är tik′yə lāt″; *adj.* är tik′yə lit) 1. *v.* to produce speech sounds by modifying the air flow with the articulators. 2. *v.* to enunciate with great clarity. 3. *v.* to express oneself using clear, expressive language. 4. *adj.* able to produce speech, as syllables, words, etc. 5. *adj.* spoken with clear enunciation. 6. *adj.* capable of using clear, expressive language. 7. *adj.* organized into an integrated whole, as *an articulated language arts program.*

articulation (är tik″yə lā′s͟hən) 1. *n.* the movement of the speech organs to modify the air flow to produce speech sounds. 2. *n.* a speech sound; specifically, a consonant sound. 3. *n.* the act of producing comprehensible speech. 4. *n.* the organization of separate ideas into a meaningful relationship. *An effective curriculum requires articulation.* 5. *n.* the joining of bones in a skeleton. 6. *n.* the development of a complete test battery to provide comparable test scores. *v.* **articulate.**

articulator (är tik′yə lā″tər) *n.* any of the fixed or movable organs used to modify the air flow in producing speech sounds. *Articulators include the tongue, lips, teeth, glottis, and hard and soft palate.* See illustration under **speech organs.**

articulatory defect inaccurate speech sound production. *Omissions, substitutions, and distortions are common types of articulatory defects.*

articulatory phonetics the study and classification of speech sounds, based on their method of production. *Cp.* **acoustic phonetics.**

artificial intelligence (AI) *the science of making machines do things that would require intelligence if done by man* — M. Minsky (1961). *Note:* Recent developments in building models of reading and the renewed interest in discourse analysis can both be traced to developments in AI.

artificial language an invented language intended for special use such as an international language, as Esperanto, or a fictional language, as Tolkien's Hobbit language.

arytenoid (ar″i tē′noid, ə rit′ᵊnoid″) 1. *adj.* having to do with a pair of small cartilages in the larynx to which the vocal cords are attached. 2. *adj.* having to do with three small muscles in the larynx.

ascender (ə sen′dər) *n.* the part of a lowercase letter that rises above its x-height, as the upper parts of b, d, f, h, i, k, l, t. *Ascenders and the upper halves of words often aid word recognition. Ct.* **descender.**

asemia (ə sē′mē ə) *n.* the loss of the ability to comprehend or use any type of symbol. *Cp.* **asymbolia.**

aside (ə sīd′) 1. *n.* an utterance by an actor to the audience, one presumably not heard by the other actors present. *In an aside, the heroine begged the audience to hiss the villain.* 2. *n.* a short comment or remark only indirectly, if at all, related to the main topic or theme; digression.

aspect (as′pekt) *n.* a term used to describe the state of verb action as beginning, in progress, completed, etc., and shown in English by the use of affixes or auxiliary words, as in *will run, is running, has run,* etc. *Cp.* **tense** (def. 1).

aspirate (*n.* as′pər it; *v.* as′pə rāt″) 1. *n.* a speech sound produced by a puff of air, unvoiced and unarticulated, as /h/ in *hat.* 2. *v.* to produce such a sound. 3. *v.* to remove something by suction.

aspirated stop a stop consonant sound released with a puff of air, as /k/, /p/, and /t/ at the beginning of a word.

aspiration (as″pə rā′s͟hən) 1. *n.* the release of a puff of air which follows some consonant sounds. See **aspirated stop**. 2. *n.* the act of breathing. 3. *n.* the act of removing something by suction. 4. *n.* a goal or objective set by a learner. See **level of aspiration**.

assessment (ə ses'mənt) *n.* the act or process of gathering data in order to better understand some topic or area of knowledge, as through observation, testing, interviews, etc.; especially, the gathering of data to include strengths and weaknesses in learning. *Note:* Some writers use the term 'assessment' to refer also to the judgments or evaluation made after the data are gathered. See also **appraisal** (def. 1); **evaluation** (def. 1). *v.* **assess.**

assessment, clinical See **clinical assessment.**

assibilation (ə sib″ə lā'shən) *n.* the change of a stop consonant to a sibilant through assimilation, as /t/ to /s/ in *admit/admission. v.* **assibilate.**

assignment (ə sīn'mənt) *n.* a task to be done, as *a study assignment.*

assimilation (ə sim″ə lā'shən) 1. *n.* the process of incorporating new ideas to make them a part of one's present knowledge, as *the assimilation of current linguistic ideas into reading theory and practice.* 2. *n.* the process of learning something so well that it becomes a part of the learner's behavior, as *the assimilation of the mechanics of reading.* 3. *n.* the psychological process of making new knowledge fit into one's experiential structure to avoid cognitive dissonance, as in the assumption by a discouraged person that all news is bad news. 4. *n.* the process by which a group becomes more like a culturally different group, as *the assimilation of Puerto Ricans in New York City.* 5. *n.* in speech production, the process of making a sound similar to or identical to a neighboring sound, as in pronouncing *grandpa* /gram' pa/. *Cp.* **assibilation.** 6. *n.* (J. Piaget) cognitive activity that incorporates, without modification, a new experience into an existing mental structure. *v.* **assimilate.** *adj.* **assimilative.**

assimilative reading reading to remember the detailed meaning of a passage; thorough reading.

associate (*v.* ə sō'shē āt″, -sē-; *n., adj.,* ə sō'- shē it, -āt″, -sē-) 1. *v.* to join together; link; correlate. *As the reader associates various textual concepts into a full sense of unity and meaning, comprehension occurs.* 2. *n.* any psychological event so linked, as *word associates.* 3. *n.* a colleague. 4. *adj.* having equal status with others, as *an associate member of a learned society.* 5. *adj.* having subordinate status, as *an associate professor as distinguished from a full professor.*

association (ə sō″sē ā'shən, -shē-) 1. *n.* a connection between any type of psychological events; specifically, a connection, or the strength of connection, between two events such that the presence of one calls forth the other: *The infant soon learns the association between the sight and sound of a dog. Note:* Associations may be formed within or between ideas, emotions, experiences, objects, etc. They may refer to a very tight relationship between specifics or to a loose one between generalities. Context must often be used to determine the exact nature of the association. 2. *n.* the process, either taught or freely experienced, by which such a connection is made. See also **conditioning.** 3. *n.* a group of people sharing a common interest, as *the International Reading Association.* 4. *n.* the statistical estimation of relationship between two or more variables.

See also **correlation** (def. 2). *Note:* Special types of association, as *free association*, are given under the describing term. *adj.* **associative.** *v.* **associate.**

associational reading 1. the process of connecting a written symbol with its meaning referent, usually a spoken word, in beginning reading. 2. the process of connecting what is presently being read to prior reading and/or experience.

association cortex those portions of the brain not primarily motor or sensory in function, but presumably integrating motor and sensory impulses. *Note:* At one time it was thought that a specific area could be identified as the association cortex. It now seems that many areas as well as simultaneous nerve excitations in several areas may have integrative functions.

association fibers See **commissural fibers.**

associative center *or* **region** See **association cortex.**

associative learning disability the failure to connect or relate two common ideas, events, etc. that are learned together and ordinarily are connected, one with the other. *Severe reading disabilities frequently involve an associative learning disorder.*

assonance (as′ə nəns) *n.* the similarity between, or repetition of, similar vowel sounds which are followed by different consonant sounds, as /a/ in *mad as a hatter. Cp.* **consonance** (def. 1).

assumption (ə sump′shən) 1. *n.* something taken, or being taken, for granted, as *a correct assumption.* 2. *n.* the acceptance of a proposition as true without proof in logical reasoning. *Careless or false assumptions in reasoning often create errors in experimental studies.* See also **postulate** (def. 1); **hypothesis.** *v.* **assume.**

assumptive teaching any instruction in which the teacher takes for granted that the students have the prerequisite experiences, skills, and vocabulary to profit from that instruction. *Assumptive teaching is the antithesis of well-planned, content-area reading instruction that guides students' acquisition of vocabulary, information, and ideas prior to and during reading assignments and lectures* — H. Herber. *Ct.* **diagnostic-prescriptive instruction; diagnostic teaching.**

astereognosis (ə ster″ē og nō′sis, ā ster″-) *n.* the loss of the ability to identify objects by touch; tactile agnosia. *Ant.* **stereognosis.**

asthenopia (as″thə nō′pē ə) *n.* any general discomfort and fatigue of the eyes, often with headache; eyestrain.

astigmatism (ə stig′mə tiz″əm) 1. *n.* an irregularity, or aberration, in the cornea and/or lens of the eye which prevents the clear focus of light rays in one or more axes of the retina. 2. *n.* a defect in vision because of such an aberration. *adj.* **astigmatic.**

asymbolia (ā″sim bō′lē ə) 1. *n.* the loss of the ability to comprehend or use certain symbols because of disease of or injury to the brain; specifically, such a loss with reference to mathematical and scientific symbols. 2. See **asemia.**

ataxia (ə tak′sē ə) 1. *n.* difficulty in voluntary muscle coordination from any of many causes, as from disease of or injury to the brain. 2. *n.* a major syndrome of cerebral palsy marked by poor muscle coordination and lack of balance, especially noticeable in walking and in using the hands. See also **locomotor ataxia.**

atherosclerosis (ath″ə rō sklə rō′sis, ath″-) *n.* the thickening and hardening of the walls of medium and large-sized arteries. *Deposits on the arterial walls may reduce the flow of arterial blood and may lead to thrombosis. Cp.* **arteriosclerosis.**

athetosis (ath″i tō′sis) 1. *n.* involuntary muscle movements, especially a slow weaving of the hands and arms, from any of many causes, as disease of or injury to the brain. 2. *n.* a major syndrome of cerebral palsy marked by continuous movement of the limbs, especially the hands, and often by facial grimaces.

atlas (at′ləs) *n.* a collection of graphic material, usually bound, relating to any given subject or subjects, commonly maps, as *a geographic atlas* or *a linguistic atlas.*

atmosphere (at′məs fēr″) 1. *n.* the general tone or mood of the setting of a story, as *the haunting atmosphere of a ghost story.* 2. *n.* the psychological effect of a situation or place, as *the prison atmosphere. adj.* **atmospheric.**

atomistic approach an instructional approach that emphasizes learning parts of a subject matter before relating these parts to the whole subject. *The alphabet method is an atomistic approach.*

atonicity (at″ənis′i tē, ā″tō nis′-) *n.* the lack, or reduction, of muscle tonus or tension; relaxation; hypotonia.

atrophy (a′trə fē) 1. *n.* the wasting away of bodily tissue, as in muscular distrophy. 2. *n.* a decline, decrease, or worsening of something. *Do inflated grades cause atrophy of scholarship?* 3. *v.* to bring about such a wasting away or decline. *Little reading may atrophy the mind. adj.* **atrophied; atrophic.**

attention (ə ten′shən) 1. *n.* the process, or result, of a selective, concentrated focus upon certain stimuli in perceiving, as *attention to text signals.* 2. *n.* the motor adjustments needed for such a focus. 3. *n.* particular notice of, and response to, another. *Each child deserves your individual attention. v.* **attend.** *adj.* **attentive.**

attention span See **span of attention.**

attenuation (ə ten″yōō ā′shən) 1. *n.* the thinning of something: either literally, as to make slender, or figuratively, as to decrease the strength, value, amount, complexity, etc., of something. *Superficial reading leads to the attenuation of comprehension.* 2. *n.* a reduction in the size of a correlation coefficient because of error in the original measures. *C. Spearman developed a formula to correct for attenuation. v.* **attenuate.**

attenuator (ə ten′yōō ā″tər) *n.* a device for reducing the intensity of an electrical signal, as the volume control of an audiometer.

attitude (at′i tōōd″, -tyōōd″) 1. *n.* a consistent, learned reaction tendency to a specific class of objects, usually with a complex pattern of emotional, intellectual, and physical involvement. *Note:* Attitude objects may range from specific objects, as food, to abstract concepts, as war, sin, and energy. 2. *n.* one's feelings about or toward someone or something, as *a negative attitude toward reading.* 3. *n.* the position or posture of the body in expressing emotion, as *a frightening attitude. adj.* **attitudinal.**

attitude scale a set of self-report items for measuring one's reactions to something to which a range of reactions is possible, as *an attitude scale toward war.*

attribute (*n.* a′trə byōōt″; *v.* ə trib′ yōōt) 1. *n.* a distinctive feature; essential quality. 2. *n.* a basic characteristic of sensation which can be discriminated. *Loudness is an attribute of pitch.* 3.

n. something used symbolically to represent a person or function. *John Bull is an attribute of the British government.* 4. *v.* to give credit to someone or something. *The lost manuscript was attributed to Dickens. n.* **attribution.**

attributive (ə trib′yə tiv) 1. *n.* an adjective or adjectival phrase that modifies a noun within a noun phrase, as *sincere* in *The students sensed the teacher's sincere efforts.* 2. *adj.* expressing a quality or characteristic, especially by an adjective in English, as *first* in *first reader.* See also **predicate adjective.**

atypical (ā tip′i kəl) *adj.* not typical; not conforming to type or norm; unusual; deviant. *Note:* Atypical is a relative concept. For example, complete inability to read as an adult is atypical in an industrial society.

audi (t) (o)- a combining form indicating *hearing, sound*; as **auditory, audiometer.**

audience reading oral reading to communicate to persons who are simply listening to the reader.

auding (ô′ding) *n.* listening with comprehension; specifically, the process of perceiving, recognizing, interpreting, and responding to oral language. *Auding is the auditory process(es) that largely parallels the visual process(es) in reading. Cp.* **rauding.**

audio (ô′dē ō″) 1. *n.* the frequencies involved in the reproduction of sound, as in radio and in the sound part of television. *Ct.* **video** (def. 1). 2. *n.* the electrical circuit which produces such sound frequencies. 3. *adj.* having to do with sound or audio frequencies.

audiogram (ô′dē ō gram″) *n.* a graph which shows the air conduction and/ or bone conduction results of an audiometric test. *Hearing loss is recorded on the audiogram in decibels at frequencies tested.*

audiolingual method (ALM) a method of teaching a second, or new, language that emphasizes oral-aural activity with much drill on pronunciation and spoken dialogue.

audiology (ô″dē ol′ə jē) *n.* the scientific study of hearing and hearing disorders.

audiometer (ô″dē om′i tər) *n.* an instrument for measuring hearing acuity in decibels for pure tones or speech. *A wide range, pure tone audiometer is usually used to determine possible hearing loss in the diagnosis of reading problems. adj.* **audiometric.**

audiometry (ô″dē om′i trē) *n.* the measurement of hearing acuity.

audiotape (ô′dē ō tāp″) *n.* a magnetic tape for recording electrical signals for sound reproduction.

audiovisual aids/materials See **educational media.**

audition (ô dish′ən) 1. *n.* the act of hearing. 2. *n.* the sense or power of hearing. 3. *n.* an opportunity to hear and see someone seeking a part in a play, dance, etc. 4. *v.* to try out for a part in a theatrical performance.

auditory (ô′di tōr″ē, -tôr″ē) *adj.* having to do with the sense of hearing, the hearing process, or the organs of hearing.

auditory acuity the keenness or sensitivity of hearing; auditory threshold. *Ct.* **auditory discrimination.**

auditory aphasia difficulty in comprehending words, as in Wernicke's aphasia; word deafness. *Note:* In auditory aphasia, hearing is unimpaired, but the person is unable to interpret or recognize the message.

auditory area *or* center the region of the cortex where the temporal lobe joins the parietal lobe; Wernicke's area; Brodmann's areas 22, 39, and 40. *Note:* The auditory area is involved in hearing and understanding sounds and language. Understanding of oral language is disrupted when the auditory area is injured. See illustration under **Brodmann's areas.**

auditory association the ability to connect several ideas or concepts presented aurally.

auditory attention *or* **memory span** See **span of attention** (def. 1).

auditory blending a sound-combining skill based on the ability to fuse discrete phonemes into recognized words. *Ct.* **auditory closure**. See also **blend** (def. 1).

auditory closure the response to and integration of aural cues into meaningful stimuli, as in the ability to hear an incomplete or distorted word or utterance, or to supply omitted elements in an utterance. *Ct.* **auditory blending.**

auditory comprehension See **listening comprehension** (def. 2).

auditory discrimination the ability to hear likenesses and differences in the sounds of phonemes and words. *Auditory discrimination is often tested in a comprehensive reading diagnosis. Ct.* **auditory acuity.**

auditory discrimination test any of many tests intended to sample competence in hearing likenesses and differences in sounds, usually speech sounds. *Note:* Commonly, these tests require same/different judgments between pairs of words, but specific tests may seek to measure competences as auditory vigilance, the detection of nonsense in a spoken message, or distinguishing differences in pitch, loudness, rhythm, etc., of either speech or non-speech sounds. *Pure tone audiometric testing is usually recommended for students who have difficulty on an auditory discrimination test.*

auditory feedback hearing one's own speech while talking. *Without auditory feedback, it is difficult to learn normal speech.*

auditory image the mental representation of something previously heard, either in memory without external cause or triggered by a present stimulus. *In word recognition, a visual word stimulus may trigger an auditory image.*

auditory masking See **masking** (def. 1).

auditory modality the use of hearing for acquiring information. *Cp.* **kinesthetic modality; visual modality.**

auditory nerve the sensory nerve for both hearing and balance; the eighth cranial nerve; acoustic nerve.

auditory perception the extraction of information from sounds, as noise, speech sounds, music, etc. See also **phonological perception; auditory discrimination; auditory processing.**

auditory processing the mental activity of receiving, understanding, weighing, ordering, remembering, and examining sounds, especially speech sounds, and considering their meanings in relationship to past experience and their future use. *Cp.* **visual processing.**

auditory scanning the process of searching a sequence of sounds, as those of speech, for a designated target.

auditory training practice in obtaining maximum information when listening; specifically, practice in discriminating and producing speech sounds; ear training.

auditory-visual integration the association of sound and sight, as of an object with its name.

auditory-vocal association the ability to make an appropriate aural response to an utterance, as to the oral analogy: *'Bark' is to 'dog' as 'meow' is to '________.'*

augmented alphabet any of a number of expanded English alphabets designed to make spelling and reading easier by the addition of letters so that each grapheme represents a different phoneme of the spoken language. See also **Augmented Roman Alphabet.**

Augmented Roman Alphabet an early name for the Initial Teaching Alphabet developed by Sir James Pitman. See **Initial Teaching Alphabet (i.t.a.).**

aural (ôr′əl) *adj.* having to do with the ear or the sense of hearing. See also **auditory.**

auricle (ôr′i kəl) *n.* the external, visible part of the ear. *Syn.* **pinna.**

author (ô′thər) 1. *n.* a person who writes; especially, the creator of a literary work. 2. *n.* the creator of any intellectual or artistic work. *Balanchine is the author of many ballets.* 3. *v.* to write; to be the writer of. *She authored a book on French cooking. Cp.* **compiler**; **editor.**

author catalog an alphabetically arranged catalog of author entries in a library card catalog. *The author catalog may also contain the names of editors, translators, etc., as added entries.*

author entry a bibliographic description of a work located in a file according to the name of its author, whether a person, agency, institution, or the like. *Cp.* **subject entry; title entry.**

author's intent *or* **purpose** the motive or reason which an author has in writing. *Writing to entertain, to inform, and to persuade are frequent intents or purposes of authors.*

autism (ô′tiz əm) 1. *n.* a severe emotional disorder in which the individual is so self-centered, or egocentric, as to be largely or wholly unable to judge reality. *Note:* In autism, social interaction, especially through language, is minimal to non-existent. Behavior patterns, as head banging, endless rocking, and eating exclusively one food, are highly repetitive. 2. *n.* the perception of the world solely to gratify one's desires; extreme or psychotic daydreaming, fantasy, or introversion. *adj.* **autistic.**

auto- a combining form indicating *self-generated, acting or directed from within*; as **autobiography, autotelic.**

autobiography (ô″tə bī og′rə fē, -bē-) 1. *n.* a person's life story written by that person. 2. *n.* the class, or genre, of such writing. *Cp.* **biography.**

autograph (ô′tə graf″, -gräf″) 1. *n.* a signature. 2. *n.* a manuscript or any document in a person's own handwriting.

auto-instructional method a general term for any learning situation in which the presentation of the material is controlled and related to the pace and success of the learner, as in most programmed learning materials.

automatic data processing (ADP) the collection, production, and analysis of information by electronic, mechanical, chemical, or some combination of these means.

automaticity (ô″tə mə tis′i tē) *n.* response or behavior without attention or conscious effort. *Automaticity in word attack permits full energy to be put into developing comprehension.*

automator (ô′tə mā″tər) 1. *n.* something that is self-acting or self-regulating. 2. *n.* something that operates without attention or conscious effort. *Skilled readers have an automator that processes punctuation. n.* **automation.**

autonomic nervous system that portion of the body's efferent nervous system which controls the endocrine glands, the heart, and the smooth muscles; visceral system. *The autonomic nervous system has two divisions, the sympathetic and the parasympathetic, which tend to work in opposition in controlling the body's involuntary functions.*

autoregulation (ô″tō reg″yə lā′s͟hən) See **self-regulation.**

autotelic system an organization or entity that in and of itself provides motivation and reward; specifically, the 'talking typewriter,' a learning system developed by O.K. Moore. *Note:* Moore's system provides an environment in which the child's natural curiosity can be met regardless of its possible future usefulness in language development.

auxiliary (ôg zil′yə rē, -zil′ə-) See **auxiliary verb.**

auxiliary verb a word used to express the time, aspect, mood, or voice of another verb, the latter usually in its infinitive or a participle form; a helping verb. *Note: Do, have,* and *will* are common auxiliary verbs, as in *do come, have been,* and *will go.* See also **modal auxiliary verb.**

AV audiovisual, as in *AV aids and materials.*

avante-garde (ə vänt′gärd′, ə vant-; *Fr.* A väN gaRd′) 1. *n.* any leading or advance group, especially in literature and the visual arts, that experiments freely in subject matter and techniques. 2. *adj.* referring to such a group, its work, or its techniques.

average (av′ər ij, av′rij) 1. *n.* a typical amount, rate, quality, etc. *Cp.* **norm** (def. 1). 2. *n.* the arithmetic mean. See **mean** (def.3). 3. *n.* a general term applied to measures of central tendency, in distributions approximating normal distribution. See also **median (Md)** (def. 1); **mode** (def. 1). 4. *v.* to find an average value for. 5. **on the average,** usually; typically. 6. *adj.* referring to an average, as *average weight.* 7. *adj.* ordinary; common; as *an average man.*

axiom (ak′sē əm) 1. *n.* a self-evident truth; maxim. *'Reading requires readiness' is an axiom.* 2. *n.* a widely accepted rule or principle, as *an axiom of law.* 3. *n.* a proposition accepted as true in order to determine its logical consequences. *Axioms are the basis of theory construction. adj.* **axiomatic.**

axon *or* **axone** (ak′son, -sōn) *n.* the portion of a neuron that carries impulses away from the cell body; the efferent part of a neuron. *Axons can be quite long, often with many branches and small end brushes. Ct.* **dendrite.**

B

DEVELOPMENT OF MAJUSCULE								
NORTH SEMITIC	GREEK		ETR.	LATIN		MODERN		
						GOTHIC	ITALIC	ROMAN
𐤁	[illegible]	B	8	[illegible]	B	𝕭	*B*	B

DEVELOPMENT OF MINUSCULE					
ROMAN CURSIVE	ROMAN UNCIAL	CAROL. MIN.	MODERN		
			GOTHIC	ITALIC	ROMAN
[illegible]	B	b	𝔟	*b*	b

The second letter of the English alphabet developed from North Semitic *beth* through Greek *beta* (β, B). The capital (B) goes back to North Semitic *beth* and particularly to Greek B, retained in the Latin monumental script. The minuscule (b) derives from cursive *ℬ*, formed by eliminating the upper loop.

babbling (bab′ling͡) *n.* a stage of early language acquisition in which an infant, usually 3-6 months of age, engages in vocal play and produces a variety of sounds, including some not found in the language environment of the child. See also **language acquisition.** *v.* **babble.**

Babinski reflex the stretching out of the toes of the foot when it is scratched or lightly stroked. *Note:* The Babinski reflex is normal in infancy, but is later replaced by a curling of the toes response. A positive Babinski reflex after infancy is a neurological sign of organic damage.

baby talk a kind of speech marked by sound distortion, syntactic simplification, and omissions, as *Baby no wanna go bye-bye?* for *You do not want to go? Note:* Baby talk is sometimes found in early language development after babbling or in the speech of indulgent adults who talk down to children.

back-formation *n.* the creation of derived word forms by analogy, either by dropping an affix, as the verb form *sedate* from *sedation*, or by creating a new base form, as *pea* from *pease*.

background (bak′ground″) 1. *n.* that part of a scene perceived as behind an occluding object. 2. *n.* a visually perceived surface which extends behind a figure. *Cp.* **figure-ground**. 3. *adj.* referring to mild sensory stimulation accompanying another activity, as *background music.* 4. *n.* the setting of a story. 5. *n.* the sum total of a person's previous learning and development; experience; as *an author's background.* 6. *n.* experiences which precede a learning situation, story, etc. *Note:* Both teachers and students need to have an appropriate background for learning: the teacher, to be able to fill in needed information for the student; the student, to be receptive to the new learning. 7. *n.* the social and historical factors preceding an event, as *a background of racial tension.* 8. *n.* a person's origin and descent, as *an Irish background.*

back-hand slant 1. handwriting with letters that lean to the left. 2. the leftward-leaning characteristic of such letters. See illustration. *Ct.* **forward slant.**

backhand slant

back *or* **backward reference** See **anaphora** (def. 2).

back vowel a vowel sound made with the highest part of the tongue retracted toward the back of the mouth, as /o͞o/ in *good*; broad vowel. See illustration under **vowel**.

backwardness in reading (*Brit.*) reading performance that is below average for a given chronological age. *The point to note about the term* backward *is that it means 'falling short of an age criterion by some specified amount ...'* — cited by A. Pilliner and J. Reid.

BAER Brainstem Auditory Evoked Response. See **brainstem audiometry**.

balanced bilingualism a hypothetical condition referring to equal proficiency in the use of two languages in all social settings.

ballad (bal′əd) 1. *n.* a narrative poem, frequently of unknown authorship, composed of short verses intended to be sung or recited, as *Lord Randal.* 2. *n.* such a poem of known authorship, as Edna St. Vincent Millay's *The Ballad of the Harp Weaver*, Coleridge's *The Rime of the Ancient Mariner*. Also called *art ballad* or *literary ballad.* 3. *n.* a popular type of folk song, as *John Henry, Casey Jones.*

ballad sheet See **broadside.**

bar (bär) *n.* a main horizontal line or stroke in a letter as in A, H, e, f, t. *Cp.* **serif.**

barbershop reading 1. the practice of having students systematically take turns reading aloud so that, as in a barbershop, each knows when his or her turn comes and often looks ahead to 'practice' the part he or she is to read. 2. the practice of having students read aloud one after the other without the students' knowing who will be called upon next.

bar graph a chart in which the length of parallel rectangular bars indicates the frequency of data represented, as a *bar graph of reading rates.* See illustration.

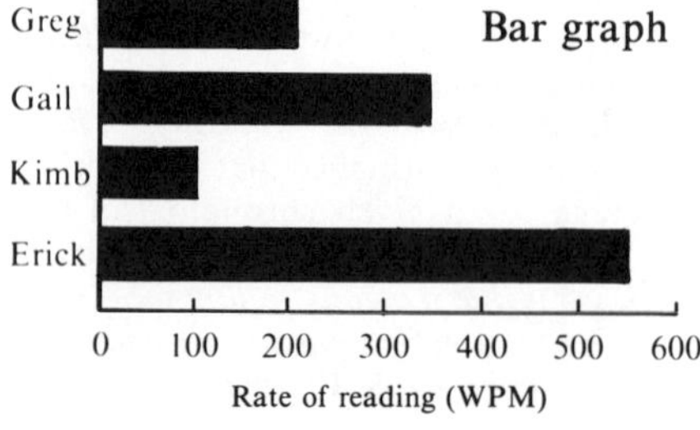

barking at print 1. discordant and usually loud word-by-word oral reading in which the reader pronounces the words but extracts and conveys little or no meaning; word calling. 2. (*Brit.*) an over-reliance on phonics instruction so that students mouth words they do not understand. *Cp.* **pickin' up corn.**

bar reader 1. a barrier that allows each eye to see only a portion of the page or target, used in testing or training binocular vision. 2. a type of reading accelerator which uses a band of light or a bar of some material that mechanically moves down the page to pace the rate of reading. See **pacer.**

basal (mental) age (bā′səl, -zəl) on the 1937 edition of the Stanford-Binet Intelligence Scale, the highest age level at which, and assumedly below which, all tests have been passed. *Basal age may be a more reliable criterion for the prediction of reading achievement than mental age...* —E. Betts, cited by H. Robinson (1946). *Note:* Partial age credits in months for tests passed above the basal age are added to the basal age in computing mental age on this test.

basal ganglia a mass of gray matter deep inside the base of the cerebral hemispheres which includes the corpus striatum and related groups of cells.

basal metabolic rate (BMR) the lowest rate of energy needed by an organism at rest to carry on its vital processes, measured by the rate of oxygen intake and heat discharge.

basal reader a text in a basal reading program or series.

basal reading program *or* **series** a comprehensive, integrated set of books, workbooks, teacher's manuals, and other materials for developmental reading instruction, chiefly in the elementary and middle school grades; (*Brit.*) reading scheme or basal reading scheme. *Note:* The rigidly controlled vocabulary and sequence of learning experiences of early basal reading programs are now often being replaced by greater vocabulary diversity and by more opportunities for pupil choice in the ordering of learning experiences.

basal *or* **basic reading vocabulary** the words introduced in basal readers, usually listed at the back of the readers.

basal reading scheme (*Brit.*) See **basal reading program** *or* **series.**

base (bās) 1. See **base word.** 2. *n.* the initial or primary component, either semantic or syntactic, of a grammar of a language or languages that is least similar to the surface structure. 3. *n.* the initial or primary component of a grammar from which a subsequent deep structure and surface structure are generated.

base component in transformational-generative grammar, the phrase structure rules and lexicon by which deep structures are generated.

base rule See **phrase structure rule.**

base word a word to which affixes are added to create related words; base; as *teach* in *teacher, teaching, teachable,* etc. *Cp.* **root** (def. 1); **stem** (def. 1).

basic instructional level See **instructional reading level.**

basic reader a beginning reading textbook for adults, usually one of a coordinated series of materials patterned after basal readers but with utilitarian content and vocabulary. *The purpose of basic readers is to develop the ability to read any material written in the vocabulary of daily usage or in the words most frequently used in adult reading material* — W. S. Gray (1956).

basic research research or study designed to generate knowledge or to validate a theoretical proposition which may or may not have direct application to curriculum and instruction in the schools. *Ct.* **action research**; **applied research.**

basic sight vocabulary *or* **words** 1. the most frequently used words in written English; specifically, those determined by word frequency counts and which pupils in beginning reading are expected to learn to recognize automatically, as the *Basic Sight Vocabulary of 220 Words* by E. Dolch. 2. a person's storehouse of immediately recognizable words.

basic skills a general term which refers to those skills, primarily cognitive and language-related, which are needed for many school learning tasks. *Speaking, reading, and mathematics, as well as listening and writing, are commonly considered to be basic skills.*

basilar membrane a thin, pliable layer of tissue in the cochlea of the inner ear. *Note:* The basilar membrane is one of the membranes that divide the cochlea into three channels and provides a base for the organ of Corti. As the fluid pulses up one channel and down the other in response to the movement of the stapes, neural impulses are generated in the organ of Corti and transmitted to the brain by the auditory nerve, thus making hearing possible.

bastard title See **half title.**

bathos (bā′t͟hos) 1. *n.* in literature, an anticlimax which abruptly shifts the general written style from the sublime to the commonplace. *Cp.* **anticlimax** (def. 3) 2. *n.* insincere and overly sentimental expression. See **sentimentalism** (def. 2).

battery, test See **test battery**. See also **achievement battery.**

battledore (bat′əl dōr″, -dôr″) 1. *n.* a paddle made of wood or cardboard used as a substitute for the hornbook. See **hornbook.** 2. *n.* an ABC.

Bayesian statistical inference a statistical procedure in which an estimate of an expected distribution of values is made before data are collected, which then serve to modify the estimate.

beast tale a story in which animals play the roles of human beings in human settings.

behavior (bi hāv′yər) 1. *n.* how one acts, as *aggressive behavior.* 2. *n.* all overt, covert, and unconscious acts, and interactions, of mind and body. 3. *n.* all overt, covert, and unconscious acts that are primarily, though not exclusively, mental; psychological activity. *v.* **behave.** *adj.* **behavioral.**

behavioral objective a statement of the nature and degree of measurable performance that is expected for a specified instructional outcome under certain conditions. *A statement for learning a comparative form of adjectives in behavioral objective terms might be phrased: Write the comparative form of red, of white, and of blue.*

behavior disorder any non-organic, disruptive conduct, often implying negative behavior which interferes with learning and social adjustment. *Extreme withdrawal, as well as extreme aggressiveness, are symptoms of behavior disorders.*

behaviorism (bi hāv′yə riz″əm) *n.* the view first advanced by John B. Watson that psychology should be limited to the study of observable behavior.

behavior modification 1. a technique to change behaviors by systematically rewarding only desirable behaviors and either disregarding or punishing undesirable behaviors. 2. the application of this technique to remedial education; precision teaching. *In essence, this approach has two main features: 1) arranging a series of learning experiences starting from what the child can already do and progressing by very small steps in which a predominance of success is assured; 2) applying effective reinforcers (rewards) to motivate and sustain effort* — A. Harris and E. Sipay (1975).

behavior problem a specific example of a behavior disorder, as truancy.

bell curve See **normal (frequency) curve.**

belles-lettres (bel le′tʀᵊ) (*pl. with sing. v.*) 1. *n.* imaginative literature (literally, 'beautiful letters'); specifically, literature that is elegant in style and is not intended to have practical application. *Lamb's 'Dissertation on Roast Pig' and Carroll's* Alice's Adventures in Wonderland *are belles-lettres.* 2. *n.* any light, witty writing.

bestiary (bes′chē er″ē, -tē- *or often* bēs′chē er″ē) *n.* a kind of literature in which the characteristics of animals become the basis for moral lessons.

best seller a book which has a very large sale. *Note:* The most widely known list of best sellers is that published by *The New York Times.*

beta rhythm *or* **wave** the brain wave pattern of relatively high frequencies, between 18 to 30 cps, and relatively low voltage. *Beta waves are associated with attention or excitement.* See also **electroencephalogram.**

beta risk the possibility of making an error of decision whereby something that is false or unacceptable is taken to be true or acceptable; the chance of making a type II error. *If, for example, it were important that no one who might fail be allowed to remain in a special program of limited size, the beta risk will be made small by using a tight acceptance level: you will not let in many who will fail, even though you might have rejected many who might have passed.* See also **type II error.** *Ct.*

alpha risk.

bi-, bin- a prefix indicating *two, twice, double*; as **bilingual, binocular.**

bias (bī'əs) 1. *n.* a preconceived tendency to accept or reject an idea, conclusion, point of view, etc., without evidence; prejudice. *The newspaper article showed a strong racial bias.* 2. *n.* the tendency to make errors in measurement in a systematic way or direction. 3. *n.* an experimental factor in research that creates errors in a systematic way or direction; constant error. 4. *v.* to cause such prejudice or error. *adj.* **biased.**

biblio- a combining form indicating *book*; as **bibliography, bibliophile.**

bibliographic tool 1. a reference aid used in preparing a bibliographic description of materials by librarians. 2. the library catalog used by patrons for information about library materials.

bibliography (bib"lē og'rə fē) *n. a list of books and/or other material by a given author or on a given subject arranged in alphabetical, chronological or classified order, or a combination of these* — L. Goman.

bibliophile (bib'lē ə fīl", -fil") *n.* one who loves books.

bibliotherapy (bib"lē ə ther'ə pē) *n.* the use of selected writings to help the reader grow in self awareness and/or solve personal problems. *Basically [bibliotherapy] involves three steps: identification, catharsis, and insight* — A. Harris and E. Sipay (1975).

bi-dialectalism (bī dī"ə lek'tə liz"əm) *n.* the relatively equal ability to communicate in several dialects of a language. *...a serious ethical problem is raised by any attempts to eradicate a child's language.... ...an effort to produce bi-dialectalism should be the goal if the child's language is to be changed* — V. Seitz (1977). *adj.* **bi-dialectal.**

bilabial (bī lā'bē əl) 1. *n.* a consonant speech sound made when both lips stop or constrict the air flow, as /p/ in *pin* or /m/ in *mom.* 2. *adj.* having to do with such a sound.

bilateral (bī lat'ər əl) 1. *adj.* having to do with two sides of the body, as *bilateral movements.* 2. *adj.* having to do with both the right and the left side. 3. *adj.* affecting both sides in a common manner, as *a bilateral treaty.* 4. *adj.* referring to descent on both parental sides. *Eye color is bilateral. Ct.* **unilateral.** *n.* **bilaterality.**

bilateral transfer the shifting of a skill learned with one side of the body to the other, as in learning to read Braille with the right hand after having learned Braille with the left hand.

bilingual (bī lin̂g'gwəl) 1. *adj.* able to speak or understand, with some degree of proficiency, another language in addition to a native language. *Note:* 'Bilingual' is sometimes improperly used to refer to individuals who speak more than two languages. *Ct.* **multilingualism.** 2. *n.* a bilingual person.

bilingual education the use of two languages as the media of instruction for an individual or group of individuals in part or all of an educational program.

bilingualism (bī lin̂g'gwə liz"əm) *n.* the ability to speak or understand, with some degree of proficiency, a second language besides one's native language. *Cp.* **multilingualism.** *Note:* The ability to read and write the second language may or may not be associated with bilingualism. See **functional bilingualism.**

bi-modal distribution a frequency distribution with two modes or high points.

bimonthly (bī munth'lē) *n.* a publication issued every two months.

binaural (bī nôr'əl, bin ôr'əl) *adj.* having to do with both ears, as *binaural hearing.*

binaural fusion the hearing of two sounds, either different or separated, as one.

bindery (bīn′də rē, -drē) *n.* a place where books, periodicals, and other materials are bound for publication.

binding (bīn′diṅg) 1. *n.* the covers and spine of a book or other material which act primarily to protect and hold together the contents. 2. *v.* the process of providing something, as a book, with a binding.

Binet *or* **Binet-Simon Scale** a series of standardized individual tests of mental ability arranged on an age scale of increasing difficulty, developed by Binet of France and first published with Simon in 1905, with revisions in 1908 and 1911. *Note:* Binet defined intelligence as...*the tendency to take and maintain a definite direction; the capacity to make adaptations for the purpose of attaining a desired end; and the power of auto-criticism* — L.Terman, cited by L. Cronbach (1970). See also **Stanford-Binet Intelligence Scale.**

Bing test an audiometric test which uses a tuning fork to distinguish between conductive and sensorineural hearing loss. *Note:* The vibrating fork is held beside the ear which is alternately blocked and left open. If there is no significant change, the loss is conductive; but if the tone is heard better with the ear blocked, then the loss is sensorineural.

binocular (bə nok′yə lər, bī-) *adj.* having to do with the use of two eyes rather than one, as *binocular vision, a binocular microscope.*

binocular coordination the smooth working together of the two eyes in visual tasks.

binocular fusion the blending into a single image of the separate images from each eye. *A test for binocular fusion is often a part of visual screening tests. Ant.* **retinal rivalry.**

binocular parallax the slightly different lines of sight of an object which each eye has because of the distance between the eyes which makes depth perception possible. *If a finger at arm's length is lined up with a point when both eyes are open, binocular parallax will make the finger jump back and forth if first one eye and then the other is closed rapidly.*

binocular rivalry See **retinal rivalry.**

binocular vision the coordinated use of both eyes to produce a single visual impression; simultaneous vision. *Fusion and stereopsis depend on binocular vision. Ant.* **monocular vision.**

bio- a combining form indicating *life*; as **biography.**

biography (bī og′rə fē, bē-) 1. *n.* the life story of a person which is written by another. 2. *n.* such a form of writing. *Cp.* **autobiography.**

biolinguistics (bī″ō liṅg gwis′tiks) *n.* the study of language in relation to the biological characteristics of humans, especially anatomy and physiology.

birth injury any damage, shock, or wound to the body or mind during the birth process. *Note:* Birth injury and birth trauma are often used as synonyms. However, some restrict a birth injury to physical damage and birth trauma to anxiety presumably originating in the stress of birth.

birth trauma See **birth injury.**

biserial correlation a correlation between two variables, both assumed to be continuous and normal in distribution, one of which has been divided into two classes, as a correlation between IQ scores and pass/fail in school. *Cp.* **tetrachoric correlation; point-biserial correlation.**

bit (bit) *n.* a *b*inary dig*it*; in information theory, the amount of information which would be obtained by receiving an answer to a question which had only two alternatives, as *yes/no* or *on/off.* See also **byte.**

bivariate (bī vâr′ē it, -āt′) *adj.* having to do with two variables, as *a bivariate distribution.*

bivariate analysis a simple form of statistical analysis applied to two variables only. *Ct.* **multivariate analysis.**

black comedy *or* **humor** morbid or bizarre elements used in modern novels, plays, and motion pictures for comic purposes. *Cp.* **theater of the absurd.**

Black English a variety of American English spoken by some Blacks, especially by those in lower socioeconomic levels. *Note:* Black English is spoken in cities and other areas as widespread as Los Angeles, Chicago, Washington D.C., New York City, and rural Mississippi. It is as highly structured and as logical as standard American English. It has characteristic lexical, phonological, and intonational patterns as well as distinctive syntactic features. Among the latter are the use of the double negative; 'be' to indicate habitual action; deletions rather than standard contractions, as 'I go' for 'I'm going;' and no possessive forms of nouns. Not all such features are necessarily present to the same extent in the speech of either an individual or of all speakers of Black English. *Cp.* **nonstandard dialect; sociolect.**

Black literature literature written by American Negro authors, often about Black people; Afro-American literature.

blank verse unrhymed verse, especially unrhymed iambic pentameter. See **iambic pentameter.**

blend (blend) 1. *v.* to combine the sounds represented by letters to pronounce a word; sound out. 2. *n.* the joining of the sounds represented by two or more letters with minimal change in those sounds, as /gr/ in *grow*, /spl/ in *splash. Syn.* **consonant cluster.** *Ct.* **digraph.** (def. 1). 3. *n.* a word made by combining elements of other words, as in combining /br/ in *breakfast* with /unch/ in *lunch* to make *brunch. Syn.* (def. 3) **portmanteau word.**

blindness (blīnd′nis) *n.* inability to see; lack or loss of useful sight. *Note: Legal blindness* is visual acuity of 20/200 or less in the better eye after correction, or reduction of the visual field to 20 degrees or less. *Absolute blindness* is lack of all perception of light. *n., adj.* **blind.**

blind spot 1. the light-insensitive point at which the optic nerve enters the retina; optic disc. See illustration under **eye.** *Note:* Normally we are not aware of the blind spot in each eye, but it is quite easy to locate. Make an x and a filled-in circle about the size of a nickel about four inches apart on a card. Using one eye, fixate on the x and move the card back and forth horizontally with the circle to the outside about 8-10 inches from the eye. When the image of the circle falls on the blind spot, the entire circle will disappear. 2. any small, irregular, light-insensitive area of the retina; scotoma. 3. something about which one is uninformed, prejudiced, or insensitive. *It is easy to have a blind spot for something one does not like.* 4. any part of an auditorium in which one cannot see or hear well. 5. an area with poor or weak radio reception.

block (blok) 1. *n.* anything that hinders or stops a function or response; obstacle. 2. *n.* an interruption of normal speech rhythm; stuttering. 3. *n.* a sudden, brief interruption of thought or memory other than the result of emotions. *Ct.* **emotional block.** 4. *v.*

to have such a block. *I block when I try to think of the name of that.* 5. *n.* a temporary or permanent interruption of a neural impulse. 6. *v.* to show how the action in a play is to be handled. *On the third reading, the director blocked the play for the actors.* 7. *v.* to plan the placement of scenery and properties on a stage for a performance. 8. *n.* a computer term for: a. a flow chart symbol for a computer operation device, or instruction. b. a section of storage locations for a particular set of instructions or data. c. a group of consecutive machine words used as a unit to guide a particular computer operation. 9. **block in, block out**, to sketch or outline broadly, without details.

blocked syllable See **closed syllable.**

blocked vowel See **closed vowel** (def. 1).

blocking (blok'ing) 1. *n.* See **emotional block**. See also **block** (defs. 1-3, 5). 2. *v.* to arrange for theater use. See **block** (defs. 6, 7).

blood pressure the force of the blood on the walls of the arteries, the maximum force being called *systolic pressure* and the least, *diastolic pressure. Note:* Blood pressure depends on the strength of the heart beat and the elasticity of the arterial walls, as well as upon many other factors, including psychological ones. See also **hypertension; arteriosclerosis; atherosclerosis.**

blown-up book (*New Zealand*) a book in which print is enlarged so as to be read by a group.

Blue-Back (-ed) Speller a popular name for Noah Webster's spelling book, first published in 1783 as *The Grammatical Institute, Part I*; retitled *The American Spelling Book* in 1787; and revised as *The Elementary Spelling Book* in 1829. *Note:* This spelling book, actually a reader and speller, was most widely used in the United States with some 100,000,000 copies being sold during its existence. The nickname comes from its blue covers.

blurb (blûrb) *n.* a description of a book prepared by the publisher and appearing on the book jacket and/or in the publisher's catalog, and sometimes in advertisements.

BMR basal metabolic rate.

boards (bordz, bôrdz) *n. pl.* any stiff material, often covered with paper or cloth, forming the covers of a book. *Covers of many early books were made of wood; hence the name boards.*

body (bod'ē) *n.* in metal typography, the main part of a printing type below the typeface. *12-point type refers to the body height, not to the typeface height, of type.*

body concept the mental picture one has of how one looks to others. *Jim's body concept improved greatly during adolescence. Ct.* **body image** (def. 1); **body schema.**

body image 1. the awareness of one's own body and its position in space at a given moment which is derived from the feedback from internal and external sensory stimulation, primarily visual and kinesthetic. *Gymnasts need to have an accurate body image at all times.* 2. body concept. *Ct.* **body schema.**

body language See **kinesics** (def. 1).

body schema the generalized concept of body image. *Note:* Body image usually comes from actual experience, while body schema is an abstracted, characteristic image of one's body, as in trying to behave in a manner consistent with one's mental picture of oneself. *Ct.* **body concept.**

body-spatial orientation the ability to manipulate one's body in an integrated manner in relation to objects located in the environment.

boldface (bōld′fās″) *n.* a heavy version of a typeface design. *Note:* Boldface is often used to emphasize parts of a text, as in dictionary entries, chapter headings, etc. *Ct.* **italic** (def. 1).

bone conduction the transmission of sound to the inner ear by vibrations of the bones of the skull, as in *a bone conduction hearing aid. Ct.* **air conduction.**

book (bo͝ok) 1. *n.* a literary composition written or printed on successive pages and bound together in a volume. 2. *n.* a notebook for writing, drawing, recording data, etc., as *a composition book, a sketch book.* 3. *n.* a major division of a literary work, as *Book I of* The Illiad. 4. *n* the text or libretto of an opera, musical play, etc. 5. **the Book**, the Bible. 6. **the book,** the telephone book. 7. *adj.* referring to book(s), as *a book catalog.* 8. *adj.* learned chiefly from books, as *book knowledge.* 9. **by the book**, in the proper form or manner, as *exercise by the book.* 10. **closed book**, something one cannot or prefers not to reveal. *Gatsby kept his past a closed book.* 11. **in one's book**, in one's opinion. *In my book, this play is a disaster.* 12. **like a book**, completely; thoroughly; as *know another like a book.*

book bank (*Brit.*) a facility which lends textbooks to students who cannot afford to buy them.

book-burning *n.* the public burning or other forms of suppressing printed materials thought by some to be unfit for other people to read. See also **censorship.**

book card a card placed in a book for circulation purposes. *The book card provides the record that the book is out of the library; when the book is in the library, the book card is kept in the book pocket.*

book club 1. a publishing plan: a. to encourage students to buy selected titles in low-cost paperback form. b. to sell books at a discount to adults. 2. an informal organization in a school, class, or library to encourage reading by its members.

book corner *or* **nook** a special place in a library or classroom for quiet, comfortable reading.

book fair a book exhibit designed to encourage the reading habit, especially in young readers, by an opportunity to browse, ask questions, etc.

book jacket a detachable paper cover intended to protect the binding and serve as an advertisement. *The lurid illustration on the book jacket was misleading.*

booklet (bo͝ok′lit) *n.* a small book or pamphlet, usually in paper cover.

booklist (bo͝ok′list″) *n.* a collection of titles of books, prepared by a teacher, librarian, professional organization, etc. Books for You *is an annotated booklist for high school students, prepared and revised periodically by the National Council of Teachers of English.*

bookmobile (bo͝ok′mə bēl″) *n.* a van or truck equipped to carry books and other library materials, serving as a traveling library, often for communities where libraries are not accessible.

bookplate (bo͝ok′plāt″) *n.* a label indicating ownership pasted inside the front cover of a book.

book report an oral or written reaction by a student to a book when read. *Note:* A book report is properly intended to stimulate a thoughtful dialogue between student and teacher.

book review a critical analysis, spoken or written, of a book.

book selection See **materials selection.**

book size *or* **format** any of the terms used to describe the height of the leaf of a book, as folio, quarto, octavo, duodecimo, twelvemo. See these terms. *Note:* These terms have their origins in the earliest days of printing and are usually imprecise in describing size: there is no universally accepted standard of usage. The terms derive from Latin, each indicating the number of leaves formed by folding, or cutting and folding, a printed sheet of paper. The greater the number of leaves obtained from one sheet, the smaller the book.

bookstall (bo͝ok′stôl″) *n.* a booth or stand at which books are sold, as *the bookstalls on the Seine in Paris.*

book talk a talk about one or more books by a teacher or librarian to introduce the books and to induce students to read them.

Book Week a week in November designated for special exhibits and programs to stimulate interest primarily in children's books and reading.

borderline defective a person of borderline intelligence. See **borderline intelligence.**

borderline intelligence mental functioning between normal and mildly retarded. *Note:* This is a broad and ill-defined category which may include the high-grade mental defective, the borderline defective, and the slow learner. See **mental retardation.**

borrowing (bor′ō ing, bôr′-) *n.* a linguistic unit introduced into a language from another language, as the English *chaise lounge* from the French *chaise.* See also **loan word.** *v.* **borrow.**

bottom-up processing a theoretical position that comprehension in reading consists of the accurate, sequential processing of text. *In bottom-up processing, comprehension is seen as text-driven: it is built up and governed by the text only, and does not involve the reader's inner experiences and expectations. Ct.* **top-down processing.** *Ct.* **interactive processing.**

bound morpheme a morpheme which may not stand alone as an independent word, as *-ing. Ct.* **free morpheme.**

boustrophedon (bo͞o″strə fēd′ən, bou″-) *n.* a method of writing in which the direction of each line of a text is alternately reversed: if the characters in one line read from left to right, the next lower line will read from right to left, and so on, alternately. *Note: Boustrophedon,* from the Greek, literally means 'as the ox turns in plowing.'

bowdlerize (bōd′lə rīz″, boud′-) *v.* to remove from any piece of writing what the censor feels is offensive or indecent; expurgate. *Note:* The term comes from Thomas Bowdler, an English physician, who removed such words from his edition of Shakespeare in the early 1800's.

brace (brās) See **bracket** (def. 1).

bracket (brak′it) 1. *n.* in popular use, one of a pair of orthographic symbols used to contain one or more words or figures, as in (*Honors*). *Note: Round or curved brackets,* or parentheses ( ), generally enclose material either inessential to a topic, undisclosed by a narrator, or inserted into a direct quotation, as in *Arthur's father (also dead) had been a railway employee. Square brackets* [ ] are used in writing, parallel to curved brackets, and are also used to enclose phonetic transcriptions, as in [sIt] for *sit. Angular brackets* < > are used to enclose a mutilated passage, an expansion of an abbreviation in a text, or a quotation or verbal expression in a reference work such as a dictionary. *Curly brackets*, or braces { }, enclose items which are considered alternative, parallel, or equivalent choices. 2. *n.* in technical use, only the square bracket. 3. *v.* to place in brackets.

brad (o) (y)- a combining form indicating *slow*; as **bradylexia**.

bradylexia (brad″i lek′sē ə) *n.* a variant of dyslexia, marked by extreme slowness in reading that is not due to either habit, low intelligence, or unfamilarity with the text. *Ct.* **tachylexia.**

Braille *or* **braille** (brāl) *n.* a writing system using patterns of raised dots to allow the blind to read by touch, developed by Louis Braille in the early 19th century. *Letters, words, numbers, or musical notes may be represented in Braille. adj.* **Braille, braille**.

brain (brān) *n.* that part of the central nervous system which lies within the skull. *The brain includes the cerebral hemispheres, the cerebellum, and the brain stem.* See illustration.

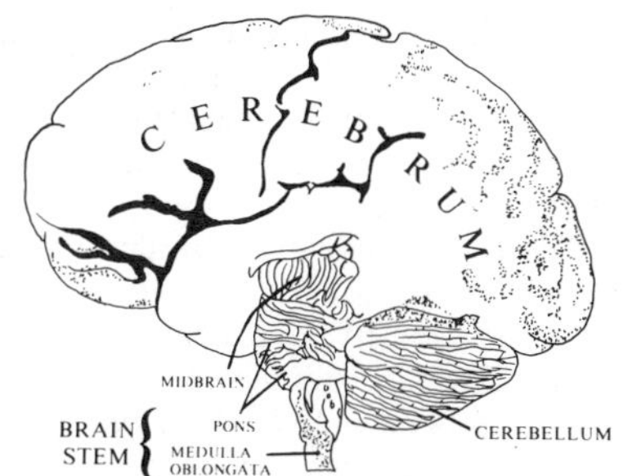

The human brain

brain damage *or* **injury** injury to brain tissue leading to poorer functioning of the central nervous system. *Brain damage can arise from accident, surgery, or disease. Cp.* **minimal brain dysfunction (MBD).**

brainstem (brān′stem″) *n.* the part of the brain composed of the midbrain, the pons, and the medulla oblongata. *Note:* The brainstem controls many involuntary activities, as breathing changes in pupil size, etc. See illustration under **brain.**

brainstem audiometry a technique for measuring hearing loss by stimulating the brainstem with rapid auditory clicks and analyzing the responses by computer. *Note:* The Brainstem Auditory Evoked Response, or BAER, thus obtained is used with infants, the cerebral palsied, and others who cannot respond to other audiometric tests.

brainstorm (brān′stôrm″) 1. *v.* to search for many ideas and/or solutions through group discussion, as *brainstorm a problem.* 2. *n.* a suddenly conceived clever idea, as *have a brainstorm.*

brainwash (brān′wosh″, -wôsh″) 1. *v.* to use drugs, tortures, and/or psychological stress to change a person's attitudes or to break down resistance. *The prisoners were brainwashed to reveal wanted information.* 2. *n.* the condition resulting from such techniques. *n.* **brainwashing.**

brain wave 1. often **brain waves**, the recorded pattern and rhythm of electrical activity in the brain. See **electroencephalogram**. 2. a sudden idea; brainstorm (def. 2).

branching program a kind of programmed instruction which provides alternative courses of action a student may take, depending on his responses. *Note:* A branching program is designed to adjust to individual differences in learning. *Ct.* **linear program.**

branching rule one of the phrase structure rules in the base component used to form tree diagrams. See **tree diagram** (def. 1).

breakthrough to literacy (*Brit.*) the

title of a reading scheme in England that makes early use of children's composing of sentences for the teaching of reading, language, and writing.

breve (brēv, brev) *n.* an orthographic symbol (˘) which is placed directly above a vowel to indicate that it has short duration or lax pronunciation, as /ă/ in *cat*, or weak stress in a metrical foot. *Cp.* **accent** (def. 2e).

brightness contrast the difference between the amount of light reflected by the paper and by the type printed on the paper. *Black type on white paper helps brightness contrast and ease of reading.*

broadsheet (brôd′shēt″) See **broadside.**

broadside (brôd′sīd) *n.* a kind of inexpensive reading matter, printed on one side of a large sheet of paper; ballad sheet; broadsheet. *Note:* Broadsides were printed from the 16th century on, and they were most popular in 18th century Colonial America. Their contents varied widely, from proclamations, both religious and civil, to comments on natural phenomena and local events.

broad vowel See **back vowel.**

Broca's aphasia See **Broca's area.**

Broca's area the speech motor area of the lower, rear corner of the left frontal lobe; Brodmann's area 44. *Brain damage to Broca's area results in expressive aphasia.* See illustration under **Brodmann's areas.**

brochure (brō s̲h̲o͝or′) *n.* a short printed work folded, stitched, or stapled together; pamphlet.

Brodmann's areas the numbered sections of a map of the cerebral cortex, developed by the neurologist Brodmann according to various arrangements of cell layers. *Note:* One of many systems of identification of cortex areas, Brodmann's map is often used as a reference for locating cerebral functions. See illustration.

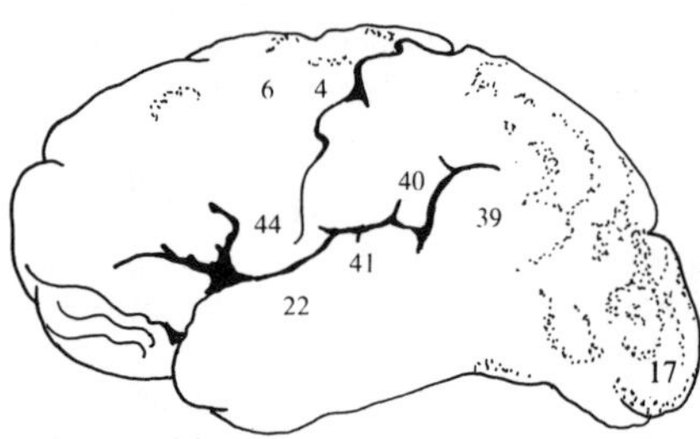

Brodmann's areas (selected)

bromide (brō′mīd, -mid) *n.* an overused, trite folk saying; cliché: *You can drive a horse to water, but you cannot make him drink.*

browse (brouz) *v.* to look over or through in an unhurried, casual way, as *browse through several new books.*

buccal (buk′əl) 1. *adj.* having to do with the cheeks. 2. *adj.* having to do with the space between the teeth and the cheeks, as *buccal cavity.*

bucolic (byo͞o kol′ik) 1. *adj.* referring to writing, usually poetry, about shepherds and rural life; pastoral (def. 1). 2. *n.* a pastoral poem. 3. *n.* a shepherd or farmer.

bulletin (bo͝ol′i tən, -tin) *n.* a periodical publication issued by a government agency, a society, an organization, etc., at regular intervals. *The state historical society's quarterly bulletin includes a list of recent acquisitions.*

burlesque (bər lesk′) 1. *n.* writing or acting that ridicules its subject by absurd exaggeration for comic effect. *Cp.* **lampoon** (def. 1); **travesty** (def. 1). 2. *n.* a parody or caricature that mocks its subject. 3. *v.* to act, write, or illustrate in such ways. 4. *n.* (also **burlesk**) a stage show with bawdy humor, slapstick, and often a strip-tease act.

byte (bīt) *n.* a unit of computer storage containing eight bits of information. *Even small home computers now have memories of several thousand bytes.* See also **bit**.

C

DEVELOPMENT OF MAJUSCULE								
NORTH SEMITIC	GREEK		ETR.	LATIN		MODERN		
						GOTHIC	ITALIC	ROMAN
7	1	Γ	ᑐ	(	C	ℭ	*C*	C

DEVELOPMENT OF MINUSCULE					
ROMAN CURSIVE	ROMAN UNCIAL	CAROL. MIN.	MODERN		
			GOTHIC	ITALIC	ROMAN
<	C	c	c	*c*	c

The third letter of the English alphabet developed from North Semitic *ghimel* and Greek *gamma* through the Etruscans, in whose language there was no meaningful distinction between the *g*-sound and the *k*-sound, and who used C for both. In Latin, C, pronounced like English K, was used mainly before A and O, and retained this sound when introduced into Britain. The capital and minuscule, which assumed their present form in Latin, were originally angular and faced to the left, as in North Semitic *ghimel* and early Greek *gamma* (⅂).

CA chronological age.

cable (kā′bəl) *n.* one or more insulated wires, often in bundles or strands, used to conduct electrical impulses, as *a telephone cable.* See also **coaxial cable.**

cacography (kə kog′rə fē) 1. *n.* poor handwriting or penmanship. *Ct.* **calligraphy** 2. *n.* poor spelling. *Ct.* **orthography** (def. 2).

caesura *or* **cesura** (si zho͝or′ə, -zo͝or′ə, siz yo͝or′ə) *pl.* **-ras, -rae** (-ē). 1. *n.* in modern usage, a break in the rhythm of language, especially a pause in the sense of the meaning within a line of verse, marked in prosody by a double vertical line. *Trust not yourself;* | | *but your defects to know*—Pope. 2. *n.* in classical Greek and Roman poetry, a pause within a metrical foot.

CAI computer-assisted instruction.

Caldecott Medal Award an annual award to the artist of the most distinguished. American picture book for children. *Note:* The Award was named after Randolph Caldecott, a 19th century English illustrator of children's books. Given first in 1938, the Award is presented by the Association for Library Service to Children of the American Library Association.

calibration (kal″ə brā′shən) 1. *n.* the adjustment of the units of a measuring instrument to agree with a standard. 2. *n.* the adjustment of an audiometer to known standards of frequency and of loudness. 3. *n.* the matching of an audiometer to a specific set of earphones. *v.* **calibrate.**

calligraphic (kal″ə graf′ik) *adj.* having to do with printed letter shapes which come from handwritten models. *Script in print is a calligraphic form.*

calligraphy (kə lig′rə fē) 1. *n.* the handwritten production of well-designed artistic letters, script, or characters; penmanship. 2. *n.* the production of line drawings or paintings having the quality of artistic penmanship.

call number a classification number assigned to library material to indicate its location within the systematic arrangement of library materials.

callosal (ka lō′səl) *adj.* having to do with the corpus callosum. See **corpus callosum.**

calque (kalk) See **loan translation.**

cant (kant) 1. *n.* a specialized vocabulary of a social or occupational group; jargon; as *poker player's cant, legal cant.* 2. *n.* argot (def. 2).

canto (kan′tō) *n.* a main section or a major division of a long poem. *Byron's* Don Juan *sets forth on his adventures in Canto II.*

capability (kā″pə bil′i tē) 1. *n.* the highest quality or ability that can be developed, as *one's capabilities for speed reading.* 2. *n.* ability. 3. *n.* capacity for use. *Poetry has great capabilities for teaching imagery.*

capacity (kə pas′i tē) 1. *n.* actual ability to do something; power to perform. *Her capacity for understanding mathematics was unlimited. He exerted himself to his fullest capacity to win the race.* 2. *n.* the potential ability to learn. *The difference may be great between a child's achievement and his capacity in reading.* 3. *n.* the greatest amount possible. *Class enrollment reached its capacity.* 4. *n.* a position; role. *In her capacity as reading supervisor, she helped teachers develop diagnostic skills.*

capacity level any assumed upper limit of some specified type of performance; commonly, listening comprehension level, as determined by a listening comprehension test.

capacity test a test which presumably measures one's potential for something. *Much misuse or misinterpretation of mental tests arises simply from the labels 'intelligence' or 'capacity', as they suggest that inborn capacity is being measured* — L. Cronbach (1970). *Only in the sense that a present behavior sample can be used as an indicator of future behavior can we speak of a test measuring capacity. No psychological test can do more than measure behavior* — A. Anastasi (1976).

capital letter a written or printed letter, larger and often differently shaped than other letters, used to begin the first word of a sentence, a proper noun, or certain abbreviations; majuscule. *Note:* A capital letter is also used for emphasis, as *Look at THAT! Cp.* **upper-case letter.** *Ct.* **lower-case letter.** *v.* **capitalize.**

caption (kap′s̱hən) 1. *n.* a heading or title, as of an article, chapter, major section, page, etc. 2. *n.* the legend or explanation for an illustration or cartoon, especially in a magazine. 3. *n.* in motion pictures, the title of a story or scene. 4. *v.* to provide such a heading, legend, or title.

card catalog an alphabetical file of bibliographic entries consisting of separate cards which provide information about books and other materials available in a specific library.

career story a narrative that tells what a person's job or professional life is like, as that of a nurse, engineer, tour guide, etc. *Note:* Career stories are sometimes of poor literary quality because the author is more interested in giving knowledge about a job than in telling an absorbing story.

caret (kar′it) 1. *n.* a proofreading symbol (‸) placed just below a line or at the margin of a line of text to indicate something either inserted or to be inserted. 2. *n.* a graphic symbol (ˇ) placed above certain consonant letters in phonetic transcription to indicate a palatal sound, as [š] for *sh* versus [s] for *s.* 3. *n.* a symbol [ʌ] used in phonetic transcription to represent a low central vowel, as in [kʌt] for *cut. Cp.* **schwa.** (def. 2).

caricature (kar′ə kə c̱hər, -c̱hŏŏr″) 1. *n.* an exaggeration or distortion of characteristics or defects of a person or thing, either in a picture or in words. *Cp.* **burlesque** (def. 1). 2. *n.* the process of producing such an exaggeration or distortion. 3. *n.* an extremely poor imitation; travesty. *The copy was a caricature of the original.* 4. *v.* to produce a distorted picture or description.

carpal age an age-equivalent measure of skeletal development, based upon the degree of growth in the small wrist bones from cartilage into hardened bones. *Cp.* **metacarpal age**. See also **anatomical age.**

carrel *or* **carrell** (kar′əl) *n.* a cubicle or

a desk with walls around three sides of its top for a person to study without distraction, usually in a library or in a specially equipped classroom.

cartographer (kär tog′rə fər) *n.* a person who draws maps or charts. *adj.* **cartographic**. *n.* **cartography.**

cartoon (kär to͞on′) 1. *n.* a satirical drawing, as that of a political figure or event. 2. See **comics**. 3. *v.* to make a satirical drawing or comic strip.

cartouche *or* **cartouch** (kär to͞osh′) *n.* an oval or oblong figure used in certain writing systems, such as ancient Egyptian, to enclose characters representing a royal name. See illustration.

Cartouche or cartouch of King Tutankhamen

cartridge (kär′trij) 1. *n.* a case or container for film or magnetic tape; especially, a case for an endless loop of motion picture film or of magnetic tape for use in a tape recorder; cassette. 2. *n.* a phonograph pickup for changing mechanical vibrations into electrical impulses.

case (kās) *n.* the relationship of a noun, pronoun, or adjective to other words in a grammatical construction, shown by word order or by prepositions in noninflected languages and by change in word form in inflected languages. *Cp.* **declension.**

casebound (kās′bound″) See **hardback** *or* **hardbound.**

case conference a meeting, formal or informal, of any or all interested parties for the presentation of an individual's case history. *Note:* The case conference may include diagnostic data, remedial procedures and results, and the development of plans for future program and/or placement.

case grammar a type of grammar developed by C. Fillmore (1968) that is used to generate linguistic constructions in terms of the relation of noun phrases to verbs.

case history *or* **study** 1. a formal and usually comprehensive report prepared about an individual, as a student with a severe reading problem, which typically contains the reason for referral, diagnostic data, remedial procedures and results, and suggestions for further efforts. 2. a type of research frequently used in education, psychology, and medicine.

cassette (kə set′, ka-) See **cartridge** (def. 1).

casual speech *or* **style** the style of discourse used when talking with friends and acquaintances. *Most dinner table conversations in a restaurant involve casual speech and would make little sense to the outsider passing by* — M. Joos (1962).

cata- a combining form indicating *repeating* (in speech pathology); as **cataphasia.**

catalexia (kat″ᵊlek′sē ə) *n.* a form of

dyslexia marked by involuntary and nonmeaningful repetition of words or phrases. *Note:* To be useful, this term should signify a lessened competency of an already smoothly acquired reading behavior.

catalog *or* **catalogue** (kat′ᵊlôg″, -ᵊlog″) 1. *n.* a list or record of materials held by a library or group of libraries arranged in a definite order, and describing the materials. *Catalogs may be card catalogs, book catalogs, microfiche catalogs, or on-line (to a computer) catalogs.* 2. *n.* a list of materials prepared for a particular purpose, as *a sales catalog, an exhibition catalog.* 3. *v.* to classify and provide bibliographic descriptions of library materials.

cataloger *or* **cataloguer** (kat′ᵊlôg″er, -ᵊlog″-) *n.* in libraries, a person who classifies library materials for use by library patrons.

cataphora (kə ta′fə rə) *n.* the use of a word or group of words as a substitute for a forthcoming group of words; forward reference; as *I, Thomas Jefferson, do solemnly swear.... Cp.* **anaphora** (def. 2). *adj.* **cataphoric.**

catastrophic reaction *or* **response** the breakdown of normal stress behavior when an individual is faced with great shock or frustration. *A catastrophic response is frequently characteristic of brain-damaged children.*

categorical (kat″ə gôr′i kəl, -gor′-) 1. *adj.* absolute; unqualified, as *a categorical denial.* 2. *adj.* having to do with a category.

categorize (kat′ə gə rīz″) 1. *v.* to organize data in groups; classify. 2. *v.* to name or label; characterize. *The poetry of T.S. Eliot is hard to categorize. n.* **categorization.**

category (kat′ə gōr″ē, -gôr″ē) *n.* a class or group that is a division of a larger classification system.

catharsis (kə thär′ sis) 1. *n.* emotional release, especially that produced by reading about or observing the tragic action of the hero in a narrative or play. 2. *n.* the treatment of emotional problems by recalling traumatic, often repressed, experiences to relive them and thereby find relief from them.

CATV Community Antenna TV.

caudal (kôd′ᵊl) 1. *adj.* having to do with the tail; towards the tail. 2. *adj.* referring to the part of the body farthest away from the head. *Ant.* **cephalic.**

causal (kô′zəl) *adj.* producing an effect. *Multiple causal factors are the rule, not the exception, in reading disability.*

causality (kô zal′i tē) 1. *n.* a cause and effect relation. 2. *n.* that which produces an effect.

causation (kô zā′shən) 1. *n.* anything which produces an effect; cause. See also **multiple-causation (theory).** 2. *n.* the relation between cause and effect, as *logical causation.* 3. *n.* the act of causing something. *adj.* **causative.**

cause (kôz) 1. *n.* anything which produces an effect. *A diagnosis of reading difficulty involves a search for causes as well as symptoms.* 2. *v.* to bring about an effect. 3. *n.* a goal or ideal sought, as *the democratic cause.* 4. *n.* a reason or basis for action; motive. *A student's persistent reading difficulties are a cause for concern.*

cause/effect relationship in a communication, a stated or implied association between some outcome and the conditions which brought it about.

CCTV closed-circuit television.

cedilla (si dil′ə) *n.* an orthographic symbol (¸) placed below a letter to indicate some distinction in pronunciation from the unmarked letter; the ç in French, Spanish, and Portuguese to indicate /s/ as opposed to /k/, as in the French *français. Note:* Certain borrowed words in English also use the cedilla in their spelling, as *façade*.

ceiling (sē'liŋ) 1. *n.* an upper limit, actual or assumed. *Many slow reading rates represent self-imposed ceilings.* 2. *n.* the highest possible score on a test. See also **ceiling effect.**

ceiling effect the failure of a test to identify fully the performance of the most competent because of a limited number of difficult test items.

censorship (sen'sər ship") 1. *n.* any attempt to limit the opportunity of others to read certain books or magazines or to see certain films or plays. *Ever since its publication, Salinger's* The Catcher in the Rye *has been an object of censorship.* 2. *n.* the acts of an official responsible for examining books, films, plays, etc., to see whether there are objectionable features, as *police censorship of films. v.* **censor.**

-cent (i)- a combining form indicating *hundredth*; as **centile, percentile**.

centile (sen'tīl) 1. *n.* any of the 100 parts of a percentile distribution of scores, or its rank order. See also **percentile**. 2. *n.* percentile. *Note:* (def. 2): Technically, an inaccurate and careless usage.

central nervous system (CNS) the brain and the spinal cord.

central tendency, measure of an indicator representing a single central value that is used to summarize a distribution of scores. See **mean** (def. 3); **median** (def. 1); **mode** (def. 1).

central thought See **main idea** (def. 1).

central vowel a vowel sound made with the tongue slightly pulled back and curved downward but near the middle of the mouth, as /u/ in *cut*. See illustration under **vowel**. *Cp.* **neutral vowel**. See also **mid vowel.**

centration (sen trā'shən) *n.* (J. Piaget) the tendency to attend to a single feature of an object or event to the neglect of other features. *Ct.* **decentration.**

-cephal (o)- a combining form indicating *head*; as **cephalic, hydrocephalus.**

cephalic (sə fal'ik) 1. *adj.* having to do with the head; towards the head. 2. *adj.* referring to the part of the body nearest the head. *Ant.* **caudal.**

-ceptor a suffix indicating *receiver*; as **receptor**.

cereb (r) (ro)- a combining form indicating *brain*; as **cerebral**.

cerebellum (ser"ə bel'əm) *n.* that part of the brain involved in fine motor coordination, lying below the occipital lobes at the back of the brain and attached to the brain stem. *Brain damage to the cerebellum results in cerebral palsy.* See illustration under **brain.**

cerebral (ser'ə brəl, sə rē'-) 1. *adj.* having to do with the brain, especially with the cerebrum. 2. *adj.* referring to the use of the intellect rather than the emotions, as *the cerebral nature of mathematics.*

cerebral cortex the outer layer of the cerebrum; specifically, its gray matter. *The cerebral cortex is involved in perception, in the higher mental functions of memory, logic, and language, and in the initiation of motor responses.*

cerebral dominance 1. the greater control of behavior by one hemisphere of the brain than by the other; hemispheric dominance; lateral dominance. *Note:* The superiority of one hemisphere of the brain over the other in cortical functions is most easily seen in the laterality of a voluntary motor function, as in handedness. There are also differences in the localization of perceptual and cognitive functions in the hemispheres, such as verbal and logical functions in the left hemisphere, and musical and holistic functions in the right hemisphere. *Cp.* **mixed cerebral dominance**. 2. the cerebral control of lower brain and spinal cord functions.

cerebral dysfunction any abnormal functioning of the brain.

cerebral hemisphere either of the halves of the cerebrum. *Note:* The hemispheres are separated front to back by a deep fissure and are connected by the corpus callosum. Each hemisphere is composed of four major lobes: frontal, occipital, parietal, and temporal. See also **cerebral dominance.**

cerebral localization 1. the mapping of areas of the cerebral cortex by types and layers of cells, by lobes and fissures, or most commonly by the sensory, motor, or association functions that seem to be related to an area. *Specific areas of cerebral localization, as those involved in speech, reading, writing, etc., are well known.* 2. attempts to determine the cause and location of defective brain functioning by various diagnostic procedures.

cerebral palsy the imperfect development of motor coordination and muscle strength because of damage to the cerebellum or motor control area of the brain. *The three major types of cerebral palsy are ataxia, athetosis, and spasticity.*

cerebrum (ser′ə brəm, sə rē-) *n.* that portion of the brain composed of the two hemispheres and the connecting corpus callosum. *The cerebrum forms almost 70 percent of the central nervous system.* See illustration under **brain.**

certification (sûr″tə fə kā′s̱hən, sə tif″ə-) 1. *n.* the process of gathering, evaluating, and approving or disapproving a person's credentials, as *teacher certification.* 2. *n.* the state of being certified, usually by means of a license. *Certification is required of public school teachers in the United States.* See also **credential** (def. 1). *v.* **certificate.**

cerumen (si ro͞o′mən) *n.* earwax.

cervical (sûr′vi kəl) *adj.* referring to the neck, the region of the neck, or any part like a neck, as the neck of a hollow organ. *n.* **cervix.**

cesura See **caesura.**

chance error See **random error.**

channel (c̱han′ᵊl) 1. *n.* in general, any medium or pathway that conducts or carries a message, as *a communication channel.* 2. *n.* a computer pathway or circuit for the flow of data or the storing of serial data. 3. *n.* a frequency band assigned to television or radio stations for their transmissions. 4. *v.* to direct or cause to move within specified lines. *Channel your energies into improving your spelling.*

chapbook (c̱hap′bo͝ok″) *n.* a modern term for small, inexpensive books sold by peddlers or, in the 16th through early 18th centuries, by chapmen. *Note:* Chapbooks in America were small, about 7.6 x 12.6 cm. (3 x 5 in.), had from 4 to 24 pages, and were often crudely illustrated. Their contents ranged from religion, romantic fiction, and biography to crime and adventure. They were at their most popular in America between 1725 and 1825, after which magazines gradually took their place.

chapman (c̱hap′mən) *n.* a traveling salesman or peddler in the early 16th to 19th centuries. *They were small chapmen's books, and cheap* — B. Franklin. See also **chapbook.**

character (kar′ik tər) 1. *n.* the totality of a person's psychological traits; personality; as *a cheerful character.* 2. *n.* a consistent, characteristic quality of an individual, especially a moral one, as *an honest character.* 3. **in character, out of character**, behavior that is typical (atypical) of a person's past behavior. 4. *n.* a person who behaves oddly; eccentric. *He is a character.* 5. *n.* a person represented in or acting in a story, drama, etc. *D'Artagnan is the central character in* The Three Musketeers. 6. *n.* a graphic symbol used to represent something. 7. *n.* the symbols, taken singly or as a whole, used in writing, printing, and computer work, as *characters on a typewriter.* 8. *n.* a symbol as part of a standard system of writing or transcription, as the *Roman alphabet* or *the International Phonetic Alphabet.* 9. *n.* the form used in writing or printing, as manuscript writing. 10. *n.* a written sign used to represent words or morphemes, as *the Chinese character for* tree: 木 *See also* **writing system; logograph.**

character disorder See **personality disorder.**

characterization (kar″ik tər i zā′shən, -tri zā′- *or esp. Brit.*, -tə rī-) *n.* the way in which an author presents a character in imaginative writing, as by description, by what the character says, thinks, and does, or by what other persons say, think, or do about the character.

characters per minute (CPM) rate of reading or speaking in terms of orthographic characters. *CPM has widely replaced words per minute in telecommunications.*

c, hard the /k/ sound represented by the letter *c* in *cake, ascot*, and *cut. The hard c usually precedes the letters a, o, and u in a syllable. Ct.* **c, soft.**

charge (chärj) 1. *n.* the record of the loan of a book. 2. *v.* to check out a book from a library.

chart (chärt) *n.* a systematic arrangement of information, often using pictures and diagrams. *Charts...symbolize rather than represent reality. They deal with generalizations and relationships rather than with the appearance of things* — E. Horn (1937).

chart, experience See **experience chart.**

checked (chekt) 1. *adj.* of a syllable, ending with a consonant sound, as *of* with /v/, *off* with /f/. See **closed syllable.** 2. *adj.* of a vowel, a vowel sound in a checked syllable, as /o/ in *Bob.* See **closed vowel.**

checked syllable See **closed syllable.**

checked vowel See **closed vowel** (def. 1).

check list items grouped together for some purpose, as a list of skills in reading, used by a teacher in observing and recording systematically a student's performance for purposes of evaluation and/or diagnosis.

child-centered (child″sen′tûrd) *adj.* emphasizing in home or school the developmental needs of the child. *A child-centered reading program attempts to consider all aspects of child development in organizing reading instruction.*

child guidance clinic an organization for the evaluation and treatment of children with behavioral problems, usually with a psychiatrist and/or psychologist in attendance. *Emotional well-being is the raison d'être for most child guidance clinics.*

child language See **language acquisition.**

children's literature the body of works written specifically for children, although often having appeal for readers beyond childhood, as E.B. White's *Charlotte's Web.*

Chi-square *n.* a statistical formula for determining whether differences between theoretical and obtained frequencies in various categories of a distribution can be considered to differ because of chance variation in sampling, as in a Chi-square test.

choral reading group reading aloud, usually to an audience.

chorea (kə rē′ə, kō-, kô-) *n.* repetitive, complex, jerky movements which may sometimes appear well-coordinated but are involuntary; St. Vitus' dance. *Chorea is a consequence of damage to the central nervous system by disease or hereditary defects.*

choreoathetosis (kōr″ē ə at͟h″ə tō′sis) *n.* a form of cerebral palsy in which slow movements are interrupted by quick jerks.

choroid (kōr′oid, kôr′-) *n.* the middle layer of the eyeball between the retina and the sclera, which furnishes a blood supply to the retina; choroid coat. See illustration under **eye.**

choroiditis (kōr″oi dī′tis, kôr″-) *n.* inflammation of the choroid.

chorus (kōr′əs, kôr′-) 1. *n.* a musical work, sung by a large group, as in a musical comedy or opera. 2. *n.* a group of singers in concert. 3. *n.* a group of singers and dancers in a musical comedy. *The story of the people in such a group is the basis for the musical comedy* A Chorus Line. 4. *n.* the part of a song following the verse; often, the most popular part of a song. 5. *n.* a dramatic convention of one or more persons who comment on the action in a play, as in Greek and Elizabethan drama. *Shakespeare used a chorus to open* Romeo and Juliet.

Christ-cross-row *n.* the alphabet, so called because of the cross placed before the alphabet in the hornbook. See illustration.

Christ-cross row

-chrom (a) (ato) (o)- a combining form indicating *color*; as **chromatic, achromatic**.

chron (i) (o)- a combining form indicating *time*; as **chronic, chronological.**

chronic (kron′ik) *adj.* continuing for a long time, as *a chronic disease. Ct.* **acute** (def. 2).

chronicle (kron′i kəl) 1. *n.* a detailed chronological record of events. *Shakespeare used Holinshed's chronicles of English history as sources for plays.* 2. *v.* to make such a record.

chronological age (CA) the number of years a person has lived, usually stated in years and months, as *a chronological age of 8-3.*

chunk (c͟hun͡gk) 1. *n.* a unit of text longer than a sentence and shorter than a paragraph that forms a discrete syntactical unit. *F. O'Hare (1971) often uses chunks in sentence-combining exercises.* 2. *v.* to integrate or otherwise organize details of information, or bits of discrete data, into larger units. See **chunking**.

chunking (c͟hun͡gk′in͡g) *n.* the process, or result, of grouping or reorganizing smaller units into larger, more meaningful ones, as *the chunking of scores to make a smooth learning curve, the chunking of a long number series to facilitate learning.*

ciliary muscle (sil′ē er″ē mus′əl) the muscle, surrounding the lens of the eyeball, that controls the shape of the lens in accommodation to permit near point and far point vision. See illustration under **eye**.

Cinderella theme a narrative that follows the basic plot of the fairy tale *Cinderella*: a young woman leads a miserable life, harrassed by a wicked stepmother and cruel stepsisters, but is at last rescued by a handsome prince.

cinema (sin′ə mə) 1. *n.* a collective term for motion pictures, often with an 'elite' connotation, as *a revival of classics from the early cinema.* 2. *n.* (*Chiefly*

Brit.) a motion picture theater. *adj.* **cinematic**.

cinquain (sin͡g kān′, sin͡g′kān) *n.* a stanza of five lines; specifically, one which has, successively, two, four, six, eight, and two syllables.

circle graph a circle that is divided in the manner of a pie to show the size of the parts of a whole; pie graph; as the distribution of one's tax dollars. See illustration.

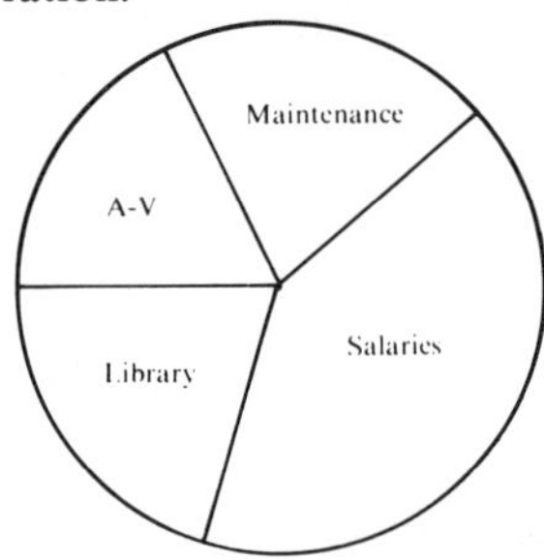

Circle graph showing the distribution of a school tax dollar

circular definition a definition in which the same term is used to define itself, as *meaning is what you mean. Note:* Dictionary entries sometimes represent circular definition: *dyslexia = reading disability*, and vice versa.

circular reasoning a series of false steps in reasoning in which one's conclusion is the same as the assumption made at the beginning of the thinking process.

circulation (sûr″kyə lā′s͟hən) 1. *n.* the transmission of something between persons or places, as *the circulation of a rumor, circulation of air.* 2. *n.* the movement of the blood through the body. 3. *n.* the lending of books and other materials from the library, including the records kept for this purpose. 4. *n.* the distribution of published material, as *a large magazine circulation, a daily newspaper circulation of 100, 000 copies. v.* **circulate.** *adj.* **circulatory.**

circumflex (sûr′kəm fleks″) *n.* an orthographic symbol (^), placed above vowel graphemes to indicate pronunciation, as in the French *bâtir.*

citation (sī tā′s͟hən) 1. *n.* the act of quoting. *She gave a citation from Huey.* 2. *n.* the quotation so made. *Huey (1908) wrote '...we read by phrases, words, or letters as we may serve our purpose best.'*

citation form ạ word form recorded in isolation from other words to serve as an example or for purposes of linguistic analysis.

class (klas, kläs) 1. *n.* a group of things which have some property in common; category. 2. *n.* a group or meeting of a group of students. 3. See **social class.** 4. *n.* an interval in a frequency distribution having no overlap with other intervals, but each of which has the same range of scores or values. *The use of classes in the analysis of data simplifies data processing. Ct.* **rank order.** 5. See **form class.** 6. *n.* a topic of study, as *the biology class.*

classic (klas′ik) 1. *n.* a literary work which has continued or will continue to appeal to readers long after the period in which it was written. Alice in Wonderland *has long been a classic. E. B. White's* Charlotte's Web *is a modern classic.* See also **adapted classic.** 2. *n.* the author of such a work. 3. **the classics**, the literature of ancient Greece and Rome. 4. *n.* a standard, model, or definitive example by which other works in a category may be judged. *A Rolls Royce is a classic of automotive engineering. adj.* **classical.**

classic, adapted See **adapted classic.**

classical conditioning the process, or result, of linking a response to a stimulus which would not otherwise produce a response; Pavlovian conditioning. *Note:* In classical conditioning, an unconditioned stimulus (food) which first produces an unconditioned response (salivation) is paired with a second stimulus (bell) to be conditioned. In time, the bell (conditioned stimulus) will produce salivation the same as, or similar to, the earlier unconditioned response. The unconditioned stimulus always precedes and brings forth the response. *Ct.* **instrumental conditioning; operant conditioning.**

classicism (klas′i siz″əm) *n.* the formal literary and artistic principles found in ancient Greek and Roman work, expressed in such qualities as simplicity, proportion, and emotional control. See also **neoclassicism.** *n.* **classicist.**

classification (klas″ə fə kā′shən) 1. *n.* the process of organizing facts, objects, or abstractions into sets or categories with common features, as dates by centuries, words by grammatical function, houses by type of construction. 2. *n.* the process of grouping languages into different types according to their historical development or to their formal relationships and similarities. 3. *n.* the act or result of placing something into an already existing category. 4. *n.* a category or scheme into which things have been or might be placed. 5. *n.* a formal scheme for arranging library materials. *The* Dewey Decimal *and* Library of Congress *classifications are widely used. v.* **classify.**

classification number See **class number.**

classified catalog a catalog arranged by subject according to a systematic classification scheme, especially a library classified catalog.

classify (klas′ə fī″) 1. *v.* to organize into groups or categories. 2. *v.* to put something into an already existing category. 3. *v.* to arrange books and other library materials according to subject and form, including the assignment of a class number. See also **classification** (def. 5).

class inclusion (J. Piaget) When a class of things (B) is composed of two parts (A and A^1) of unequal size ($A > A^1$), the understanding is that A is not greater than B.

class interval the range of scores in a class; the size of an interval in a frequency distribution. *All of the scores that fall within the boundaries of a class interval are tallied in that class.*

class noun a noun with sub-classes; generic term. *'Dog' refers to the class of animals known as 'dogs,' which has sub-classes such as Airedales, spaniels, and collies.*

class number a number used to designate a specific division of a classification scheme which is symbolized entirely or partly by numerals. *The class number for fairy tales in the Dewey Decimal Classification is 398.2.*

classroom climate the interpersonal tone of a classroom.

classroom library a collection of books located in a classroom, often changed several times a year. *A student committee helped the teacher select books from the school's main library for their classroom library.*

clause (klôz) *n.* a group of words with a subject and a predicate, used either to form a part of or a whole sentence. *Ct.* **phrase** (def. 1). *Note:* Special types of clause, as *dependent clause*, are given under the describing term. *adj.* **clausal.**

claustrophobia (klô″strə fō′bē ə) *n.* an abnormal fear of small, closed places.

cleft lip a congenital split lip, usually the upper lip; harelip. *A cleft lip is caused by failure of the right and left* *halves of the lip to grow together.*

cleft palate a congenital opening in the hard and/or soft palate which sometimes extends into a cleft lip. *A cleft palate makes speech difficult and usually requires surgery.*

cliché (klē shā′, kli-) 1. *n.* an expression used so often that it has lost its original freshness, as *blind as a bat, cold as ice.* 2. *n.* an overused form, character, plot, etc., as melodrama, the character of Shylock, the boy-meets-girl plot.

client (klī′ənt) *n.* one who gets help from a professional person or agency, as in a psychological clinic or a reading clinic.

client-centered therapy a non-directive approach to the resolution of psychological problems developed chiefly by Carl Rogers. *Note:* In client-centered therapy the client is responsible for trying to understand and solve personal problems. The therapist's role is to accept and support the client and to reflect back what the client says. The approach is sometimes called 'Mmm' therapy to emphasize the noncommittal role of the therapist. *Ct.* **(ego) supportive therapy**.

climax (klī′maks) 1. *n.* the major turning point in the action of a story. See also **action** (def. 2); **plot** (def. 1). 2. *n.* the point at which the reader or audience is most involved and has the greatest emotional response to a literary work or dramatic performance. 3. *n.* the development, and highest point, of ideas of greater and greater force in a rhetorical argument. *adj.* **climactic.**

clinic (klin′ik) 1. *n.* a place, or process, using specialized resources for evaluating and treating patients, clients, or students on an out-patient or visiting basis, as *a hospital eye clinic.* 2. *n.* courses or locations that offer assistance for specific problems, as *a writing clinic.*

clinical (klin′i kəl) 1. *adj.* having to do with experience in direct observation and actual treatment. *The clinical picture of Dale's reading problem was quite different from theoretical expectations.* 2. *adj.* analytical; objective; as *perceptive clinical judgment.*

clinical assessment a diagnostic or prescriptive evaluation which may involve both the administration of formal tests and the observation of behaviors exhibited by the person being assessed.

clinical method 1. an in-depth, structured study of individuals, using systematic diagnostic and treatment procedures. 2. the procedure(s) used in a clinic setting. 3. (J. Piaget) a. in his earlier work, an interview procedure for exploring children's cognitive processes. b. in his later work, a combination of interview and experimental procedures called 'critical exploration.'

clinical psychology a branch of psychology dealing with the study of, research in, and actual practice of the prevention, diagnosis, and treatment of psychological and behavioral disorders.

clinician (kli nish′ən) *n.* a specialist who works directly with subjects, usually in a clinic setting, as *a reading clinician.*

clipping (klip′ing) *n.* the shortening of a word to a new form with the same meaning, as *math* (or in some English-speaking nations, *maths*) for *mathematics.*

clonic (klon′ik, klō′nik) *adj.* shifting rapidly from muscle tension to muscle relaxation, as *a clonic spasm. Ct.* **tonic** (def. 1).

clonic block in stuttering, the rapid

and prolonged repetition of sounds. *Ct.* **tonic block.**

closed-circuit television (CCTV) private rather than general public television used as an instructional aid in the classroom, as a monitoring device in business, as a sporting event telecast in a theater for a selected audience, etc.

closed stacks a library bookshelving area not personally available to most users. *Ct.* **open stacks.**

closed syllable a syllable ending with one or more consonants, as in *mat, hand*; blocked syllable; checked syllable. *Ct.* **open syllable.**

closed vowel 1. a vowel in a syllable or morpheme that ends with a consonant, as /a/ in *hat*; checked vowel; blocked vowel. 2. a vowel produced while the lips and jaw are held in a relatively close and tense position, as /o͞o/ in *boot. Ct.* **open vowel.**

close juncture See **juncture.**

closet drama a play, often in verse, written to be read rather than acted.

closure (klō'zhər) 1. *n.* the tendency to perceive things as wholes, even if parts are missing or there are gaps in continuity, as *auditory closure, grammatical closure, visual closure.* 2. *n.* the temporary blocking of the air stream in voice production. 3. *n.* the completion of a physical or mental activity.

cloze procedure 1. any of several ways of measuring a person's ability to restore omitted portions of an oral or written message from its remaining context. *Note:* W. Taylor coined the term 'cloze' in 1953 to reflect the gestalt principle of 'closure,' the ability to complete an incomplete stimulus. In reading practice, a standardized procedure and set of scores have been developed to differentiate frustration/instructional reading levels and instructional/independent reading levels. *Ct.* **maze** (def. 1). 2. the use of this procedure as an instructional strategy, as in reading, in listening comprehension, in developing style sensitivity, and in aiding attention during extended reading passages.

cluster (klus'tər) 1. *n.* a linguistic sequence: a. of sounds, as *the consonant cluster /sp/.* b. of parts of speech, as *the verb cluster 'might have been.'* 2. *n.* a group of languages or dialects whose common features may be explained geographically. 3. *n.* a sub-group of highly correlated variables. 4. *v.* to group or be grouped in some way.

cluster analysis any of several statistical procedures for detecting a cluster in a correlation matrix.

cluster phonics a synthetic phonics approach that emphasizes the identification of phonograms, as *ate* in *mate, date,* and *berate. Ct.* **letter phonics; whole word phonics.**

cluttering (klut'ər ing) *n.* rapid, incomplete speech that is often jerky, slurred, spoken in bursts, and difficult to understand; 'nervous' speech. *Cluttering, unlike some stuttering, may frequently be controlled by slow, careful speaking.*

CNS central nervous system.

co (l) (m) (n)- a prefix indicating *with, together*; as **coefficient, collate, component, congenital.**

co-author (kō ô'thər, kō'ô"-) *n.* one of two or more authors who together produce a written work; joint author. *Note:* In some cases, the contribution of each author cannot be separately identified; in others, the contributions of each are specifically identified.

coaxial cable an insulated cable which conducts high frequency signals and which is shielded by a network of thin braided wires.

co-basal reader *or* **series** a basal reader or reading series used in connection with another basal reading program.

cochlea (kok′lē ə) *n.* the part of the inner ear in which vibrations are received by the organ of Corti and neural impulses leave via the acoustic nerve. See illustration under **ear**.

code (kōd) 1. *n.* the storable information which enables one to send or understand a message in communication. *Phonological distinctive features, as rounded, high, voiced, etc., are a code.* 2. *n.* a system of signals used to represent letters and numbers in transmitting information, as *Morse code.* 3. *n.* a system of symbols involving sounds, letters, words, or other oral or graphic devices used in transmitting messages requiring secrecy, as *secret code.* 4. *v.* to change information into a code. *Cp.* **encode** (def. 1).

coefficient of alienation (k) a statistical measure that shows the degree to which two or more variables are unrelated. *Ct.* **coefficient of correlation.**

coefficient of concordance a statistical measure of the degree of agreement among several rankings.

coefficient of correlation any one of several statistical measures that show the degree to which two or more variables are related, as *a product-moment coefficient.* See **product-moment coefficient (r).** *Ct.* **coefficient of alienation (k).**

cognate (kog′nāt) 1. *n.* a word related in meaning and form to a word in another language; etymon. *English 'grow' has among its cognates Old High German 'gruoen- and Old Norse 'grōa.'* 2. *adj.* referring to such a form.

cognition (kog nish′ən) *n.* knowing; specifically, the process, or result, of recognizing, conceiving, judging, and reasoning. *Note:* Perceiving is considered a part of cognition by some psychologists, but not by others.

cognitive clarity the understanding that printed text is a form of language; i.e., that it has a communicative purpose and that features of spoken language are represented by written signs. *Cognitive clarity is essential in learning to read.* See also **linguistic awareness; metalinguistic awareness.**

cognitive deficit a perceptual/conceptual difficulty that affects intellectual functioning.

cognitive dissonance a term coined by Leon Festinger to describe a perceived inconsistency between one's attitudes and one's behavior, producing a conflict which needs to be resolved. *Cognitive dissonance may arise in a student who has high self-esteem but negative feelings about being assigned to a remedial reading class.*

cognitive domain the psychological field of intellectual activity. *Ct.* **affective domain; psychomotor domain.**

cognitive entry in reading a literary work, the ability to participate actively in, and relate to one's experience, the cognitive behaviors of knowing, comprehending, applying, analyzing, synthesizing, and evaluating. *Cp.* **imaginative entry.**

cognitive map a concept, first advanced by E.C. Tolman in studies of maze learning by rats, referring to a pattern of relationships formed in the mind to explain learning in problem-solving tasks.

cognitive meaning that part of meaning which is directly related to objects and events and is free of emotional content; denotation; lexical meaning. *Ct.* **affective meaning; connotation.**

cognitive psychology See **cognition.**

cognitive representation a way of

thinking about an object of thought or a language referent; specifically, any of three ways so used in Jerome Bruner's concept of cognitive functioning: *enactive representation* (motor), *iconic representation* (perceptual), *symbolic representation* (cognitive).

cognitive strategy the intellectual plan or operation used to study, solve a problem, cope with a situation, etc.

cognitive structure the organization of thinking into a consistent system. *Changes in cognitive structure are characteristic of mental development.*

cognitive style the theoretical assumption that individuals have a consistent approach to problem-solving or to general learning activities, as, for example, an analytic or holistic approach. *Cognitive style is of interest to teachers when a student's approach to an assignment is incongruent with the demands of the task.*

coherence of text the subjective interpretation by the reader of the degree of cohesion in text; the degree to which ideas appear to 'hang together' in a clear, unified pattern. *Cp.* **cohesiveness in text.**

cohesion (kō hē′zhən) *n.* in discourse or text, features which link component parts, as back reference of pronouns to nouns, or the degree to which the parts of the discourse or text are related.

cohesiveness in text the links or ties that connect text elements to provide unity and clarity, either within or between sentences, and contribute to the reader's impression of text coherence. *Cp.* **coherence of text**.

coinage *or* **coined word** *n.* a word deliberately created for a particular purpose, as *Kodak*.

collaborator (kə lab′ə rā″tər) *n.* a person who joins with one or more associates in producing a work. *The artist and the research assistant were collaborators with the author in a new history of the Aztecs. v.* **collaborate.**

collateral reading reading(s) in addition to and supplementing the basic text(s) for a unit or a course. *Collateral reading in a history course may include the poetry and fiction of the period.*

collation (ko lā′shən, kə-, kō-) *n.* the part of the library catalog entry which describes the physical properties of the book, such as number of pages, size, type of illustrations, etc. *v.* **collate.**

collective noun a noun that refers to a group of persons or things but is singular in form, as *herd, jury, clergy.*

collocation (kol″ə kā′shən) *n.* the habitual occurrence of two or more words with each other in a given language. *In English, 'green,' 'white,' and 'red' are frequently in collocation with 'grass,' 'snow,' and 'roses,' respectively. adj.* **collocable.** *v.* **collocate**.

colloquial (kə lō′kwē əl) 1. *adj.* referring to a language expression or style of use that is appropriate in informal situations but inappropriate in formal ones. *Most dictionaries are written in a formal rather than in a colloquial style.* 2. *adj.* referring to a language expression or style that is old-fashioned or folk-like, as *Will Rogers' colloquial speech. n.* **colloquialism.**

colon (kō′lən) 1. *n.* a punctuation mark (:) used to separate the main part of a sentence from an explanation, example, quotation, list, etc., and after the salutation of a formal letter. 2. *n.* the graphic mark used to separate parts of certain numerical expressions such as time, ratio, or journal number information, as in 12:45 p.m. or Science 2:6. *Cp.* **semicolon; comma** (def. 1); **dash** (def. 1).

colophon (kol′ə fon″, -fən) 1. *n.* a statement at the end of a book giving information about its publication, such as the name of the printer or publisher, the place and date of publication, and often the name of the type style and the typographer. 2. *n.* the emblem of the printer or publisher.

color blindness any deviation from the normal in the perception of color. *Note: Color-blindness probably interferes very little with reading except in the first grade or two.... Color-blind children may have more difficulty interpreting the color pictures now so widely used in beginning reading materials* — A.I. Gates (1947). *Ct.* **color perception.**

color coding the use of color cues to indicate the relationship between specific letters or graphemes and the sounds they represent.

color perception the differentiation of light rays of varying wave lengths. *The cones of the retina are the receptors in color perception. Ct.* **color blindness.**

combinatorial reasoning (J. Piaget) that characteristic of formal operational thought which enables the individual to logically combine concepts in all possible combinations.

combined method a way of communicating used by the hard of hearing that combines speech with signing. *Ct.* **manual method; oralism** *or* **oral method.**

combining form a root with which other roots and/or affixes may be combined to form compounds or derivatives, as *-ego-*, a combining form indicating *self: egocentric, superego, egomania.*

comedy (kom′i dē) 1. *n.* a play, motion picture, or the written form of either, in which the author's intent is to amuse the audience or reader, and in which the ending is usually satisfactory for the chief characters. 2. *n.* a dramatic form of this nature. 3. *n.* the comic element, as in literature or life. See also **wit** (def. 1); **humor** (def. 1). 4. *n.* any comic incident. *Note:* Comedy exists in many forms and degrees, sometimes containing tragic aspects, and sometimes dealing with realistic social concerns that are treated in a light or satirical way.

comedy of manners drama which satirizes the manners and customs of a highly sophisticated society or social class, focusing especially on their amorous or immoral affairs. *Oscar Wilde's* Lady Windemere's Fan *is a comedy of manners.*

comic (kom′ik) 1. *adj.* characterized by comedy, as *a comic situation.* 2. *adj.* acting in or writing comedy, as *a comic writer.* 3. *n.* an actor in a comedy; comedian. 4. See **comics.** *adj.* **comical.**

comic book a long story in comic strip form, often with characters first introduced in comic strips, as Peanuts, Dennis the Menace, etc.

comic relief a brief humorous scene in an otherwise serious drama or novel which gives the audience relief from the emotional intensity of the situation. *Note:* A classic example of comic relief is the gravediggers' scene in *Hamlet.*

comics (kom′iks) *n. pl.* stories or incidents told largely through a series of pictures; comic strips; funnies. *Note:* Comics appear in newspapers, usually together on a page which carries eight or ten different stories with two or four pictures each, as Gasoline Alley, Dick Tracy, etc. In Sunday editions, the comic strip is expanded, in color, to a larger space, six to twelve pictures which occupy from one-fourth to a half page. Though the term suggests lightness and humor, many comics are not, but may deal with action and adventure (Steve Canyon), life's problems (Rex Morgan, M.D.), or politics (Doonesbury).

comic strip See **comics.**

comma (kom'ə) 1. *n.* a punctuation mark (,) used to separate two or more distinct but related ideas such as a series, as in *nuts, bolts, or screws,* or to enclose a word, phrase, or clause within a sentence, as *Mrs. Sawchuk, who's from Moosejaw, missed the snow. Cp.* **dash** (def. 1); **semicolon.** 2. *n.* a pause or breathing point in a line of poetry or song.

comma fault *or* **splice** the improper use of a comma between two independent clauses not connected by a conjunction, as *My dog came running, he was glad to see me.* See also **run-on sentences.**

commissural fibers the microscopic, threadlike nerve structures that connect the two sides of the central nervous system; association fibers. *Note:* The cerebral commissural fibers are part of the white matter of the cerebrum and are collectively known as the corpus callosum.

common noun a noun denoting a class or class member rather than a unique thing, as *hill, salt, people,* as opposed to *Paris, Abraham Lincoln, The Folies Bergère.*

common word a word form with the same or similar meaning in different contexts. *Common words, as 'like,' 'next,' 'hope' are the familiar words used in informal everyday communication. Ct.* **technical word.**

communality (kom″yo͞o nal'i tē) 1. *n.* that part of the variance of a single test that is shared with another test. 2. *n.* the sum or average of the communalities of single tests.

communication (kə myo͞o″nə kā'shən) 1. *n.* the sharing of information or ideas. 2. *n.* the process or results of conveying information. *Note* (def. 2): Communication may take place between social units such as persons or groups, between persons and mechanisms such as computers, or between such mechanisms. 3. *n.* transmission, or transmission and reception, of information by means of gestures, words, or other symbols, as *communication between persons and animals.* 4. *n.* information which has been, is being, or is to be transmitted, as the content of a telegram. 5. *n.* a dynamic interdependence or relationship between individuals. *She enjoyed close communication with her mother.* 6. **communications,** *a.* a branch of study relating to media production and use. *b.* a means used for conveying information, as the telephone. *v.* **communicate.** *adj.* **communicative.**

communication arts 1. aspects of the curriculum which emphasize verbal, nonverbal, and visual processes for conveying meaning. *The communication arts include radio, television, drama, and dance.* 2. language arts.

communication channel See **channel** (defs. 1, 3).

communication disorder a speech handicap or learning disability which interferes with the reception and/or expression of thoughts, ideas, etc.

communication(s) theory the study of all aspects of communication, especially those that reveal parallels in humans, animals, and machines. *Cp.* **information theory.**

communicative competence the ability to use language that is appropriate to the demands of social situations. *Note:* In a literate society, communicative competence also includes reading and writing ability.

community (kə myo͞o′ni tē) 1. *n.* a group of persons, often with similar cultural patterns, who live near each other. 2. *n.* a group of persons with similar interests, as *a community of writers, the reading community.*

Community Antenna TV (CATV) a form of closed circuit TV linked by cable to various locations, as homes and offices, in a community.

comparable form 1. any of two or more forms of a test that are similar in content, item difficulty, and test results; equivalent form; parallel form. 2. any of several successive levels of a test series.

comparative degree the form of an adjective or adverb that shows a greater or lesser degree in quality, quantity, or intensity in comparison to some other referent or quality. *Note:* In adjectives, the comparative degree is shown by the morpheme *-er*, as in *older*; or, in adverbs, by *more* or *less*, as in *more rapidly, less rapidly. Cp.* **positive degree; superlative degree.**

comparative reading the study of reading instruction in two or more countries to identify likenesses and differences, trends, and issues in the theory and practice of reading.

comparison (kəm par′i sən) 1. *n.* the change of an adjective or an adverb to show greater or lesser degree, as *sad, sadder, saddest, most sad, least sad.* 2. *n.* a literary technique of placing together like, or unlike, characters, situations, or ideas for emphasis or clarity. See also **contrast** (def. 3). *adj.* **comparative.** *v.* **compare.**

compendium (kəm pen′dē əm) *pl.* **-diums, -dia.** 1. *n.* a condensation or abridgment of a longer work. 2. *n.* a list or inventory.

compensation (kom″pən sā′shən) 1. *n.* any effort of an organism to restore a normal state of balance or equilibrium. 2. *n.* a psychological defense mechanism in which a person tries to offset a deficiency by emphasizing a substitute ability or trait, often with inappropriate results. *Boasting is a frequent compensation for feelings of insecurity.* 3. *n.* a process in which stimuli cancel or partially cancel each other; masking. *adj.* **compensatory.** *v.* **compensate.**

compensatory class *or* **education** a class or program for economically disadvantaged persons that provides needed experiences and skills for further educational development.

compensatory eye movements reflex adjustments of the eyes made to follow or hold a visual target steady in single binocular vision, accomplished by moving the eyes simultaneously in a direction along with or opposite to the target.

compensatory reading (*Brit.*) remedial reading.

competence (kom′pi tᵊns) 1. *n.* the ability to perform a given task adequately. 2. *n.* linguistic competence; specifically, in transformational-generative grammar, *the speaker-hearer's knowledge of his language* — N. Chomsky (1970). *Note* (def. 2): This knowledge, or competence, is not a collection of facts, but a system of processes which can create, or generate, an infinite number of new sentences. A grammar in such a theory is not a description of sentences produced by speakers but is a description of the generative processes by which any sentence can be produced for a given language. *Cp.* **performance** (def. 5). 3. *n.* legal responsibility for one's actions and affairs, meeting the minimum legal requirements for age, citizenship, mental ability, sanity, etc. *Ant.* (defs. 1, 3), **incompetence.** *adj.* **competent.** See also

communicative competence.

compilation (kom″pə lā′shən) *n.* a work consisting of material gathered from a variety of sources.

compiler (kəm pī′lər) *n.* a person who assembles, into a single book, selections from the works of various authors or from a single author, or produces a bibliography. *Cp.* **author** (def. 1); **editor** (def. 1). *v.* **compile.**

complement (*n.* kom′plə mənt; *v.* kom′ plə ment″) 1. *n.* the word(s) that complete(s) the predicate, or verb phrase, of a sentence, as *a policeman* in *Tom is a policeman. Note:* While an object, a predicate noun, or predicate adjective usually acts as a complement, the predicate may also be completed by an adverb, as *often* in *It happens often*, or by an infinitive phrase, as *to win* in *He likes to win.* 2. *v.* to so complete a grammatical construction.

complementarity (kom″plə men târ′i tē) *n.* the relationship between words whose meanings are mutually exclusive, as *single/married, father/mother.*

complementary distribution a condition in which two linguistic elements are mutually exclusive in a given context. *In English, the plural markers '-s' and '-en' attach to different sets of nouns and are in complementary distribution. Ct.* **free variation.**

complete predicate the verb in a syntactical construction along with all its modifiers, complements, and/or subordinate parts, as *is going home* in *Dale is going home.*

complete subject the principal noun along with all its modifiers that is in a construction with a verb and determines the number of the verb, as *five white-bearded men* in *Five white-bearded men dozed away. Cp.* **subject** (def. 3).

completion item a test item in which the omitted part(s) must be filled in. See also **cloze procedure** (def. 1).

complex sentence a sentence with one independent clause and one or more dependent clauses: *I knew* (independent clause) *when you came in* (dependent clause).

component (kəm pō′nənt) 1. *n.* a part of something else. *Reading models have several components.* 2. *adj.* serving as such a part.

composite score the sum or average of different measures, often weighted, of the same individual or object. *The regression equation is a means of combining different measures of the same object in order to derive a composite measure or score.*

composition (kom″pə zish′ən) 1. *n.* the process of putting parts together to form a unified whole, especially an artistic whole. *The composition of the mosaic required many small pieces.* 2. *n.* the result of such a process. 3. *n.* the way in which something is made or structured. *The composition of the cement was faulty.* 4. *n.* the process of putting words together according to an organized plan to form an effective and usually grammatical message or artistic work in speech or writing. *The four major forms of composition are argumentation, description, exposition, and narration. Cp.* **writing** (defs. 4, 6). 5. *n.* a short school essay. 6. *n.* the art of writing music. 7. *n.* a piece of music. 8. *n.* the setting up of type for printing. *v.* **compose.**

compound bilingualism the ability to use two languages, but with considerable reliance upon one's native language to determine word meaning and make semantic distinctions.

compound-complex sentence a compound sentence with one or more dependent clauses: *Teachers speak and students listen* (compound independent clauses) *when both are motivated* (dependent clause). *Cp.* **compound sentence.**

compound noun a group of two or more nouns treated as a unit, as *student teacher, blueprint, apartment house, flagpole.*

compound phonogram two or more letters that represent a phonic unit but do not make a word, as *gr, aw, ing.*

compound predicate a predicate consisting of two or more verb phrases, as *Charlie enjoys swimming daily and diving occasionally. Ct.* **simple predicate.**

compound sentence a sentence with two or more coordinate independent clauses but no dependent clause: *George walked,/ and Harry ran. Cp.* **compound-complex sentence.**

compound subject the complete subject, or noun phrase, formed by two or more simple subjects.

compound word a word formed by combining two or more words, as *bookstore, flyleaf, true-false,* etc.

comprehensibility (kom″pri hen″sə bil′i tē) *n.* the quality of written or oral language that makes it easy to understand. *Cp.* **readability** (def. 1). *adj.* **comprehensible.**

comprehension (kom″pri hen′s̱hən) 1. *n.* the process of getting the meaning of a communication, as in a personal letter, speech, sign language. 2. *n.* the knowledge or understanding that is the result of such a process. 3. See **reading comprehension.** 4. *n.* all that a word or concept implies; connotation; as *one's comprehension of equality. Ct.* **denotation.** 5. *n.* the direct, immediate awareness or apprehension of concrete objects, events, etc., as *sudden comprehension of the danger. Note:* This definition is more restrictive than defs. 1-4, especially with respect to the degree of meaning or understanding involved. *v.* **comprehend.**

comprehension processes any of the ways by which one acquires meaning.

comprehensive school a secondary school that includes courses of study in many areas, often with academic, technical, commercial, and trade curriculums. *Note:* The comprehensive school is the most common type of high school in the United States.

compressed speech a re-recorded audiotape in which very short portions, a few milliseconds in length, of the original signal have been randomly omitted so that the message sounds faster but not higher in pitch. *Note:* The number of omissions made per unit of time determines the amount of audio-tape compression. A mild amount of compression appears to improve listening comprehension. Time-compressed tapes are now widely used by the blind and are beginning to be used for the regular presentation of instructional materials in schools.

compulsion (kəm pul′s̱hən) *n.* a force or impulse that makes one behave contrary to one's desires.

compulsive (kəm pul′siv) 1. *adj.* overly task-oriented, especially toward details; perfectionistic. *Cp.* **impulsive.** 2. *n.* one so oriented. 3. *adj.* excessively concerned with morality, appearances, standards, rules, etc. 4. *n.* one so concerned. See also **obsessive-compulsive.**

compulsiveness (kəm pul′siv nis) *n.* the tendency to perform repeatedly an action that is neither overtly logical nor necessary. *Compulsiveness may become an irrational ritual which the individual cannot resist.*

computer (kəm pyo͞o′tər) *n.* a mechanical or electronic machine which can accept (input) data, process the data, and produce (output) the resulting data at very high speeds. *The computer* *must be guided in its operations by proper programming. v.* **computerize.**

computer-assisted instruction (CAI) 1. an automated program presented step-by-step by a computer with responses from the learner indicated as correct or not and with options for the learner to follow. 2. a computer program which gives individualized lessons, tests, periodic reports, etc.

computer-based instruction teaching/learning activities which use a computer.

computer printout the report, or output, of a computer, usually printed on one continuous sheet of paper.

computer program a set of specific operational instructions fed into a computer to solve a problem, process data, etc. *A computer output is no better than the computer program: 'junk in',...'junk out'.*

computer tape a magnetic tape for computer use.

computer terminal 1. a unit which can send data to, or receive data from, a computer. 2. a control unit in a computer system to which one or more sending/receiving devices can be connected.

concatenation (kon kat″ᵊnā′s̲hən) *n.* the linking of syntactic elements in a sequence to form phrases, clauses, or, in transformational-generative grammar, strings.

concave lens a lens which spreads out light waves. *Syn.* **minus lens.** *Ant.* **convex lens.** See illustration under **lens.**

conceit (kən sēt′) 1. *n.* a fanciful and often witty notion or idea, especially in poetic images: *And the sabbath rang slowly/in the pebbles of the holy stream* — D. Thomas. 2. *n.* a far-fetched, over-elaborate metaphor: *Our eyebeams twisted, and did thread/Our eyes upon one double string* — J. Donne. 3. *n.* a too great opinion of oneself, as *full of conceit. adj.* **conceited.**

concentric method *or* **curriculum** (*Brit.*) See **spiral curriculum.**

concept (kon′sept) 1. *n.* an abstract idea; general meaning; specifically, the result of identifying and abstracting a distinguishing quality or characteristic from sensory and/or ideational data and of generalizing its application to several other examples and/or classes of data. *A concept is not an isolated, ossified, changeless formation but an active part of the intellectual process, constantly engaged in serving communication, understanding, and problem-solving* — L. Vygotsky (1962). *Note:* Concepts tend to develop slowly and often remain incomplete. For example, the concepts of *redness* or *justice* develop only after much experience with their referents. After many years of professional discussion, the concept of *dyslexia* still remains a fuzzy theoretical construct. 2. *n.* a generalized idea derived from all the objects or events in a class and applicable to all members of the class; abstract concept; as intelligence in primates. 3. *n.* a characteristic applicable to a specific object or event; concrete concept; as the dog's falsetto bark. 4. *n.* in popular usage, any thought, idea, or notion. See also **meaning** (def. 10). *Note:* Words, symbols, and signs are often used to refer to concepts; but they are not the concepts, they merely represent the concepts. *adj.* **conceptual.** *v.* **conceptualize.**

concept attainment the development and acquisition of a given level of understanding of a concept, especially as a result of intensive intentional thinking. *Cp.* **concept formation.**

concept book a book in which examples and comparisons are used to present an abstract idea or ideas in concrete and understandable ways.

concept burden See **concept load** *or* **density**.

concept formation the process of, or stages in, the development and acquisition of understanding of an abstract idea; a cognitive system for integrating and organizing information based on common relationships. *Cp.* **concept attainment**.

concept load *or* **density** 1. the proportion of different ideas in relation to text length; proposition density. 2. a factor incorporated into some early readability estimates, as the number of abstract words, the degree of abstractness of the words or ideas presented, or the proportion of items of information to the length of the passage. *Cp.* **vocabulary burden** *or* **load.**

conceptual (kən sep′ch͟o͞o əl) *adj.* having to do with abstract ideas or theoretical constructs.

conceptual frame *or* **framework** a theoretical scheme or pattern of ideas used to form hypotheses, models, etc. *Language acquisition theory provides one conceptual frame for beginning reading instruction.*

conceptualize (kən sep′ch͟o͞o ə līz) *v.* to form a concept of something; think at an abstract level; as *conceptualize a strategy of war. n.* **conceptualization.**

conceptual learning the acquisition of new concepts or the alteration of old concepts.

conceptually-driven See **top-down processing.**

conceptual model a simplified representation of abstract ideas, relationships, etc., presented in a concrete way, as in a diagram, flow chart, or physical display.

conclusion (kən klo͞o′zh͟ən) 1. *n.* outcome; result. 2. *n.* a judgment inferred or deduced from evidence; inference. *The ability to draw conclusions is sometimes given as an objective in reading instuction. Note:* Not all inferences are conclusions. 3. *n.* the final part of anything; end; as the closing statement in a composition or speech. 4. **in conclusion**, finally. *v.* **conclude.** *adj.* **conclusive.**

concord (kon′kôrd, koŋ′-) *n.* the grammatical correspondence, or agreement, of two or more items in a sentence or proposition; especially, the agreement in number, gender, and person between a subject and a predicate.

concordance (kon kôr′dᵊns, kən-) *n.* an alphabetical list of words in the Bible or other works giving the location in the text and usually some part of the context.

concrete (kon′krēt, koŋ′-, kon krēt′) 1. *adj.* not abstract. *This book is concrete; literature is abstract.* 2. *adj.* actual; real; not hypothetical; as in breaking a window. 3. *n.* a term with an actual or existing referent. *This definition is a concrete. v.* **concretize.**

concrete noun a noun with a material referent, as *house, coat, book. Ct.* **abstract noun.**

concrete operations (J. Piaget) the first organized system of logical thought in mental development, usually from about 7-11 years, that is dependent upon direct interaction with the real, concrete world. *The child who can develop a hierarchy of classes of objects that he can see, but cannot do so for absent objects, is using concrete operations. Note:* Concrete operations are characterized by reversibility, as in conservation, and other groupings. *Ct.* **formal operations.** See also **operations; pre-operational thought; infralogical operations.**

concrete poetry poetry in which graphic physical arrangements of words, rather than standard poetic forms, are used to help suggest the author's meaning or theme. *Note:* Dylan Thomas and e.e. cummings have written modern concrete poetry, although this type of poetry goes back to ancient times. George Herbert's 'The Altar' composed in the shape of an altar, is a 17th century example of concrete poetry in English.

concrete thinking a form of thinking found in some brain-injured persons that is characterized by such symptoms as inability to shift mental set, form gestalts, plan for the future, etc. *Cp.* **abstract reasoning** *or* **thinking**.

concrete word 1. a word with a specific, material referent. *Bicycle is a concrete word.* 2. a word that refers to something which can be experienced through the senses, directly or through imagery, as raw silk, soft as silk, etc. *Ct.* **abstract word**.

concretism (kon′krēt″izəm) 1. *n.* the theory and practice of concrete poetry. 2. *n.* using specific examples of things and experiences in real life to illustrate abstract concepts and qualities.

concurrent validity evidence of validity gained by correlating test scores with performance at approximately the same time on some external criterion, as correlating test scores with cumulative grade point average for the same students. See also **validity** (def. 3).

conditional clause a clause that expresses a condition, or supposition, usually introduced by the word *if,* as *If I were king,* . . . .

conditioning (kən dish′ə ning) *n.* the process, or result, of linking a stimulus with a response originally caused by a different stimulus, as in classical, instrumental, and operant conditioning.

conduction deafness a hearing loss which occurs when sound is hindered in transmission through the outer and/or middle ear. *Ct.* **sensorineural deafness**.

cone of experience *a pictorial device [or]...visual analogy...set up to show the progression of learning experiences from direct, firsthand participation to pictorial representation and on to purely abstract, symbolic expression*—E. Dale (1969).

cones (kōnz) *n. pl.* light-sensitive cells in the retina which are needed especially for color vision and for fine visual discrimination. *Cp* **rods**.

confidence interval the limits in a sample distribution between which the population value is expected to lie with a particular degree of confidence; specifically, the distance in standard deviation units from the mean that determines such limits.

confidence level the percentage of times that a sample would be expected to fall by chance outside the confidence interval; risk level. *At the .05 confidence level, only five percent of the time would a person's true score fall outside the confidence interval.*

configuration clue the use of an identifiable shape or outline of a word as an aid to word identification, especially the pattern the letters make above and below the x-height of the word, as jolly, general, reading.

confirmation (kon″fər mā′shən) 1. *n.* in reading or listening, the verification of predictions by later information about a writer or speaker's meaning or use of language. *Ct.* **disconfirmation**. 2. *n.* in linguistics, the use of a tag question to imply verification of the preceding statement, as *wasn't he* in *The weatherman was wrong again,* *wasn't he?* See **tag question.**

conflict (*n.* kon′flikt; *v.* kən flikt′) 1. *n.* opposing forces in a drama, a novel, or a short story which create interest in the plot and characters. *Note:* The hero or protagonist may oppose other characters, nature, society, some element within himself, or a combination of these forces. 2. *n.* a physical struggle between opposing forces, as *a conflict in war.* 3. *n.* a struggle between opposing ideas or desires, or between incompatible responses to impulses, as *a conflict of theories, a conflict of wills, mental conflict.* 4.*v.* to oppose.

confusion (kən fyo͞o′zhən) 1. *n.* the failure to make accurate discriminations; especially, such failure in the language activities of reading and listening and in the recall of verbal material. *In reading, failure to follow directions, reversals, or a semantic problem are evidences of confusion.* 2. *n.* mental or emotional discomfort great enough to interfere with learning or other normal functions. 3. *n.* temporary or chronic disorientation in time, place, or consciousness of self. *n.* **confusability**; *v.* **confuse.**

congenital (kən jen′i tᵊl) *adj.* present at birth. *Note:* The term 'congenital' does not imply hereditary or other causation. *Cp.* **innate** (def. 1).

congenital alexia See **dyslexia** (def. 1). *Note: Congenital alexia is an incorrect term, because it has never been shown that children (other than severely subnormal) are congenitally incapable of learning to read*— M. Vernon (1978).

congenital word blindness See **dyslexia** (def. 1).

conjoin (kən join′) *v.* to connect two or more parallel syntactic units with coordinating conjunctions to form compound predicates, etc.

conjugation (kon″jə gā′shən) 1. *n.* the inflection of verbs; specifically, a set of all possible inflected forms of a verb as *sing, sings, singing, sang, sung* for the verb *sing.* 2. *n.* a class of verbs with the same inflection markers. See also **paradigm** (def. 2). *v.* **conjugate.**

conjunction (kən jungk′shən) 1. *n.* a word used to connect words, phrases, clauses, or sentences; connective; as *and* in *she and I* or *When* in *When you are ready, we will go. Note:* A *coordinating conjunction* connects two equivalent grammatical elements. When they are used in pairs, as *either... or*, they are called *correlative conjunctions.* A *subordinating conjunction* introduces a dependent clause, connecting it to an independent clause. 2. *n.* the process, or result, of so connecting. See also **conjoin.**

conjunctive (kən jungk′tiv) 1. *adj.* related; linked; as *a conjunctive array of stimuli. Ct.* **disjunctive** (def. 1). 2. See **conjunction** (def. 1).

conjunctive adverb an adverb, as *however, nonetheless, therefore,* used to introduce or connect clauses.

conjunctive thought a form of logical thinking in which logical relations are identified, as the member of a class, a sequence, etc. *Cp.* **disjunctive thought; relational thought.**

connective (kə nek′tiv) See **conjunction** (def. 1).

connotation (kon″ə tā′shən) *n.* an implied, suggested, non-literal meaning of a word or group of words. *The term 'comprehension' has many connotations. Ct.* **denotation**; **cognitive meaning**. *adj.* **connotative**. *v.* **connote.**

consecutive interpretation the rendition, in another language, of a speaker's message in long segments, as one or more sentences, paragraphs, idea units. *Note:* The interpreter may take brief notes if the segment is especially long; then, when the speaker halts, orally summarizes what has been said as accurately as possible. *Cp.* **simultaneous interpretation**.

conservation (kon″sər vā′s̲h̲ən) *n.* (J. Piaget) the logical thinking ability to keep an invariant property of something in mind under changing perceptual conditions. *Ant.* **non-conservation**. *Note:* Piaget conducted several famous experiments in conservation, as by distorting the shape of a plasticine ball or by pouring the same quantity of water into markedly different-shaped containers and asking children in each case whether the quantity was the same or different.

consonance (kon′sə nəns) 1. *n.* the repetition of the final consonant sound in words which do not use the same vowel; consonant rhyme; as *ham-hum*. *Cp.* **assonance**. 2. *n.* agreement or unity. 3. *n.* a blending of harmonious musical sounds. *Ant.* **dissonance.**

consonant (kon′sə nənt) 1. *n.* a speech sound made when one or more of the articulators constricts, stops, diverts, or obstructs the air flow. *Note:* This modification of the air flow distinguishes consonants from vowels physiologically. Consonants may also be classified by the way in which they are formed, as *fricative,* and by the articulators involved, as *bilabial.* Such distinctions are given under the describing term. 2. *n.* any speech sound in a syllable which is not the sound of greatest loudness and/or resonance, as the *t* and *d* of Ted. *Note:* This contrast of the sound value distinguishes consonants from vowels phonetically. 3. *n.* a letter representing any of these sounds. *adj.* **consonantal.**

consonantal (kon″sə nan′tᵊl) 1. *adj.* having to do with one of the distinctive features used to differentiate one phoneme from another; specifically, that the air flow include a stoppage or constriction. 2. *adj.* having to do with the graphic signs in a writing system, such as the Arabic alphabet, which does not have distinctive letters or graphemes for vowels.

consonant blend See **consonant cluster**.

consonant cluster a sequence in a syllable of two or more distinguishable consonant sounds before or after a vowel sound, as /skr/ and /mz/ in *screams;* in teaching practice, often called *consonant blend. Note:* Consonant cluster in this sense refers only to sounds, not to letters representing sounds. *Cp.* **blend** (def. 2).

consonant digraph a combination of consonant letters representing a single speech sound, as *gn* for /n/ in *gnat*, or *gh* for /f/ in *rough. Ct.* **blend** (def. 2).

consonant letter an alphabet letter used singly or with other such letters to represent a consonant sound, as *t* in *t*ea or *s* in *sea. Ct.* **vowel letter**. See also **consonant** (def. 3).

consonant substitution a word identification technique in which a known consonant sound, primarily in the initial or final position, is combined with a known word part, or phonogram, to arrive at the pronunciation of unknown words. *If a student knows the phonogram 'ole' as in 'hole' and 'pole,' and has now learned the initial sounds /r/ and /m/, consonant substitution will help the student identify the new words 'role' and 'mole.'*

consonant-vowel-consonant sequence (CVC) a pattern of sounds that represents one of the most common sequences of sounds in the syllables of English words, as /sak/ in *sack*.

constancy of the IQ the degree to which an individual's IQ changes on repeated testing with the same or similar test over a substantial time span. *The concept of constancy of the IQ does not imply that intelligence is or should remain the same.*

constancy, perceptual See **perceptual constancy**.

constant error a consistent error in one direction. *The subject, experimenter, or treatment, singly or together, may cause a constant error.* See also **error.**

constituent (kən stich′o͞o ənt) *n.* a member of a linguistic construction. *A noun is a constituent of a noun phrase. Cp.* **immediate constituent**.

constraint (kən strānt′) *n.* a restriction or limitation placed on language production or use. *Black English has a constraint against forms of the type 'I don't have any,' rejecting this for 'I don't have none.'* See also **contextual constraint.** *v.* **constrain.**

construction (kən struk′shən) 1. *n.* arrangement of two or more forms that make up a grammatical unit, as morphemes, constituent words, or word phrases, constituent clauses, etc. *Note: Cookhouse* is a construction of the morphemes *'cook'* and *'house;' 'The cat ate the rat'* is a construction of a subject and a predicate. 2. *n.* a group of words or morphemes governed by a grammatical rule. *v.* **construct**; *adj.* **constructive**.

constructive cue system 1. in reading, significant linguistic data that a reader can use in creating meaning from text. 2. in speaking, acoustic and articulatory information that is used in creating meaning from speech.

construct validity evidence of validity gained by showing the relationship(s) between a theoretical construct, as anxiety, and a test which proposes to measure the construct. *The greater the evidence of the relationship(s), the greater the construct validity of the test.* See also **validity.**

consultative speech *or* **style** the informal style of discourse commonly used when speaking to strangers or others who do not have the background of shared experiences required for casual speech. *Telephone business conversations would be meaningless without the listener feedback provided in consultative speech* — M. Joos (1962).

consumable material teaching and testing material that is meant to be used and discarded, as most reading workbooks, rather than saved and used again.

contemporary literature *or* **fiction** 1. literature of the present time or period; modern literature. *Note:* This use of the term 'contemporary' is an elastic one, subject to revision from time to time. A current authority defines it as literature since the beginning of the first World War in 1914. 2. imaginative writing in which the author deals with his own time rather than with some earlier period. Uncle Tom's Cabin *is an example of contemporary fiction, but* Ivanhoe *is not* — E. Horn (1937).

content (kon′tent) 1. *n.* the ideas or subject matter found in a communication source, especially printed or written, as *editorial content, the content of a book.* 2. **contents**, the major headings of a printed source, as *the table of contents of a book.* 3. *n.* significance. *The play was supposedly serious but lacked any real content.* 4. *n.* the substance or subject matter of cognition as distinguished from its form. *Content includes all the essential qualities of a given conception.*

content analysis the analysis of the expressed and hidden meaning of a communication to find out its purpose and judge its potential effects. *Content analysis has been widely used to study most aspects of newspapers and to discover the amount of sexism and racism in reading textbooks.*

content area *or* **field** an organized body of knowledge, or discipline, that is reflected in its technical vocabulary, as mathematics, social studies, literature, science. *Note:* Reading, an instrumental or tool subject which cuts across all content fields, is ordinarily not considered a content field.

contentive (kən ten′tiv) See **content word.**

content reading reading in subject-matter areas as history, science, mathematics, etc., usually for study purposes.

content-referenced measurement measurement with items that are selected from specifics in a content domain, often a set of specific behaviors. *Note:* Most tests which have good content validity represent content-referenced measurements.

contents, table of See **table of contents.**

content validity evidence of validity gained by showing that the test content is representative of a specified behavior domain. *Cp.* **curriculum validity.**

content word a word having lexical meaning, as *cat, duty, house. Ct.* **function word.**

context (kon′tekst) 1. *n.* the sounds, words, or phrases that surround a spoken or written language unit, often influencing its meaning and effect; linguistic environment. See also **context (-ual) clue.** 2. *n.* the set of circumstances that surround a spoken or written message and form a framework for its interpretation; broader context. *Note:* The broader context may involve any one or a combination of social, emotional, intellectual, or physical factors. For example, one must understand the broader context of Athenian democracy to understand how it differed from American democracy. See also **pragmatics** (def. 1). 3. *n.* the psychological processes that are related to and give meaning to a given mental process, thus making the significance of a given mental event theoretically dependent upon its context. 4. the social or cultural situation in which a spoken or written message occurs. *adj.* **contextual.**

context-bound *or* **-sensitive** *adj.* referring to the dependence of the content of phrases or phrase elements upon the surrounding context, such that rewrite rules in phrase structure grammar must be adjusted. *Ct.* **context-free.**

context (-ual) clue an item of information from the immediate setting in which a word or group of words occurs, as surrounding words, phrases, sentences, illustrations, syntax, typography, etc., that might be used to help determine the meaning and/or pronunciation of the word or word group in question: *'Happy __________,' the children sang, as the cake with lighted candles was brought in.*

context-free *adj.* referring to the independence of phrases or phrase elements from the surrounding context, such that rewrite rules in phrase structure grammar can be freely applied. *Ct.* **context-bound** *or* **-sensitive.**

contextual analysis 1. the search for the meaning of an unknown word through an examination of the surrounding context. 2. the study of the context to determine as exactly as possible what the author means. *Contextual analysis is a major concern in literary criticism.* 3. the use of a larger linguistic unit to determine the meaning of a smaller unit.

contextual constraint any limitation on the nature and amount of information available in a communication for processing in reading or listening; textual constraint. *Note:* Redundancy is a common type of contextual constraint. In propaganda and other forms of persuasive communication, the use of contextual constraint is a deliberate attempt to achieve the author's purpose. See also **constraint.**

contingency table a classification table with different categories on each of the two axes, forming cells into which numbers may be entered to show frequency of occurrence. *Note:* Such a table might show how many boys and girls are either slow, average, or fast readers.

continuant (kən tin′yo͞o ənt) *n.* a speech sound produced as a continuous, uninterrupted air flow, as vowels and some consonants in English. *Ct.* **stop** (def. 2).

continuation school a public adult education school in the United States for working people who may take general education and/or vocational courses on a part-time basis.

continuous progress plan a curriculum plan in which students advance at their own rate of achievement rather than at a rate set by age or grade standards.

contoid (kon′toid) *n.* a phonetic term for a consonant sound. *Note: Cp.* **consonant** (defs. 1, 2) which is a phonological term for the consonant phonemes and written letters of a language.

contraction (kən trak′s̱hən) 1. *n.* the process of becoming smaller, tighter, shorter, etc., or the resulting condition. *A synopsis is a contraction of a longer literary work.* 2. *n.* the shortening and thickening of a muscle under tension. 3. *n.* the shortening of a written or spoken expression by the omission of one or more letters or sounds, as *can't* for *cannot. Cp.* **abbreviation.** See also **aphesis; apocope; syncope** (defs. 1, 2). 4. *n.* a Braille sign representing a word or part of a word. *v.* **contract.** *adj.* **contractive.**

contralateral (kon″trə lat′ər əl) *adj.* referring to a different side of the body; especially, when a motor or sensory disorder occurs on the side of the body opposite to the source of the nerve damage causing the disorder. *Ct.* **ipsilateral.**

contrast (*n.* kon′trast; *v.* kən trast′) 1. *n.* a difference or degree of difference. *Contrasts in form are distinctive features of letters.* 2. *v.* to note differences in. *Contrast the settings of* Anna Karenina *and* Fathers and Sons. 3. *n.* a literary technique for placing together unlike ideas, situations, or characters for emphasis or clarity. See also **comparison** (def. 2). 4. *n.* the art of using this technique.

control group in experimental design, a comparison group of subjects that is as like the experimental group as possible and receives the same treatment conditions save that of the experimental variable.

controlled reading reading done under any of a wide variety of conditions designed to guide eye-movements, fixations, and/or rate of reading, as in the use of a reading pacer.

controlled vocabulary 1. See **vocabulary control.** 2. See also **simplified vocabulary.**

controlling eye 1. the eye which seems to control binocular visual perception. *Cp.* **sighting eye.** 2. the eye which usually fixates in alternating vision or strabismus; dominant eye (def. 3).

convention (kən ven′shən) 1. *n.* common usage in a language. 2. *n.* an accepted way of creating an effect, as the soliloquy in the theater, flashback in fiction, foreshortening in painting, etc. 3. *n.* one of a set of rules for the behavior of a group; custom. *adj.* **conventional.**

convergence (kən vûr′jəns) 1. *n.* a coming together of ideas, objects, events, behaviors, etc., so as to focus on one thing or to produce a common result, as *the convergence of medical and educational research on mental retardation.* 2. *n.* the bending of light rays to a focus as they pass through the crystalline lens of the eye or through any convex, or plus, lens. 3. *n.* the turning in of the lines of sight by both eyes from far to near points so that, together with accommodation, images of nearby objects fall on corresponding parts of the foveal areas of the retinas to permit binocular fusion. *Cp.* **accommodation** (def. 3). 4. *n.* the innervation of a single cell by synaptic junctions from more than one nerve cell. *Ant.* **divergence.** *adj.* **convergent.** *v.* **converge.**

convergence, accommodative See **accommodative convergence.**

convergent squint *or* **strabismus** crossed eyes; specifically, a form of strabismus in which the line of sight of the deviant eye crosses in front of that of the fixating or controlling eye; inturning. *Syn.* **esotropia.** *Ant.* **divergent squint** *or* **strabismus.**

convergent thinking the ability to analyze and integrate in order to infer reasonable conclusions or specific solutions from given information. *Multiple-choice tests require convergent thinking.* *Ct.* **divergent thinking.**

convergent validity a type of construct validation; specifically, the process, or result, of finding that two or more indicators thought to assess the same variable correlate with each other. *Ct.* **discriminant validity.**

conversational analysis the study of the contextual and social dimensions of knowledge as revealed in conversation. *Note:* The assumption is made in conversational analysis that natural conversations are frequently incomplete or ambiguous; therefore, they are understandable only in relation to the social situation in which they occur. See also **discourse** (defs. 1, 3); **discourse analysis; context** (def. 4).

conversion (kən vûr′zhən, -shən) See **functional shift.**

conversion reaction the appearance of a physical symptom, such as paralysis or anesthesia, as a result of psychic conflict.

conversion table a table for changing one set of scores or values into another set, as for changing raw scores into standard scores.

converted hand dominance preference for the hand other than that originally preferred, usually a shift in preference from left-handedness to right-handedness.

converted score See **derived score.**

convex lens a lens which causes light waves to come together. *Syn.* **plus lens.** *Ant.* **concave lens.** See illustration under **lens.**

co-occurrence (kō″ə kûr′əns, -ə kur′-) *n.* the relationship needed or allowed between different word forms that make a sentence, as, for example, the noun/verb relationship in subject/predicate, the article/noun relationship, etc. *adj.* **co-occurrent.** *v.* **co-occur.**

cooperating center any of the several

agencies offering specialized services and facilities for an adult education program, as churches, museums, libraries, etc.

coordinate bilingualism the ability to use two language systems independently, with or without reference to each other.

coordinate clause any of two or more independent clauses joined by a conjunction.

coordination (kō ôr″dᵊ nā′shən) 1. *n.* the smooth neuromuscular integration and sequencing of parts of the body to produce an action. *Ballet dancing requires superior coordination.* 2. *n.* a harmonious working together of functions or parts, as *team coordination.* 3. *n.* a proper order or relationship. *Military plans require coordination.* 4. *n.* the linking of words by use of coordinating conjunctions, as *You* and *I* in the phrase. *You and I.* *v.* **coordinate.**

coping behavior an action or action pattern that allows one to 'get along'; problem-solving or adaptive behavior. See also **adjustment** (def. 1); **accommodation** (def. 1).

copula (kop′yə lə) See **linking verb.**

copying (kop′ē ing) 1. *n.* loosely, any act of reproducing or duplicating something. 2. *n.* technically, the reproduction of original text and/or illustrative material by writing or drawing without photography and without the use of a mimeograph or ditto stencil.

copyright (kop′ē rīt″) 1. *n.* exclusive legal right to publish and control the reproduction and sale of a literary, musical, or artistic work for a certain number of years. *When a copyright has expired, the work is said to be in the public domain.* 2. *v.* to so publish and control.

copyright page the reverse, or verso, of the title page where copyright information usually appears. *The copyright page may also include other information, as the edition, cataloging particulars, etc.*

core curriculum 1. the school subjects which all students must study regardless of other subjects taken. 2. in the United States, a particular subject matter, as social studies, to which other subjects are related. *Cp.* **correlated curriculum.**

core vocabulary the words and meanings needed to understand a special field, textbook, topic, etc.

cornea (kôr′nē ə) *n.* the clear part of the outer layer of the eyeball in front of the iris and lens. See illustration under **eye.** *adj.* **corneal.**

corneal-reflection method a technique for studying eye movements by observing or photographing light reflected from the cornea. See also **eye-movement camera.**

corollary (kôr′ə ler″ē, kor′-) 1. *n.* something which may be reasonably deduced or inferred. *Her good grades were a corollary of good study habits.* 2. *n.* a natural result. *Art is a corollary of culture.* *adj.* **corollary.**

coronal (kə rōn′ᵊl, kôr′ə nᵊl, kor′-) *adj.* referring to sounds which are produced with the tongue tip close to or touching the alveolar ridge behind the front teeth. *Note:* In English, coronal consonants include /t/ and /ch/.

corpus (kôr′pəs) *pl.* **-pora** (pərə). *n.* a set of linguistic data that represent a sample of any type of linguistic material for a given language, normally presented in writing or on audiotape.

corpus callosum (kôr′pəs ka lō′səm) a bundle of nerve fibers which connects the cerebral hemispheres.

corpus striatum (kôr′pəs strī ā′təm) a striped mass of gray matter that is part of the basal ganglia at the base of the cerebral hemispheres.

correction (kə rek′shən) 1. *n.* any change which makes something wrong into something right, as *the correction of juvenile offenders through training programs, the correction of false rumors.* 2. *n.* a change intended to remove an error; revision; alteration. *Proofreader's marks tell the printer what corrections to make.* 3. *n.* the statistical handling of data by some accepted procedure to reduce distortions of design or the effects of random error. 4. *n.* a quantity used to correct data or to reduce error, as *a statistical correction.* 5. *n.* a visual prescription made by an eye specialist which tells the refractive characteristics of a lens or lenses needed to improve a patient's vision. *adj.* **corrective.** *v.* **correct.**

correction for chance *or* **guessing** in some objective tests, a scoring formula that varies with the number of choices and is used to recognize that some students answer many items when in doubt but that others do not. *The basic assumption is incorrect, and the formula does not truly 'correct for guessing'* — L. Cronbach (1970).

correction strategy the use of a reader's or speaker's knowledge of language and the context in which it is used to correct errors; self-correction. *Note:* A child may deviate from the text *The children became quiet* and read it *The children came quiet;* then, recognizing that *came quiet* is grammatically incorrect, self-correct it.

corrective reading supplemental, selective instruction for minor reading difficulties, often within a regular classroom by the regular teacher, an aide, or peer tutor. *Corrective reading instruction is more specific than developmental instruction, but less intensive than remedial reading instruction.*

correctness (kə rek′nis) *n.* language usage that meets an accepted standard; specifically, the degree to which language usage is acceptable in a sociolect or dialect. *Note:* Language usage that is correct and appropriate in a given dialect and/or social setting may not be considered correct in another dialect or setting. While grammarians have historically tended to judge one dialect of a language to be correct and others to be wrong, linguists often avoid such absolute value judgments.

correlate (kôr′ə lāt″, kor′-) 1. *v.* to connect or relate something to something else. 2. *v.* to show relationship between items or behaviors; specifically, to compute a correlation coefficient. 3. *v.* to be so connected or related. *The test results correlated as expected.* 4. *n.* something that is logically or empirically related to something else. *Verbal fluency is a correlate of intelligence.*

correlated curriculum a curriculum in which ideas, processes, skills, etc., common to different subjects are developed in each subject in relation to the others, as *a correlated curriculum in history, literature, and art. Cp.* **core curriculum.**

correlation (kôr″ə lā′shən, kor″-) 1. *n.* a mutual or interdependent relationship, as *a correlation between will to live and aging.* 2. *n.* a statistical procedure for analyzing the extent to which two or more variables tend to vary together and which yields a coefficient expressing the degree of relationship. *Note:* Special types of correlation, as *rank-order correlation,* are given under the describing term. 3. See **coefficient of correlation.** 4. See

correlated curriculum.

correlational research research designed to examine through the statistical process of correlation the extent to which two or more variables tend to vary together.

correlation coefficient See **coefficient of correlation.**

correlative (kə rel′ə tiv) 1. *n.* a pair of co-ordinating conjunctions, as *either/or.* 2. *adj.* referring to such a pair.

cortex (kôr′teks) *pl.* **cortices.** *n.* the outer layer of something, as of a body organ or structure; specifically, the outer layer of gray matter of the cerebellum and the cerebrum. *The cortex of the cerebrum is involved in perception, memory, logic, and language. adj.* **cortical.**

cortical blindness loss of sight from a cerebral lesion.

cortical deafness loss of hearing from a cerebral lesion.

cortical localization See **cerebral localization** (def. 1).

cost effectiveness the study of how much money and other resources it takes to get expected results; specifically, how much to reach the objectives of a given program, or how much to reach alternative or competing objectives. *A cost effectiveness study of two Right to Read programs producing equal results might show one to be more economical than the other.*

counter- a combining form indicating *against;* as **counteract, counter-argument.**

counting book a book in which pictures of objects are used to build the concept of numbers, one to ten.

count noun a noun that refers to things that can be counted, as *apple, table, book. Note:* In English, count nouns may be used with the indefinite article and in the plural, as *the book, some books. Ct.* **mass noun.**

couplet (kup′lit) *n.* a stanza of two lines which rhyme; especially, two rhyming lines of verse which have the same length: *The learn'd is happy nature to explore,/The fool is happy that he knows no more* — A. Pope.

covariance, analysis of See **analysis of covariance.**

covert (kuv′ərt, kō′vərt) *adj.* unobservable; concealed. *Most silent reading processes are covert. Ant.* **overt.**

cover test a test of the presence of oculomotor imbalance such as a phoria or strabismus. *Note:* The subject fixates a target with both eyes. The examiner interrupts fusion by covering first one and then the other eye. If the eye moves when uncovered to refixate the target, oculomotor imbalance is indicated.

CPM characters per minute.

cps, c.p.s. cycles per second, a measure of speed of vibration; Hertz (Hz); as in frequency of sound waves.

creative reading the process of gaining new insights in reading by identifying salient ideas, recombining them in novel ways, and relating them imaginatively to experience. *Creative reading emphasizes comparison and relationships, the recreation of known ideas into new combinations and patterns, and flexibility on the part of the reader* — H. Huus. *Ct.* **critical reading.**

creative thinking 1. thought processes characterized by unique powers of problem identification, hypothesis formation, and solution evaluation. 2. divergent thinking. See **creativity.**

creative writing writing that expresses the writer's thoughts and feelings imaginatively, often uniquely and poetically, primarily through relational patterns of language and thought. *Note:* Presumably, creative writing is guided more by the writer's need to express feelings and ideas in an idiosyncratic yet formal way than by the often restrictive demands of factual accuracy and the logical progression of ideas characteristic of expository writing. See also **poetic writing**. *Ct.* **exposition** (defs. 1, 2).

creativity (krē″ā tiv′i tē) *n.* inventiveness; originality; the development of a new thought or artistic effort. *Note:* To be of real interest to society, creativity needs to be new to all; but one may speak of creativity in an individual when the thought or artistic production is fresh and new to the individual. While creativity is based on divergent thinking, it needs the intellectual control of convergent thinking in evaluating the effectiveness of the divergent productions. See also **imagination.** *adj.* **creative.**

credential (kri den′shəl) 1. *n.* a statement, usually in the form of a license, used for evidence of certification. See also **certification** (def. 2). 2. **credentials**, evidence of authority, rights and privileges, etc., usually in writing. *The ambassador presented his credentials.*

creole (krē′ōl) 1. *n.* a pidgin language developed from two or more languages which eventually comes to be used as a native language. *Close social contact of different language groups often produces creole, or a creolized language. Cp.* **patois** (def. 2); **pidgin; lingua franca**. 2. *n.* (*Cap.*) a patois, principally French, spoken chiefly in parts of Louisiana and the West Indies, especially Haiti. 3. *n.* (*Cap.*) a person born in the West Indies or Latin America but of European, especially Spanish, ancestry. 4. *n.* a person of mixed Spanish and Negro, or French and Negro, ancestry. *adj.* **creole; Creole.** *v.* **creolize.**

cretinism (krēt′ənizʺəm) *n.* a congenital thyroid deficiency with severe retardation of both physical and mental growth; infantile hypothyroidism. *n.* **cretin.**

crisis (krī′sis) 1. *n.* the point of greatest conflict, as in drama or fiction; the turning point of the action; climax (def. 1). 2. *n.* the turning point in a serious disease, leading to recovery or death. 3. *n.* an unstable social condition requiring decisive action, as *the crisis of inflation.*

criterion (krī tēr′ē ən) *pl.* **-ria, -rions.** *n.* a level, degree, or standard used for evaluating something, as performance on a test, the student product of an activity, standard, etc.

criterion level the score which a person must make on a test to meet a predetermined standard of performance.

criterion-referenced measurement the assessment of performance on a test in terms of the kind of behavior expected of a person with a given score. *Ct.* **norm-referenced measurement.** *Note: During most of the history of psychological testing, test specialists have emphasized norms, but criterion reference and norm reference are both useful. The former tells what a person is able to do; the latter tells how he compares with others. The former is useful in judging him as an isolated individual; the latter in judging his ability to compete* — L. Cronbach (1970).

criterion score a specific performance score or score range on a measurement which is used to indicate a particular criterion level. *Note:* A criterion score can be used as a dependent variable in research.

critic (krit′ik) 1. *n.* one who judges and evaluates. 2. *n.* one who does this professionally, especially for literary or artistic works, as *a book critic, theater critic, TV critic.*

critical analysis a study of a literary or other artistic work according to certain principles of criticism.

critical evaluation 1. the process of arriving at a judgment of the worth of a selection by examining the extent to which its content, form, and style achieve the author's desired purpose; internal evaluation. 2. the process of judging the worth of a selection by comparing it to other selections that are similar in purpose and of known quality; external evaluation. 3. the judgment resulting from internal evaluation and/or external evaluation. See also **critical reading**.

critical exploration See **clinical method** (def. 3).

critical period a relatively short span of time in which the individual has the greatest readiness for some specific learning or type of learning. *Note:* The concept implies that if learning does not take place during this time, it will either not take place or be less effective. Research has neither substantiated nor disproved that such a period, extended by analogy from behavior in lower animals, exists in humans.

critical ratio (CR) a test of the level of significance of a particular statistic; specifically, a ratio of the statistic divided by its own standard error.

critical reading 1. the process of making judgments in reading: *evaluating relevancy and adequacy of what is read* — E. Betts, cited by N.B. Smith (1965). 2. an act of reading in which a questioning attitute, logical analysis, and inference are used to judge the worth of what is read according to an established standard. *Critical reading is the judgment of validity, or worth of what is read, based on sound criteria or standards developed through previous experiences* — H.M. Robinson (1970). *Note:* N.B. Smith (1965) has pointed out that Betts was the first to use the term 'critical reading,' so the term is of fairly recent origin. W.S. Gray, D. Russell, and others endorsed the critical function in reading because they believed that the thinking processes used in reacting to what was read formed a complete psychological unit; i.e., reading. In this way, critical reading came to be thought of as an extension of reading beyond the literal and interpretative levels. Although fragmentary descriptions of critical reading exist, the principal focus has been on the evaluative aspect of reading. Critical reading may involve internal and/or external critical evaluation. (See **critical evaluation**). Among the identified skills of critical reading involved in making judgments are those having to do with the author's intent or purpose; with the accuracy, logic, reliability, and authenticity of the writing; and with the literary forms, components, and devices identified through literary analysis.

critical score that point on a scaled distribution of scores that divides them for some useful purpose, as *a critical score for passing a test. Cp.* **cutting score.**

criticism (krit'i siz"əm) 1. *n.* the act of analyzing and judging a literary work, a dramatic performance, and other works of art. See also **literary criticism** (def. 1). 2. *n.* the act of making a severely negative judgment; finding fault. *Constant criticism cramps creativity.* 3. *n.* a critical reaction, orally or in writing; critique. *The students offered their criticisms of the poem.* 4. *n.* any of several methods for verifying, dating, and reconstructing texts. *Scholars use the tools of literary criticism to identify unsigned manuscripts. v.* **criticize.**

critique (kri tēk') 1. *n.* a critical review,

usually in essay form. 2. *n.* a critical comment made in passing judgment. 3. *v.* to review or analyze critically.

cross-age tutoring the instruction of a student on an individual basis by a knowledgeable student of another age group, usually older.

cross-cultural method the scientific study of what effects, if any, a particular environmental situation has upon persons in two or more cultures, as in a study of early formal reading instruction in the United States and England.

crossed dominance 1. motor preferences not confined to one side. 2. a theory which states that unless all of one's motor preferences are unilateral, as right-handed, right-eyed, and right-footed, neurological development is incomplete or immature. *Note:* Research has failed to support this reductionistic theory as a cause of reading failure. *Cp.* **cerebral dominance.**

cross-modal integration the association of information from two or more modalities, as visual-auditory-kinesthetic (VAK); intersensory integration.

cross reference a direction to consult another entry or heading, as a different or related term, variant spelling, etc.

cross-section (al) method a way of studying behavior or development by taking a large-scale, representative measure on one or more variables at one time. *Ct.* **longitudinal method.**

cross validation the application of a prediction formula or composite scoring rule developed in connection with one sample to another sample.

crypt (o)- a combining form indicating *hidden, concealed*; as in **cryptogram.**

cryptogram (krip′tə gram″) *n.* a message or passage written in a secret code; crypotograph.

cryptography (krip tog′rə fē) 1. *n.* the study of secret codes. 2. *n.* the creation and/or the breaking of a code. *n.* **cryptograph.** *adj.* **cryptographic.**

crystalline lens the convex lens near the front of the eyeball which brings light rays together to focus on or near the retina.

crystallized abilities abilities developed to a high degree through practice or instruction. *Ct.* **analytic abilities.**

c, soft the /s/ sound that the letter *c* represents in *cell, cymbal,* and *percent. The soft c usually precedes the letters e, i, and y in a syllable. Ct.* **c, hard.**

cue (kyo͞o) 1. *n.* a hint. 2. *n.* a distinctive signal to which one has learned to respond. *The sound of the bell was a cue for the students to change classes.* 3. *n.* any part of a perceptual pattern which helps one to discriminate or recognize that pattern. *In rapidly skimming familiar content, few cues are needed to provide meaning.* 4. *n.* a signal to begin an action or speech, or start again, especially in drama or music. 5. *v.* often **cue in**, to prompt in drama or music. 6. *n.* a direction in a written script, as *a lighting cue, a camera cue.*

cued speech an aural reeducation program which includes the use of lip reading and manual signing to distinguish between confusing mouth positions.

cue reduction a process by which the perception of fewer and fewer aspects of a stimulus field are needed to set off the learned response.

cultural determinism the belief that all aspects of human life, including one's personality, are shaped by one's culture.

culturally deprived *or* **disadvantaged** See **disadvantaged.** *Note: These terms seem to be used more or less synonymously to refer to children whose cultural environment appears to be less* *favorable to their cognitive development than that of middle-class white Americans, British* — M.A. Vernon (1978). *Cultural deprivation is an impossibility — unless we all agree that all people are culturally deprived in certain situations and at certain times* — Y.A. Goodman.

culture (kul′chər) 1. *n.* all behavior patterns and products of a social group which are passed on to others, often with symbolic meaning. *Language, cooking pots, and customs are all parts of culture.* 2. *n.* persons with common customs, values, etc., as *teenage culture.* 3. *n.* the development of intellectual and esthetic qualities to a higher degree, as *the culture of the Renaissance. adj.* **cultural.**

culture-fair test a test which attempts to use items as free as possible from specific cultural or class bias, such as language, customs, etc. *Note:* While the term 'culture-free' is sometimes used as a synonym for 'culture-fair', no test is completely free of cultural bias.

cumulative frequency curve *or* **distribution** a curve showing the summed number or percentage of scores or values falling at and below, or at and above, each plotted point. *The cumulative frequency curve is a flattened s-shape, or ogive.*

cumulative index an index issued periodically that combines at regular intervals new entries with those in earlier numbers.

cumulative school record an individual, chronological record of schooling, often including data on intellectual, socio-emotional, and physical development as well as on the educational development of a student. *The cumulative school record is kept throughout the student's school years.*

cumulative spelling spelling a word by syllables, adding each syllable cumulatively to the preceding syllable, as '...a-d *ad,* m-i *mi, admi,* r-a *ra, admira,* t-i-o-n *shun, admiration.*' (Barnard, 1863). *Cp.* **alphabet method** (def. 1).

cumulative tale a story with many details repeated again and again until the climax, as *The House that Jack Built.*

cuneiform (kyo͞o nē′ə fôrm″, kyo͞o′nē ə-) 1. *n.* a non-alphabetic writing system developed by the Sumerians, composed of wedge-shaped characters pressed into clay. 2. *n.* the cuneiform alphabet.

curricular (um) validity evidence of validity gained by showing that the test content is representative of the behavior domains of the curriculum. *Cp.* **content validity.**

curriculum (kə rik′yə ləm). *pl.* **-la, -lums. 1.** *n.* all the experiences sponsored by a school. 2. *n.* the total program of studies of a school. 3. *n.* a particular part of the program of studies of a school, as *the English curriculum, the reading curriculum. adj.* **curricular**.

curriculum guide a written plan describing the curriculum of a school or school system. *Note:* Curriculum guides vary in scope and detail, but usually give the philosophy, specific objectives, and ways of carrying out the program of studies.

curriculum laboratory an instructional materials center for teacher use; resource center.

cursive writing a type of handwriting in which all or most letters are joined together within each word. See illustration. *Ct.* **manuscript writing; print** (def. 7); **shorthand.**

This is cursive writing.

cursory reading quick reading of material which would give, at most, its general significance; skimming.

curvilinear (kûr″və lin′ē ər) *adj.* referring to forming, or being bounded by, a curved line. *Many variables reveal a curvilinear form when plotted on a graph.*

cutaneous sense the sense of touch, on or just below the skin, including the sensations of pressure, heat, pain, etc.

cutting score a score on an ordered series of test scores that divides subjects into different treatment groups. *The cutting score for passing the courses is 75. Cp.* **critical score.**

C-V-C a consonant-vowel-consonant sequence.

cybernetics (sī″bər net′iks) *n.* the study of communications and of the control of communication processes in people, in machines, and in the interactions between people and machines. *Note:* The term was coined by N. Weiner to refer to the regulation of behavior by messages. Feedback is the best-known form of message for controlling an ongoing process. See also **information theory.** *adj.* **cybernetic.**

cyclophoria (sī″klō fôr′ē ə) *n.* a turning of the eyes from a common line of sight because of eye muscle imbalance; imbalance, but in a rotational manner.

cylinder *or* **cylindric lens** a lens with more refractive power in one axis of the eye than another, used to correct astigmatism.

Cyrillic alphabet the alphabetic writing system used in Russian and in certain other Slavonic languages, based on old Greek letters and developed by Cyril, a Greek Christian missionary, in the 9th century A.D. for use among the Slavs of Central Europe.

D

DEVELOPMENT OF MAJUSCULE									
NORTH SEMITIC	GREEK		ETR.	LATIN		MODERN			
						GOTHIC	ITALIC	ROMAN	
Δ	Δ	Δ	ɑ	ɑ	D	𝔇	*D*	D	

DEVELOPMENT OF MINUSCULE					
ROMAN CURSIVE	ROMAN UNCIAL	CAROL. MIN.	MODERN		
			GOTHIC	ITALIC	ROMAN
ꝺ	ð	d	𝔡	*d*	d

The fourth letter of the English alphabet developed from North Semitic ***daleth*** and Greek ***delta***. The capital (D) corresponds generally to the North Semitic ***daleth*** and Greek ***delta*** (Δ), arriving at its present form in Latin. The minuscule (d) corresponds closely to the Greek ***delta*** (δ), acquiring its present form from the Roman cursive ***d***.

dactyl (dak′t[ə]l, -til) *n.* a metrical foot in verse which has three syllables: an accented syllable followed by two unaccented syllables: *This is the forest primeval, the murmuring pines and the hemlock* — H.W. Longfellow. *adj.* **dactylic.**

dactylology (dak″t[ə]lol′ə jē) See **finger spelling.**

daily (dā′lē) *n.* a serial publication issued every day, or every day except Sunday.

Dale-Chall readability formula a method of estimating the difficulty level of reading material developed by E. Dale and J. Chall that is based upon the percentage of words not on the *Dale List of 3,000 Familiar Words* and upon the average number of words in the sentences in 100-word samples of the material. *Note:* This method predicts 50 percent comprehension, with a table yielding corrected reading grade levels. A considerable number of modifications, extensions, and special uses of the formula have been suggested since its first publication in 1948, but the formula continues to be used primarily as originally published. *Cp.* **Flesch readability formula; Fry readability graph (scale); Spache readability formula.**

dame school up to early 19th century in Great Britain and the United States, an informal school in a woman's home. *Note:* The 'dame' would teach children, from the ages of three to six, their letters and the rudiments of reading. *Cp.* **reading school.**

damping effect the mechanical or electronic reduction of vibration amplitude. *Acoustic tile has a damping effect. v.* **damp; dampen.**

dangling modifier *or* **participle** a participle or participial phrase which, as it is placed, modifies the wrong object: *Dangling in midair, the volcano was viewed by the balloonist.*

dash (dash) 1. *n.* a. a punctuation mark (—), longer than a hyphen, indicating an omission, as *d_n* or *my friend M_;* b. a bond, as between proper names, the beginning and the end of a series such as *A-Z*, or a citation and its author; c. a break in the structure or train of thought of a sentence, paragraph, or letter, as *Followed — you mean from —? Note:* Interruptions or supplementary words may be enclosed in dashes, as in *After all — I say — we can't leave now!* 2. *n.* a straight stroke of a pen, as through or below a word. *Cp.* **hyphen; comma** (def. 1).

data (dā′tə, dat′ə, dä′tə) 1. *n.* (*pl. but often sing. in use*) a collection of facts, observations, scores, etc.; information. *Good decisions require good data.* 2. *adj.* referring to gathered information, as *data storage.*

databank (dā′tə bangk″, dat′ə-, dä′tə-) *n.* the store of information in a computer retrieval system that may be displayed on an electronic viewing screen.

data-driven See **bottom-up processing.**

data processing a series of systematic operations in collecting, producing, and analyzing data, especially by machine; information processing.

dative case 1. in English, the case of an indirect object of a verb, indicated by word order, or, in inflected languages, by a change in word form. *Note: Tom* is in the dative case in *Give Tom the book. Cp.* **indirect object**. 2. in case grammar, the case of that which is affected by a verb action or state, as *The kitten* in *The kitten was given away.*

datum (dā′təm, dat′əm, dä′təm) *n.* the little-used singular form of **data.**

dB decibel.

de- a prefix indicating *out of, from, without*; as **deductive, dependent, deformity.**

dead language a language which exists now only in historical records, and is no longer spoken, as Hittite, or is spoken only by language specialists and/or by participants in some ritualistic use of language, as Latin or Sanskrit by priests. *Ct.* **living language.**

dead metaphor a metaphor so common and habitual that it is no longer thought of as a metaphor, as *sitcom, hardware,* and *software* in educational media.

deaf (def) 1. *adj.* unable to hear. 2. *adj.* unwilling to listen, as *deaf to all requests.* 3. *n.* one who is unable to hear.

deaf-mute *or* **deaf mute** (def′myo͞ot″, -myo͞ot′) 1. *n.* a person who can neither hear nor speak. 2. *adj.* unable to hear or to speak.

deafness (def′nis) *n.* the inability to hear. *Deafness means a degree of hearing loss that causes communication problems, even with amplification. Note*: Special types of deafness, as *conduction deafness,* are given under the describing term.

Deanol (de′a nôl) *n.* a trade name for deanol acetamidobenzoate, a central nervous system stimulant. *Note:* Deanol was proposed for extending the attention span of some learning disabled children. However, side effects limit its general use.

decalage (dā′kə lAzh″) *n.* (J. Piaget) a time lag that occurs in the intellectual growth of a child: a. **horizontal décalage**, the time lag between a child's ability to apply a cognitive scheme or structure to one concept and the ability to apply it to another, as the ability to conserve mass before conserving weight. b. **vertical décalage**, the time lag between a simple and a complex intellectual task, as the difference in the ability of a child in the preoperational stage to find his way around a museum room and the later ability in the concrete operations stage to draw a map of the room.

decentration (dē″sen trā′shən) *n.* (J. Piaget) the ability to take account of several aspects of an object or event at the same time. *Ct.* **centration.**

decibel (dB) (des′ə bel″) *n.* the standard unit for measuring sound loudness or intensity in audiometric testing. *Note:* The decibel is used to express a logarithmic ratio of sound intensity, power, or pressure. Hearing loss is expressed in decibels to indicate the difference between expected normal hearing level and the intensity needed for the sound to be heard by the subject.

decile (des′il, -īl) *n.* the division of a distribution of scores into parts so that one tenth of the scores fall in each division. *A score in the sixth decile on a reading test is slightly above average. Cp.* **centile.**

decimal classification any classification scheme whose notation consists of numbers constructed and expanded by orders of ten, as *the Dewey decimal classification.*

declarative mood See **indicative mood.**

declarative sentence a sentence that makes a statement: *Tracey likes pizza.*

declension (di klen′shən) 1. *n.* the set of inflections of a noun, pronoun, or adjective, as *man, men, man's, men's* for the noun *man*; paradigm (def. 2). 2. *n.* a word class with the same inflection forms. *v.* **decline.**

decode (dē kōd′) 1. *v.* to change communication signals into messages; especially, to get the intended meaning from an analysis of the spoken or graphic symbols of a familiar language, as *decode a word in one's mother tongue. Note:* To learn to read, one must learn the conventional code in which something is written in order to decode the written message. In reading practice, the term is used primarily to refer to word identification rather than to higher units of meaning. We also speak of *decoding Morse code signals, decoding body language.* 2. *v.* to translate an unfamiliar code of symbols into a familiar one, as *decode a secret message.* See also **encode** (def. 1); **recode** (def. 1). *n.* **decoding.**

decussation (dē″kə sā′shən, dek″ə-) *n.* a crossing over of nerves or structures in an X form, as *the motor decussation in the medulla.* See also **optic chiasma.**

deduction (di duk′shən) 1. *n.* the process of logical reasoning from principles to specific instances. *Ct.* **induction** (def. 1). 2. *n.* a conclusion drawn or inferred from something known. *Sherlock Holmes is famous for his deductions from evidence. v.* **deduce.** *adj.* **deductive.**

deductive method a teaching-learning method in which a generalization or rule is first considered and then is applied to specific examples. *A phonics approach which states a phonics generalization followed by illustrative exercises is a deductive method. Ct.* **inductive method.**

deductive phonics See **analytic phonics.**

deductive reasoning See **deduction** (*def. 1*).

deep meaning See **deep structure.**

deep structure meaning; specifically, in transformational-generative grammar, the meaning to which a spoken or written sentence refers which may not be apparent from its surface structure until verified by sentence transformation. *Note:* While the surface structure of these two sentences is the same, the deep structure or meaning is different: *Mary invited Anne to come home. Mary ordered Anne to come home.*

defect (dē′fekt, di fekt′) 1. *n.* a fault in structure or function, as *a speech defect.* 2. *n.* a lack of something thought important. *Lou's only defect was lack of motivation. adj.* **defective.**

defense mechanism 1. a psychological strategy characteristically used to reduce or avoid anxiety, fear, or guilt. *Defense mechanisms, as withdrawal, rationalization, and sublimation, are many, varied, and used in different combinations.* 2. any action or response, as flight, aggression, or submission, used as protection from a physical or emotional threat. 3. in Freudian theory, any system used by the ego to suppress the id and occasionally the excessive demands of the superego.

deficit (def′i sit) *n.* a lack, usually in some aspect of development that interferes with learning, as *language deficit.*

deficit theory of language a proposed explanation of poor language development as lack of verbal stimulation leading to impaired cognitive development. *The deficit theory appears as the concept of 'verbal deprivation'*— W. Labov (1973).

definite article See **article** (def. 2).

definition (def″ə nish′ən) 1. *n.* a statement of meaning; a precise explanation or example of the meaning of a word or phrase. *A dictionary is a book of definitions.* See also **connotation; denotation.** 2. *n.* the clarity or distinctness of a sound or shape, as *tape-recorder definition, optical definition.* *v.* **define.** *adj.* **definitive.**

deformity (dif ôr′ mi tē) 1. *n.* anything that is distorted or flawed, as *a character deformity.* 2. *n.* an abnormally formed part of the body, as *a spinal deformity.* 3. *n.* anything that is made ugly. *Highway litter is a deformity of nature.* *v.* **deform.** *n.* **deformation.**

degree (de grē′) *n.* one of three forms of adverbs and adjectives that show difference in quality, quantity, or intensity. See **positive degree; comparative degree; superlative degree.**

degrees of freedom (df) the number of observations or statistical values that are free to vary; usually, the total number of values minus the fixed constraints. *Given a sample of readers and non-readers, there is only one degree of freedom beyond the category of readers — the category of non-readers.*

deictic (dīk′tik) 1. *adj.* pointing out. *The word 'this' is a deictic sign.* 2. *n.* a word which has a pointing or locating function, as the demonstrative words *this* or *that,* or the location words *here* or *there.* *n.* **deixis.**

delayed auditory feedback a slight delay in hearing one's own voice, experimentally controlled by a tape recorder, used to study speech problems and to test for functional hearing loss.

delayed recall the retelling of material some time after study, as required in most school tests. *Ct.* **immediate recall.**

delayed speech the later than normal acquisition of spoken language due to one or more developmental factors, as maturation, experience deprivation, psychological and/or physiological difficulties, etc.

deletion (di lē′shən) *n.* the omission of an expected word, phrase, sentence, etc., in speech or writing. *Note:* A deletion may be accidental, a part of systematic language change, or the result of censorship. *v.* **delete.**

delinquent, juvenile See **juvenile delinquent.**

delirium (di lēr′ē əm) *pl.* **iums, -ia.** *n.* a confused mental condition, usually the result of shock or fever, with delusions, illusions, hallucinations, and incoherence.

delta rhythm *or* **wave** a brain wave pattern of very low frequencies, between .5 and 4 cps. *Delta waves are normal in sleep, but abnormal during periods of wakefulness.* See also **electroencephalogram.**

demo- a combining form meaning *people*; as **demographic.**

demographic (dē″mə graf′ik, dem′ə-) *adj.* having to do with the statistical study of populations. *n.* **demographics; demography.**

demonstration (dem″ən strā′shən) 1. *n.* the act of attempting to prove, as by reasoning, experiment, or show of evidence. *The demonstration showed that diet A produced healthier mice than did diet B.* 2. *n.* the use of materials to illustrate a process or principle, or to serve as an example of how to do something, as *a cooking demonstration.*

demonstrative (de mon′strə tiv) 1. *n.* a word that points out something specific; deictic (def. 2). *Note:* In English, these include *this, that, these, those,* and *such a,* as in *Such a man would make a good friend.* 2. *adj.* referring to such a word.

dendrite (den′drīt) *n.* the portion of a neuron that carries impulses towards the cell body; the afferent part of a neuron. *Dendrites tend to be very short with complicated end brushes. Ct.* **axon** *or* **axone.**

denotation (dē″nō tā′s̬hən) *n.* the direct, explicit meaning of a word or phrase, as in a basic dictionary definition; lexical meaning. *Ct.* **connotation; affective meaning**. *adj.* **denotative.** *v.* **denote.**

denouement (dā″no͞o mäN′) 1. *n.* the final outcome of a plot, as in drama or fiction; the action following the climax. 2. *n.* the point at which this action occurs. 3. *n.* the unraveling or untying of any complicated situation.

dental (den″tᵊl) 1. *adj.* having to do with the teeth. 2. *n.* a consonant speech sound in which the teeth and lips are used to constrict the air flow, as /f/, /v/, and /t̷h̷/ or /*th*/. 3. *adj.* having to do with a sound made using the teeth and lips.

dependency (di pen′dən sē) 1. *n.* the need to be taken care of, especially physically and economically, as *infant dependency, old-age dependency.* 2. *n.* an emotionally submissive relationship, often unhealthy beyond early childhood, that is satisfying to the submissive person. 3. *n.* the psychophysiological need for drugs, as in drug addiction. *adj.* **dependent.** *n.* **dependence.**

dependent (di pen′dənt) *n.* one who receives financial or other kinds of help from another person or agency.

dependent clause a clause that modifies the main or independent clause to which it is joined; subordinate clause; as *until you leave* in the sentence *I will wait until you leave. Cp.* **independent clause.**

dependent variable the response variable(s) in an experiment affected by the manipulation of the independent variable(s). *Ct.* **independent variable.** See also **intervening variable.**

depressant (di pres′ənt) 1. *n.* something that reduces nervous and/or physical activity; sedative. *Ct.* **stimulant.** (def. 1). 2. *adj.* lowering one's spirits. *An unannounced examination may have a depressant effect.*

depression (di pres̬h′ən) 1. *n.* chronic, severe, emotional dejection, often with unrealistic feelings of inadequacy. *Depression may be induced by or lead to physiological dysfunctioning.* 2. *n.* occasional feelings of mild dejection. 3. *n.* a place or part that is lower than its surroundings, as *the foveal depression in the retina.* 4. *n.* a function, operation, or period that is less than normal, as *an economic depression.*

deprivation (dep″rə vā′s̬hən) *n.* the act, or condition, of having something desired or needed taken away, as *deprivation of food. Cp.* **frustration.** *v.* **deprive.**

depth perception 1. the detection of relative distance. 2. the detection of three-dimensional aspects of space and its objects; stereopsis. *Note:* Depth perception is a complex achievement which may involve binocular vision and motion parallax as well as such information as shadow, perspective, and especially occlusion.

derivation (der″ə vā′s̬hən) 1. *n.* the use of affixes to build new words from a root or base word, often with a change in the form class of a word, as in the verb *predict* becoming the noun *prediction.* 2. See **etymology**. 3. *n.* in syntax: a. the division of a grammatical structure into its component parts, as the derivation of an article-adjective-noun construction from a noun phrase. b. the grammatical structure of the surface level of a sentence obtained by rules from more abstract levels, or the process of rule application by which the surface structure is obtained. *v.* **derive.** *adj.* **derivational.**

derivational affix a prefix or suffix added to a root or stem to form another word, as *re* in *reread, ness* in *likeness*; and, if a suffix, often changing the word into a new part of speech, as *-ness* changes the adjective *like* to a noun. *Cp.* **inflectional affix.**

derivative (di riv′ə tiv) *n.* a word formed by adding a prefix and/or suffix to a root word or stem; derived form; as adding *pre* before *fix* to make *prefix.*

derived meaning 1. the new meaning acquired when a prefix or suffix has been added to a word or stem. *Cp.* **word formation** (def. 1). 2. new meaning acquired by a term when it is applied in a situation other than the one in which it is usually used, as '*I must get my bearings amid all this paperwork.*' *Cp.* **etymology.**

derived score a unit into which a score, usually a raw score, is changed. *Standard scores, mental age, and percentile rank are derived scores.*

derived sentence in early transformational-generative grammar, a sentence produced by applying transformational rules to a kernel or base sentence; kernel sentence (def. 1). See also **transformation** (def. 2); **transformational rule.**

descender (di sen′dər) *n.* the part of a lowercase letter that falls below its x-height, as in *g, j, p, q, y. Descenders sometimes aid word recognition. Ct.* **ascender.**

description (di skrip′shən) 1. *n.* one of the four traditional forms of composition in speech or writing. *Cp.* **argumentation** (def. 2); **exposition** (def. 1); **narration** (def. 1). 2. *n.* a picture in words, especially words rich in sensory images, of a character, a happening, or a setting in a story. *adj.* **descriptive.**

descriptive (di skrip′tiv) 1. *adj.* referring to an adjective or other modifier that expresses the quality of something, as *good* in *a good reader.* 2. *adj.* non-limiting with reference to a modifying clause; non-restrictive; as *whoever he was* in *The man, whoever he was, took our picture. Note:* In English, a descriptive clause is usually set off by commas.

descriptive grammar a grammatical system based upon usage rather than upon prescription. *Ct.* **prescriptive grammar** (def. 2).

descriptive linguistics 1. language study that describes the structure and function of aspects of a single language at a certain stage of its development; synchronic linguistics. 2. American structural linguistics prior to transformational-generative linguistics in the late 1950's.

descriptive research an investigation, often of a survey type, which attempts to describe accurately and factually a subject or an area.

desegration (dē″seg rə gā′shən, dē seg″-) *n.* See **integration** (def. 3). *Ant.* **segregation.**

design (di zīn′) 1. *n.* a plan of action or structure, as *an experimental design, an architectural design.* 2. *v.* to make such a plan. 3. *v.* to have as a purpose. *Paperbacks are designed to be easy to carry about and use.* 4. *n.* a representation of something, especially in drawing: a. a schematic drawing or outline, as *a flow-chart design.* b. an artistic sketch, as *a dress design.* 5. *v.* to make such a representation. 6. *n.* the formal elements of an artistic work. *The identification of various rhetorical designs is a literary analysis skill.* 7. **designs**, selfish or evil intentions, as *subversive propaganda designs.*

details, reading for See **reading for details.**

determinant (di tûr′mə nənt) 1. *n.* something which causes a later event to happen; determiner. *The search for a single determinant of reading difficulties has not been successful.* 2. *n.* a characteristic which distinguishes. *The height of the ascender is the determinant which separates an 'h' from an 'n' in printing. adj.* **determinant; determinate.** *v.* **determine.**

determiner (di tûr′mə nər) *n.* a word which specifies or points to what is being referred to, as definite and indefinite articles *a, the, some*, demonstrative adjectives *this, that*, and other words having this function.

determining letter(s) any letter(s) which provide(s) a person with clues for identifying a particular word. *Note:* Any letter may serve a particular person as a determining letter. Most often, however, these are letters with maximal differences, as ascenders or descenders, double letters, or the first letters of a word.

deus ex machina (de′o͞os eks mä′ki nä″) the introduction of a highly improbable person or event to resolve a plot difficulty that has no obvious solution. *Note:* The term, meaning 'the god from the machine,' comes from the ancient Greek and Roman practice of lowering a god from overhead to help characters in a play to resolve a difficult situation. In current usage, the term refers to those who unexpectedly solve a difficult situation, or to devices used by writers who are careless in constructing believable plots.

developmental age level of growth and/or development, either specific or general, stated as an age equivalent, as *carpal age, social age.*

developmental alexia the complete inability to read, presumably due to defective or delayed brain growth, without demonstrable brain damage. Cp. **alexia; acquired alexia.**

developmental aphasia disturbance(s) in language processing, presumably due to defective or delayed brain growth, without demonstrable brain damage.

developmental dyslexia 1. a mild form of alexia, presumably neurological in origin, shown by deviations from normal developmental rates or mastery levels; selective or specific reading disability. *Ct.* **acquired dyslexia.** See also **dyslexia** (def. 1). 2. a reading difficulty assumed to be hereditary or congenital in nature.

developmental lag a delay in the maturity of one or more areas of normal growth, but not in all areas; developmental imbalance. *Note:* The implication of the term is that the delay is temporary. See **organismic age.**

developmental method the study of the sequence of change in a person's development, particularly in maturation, to gain psychological understanding. *Cp.* **historical method.** *Ct.* **ahistorical method.**

developmental psychology the branch of psychology that deals with the course of development over the life span; particularly, with mental and social-emotional processes from birth to early childhood.

developmental reading 1. reading instruction, except remedial, for students at all levels. 2. reading instruction, except remedial, for all students beyond the elementary school level. *Note:* According to N.B. Smith (1965), this is the earliest meaning of the term in the reading literature. 3. a comprehensive ing literature. 3. a comprehensive school program of remedial and nonremedial reading instruction for all students. 4. remedial reading instruction in high school and college, a misuse of the term.

developmental task a term popularized chiefly by R.J. Havighurst, indicating a specific responsibility that the individual faces at certain life stages in order to be well-adjusted. *Developmental tasks grow out of the interaction of physical maturation, social demands, and the values and aspirations of the individual.*

developmental testing the tryout of instructional methods and materials to determine which parts need revision.

deviant (dē′vē ənt) 1. *adj.* having to do with behavior that is unexpected, or does not fit a norm or standard. 2. *n.* one who varies in attitudes and/or behavior from the norm or an accepted standard.

deviate (*n., adj.,* dē′vē it, *v.* dē′vē āt″) *n.* one whose behavior is markedly different from group norms; social deviate. *adj.* **deviate.** *v.* **deviate.**

deviation (dē″vē ā′shən) 1. *n.* any departure from a standard or norm, as *deviation in behavior.* 2. *n.* in statistics, the difference between one set of values and some reference point, usually the mean.

deviation IQ a standard score in which the mean is taken as 100 and the standard deviation as 15, or approximately so.

Dewey decimal classification the library classification scheme designed by Melvil Dewey which divides all knowledge into ten major groups by subject, each of which can be subdivided indefinitely. *Note:* This scheme, or modifications of it, is widely used in school, public, and smaller-sized libraries. *Cp.* **Library of Congress classification (LC); Universal decimal classification.**

dexterity (dek ster′i tē) 1. *n.* skill, ease, and cleverness in using the hands, body, or mind. 2. *n.* right-handedness. *Note:* Dexterity comes from the Latin *dexter* which means 'on the right hand or side,' the direction from which the Romans believed favorable omens came. *Ct.* **sinister; gauche.** See also **ambidextrous.**

dextral (dek′strəl) 1. *adj.* having to do with the right side; moving from the left to the right. *English, which is written and read from left to right, is a dextral language.* 2. *n.* a person who consistently chooses to use the right side, right hand, etc. See also **dexterity** (def. 2). *Ant.* **sinistral.** *n.* **dextrality.**

df degrees of freedom.

di (a)- a prefix meaning *separate, double,* as **divergent, dialogue**; or, *negation, lack,* as **dichromatism.**

diachronic (dī″ə kron′ik) *adj.* referring to language changes over time; historical; as *diachronic linguistics. Ct.* **synchronic.**

diacritic *or* **diacritic (-al) mark** (dī″ə krit′ ik *or* dī″ə kri′ti kəl) *n.* a mark added to a grapheme to indicate a specific pronunciation. *Note:* Diacritic marks are generally used to augment an alphabet so that a unique symbol is available for each speech sound or phoneme in a particular language; so that a dictionary may describe the preferred or existing pronunciations of each entry or word in a non-technical but clear fashion; or so that a unique symbol is available for each phonetically-distinct speech sound of a phonetic alphabet. Common diacritics include: *acute accent; apostrophe; caret; cedilla; circumflex; diaeresis; grave accent; macron; tilde; umlaut.* See these terms. *Cp.* **accent** (def. 2).

diadochokinesia (dī ad″ə kō ki nē′zhə, -zhē ə, zē ə, -kī-) 1. *n.* the ability to make opposing motor movements, as flexing and extending the arm or the jaw. 2. *n.* the ability to make rapid, repetitive movements of the articulators, as by quickly repeating /p/ /t/ /k/ in order several times. *Ant.* **adiochokenesia.**

diaeresis *or* **dieresis** (dī er′i sis) *pl.* **-ses** (sēz″). 1. *n.* the graphic symbol (¨) placed above the second of adjoining vowel letters to indicate a separate syllable, as aërial, oögenesis. *Ct.* **umlaut** (def. 3). 2. *n.* the separation of adjoining vowels to make two syllables, as *po′et.* 3. *n.* a pause, or caesura, in a line of verse when a word ends a metrical foot.

diagnosis (dī″əg nō′sis) 1 *n.* the act, or result, of identifying disorders from their symptoms. *Note:* Diagnosis technically means only the identification and labeling of a disorder, but as the term is used in education, it often includes the planning of instruction based on the evaluation of the problems and consideration of their causes. *There are different levels of diagnostic study, ranging from a casual observation that a student appears to be nearsighted to a clinical detection of aniseikonia; from a vague realization that a student is having difficulty in reading to an astute analysis of the process by which he gains meaning, significance, enjoyment, and value from printed sources* — R. Strang. 2. *n.* the classification of people or things into established categories, as *an educational diagnosis.* 3. **negative diagnosis**, the identification of a disorder by the recognition of what it is not. *A diagnosis of dyslexia is usually a negative diagnosis; i.e., there is no alternative explanation of the reading difficulty.*

diagnostic-prescriptive instruction instruction which is preceded by and adjusted to careful diagnosis. *Cp.* **diagnostic teaching.**

diagnostic teaching instruction in which diagnosis and instruction are fused into a single on-going process. *Cp.* **diagnostic-prescriptive instruction.** *Ct.* **assumptive teaching.**

diagnostic team a group of specialists, often school personnel, that studies and recommends treatment for more severe student problems that do not respond to ordinary classroom procedures. *A diagnostic team may include a psychologist, a psychometrician, a social worker, a speech therapist, and a nurse and/or doctor.*

diagnostic test a test designed to analyze strengths and weaknesses in content-oriented skills. *Note:* Diagnostic tests may permit comparison among several sub-abilities of the same individuals and sometimes comparisons of strong and weak points of a group or class. *Available instruments for the diagnosis of reading difficulties vary widely in the thoroughness of analysis they permit and in the specific procedures followed. ...Among the most common weaknesses of diagnostic reading tests are inadequate reliabilities coupled with high intercorrelations of the subtests from which separate scores are derived* — A. Anastasi (1976).

diagram (dī′ə gram″) 1. *n.* a drawing used to illustrate concepts, relationships, or processes usually more concretely than in a graph. See illustration. 2. *v.* to prepare such a drawing.

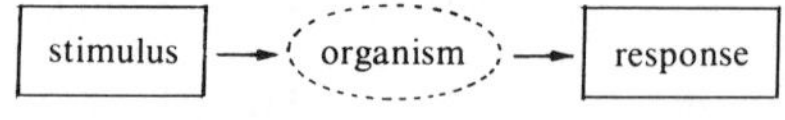

Example of a diagram

diagraming (dī′ə gra″miŋ) 1. *n.* the process of analyzing sentences by making a linear chart to help visualize the relationships of sentence components, sometimes used in teaching traditional grammar. *Note:* The sentence *The lively little boy tossed the red balloon high* *into the air* might be shown as in the illustration. 2. See **tree diagram** (def. 1).

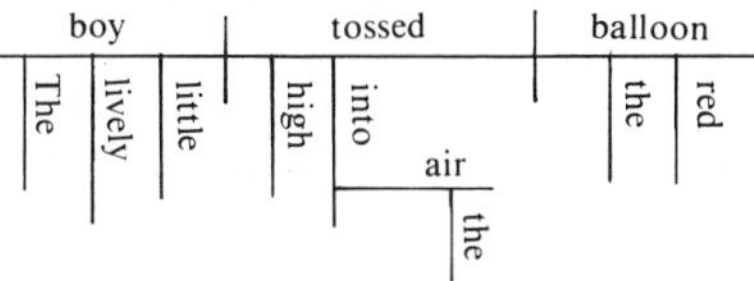

Diagraming: The lively little boy tossed the red balloon high into the air.

dialect (dī′ə lekt″) 1. *n.* a variety of the language of a speech community differing enough from other varieties of that language in pronunciation, grammar, and vocabulary to be considered a distinct type, but not a separate language because there is mutual understandability. *Ct.* **idiolect**. 2. *n.* a regionally limited, spoken variety of a given language. See also **non-standard dialect; regional dialect; social dialect; prestige dialect; standard dialect.**

dialectic (-al) (dī″ə lek′tik, -ti kəl) 1. *adj.* having to do with logic and with deductive reasoning, as opposed to intuition or inductive reasoning. 2. *n.* the practice of logical discussion. 3. **dialectics**, logic or one of its branches.

dialectology (dī″ə lek tol′ə jē) *n.* the study of regional, social, and temporal varieties of a language to determine how these varieties differ in pronunciation, grammar, and vocabulary in terms of their geographical distribution.

dialogue *or* **dialog** (dī′ə lôg″, -log″) 1. *n.* a conversation between two or more persons, or between a person and something else, such as a computer. 2. *n.* a conversation between characters in a play, novel, or short story 3. *n.* a literary work written as conversation, as *Plato's Dialogues.* 4. *n.* a friendly exchange of ideas, especially on social issues, in search of agreement, as *political dialogue.* 5. *n.* a drill technique used in teaching English as a second language or in foreign language instruction.

diaphragm (dī′ə fram″) 1. *n.* the muscular wall which separates the chest and abdominal cavities. *The diaphragm is used to control breathing and voice production.* 2. *n.* a thin disc that vibrates from sound waves, as in the eardrum or telephone. 3. *n.* a thin disc with a center hole, often adjustable in size, which is used with an optical lens to control the amount of light, as in a camera.

diary (dī′ə rē) 1. *n.* a record of a person's own experiences and thoughts, usually kept daily; journal. 2. *n.* a book for such a record. 3. *n.* (*Brit.*) an engagement calendar.

diastolic pressure (dī″ə stol′ik) the lowest blood pressure level in the arteries, occurring when the heart is most relaxed and the chambers are filled with blood, but before the heart muscles contract to pump the blood through the body. *Ct.* **systolic pressure.**

diazo process (dī az′ō, -ā′zō) a duplicating process especially useful in making overhead transparencies in which the master image is placed between a film or paper specially treated with a dye compound and ultraviolet light, the exposed film or paper being then processed chemically to produce an image.

dich (o)- a combining form indicating *split, separated into two*; as **dichotic**.

dichotic listening the simultaneous stimulation of both ears with different sounds such as tones or words. *Note:* The way in which competing messages are perceived in dichotic listening is of interest in severe reading disability since auditory rivalry is theoretically related to cerebral dominance.

dichromatism (dī krō′mə tiz″əm) *n.* partial color blindness; specifically, defective color vision in which only two of the three primary colors are seen. *Dichromatism is more commonly described by the missing color, as in red blindness. adj.* **dichromatic**.

diction (dik′shən) 1. *n.* clarity of speech or singing: enunciation. 2. *n.* the careful choice of words in speaking or writing in order to communicate clearly.

dictionary (dik′shə ner″ē) 1. *n.* a book listing words of a language, usually in alphabetical order, and giving spelling, pronunciation, and meaning(s), and often information about word origin and usage. 2. *n.* such a book, often with less complete information, giving word meanings in a special field, as *a medical dictionary*, or word meaning equivalents in another language, as *a German-English dictionary.*

didactic (-al) (dī dak′tik, -ti kal) 1. *adj.* intended to teach, as *didactic poetry.* 2. *adj.* inclined to moralize. 3. **didactics**, the art or science of teaching.

dieresis See **diaeresis**.

differential diagnosis diagnosis which attempts to distinguish among symptoms that have similar characteristics, as in primary vs. secondary reading retardation.

differential validity the degree to which a classification battery of tests yields a set of scores that predict in which of two situations a person will perform best.

differentiated reading instruction the provision of varied learning situations such as whole class, small group, and individual instruction to meet the needs of students of different levels of reading competence.

differentiation (dif″ə ren″shē ā′shən) 1. *n.* the process of becoming separable from something else or from a former condition. 2. *n.* the process of distinguishing among stimuli; specifically, the process of breaking down a homogeneous perceptual field or array into parts that can be distinguished. 3. *n.* a conditioning or discrimination learning procedure for learning to distinguish one set of stimuli from another set, or to make an appropriate response to one of two or more sets of stimuli. 4. *n.* specialized biological change, of increasing specificity. *v.* **differentiate**.

difficulty value the degree to which a test item discriminates in a given group, usually expressed as the per cent answering correctly. See also **item analysis**.

diffusion (di fyōō′zhən) 1. *n.* the spread of news, as by the newspaper, TV, or radio. 2. *n.* cultural spread from one area or group to another by borrowing of social customs and by adaptation. 3. *n.* spread of one cultural group, by migration, into geographic regions formerly inhabited mainly by the other. *v.* **diffuse**.

digest (*n.* dī′jest; *v.* di jest′, dī-) 1. *n.* a short condensed version of a longer work, as *a book digest.* 2. *n.* a collection of materials in shortened form, as *a digest of state laws.* 3. *v.* to assimilate, literally or figuratively. *He slowly digested her meaning.* 4. *v.* to think over, as *digest a proposal.* 5. *v.* to arrange or reduce by classifying; condense.

diglossia (dī glôs′ē ə, -glos′-) *n.* the presence of a high and low style or standard in a language, one for formal use in writing and some speech situations and one for colloquial use, as in modern Greek or Arabic. *Note:* The two styles or standards are usually so different that the formal type requires special study to master it. *adj.* **diglossic**.

digraph (dī′graf, -gräf) 1. *n.* two letters which represent one speech sound, as *ch* for /ch/ in *chin.* 2. *n.* a grapheme resulting from the fusion of two letters into one, as in œ, Æ, etc.; ligature. *Cp.* **trigraph.** *adj.* **digraphic.**

digression (di gresh′ən, dī-) *n.* a wandering away from the main point, theme, or plot in writing and speaking. *Dickens makes many digressions in* Oliver Twist. *adj.* **digressive.**

Dilantin (di lan′tin) *n.* a trade name for diphenylhydantoin, a drug used to control epilepsy.

dime novel a melodramatic paperback romance or adventure book, cheaply produced and widely sold from the mid-19th through the first quarter of the 20th century. *Note:* The first dime novel, ***Beadle's Dime Novels no. 1,*** appeared in 1860 and was the American counterpart of the British penny dreadful. 2. a cheap, sensational novel; potboiler.

diminutive (di min′yə tiv) 1. *adj.* small. 2. *n.* a word or suffix used to describe something small, youthful, fragile, feminine, etc. *Note:* In English, the suffix *-let*, as in *booklet, piglet, eyelet*, often functions as a diminutive.

diopter (dī op′tər) *n.* the standard unit for expressing the refractive power of a lens; specifically, a unit in which one diopter represents the power of a lens that will focus parallel light rays at a distance of one meter. *Note:* The power of a lens in diopters is computed by dividing the focal length of the lens, in meters, into 1.00.

diorama (dī″ə ram′ə, -rä′mə) *n.* a three-dimensional scene often created by placing figures or objects in front of a two-dimensional backdrop, as in many museum displays.

diotic (dī ō′tik, -ot′ik) *adj.* having to do with stimulating each ear in the same way; binaural. *Ct.* **dichotic listening.**

diphthong (dif′thông, -thong, dip′-) 1. *n.* a vowel speech sound or phoneme that begins with one vowel sound and, by a change of tongue position, moves toward another vowel or semi-vowel position in the same syllable; as any of the vowel sounds in *bee, bay, boo, buy, boy,* and *bough.* See also **rising diphthong, falling diphthong; wide diphthong; narrow diphthong.** 2. *n.* a graphic symbol of two adjacent letters in brackets used in phonetics to represent diphthongs, as [ay].

dipl (o)- a combining form indicating *double*; as **diplopia.**

diplopia (di plō′pē ə) *n.* the seeing of two objects when only one is present; double vision.

direct discourse an exact quote of speech or writing, as the announcement by Calvin Coolidge: *I do not choose to run. Ct.* **indirect discourse.**

directed reading activity (DRA) 1. a step-by-step process of dealing with a reading lesson under the guidance of a teacher; developmental reading lesson. *The DRA is a specific example of a directed teaching activity used in the content fields.* 2. a lesson plan which involves *a.* preparation/readiness/motivation for reading a lesson; *b.* silent reading; *c.* vocabulary and skills development; *d.* silent and/or oral re-reading; and *e.* follow-up or culminating activities. *Note:* The directed reading activity changes in detail from one writer to another, but the underlying concept remains the same. A further step in this process is the *directed reading-thinking activity (DRTA)* in which the chief elements are prediction and verification. Students in the pre-reading stage set their own purposes for reading by making predictions; in the reading stage they verify their predictions; and in the discussion stage they check their verifications.

direct experience the actual participation and the personal observation of actions, conditions, events, etc., as going to a circus, meeting an author, taking a trip, etc. *Ct.* **vicarious experience**.

directional confusion a weak or nonexistent ability to perceive spatial orientation accurately. *Ct.* **directionality**. 2. uncertainty or inconsistency in left-right directions or movements, as in attempting to read or write English from right to left.

directionality (di rek″shə nal′i tē, dī-) *n.* the ability to perceive spatial orientation accurately, as up-down, right-left, front-back; directional orientation. *Note:* Kephardt and others believe that directionality is a projection of one's concept of laterality into the external world. *Ct.* **directional confusion**. (def. 1).

direct object the person or thing that receives the action or is affected by the action of a transitive verb in a sentence, as *John* in the sentence *Tom hit John*. *Cp.* **indirect object**.

dirge (dûrj) 1. *n.* a funeral hymn. 2. *n.* a song or verse of sorrow. 3. *n.* a mournful sound.

dis- a prefix indicating *negation, lack*; as **disorder**.

disability (dis″ə bil′i tē) 1. *n.* the loss of, or injury to, a body part or its function. *Blindness is a visual disability*. 2. *n.* any handicap that puts one at a disadvantage. See **reading disability**. *v.* **disable**.

disabled reader one whose performance in reading is markedly below his or her intellectual ability.

disadvantaged (dis″əd van′tijd, -vän′-) *n.* a person or group whose socioeconomic and/or cultural status is thought to be lower or less favorable by the dominant culture in a society, often because of poorer performance in academic learning. *adj.* **disadvantaged**.

disconfirmation (dis″kon fər mā′shən) *n.* in reading or listening, the failure of later information to verify earlier predictions. *Ct.* **confirmation** (def. 1).

discourse (*n.* dis′kōrs, -kôrs, dis kōrs′, -kôrs′; *v.* dis kōrs′, -kôrs′) 1. *n.* a formal presentation on a subject, either written or spoken, as *Plato's discourses on philosophy*. 2. *n.* in linguistics, any form of oral or written communication more extended than a sentence. 3. *n.* conversation. 4. *v.* to converse. 5. *v.* to make a formal presentation, either written or spoken. *He discoursed with enthusiasm on the new treaty*.

discourse analysis the study of the function and structure of language units larger than a sentence, as stories, speeches, and conversations. *Discourse study [analysis]...is the study of the situational uses of the potentials of the language* — J. Kinneavy (1971). *Cp.* **rhetoric** (def. 1).

discriminability (di skrim″ə nə bil′i tē) *n.* the characteristic of being distinguishable, as *the discriminability of distinctive letter features. adj.* **discriminable**.

discriminanda (di skrim″ə nän′də) See **determinant** (def. 2, *pl.*).

discriminant validity a type of construct validation; specifically, the process, or result, of finding that two or more indicators thought to assess the same variable fail to correlate with each other.

discrimination (di skrim″ə nā′shən) 1. *n.* the process of noting differences between stimuli, as *sensory discrimination. Note:* In reading practice, teachers often use the term to refer to the noting of likenesses and differences. *Cp.* **differentiation** (def. 2). *Ct.* **acuity** (def. 2). *Note:* Special types of discrimination, as *word discrimination,* are given under the describing term. 2. *n.* learning to react differently to different stimuli, as *discrimination as a type of learning.* 3. *n.* the ability to make discerning judgments based on fine distinctions, especially in the arts. 4. *n.* biased actions or feelings, usually unfavorable, toward a group of individuals, as *racial discrimination, social discrimination. v.* **discriminate.**

discriminator (di skrim′ə nā″tər) 1. *n.* a distinctive orthographic feature of a letter, word, or phrase that aids identification, as the use of capital letters in the acronym *UNESCO.* 2. *n.* one who can distinguish one thing from another. 3. *n.* an electronic device that can distinguish among different sorts of signals.

discursive (di skûr′siv) *adj.* rambling; digressive. *Discursive writing wanders from digression to digression with no apparent direction. Ct.* **non-discursive**.

disinhibition (dis in″i bish′ən, -in″hi-, dis″in-) 1. *n.* the temporary loss of an inhibition; inhibition of an inhibition. 2. *n.* the revival of an extinguished conditioned reflex by a new and different stimulus. 3. *n.* the lack of physical or social restraint; impulsiveness; as in a temper tantrum, in making uncalled-for remarks, etc. *adj.* **disinhibitory.** *v.* **disinhibit**.

disjunctive (dis jungk′tiv) 1. *adj.* unrelated; separated; as *a disjunctive array of stimuli. Ct.* **conjunctive** (def. 1). 2. *adj.* referring to expressions in opposition to each other. *The statement 'You may read the text, but not your free-reading book' is a disjunctive statement.*

disjunctive thought a form of logical thinking in which logical elements that are unrelated are identified, as opposites, distinctive features, etc. *Cp.* **conjunctive thought; relational thought**.

disorder (dis ôr′dər) 1. *n.* disease. *Schizophrenia is a mental disorder.* 2. *n.* marked deviation from the norm in structure or function, as *a speech disorder. Note:* Special types of disorder, as *behavioral disorder,* are given under the describing term.

dispersion (di spûr′zhən, -shən) *n.* the extent to which observations or events vary among themselves or deviate from some reference point, as the mean. *The standard deviation is a statistical measure of dispersion.*

dissertation (dis″ər tā′shən) 1. *n.* any formal scholarly presentation, usually in writing. 2. *n.* a formal paper or essay reporting on one's own research. *A dissertation is usually required for the doctoral degree. Cp.* **thesis** (def. 1).

dissimilation (di sim″ə lā′shən) *n.* the process, or result, by which two neighboring speech sounds become less alike, usually for ease of pronunciation, as in the change in sound of *r* to *l* in the borrowing of the French *marbre* into English as *marble. v.* **dissimilate.**

dissociation (di sō″sē ā′shən, -shē ā′-) 1. *n.* the neurotic or pathological separation of a specific set of behaviors from general psychological functioning: compartmentalization; as *dissociation in multiple personality.* See also **schizophrenia**. 2. *n.* the separation of a behavior or set of behaviors from conscious control, as *dissociation under hypnosis.*

dissonance (dis′ə nəns) 1. *n.* a mixture of harsh, inharmonious sounds. 2. *n.* an inconsistency. *In cognitive dissonance, one's beliefs and one's actions are not the same. Ant.* **consonance.** *adj.* **dissonant**.

distal (dis′tᵊl) *adj.* away from the center of the body, or from the point of origin or attachment, as of an organ or bone. *The ear lobe is the distal part of the ear. Ant.* **proximal.**

distance vision the ability to see objects that are far away rather than near. *Note:* The visual acuity of distance vision is usually measured by having the subject identify the smallest possible target at a distance of six meters (20 ft.) or more.

distinctive feature 1. a distinguishing characteristic of a perceptual object or field; especially, a characteristic that contrasts noticeably with another perceived characteristic. *The letter forms A and O differ in distinctive features.* 2. any aspect of speech sound description used to differentiate one phoneme from another. 3. the theoretical system for describing such aspects. *Distinctive features may be based on acoustical, articulatory, or perceptual data.*

distractibility (di strak″ti bil′i tē) *n.* the inability to maintain attention to relevant rather than irrelevant stimuli. *Extreme distractability is a common symptom of hyperactivity.*

distractor (di strak′tər) *n.* any incorrect alternative in a multiple-choice or matching item.

distribution (dis″trə byo͞o′s̱hən) 1. *n.* the act, or result, of grouping elements into classes, as by dividing sounds by the manner of their formation into consonants or vowels. 2. *n.* the result of grouping data into classes or categories. *Statistical distributions are often expressed as tables or graphs.* 3. *n.* the frequency and/or geographic location of a linguistic item. *The distribution of the term 'ain't' is wide; the distribution of Pennsylvania Dutch is limited.* See also **complementary distribution.** *v.* **distribute.**

disyllable *or* **dissyllable** (dī′sil ə bəl, di sil′-) *n.* a word with two syllables. *adj.* **disyllabic** *or* **dissyllabic.**

ditto delirium See **purple curriculum.**

divergence (di vûr′jəns, dī-) 1. *n.* a difference or separation in ideas, objects, events, behaviors, etc.; deviation; as *a divergence of opinion, a divergence in course of action.* 2. *n.* the bending of light rays away from each other as they pass through a concave, or minus, lens. 3. *n.* the normal turning out of the eyes as the distance to their point of fixation increases. 4. *n.* the abnormal turning out of one eye relative to the other. See **divergent squint** *or* **strabismus.** 5. *n.* the innervation of several cells by the multiple synaptic junctions of a single nerve cell. *Ant.* **convergence.** *v.* **diverge.** *adj.* **divergent.**

divergent squint *or* **strabismus** walleyes; specifically, strabismus in which the line of sight of the deviant eye does not converge enough to meet that of the fixating or controlling eye. *Syn.* **exotropia.** *Ant.* **convergent squint** *or* **strabismus.**

divergent thinking the ability to elaborate and expand in order to generate new ideas or alternative interpretations of given information. *Some essay tests stimulate divergent thinking. Ct.* **convergent thinking.**

document (*n.* dok′yə mənt; *v.* dok′yə mənt″) 1. *n.* a written, printed, or otherwise recorded item that gives information or evidence, as a passport, a deed, a tape recording of a conversation. 2. *n.* a government publication. 3. *v.* to provide information or evidence through the use of supporting documents.

documentary (dok″yə men′tə rē) *n.* a film based primarily on fact rather than on fiction. *A true documentary shows events as they occurred.*

documentation (dok″yə men tā′shən) *n.* the verification, selection, and use of documents to establish authenticity.

doggerel (dô′gər əl, dog′ər-) 1. *n.* a form of verse, often trivial and sentimental, usually of irregular rhythm, and sometimes comic or burlesque in intent. *She kissed the hairbrush / By mistake, / She thought it was / Her husband Jake.* 2. *adj.* referring to such verse or its characteristics.

domain (dō mān′) 1. *n.* broadly, any field of action, knowledge, or influence. *The lexicographer's domain is the written word.* 2. *n.* a particular behavioral field: cognitive, affective, psychomotor.

domain-referenced measurement the assessment of learning in a sample from a specific domain such as the vocabulary of all first grade readers.

Doman-Delacato method a remedial reeducation program based on the assumption that severe learning problems are due to a defect in neurological development as seen in the failure to establish lateral dominance. *Note:* The method has failed to produce predicted results in controlled experimentation, but anecdotal reports of extraordinary results continue.

dominant eye 1. in normal vision, the consistent use of one eye in some sighting or motor task. 2. the preference for using one eye over the other, a preference possibly important in looking through the viewfinder of a camera. 3. the eye that fixates most often in alternating vision.

dominant hemisphere the cerebral hemisphere that exercises preferential control over a specified behavior. *A dominant hemisphere controls laterality.* See **cerebral dominance** (def. 1).

dominant letter a letter in a word that is easy to distinguish and aids word identification, usually extending above or below the x-height of a lower-case letter. *The word 'Jeopardy' has the dominant letters J, p, d, and y.* See also **configuration clue**.

dorsal (dôr′səl) 1. *adj.* having to do with, on, or at the back; posterior. 2. *adj.* behind the backbone or towards the back of he body. *Ant.* **ventral.**

double entendre (dub′əl än tän′drə, tänd′; *Fr.* dōō bläɴ -täɴ′dʀᵊ) 1. a word or phrase that has two meanings, one of which is suggestive or risqué, possibly indecent. 2. a double meaning; ambiguity. See also **pun** (def. 1).

double negative the use of two negative words in the same clause to express a single negation, as *never* and *nobody* in *He never saw nobody work so hard. Note:* A double negative, although usually considered non-standard in English, is accepted as standard in a sentence such as *She is not unlikely to be home.* It is also required in certain languages, as French and Russian.

double vision See **diplopia**.

Down's syndrome a congenital abnormality with mild to severe mental retardation, a flattened head with broad nose and slanted eyes, and stubby fingers; formerly called mongolism.

DRA directed reading activity.

drama (drä′mə, dram′ə) *n.* a story in dramatic form that emphasizes conflict of characters and that is written to be performed by actors; play.

dramatic irony a situation in which a character says or does something, the full meaning of which he does not understand but which the audience does. *Note:* A famous example of dramatic irony occurs in Shakespeare when Othello calls the villain 'honest Iago.' See also **irony** (def. 2).

dramatic poetry the use of one or more techniques of drama, such as characters, dialogue, conflict, etc., in poetry. *The personalities of characters in dramatic poetry are often revealed through dialogue and conflict rather than through description.*

dramatization (dram″ə ti zā′shən, drä″ mə-) 1. *n.* the acting out of a story, play, incident in a novel, etc., in whole or in part. 2. *n.* the change of a story, novel, etc., into dramatic form. 3. *n.* the version so changed. *v.* **dramatize**.

drill (dril) 1. *n.* a methodical repetition of knowledge or behavior, presumably for learning, as *multiplication table drill.* 2. *n.* specific language learning exercises, as *phonetic, vocabulary, and grammar drills.* 3. *v.* to repeat through systematic practice. *The teacher asked Carol to drill Lee on spelling.*

drive (drīv) 1. *n.* an inner force that stimulates or prevents action: *the energy of behavior*—P.T. Young. 2. **drive state**, a. the general energy condition of an organism. b. the physiological factors involved in a given learning sequence.

DRTA See **directed reading activity (DRA)** (def. 2. *Note*).

duality (do͞o al′i tē, dyo͞o-) *n.* the property of having two simultaneous systems, as language having grammatical and phonological systems. *n.* **dualism**. *adj.* **dualistic**.

duct (dukt) *n.* a tube or canal through which a gland secretes body fluids.

duction (duk′shən) 1. *n.* for a single eye, the movement of the eyeball by any of the extraocular muscles. 2. *n.* for both eyes, convergent or divergent ocular movements to maintain single binocular vision. *Duction tests are used to estimate the subject's ability to compensate for various types of oculomotor imbalance.*

ductless gland See **endocrine gland**.

dull-normal *n.* a person with an IQ score between normal and mild retardation; slow learner. See **mental retardation**.

duodecimo (do͞o″ə des′ə mō″, dyo͞o″-) *n.* a book often measuring approximately 17.5 to 20 cm. (about 5x7½ in.) in height, printed on sheets folded to make 12 leaves or 24 pages; twelvemo. See also **book size** *or* **format.**

duplicate (do͞o′plə kit, dyo͞o′-) *n.* any one of two or more copies of a book, periodical, or other material in a library; usually called *dup.*

duplicating (do͞o′plə kā′ting, dyo͞o′-) 1. *n.* loosely, the act of copying or reproducing something. 2. *n.* technically, the reproduction of original copy by the use of a master copy or stencil rather than by photography. *adj., v.* **duplicate**.

duration of fixation the length of time that the eyes pause during visual inspection. *The average duration of fixation during reading is about one fifth of a second.* See illustration under **eye-movement pattern**.

dust jacket See **book jacket**.

dyad (dī′ad) *n.* two; a pair; especially, two individuals who relate to each other as a unit, as mates, mother and child, etc. *Note:* There are also *monads* (ones), *triads* (threes), *quads* (fours), etc. *adj.* **dyadic.**

dys- a prefix indicating *bad, difficult*; as **dysgraphia**.

dysacusis (dis″ə kyo͞o′sis) 1. *n.* difficulty in understanding speech caused by disturbances in pitch or in loudness perception rather than sensitivity to sound; auditory agnosia. 2. *n.* pain caused by sound, particularly when the sound is at normal levels.

dysarthria (dis är′thrē ə) *n.* poor speech articulation because of lack of control of speech muscles by the central nervous system. *Ct.* **dyslalia**. See also **anarthria**.

dyscalculia (dis″kal kyo͞o′lē ə) *n.* extreme difficulty in performing mathematical calculations.

dysfluency (dis flōō'ən sē) *n.* repetitious, hesitant speech. *adj.* **dysfluent.**

dysfunction (dis fuṅgk'shən) 1. *n.* the faulty operation of a body organ or process, as *an eye dysfunction, a circulation dysfunction.* 2. *n.* a faulty social adjustment characteristic, as *a personality dysfunction.*

dysgraphia (dis graf'ē ə) *n.* a mild form of apraxia involving difficulty in producing handwriting because of disease of or injury to the brain.

dyslalia (dis lā'lē ə) *n.* poor speech articulation for any reason other than lack of control by the central nervous system, as defective articulators, hearing loss, faulty learning, etc.; functional speech defect. *Ct.* **dysarthria.**

dyslexia (dis lek'sē ə)

The concept of dyslexia, like that of learning disability, has a long history of differing interpretations. The medical profession tends to regard it as a disease for which there is a causative factor; the psychological profession, a serious problem of unspecified origin. The education profession has wavered between these positions.

1. *n.* a medical term for incomplete alexia; partial, but severe, inability to read; historically (but less common in current use), word blindness. *Note:* Dyslexia in this sense applies to persons who ordinarily have adequate vision, hearing, intelligence, and general language functioning. *Dyslexia is a rare but definable and diagnosable form of primary reading retardation with some form of central nervous system dysfunction. It is not attributable to environmental causes or other handicapping conditions — J. Abrams (1980).* 2. *n.* a severe reading disability of unspecified origin. 3. *n.* a popular term for any difficulty in reading of any intensity and from any cause(s). *Note:* Dyslexia in this sense is a term which describes a symptom, not a disease. Due to all the differing assumptions about the process and nature of possible reading problems, dyslexia has come to have so many incompatible connotations that it has lost any real value for educators, except as a fancy word for a reading problem. Consequently, its use may create damaging cause and effect assumptions for student, family, and teacher. Thus, in referring to a specific student, it is probably better that the teacher describe the actual reading difficulties, and make suggestions for teaching related to the specific difficulties, not apply a label which may create misleading assumptions by all involved. See also **learning disability.** *adj., n.* **dyslexic.**

dyslogia (dis lō'jə, -jē ə) 1. *n.* difficulty in speaking because of brain damage or dysfunction; aphasia. *Note:* Dyslogia is usually considered less severe than alogia. *Cp.* **alogia** (def. 1). 2. *n.* difficulty in speaking because of mental retardation or extreme mental confusion.

dysnomia (dis nō'mē ə) *n.* a mild form of anomia involving difficulty in recalling names of objects, people, events, etc.

dysphasia (dis fā'zhə, -zhē ə, -zē ə) *n.* a mild form of aphasia involving difficulty in understanding or using language because of disease of or injury to the brain.

dysphemia (dis fē'mē ə) *n.* a speech disorder, often involving stuttering, because of illness or emotional stress.

dysphonia (dis fō'nē ə) *n.* any difficulty in voice production; partial loss of voice. *Cp.* **aphonia.**

dyspraxia (dis prak'sē ə) *n.* general clumsiness; specifically, a mild form of apraxia involving difficulty in making coordinated muscle movements because of disease of or injury to the brain.

dysrhythmia (dis rith'mē ə) 1. *n.* irregular fluency in speech production. See also **stuttering** (def. 1). 2. *n.* an irregular wave pattern on an electroencephalogram, or EEG.

dystonia (dis tō'nē ə) *n.* an abnormal muscle tension state, as in cerebral palsy, in which the muscles may be either too tight or too lax.

E

DEVELOPMENT OF MAJUSCULE								
NORTH SEMITIC	GREEK		ETR.	LATIN		MODERN		
						GOTHIC	ITALIC	ROMAN
Ǝ	Ǝ	E	Ǝ	Ǝ	E	𝕰	*E*	E

DEVELOPMENT OF MINUSCULE					
ROMAN CURSIVE	ROMAN UNCIAL	CAROL. MIN.	MODERN		
			GOTHIC	ITALIC	ROMAN
ɛ	ϵ	e	𝔢	*e*	e

The fifth letter of the English alphabet developed from North Semitic *he*. Originally a consonant with an *h*-sound, it was transformed into a vowel in Greek, although in Classical Greek and in certain local alphabets North Semitic *heth* (see H) was used to represent *eta* (long e). The minuscule (e) was derived from the capital (E) through the uncial form.

ear (ēr) 1. *n.* the organ of hearing and balance, composed of the external ear, the middle ear, and the inner ear. See illustration 2. *n.* the visible external ear; auricle. 3. *n.* the sense of hearing in general, as *pleasing to the ear*. 4. *n.* the sensitive perception of sounds, especially musical sounds, as *have a good ear*. 5. *n.* attention, as in *lend me your ear*.

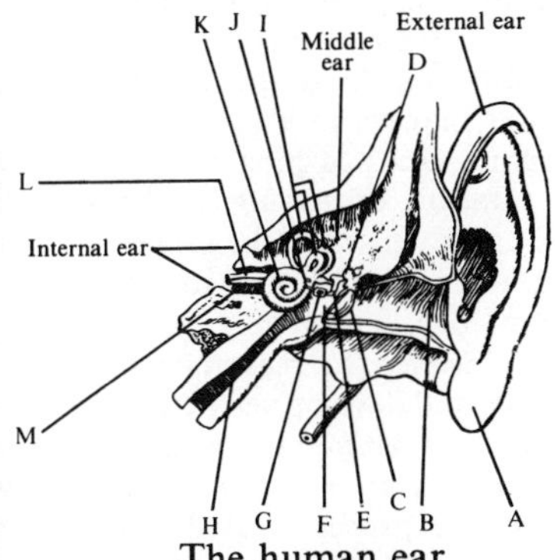

The human ear

External ear: A, Lobe; B, External auditory meatus. Middle ear: C, Tympanic membrane; D, Malleus; E, Incus; F, Tympanic cavity; G, Stapes; H, Eustachian tube. Internal ear: I, Semi-circular canals; J, Vestibule; K, Cochlea; L, Auditory nerve; M, Internal auditory meatus.

eardrum (ēr′drum″) *n.* a thin membrane which transmits vibrations from the outer ear to the middle ear; tympanic membrane. See illustration under **ear**.

early childhood education (ECE) infant, preschool, and other educational programs ordinarily for children prior to entrance to the primary grades.

early reading 1. reading ability that is either self-taught or learned from others before formal instruction in school. 2. teaching children to read before the usual entrance age to school, as at ages 3 and 4.

ear training specific articulation training in which one compares one's own speech to model speech, thus learning to differentiate the sounds and then to produce the model sound.

ECE early childhood education.

echo- a combining form indicating *repetition*; as **echophrasia**.

echoic reading oral reading in which students imitate or repeat another's reading.

echolalia *or* **echophrasia** (ek″ō lā′ lē ə; ek″ō frā′zhə, -zhē ə, -zē ə) 1. *n.* in the early stages of language development, an infant's normal repetition of the vocal sounds made by others. 2. *n.* echo speech; *the parrot-like repetition of words just spoken* — M. Vernon (1978). *Note:* Such repetition is often found to an extreme degree in autistic children. It is also considered abnormal when it persists into later ages when it may be either a functional disorder or a result of brain damage.

eclectic (i klek′tik) 1. *adj.* selecting, or made up from, various sources; specifically, selecting and using the best from several systems, as *an eclectic reading* *program.* 2. *n.* one who behaves in an eclectic manner. *n.* **electicism.**

eclectic approach *or* **method** 1. a systematic way of teaching reading that combines features of the analytic, or global, and the synthetic approaches or methods. 2. any approach or method of teaching reading that draws upon and combines features from other approaches or methods. *Note:* Often, an eclectic approach or method implies no method at all, in that pieces and parts of many programs may be taken up and dropped with no overriding philosophy or sequence.

eclectic reader any of several series of readers of the mid-19th century which introduced varied content to replace the earlier religious and patriotic emphases in American readers. *The McGuffey readers were eclectic readers. Note:* The term 'eclectic' was actually a popular catchword in the mid-19th century, and used in connection with textbooks in other subjects, as eclectic music, etc.

edema (i dē′mə) *n.* too much fluid in body tissues or cavities, causing swelling.

edit (ed′it) 1. *v.* to make needed changes in a manuscript; revise. 2. *v.* to gather and prepare materials for publication. 3. *v.* to oversee the selection and presentation of content in some media as print, film, etc. 4. *v.* to cut out portions of print, film, tape, etc.

edition (i dish″ən) 1. *n.* one of a series of like printings of a publication. 2. *n.* the total number of copies printed from one set of type at one time. 3. *n.* the format of a published written work.

editor (ed′i tər) 1. *n.* a person who collects, prepares, and arranges material for publication in print, films, etc. *Note:* Editors may be staff members of a publishing house, or may be professional consulting editors, as a college professor who edits an anthology. 2. *n.* a person with managerial and sometimes a policymaking role in those parts of a publication which give the publisher's opinion. 3. *n.* the supervisor of a department of a publication, as *the travel editor. Cp.* **author** (def. 1); **compiler.**

editorial (ed″i tōr′ē əl, -tôr′-) *n.* an essay on some topic in a newspaper or other media that reflects the opinion of the publisher, producer, or one or more of the editorial staff.

educable mentally retarded (EMR) a person with an IQ between two and three standard deviations below the mean, usually between 55 and 70; high-grade mental defective; moron. *EMRs are usually able to maintain themselves socially and economically in the community.* See also **mental retardation.**

education (ej″o͝o kā′shən, ed″yo͝o-) 1. *n.* the changes in a person caused by teaching and learning rather than by maturation, as *reading education.* 2. *n.* in a broad sense, the processes used in teaching and learning to produce the knowledge and highly generalizable skills needed to reason, make judgments, and develop aesthetic appreciation. *Wide reading is the hallmark of a liberal education.* 3. *n.* in a narrow sense, the processes used in teaching and learning to gain specific practical skills; training. *Learning to type was part of his education.* 4. *n.* a level or degree of schooling, as *a college education.* 5. *n.* teaching; pedagogy. 6. *adj.* having to do with teacher preparation, as *an education student. adj.* **educational.** *v.* **educate.**

educational measurement 1. the act of assessing school learning and its effects, usually with a view to improving instructional practices, as the National

Assessment of Educational Progress. 2. the results of such assessment.

educational media the various means of communicating material to be learned, such as motion pictures, filmstrips, photographs, recordings, television, printed materials, graphics, computer-based instruction, etc. *Educational media is a more recent term for audio-visual aids or materials.*

educational objective See **objective** (def. 2.).

educational psychology a branch of psychology devoted to the study of educational problems, procedures, and practices in order to improve educational productivity.

Educational Resources Information Center (ERIC) any one of several federally-supported agencies which examines, evaluates, collects, and distributes information related to research and instruction, as *The Center for Reading and Communicating Skills (ERIC/RCS); The Center for Language and Linguistics; The Center for Teaching Education; The Center for Handicapped and Gifted Children; The Center for Tests, Measurement, and Evaluation;* etc. *Note:* The centers are important storehouses, especially of fugitive materials, as speeches, that otherwise might be lost.

educational technology the use of educational resources of all types, material and human, in human learning. *Note:* Beyond media hardware and software, educational technology involves the institutional management of learning processes through instructional systems.

educational television (ETV) educational or informational programs transmitted by non-commercial stations, including public television, instructional television, school television, etc. *Note:* ETV does not ordinarily apply to closed-circuit television (CCTV).

EEG electroencephalogram.

effects of reading 1. the results upon the reader of the act of reading 2. specifically, what motivations and to what extent the motivations of the reader are satisfied by what is read. *Any effects of reading imply interaction between the reader's predispositions and the content of the publication* — D. Waples and others (1940). *Note:* Waples identified five primary effects of reading — *aesthetic, instrumental, prestige, reinforcement,* and *respite effects.* See these terms for definitions.

efferent (ef′ər ənt) *adj.* away from the center of the body or a body part. *An efferent nerve carries impulses from the central nervous system out towards a muscle. Ct.* **afferent**.

efferent reading a type of reading ...*in which the primary concern of the reader is what he will carry away from the reading...or...what will remain as the residue* after *the reading — the information to be acquired, the logical solution to a problem, the actions to be carried out* — L. Roseblatt (1978). *Cp.* **aesthetic reading**. See also **effects of reading**.

efficiency, reading See **reading efficiency**.

e, final 'silent' *e*; the spelling pattern in English in which *e* is the last letter in a word and does not represent a final sound, but which often signals a long vowel sound for the preceding vowel letter, as *e* in *hate, rote, fire.* See also **silent letter**.

-ego- a combining form indicating *self*; as **egocentric, superego**.

ego (ē′gō, eg′ō) 1. *n.* the uniqueness of the person or the self; self-assertion, without implying selfishness: *I am I.* 2. *n.* in Freudian theory, the conscious and reality-driven sense of self that is part of the psyche. *Ct.* **id; superego.** 3. *n.* selfishness or conceit. *n.* **egoist** (def. 3); *adj.* **egotistic** (def. 3).

egocentric (ē″gō sen′trik, eg″ō-) 1. *adj.* self-centered with relative indifference to others, but not necessarily selfish. 2. *n.* a self-centered person. 3. See **egocentrism.** See also **autism; introversion.**

egocentric language *or* **speech** (J. Piaget) speech which is unadapted to the point of view of others and/or is not specifically directed to others, as children's monologues and songs while playing.

egocentric logic (J. Piaget) a mode of thinking that is more intuitive than deductive, with little value attached to proving or checking propositions. See also **syncretism** (def. 4).

egocentrism (ē″gō sen′triz əm, eg″ō-) 1. *n.* the characteristic of being egocentric 2. *n.* (J. Piaget) *the child's inability to take another's point of view. [Note:] It is not a pejorative term with respect to the child since the child does not take another's point of view because he cannot as opposed to the egocentric adult who can take another's point of view but will not* — D. Elkind.

(ego) supportive therapy an approach to psychological problems in which the therapist provides acceptance, encouragement, and direct help in analyzing the client's problems and in planning improved future functioning. *Ct.* **client-centered therapy.**

eidetic imagery (ī det′ik) the vivid and detailed mental picturing of something previously seen, as the page of a text, an illustration, etc.; the ability to so picture. *Note:* An eidetic image is clear and more accurate than a memory image and may be projected like an afterimage onto a screen. Eidetic imagery is believed by some to be a common occurrence in children but lessens with age.

elaborated code a term coined by the British sociologist B. Bernstein to describe the structurally complex speech used by privileged members of a speech community. *Note:* An elaborated code tends to rely more on complex syntactic patterns to fully express meaning than on a common context or background of experience among those to whom it is addressed. *Ct.* **restricted code; public language.** See also **formal speech** *or* **style.**

elaboration (i lab″ə rā′shən) 1. *n.* the process, or result, of expanding in detail or complexity a simpler object or idea. *Your theme is excellent but needs elaboration.* 2. *n.* the 'extra processing' of text done by a reader: *the more extra processing one does that results in additional, related, or redundant propositions, the better will be the 'memory' for the material processed* — L. Reder (1980). *v., adj.* **elaborate.**

electroencephalogram (EEG) (i lek″ trō en sef′ə lə gram″) *n.* a graphic record of electrical brain activity made by placing small electrodes on the scalp and recording changes in electrical activity occurring within the brain. *Note:* The EEG is used to identify and locate abnormalities within the brain such as tumors. Several regularly occurring rhythms or waves are known and are correlated with normal states of concentration or sleep: alpha, beta, delta, and theta waves. A flat EEG pattern indicates no brain activity and is one means used to determine legal death. The EEG patterns preceding and during epileptic attacks are both dramatic and diagnostic. *n.* **electroencephalo-**

graphy. *adj.* **eletroencephalographic.**

electromyogram (EMG) (i lek″trə mī′ə gram″) *n.* a graphic record of electrical currents associated with muscle activity. *Note:* The EMG may be made from electrodes placed on the skin or inserted directly into the target muscle, and may be made while the muscle(s) is (are) resting, under voluntary or involuntary contraction. Electromyography is used to study eye movements and subvocal responses during reading.

electro-oculogram (i lek″trō ok′yə lə gram″) 1. *n.* a record of differences in electropotentials in the eye, as found in measuring eye movement activity 2. *n.* any printed record of eye movements, as by electrographic tracing, photography, etc. *n.* **electro-oculography.**

elegy (el′i jē) 1. *n.* a formal poem, mournful or melancholy, often a lament for the dead, as Gray's *Elegy Written in a Country Churchyard.* 2. *n.* a mournful musical composition, usually short.

element (el′ə mənt) *n.* that part of a larger grammatical construction which can be identified and analyzed, as words in a sentence or phonemes in a word.

elementary school in the United States the school which most children of 5 or 6 to 11 or 12 years attend; grade school. *Note:* The elementary school may include kindergarten and extend through grades 4, 6, or even 8. See also **middle school.**

elision (i lizh′ən) 1. *n.* the omission of a sound in a word in pronunciation, as in *e'er, I'll, doesn't.* 2. *n.* in verse, the dropping of a vowel for a metrical purpose: *Though fair th' extended Vale, and fair to view....* — Coleridge. 3. *n.* omission of a passage in a written work. *v.* **elide.**

elite (i lēt′, ā lēt′) *n.* a rather small type size, popular for typewriters. *Ct.* **pica** (def. 2).

ellipsis (i lip′sis) *pl.* **-ses** (sēs). 1. *n.* the omission of a part of a sentence that is not needed for meaning: *I don't want to go, but you can if you want to,* becomes *...can [go] if you want to [go].* 2. *n.* an orthographic symbol of three or more dots (...) used to show an omitted part of a passage.

elocution (el″ə kyōō′shən) *n.* the training in, or use of, effective public speaking.

em-, en-, end (o), ento- a prefix indicating *in, within, into*; as **embedding, encode, endocrine.**

em (em) 1. *n.* a unit of measurement in typographic design, about 2.7 mm. (1/6 in.) in length. *Indent one em.* 2. *n.* the square of any type size. *Ct.* **en.**

embedded figure a shape partially hidden by its surrounding context, or ground, often making immediate recognition somewhat difficult. See illustration. See also **figure-ground.**

Embedded figure: A

embedding (em bed′ing) *n.* a sentence-combining process in which one clause is contained inside another, as *The dog won the show* may be combined or embedded with *The dog was a wolfhound* to form *The dog that won the show was a wolfhound. Note:* The embedded sentence is often signalled by *that, which, who,* etc. *Cp.* **recursiveness.**

embolism (em′bə liz″əm) *n.* the stoppage of circulation in a blood vessel by matter coming from another part of the circulatory system. *Cp.* **thrombosis.**

EMG electromyogram.

emmetropia (em″i trō′pē ə) *n.* normal vision; specifically, the ideal refractive condition in which, without accommodation, an object six meters or more away is focused clearly on the retina. See illustration. *Ct.* **myopia; hyperopia; astigmatism.** *n.* **emmetrope.** *adj.* **emmetropic.**

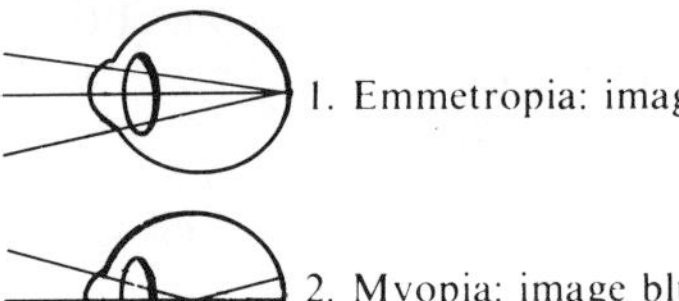

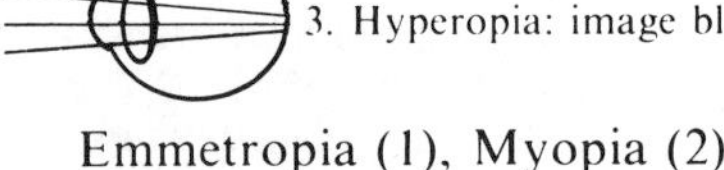

Emmetropia (1), Myopia (2), Hyperopia (3)

emotional block 1. the recurring inability to respond appropriately, especially to think clearly, as a result of fears or other powerful emotions. *Ct.* **block** (def. 3). 2. in psychoanalytic theory, a term indicating the repression of emotion(s). *Note:* Emotional block is often loosely used by lay persons to explain relatively minor emotional problems.

emotional disorder a chronic emotional response pattern, either too intense or too lacking in emotion for normal functioning. See also **anxiety hysteria; personality disorder.**

emotionally disturbed 1. an emotionally unstable person with diminished ability to learn and to cope with the environment. 2. referring to such a person. *Cp.* **emotional disorder.**

emotive language language, oral or written, which arouses emotional involvement and associations in the listener or reader by the use of emotionally-charged words, dramatic intonation, or syntax, etc. *An evangelist often uses emotive language to inspire the audience.*

emotive meaning See **affective meaning.**

empathy (em′pə thē) 1. *n.* identification with another person's feelings, thoughts, and ideas, leading to their understanding and acceptance, as *empathy for a student's difficulties. Note:* A distinction is usually made between *empathy* and *sympathy*: in *empathy*, emotion is intellectually controlled and differs from that of the subject; in *sympathy*, persons presumably share the same emotion. See also **identification** (def. 2). 2. *n.* the imaginative attribution of one's own feelings to an object, animal, character in literature or the theater, etc. *Note:* Writers, especially poets, make frequent use of empathy, as in Keats' *Ode to a Grecian Urn* or Shelley's *To a Skylark.* Readers likewise frequently use empathy as they react to characters in their reading. *v.* **empathize.**

emphasis (em′fə sis) 1. *n.* the stress given to a spoken word to show its special importance. *He spoke slowly, with emphasis on each word.* 2. *n.* the relative importance attached to anything, as *emphasis upon correct spelling.* 3. *n.* something to which importance is attached. *Neatness was given emphasis.* 4. *n.* prominence of form or outline. *The spotlight gave emphasis to the actor's face. v.* **emphasize.**

emphatic (em fat′ik) *adj.* referring to a word, pitch, or stress used to give special force or emphasis to speech or writing, as the use of *did* in *I did go.*

empirical (em pir′i kəl) 1. *adj.* coming from or guided by observation or experiment. 2. *adj.* verifiable only by data or observation. *The principal* *used test scores for empirical evidence of reading gains.*

empirical validity validity that can be verified by observed facts or experience.

EMR educable mentally retarded.

en (en) *n.* half of an em.

enactive representation See **cognitive representation.**

encephal (o)- a combining form indicating *brain*; as **encephalogram.**

enchantment (en chant'mənt, -chänt'-) 1. *n.* a motif in folklore, as *Merlin's use of enchantment in the King Arthur tales.* 2. *n.* the use of supernatural powers to make possible the impossible, such as the long sleep of Snow White in the Grimms's story, *Snow White and the Seven Dwarfs.*

encode (en kōd') 1. *v.* to change a message into symbols, as *encode oral language into writing, encode an idea into words,* or *encode a physical law into mathematical symbols.* See also **decode** (def. 1); **recode** (def. 1). 2. *v.* to give a deep structure to a message. *Encoding starts with meaning...You start out with a message; then you assign a deep structure* — K. Goodman (1971). *n.* **encoding.**

enculturation (en kul″chə rā'shən) See **socialization.**

encyclopedia (en sī″klə pē'dē ə) 1. *n.* an extensive collection of articles about subjects in important areas of knowledge, usually arranged alphabetically, as the *Encyclopedia Britannia.* 2. *n.* a similar work limited to a special field or subject, as *an encyclopedia of music and musicians.*

end matter all those parts of a book following the body, or text, as index, addenda, supplements, etc.; back matter.

endocentric (en″dō sen'trik) *adj.* referring to a construction or compound that has the same syntactic function as its head term. *'Cold water' is an endocentric construction for 'water.' Ct.* **exocentric.**

endocrine gland any of several body glands that secrete inside the body rather than into an outside opening or duct of the body; ductless gland. *The adrenals are endocrine glands.*

endogenous (en doj'ə nəs) *adj.* beginning or coming from within; specifically, referring to growth and/or conditions caused by genetic or hereditary factors, as *endogenous mental retardation. Ant.* **exogenous.**

end paper *n.* a sheet of paper at each end of a book, half of which is pasted to the inside of the cover, the other half of which is free and forms the flyleaf; end sheet. *Note:* End papers, whether blank or decorative, have a structural function, helping to attach the contents to the covers and forming part of the hinge or joint.

end rhyme the rhyming of ends of lines of verse, the most typical place for rhyme in English verse.

English (ing'glish, -lish) 1. *n.* the native language of several hundred million speakers in the British Commonwealth nations, the United States, and many former British colonies. 2. *adj.* referring to England, its people, institutions, etc., as *English law.* 3. *adj.* referring to something spoken or written in England, as *English pronunciation.* 4. *n.* the course of study in schools and colleges which includes specific instruction in English grammar and in American and British literature, as well as in the language and communication arts. *Note:* Special types of English, as *nonstandard English,* are given under the describing term.

English as a Foreign Language (EFL) the teaching of English language skills in a non-English speaking community or country. *Ct.* **English as a Second Language (ESL)**

English as a Second Language (ESL) a program for the teaching of English language skills (speaking, listening, reading, and writing) to persons in an English-speaking environment whose native language is not English. *Note:* The acronym ESOL (English to Speakers of Other Languages) is sometimes used instead of ESL.

English school a form of secondary education that developed in the United States in the 18th century for students who needed a practical and vocational education rather than a classical one. *Note:* Girls as well as boys were admitted to some English schools. Courses such as English, mathematics, accounting, bookkeeping, letter writing, navigation, and modern languages were offered. *Cp.* **Latin grammar school**.

engram (en′gram) *n.* a specific physical change in nerve tissue assumed to take place in response to stimulation. *Note:* Although the engram, a hypothetical construct postulated by S.T. Orton (1929), is often used to explain memory, there is little research evidence to confirm it.

enlarger (en lär′jər) *n.* a device for projecting images from a photographic negative to increase or reduce their size on paper or film. *v.* **enlarge.** *n.* **enlargement**.

enrichment (en rich′mənt) *n. the provision of some form of additional educational experience which supplements regular classroom activities* — M.D. Vernon (1978). *Special provisions for the disadvantaged and the gifted as well as such activities as supplementary reading in the classroom are forms of enrichment. Note:* Enrichment is sometimes applied only to activities which expand skills or knowledge after competence is reached, thus excluding drill or review activities.

entering behavior a description of the skills and concepts needed to begin a learning activity.

entr'acte (än trakt′; *Fr.* än tʀakt′) *pl.* **-tr'actes** (-trakts′; *Fr.* -tʀakt′). 1. *n.* the time between two acts of a play, opera, or musical comedy; interval. 2. *n.* entertainment presented at this time.

entropy (en′trə pē) 1. *n.* a measure of randomness. *Complete uniformity in anything would be zero entropy.* 2. *n.* in information theory, uncertainty. *Note:* The construction 'either...or...' has less uncertainty and thus contains more information than does the construction 'etc.,' which is highly uncertain and contains little information.

entry (en′trē) 1. *n.* a term listed alphabetically, usually in boldface, in a dictionary or glossary; vocabulary entry. 2. *n.* the record of a book or other material in a bibliographic tool such as a library catalog. *Note:* The entry should be distinguished from the library card that carries the entry. 3. *n.* an item recorded in a particular place, as in a statistical tabulation.

enunciate (i nun′sē āt″, -shē-) 1. *v.* to speak, especially with distinct articulation. 2. *v.* to make a statement or announcement. *n.* **enunciation**.

enuresis (en′yə rē′sis) *n.* uncontrolled bed-wetting, usually occurring while asleep. *adj.* **enuretic**.

environment (en vī′rən mənt, -vī′ərn-) 1. *n.* the totality of external things, conditions, and influences which may affect the individual, as *the physical environment, social environment, intellectual environment.* 2. *n.* in linguistics, the context or domain to which a grammatical rule may be applied. *adj.* **environmental**.

environmental validity the extent to which an experimental finding maintains its value later among the uncontrolled variables in a real situation; practical rather than statistical significance.

ephemera (i fem′ər ə) *pl.* **-eras, erae** (-ə rē″). See **fugitive material.**

epic (ep′ik) 1. *n.* a long narrative poem, usually about a hero and his great deeds, stated in lofty, elevated language. *Homer's* Odyssey *is a great epic.* 2. *adj.* referring to this kind of poem. 3. *adj.* great or awesome, as *epic events of the atomic age.*

epiglottis (ep″ə glot′is) *n.* a thin flap of cartilage that closes off the larynx during swallowing to keep the airway clear.

epigram (ep′ə gram″) 1. *n.* a brief saying, witty and pointed. *Wedding is destiny,/And hanging likewise* — John Heywood. 2. *n.* a short poem, often with a satirical twist, related historically to the epitaph: *Underneath this stone doth lie/As much beauty as could die;/Which in life did harbour give/To more virtue than doth live* — B. Jonson. *adj.* **epigrammatic.**

epigraph (ep′ə graf″, -gräf″) 1. *n.* an engraved inscription, as on a monument, building, work of art, etc. 2. *n.* a quotation at the beginning of a book, chapter, etc. *adj.* **epigraphic.**

epigraphy (i pig′rə fē) *n.* that field of study which deciphers and interprets ancient engraved or molded inscriptions, as runic and cuneiform writing. *Cp.* **paleography** (def. 2).

epilepsy (ep′ə lep″sē) *n.* a broad syndrome of periodic brain dysfunctions with motor, sensory, autonomic, and psychological symptoms, often including changes in consciousness and seizures ranging from small spasms to large convulsions. *Note:* Electroencephalographic patterns usually show dramatic pattern changes during seizures. These may be set off by activity within the brain, or by lights, sounds, or even stress. The most common acquired cases of epilepsy are birth injuries, anoxia, tumors, and metabolic disorders. It is now possible to predict and control most seizures by medication. See **petit mal; grand mal.**

epilogue *or* **epilog** (ep′ə lôg″, -log″) 1. *n.* a final speech by one or more characters in a play, usually to tie up any loose ends. *Many television plays include an epilogue.* 2. *n.* a brief concluding addition to a written work. *Ct.* **prologue** *or* **prolog** (def. 1).

episode (ep′i sōd″, -zōd″) 1. *n.* an incident in a person's life, as *a childhood episode.* 2. *n.* in writing, an incident, often a digression, which the author may or may not link to the plot or theme. *Many early novels are merely a series of episodes.* 3. *n.* one of the parts of a serial in a magazine or a mass media production. 4. *n.* in ancient Greek tragedy, the dramatic action between two choruses.

episodic (ep″i sod′ik, -zod′-) *adj.* a style of narrative or storytelling that describes a chain of incidents, as in Henry Fielding's *Tom Jones.*

epistemology (i pis″tə mol′ə jē) *n.* the branch of philosophy having to do with the nature of knowledge and of knowing. *adj.* **epistemological.**

epistle (i pis′əl) 1. *n.* a letter, generally written in formal and sometimes didactic style. 2. *n.* (*Cap.*) one of the books in the New Testament, or a section from it, written as a letter by an apostle. 3. *n.* a letter of dedication in a book.

epitaph (ep′ə taf″, -täf″) *n.* a brief memorial statement for a dead person, often inscribed on a tombstone or found in literary works. *The epitaph for Rich-*

ard Burbage, a famous Skakespearean actor, was 'Exit Burbage.'

epithet (ep′ə thet″) 1. *n.* any word or brief phrase used to characterize a person or thing, as *Theodore Roosevelt's epithet,* 'The Roughrider.' 2. *n.* a word or remark that expresses contempt or abuse.

eponym (ep′ə nim) *n.* a name of a real or imaginary person given to an institution, place, event, etc., as *Pennsylvania, Buckingham Palace.*

equi- a combining form indicating *equal;* as **equivalent.**

equilibration (ē″kwə lə brā′shən, i kwil″ə-) *n.* (J. Piaget) a principle which refers to the dynamic balance between accommodation and assimilation in the process of mental development. *With heredity, environment, and social transmission, equilibration makes possible the acquisition of more complex mental structures.*

equilibrium (ē′kwə lib′rē əm) 1. *n.* a balance between opposing forces in the body, as the physiological condition of homeostasis, or evenness in emotional mood. 2. *n.* the balanced, upright posture that is aided by the semicircular canals of the inner ear. 3. *n.* (J. Piaget) adaptive interaction between an organism and its environment, or between the factors in cognitive structure. *Equilibrium is mobile and dynamic, fleeting in the elementary cognitive functions such as perception, and more stable for the higher mental functions.*

equivalent form See **comparable form** (def. 1).

equivocation (i kwiv″ə kā′shən) 1. *n.* the use or occurrence of a word or phrase that has two or more possible meanings; ambiguity. 2. *n.* a deliberate form of ambiguity. *Politicians are fond of equivocation.* 3. *n.* the occurrence of two words identical in spoken and/or written form but different in meaning, as *figure* in *the figure one, a shapely figure.* 4. *n.* intentional lying. 5. *n.* in logic, a fallacy resulting from having more than one meaning for the same term in a formal argument, as the term 'right' in the following argument: *A person ought to do what is right. A person has a right to eat as much as he wishes. Therefore, a person ought to eat as much as he wishes.*

ERIC Educational Resources Information Center.

errata (i rā′tə, i rä′-) *sing.* **erratum.** *n. pl.* a list of typesetting errors and their corrections which, if needed, are usually put on a separate sheet inserted in a publication.

error (er′ər) 1. *n.* a mistake, as *an error in reading.* 2. *n.* a mistaken opinion or belief, as *an error of faith.* 3. *n.* a belief in something not true, as *in error about the right time.* 4. *n.* a wrongdoing. *Mend the error of your ways.* 5. *n.* deviation from a true score or value. See also **standard error (SE, S.E.).** 6. *n.* in an experiment, any uncontrolled quantitative variation due to the experimenter and/or to experimental conditions. *Note:* Special types of errors, as *constant error,* are given under the describing term. *v.* **err.**

error of estimate 1. when using a regression equation, an error in judging the value of one variable from another. 2. standard error of estimate.

error of measurement a measure of the extent to which data fit within the limits of sampling error.

escape reading reading of any type that provides the reader with relief from tension. See **respite effect.** *Note:* While escape reading is often identified with certain characteristics of reading material, as fantasy, adventure, and humor, its function as escape depends on the effect upon the reader.

e, silent See **silent letter; e, final.**

ESL English as a Second Language.

eso- a prefix indicating *inner, inward*; as **esophoria.**

ESOL English to Speakers of Other Languages. See **English as a Second Language (ESL); English as a Foreign Language (EFL).**

esophoria (es″ə fōr′ē ə, -fôr′-) *n.* a heterophoria in which one eye turns inward when fusion is broken. *Cp.* **esotropia.** *Ant.* **exophoria.** *adj.* **esophoric.**

esotropia (es″ə trō′pē ə) *n.* crossed eyes; specifically, a heterophoria in which one eye clearly turns inward; convergent squint or strabismus. *Cp.* **esophoria.** *Ant.* **exotropia.** *adj.* **esotropic.**

Esperanto (es″pə rän′tō, -ran′-) *n.* an artificial language based upon major European languages. *Esperanto was created by L.L. Zamenhof in the hope that it would become an international language.*

essay (*n.* es′ā for def. 1; es′ā, e sā′ for def. 2; *v.* e sā′) 1. *n.* a relatively brief literary composition, usually in prose, giving the author's views on a particular topic. *Note:* The essay has so many varieties, formal and informal, that it defies more specific definition. It has been an important form and force in literature since Montaigne first used the term to describe the written expression of his views. 2. *n.* an attempt to do something, as *an essay at speaking.* 3. *v.* to try; attempt.

essay examination *or* **test** a test requiring written response, usually at some length, to one or more questions or topics. *Cp.* **objective test.** *Note:* The essay examination or test is often regarded as a highly subjective test in comparison with objective tests. Numerous studies have shown, however, that a relatively high degree of objectivity may be introduced in the essay test by proper construction of test items and by the training of test scorers.

-esthesia, -esthesis a combining form indicating *sensation, perception*; as **synesthesia.**

ethn (o)- a combining form indicating *race, people*; as **ethnographic.**

ethnic (et͟h′nik) 1. *adj.* similar or alike in racial and cultural background. *Indians are an ethnic minority in the United States.* 2. *adj.* similar or alike in a specific cultural trait, as dialect or language, costume, etc. *n.* **ethnicity.**

ethnocentrism (et͟h″nō sen′triz əm) *n.* the use of one's own social group in making judgments about other groups; especially, judgments of superiority to other groups, cultures, or races. *adj.* **ethnocentric.**

ethnographic (et͟h″nə graf′ik) *adj.* referring to the scientific study of individual cultures represented in ethnic groups. *Note:* Ethnographic research in education refers to on-site, naturalistic studies of classroom teaching/learning situations. *n.* **ethnography.**

ethnography of communication a description of a communicative situation in terms of the physical and social relationships between a speaker or writer and their context.

ethos (ē′thos, eth′os) 1. *n.* the basic spirit of the culture of a people, as *the classic ethos of ancient Greece.* 2. *n.* the moral element in dramatic literature that determines what a character will do. *A spiritual ethos guides Joan in Shaw's* St. Joan. 3. *n.* the spirit or character of a person, group, etc., as *the ethos of environmentalists.*

etiology (ē″tē ol′ə jē) 1. *n.* the study of the causes of diseases or disabilities. 2. *n.* a euphemism for the cause(s) or origin of a disease or disability. *adj.* **etiological.**

ETV educational television.

etymological spelling the respelling of a word so as to indicate its language of origin, as respelling Middle English *dette* as *debt*, after the Latin *debitum*.

etymology (et″ə mol′ə jē) *n.* the study of the origins and development of the structure and meanings of words. *adj.* **etymological.**

etymon (et′ə mon″) See **cognate** (def. 1).

eu- a combining form indicating *good, well*; as **eulogy.**

eulogy (yo͞o′lə jē) 1. *n.* formal praise, especially in honor of the dead, as *the minister's funeral eulogy.* 2. *n.* high praise, as *eulogy for an Olympic victor.* *v.* **eulogize.** *adj.* **eulogistic.**

euphemism (yo͞o′fə miz″əm) 1. *n.* the substitution of a mild or inoffensive expression for a blunt or harsh one. 2. *n.* the expression so substituted. *'Passed away' is a euphemism for 'died.'*

euphony (yo͞o′fə nē) 1. *n.* a pleasing sound effect, especially in combinations of speech sounds. 2. *n.* the changing of speech sounds to simplify pronunciation, as /wo͝os′tər/ for *Worchester.* *adj.* **euphonic.**

euphuism (yo͞o′fyo͞o iz″əm) 1. *n.* an ornate writing style popular in late 16th-century England that is characterized by many similes, rhetorical questions, and use of alliteration, as in John Lyly's *Euphues.* 2. *n.* such a style of expression. *adj.* **euphuistic.**

Eustachian tube (yo͞o stā′shən, -stā′kē ən) a narrow air canal which connects the middle ear and the nasal part of the throat. *The Eustachian tube allows the air pressure inside the middle ear to balance that outside whenever one yawns or swallows.* See illustration under **ear.**

evaluation (i val′yo͞o ā′shən) 1. *n.* judgment of performance as product or process of change. *Note:* Evaluation is an attempt to understand a process that is sometimes guided by pre-set objectives but at other times involves objectives added during the evaluation process. 2. *n.* the process of testing, appraising, and judging achievement, growth, product, process, or changes in these, frequently using formal and informal tests and techniques. *Note* (def. 2): The process of evaluation is global in conception and application. It represents a broad concept that may be distinguished from the concerns of measurement, appraisal, and assessment in that the latter operations can form the basis for evaluation, but not the reverse. 3. *n.* a synthesis of appraisals as by test scores, interviews, etc., in a case study. *v.* **evaluate.** *adj.* **evaluative.**

evaluator (i val′yo͞o ā″tər) *n.* a person who determines whether objectives have been met, as in an instructional program, or who tries to better understand something, as a process of change. *Note:* An *inside evaluator* is someone who has participated in some aspect of that which is being evaluated (as a staff member); an *outside evaluator* is one who has not been identified with that which is being evaluated in any way and is, therefore, presumed to be wholly objective in the sense of having no conflict of interest.

ex (o)- a prefix indicating *out of, beyond*; as **extension, exocentric.**

examination (ig zam″ə nā′shən) 1. *n* the act of testing. *A written examination was conducted.* 2. *n.* a test, as *an English examination.* 3. *n.* test answers. *She handed in her examination* 4. *n.* an inquiry; investigation. *Holmes made a careful examination of the scene* *of the crime.* 5. *n.* subjected to testing, as *physical examination.* 6. *adj.* referring to a test, as an *examination question.* *v.* **examine.** *n.* **examiner.**

exceptional child a general term for a child who is very different from the usual child in one or more aspects of development — physical, intellectual, social, or emotional. *Note:* In the statistical sense, exceptional refers to significant deviations from the norm in either direction: both the gifted and the retarded child represent exceptional mental functioning. Commonly, however, the term is a euphemism for a child with some deficit or handicap.

exclamation mark a punctuation mark (!) placed at the end of a sentence to indicate that the speaker or writer is surprised, or that the message should be emphasized, as *You don't say!*

exclamatory (ik sklam'ə tōr"ē, -tôr"ē) 1. *n.* a grammatical construction expressing strong opinion or emotion, often punctuated by an exclamation point or marked by intonation, as *What a fantastic play!* 2. *adj.* referring to such a construction.

exemplar (ig zem'plər, -plär) *n.* something that serves as an example, model, or ideal. *Names are exemplars of the class of proper nouns. He is a perfect exemplar of a gentleman.* *adj.* **exemplary.**

exhalation (eks"hə lā'shən, eg"zē-) 1. *n.* the process of breathing out. *English speech depends on exhalation. Ant.* **inhalation.** 2. *n.* the result of breathing out. *v.* **exhale.**

exhibit (ig zib'it) 1. *n.* a collection of books, objects, or materials arranged for others to see and sometimes handle. 2. *v.* to show such a collection. *n.* **exhibition; exhibitor.**

existentialism (eg"zi sten'shə liz"əm) *n.* a set of philosophic ideas which share the assumption that each person is a uniquely important, free, and responsible individual in the universe. *Note:* Existentialism has been expressed in various forms, especially in literature by Jean-Paul Sartre and in religion by S. Kierkegaard and others. Although many playwrights and novelists have emphasized the loneliness and despair of free man in a hostile world, the existential writings of theologians elaborate the positive nature of the responsibility that the individual's freedom of choice brings. In teaching, an existential point of view leads a teacher or clinician to adopt a role as a reality-mirror, showing students the implications and probable consequences of their behavior, but allowing them to make their own decisions. *adj.* **existential.**

existential sentence a sentence which states that something exists or is situated at a specific place or time: *There's a man at the door.* *Ct.* **predicative sentence.**

exocentric (ex"sō sen'trik) *adj.* referring to a construction or compound which functions differently from its elements. *Behind the building* is an exocentric construction because, although none of its elements is an adverb, it may function as an adverb. *Ct.* **endocentric.**

exogenous (ek soj'ə nəs) *adj.* beginning or coming from without; specifically, referring to growth and/or conditions caused by congenital or post-natal factors, as *exogenous kidney failure. Ant.* **endogenous.**

exophoria (eks"ō fōr'ē ə, -fôr'-) *n.* a heterophoria in which one eye turns outward when fusion is broken. *Cp.* **esotropia.** *Ant.* **esophoria.** *adj.* **exophoric.**

exotropia (ek"sə trō'pē ə) *n.* wall-eyes;

specifically, a heterotropia in which one eye turns outward; divergent squint or strabismus. *Cp.* **esophoria**. *Ant.* **esotropia**. *adj.* **exotropic**.

expansion (ik span′shən) *n.* the extension of a grammatical structure by adding further elements without changing its basic form, as adding *little, blonde-haired* to *Susan has a (little, blonde-haired) brother*.

expansion rule in transformational-generative grammar, a rewrite rule for indicating the expansion of a sentence.

expected response in miscue analysis, an accurate oral reading of a text.

experience (ik spēr′ē əns) 1. *n.* a specific instance of undergoing some event, as *one's first experience in reading a book*. 2. *n.* the total effect of all events thus undergone, as *a person of considerable experience*. 3. *n.* the effect of selected events thus undergone, as *a background of experience for studying algebra*. 4. *v.* to undergo; feel; as *experience pain*. *adj.* **experiential**.

experience approach *or* **method** 1. a way of teaching reading in which reading materials are created from student experiences and vocabularies. *Note:* E. Huey (1908) cites this example: *After performing some experiment, or perhaps working in the garden or observing things in nature, the children gather to tell what has been done, and the teacher writes their statements on the board. They read and correct their own statements, and often these are printed by some of the older children and returned as a printed story of what has happened. The child can read these, knowing the gist of it...* 2. an instructional program based upon student needs and interests rather than upon preplanned curriculum materials.

experience chart a dictated account by students about a common experience, usually transcribed by the teacher on a large chart or chalkboard for group use.

experience, cone of See **cone of experience**.

experiment (*n.* ik sper′ə mənt; *v.* ek sper′ ə mənt″) 1. *n.* a trial procedure; specifically, the formal observance of experimental design conditions. 2. *v.* to conduct a trial procedure in order to determine cause and effect relationships.

experimental design the plan(s) for conducting a specific piece of research; specifically, the plan(s) for selecting subjects, manipulating dependent variables, and collecting and analyzing the data.

experiment book an information or factual type of book for children which features activities, demonstrations, and experiments.

explanation (ek″splə nā′shən) 1. *n.* the process of making something simple, clear, and easy to understand. 2. *n.* a clarifying statement; exposition. 3. *n.* a meaning or interpretation. *What is the explanation of this?*

expletive (ek′splə tiv) 1. *n.* an interjection of frustration or anger, commonly a swear word. 2. *n.* a substitute or added word or phrase used in a sentence, as *It* in *It is his duty to go* instead of the construction *His duty is to go*.

explication de texte (ek splē kä syôɴ de tekst′) *pl.* **explications de texte** (ek′splē kä syôɴs de tekst′). (*French*) 1. a very close and detailed method of analyzing literature, developed first in France. 2. an approach to literary criticism that uses such a method.

explicit (ik splis′it) 1. *adj.* clear, specific, and unambiguous, as *explicit directions*. *Ant.* **ambiguous**. 2. *adj.* outspoken, as *an explicit remark*. 3. **explicit definition**, definition by synonyms; denotation. *Ant.* **implicit definition**. 4. *adj.* overt; visible; as *the ex-*

plicit signs of measles.

exponent (ik spō′nənt, ek′spō nənt) 1. *n.* one who explains; interpreter. 2. *n.* a person or thing that is representative or symbolic of something. *George Washington is the exponent of honesty in American lore.*

exposition (ek″spə zish′ən) 1. *n.* one of the four traditional forms of composition in speech and writing. *Note:* The primary purpose of exposition is to set forth or explain. Good exposition in speech or writing is clear in conception, well-organized, and understandable. It may include limited amounts of argumentation, description, and narration to achieve this purpose. *Cp.* **argumentation** (def. 2); **description** (def. 1); **narration** (def. 1). 2. *n.* the act of explaining or setting forth, as *a skilled exposition of ideas.* 3. *n.* display, as in a public exhibition, show, or fair. *adj.* **expository**.

expression (ik spresh′ən) 1. *n.* the act or result of setting forth something in words; utterance. 2. *n.* a particular word or wording, as *I don't believe it. Cp.* **idiom** (defs. 1-3). 3. *n.* wording, as *an awkward expression.* 4. *n.* modulation and pacing in the use of the voice to convey meaning and feeling. 5. *n.* the quality of feeling shown, as *read with expression, the minister's stern expression.* 6. *n.* an action or act representative of an organism. *Thinking is an expression of the higher mental process.* 7. *n.* a response indicating emotion, as *an expression of joy.* 8. *n.* a symbolic representation, as *a mathematical expression. v.* **express.** *adj.* **expressive.**

expressionism (ik spresh′ə niz″əm) *n.* (*often Cap.*) an artisitc movement prominent in the 1920's; specifically, an emphasis upon the intentional distortion of objective reality in the fine arts, literature, and drama through symbolism and emotional content, as in Picasso's *Guernica*, James Joyce's *Ulysses*, and Eugene O'Neill's *The Emperor Jones. Cp.* **impressionism.** *adj.* **expressionistic**.

expressive aphasia 1. difficulty in producing syntactic speech, and often writing, because of brain injury or disease. 2. difficulty in recalling the sequence of words needed to say what one wishes to say, as in Broca's aphasia.

expressive language 1. language whose function is to state something rather than to persuade or exchange pleasantries. 2. language which is vivid and colorful, metaphorical, rich in connotations, etc. 3. speaking and writing. *Ct.* (def. 3) **receptive language**.

expressive objective an aim or purpose of some process of change, as instruction, stated in terms of the nature and/or the number of activities to be introduced.

expressive writing a term used by J. Britton and others (1975) to describe highly personal writing, as in diaries, personal letters, autobiographies, etc. *Note:* Expressive writing is seen as having its origin in the intimate, direct, expressive utterances of children as described by E. Sapir, out of which one type of writing develops which is *a form of written-down expressive speech* — J. Britton. *Cp.* **poetic writing; transactional writing**.

expurgate (ek′spər gāt″, ik spûr′gāt) *v.* to censor, 'cleanse,' by removing objectionable, erroneous, or obscene parts of material before presentation or publication, as *expurgate a memoir. Cp.* **bowdlerize**; **censorship**.

extension (ik sten′shən) 1. *n.* the class of things to which a term applies; denotation. *Ct.* **intension**. 2. *n.* the process, or result, of stretching out, as of time, space, influence, etc. 3. *n.* anything added to something else; specifically, the adding of referents to which a term may apply, as *the extension of 'foot' to the term 'zipper-foot.'* *v.* **extend.** *adj.* **extensional.**

extensive reading a reading program in which students read widely without restraints, with emphasis on broadening the scope of materials read. *Extensive reading contributes to one's breadth of vicarious experience.* *Ct.* **intensive reading.**

extensor (ik sten'sər, -sôr) *n.* a muscle that tends to straighten a limb, open a joint, or extend an organ on contraction. *Ant.* **flexor.**

external auditory meatus the canal in the external ear which carries sound pressure to the eardrum. See illustration under **ear.**

external ear the visible part of the ear which carries sound waves to the middle ear; outer ear. *The external ear includes the auricle, the external auditory meatus, and sometimes the tympanic membrane, or eardrum.* See illustration under **ear.**

exteroceptor (ek"stər ə sep'tər) *n.* a sense organ or sensory nerve terminal chiefly in the skin, the mucous membranes, and the eye and ear, which receives stimulation from the external environment. *Exteroceptors in the skin are sensitive to pressure.* *Cp.* **interoceptor; proprioceptor.**

extra-, extro- a combining form indicating *outside, beyond* (a boundary or scope); as **extraocular, extroversion.**

extraocular muscles the six intrinsic muscles attached to the outside of the eyeball which serve to turn and rotate it in its socket. *Ct.* **intraocular muscles.**

extrapolate (ik strap'ə lāt", ek'strə pə-) 1. *v.* to infer something unknown from the known,; conjecture; as *extrapolate future trends from historical data.* 2. *v.* to estimate the value of a variable beyond its known range from available data, as *extrapolate the norms for a test.* *Ct.* **interpolate** (def. 2.). *n.* **extrapolation.**

extraversion (ek"strə vûr'zhən, -shən, ek'strə- vûr"-) *n.* the process of turning outward; specifically, a normal type of behavior focused on social interaction and on sociability rather than oneself. *Ant.* **introversion.** *n.* **extravert.**

extrinsic (ik strin'sik) 1. *adj.* coming from without; non-essential; extraneous; as *extrinsic motivation.* 2. *adj.* having to do with something, especially muscles and nerves, originating outside of the part of the body that it affects. *Extrinsic eye muscles rotate the eyes.* *Ct.* **intrinsic.**

extrinsic method a teaching-learning approach in which goals and rewards come from the teacher, not the student. *Ct.* **instrinsic method.**

extrinsic motivation 1. behavior directed toward satisfaction through anticipated reward or punishment. 2. the control of such behavior, as through gold stars, grades, and token gifts. *Note:* Properly guided and controlled, extrinsic motivation may lead to intrinsic motivation. *Ct.* **intrinsic motivation.**

extrinsic phonics any phonics approach that is taught as a supplemental learning aid rather than as an integral part of the program of reading instruction, often in separate workbooks during special time periods. *Ct.* **intrinsic phonics.**

extroversion (ek"strō vûr'zhən, -shən ek'strō- vûr"-, -strə-) See **extraversion.**

eye (ī) 1. *n.* the organ of vision, especially that part in the eye socket of the skull: the eyeball and the retina. See illustration. 2. *n.* that part of the eye most easily seen; especially the pupil the iris which gives the eye its color and the white sclera which may redden if irritated. 3. *n.* the structures surrounding, supporting, and protecting the eye, as the eyebrow. 4. *n.* sensitive and discriminating visual perception, as *an eye for beauty*.

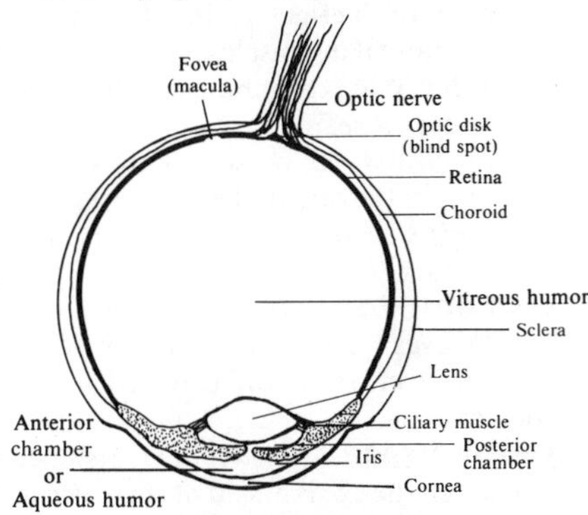

The human eye

eye coordination the working of the eyes together rather than against each other, as in efficient and comfortable vision.

eye-dialect (ī″ di′ə lekt″) *n.* written language spelled according to regional/social pronunciation and intended to convey such pronunciation: 'We's safe, Huck, we's safe! Jump up and crack yo' heels! Dat's de good ole Cairo at las', I jis knows it is! — Jim in Mark Twain's *Adventures of Huckleberry Finn*.

eyedness (īd′nis) *n.* the consistent preference for one eye over the other in monocular tasks such as sighting a gun. See **dominant eye**.

eye dominance See **dominant eye**.

eye fixation See **fixation** (defs. 1, 2).

eye-hand coordination the smooth integration of visual with tactile and/or kinesthetic sensory information to make fluent, accurate hand movements: *the mind's eye steering the hand* — G. Kaluger and C. Colson (1978).

eye-hand dominance a theoretical assumption that the controlling hand and dominant eye should be on the same side for effective coordination. *Note:* The assumption is suspect. See **cerebral dominance** (def. 1).

eye-movement camera an instrument for photographing eye movements, especially while reading. *Note:* For many years, a corneal reflection method was used to record eye-movements photographically. Later, heat sensitive paper and electric pens allowed a direct print-out of such movements, by-passing the need to develop the film. Most recently, TV cameras and computer analysis of movements have been used in the study of eye-movements. See also **eye-movement pattern**.

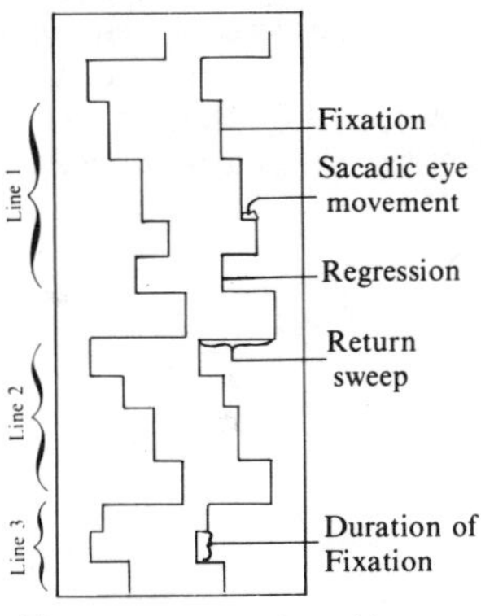

Eye-movement pattern

eye-movement pattern 1. the corneal reflection eye-movement pattern, especially that revealed in reading, as the number and direction of fixations, regressions, loss of fusion, etc. See illustration. 2. eye-movement patterns recorded and analyzed by TV cameras linked to computers. *Note:* The increased accuracy and sophistication of these newer patterns provide all of the corneal reflection data plus other information which appears to hold promise for early detection of visual or neurological dysfunction. See also **eye-movement record; eye-movement camera.**

eye-movement photography See **eye-movement camera.**

eye-movement record any record of eye-movements during reading or other visual inspection tasks. *Common eye-movement records include film, TV/computer printouts, and peephole observations.* See also **eye-movement pattern; Miles peephole method.**

eye movements 1. for eye specialists, any changes in position of the eyes, as nystagmus, pursuit, etc. 2. for reading specialists, the ways the eyes appear to move in reading, as fixations, regressions, return sweeps, saccades, etc. *Note:* Eye movements are symptoms, not causes, of fundamental reading processes. *The classroom teacher needs to be concerned with movements of the eyes little more than with the movements of the bones of the inner ear* — E. Horn (1937).

eye muscle imbalance a deviate eye condition caused by abnormal development or ineffective functioning of the extraocular muscles.

eye preference the choice of the dominant eye in seeing.

eye specialist a person with special training in the care of the eyes. *Ophthalmologists and optometrists are eye specialists.*

eyestrain (ī'strān) *n.* tiredness or stress of the eyes, primarily from their overuse or from some uncorrected visual defect.

eye-voice span the average distance by which the eye is ahead of the voice in oral reading. *A wide eye-voice span allows the reader to anticipate meaning, phrase in thought units, adjust intonation and breathing, and check pronunciation before speaking.*

F

DEVELOPMENT OF MAJUSCULE								
NORTH SEMITIC	GREEK		ETR.	LATIN		MODERN		
						GOTHIC	ITALIC	ROMAN
Y	ꟻ	—	ꟻ	ꟻ	F	𝔉	*F*	F

DEVELOPMENT OF MINUSCULE					
ROMAN CURSIVE	ROMAN UNCIAL	CAROL. MIN.	MODERN		
			GOTHIC	ITALIC	ROMAN
F	F	ſ	𝔣	*f*	f

The sixth letter of the English alphabet developed from North Semitic *waw,* denoted by a symbol resembling Y. A variant (see **U**) was adopted by the Greeks as *digamma* (ϝ), which had a *w*-like sound, but later dropped out of use as an alphabetic character, surviving only as a numeral. In early Latin, the *f*-sound was represented by *fh;* but the *h* was soon discontinued. The minuscule (**f**) is a scribal variant of the capital.

F See **F test** *or* **value.**

fable (fā′bəl) 1. *n.* a short tale in prose or verse to teach a moral; especially, a tale using animals and inanimate objects as characters. *Cp.* **allegory**. 2. *n.* a myth or a legend. 3. *n.* a lie or falsehood. 4. *v.* to state falsely; lie.

face (fās) See **typeface** (def. 1).

face validity the degree to which a test appears reasonable and usable; test content that is superficially valid in appearance but not necessarily so in a technical sense. *Note:* Face validity refers only to test user acceptability, not to content validity. For this reason a test with face validity alone is a poor test, but one with high face validity *and* content validity may be very good and widely used.

factor (fak′tər) 1. *n.* anything that combines with other things, as events, ideas, etc., to produce a result. *Many factors influenced the school closing.* 2. *n.* any of the mathematical units which, when multiplied together, will give a stated product. *Both 3 and 4 are factors of 12.* 3. *v.* to break down a product into its mathematical units; factoring. 4. See **factor analysis**.

factor analysis any of several methods for analyzing the intercorrelations of tests; a type of multivariate analysis. *Note:* When a factor is located in factor analysis, it is interpreted as a source of communality that is often given a name. *'Rate of reading' is a factor found in many different factor analyses and is therefore understood to exist independently of the particular reading test used.*

factorial design any experimental design that involves the systematic variation, or possible combination, of two or more independent variables in relation to the dependent variable, as a study of the effect of phonic skills and vocabulary knowledge upon rate of comprehension.

factor loading the relationship expressed as a correlation in multivariate analysis between a factor and a test: the higher the factor loading, the more adequately the factor accounts for scores on the test, and vice versa.

factor score in multivariate analysis, the weighted sum of scores on the tests, designed to give a score maximally correlated with the underlying factor.

factual question a type of question used to explore a person's understanding of what is read or heard but limited to the recall of information in the passage.

fairy tale a folk story about real life problems, but usually involving imaginary characters and magical events. *Cp.* **folk tale** *or* **story; myth**.

fallacy (fal′ə sē) 1. *n.* any unsound argument or form of reasoning, as *the fallacy of circular reasoning.* 2. *n.* a false or deceptive notion, idea, etc. *adj.* **fallacious**.

falling diphthong a diphthong in which the initial vowel is dominant, as /ī/ in *buy*. *Ct.* **rising diphthong**.

falsetto (fôl set′ō) *n.* a high-pitched, thin voice, especially in singing, which is less full and powerful than the normal voice.

family constellation the characteristics of members of a family, as their number, order of birth, interrelationships, etc.

family therapy treatment by a psychotherapist to any or all members of a family as a group to work on conflict situations. *Cp.* **play therapy**. See also **group therapy**.

fantasy (fan′tə sē, -zē) *n.* a highly fanciful story about characters, places, and events that while sometimes believable, do not exist. *Ct.* **realistic fiction**.

farce (färs) 1. *n.* a light, humorous play emphasizing improbable situations rather than characterization. 2. *n.* humor of the type found in such plays. 3. *v.* to stuff writing and speaking with humor and wit. *Note:* Historically, farce was the injection of a play with jokes and gags. 4. *n.* a sham; mockery. *The actor's interpretation of the serious role was a farce. adj.* **farcical**.

far point an accepted distance of about six meters (20 ft.) or more for measuring visual acuity and the vision function at a distance. *Ct.* **near point**.

far point acuity visual acuity for distance vision. See **distance vision**.

far point of accommodation the distance from the eyeball at which a point source of light will focus on the retina when the accommodation of that eye is inoperative. *Note:* For a normal or emmetropic eye, this distance is optical infinity or about six meters (20 ft.) or more. *Ct.* **near point of accommodation**.

far point of convergence the real or assumed point where the lines of sight from the two eyes cross when convergence is relaxed. *Ct.* **near point of convergence**.

farsightedness (fär′sī″tid nis) See **hyperopia**.

fatigue (fə tēg′) 1. *n.* lowered ability to continue mental or physical work. *Long hours of continuous work may produce fatigue. Note:* Reading fatigue may be physical as in the exhausting use of the ciliary muscles when problems of accommodation exist, or more commonly it may be lack of interest in what is being read. *Reading fatigue is mainly fatigue of mind and not of eye* — E. Huey (1908). 2. *n.* lowered physiological functioning from overexertion or stimulation. *Note:* Extreme muscle fatigue may put an end to a motor task. 3. *n.* the perception of tiredness; weariness. *Monotonous tasks may produce fatigue.* 4. *v.* to make tired. *The long run fatigued the joggers.*

feature (fē′chər) *n.* a distinctive property of something; specifically, in linguistics, a distinctive speech sound, grammatical structure, or semantic characteristic that is useful in linguistic analysis. *Cp.* **distinctive feature** (defs. 1, 2).

feature analysis a method of analysis which describes qualities of linguistic components, as the 'voiced' versus 'voiceless' characteristics of consonants.

feeble-minded 1. *adj.* referring to any degree of mental retardation 2. *adj.* (*Brit.*) referring to the educable mentally retarded (EMR). *Note:* The term has been replaced by others in current usage. See **mental retardation**. *n.* **feeble-mindedness**.

feedback (fēd′bak″) 1. *n.* any information used to judge and/or change a process, result, etc. *A speed governor on an engine, student course evalua-*

tions, and directions by a coach are examples of feedback. 2. *n.* impulses from proprioceptors used to guide motor movements. 3. See **acoustic feedback.**

feedback loop the pathway by which information about the results of a process is sent back to modify or control the process. *Auditory feedback is an example of a feedback loop.*

feltboard (felt′bōrd″, -bôrd″) See **flannelboard.**

felt need a need which one is aware of and sensitive to.

feminine gender See **gender.**

feminist literature 1. writings by and about women. 2. a reappraisal by women of the historical, sociological, and psychological status and role of women that was analyzed initially by men. *Note:* Much of this literature expresses points of view about the stereotyping of women, and is especially directed toward removing sexism in language, including the language of dictionaries, in occupational and educational opportunity, and in the home. 3. writings from the feminist movement advocationg social, economic, and political rights for women equal to those of men.

fenestra (fi nes′trə) *pl.* **-trae.** *n.* a small opening or window, as in a bone or membrane.

fenestra ovalis See **oval window.**

fenestra rotunda See **round window.**

fenestration (fen″i strā′shən) *n.* a surgical operation to replace the round and/or oval window with a new opening into the cochlea to improve hearing.

Fernald (-Keller) approach *or* **method (VAKT)** a technique for learning words that involves looking at a word (*V*isual) while saying it (*A*uditory) and tracing it (*K*inesthetic, *T*actile), described at length in G. Fernald's *Remedial Techniques in Basic School Subjects. Note:* The technique is usually one part of a more comprehensive instructional method, often in remedial settings. *Cp.* **Gillingham Method.**

fiction (fik′shən) 1. *n.* imaginative narrative writing designed to entertain, as distinguished from that which is designed primarily to explain, argue, or merely describe; specifically, a type of literature, especially prose, as novels and short stories, but also including plays and narrative poetry. *Note:* Fiction, or a fictional element, is found in many specific literary forms, as historical fiction, fables, fairy tales, folklore, legends, and picture books. Elements of fiction may also be found in some biographies, autobiographies, and other forms of nonfiction. *Ct.* **nonfiction.** 2. *n.* a falsehood.

fictionalized biography the life story of a person, based partially on fact, partially on the imagination of the writer. *Jean Lee Latham has written many fictionalized biographies for young readers.*

field dependent referring to perception in individuals who show *relatively passive submission to the domination of the background, and inability to keep an item separate from its surroundings*—H.A. Witkins (1959).

field experience *or* **work** any type of off-campus work, usually of a practical nature, sponsored by a school or college.

field independent referring to perception in individuals who have *a capacity to differentiate objects from their backgrounds* — H.A. Witkin (1959).

field of discourse topically-related language. *The field of discourse of word analysis is much different from that of children's literature.*

field of vision See **visual field.**

field research *or* **study** research that,

unlike laboratory research, takes place in more natural and less controlled settings. *Ct.* **laboratory research**.

field testing the tryout of something in well-developed form in appropriate situations to find out what final changes may be needed. *Field testing is commonly used for new reading materials.*

field trip a visit to a place outside the regular educational setting for first-hand study of persons, places, or events, as *the local fire station, a museum, a book fair, a newspaper printing plant, etc.*

figurative knowledge (J. Piaget) perceptual and symbolic knowing attained directly from language, gesture, mental imagery, and perceptual recognition; static concepts representing external or figural aspects of objects and events, as in learning to identify and write letters and words. *Ct.* **operativity**.

figurative language language enriched by word images and figures of speech: *The dusky night rides down the sky,/ And ushers in the morn* — H. Fielding. See **figure of speech**; **image** (def. 8).

figure (fig′yər) 1. *n.* any written symbol other than a letter. 2. **figures**, arithmetic. 3. *n.* a visual form, shape, or outline. 4. *n.* a two- or three-dimensional representation of a form, especially the human form. 5. *n.* a text drawing, other than a table, graph, or diagram, as *a figure showing a learning curve* (usually abbreviated: *Fig.*). 6. *n.* a figure of speech. 7. *n.* a person who represents a certain role, as *a father figure*. 8. *v.* to work with numbers, as *figure a sum. adj.* **figural**.

figure-ground *n.* the perception or awareness of a distinctive form (figure) on a relatively formless background (ground), as the perception of an embedded figure or the awareness of a familiar voice in a noisy room. *Note:* Figure and ground interact, one influencing the other and sometimes becoming the other, as in a reversible figure.

figure of speech the expressive, nonliteral use of language for special effects, usually through images, as in metaphor and personification. *Note:* While many types of figures of speech make comparisons, others, as irony and hyperbole, do not.

film (film) 1. *n.* what photographic negatives and positives are recorded on. 2. *n.* a motion picture. 3. **films**, motion pictures, collectively. 4. *v.* to be appropriate for a motion picture. *This scene will film well.* 5. *v.* to take motion pictures of, as *film a novel. adj.* **filmic**.

filmloop (film′lo͞op″) See **loop**.

filmstrip (film′strip″) *n.* a short strip of film containing a series of positive prints for projection onto a screen, one at a time.

filmstrip projector a device to project filmstrips.

filter (fil′tər) 1. *n.* a material or process for screening out. *A hearing aid is not only an amplifier but an acoustic filter.* 2. *v.* to selectively screen out something from its surroundings, as to *filter water through charcoal, filter out sensitive information.*

final glide See **off-glide**.

fine motor coordination the control of small sets of voluntary muscles, as in writing, in grasping small objects, or in controlling eye movements.

finger spelling communicating ideas by finger movements which stand for letters or letter combinations in conventional spelling, as in the manual alphabet of the deaf; dactylology. *Cp.* **sign** (def. 4).

finite verb a verb form which shows, or potentially shows, person, number, and tense, as *opens* in *She opens the door. Ct.* **infinitive**.

first edition 1. the total number of copies of the first printing of a work. See also **limited edition**. 2. a single copy of this number.

first person 1. referring to the persons speaking, as *I* in *I hope it rains*, or *we* in *Will we be on time?* 2. a passage written from the point of view of the main character. *Ct.* **second person**; **third person**. See also **person**.

fis phenomenon the inability of children to recognize how their own speech deviates from adult norms, as the child who says 'No, not fis, but *fis*' in response to an adult's attempt to mimic the child's pronunciation of *fish*.

fissure (fish'ər) *n.* a deep furrow, crack, or groove, especially between the major divisions of an organ such as the liver or the brain. *Cp.* **sulcus**. See illustration under **lobe**.

fissure of Rolando the deep groove that separates the frontal lobe of the cerebrum from the parietal lobe; central cerebral sulcus. See illustration under **lobe**.

fissure of Sylvius the deep groove that separates the temporal lobe of the cerebrum from the parietal and frontal lobes; lateral cerebral fissure. See illustration under **lobe**.

fit (fit) 1. *n.* a sudden, severe attack that produces convulsions or unconsciousness; seizure; as *an epileptic fit*. 2. *n.* a strong but passing physical disturbance; spell; spasm; as *a fit of coughing*. 3. *n.* any sudden emotional reaction, as *a fit of jealousy*. 4. *adj.* healthy, as *fit exercise*. 5. *adj.* adapted; suited; ready; as *fit to eat*. 6. *adj.* proper, as *a fit book for children*. 7. *adj.* competent, qualified; worthy; as *a fit candidate*. 8. *v.* to be suitable for; match. *His name fit him perfectly*. 9. *v.* to conform to: *Some statistical procedures require obtained data to fit a theoretical distribution*. See also **goodness of fit test**. 10. *v.* to equip or make ready. *Mrs. James fit the books with bookcovers*. 11. *v.* to make a place for, as *fit all students in the bus*. 12. **by fits and starts**, irregular; impulsive; as *read by fits and starts*. 13. **fit to be tied**, very angry, furious.

fixation (fik sā'shən) 1. *n.* the observable stops in eye movements, as when viewing a picture, looking around the environment, or reading a line of print. *Visual perception seems to occur during, not between, fixations*. See illustration under **eye-movement pattern**. 2. *n.* the adjustments internally and in the position of the eyes to achieve clear vision. 3. *n.* a preoccupation to the point of obsession with some idea(s) or action(s). *Hamlet's fixation was to avenge his father's death*. 4. *n.* in psychoanalytic theory, a strong and lasting emotional attachment which prevents the making of new relationships or new response patterns. 5. *n.* a habit which has outlived its former usefulness, as washing dishes thoroughly before putting them into an automatic dishwasher. 6. *n.* the strengthening of a motor behavior or memory through practice and review. *v.* **fixate**.

fixation pause 1. an eye-movement stop. 2. duration of an eye-movement fixation.

fixation point a target to which the eye(s) is directed, usually to get a foveal image to maintain single binocular vision. *Fixation points are linked by saccades*.

flaccid (flak'sid) 1. *adj.* soft; flabby; lax; loose; as *a flaccid chin*. 2. *adj.* loose muscles and absence of tendon reflexes; hypotonic; as *flaccid paralysis*. *Ant.* (def. 2) **spastic**.

flannelboard (flan′ᵊl bōrd″, -bôrd″) *n.* a stiff display board covered with felt or flannel for displaying pictures, symbols, cutouts, etc., for instructional purposes; feltboard.

flashback (flash′bak″) *n.* the technique of returning to an earlier time in the course of a narrative to introduce prior information, as in Wilder's *Bridge of San Luis Rey. Note:* Flashback is also widely used in drama, TV, film, and radio.

flash card *or* **device** 1. a teaching technique by which numbers, letters, words, etc., are exposed to view on cards for a very brief moment. 2. any short exposure device using cards or slides for a pre-determined amount of time, often a fraction of a second; tachistoscope.

Flesch readability formula a method of estimating the difficulty level of adult reading material developed by R. Flesch and published in 1943, orginally based upon sentence length in words, the number of affixes, and the number of personal references in 100-word samples of material. *Note:* The formula has undergone several revisions. A 1948 revision called the Reading Ease formula, based upon number of syllables per 100 words and sentence length in words, is widely used. *Cp.* **Dale-Chall readability formula; Fry readability graph (scale); Spache readability formula.**

flexibility, reading See **reading flexibility**.

flexor (flek′sər) *n.* a muscle that tends to close a limb back upon itself, to bend a joint, or to retract an organ on contraction. *Ant.* **extensor**.

flip chart one of a collection of large sheets of paper that are hinged at the top so that they can be turned over, one by one, often used to display illustrations and/or the language of children in stories about their experiences.

flow chart a schematic drawing showing the steps in and/or routes through any complicated process, as *a flow chart of the reading process.*

fluency (flo͞o′ən sē) 1. *n.* the clear, easy, written or spoken expression of ideas in writing or speech. *Winston Churchill wrote with great fluency.* 2. *n.* freedom from word identification problems which might hinder expression of ideas during oral reading. 3. *n.* the ability to speak, write, or perform smoothly, easily, and readily. *Good debators and dancers have fluency.* 4. *n.* the ability to produce words, or larger language units, in a limited time interval. *Word fluency is often tested in a comprehensive reading diagnosis. adj.* **fluent**.

fluid abilities See **analytic abilities**.

flyleaf (flī′lēf″) *pl.* **-leaves**. *n.* the leaves at the beginning and end of a book, hinged to the end papers. See also **end paper**.

fly title See **half title**.

focal length the distance from the center of a lens, or the midpoint of a mirror, which parallel rays must travel to come to a focus. See illustration under **lens.** See also **diopter**.

focus (fō kəs) *pl.* **-cuses, -ci** (-si). 1. *n.* the point at which rays, as light, heat, sound, etc., meet or appear to meet after refraction or reflection; focal point, as of a lens. 2. See **focal length**. 3. *v.* to adjust a system of lenses, mirrors, or electromagnetic force to bring energy rays to a convergence point that is clear and sharply defined, as *focus a camera lens.* 4. **in focus**, with a clear, well-defined image. 5. *n.* the site of origin or major concentration of a disease or injury, as *a focus of infection.* 6. *n.* a center of interest or attention, as *the* *focus of the book review tonight is....* 7. *v.* to concentrate on or attend carefully to something, as *focus on a study assignment.*

foil (foil) 1. *n.* a person, or sometimes a thing, that makes another person appear better by contrast, as *one comedian being a foil to another.* 2. *v.* to contrast. 3. *n.* a four-sided fencing sword with a blunt point. 4. *n.* an item in a multiple-choice or matching test that is plausible but incorrect; distractor.

folio (fō'lē ō") 1. *n.* a sheet of paper folded once to make 2 leaves, or 4 pages. 2. *n.* a volume with pages of the largest size, especially one more than 30 cm. (12 in.) See also **book size** *or* **format**.

folk etymology the false and often unwitting modification of a word or phrase whose origin is little understood, as *Welsh rarebit* for *Welsh rabbit*, or *asparagus* for *sparrow-grass.*

folklore (fōk'lōr", -lôr") *n.* the traditions and beliefs of the people of an age, reflected in tales — first oral, later written — passed from generation to generation.

folk tale *or* **story** a story of unknown origin but well-known through repeated story telling, as *Paul Bunyan folk tales. Cp.* **myth**; **fairy tale**; **legend** (def. 1).

foot (fo͝ot) *pl.* **feet.** 1. *n.* a unit of rhythm in verse which has usually one stressed syllable and one or more unstressed syllables; metrical unit. 2. **foots,** footlights in a theater.

footcandle (fo͝ot'kan'dᵊl) *n.* a unit for measuring light intensity, as in legibility research. *A footcandle is about the light intensity on a small area of surface held vertically one foot from an ordinary candle* — M. Tinker (1965).

footedness (fo͝ot'id nis) *n.* consistent preference for either the left or the right foot, as in kicking.

footnote (fo͝ot'nōt") 1. *n.* added information or credit given in a text in a statement or reference at the bottom of a page or the end of a chapter. *Footnotes are often set off on the page and keyed to the text by an asterisk or superscript number or letter.* 2. the symbol referring to a footnote. 3. *n.* information added to a main passage, often as an afterthought. 4. *v.* to add footnotes to, or annotate, a text.

forced-choice item a test item containing several plausible choices to which one must respond. *Forced-choice items are often used in personality inventories where the answers selected may reflect emotions or abilities rather than fact or knowledge.*

fore-glide See **on-glide**.

foreign accent the influence of the speech sounds of a previously learned language on another language later acquired.

foreshadowing (fōr s͟had'ō iṉg, fôr-) *n.* the technique of giving clues to coming events in a narrative; 'arrows pointing ahead.' *The picking up of rocks by the boys in the opening scene of Shirley Jackson's 'The Lottery' is a foreshadowing of the ending. v.* **foreshadow**.

foreword (fōr'wûrd", -wərd, fôr'-) See **preface**.

forgetting curve See **retention curve**.

form (fôrm) 1. *n.* shape; outline; configuration; especially, of a linguistic unit, as *word form, grapheme form, phoneme form. Note:* Form in this sense of outward structure is often contrasted with function, as in *form* vs. *function.* 2. *v.* to give shape to; arrange; as *form letters in handwriting, form a sentence.* 3. *n.* any linguistic structure by which meaning is transmitted, as through the shape and sound of a word, the grammatical structure of a sentence, etc. 4. *n.* an inflectional variant of a word. 5. See **literary form**. 6. *n.* a variant way of writing or pronouncing a term. *In the construction 'we'll', 'll' is a form of 'will.'* 7. *n.* something perceived as a psychological whole; gestalt; as *an ink blot form.* 8. *n.* the philosophic concept of the underlying structure, pattern, or nature of a thing; essence. *What is the form of knowledge?* 9. *n.* technical style. *In the 1960's, Tenneesee Williams was not in top form.* 10. *n.* a document to be completed in writing, as *a questionnaire form.* 11. *n.* a frame into which type is locked for printing. 12. *n.* (*Mostly Brit.*) a grade in which a student is placed in school, as *the fourth form.*

formal operations (J. Piaget) an organized system of logical thinking ability which usually appears in the process of mental development between about ages 11-15, involving abstract reasoning and the setting up and testing of verbal hypotheses. *The person who can formulate an hypothesis about the nature of thinking is using formal operations. Ct.* **concrete operations**. See also **operations; preoperational thought; infralogical operations.**

formal speech *or* **style** a style of speaking used to inform an audience in impersonal terms, marked by careful attention to organization of content and to grammatical structure and pronunciation. *Professional lectures are often delivered in a formal style. Cp.* **frozen speech** *or* **style**.

formant (fôr′mənt) *n.* in voice spectrograms, one of several acoustic frequency bands used to identify the characteristic patterns of resonance in vowels and in some consonants.

format (fôr′mat) 1. *n.* the physical appearance of a publication, including size, shape, binding, paper, type, margins, illustrations, etc. *An attractive format helps to make a book readable.* 2. *n.* the size and shape of a publication, depending on how many times a printed sheet is folded to make leaves. See **book size** *or* **format**.

formative (fôr′mə tiv) See **bound morpheme**.

formative evaluation evaluation usually of an instructional process as it is taking place in order to monitor the progress of participants, as students in a program, to study the process and its functions. *Cp.* **summative evaluation.**

form class 1. a class of all words which are used in the same way in all sentences of a language, as nouns, verbs, adjectives, adverbs, etc. 2. a class of all the linguistic forms that can fill a given position in a sentence: as *Mary* or *She* in completing the sentence: ____ *likes to play basketball.*

form perception the perception of shapes, outlines, and wholes, as *word form perception.* See also **visual discrimination**.

formula, readability See **readability formula**.

formula story a narrative written according to a set of predictable events, as if the author were following a set of directions, as in the love-versus-loyalty and boy-meets-girl formulas.

forward slant 1. handwriting with letters that lean to the right, the standard handwriting style for American English. See illustration. 2. the rightward-leaning characteristic of such letters. *Ct.* **back-hand slant**.

fotonovel (fō′tō nov″əl) *n.* a book, usually a paperback, in which photographs, as those from a motion picture, supplemented by dialogue in captions and balloons, tell the story.

fovea (centralis) (fō'vē ə) (sen trā'lis) *n.* a small area of cones near the center of the retina in which, under well-lighted conditions, vision is sharpest. See illustration under **eye**. *The fovea centralis is in the center of the macula lutea.* See also **macula (lutea)**. *adj.* **foveal**.

foveal vision 1. normal vision in which the line of sight falls on the fovea centralis. *Ct.* **peripheral vision**. 2. vision which uses the central macular area. 3. vision which allows maximum clarity and color sensitivity.

fragment (frag'mənt) *n.* an incomplete grammatical construction.

frame (frām) 1. *n.* a single picture on a film strip or motion picture film. 2. *n.* a single unit of programmed instructional material to which a learner must respond, as *information, response, and feedback frames.* 3. *n.* in language teaching, each blank in a lesson on grammar: *'verb' would fit in the frame, 'A ____ shows a state of being or action.'* 4. *n.* box-like lines to set off printed material on a page.

frame of reference a cognitive structure or scheme to which ideas, information, etc., may be related; schema.

F-ratio an index of the significance of the difference between two variances. *Note:* The larger variance is divided by the smaller one. The ratio may be interpreted by means of a standard F-ratio table based on the degrees of freedom of the two statistics.

free association an unstructured and uncensored flow of ideas, impressions, or words. *Free association to a question is often an effective first step in writing essay examinations.* See also **stream of consciousness** (def. 1).

free association test See **word association test**.

free morpheme a morpheme which can stand alone as an independent word, as *cat. Ct.* **bound morpheme**.

free reading student-selected rather than teacher-assigned reading activities.

free-response test a test in which a person states answers in his own words rather than by selecting given responses. *An essay examination is a free response test.*

free translation a non-literal, idiomatic translation of something from one language to another that is intended to reflect the communicative function and spirit of the original; for example, *I'm ten years old* for the strictly literal *I have ten years* of the French sentence *J'ai dix ans. Ct.* **literal translation**.

free variation the possibility that two linguistic elements can occur in the same context without change in meaning or function, as tə mā'tō/tə mä'tō, or the sounds /d/ and /t/ that form the past tense [-D] as in *spelled* and *spelt. Ct.* **complementary distribution**.

free verse verse with an irregular metrical pattern and length of line. *Note:* Free verse, or *vers libre*, arose in a 19th century literary movement in France to free poetry from the strict metrical rules of that time.

free vowel in English, vowel sounds that can occur both finally and before consonants in a syllable or morpheme, as /o͞o/ in *boot, shoe. Ct.* **closed vowel** (def. 1).

frenulum (fren'yə ləm) *pl.* **-la** (-lə). *n.* the vertical membrane on the underside of the tongue restricting the elevation and extension of the tongue tip.

frenum (frē'nəm) *pl.* **-na** (-nə). *n.* a fold of membrane which limits the movements of some organ or part; frenulum.

frequency (frē'kwən sē) 1. *n.* the number of times some event occurs in a given category. 2. *n.* the number of cycles per second (Hz) of a sound wave or of a light wave. *Ct.* **amplitude** (defs. 1, 2).

frequency curve a graphic form of a frequency distribution in which the midpoint frequency of each successive class interval is joined by a continuous line, usually smoothed. See illustration under **frequency distribution**. See also **frequency polygon**; **histogram**.

frequency distribution the number of times each of the possible events occurs in each of the possible categories, as *the frequency distribution of student scores at each grade level.* See illustration.

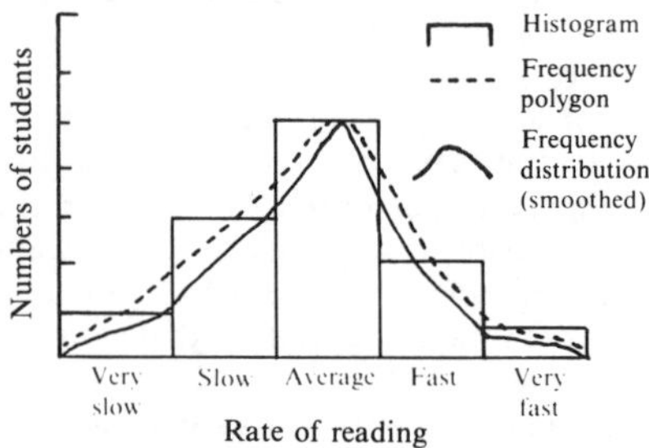

Frequency curve or distribution

frequency modulation a form of radio transmission in which the power output remains the same but the frequency of the waves carrying the signal varies.

frequency polygon a graphic form of a frequency distribution which is plotted at the mid-point frequency of each class interval. See illustration under **frequency distribution**. See also **frequency curve**; **histogram**.

fricative (frik′ə tiv) *n.* a consonant speech sound made by constricting but not stopping the air flow; spirant; as /z/ in *zero.*

frontal lisp the substitution of a /th/-like sound for the sibilant sounds /s/ or /z/ when the tongue blocks the usual air flow between the teeth; interdental lisp.

frontal lobe that portion of the cerebral hemisphere in front of the fissure of Rolando, roughly the forward half of the hemisphere. See illustration under **lobe**.

frontal plane any imaginary surface or plane which passes vertically through the body from side to side at right angles to the median plane. See also **median plane**; **sagittal plane**.

frontispiece (frun′tis pēs″, fron′-) *n.* an illustration facing the title page of a book.

front matter all those parts of a book preceding the body, or text, as table of contents, preface, dedication, etc. *Front matter is usually paginated in lower case Roman numerals.*

front vowel a vowel sound made with the highest arched portion of the tongue near the front of the mouth, as /ē/ in *feet.* See illustration under **vowel**.

frozen speech *or* **style** an extremely formal style of speech or writing; especially, writing of such subtlety and quality that rereading gives the reader fresh meaning and insights. *Great classics are written in frozen style. ...in frozen style the writer who is dedicated can enable the reader to educate himself indefinitely far beyond what the writer put into the text in the first place* —M. Joos (1961). *Cp.* **formal speech** *or* **style.**

frustration (fru strā′s͟hən) 1. *n.* interference with the attainment of a desired goal. *Lack of reading materials may be a source of frustration in reading development. Note:* Competing desired goals may also lead to frustration. 2. *n.* the feelings of failure, futility, and fury arising from such interference, often leading to disappointment, dissatisfaction, and discouragement. *In attempting to avoid frustration in their students, some teachers fail to challenge student abilities and thus lead to* *unintended boredom.* 3. *n.* something which interferes with one's desire to achieve. *Carping criticism can be a frustration. v.* **frustrate**.

frustration reading level the readability or grade level of material that is too difficult to be read successfully by a student, even with normal classroom instruction and support. *At the frustration reading level, according to E. Betts (1957), the student has great difficulty in word identification and in passage comprehension, often revealing tenseness, withdrawal, and sometimes hostility. Note:* Less than 90 percent word attack accuracy and less than 50 percent comprehension are often used as standards in judging this level. The concept of excessive difficulty is perhaps more useful in avoiding a mismatch of students and materials than in determining a specific level of frustration. See also **informal reading inventory (IRI); independent reading level; instructional reading level**.

Fry readability graph (scale) a method of estimating the difficulty level of reading material developed by E. Fry and based upon the number of syllables and the number of sentences in 100-word samples, with grade level values read from a graph or (more recently) a sliding scale. *Note:* A number of modifications have been proposed since original publication in 1965, chiefly in extending the values downward to preprimer levels and upward to college levels. *Cp.* **Dale-Chall readability formula; Flesch readability formula; Spache readability formula**.

F test *or* **value (F)** a statistical test for the significance of the difference between the variances of two samples of behavior. *Note:* The F test is useful in showing the homogeneity of variance in different samples; i.e., the extent to which the variance of test scores in the samples is stable.

fugitive material material printed in limited quantities and usually of timely interest only; ephemera. *Theater programs and circus posters are fugitive materials. Note:* ERIC is a rich source of fugitive materials.

function (fuŋk′shən) 1. *n.* purpose; role; as *to have a dramatic function.* 2. *n.* the intended use or effect of language: *We may exhort, beg, wheedle, needle, order, command, demand, question, assert, and sometimes just plain fool around. We vary the function of language to fit our goal* — J. De Stefano (1980). 3. *n.* the grammatical role of a linguistic form in a given construction, as a noun used as the subject of a sentence. 4. *adj.* referring to such a role. 5. *n.* a factor related to or dependent upon another factor, as *x is a function of y. adj.* **functional**.

functional (fuŋk′shə nəl) 1. *adj.* having to do with a given purpose or function, as *functional architecture.* 2. *adj.* without known organic cause or structural change; psychogenic. *A neurosis is a functional disorder. Ct.* **physiogenic**.

functional bilingualism the ability to understand, speak, read, and write in both one's native language and a second language. See also **bilingualism**.

functional disorder a disturbance in function or behavior without an organic basis. *Loss of speech is sometimes a functional disorder due to an emotional upset. Ct.* **organic disorder**.

functional hearing loss the loss or reduction of hearing acuity without a known organic cause.

functional literacy a level of competence in reading, writing (and sometimes arithmetic and vocational skills) essential for working and living; survival reading skills. *Note:* Functional literacy standards vary from country to country, within countries, and among different groups within a country. *A person is functionally literate when he has acquired the knowledge and skills in reading and writing which enable him to engage effectively in all those activities in which literacy is assumed in his culture or group* — W.S. Gray (1956).

functional reading 1. reading for practical purposes, as to get information. 2. the level of reading skill needed to get along in a society. See **functional literacy**. 3. printed media met in daily living.

functional shift the extension of the use of a word to another grammatical category; conversion; as *package* (noun) to *package* (verb) in *He packaged the book for mailing.*

function word a type of word that has a grammatical, but not a lexical meaning, as *in, the, or. Function words are sometimes called service words, structure words, or high-frequency words. Ct.* **content word**.

functor (fuñgk′tər) See **function word**.

funnies (fun′ēz) See **comics**.

fusion (fyo͞o′zhən) 1. *n.* the bringing together, or merger, of separate things into a whole that functions as a unit in which the original parts tend to lose their identity. *The traveller's report was a fusion of all his impressions.* 2. **sensory fusion** the blending of several sensations, as of the images from the two eyes, the impressions from the two ears, or the touch from two or more points on the skin, into one sensation. 3. **flicker fusion**, the perception of rapidly blinking light as steady. 4. *n.* the surgical operation of making a joint immovable, as *spinal fusion.* 5. *n.* in psychoanalysis, the balance between the instinct to live and to die that is present in a normal personality. 6. *n.* in linguistics, the merging: a. of speech sounds, as in a diphthong; b. of morphemes, as adding *th* to *grow* to make *growth*; c. of words, as in *actor-director*.

futhork *or* **futhark** (fo͞o′th ôrk; fo͞o′th ärk) *n.* the runic alphabet, developed in the 2nd or 3rd century from the Greek and Roman alphabets, that was used for Old Scandinavian and other northern European languages, characterized by angular letters especially suitable for easy carving in wood or stone; runic alphabet. *Note:* The name *futhork* is made up of the phonetic values of the first five letters of this alphabet. See illustration. See also **rune** (def. 1).

The runic alphabet

By permission. From Webster's New Collegiate Dictionary, ©1980 by G. & C. Merriam Co., Publishers of the Merriam-Webster Dictionaries.

future aspect (tense) a verb aspect that indicates an action or state that will take place later in time, usually indicated in English by the modal auxiliary *shall* or *will*, as in *She will order it. Note:* Strictly speaking, there is no future *tense* in English. The complex verb form refers to future *time*. The only two *tenses* are past and non-past.

future perfect aspect (tense) a verb aspect in English that indicates a completed action or state at a time later than the utterance and marked by the modal auxiliary *will have* plus a past participle: *I will have prepared dinner before you come home.*

future progressive aspect (tense) a verb aspect in English that indicates an action or state that will be going on and is marked by *will be* and a gerund: *The new factory will be operating Tuesday.*

G

DEVELOPMENT OF MAJUSCULE						
NORTH SEMITIC	GREEK	ETR.	LATIN	MODERN GOTHIC	MODERN ITALIC	MODERN ROMAN
SEE LETTER C			Ꞓ	𝔊	*G*	G

DEVELOPMENT OF MINUSCULE					
ROMAN CURSIVE	ROMAN UNCIAL	CAROL. MIN.	MODERN GOTHIC	MODERN ITALIC	MODERN ROMAN
ʒ	ς	ᵹ	𝔤	*g*	g

The seventh letter of the English alphabet developed from North Semitic *ghimel* and Greek *gamma* (see **C**). The Etruscans, having no meaningful distinction between the *g*-sound and the *k*-sound in their language, used this symbol for both. When the distinction again had to be made in Latin, the small stroke was added to the lower curve of the C. Thus, a new letter was created (G) and was given the position of the Semitic and Greek Z, which was dropped (see **Z**). The minuscule (g) is a scribal variant of the capital.

g *or* **g factor** See **general factor**.

galley proof a trial printed impression made after type is set but before it is made up into pages. *Note:* Galley proof gets its name from the tray used to hold type as it is first set and before it is made up into pages. *Cp.* **page proof**.

galvanic skin response (GSR) the changes in electrical resistance of the skin measured by a galvanometer. *Note:* These changes in resistance, as in a lie detector test, are affected by many situational factors and are difficult to interpret.

ganglion (gang̃' glē ən) *pl.* **-glea**. *n.* a group of nerve cell bodies located, in current usage, outside the central nervous system. *adj.* **ganglionic**; **gangliar**; **ganglial**.

gatekeeper (gāt'kē"pər) 1. *n.* in journalism, an editor who decides specifically what news shall and what shall not be included in a news edition. *The concept of 'gates' and 'gatekeepers' in such a communication channel as the newspaper was suggested by K. Lewin.* 2. *n.* a controlling influence such as standardized tests in determining who shall receive schooling. *n.* **gatekeeping**.

gauche (gōsh) *adj.* socially awkward or clumsy. *Note:* Literally, gauche means 'on the left' in French. *Cp.* **sinister**. *Ct.* **dexterity** (def. 1).

gazetteer (gaz"i tēr') *n.* a geographical dictionary.

geminate (*adj., n.* jem'ə nit, -nāt"; *v.* jem'ə nāt") 1. *adj.* arranged in pairs. 2. *n.* the prolonging of the sound represented by doubled consonant letters; doubling; as in *mamma*. 3. *n.* in orthography, a pair of adjacent identical letters, as *pp* in *happy*. 4. *n.* the production of the same speech sound twice in succession, as /*k*/ and /*k*/ in *bookkeeper*. 4. *v.* to produce such a succession of sounds. 5. *v.* to repeat immediately, when speaking or writing, a word or phrase for emphasis.

gender (jen'dər) *n.* a class, or set of classes, governing the forms of nouns, pronouns, adjectives, and articles; specifically, in English, the masculine and feminine genders. *Note:* Gender terms and forms do not refer to biological gender. The terms used to indicate gender vary, as in the Dutch common gender or the animate and inanimate genders of certain American Indian languages. Gender is indicated in English in the third person singular personal pronouns as the feminine *she*, the masculine *he*, and the neuter *it*. The third person singular may or may not match sexual gender, as references to a ship as *she* indicate, or to *he* as an indefinite person.

gene (a) (o)- a combining form indicating *birth, origin*; as **genetic, heterogeneous**.

general factor (g) 1. a factor hypothesized by C. Spearman (1904) to be common to all tests of mental ability. 2. in factor analysis, a factor common to all tests being factor analyzed.

generalization (jen″ər ə li zā′s̲h̲ən) 1. *n.* the inductive process of inferring from a limited sample of objects, ideas, etc., a principle or conclusion which applies to the entire class of the sample, as *statistical generalization.* 2. *n.* the principle or conclusion thus inferred. *v.* **generalize.**

general semantics a movement, initiated in the 1930's and 1940's, seeking to improve communication by emphasizing the treatment of words as conventional symbols only, and the recognition of the non-causal, arbitrary relation between words and things: *the word is not the thing.*

generate (jen′ə rāt) *v.* to produce sentences and the grammatical structures related to them.

generative grammar 1. a form of grammar which generates, or predicts by rules, all the possible sentences of a language. 2. the study of such grammars. 3. transformational-generative grammar.

generative phonology the study of phonology which seeks to determine the phonological rules which govern the possible phonetic or phonemic features of a language or languages.

generative semantics a grammatical theory, developed in the late 1960's and the 1970's, which assumes that the underlying structure of language is the semantic structure; therefore, only one set of rules is necessary to arrive at the surface structure of a given sentence. *Ct.* **tranformational-generative grammar.**

generative-transformational grammar See **transformational-generative grammar.**

generic term See **class noun.**

genetic (jə net′ik) 1. *adj.* having to do with genes, or with the behaviors or conditions which are produced or influenced by the composition of genes in an organism. *Eye color is a genetic trait.* 2. *adj.* having to do with the origin and development of organisms, or with something that may be likened to an organism. *The genetic study of languages leads to an understanding of the development of modern languages. Cp.* **congenital.**

genitive (jen′i tiv) *n.* a case form in some inflected languages that indicates relationships such as possession or source. *Note:* In written English, this relationship is marked by the apostrophe, as in *my father's car*, or by the preposition *of* as in *the report of the committee.* See also **possessive** (def. 2).

genius (jēn′yəs) 1. *n.* the highest category of intelligence, usually considered to be at least three or more standard deviations above the mean. *Geniuses with IQ's of 180 and 200 are exceptional.* 2. *n.* a person in this category. 3. *n.* a person especially gifted in creative, artistic, musical, or inventive performance. *He is failing school, but is a genius at chess.* See also **gifted.** 4. *n.* natural ability, as *a genius for work.* 5. *n.* a person who exercises strong power over others or on events whether for good or evil, as *an evil genius, a protective genius.*

genre (z̲h̲än′rə) 1. *n.* a form or type of literary and other artistic content, as a novel, tragedy, comedy, poem, etc. 2. *n.* paintings which are realistic, portraying everyday life scenes.

Gerstmann's syndrome a pattern of behaviors marked by finger agnosia, confusion of left and right, agraphia, and acalculia, and caused by lesions of the angular gyrus.

gerund (jer′ənd) *n.* a verbal form used as a noun while still suggesting the meaning of a verb, formed in English by adding *-ing* to the basic verb, as *Running* in *Running is great exercise.* See also **present participle**.

gestalt *or* **Gestalt** (gə s̲h̲tält′) *pl.* **gestalten, gestalts**. 1. *n.* any organized whole that is different from and greater than the sum of its parts and their relationships, as a word, melody, theory, face, etc. *Note:* Gestalt arose from and refers to a psychological theory based chiefly upon the experimental investigation of part-whole relationships in perception. 2. *adj.* referring to a gestalt or to gestalt theory.

gesture (jes′c̲h̲ər, jes̲h̲′-) *n.* any movement of some part of the body used to communicate, as in waving goodbye or nodding in agreement.

g, hard the /g/ sound that the letter *g* represents as in *gate, gone,* and *gun. Ct.* **g, soft**.

gifted (gif′tid) 1. *adj.* having special talents or skills, as *a gifted orator.* 2. *adj.* having superior intellectual functioning or potential. *'Genius' represents the topmost level of gifted persons.* 3. *adj.* having so much intellectual, creative, artistic, or athletic potential as to need distinctive educational programs or services. *Note:* Opinions vary about how superior one needs be to be called gifted; for example, the lower limit for the gifted may be considered the top ten percent, the top two percent, more than two standard deviations above mean, or at some specific IQ score, sometimes as low as 130 IQ.

Gillingham method a synthetic phonics system reinforced by intensive writing and spelling practice. *Cp.* **Fernald (-Keller) approach** *or* **method**.

gingerbread method a 17th and 18th century practice, more written about than used, in which the letters of the alphabet were made of gingerbread, and the child could eat the letters when able to name them: *'And that the Child may learn the better,/ As he can name, he eats the letter;/ Proceeding thus with Vast Delight,/ He spells, and gnaws from Left to Right'*— Matthew Prior (1696).

gist (jist) *n.* the essential or central meaning of a communication aside from details. *The ability that is probably required most frequently of high school students is the ability to get the 'gist' of the author's meaning* — R. Strang (1967).

glare (glâr) *n.* strong light which makes the eyes tired, either by shining directly into the eyes or by reflection from a page or other surface.

glide (glīd) 1. *n.* a sound produced during the transition of the articulators from one position to another, as the /y/ sound between /ī/ and /i/ in some pronunciations of *quiet* /kwī(y)it/. 2. *n.* a speech sound made while the articulators involved are moving, as /r/. 3. *n.* a speech sound which has the characteristics of both vowels and consonants, as /y/ in *your*; semivowel (def. 1). 4. *n.* the transitional sound of a diphthong, as the latter part of /oi/ in *coin*.

global approach *or* **method** an early term for the look-and-say approach; reading instruction that emphasizes the immediate recognition of whole words, not analysis of word parts. *Note:* Occasionally, the term was used for the sentence method and the story method.

globe (glōb) 1. *n.* a sphere which shows a map of the earth or the heavens. *The size, shape, and location of the earth is shown more accurately on a globe than on a two-dimensional map.* 2. **the globe**, the earth. 3. *n.* a planet. *adj.* **global**.

-gloss (a) (o)- a combining form indicating *tongue*; as **glossal**. See also **glott (i) (o)-**.

gloss (glos, glôs) 1. *n.* a brief explanation of printed text, usually in the margin or in an appendix. 2. *v.* to make such an explanation. 3. **gloss over,** to make an explanation that is beside the point, as *gloss over careless thinking with a flurry of words.* 4. *n.* a glossary.

glossal (glos'əl, glô'səl) *adj.* having to do with the tongue.

glossary (glos'ə rē, glô'sə-) *n.* an alphabetical listing, usually at the back of a book, of selected words with their definitions, often with other identifying information as that found in a dictionary.

-glott (i) (o)- a combining form indicating *tongue*; as **epiglottis**. See also **-gloss (a) (o)-**.

glottal (glot'ᵊl) *adj.* having to do with the glottis; laryngeal.

glottal stop the stopping and quick release of the air flow made by closing the glottis, as in the transition between the first and second syllables of the negative *unh-uh.*

glottis (glot'is) *n.* the true vocal folds and the variable opening between the vocal folds in the larynx. *The glottis makes it possible to produce voice.*

-gnosia, -gnosis a combining form indicating *knowledge*; as **agnosia, diagnosis.**

goal (gōl) 1. *n.* the general purpose or end toward which behavior is directed, as *one's goal in life.* 2. *n.* a specific target to be achieved, as writing a poem, putting a basketball through the hoop. 3. *n.* a successful, satisfying response, as *reaching the goal of an experiment and receiving a reward.*

goodness of fit test any of several statistical measures which test the degree to which obtained scores agree with a theoretical set of expected scores.

Gothic novel 1. a style of novel, especially popular in the late 18th and early 19th century, characterized by mysterious settings, an atmosphere of gloom and terror, supernatural happenings, and often violence and horror. *Mary Shelley's* Frankenstein *is a classic Gothic novel.* 2. a modern story written in that style.

GPA grade point average.

graded word list any of many lists constructed with the words usually ranked by grade level or reader level. *Graded word lists are often used to assess word recognition, vocabulary power, and spelling competence.*

grade equivalent a type of derived score based on the grade of a test-standardized population at which the average person earns a given score. *Note:* Test authorities as A. Anastasi and L. Cronbach strongly condemn such a conversion in educational practice, chiefly because the individual is compared to members of another group which may be very dissimilar, and because such comparisons have led to unfortunate educational policy decisions. *Cp.* **age equivalent**. See also **grade norm**.

grade level 1. successive levels of an educational program into which students are divided according to age and/or achievement; grade. 2. achievement level in relation to age. *Students may perform at, below, or above grade level.* 3. a designated level of text difficulty determined by a readability formula. 4. a reader's level of reading performance on a standardized reading test as compared to a norming population. 5. the class to which a student has been assigned on the basis of age.

grade norm the mean raw score obtained by students in a particular grade, as in *a table of grade norms. Cp.* **grade equivalent**.

grade point average (GPA) the average of numerical values assigned to grades in school courses. *Note:* The usual practice is A=4, B=3, C=2 grade points, etc. The GPA is often used as a tool for predicting scholastic success and as a criterion measure for school and college admission.

grade scale a standardized scale of grade norms or equivalents for measuring development.

grade school See **elementary school**.

gradient (grā′dē ənt) 1. *n.* a uniform change in response from high to low, or vice versa. 2. *n.* a change in motivational strength resulting from a change in condition(s) of stimulation.

graffiti (grə fē′tē) *n. pl.* writing and/or drawings made in public places, as on the walls of restrooms, subways, etc.

-gram a combining form indicating *written, drawn*; as **anagram**. See also **-graph**.

grammar (gram′ər) 1. *n. a linguistic description of some language — a set of statements saying how a language works* — Langacker (1973). *Note:* In this usage, the grammar includes the phonological, morphological, syntactic, and semantic description of both the language's structure at a given time and its evolution over time. 2. *n.* the morphology and syntax of a language. 3. *n.* the descriptive study of a language or languages. 4. *n.* what one knows about the structure and use of one's own language that leads to its creative and communicative use.

grammar school 1. (*Brit.*) an eight-year secondary school, funded by public funds, for college-bound children who enter at age 11 upon passing a competitive examination. *Note:* The British Education Act of 1944 set up a tripartite educational system, from which the grammar school and the modern secondary school survive. Since 1947, many of these have combined into comprehensive schools. 2. (*Brit.*) after 1580, a secondary school with a classical curriculum; the forerunner of today's 'Public' schools such as Eton. 3. See **Latin grammar school**. 4. (*An old use.*) in the United States, an elementary school.

grammaticality (grə mat″i kal′i tē) *n.* the degree to which a written or spoken utterance follows the grammatical rules of the language to which the utterance belongs. *Note:* The grammaticality of a certain sentence can be controversial, as in *Drive slow*. Grammaticality is often considered to be correctness in language usage according to prescriptive grammar, although linguists tend to support that usage favored by a majority.

grammatical meaning meaning which is dependent upon syntactical relationships, as the meaning of the subject or object of a sentence. *Ct.* **lexical meaning**.

grammatic closure the tendency to fill in missing or unclear syntactical and/or grammatical information in comprehending a message. *Grammatic closure often enables a listener to anticipate the next word of a speaker.*

grand mal (gran′ mal′; *Fr.* grän mal′) a violent epileptic seizure with a sudden loss of consciousness followed by severe convulsions. *Cp.* **petit mal**. See also **epilepsy**.

-graph (o)-, -graph (y)- a combining form indicating *written, drawn*; as **grapheme, ophthalmograph**. See also **-gram**.

graph (graf, gräf) 1. *n.* any graphic symbol. 2. *n.* in orthography, a particular letter or group of letters recurring as a unit and representing a particular phoneme, such as *ea* for /ē/ in *beat*. 3. *n.* an allograph (def. 1). 4. See **line graph**; **bar graph**.

grapheme (graf'ēm) *n.* a written or printed orthographic representation of a phoneme, as *b* and *oy* for /b/ and /oi/ in *boy*. *Note:* In English, a grapheme may be a single alphabet letter or a group of letters as in *boy* above, and includes all of the ways in which it may be written or printed. *Cp.* **allograph** (def. 1). *adj.* **graphemic**.

grapheme-phoneme correspondence the relationship between a grapheme and the phoneme(s) it represents; letter-sound correspondence, as *c* representing /k/ in *cat* and /s/ in *cent*. *Phonics as a teaching device concerns grapheme-phoneme correspondences: how to pronounce words when seen in print.* *Note:* Technically, grapheme-phoneme correspondence refers to letter-to-sound correspondence, not vice versa. *Ct.* **phoneme-grapheme correspondence**.

graphemics (gra fē'miks) *n.* (*with sing. v.*) the study of the use of orthographic signs in a writing system; graphology. *Ct.* **graphetics**.

graphetics (gra fe'tiks) *n.* (*with sing. v.*) the study of the general function and shape of orthographic symbols irrespective of their particular use in a writing system. *Ct.* **graphemics**.

graphic (graf'ik) 1. *adj.* characterized as legible or meaningful, as a drawing, a string of letters, or a mathematical model or figure. 2. See **graphics**. See also **graphetics**.

graphic display the visual marks and signs used in a language to represent the written language. 2. the printed or written text produced from writing.

graphic feature an identifying feature, represented in writing, drawing, painting, etc.

graphics (graf'iks) 1. *n. sing.* the art of drawing. 2. *n. pl.* drawings or reproductions of drawings, photographs, maps, charts, diagrams, etc.

graphology (gra fol'ə jē) 1. *n.* See **graphemics**. 2. *n.* the study of handwriting, especially for the purpose of discovering the character and personality of the writer. *adj.* **graphological**.

grapho-phonic (gra″fo fon'ik) *adj.* referring to the phonic relationships between the phonology and orthography of a language.

graphotactics (graf″ō tak'tiks) *n.pl.* 1. the permissible arrangements of orthographic symbols in forming morphemes and words of a language or languages. 2. the study of such arrangements. *adj.* **graphotactic**.

grave accent (grāv', gräv') 1. a graphic mark (`) placed directly above a vowel spelling to indicate that the vowel sound is falling in pitch (Greek), open or lax (French), or secondarily stressed (English), as in *Súndày*. See **secondary accent** (def. 2). 2. in English, a mark (`) placed above a normally unpronounced *e* to indicate that it is to be pronounced as the central vowel /ə/, as *hallowèd*. *Cp.* **acute accent**.

gray matter 1. those portions of the brain and spinal cord made up mostly of nerve cell bodies and dendrites. *Most of the cortex, specific cell areas of the brain, and nearly all of the spinal cord are gray matter.* 2. (*Informal.*) brains; intellect. *Thinking requires the use of gray matter.*

Great (English) Vowel Shift a change in certain vowel sounds in late Middle English, as from Middle English *hūs* to present *house*. *Note: These vowels took a clockwise turn in the height dimension: low vowels became mid, mid vowels became high, and high vowels became low...* — S. Schane (1973).

Greek alphabet an alphabet developed by the Ancient Greeks, which extended the Semitic alphabet by adding vowel letters and served as the source for the Roman, Coptic, and Cyrillic alphabets, and for various symbols used in mathematics, linguistics, etc., as ä, ß, ɣ.

gross motor coordination the control of large sets of voluntary muscles, as in running, jumping, skipping, or in gymnastics. *At about ages 5 to 7, children can normally demonstrate gross motor control by balancing on their tiptoes, skipping on alternate feet, or making large letters or drawings on a chalkboard.*

groupements (gro͞op′moɴz) See **grouping** (def. 3).

grouping (gro͞op′iŋg) 1. *n.* the division of students for instruction into classes chiefly by age and ability; interclass grouping; as *homogeneous grouping, heterogeneous grouping. Note:* The many varieties of grouping also include cross-age grouping and cross-class grouping outside of the regular classroom. 2. *n.* the division of students for instruction within classes on one or more criteria such as achievement, reading ability, or interests; intraclass grouping. 3. **groupings** (J. Piaget), a set of inferred logical structures — cloure, reversibility, associativity, identity, and repetition — that underlie and make possible the concrete logical operations.

groups (gro͞ops) *n. pl.* (J. Piaget) logical models that represent the classificatory and relational thinking of children in the concrete operations period.

group test of mental ability an ability test that may be given to several persons, as in a class, at the same time by one person.

group therapy treatment by a psychotherapist of two or more clients at one time even though they may have different problems. See also **family therapy**; **psychodrama**; **role-playing** (def. 3).

growth (grōth) 1. *n.* a normal increase in size, complexity, or differentiation of an organism or of any of its parts. 2. *n.* an increase in the size and/or scope of a functional ability, as *reading growth.* 3. *n.* size or stage of development. *The school reached its maximum growth.* 4. *n.* an abnormal multiplication of cells. *A tumor is a growth.* 5. *n.* something that has grown naturally, as *a growth of trees.* 6. *adj.* having to do with increases in size or amount, as *a growth chart.*

grunt-and-groan method See **spit-and-cough method**.

g, soft the /j/ sound that the letter *g* represents, as in *gentle, giant,* and *gyro. Ct.* **g, hard**.

GSR galvanic skin response.

guessing, correction for See **correction for chance** *or* **guessing**.

guide card a card with a projecting tab or edge higher than the material with which it is used, inserted in a file to divide it into sections and help locate material, as in a library card catalog, filing cabinet, etc.

guided reading reading instruction in which the teacher provides the structure, including the purpose, for reading and for responding to the material read. *Most basal reading programs have guided reading lessons.* See also **directed reading activity**.

guide, teacher's See **teacher's guide** *or* **manual**.

guide words words appearing at the top of each page of an encyclopedia dictionary, telephone book, etc., indicating the first and last entry words on a page. *The guide word at the top left of the page is the same as the first word on the page; the guide word at the top right of the page is the same as the last* *word on the page.*

guttural (gut′ər əl) 1. *adj.* having to do with the throat. 2. *adj.* harsh, throaty. 3. *adj.* having to do with a sound made at the back of the mouth. 4. *n.* a sound so made. *Syn.* **velar**.

gymnasium (jim nā′zē əm; gim nä′zē o͝om″) *pl.* **-siums, -sia**. *n.* a classical school in continental Europe, especially Germany, which prepares students for university work.

gyrus (jī′rəs) *pl.* **gyri**. *n.* a small fold or convolution of the brain, smaller than a lobe. *Cp.* **lobe** (def. 1).

gyrus of Broca See **Broca's area**.

H

DEVELOPMENT OF MAJUSCULE								
NORTH SEMITIC	GREEK		ETR.	LATIN		MODERN GOTHIC	MODERN ITALIC	MODERN ROMAN
𐤇	⊟	H	𐌇	⊟	H	ℌ	*H*	H

DEVELOPMENT OF MINUSCULE					
ROMAN CURSIVE	ROMAN UNCIAL	CAROL. MIN.	MODERN GOTHIC	MODERN ITALIC	MODERN ROMAN
h	h	h	𝔥	*h*	h

The eighth letter of the English alphabet is traceable to North Semitic origins. In that early alphabet its pronunciation was similar to that of Scottish *ch*. In Classical Greek, the symbol came to represent *eta* (written H). In English, this letter represents an aspirate sound, but in most Indo-European languages it has seldom been used in this way.

habit (hab′it) 1. *n.* a consistently-used, acquired behavior pattern with a minimum of voluntary control, as recognizing familiar words, cleaning the chalkboard. 2. *n.* consistently used, acquired behavior pattern nearly or completely involuntary, as walking. 3. *n.* the tendency to repeat a given response to a stimulus. *Children have a fairly predictable habit of coming to the kitchen when they smell cookies.* 4. *n.* a compulsive practice or use, as *a drug habit. adj.* **habitual.**

haiku (hī′kōō) 1. *n.* a major type of Japanese poetry; specifically, a form of verse written in seventeen syllables with three lines of five, seven, and five syllables, respectively, to express a single thought and to call forth a specific response. 2. *n.* a poem written in this manner.

hair space the thinnest space used to separate elements of type. *A metal spacer is used to make a hair space between hand-set type.*

half title a brief title printed on a separate leaf preceding the title page; bastard title; fly title.

hallucination (hə lōō″sə nā′shən) *n.* a perception for which relevant and adequate stimuli are lacking; false perception; as *Macbeth's hallucination of the dead Banquo in Shakespeare's play* Macbeth. *v.* **hallucinate.**

halo effect the tendency to allow one impression, either specific or general, good or bad, to filter through and color other impressions of an individual.

handbook (hand′bŏŏk″) *n.* an instructional guide, manual, or reference tool, usually small and designed for quick and easy use, as *a bird watcher's handbook.*

handedness (hand′id nis) *n.* preference for either the left or right hand, as in writing, throwing, etc.

handedness test any task intended to determine handedness or the preferred hand, as the hand chosen for handwriting, eating, etc.

hand-eye dominance See **eye-hand dominance.**

handicapped (han′dē kapt″) 1. *n.* a person who because of physical and/or mental limitations has difficulty but not complete inability in the performance of specific tasks, as in schooling, employment, etc. See also **multiply handicapped**. *Note:* Special types of handicapped, as *orthopedically handicapped,* are given under the describing term. 2. *adj.* referring to such a person or condition. 3. **the handicapped** (*with pl. v.*), the handicapped as a group.

handwriting (hand′rī″ting) 1. *n.* writing that is done by hand rather than by mechanical means such as a typewriter. See **cursive writing; manuscript writing.** 2. *n.* a person's individual style of writing; penmanship. *Sue's handwriting is very clear.*

handwriting scale a scaled set of

handwriting specimens used for judging the legibility of handwriting. *Note:* Since handwriting varies greatly in size, slant, and letter formation, as well as in the rater's bias for a particular style of handwriting, exact judgments of handwriting legibility are difficult.

hanger (haŋ'ər) (*Brit.*) *n.* (*An old use.*) a double-curved stroke (ʔ) practiced in beginning handwriting instruction, usually in the phrase *pothooks and hangers: His skill in making pothooks and hangers with a pencil. . . .* — W. Irving (1849).

Hans Christian Andersen Award an international award given every two years to an author and to an illustrator for their entire body of work for children. *Note:* The award for an author was established by the International Board on Books for Young People in 1956. In 1966 an award for an illustrator was added.

haptic (hap'tik) 1. *adj.* referring to the sense of touch and muscular sensitivity. 2. **haptics,** the study of active touch.

hardback *or* **hardbound** (härd'bak″; härd'bound″) 1. *n.* a book with stiff or hard covers; casebound. 2. *adj.* referring to such a book. *Ct.* **paperback.**

hard consonant a voiced consonant, one produced by the vibration of the vocal cords, as /d/ in *dog* and /g/ in *gas.*

hard neurological sign firm evidence of organic damage to the brain and/or central nervous system gathered from changes in reflexes, sensations, or muscular strength and coordination. *Ct.* **soft neurological sign.**

hard of hearing a person who has a measurable hearing loss of some degree but who is still able to communicate aurally and orally, with or without a hearing aid. *adj.* **hard-of-hearing.**

hard palate the bony front part of the roof of the mouth.

hardware (härd'wâr″) *n.* the equipment or devices of a computer and/or educational system, as distinguished from the materials used or consumed in such a system. *Ct.* **software.**

harelip (hâr'lip″) See **cleft lip.**

Hawthorne effect an increase in effort because of the motivating effect of receiving special attention. *Note:* The Hawthorne effect was first noted in an experiment to increase productivity in an industrial plant of the Western Electric Company. Control groups are now routinely used in experimental situations to provide information to offset a possible Hawthorne effect.

head (hed) 1. *n.* a word in a phrase which determines the syntactic classification of the entire phrase, as *car* in *older cars* or *tired* in *unusually tired.* 2. *adj.* referring to such a word or phrase.

heading (hed'iŋ) 1. *n.* a word or phrase at the head of a page or at the top of an entry in a card catalog. 2. *n.* a rubric.

headmaster *or* **headmistress** (hed'mas″tər, -mä'stər; hed'mis″tris) 1. *n.* in the United States, a title often used for the principal of a private or independent school, or occasionally of a public school. 2. *n.* (*Brit.*) the appointed academic and executive chief of a school.

health, mental See **mental health.**

hearing (hēr'iŋ) 1. *n.* the sense used to perceive sound. 2. *n.* the perception of sound.

hearing aid a device to increase hearing efficiency by focusing and/or amplifying sound waves, thus stimulating the inner ear by air conduction or bone conduction. *Note:* Modern hearing aids are small electronic units capable of powerful and selective amplification. Rapid progress is being made in the fitting of hearing aids to very young children with severe hearing loss.

hearing comprehension See **listening comprehension** (def. 2).

hearing conservation the programs and specific steps taken to prevent damage to hearing, usually by some sort of sound reduction, as by the muffs worn by ground personnel working near jet aircraft.

hearing handicapped See **hearing impaired.**

hearing impaired a person with a hearing loss of any degree from a very mild to a complete hearing loss; hearing handicapped.

hearing loss a reduction in auditory acuity, usually measured in decibels (dB). *Note:* The amount of hearing loss is often categorized as: *mild* — up to 40 dB; *moderate* — up to 55 dB; *moderately severe* — up to 70 dB; *severe* — up to 90 dB; and, *profound* — above 90 dB.

hearing test an audiometric examination to determine the hearing threshold for pure tones and/or speech.

hearing threshold 1. the lowest intensity in decibels (dB) at which a tone can be distinguished from silence during audiometric examination. 2. the lowest intensity at which speech sounds or words can be accurately identified 50 percent of the time.

hearing vocabulary See **listening vocabulary**.

hemi- a prefix indicating *half;* as **hemiplegia.**

hemianopia *or* **hemianopsia** (hem″ē ə nō′pē ə; hem″ē ə nop′sē ə) *n.* full or partial blindness in one half of the visual field of one or both eyes.

hemiplegia (hem″i plē′jē ə, -jə) *n.* paralysis of one side of the body. *Ct.* **paraplegia**. See **paralysis** (defs. 1, 2).

hemispheres (hem′i sfērz″) *n. pl.* 1. the cerebral hemispheres. 2. the cerebellar hemispheres. 3. the halves of any sphere, as *the north and south hemispheres of a globe.*

heredity (hə red′i tē) *n.* the genetic characteristics and traits, including genes, passed from the parents to children. *Cp.* **innate** (def. 1). *adj.* **hereditary.**

hereditary predisposition the theory that inherited characteristics include a number of tendencies that may or may not develop, depending upon the stresses and strains in the individual's environmental situation.

hero *or* **heroine** (hēr′o; her′ō in) 1. *n.* the chief character in narrative or dramatic literature; protagonist. 2. *n.* a person admired for noble qualities. *adj.* **heroic**.

heroic couplet a pair of lines of iambic pentameter poetry: *What dire offense from amourous causes springs!/ What mighty contests rise from trivial things!* — A. Pope.

Hertz (Hz) (hûrts) *n.* an international unit of frequency measurement equal to one cycle per second (cps).

hesitation (hez″i tā′shən) *n.* a halt or pause in speech or oral reading. *Note:* In discourse, hesitations often serve as place-markers while one collects one's thoughts. However, hesitations of a given length on some oral reading tests are scored as errors, while actually reflecting one's nervousness or a general state of doubt or uncertainty of meaning rather than the breakdown of word attack skills. The significance of a hesitation when reading orally has not been precisely determined.

hesitation phenomenon the habitual insertion of neutral sounds in natural speech, as *um...um, er, mmm....*

heter (o)- a prefix indicating *different,*

other; as **heteronym.**

heterogeneous grouping the inclusion of students of differing levels of intelligence and/or achievement in one or more skills or subjects, either within classes or within schools. *Ant.* **ability grouping; homogeneous grouping;** (Brit.) **streaming.**

heterograph (het′ər ə graf″, -gräf″) *n.* a word identical to another word in meaning and perhaps in pronunciation but different in spelling, as *inquiry/enquiry. adj.* **heterographic.**

heterography (het″ə rog′rə fē) 1. *n.* an orthography that contains the same letter or letter groups to represent different sounds; polyphony: as, in English, *c* in *face* and *came. Ct.* **one-to-one correspondence** (def. 2). 2. *n.* any nonstandard spelling, as *nite* for *night.*

heteronym (het′ər ə nim″) 1. *n.* a homograph. 2. *n.* in popular usage, a word with the same spelling as another word, but with a different pronunciation and meaning, as *lead* /led/ versus *lead* /lēd/. *Ct.* **homonym.**

heterophoria (het″ər ə fōr′ē ə, -fôr′-) *n.* a general term for oculomotor imbalance, the tendency for the eyes to deviate from one another in their line of sight. *Note:* Heterophoria may cause fusion to be broken and produce double vision. Efforts to restore binocular vision may create fatigue, discomfort, and eyestrain.

heterotropia (het″ər ə trō′pē ə) *n.* a general term for the deviation of one eye from the point of fixation of the other, as in exotropia, esotropia, etc. *Note:* Heterotropia refers to all such deviate eye conditions in any direction, whether caused by refractive, muscular, neurological, or hysterical conditions, and whether present permanently or occasionally.

heuristic (hyo͞o ris′tik) 1. *adj.* helpful in leading to further investigation. *Theoretical models of the reading process have heuristic value.* 2. *adj.* encouraging the student to learn for himself. *The Socratic method of questioning is a heuristic method of teaching.* 3. *n.* a process of conscious inquiry. *Learning to write abstracts is a practical heuristic.*

hexameter (hek sam′i tər) *n.* a line of poetry with six metrical feet, used extensively in classical Latin and Greek poetry, but rarely in English.

hiatus (hi ā′ təs) *pl.* **-tuses, -tus.** 1. *n.* the pause in speech between two words when the vowel at the end of the first word and the vowel at the beginning of the second are both carefully enunciated, as *be eager.* 2. *n.* any gap or interruption in knowledge, series of events, etc., as *a hiatus in Mayan history, a hiatus in the plot.*

hierarchy (hī′ə rär″kē, hī′rär′) *n.* an ordered arrangement in which lower ranks or levels are subordinate to higher ones, as *a hierarchy of abilities. adj.* **hierarchical.**

hieroglyph (hī′ ər ə glif″, hī′ rə-) *n.* a graphic symbol used in ancient Egyptian writings in which conventionalized pictures represented ideas, words, and syllables. *Cp.* **logograph; ideograph.**

hieroglyphic (-ical) hi′ər ə glif′ik, hi′rə-, hi′ər ə glif′i kəl) 1. *adj.* written in or referring to the graphic symbols used in the ancient Egyptian writing system. 2. *adj.* written with such symbols. 3. *adj.* hard to read or decipher.

hieroglyphics (hī″ər ə gli′fiks, hī″ rə-) 1. *n.* a writing system, especially ancient Egyptian, Hittite, or Mayan, in which pictures of objects represented words, ideas, or syllables. *Cp.* **logosyllabic writing; ideography; logography; syllabary** (defs. 1, 3). 2. See **hieroglyph.**

higher mental processes any form of thinking, especially of a logical and abstract type.

higher-order structure 1. a topic or heading under which related information is grouped, as 'voice,' under which voice production, articulation, quality, etc., may be placed. 2. in structural grammar, a level of increasing abstraction. *A phoneme is a higher-order structure than a phone.*

high frequency loss a hearing loss for frequencies above 2000 Hz. *The sounds of sibilants, as /s/, and fricatives, as /f/, may not be heard in high frequency loss.*

high-frequency word See **service word.**

high-grade mental defective an educable mentally retarded person; moron. See **mental retardation.**

high interest / low vocabulary book a book with high story appeal to hold the attention of poor readers, slow learners, and/or the culturally disadvantaged, written with a limited vocabulary they can understand.

high school See **secondary school.**

high school equivalency examination a test given to determine whether or not a person has, by experiences of various kinds, an education equal to that provided in high school.

high vowel a vowel sound made with the highest arched portion of the tongue near the roof of the mouth, as /ē/ in *feet.* See illustration under **vowel.**

hiragana (hēr″ə gä′nə) *pl.* **hiragana, hiraganas.** 1. *n.* the Japanese cursive syllabary used to represent affixes, grammatical words, and content words not represented by Chinese characters. 2. *n.* a character of this writing system. *Cp.* **katakana; kanji.**

histogram (his′tə gram″) *n.* a graphic form of a frequency distribution which uses rectangular bars the width of the class interval to show the height of the frequency of each class interval. See illustration under **frequency distribution.** See also **frequency curve; frequency polygon.**

historical fiction *or* **novel** a long narrative of past events and characters, partly historical but largely inspired by the imagination of the author. *Margaret Mitchell's* Gone With the Wind *is an historical novel. Note:* It is a problem for the reader as to what is historical fact and what is the author's imagination. Conversations between Queen Elizabeth I and Sir Francis Drake may be based on fact, but the conversation itself comes from the imagination of the author.

historical linguisitics the study of language change over time, as by comparing related languages at different points in their development and from examining the internal structure of the language as it exists today; diachronic linguistics.

historical method the methods used by researchers to reconstruct and interpret the past as contrasted with the experimental or scientific method. *Cp.* **historical research.**

historical research the techniques used by historians to reconstruct and interpret the past. *Note:* The data for historical research are the spoken, written, and printed sources, or other material, originating from those who participated in or witnessed the events studied. The historian must evaluate these data for authenticity, bias, and generalizability, and draw conclusions from the data as to what happened, and why. *Cp.* **historical method.**

hol (o)- a combining form indicating *whole, entire*; as **hologram.**

holistic (hō lis′tik) 1. *adj.* having to do

with a psychological approach which represents the belief that the whole is different from and greater than its parts; gestalt. *A poem is a holistic creation.* 2. *adj.* in word recognition, referring to the recognition of a word as a single unit separate from its letter components.

holistic approach a teaching-learning approach that emphasizes wholes of subject matter and the integration of parts with wholes.

hologram (hō′lə gram, hol′ə-) *n.* an image which gives the illusion of three dimensions, created by a photographic technique that uses a laser beam.

holophrase (hol′ə frāz″, hō′lə-) *n.* a single word that is used to express the meaning of a sentence. *Note:* The term is usually applied to a stage of language acquisition during which a child may say *shoe* for *I want my shoes, Where are my shoes*?, etc. *adj.* **holophrastic.**

homeostatic (hō″mē ə stat′ik) *adj.* referring to a balanced condition or state of equilibrium, especially in body processes. *n.* **homeostasis.**

home study program a course of study conducted by correspondence or other means at one's home, especially for adults and handicapped persons.

home visitation program a course of study monitored by visiting teachers, especially for those who are handicapped or live in remote areas.

homo-, homeo- a combining form indicating *alike, resembling;* as **homonym, homeostasis.**

homogeneity (hō″mə jə nē′i tē, hom″ə-) 1. *n.* the quality of sameness or likeness in a set of persons, items, etc. 2. *n.* such a quality in a test in which test items measure a single variable. *adj.* **homogeneous.**

homogeneous grouping See **ability grouping.**

homograph (hom′ə graf″, -gräf″) *n.* a word with the same spelling as another word, whether or not pronounced alike, as *pen* (a writing instrument) vs. *pen* (an enclosure), or *bow* (and arrow) vs. *bow* (of a ship). *Ct.* **homophone.**

homonym (hom′ə nim) 1. *n.* technically, a word with the same oral or written form as another word, as *bear* (an animal) vs. *bear* (to support) vs. *bare* (exposed), or *row* (to propel a boat) vs. *row* (a line) vs. *row* (a brawl). *Note:* In this sense, *homonym* is a cover term which, as its literal meaning indicates, includes both homophones and homographs—words with the same name, whether spoken or written, or both. The different spellings and/or pronunciations of homonyms are due to differing origins of these words. 2. *n.* in popular usage, a word with the same pronunciation and spelling as another word, but different in meaning, as *bay* (a body of water), *bay* (part of a window). *Cp.* **heteronym.**

homophone (hom′ə fōn″, -hō′mə-) 1. *n.* technically, a word with the same pronunciation as another word, whether or not spelled alike, as *hare* and *hair*, or *scale* (of a fish) and *scale* (a ladder). 2. *n.* in popular usage, two or more different graphemes that represent the same sound, as /k/ spelled *c* in *candy, k* in *king, ch* in *school. Ct.* **homograph.**

Horatio Alger story a story with a rags-to-riches theme. *Note:* Horatio Alger was the author of a long series of such books, as *Strong and Steady* and *Strive and Succeed.*

hornbook (hôrn′bo͝ok″) *n.* a single page fastened to a small hand-held paddle, designed to introduce the child to reading and to Christian prayers. See illustration. *Note:* Made of wood or metal, with the page tacked or glued on, hornbooks were in use from the mid-15th through the mid-18th century in England and in the American colonies. The term is derived from a transparent sheet of horn which originally protected the text. The page regularly consisted of the alphabet, normally preceded by a cross (see **Christ-cross-row**); part of the syllabarium (up to *ad ed id od ud*); the invocation; and the Our Father. The hornbook was the child's first text in a sequence of texts which combined reading instruction with instruction in Christian worship... *the ordinary road of the hornbook, primer, Psalter, Testament and Bible* — Locke (1693). *Cp.* **battledore** (def. 1).

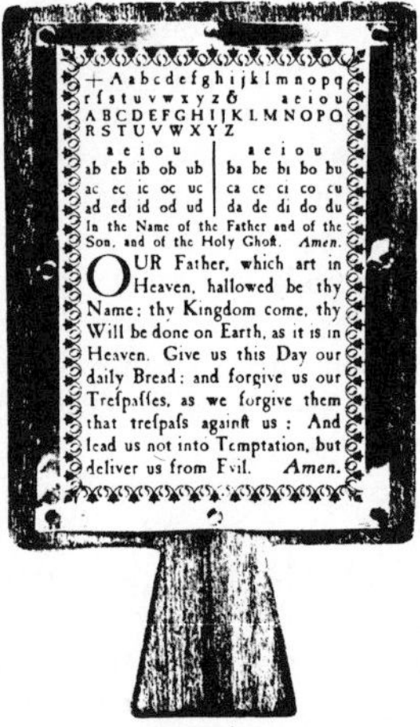

From a photograph in A Little History of the Horn-Book *by Beulah Folmsbee. The Horn Book, Inc., 1942.*

Hornbook

humanism (hyo͞o′mə niz″əm, *often,* yo͞o′-) 1. *n.* a way of thinking or an attitude that is concerned with the cultivation of human values, interests, and worth today rather than theological promises of salvation tomorrow. 2. *n.* (*sometimes cap.*), belief or study in the humanities; especially, the Renaissance movement of reawakening interest in human capabilities that was stimulated by the rediscovery of classical Greek and Roman culture. *n.* **humanist.**

humor (hyo͞o′mər, *often,* yo͞o′-) 1. *n.* a comic quality which amuses, often arising from some incongruity in character, behavior, or situation, as in *Charlie Chaplin's humor.* 2. *n.* the ability to note and appreciate the amusing. *He lacks a sense of humor.* 3. *n.* comic writing or talk, as *put humor into a speech.* 4. *n.* disposition. *She is usually of a pleasant humor.* 5. *n.* a sudden whim. *Come, I'm in a humor to buy a new dress.* 6. *n.* a temporary mood, as *be in bad humor today.* 7. **the humors,** the four body fluids — blood, phlegm, yellow bile, and black bile — believed by early physiologists to determine one's disposition and health. *Note* (def. 7): In Elizabethan literature and plays, people were often characterized by their dominant humor

The humors: (top) sanguine, choleric, (at bottom) phlegmatic and melancholic.

Reprinted as it appeared in the *Smithsonian,* November 1980, from *Physiognomy* by Johann Casper Lavater, London, 1806.

as sanguine, phlegmatic, choleric, or melancholic. Disease was thought to be caused by an imbalance of the humors. See illustration. See also **wit** (def. 1); **comedy**. *adj.* **humorous**.

hybrid word (hī′brid) a word formed from morphemes derived from more than one language; as *television*, in which *tele-* has a Greek source, and *-vision* has a Latin one. *n.* **hybridization**. *v.* **hybridize**.

hydrocephalus (hī″drə sef′ə ləs) *n.* abnormal and excessive fluid in the brain ventricles or within the skull. *Note:* Hydrocephalus may be caused by disease, injury, or congenital conditions. It may be present at birth or develop very slowly, or suddenly. Hydrocephalus can often now be treated surgically to reduce or prevent brain damage. *adj., n.* **hydrocephalic**.

hygiene of reading the study of the physical factors which affect the legibility of reading materials and cause fatigue; specifically, such factors as type size, thickness, and spacing; leading; letter form; length of line; quality and level of illumination; book size; reading posture and distance.

hypacusis (-sia) *or* **hypoacusis (-sia)** (hip″ə kyo͞o′sis, -ko͞o′-, hi″pə-; -zhə, --zē ə; hi″pō ə kyo͞o′sis, -ko͞o′-; -zhə, zē ə) *n.* loss in hearing perception; hard of hearing. *Ant.* **hyperacusis**.

hyper- a prefix indicating *over, above, in excessive amount;* as **hyperkinesis**.

hyperactive (hī″pər ak′tiv) 1. *adj.* having an unusual, pathological degree of motor activity; hyperkinetic. *Note:* Hyperactive students are usually impulsive, distractible, and restless, with low frustration tolerance. As a result, they may have difficulty in school learning tasks. 2. *adj.* referring to any activity carried to an unusual degree, as *a hyperactive imagination.*

hyperactivity (hī″pər ak tiv′i tē) 1. *n.* a greater than normal level of activity. *The coming wedding led to hyperactivity in the bride-to-be's family.* 2. *n.* chronic distractability, instability, and excessive motion, usually with a low tolerance for frustration; hyperkinesis. *Many factors, singly or in combination, may cause hyperactivity.* 3. *n.* the normal fast-paced exploration, investigations, and activity-changing behavior of young children. *Ct.* **hypoactivity**.

hyperacusis (-sia) (hī″pər ə kyo͞o′sis, -ko͞o′-; -zhə, zē ə) *n.* extreme sensitivity of hearing. *Ant.* **hypacusis (-sia)** *or* **hypoacusis (-sia)**.

hyperbole (hī pûr′bə lē) *n.* an intentionally exaggerated figure of speech: *I have told you a million times.*

hypercorrection (hī″pər kə rek′shən) *n.* the use of a word, pronunciation, inflectional pattern, or grammatical construction mistakenly assumed to be more correct than that which it replaces; overcorrection; as *Whom* for *Who* in *Whom do you think you are?*

hyperdistractibility (hī″pər di strak″tə bil′ə tē) *n.* hyperactive attention to stimuli resulting in the inability to direct and maintain attention to given stimuli.

hyperglycemia (hī″pər glī sē′mē ə) *n.* higher than normal sugar levels in the blood. *Hyperglycemia is often the result of diabetes and is frequently serious.*

hyperkinesis (hī″pər ki nē′sis, -kī-) *n.* hyperactivity. *adj.* **hyperkinetic**.

hypermetropia (hī″pər mi trō′pē ə) *n.* farsightedness. See **hyperopia**.

hyperopia (hī″pə rō′pē ə) *n.* farsightedness; hypermetropia; specifically, a refractive condition in which the principal focus of retinal images is behind the retina so that objects may be unclear, either because the light rays do not converge sufficiently or because the eye itself is too short from front to back. See illustration under **emmetropia**. *Persons with uncorrected hyperopia may experience difficulty in distance seeing as well as in reading comfortably at the near point. n.* **hyperope**. *adj.* **hyperopic.**

hyperphoria (hī″pər fōr′ē ə, -fôr′-) *n.* the tendency for an eye to turn up; specifically, a vertical heterophoria in which the line of sight of one eye turns up when fusion is broken.

hypertension (hī″pər ten′shən) *n.* high blood pressure.

hyperthyroidism (hī″pər thī′roi diz″əm) n. too great secretion of thyroid, with such symptoms as distractability, excitability, restlessness, heightened basal metabolism, goiter, and various problems of the nervous system. *Severe, untreated hyperthyroidism may result in death.*

hypertonic (hī″pər ton′ik) *adj.* having excessive tension in skeletal muscles; resistance to passive stretching of muscles. *Hypertonic muscles are often seen in cerebral palsy. n.* **hypertonicity**.

hypertropia (hī″pər trō′pē ə) *n.* a vertical heterotropia in which one eye turns up relative to the other; vertical strabismus.

hyphen (hī′fən) *n.* a punctuation mark (-), shorter in length than a dash, used to separate parts of a word when one part must be carried over to another line, to connect parts of a compound word, as *mother-in-law*, to separate letters indicating halting speech, or to show the spelling out of a word, as *s-p-e-l-l*, etc. *Cp.* **dash** (def. 1). *v.* **hyphenate**. *adj.* **hyphenated**.

hypnagogic image (hip″nə goj′ik) one of the shadowy, sensory images often seen in the daydreaming condition between wakefulness and sleep. *Dull lectures or a boring book may lead to drowsiness and hypnagogic images.*

hypo- a prefix indicating *under, below, to a lesser degree than normal*; as **hypothyroid**.

hypoactivity (hi″pō ak tiv′i tē) 1. *n.* a less than normal level of activity; hypokinesis. 2. *n.* a chronic state of inaction, lethargy, and apathy which may be caused by many factors, singly and in combination. *Ct.* **hyperactivity**. *adj.* **hypoactive**.

hypochondriac (al) (hī″pə kon′drē ak″, hī″pō kon drī′ə kəl) *adj.* showing too great concern for one's own health, with a decided tendency to believe in imaginary diseases; pessimistically exaggerating minor health problems. See also **malingering**. *n.* **hypochondria**.

hypoglycemia (hī″pō glī sē′mē ə) *n.* below normal sugar levels in the blood.

hypokinesis (hī″pō ki nē′sis, -kī-) *n.* an abnormal decrease in motor activity and body movements; hypoactivity. *adj.* **hypokinetic**.

hyponym (hī′pə nim, -pō-) *n.* a member of a set of terms that are a part of a larger and more general term. *'Crimson,' 'scarlet,' and 'pink' are hyponyms of 'red.' n.* **hyponomy**. *adj.* **hyponymous**.

hypophonia (hī″pə fō′nē ə) *n.* a form of dysphonia in which one can use only a whispered voice.

hypophoria (hī″pə fōr′ē ə, -fôr′-) *n.* the tendency for an eye to turn down; specifically, a vertical heterophoria in which the line of sight of one eye turns down when fusion is broken.

hypopituitarism (hī″pō pi to͞o′i tə riz″əm, -tyo͞o′-) *n.* a deficiency of normal pituitary gland hormones resulting in low basal metabolic rate, stunted growth, disinterest in sex, and slow mental processes.

hypothalamus (hī″pə thal′ə məs) *pl.* **-mi** (mi″). *n.* an area at the base of the brain that is involved in the autonomic nervous system, in general endocrine activity, and in many body control activities, such as water retention, hunger, temperature control, etc.

hypothesis (hī poth′i sis, hi-) *pl.* **-ses** (sēz″). 1. *n.* a tentative assumption made to be tested, as *an experimental hypothesis.* 2. *n.* an assumption made in an argument. 3. *n.* a guess or conjecture. *v.* **hypothesize**.

hypothyroidism (hī″pə thi′roi diz″əm) *n.* too little secretion of thyroid, with such symptoms as lowered mental functioning, emotional disorders, lowered basal metabolism, lethargy, sensitivity to cold, and menstrual problems. *Untreated, hypothyroidism can lead to cretinism or other severe disorders.*

hypotonia (hī″pə tō′nē ə, hi″pō-) See **atonicity**.

hypotropia (hī″pə trō′pē ə) *n.* a vertical heterotropia in which one eye turns down relative to the other; vertical strabismus.

hysteria (hi stēr′ē ə, -ster′-) *n.* a neurosis characterized by emotional instability, repression, dissociation, and a variety of psychogenic symptoms. See also **anxiety hysteria**.

hysterical (hi ster′i kəl) 1. *adj.* expressing behavior characterized by hysteria, as *hysterical crying*. 2. *adj.* indicating a functional disorder when the organic system is intact, as *hysterical paralysis*.

Hz Hertz.

I

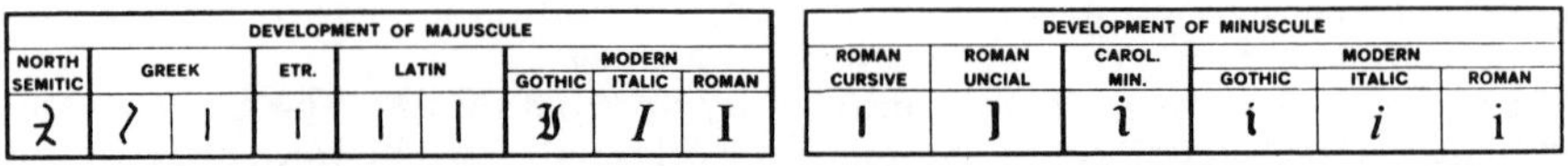

DEVELOPMENT OF MAJUSCULE								
NORTH SEMITIC	GREEK		ETR.	LATIN		MODERN		
						GOTHIC	ITALIC	ROMAN
ʐ	ʔ	I	I	I	I	𝕴	*I*	I

DEVELOPMENT OF MINUSCULE					
ROMAN CURSIVE	ROMAN UNCIAL	CAROL. MIN.	MODERN		
			GOTHIC	ITALIC	ROMAN
I	I	i	i	*i*	i

The ninth letter of the English alphabet developed from North Semitic consonant *yodh* (y) which became the Greek vowel *iota* (ι). Originally, it was much like a Z in form, acquiring its present shape in Greek. The minuscule (i) was first written with a dot in early Medieval Latin to distinguish it from the *u* (written ıı), the *m* (written ııı), and other letters written with similar vertical strokes.

-ia a suffix indicating *disease, disorder* (in medicine); as **alexia, dyslalia.**

iamb (ī'am, ī'amb) 1. *n.* metrical foot of two syllables, the first unstressed, the second stressed: *Wherein Leander on her quivering breast* — C. Marlowe. 2. *n.* referring to satirical verse written in this meter. See also **iambic pentameter**. *adj.* **iambic**.

iambic pentameter a metrical scheme in poetry with five iambs in each line. *The greater part of a Shakespearean play is written in iambic pentameter.*

iatrogenic (ī a″trə jen'ik, ē a″-) 1. *adj.* brought about by, or related to, the professional duties of a physician or surgeon; specifically, functional behavior illnesses or disorders thought to be caused by autosuggestion during a medical examination. 2. *adj.* referring to any worsening of a condition by the treatment thereof, or to the development of general or specific problems as a result of the treatment of some other problem. *Note:* Remedial treatments may have iatrogenic aspects: to enter a remedial reading room may stigmatize the student in the eyes of his peers; to be referred for psychiatric evaluation often haunts a student's school life, even if the report is negative.

-ic a suffix indicating *referring to, having to do with*; as **iconic, poetic.**

iconic representation See **cognitive representation.**

iconic sign (ī kon'ik) 1. a representation or picture of some object; a picture of a dog for 'a dog.' 2. an orthographic character which is pictographic. *Note:* In number usage, the Roman numeral *II* is an iconic sign, but *2* and *two* are symbolic. *Cp.* **logograph; ideograph.** See also **pictograph.**

id (id) *n.* in Freudian theory, the unconscious, instinctual, and primitive part of the psyche that is body-driven and seeks immediate gratification and self-preservation, as in eating. *Ct.* **ego**; (def. 2); **superego**.

idea (ī dē'ə, ī dēᵊ') 1. *n.* any mental process, notion, or image which is a result of cognition rather than sensation; thought; concept; as *verbal ideas, an idea for a theme.* 2. *n.* a tentative plan of action; intention; as *an idea to save energy.* 3. *n.* a hint or clue. *I have no idea where to find it.* 4. *n.* an impression. *Give me an idea of what you want.* 5. *n.* a phantasy. *What a silly idea! adj.* **ideational.** *n.* **ideation.**

idea density See **concept load** *or* **density** (def. 1).

identification (ī den″tə fə kā'shən, i den'-) 1. *n.* the act or process of recognizing or assigning meaning, as *word identification.* 2. *n.* the projection of oneself into the person of another, real or imaginary, so as to share another's qualities, problems, etc., as *a boy's identification with his father, identi-*

fication with the heroine of a story. Cp. **empathy** (def. 1). *Note* (def. 2): Identification may operate as a defense mechanism in disturbed persons to relieve severe psychological stress. 3. *n.* assuming the values and interests of a social group; social imitation. 4. *n.* an aid to recognition or meaning, as *fingerprint identification.* 5. *n.* the use of a form of the verb 'to be', as in *I am Jane*, to show that *I* and *Jane* are one and the same. *v.* **identify.**

identification book an information book; *a naming book at its simplest level* — C. Huck (1976).

identity (ī den′ti tē, i den′-) *n.* (J. Piaget) the recognition that an object remains basically the same across transformations. *The identity of a quantity does not change in a mental manipulation if nothing has been added or taken away.*

ideo- a combining form indicating *idea;* as **ideograph.**

ideograph (id′ē ə graf″, - gräf″, ī′dē-) 1. *n.* a graphic symbol that represents an idea or object rather than a speech sound or word; ideogram. 2. *n.* a conventionalized graphic symbol which conveys by association the idea, object, or event represented, as the Japanese ideograph (子) for child. *Note* (def. 2): A particular ideograph may represent the same idea in two languages, such as Chinese and Japanese, but will be read as different words, depending on the language or dialect. 3. *n.* any graphic symbol representing an idea or word or morpheme; a logograph. *Cp.* **pictograph.** *n.* **ideography.** *adj.* **ideographic.**

ideography (id″ē og′rə fē, ī″dē) 1. *n.* a writing system that uses orthographic symbols to represent ideas, events, or objects without necessarily representing sounds or words of language. 2. *n.* a writing system composed only of ideographs, as Chinese, or Japanese Kanji. See **ideograph** (def. 1). *Cp.* **logography; pictography.** *Ct.* **syllabary** (defs. 1, 3); **alphabet** (def. 2).

idio- a combining form indicating *individual, one's own, peculiar;* as **idiolect.**

idioglossia (id″ē ə glos′ē ə, -glô′sē ə) *n.* a great distortion of normal language, especially by substitutions; a unique language. *Idioglossia may be related to mental retardation but is also sometimes used as an invented language by twins.*

idiolect (id′ē ə lekt) *n.* an individual's speech habits in a speech community, including pronunciation, grammar and vocabulary; one's distinct way of using language. *Ct.* **dialect** (def: 1).

idiom (id′ē əm) 1. *n.* an expression that does not mean what it literally says: *to have the upper hand* has nothing to do with 'hands' but means *to have an advantage. Note:* Idioms are language constructions peculiar to a given language. They usually cannot be translated literally into another language. For this reason, languages especially rich in idioms as English, French, German, and Russian are difficult to translate. 2. *n.* a language, dialect, or style of speaking peculiar to a people, as *New England idiom.* 3. *n.* a construction or expression peculiar to a given language (from the point of view of another language.) *The French use the idiom 'J'ai faim' ('I have hunger') to express the American idiom 'I am hungry.'* 4. *n.* a distinctive, individual style or character, especially in music and art, as *the Beethoven idiom, the Rembrandt idiom.* 5. *n.* a password; secret signal; as 'open sesame.' *adj.* **idiomatic.**

idiopathic (id″ē ə path′ik) 1. *adj.* referring to a disease of unknown origin. 2. *adj.* referring to a diseased condition or sympton whose origin is within the organ involved and not the result of something external to the organ.

idiosyncratic (id″ē ō sin krat′ik) *adj.* characteristic of an individual, as *an idiosyncratic notion. n.* **idiosyncracy.**

idiot (id′ē ət) 1. *n.* profound mental retardation; specifically, a person with an IQ five or more standard deviations below the mean, or not above 25. *Idiots need constant supervision since they are unable to learn connected speech or even to care for themselves.* See **mental retardation**. 2. *n.* an utterly foolish person who acts as though without sense; fool; dunce. *Stop acting like an idiot.* 3. *n.* a jester; clown. 4. **idiot savant**, a person with very low general intelligence but with some special competence, as in calculating. *n.* **idiocy.** *adj.* **idiotic.**

idyll (īd′ᵊl) 1. *n.* a short poem or prose narrative describing the simple life and its times in a romantic and sometimes pastoral way, as Whittier's *Maud Muller.* See also **pastoral** (defs. 2, 3). 2. *n.* a long narrative poem idealized in subject, tone, and mood, as Tennyson's *Idylls of the King.* 3. *n.* material for such writing. *adj.* **idyllic.**

illiteracy (i lit′ər ə sē) 1. *n.* the inability to read and/or write a language. 2. *n.* lack of education. 3. *n.* a mistake in the expected use of language. *Ant.* **literacy.** *adj.* **illiterate.**

illiterate (i lit′ər it) 1. *adj.* unable to read. 2. *adj.* unable to read and write. 3. *adj.* not meeting the educational expectations of a social group, usually the dominant group; unschooled. 4. *adj.* uncultured; unread, especially in literature. 5. *adj.* without competence in a content field, as *being illiterate in mathematics. Ant.* **literate.** *n.* **illiterate.**

illumination (i lo͞o″mə nā′s̲hən) 1. *n.* the light falling upon some surface such as a page. *The proper level of illumination for reading depends upon the 'intensity, color, and distribution of light in relation to vision'* — M. Tinker (1965). 2. *n.* the decoration of manuscript, page, letter, etc., with designs and often color, as in the illumination of medieval manuscripts. *v.* **illuminate.**

illustration (il″ə strā′s̲hən) 1. *n.* a picture, photograph, or other visual image, as *a textbook illustration.* 2. *n.* an explanation; a clarification, as by an example. *Humorous illustrations enliven a dull lecture. v.* **illustrate.**

illustrative (i lus′trə tiv, il′ə strā″tiv) *adj.* explanatory or clarifying, as *an illustrative argument.*

image (im′ij)

Image is a general term with many shades of meaning, but usually meanings that imply a physical or mental resemblance, as between or among persons or things. An image may be concrete or abstract. It may be based on experience or imagination. It may refer to sensory experiences, especially visual ones, or to any physical or ideational representation of such experiences.

1. *n.* a physical likeness or representation of something in painting, sculpture, photography, etc., as *Michelangelo's image of David.* 2. *n.* a mental representation of something usually incomplete; impression. *As she read on, the image of the heroine became clearer.* 3. *n.* an optical representation formed by refraction or reflection, as *a mirror image, a camera image.* 4. *n.* form, as *an idol in the image of a god.* 5. *n.* typical example. *He was the very image of fear.* 6. *n.* copy. *That child is the image of her*

mother. 7. *n.* a description in speech or writing. *Sir Walter Scott's writing contains many nature images.* 8. *n.* a figure of speech, especially a simile or metaphor. 9. *v.* to represent, make, project, conceive, visualize, etc., an image, as *image a thought. Note:* Special types of image, as *retinal image*, are given under the describing term. *adj.* **imaginal.**

imagery (im′ij rē, im′ij ə rē) 1. *n.* the process of imagining. 2. *n.* imaginative mental images formed while reading or listening to a story, perceiving, etc. 3. *n.* the use of language to create sensory impressions. 4. *n.* collectively, the figurative language in a work. 5. *n.* in literature, the study of image patterns as clues to the author's deeper meaning(s).

imagination (i maj″ə nā′shən) 1. *n.* the process, or result, of forming mental patterns of something not present to the senses, as in thinking 'what if' rather than 'what is.' *The sphinx is the product of the imagination.* 2. *n.* the power to create ideal works, especially in literature and the arts, that also have realistic elements, as *the satiric imagination of Jonathan Swift.* 3. *n.* the process or power of imagining or phantasizing. *Children's imagination sometimes replaces reality.* 4. *n.* resourcefulness; ingenuity. *A little imagination often helps solve problems.* See also **creativity.** *v.* **imagine.** *adj.* **imaginative; imaginary.**

imaginative entry the ability to relate to, or empathize with, the vicarious experience of characters, situations, and mood of a literary work by finding parallels in one's own experience. *All students are capable of imaginative entry into vicarious experiences merely because they are human and have had many experiences* — D. Burton (1964). *Cp.* **cognitive entry.**

imaginative literature literary creations formed and ordered through the minds of their authors.

imbecile (im′bi sil, -səl) 1. *n.* See **trainable mentally retarded (TMR).** See also **mental retardation.** 2. *adj.* referring to trainable mentally retarded. 3. *adj.* absurd; silly; as *an imbecile remark. adj.* **imbecilic.**

IMC instructional materials center.

imitation (im″i tā′shən) 1. *n.* the modeling of one's behavior on the observed behavior of others. *Imitation is a critical part of language acquisition.* 2. *n.* the result of such modeling. 3. *n.* a copy, rather than the original. *The expensive edition of the book proved to be an imitation.* 4. *n.* a literary style similar to another's, as *an imitation of Henry James.* 5. *n.* the aesthetic concept of realistic representation, as *a noble imitation of nature. v.* **imitate.** *adj.* **imitative.**

immaturity (im′ə to͝or′i tē, -tyo͝or′-, -cho͝or′-) 1. *n.* incomplete development in one or more ways of an organism, as *reading immaturity.* 2. *n.* relatively delayed development in a function or trait for a given age, as *physical immaturity, emotional immaturity. Ct.* **maturity.** *adj.* **immature.**

immediate comprehension *or* **knowledge** See **apprehension** (def. 1).

immediate constituent part of a linguistic construction resulting from one division of a sentence, phrase, or word into its component parts, the first and largest of such divisions being the immediate constituents. *In the sentence, 'Orange juice tastes good,' the subject 'Orange juice' and the predicate 'tastes good' are the immediate constituents.* See also **immediate constituent analysis.**

immediate constituent analysis the

separation of a linguistic construction into its main component parts: *'Poor John ran away' contains the immediate constituent parts 'Poor John'* and *'ran away.'* See **immediate constituent.** *Note:* This method of analysis of linguistic units, introduced by L. Bloomfield (1933), results in a description of a phrase, clause, or sentence as one of a hierarchy of grammatical categories assigned to the linguistic units.

immediate recall the retelling of material very soon after study, as in recall of details after reading a selection. *Ct.* **delayed recall.**

immunization (im″yə nī zā′s̲h̲ən) *n.* in studies of the effects of persuasive reading materials on reader attitudes, the use of selections designed to make the reader less likely to change an attitude, as in reading an article on the contributions of labor to industry before reading one on labor strikes.

impedance (im pēd′ᵊ ns) *n.* opposition to the flow of energy; specifically, the opposition of a membrane, as the eardrum, to sound wave vibrations.

impedance audiometry the physical measurement of the opposition of the middle ear system to sound wave vibration.

imperative mood 1. a verb form that expresses a command, request, prohibition, etc., as *run* in *Run! Please run away. Don't run.* 2. referring to such a verb form.

imperfect tense a verb tense or aspect in English that shows a continuous or habitual action that has occurred in the past, as *was always whispering* in *Frank was alwaying whispering. Ct.* **present perfect aspect (tense); past tense.**

impersonal pronoun a pronoun with an indefinite referent, as *It* in *It seems to me*... and *Such* in *Such is life. Ct.* **personal pronoun.**

implication (im″plə kā′s̲h̲ən) *n.* any of the conclusions, inferences, expectancies, etc., that may be logically implied or understood, but not directly stated, from the author's argument in a text or utterance. *The implication was clear from the president's reasoning in his address that his country intended to keep the peace. Note:* Reading for implications is a major objective of reading instruction. It is especially valuable in learning to test the adequacy of an author's conclusions by logically projecting what would happen if those conclusions were carried out.

implicit (im plis′it) 1. *adj.* implied rather than expressly stated. *Concern was implicit in her voice.* 2. *adj.* unquestioning, as *implicit faith.* 3. **implicit definition,** definition by context; connotation. *Ant.* **explicit definition.** (See **explicit** (def. 3).)

implicit speech internal or silent speech; covert symbolic language activity inferred from reports of the mental rehearsal of ideas; inner speech. *Ct.* **subvocalization.**

implied meaning See **inferred meaning.**

implosion (im plō′z̲h̲ən) 1. *n.* the inward movement of air when a stop consonant is released, as /t/ in *meeting.* 2. *n.* a sound so made as the air rushes in when a stop consonant is released; especially, a clicking sound used as a phoneme, as in several African languages. *Common nonphonemic uses of implosions are the clicks used to call a horse or to indicate displeasure.* 3. See **implosive therapy.**

implosive therapy a behavior therapy technique used chiefly in the treatment of a phobia; implosion. *Note:* The client is flooded with imagined or real exposure to the feared object or event until the defenses weaken. When the client accepts the continued exposure after the defenses are down, the phobia dissipates. *Cp.* **systematic desensitization.**

imply (im plī′) 1. *v.* to suggest or indicate indirectly by word or action. *Aggressive speech and action imply anger or frustration.* 2. *v.* to show as a necessary condition. *A library implies reading and listening materials.*

impression (im presh′ən) 1. *n.* a particularly strong psychological reaction to stimuli. *The unwelcome propaganda created a negative impression.* 2. *n.* any immediate and somewhat generalized reaction to something read, heard, experienced, etc. *She browsed through the book to get an impression of its contents.* 3. *n.* a belief, as *the impression it was true.* 4. *n.* the effect of stimulation on nerve activity. *Note:* The effect may range from a vague awareness of something seen or heard to a sharp, specific percept. 5. *n.* a printed copy. 6. *n.* all copies made from the same type at one printing operation. *Several impressions may be needed for one edition of a popular book. Cp.* **edition.** *v.* **impress.**

impressionism (im presh′ə niz″əm) 1. *n.* (*usually cap.*) a painting style begun in the 19th century by Monet and others to show subjectively their momentary perceptions, especially in terms of the effects of light upon objects rather than upon their representation in realistic detail. 2. *n.* a highly personal writing style in which the momentary perceptions of the author are presented without intentional distortion, as in L. Durrell's *Alexandria Quartet. Cp.* **expressionism.** *adj.* **impressionistic.**

imprint (im′print) *n.* the place and date of publication and the name of the publisher and/or printer, usually printed at the bottom of the title page.

imprinting (im prin′ting) *n.* learning which takes place quickly and early in life, and which remains difficult to extinguish or to forget. *v.* **imprint.**

impulse (im′puls) 1. *n.* an immediate, unconsidered response to stimulation, as *act on impulse.* 2. *n.* the psychoanalytic concept of an instinctual act controlled by the id. 3. *n.* a progressive wave of electrical stimulation along a nerve or muscle fiber. 4. *n.* any brief, intermittent surge of power. *Electric counters tally another count each time they receive an impulse.*

impulsive (im pul′siv) *adj.* acting without deliberation or reflection. *Childhood play tends to be impulsive. Cp.* **compulsive.**

impulsiveness *or* **impulsivity** (impul′siv nis; im pul si′vi tē) *n.* the inability to restrain or reflect upon one's responses; the tendency to make hasty actions, as in speaking before thinking.

in-, il-, im-, ir- a prefix indicating *into, within,* as **incorporation**; or *not, without,* as **incoordination, illiteracy, impersonal, irregular.**

incentive (in sen′tiv) 1. *n.* motive; especially, a motive in the form of an external reward which encourages the subject to reach the main goal, as *the incentive induced by school emblems and trophies.* 2. *n.* the external reward which serves such a purpose.

incidental learning the acquisition of knowledge not directly taught or sought. *When one seeks specific information in a text, other information gained while reading the text is considered incidental learning. Note:* Ernest Horn's comment on the educational value of incidental learning: *While incidental learning does take* *place, it is not to be trusted in important matters* (1937).

incidental memory the process, or result, of recalling, without direct effort, material while trying to remember something else. *Cp.* **incidental learning.**

incidental method an unstructured way of teaching; specifically, a reading approach that is based upon student experiences and the reading needs identified by the teacher rather than upon a preplanned reading lesson or program.

incompetence (in kom′pi təns) 1. *n.* the inability to perform a given task adequately. 2. *n.* lack of legal responsibility for one's actions and affairs; inability to meet the minimum legal requirements for age, citizenship, mental ability, sanity, etc.; mental defectiveness. *Ct.* **competence** (defs. 1, 3). *adj.* **incompetent.**

incoordination (in″kō ôr″dᵊ nā′shən) *n.* the lack of harmony in the working of the parts of an organism, especially in the lack of balance or timing of different muscles or muscle groups which causes complex actions to be clumsy or impossible; ataxia.

incorporation (in kôr″pə rā′shən) 1. *n.* taking something in as a part of oneself, as in the process of including new learning in the cognitive structure. 2. *n.* the process of taking on the attributes of another person as a model and making them one's own, an extension of a psychoanalytic concept based upon the act of eating and digesting. *v.* **incorporate.**

increment (in′krə mənt, ing′-) 1. *n.* an addition or increase, as *an increment in the number of school library books.* 2. *n.* the process of so adding to or increasing. 3. *n.* a change in an independent variable. *adj.* **incremental.**

incremental repetition the repeating, with variation, of a refrain or other part of a poem, especially in popular ballads: *O what will you leave to your father dear?/ The silver-shod steed that brought me here./ /What will you leave to your mother dear?/ My velvet pall and my silken gear. Note:* In this ballad, the incremental repetition refers to the way in which successive dialogue patterns reflect earlier ones. *Ct.* **parallel repetition.**

incus (ing′kəs) *pl.* **incudes** (in kyōō′dēz). *n.* the middle of the three bones, or ossicles, in the middle ear. See illustration under **ear**. *The incus is shaped roughly like a blacksmith's anvil, whence its name.*

indefinite article See **article** (def. 2).

indefinite pronoun a pronoun without a specific referent, as *whoever, anybody, something.*

indention *or* **indentation** (in den′shən; in″den tā′shən) *n.* the moving in from the normal margin of print, as *the indention of a paragraph. v.* **indent.**

independent clause a clause that can stand alone as a complete grammatical construction; specifically, a clause containing a complete subject and a complete predicate, which may be introduced by a coordinating conjunction as *but* or *therefore*, but not by a subordinating conjunction, as *when* or *since*; main clause. *Cp.* **dependent clause.**

independent groups design an experimental design with separate control and experimental groups in which each subject gets only one treatment; independent sample design. *Ct.* **repeated measures design.**

independent reading level the readability or grade level of material that is easy to read fluently with few word attack problems and high comprehension: the student is on his own. *Note:*

Better than 99 percent word attack accuracy and better than 90 percent comprehension are often used as standards in judging this level. The concept of great ease of reading is especially useful in the selection of material for leisure reading. See also **informal reading inventory (IRI); frustration reading level; instructional reading level.**

independent school a privately-controlled school that relies upon tuition and gifts for support rather than upon government funds; private school.

independent study an arrangement by which a student works on a paper or project on his own as a part of, or instead of, a formal course, conferring with one or more faculty members for suggestions and guidance.

independent variable the stimulus variable(s) manipulated in an experiment to observe the effect upon one or more (dependent) variables(s). *Ct.* **dependent variable.** See also **intervening variable.**

index (in′deks) 1. *n.* a guide to the contents of a publication through some systematic arrangement of proper names, subject terms, dates, etc. 2. *n.* a separate volume or volumes containing such information. *Every year Elodie buys the cumulative index to* Gourmet *magazine.* 3. *v.* to make an index.

indicative mood a verb form that makes a simple statement or question, usually factual in nature; the declarative mood; as *is* in *He is here*, and the interrogative mood, as *Is* in *Is he here?*

indirect discourse a paraphrase of speech or writing: *He is believed to have said 'No.' Ct.* **direct discourse.**

indirect object the person or thing to whom or for whom the action of a transitive verb in a sentence is performed, as *me* in *Please give me the salt. Note:* In English, the indirect object usually comes between the verb and the direct object. *Ct.* **direct object.**

indirect vision peripheral vision; specifically, sight from visual stimulation outside the macular area of the retina.

individual differences any differences between people in one or more dimensions of growth or performance, as in age or in arithmetic skills.

individualization (in″də vij″o͞o ə lī zā′s̬hən) *n.* the adjustment of teaching-learning activities to student needs, either on an individual or group basis. *adj.* **individualized.** *v.* **individualize.**

individualized reading an approach to reading instruction, originated in the 1950's as an alternative to basal reading programs, which emphasizes student self-selection of reading materials, largely trade books, and self-pacing in reading, with the teacher adjusting instruction to student needs in small group work and in individual conferences. *Note:* The specific application of the term 'individualized reading' to one instructional approach has caused confusion. For a more general and widely used concept of individualizing reading instruction, see **individualization.**

individually prescribed instruction (IPI) a series of lessons, planned for an individual, based on the person's responses in a diagnostic testing program.

individual test a test designed to be administered to one person at a time by a trained examiner, as *the Stanford-Binet Intelligence Scale.*

indoctrinate (in dok′trə nāt″) 1. *v.* to teach or teach about certain principles, often for the purpose of uncritical acceptance. 2. *v.* to train persons in the particular behavior patterns of a group. *n.* **indoctrination.**

induction (in duk′s͟hən) 1. *n.* the process of determining principles by logic and/or observation from data; reasoning from part to whole; inductive reasoning. *Ct.* **deduction** (def. 1). 2. *n.* the leading into a new condition, state, or behavior, as *the induction of sleep through anesthesia.* 3. *n.* the process by which some cell tissues stimulate and direct the growth of other developing embryonic cells. 4. *n.* the process of creating an electrical current or magnetic field in a body by the action of another body with such current or field, even though there is no direct connection. 5. *n.* an initial experience or formal ceremony to introduce someone into an organization or to an activity, as *induction into an honorary society. adj.* **inductive**.

inductive learning learning by example, ultimately resulting in a rule or generalization. See **inductive method.**

inductive method a teaching-learning method in which specific examples are first examined to identify a common characteristic and then used to develop a generalization or rule. *A phonics approach which gives many examples of a phonic pattern before stating the phonics generalization is an inductive method. Ct.* **deductive method.**

inductive phonics See **synthetic phonics.**

inductive reasoning See **induction** (def. 1).

inevitabilty (in ev″i tə bil′i tē) *n.* something that cannot be avoided or escaped, especially in narrative and dramatic writing, as *the obvious inevitability of the outcome of the story. adj.* **inevitable.**

infant reader *(New Zealand)* a beginning reading book.

infant school *(Brit.)* 1. a school for children aged 5-7. 2. a school for children aged 5-7, plus nursery classes for younger children aged 3-4.

inference (in′fər əns, -frəns) 1. *n.* the process of judging or concluding in reasoning, as *reasoning by inference from given premises.* 2. *n.* the result of such a process; inferred meaning *(def. 1). v.* **infer.** *adj.* **inferential.**

inferential statistics See **statistics** (def. 1). See also **Bayesian statistical inference.**

inferior (in fēr′ē ər) 1. *adj.* lower in place, as *the inferior rung on a ladder.* 2. *adj.* referring to the lower half of the body. See also **caudal** (def. 2). 3. *adj.* lower in status or degree, as *an inferior job, an inferior reading score.* 4. *adj.* lower in importance or value, as *inferior self-esteem, an inferior jewel.* 5. *n.* a person lower in rank or worth than another. *Ant.* (defs. 1-5) **superior** (defs. 1-4, 9). 6. *n.* a subscript, as the *2* in H_2O. *Ct.* **superior** (def. 10). *n.* **inferiority.**

inferred meaning 1. a meaning which leads to an unstated conclusion. 2. *(Informal.)* implied meaning. *Note:* While 'imply' is sometimes used as a synonym for 'infer,' many distinguish between these terms: *the author implies; the reader infers* —O. Niles (1979).

infinitive (in fin′i tiv) *n.* the uninflected or base form of the verb, as *to go. Note:* It may be used in a verb phrase, as *go* in *He may go,* or as a substantive, as *To err* in *To err is human* — Pope. *Ct.* **finite verb.**

inflected form 1. a suffix which changes the form or function of a word but not its basic meaning, as *-ed* in *sprayed,* or *-ing* in *following.* 2. a root, derived form, or compound that takes an inflectional ending to mark the plural, tense, case, etc., as *toast* + *s* in *toasts.* See also **inflection** (defs. 1, 2).

inflection (in flek′s͟hən) 1. *n.* the process, or result, either of changing the form of a word, or of adding suffixes to express a syntactic function without changing the form class of a word, as adding *-s* to form regular noun plurals or adding *-ed* to form the regular verb past tense. *Note:* Forms of pronouns are inflected to show number, case, and gender. Verbs are inflected to show voice, mood, time, aspect, number, and person. 2. *n.* a word part, as *-s,* added in inflection. 3. *n.* changes in voice pitch and stress; modulation.

inflectional suffix in English, a suffix that, when added to a noun, expresses plurality or possession; when added to a verb, expresses tense; and when added to an adjective and some adverbs, expresses comparison.

informal assessment *or* **test** any nonstandardized sampling of ability or performance. *The value of informal tests is directly proportional to the objectivity and competence of the examiner.*

informal English the style of English used in casual speech or writing, such as in personal letters. See also **casual speech** *or* **style.**

informal reading inventory (IRI) the use of a graded series of passages of increasing difficulty, usually taken from basal readers, to make an informal diagnosis of one or more levels of reading performance. *Note:* This technique was first described at some length by E. Betts in a 1946 publication as a way of identifying several levels of student functioning in reading: independent, instructional, and frustration levels. The technique is adaptable to the rough assessment of oral reading skills and comprehension, as well as of silent reading. In addition, if passages are read to the student, some indication of level of listening comprehension (def. 2) may be gained. See also **frustration reading level; independent reading level; instructional reading level.**

informal writing writing that is casual or familiar, as that for friendly letters, creative writing, or writing for one's own use, rather than the formal writing of business letters, official reports, professional documents, etc.

informatics (in″fər ma′tiks) *n.* the scientific study of information, its processing, and its products.

information (in″fər mā′shən) 1. *n.* knowledge of a particular sort that is communicated or received; news. *What new information do you have?* 2. *n.* such knowledge gained through instruction or research. 3. *n.* that aspect of stimulation that specifies properties of things and events for perception. 4. *n.* in information theory, an indication of the number of possible alternative messages that may be sent or received. 5. *n.* in communication(s) theory, the content of something transmitted from source to receiver which is new, unexpected, and non-redundant. See also **entropy** (def. 2); **bit; byte.**

information book a nonfiction book of facts about a subject.

information density the amount of information content in a given communication.

information processing 1. the process of organizing and handling data, either by the human mind or by mechanical or electronic means. 2. the study of such a process; informatics.

information retrieval 1. the process of recovering data either from human memory or from mechanical or electronic storage, as in a library or in a computer bank. 2. the study of such a process.

information storage the placing of data in memory or in a databank for later use.

information theory the study of communications; especially, the application of probability estimates to the encoding, transmission, and reception of communications, most fully developed by C. Shannon and N. Wiener; cybernetics. *Information theory has led to mathematical statements of the amount of information in a statement. Cp.* **communication(s) theory.**

infralogical operations (J. Piaget) operations such as distance, time, rate, action, space, geometry, movement, speed, and causality that are parallel to and are synchronous with concrete and formal operations.

inhalation (in″hə lā′s̲h̲ən) *n.* the process of breathing in. *Ant.* **exhalation** (def. 1). *v.* **inhale.**

inhibition (in″i bis̲h̲′ən, in″hi-) 1. *n.* the stopping or limiting of body or physical processes, as *the inhibition of heart rate by meditation, inhibition of rust by paint.* 2. *n.* the stopping or limiting of a psychological process by countering forces, as in the normal restraint of impulses with socialization. 3. *n.* in psychoanalysis, the action of the superego in preventing instinctual processes from becoming conscious processes. 4. *n.* a state of reduced excitability at a synapse due to prior stimulation. 5. *n.* the state resulting from such interference. *v.* **inhibit;** *adj.* **inhibitory.**

initial blend 1. the joining of two or more consonant sounds, represented by letters, that begin a word without losing the identity of the consonant sounds, as /bl/ in *black*, /skr/ in *scream.* 2. the joining of the first consonant and vowel sounds in a word, as /b/ and /ā/ in *baby. Note:* This process is regarded by some in reading practice to be one of the most crucial steps in learning phonics.

initial glide See **on-glide.**

initial sight words in beginning reading, words which are to be learned as wholes rather than by phonic or structural analysis.

initial teaching alphabet (i.t.a.) 1. the current name for Augmented Roman Alphabet. 2. an elementary reading program using the Augmented Roman Alphabet. 3. the materials so used. See illustration.

h œ p

The word 'hope' in i/t/a

initiation rites 1. See **rites of passage.** 2. ceremonies used in introducing a new member to an organization.

in medias res (in me′di äs″ Res′); *Eng.* (in mē′ dē as″ rēz, in mā′ dē äs″ rās′) literally, Latin for 'in the middle of things': the technique of opening a story or play in the middle of the action, with flashbacks later to earlier parts.

innate (i nāt′, in′āt) 1. *adj.* present from birth; inborn; native; hereditary; as *an innate defect. Cp.* **congenital.** 2. *adj.* belonging to the character of something. *Gesture is an innate part of mime.* 3. *adj.* conceived by the mind without benefit of experience, as *innate knowledge.*

innate (-ness) theory See **nativistic theory.**

inner-city/inner city *adj.* having to do with the older and usually central part of a city, especially that part in which low income persons live in unfavorable, crowded conditions, often a ghetto containing persons of a single ethnic heritage.

inner ear the part of the ear deepest in the head; internal ear; specifically, the sensory organ which changes the mechanical energy of sound waves into electrical energy in the cochlea to permit hearing, and which regulates body balance by means of the semicircular canals. See illustration under **ear.** *Syn.* **labyrinth.**

inner speech See **implicit speech.**

innervation (in″ ər vā′s̲h̲ən) 1. *n.* the supply and pattern of distribution of efferent nerves to muscles or glands. 2. *n.* the excitation of such nerves. 3. **double innervation,** the condition of being supplied with nerve fibers from both the sympathetic and the parasympathetic nervous systems, as in the heart. 4. **reciprocal innervation**, the condition in which the nerve supply to pairs of opposing muscles, particularly around joints, allows one of the pair to contract while the opposing one relaxes. *Reciprocal innervation makes skeletal movement possible. v..* **innervate.**

in print available from the publisher.

input (in′po͝ot″) 1. *n.* something that enters from without; stimulus; as *energy input, information input.* 2. *n.* the act of so entering. 3. *v.* to enter something into a communications system, as *to input data into a computer.* 4. *n.* information which acts on a communications receiver, as *computer input.* 5. *n.* data available for solving a problem. *I need all the input I can get.* 6. *adj.* referring to a communications device for entering information, as into a computer. *Ct.* **output.**

INRC group (J. Piaget) the *I*dentity, *N*egation, *R*eciprocity, *C*orrelative transformations which work together as a system to form the structure which makes possible the highest level of logical thought, that of formal operations.

insertion (in sûr′s̲h̲ən) 1. *n.* the addition of one or more words in the oral reading of text; one of several types of oral reading errors commonly recorded in testing oral reading. See also **mispronunciation; substitution** (def. 2). *Ct.* **omission.** 2. *n.* that which is put in. *Proofreader's marks are insertions in text.* 3. *n.* the attachment or place of attachment of a body part or organ. *Cp.* **origin** (def. 3). *v.* **insert.**

inservice education education for employed teachers, often offered by a school district.

inside-out theories See **top-down processing.**

insight (in′sīt″) 1. *n.* the clear, immediate understanding of the nature of something; apprehension; intuition. *The teacher had keen insight into the nature of Fred's problem.* 2. *n.* the learning process, or result, of noting, through perceptual reorganization, those relationships that lead to problem solution. *Note:* This gestalt concept originally specified the suddenness of perceptual reorganization in perceptual problem-solving tasks. The concept has now been extended to cover a more gradual understanding of relationships and a wide range of types of problem-solving tasks. 3. *n.* in psychotherapy, the patient's understanding or awareness of his thoughts, feelings, and actions; self-knowledge. *The effectiveness of psychotherapy depends upon the patient's insight.* 4. *n.* a mystical revelation. *adj.* **insightful.**

instantiation (in stan″s̲h̲ē ā′s̲h̲ən) *n.* a concrete representation of some abstract idea. The Gift of the Magi *is an instantiation of love.*

instruction (in struk′s̲h̲ən) 1. *n.* a systematic, guided series of steps, procedures, or actions intended to result in learning or in the reaching of a desired goal by students; teaching; education. 2. *n.* the general or specific content of what is taught. 3. *n. (usually pl.)* orders or directions. 4. *n.* the operational code which guides computer processes. *adj.* **instructional.** *v.* **instruct.**

instructional framework the conceptual structure used to design and analyze teaching.

instructional materials center (IMC) a place in a school which includes the educational media center and usually the library, containing materials and equipment which permit a variety of individual and group learning experiences. *Cp.* **resource center; media center.**

instructional objective See **objective** (def. 2).

instructional reading level the readability or grade level of material that is challenging, but not frustrating for the student to read successfully with normal classroom instruction and support. *At the instructional reading level, the number of new words and the demands upon comprehension stimulate rather than block reading progress. Note:* Better than 95 percent word attack accuracy and better than 75 percent comprehension are often used as standards in judging this level. The concept of matching students with challenging but possible reading materials is especially significant for reading growth. See also **informal reading inventory (IRI); frustration reading level; independent reading level.**

instructional sequence the order in which something is taught, based on a rationale involving objectives, the learner, and the material.

instructional system a pattern of teaching/learning components organized to lead to specific goals.

instrumental conditioning the process, or result, of linking a response to a stimulus that otherwise would not produce a response, depending upon the subject's response behavior to secure a reward or to avoid punishment. *Note:* For example, in instrumental conditioning, a button (conditioned stimulus) is pressed (conditioned response) to open a food box (unconditioned stimulus or reinforcement) and allow eating the food (unconditioned response). In instrumental conditioning, the unconditioned stimulus always follows the conditioned response. *Ct.* **classical conditioning**. See also **operant conditioning.**

instrumental effect an effect of reading noted by D. Waples and others (1940); specifically, one which adds to the reader's knowledge, often with the intent to use such knowledge in a practical way. *Cp.* **effects of reading.**

instrument visual screening a set of procedures used with a special instrument to quickly survey selected visual functions, as in schools, for possible referral to an eye specialist. *Note:* Typical visual functions measured are acuity, stereopsis, and muscular imbalance.

intake counselor a skilled person who has the initial interview with someone entering an academic program, a special care facility, etc.

integrated method *the use of reading as a tool in furthering the interests and activities of the children, and both reading and the other subjects are drawn upon as they are needed and as they enter naturally into the children's in-school and out-of-school enterprises*— N. B. Smith (1965).

integration (in″tə grā′shən) 1. *n.* the combining of separate parts, traits, etc., into a unified, functioning whole, as the integration of history and literature, personality integration, etc. 2. *n.* the working together of different cultural and/or racial groups without prejudice. 3. *n.* the formal breaking down by law of separate facilities for different races; desegregation. *adj.* **integrated.** *v.* **integrate.**

intellect (in′tᵊ lekt″) 1. See **cognition.** 2. *n.* ability to think, as *a weak intellect, a brilliant intellect.*

intellectual (in″tᵊlek′cho͞o əl) 1. *adj.* having to do with cognition. 2. *adj.* having to do with high mental ability. 3. *n.* a person of high mental ability. 4. *n.* a person who is primarily interested in ideas and enjoys thinking about them. *Note:* The term is sometimes used sarcastically to indicate an impractical person. 5. *n.* one who is extremely rational rather than emotional.

intellectual realism (J. Piaget) in the egocentric thought of children and primitive people, the representation of the environment as it is thought to be rather than as it is directly perceived.

intelligence (in tel′i jəns)

Intelligence is a hypothetical notion which has been wooed by many definitions but which remains elusive. The old conception that intelligence is solely an inherited quality unaffected by environment (def. 3) has now largely been abandoned by authorities in tests and measurement but still lingers in educational practice. Although there is still the popular operational conception that intelligence is what an intelligence test measures (def. 2), current views about intelligence tend to emphasize information processing skills. *Note:* For Binet's concept of intelligence, see **Binet** *or* **Binet-Simon Scale.** See also **general factor (g)** (def. 1); **specific factor(s).**

1. *n.* the skills by which a person processes information. 2. *n.* general mental ability as measured by a standardized intelligence test; brightness; scholastic aptitude. 3. *n.* inherited mental ability. 4. *n.* (J. Piaget) a balanced or equilibrated system of operations resulting from the individual's interactions with objects and events in the environment; the development and adaptation of cognitive structures to reality. *Note:* In Piaget's conception of intelligence, it would be defined differently for each of his stages of development. 5. *n.* evidence of mental ability, as *a woman of intelligence.* 6. *n.* understanding. *He displayed intelligence of my needs.* 7. *n.* information; news. *What secret intelligence do you have? adj.* **intelligent.**

intelligence quotient (IQ) the ratio between mental age and chronological age, or between mental age and the mental age normal for a given chronological age, multiplied by 100. *Cp.* **deviation IQ.** *Note:* The ratio IQ was first used in the 1916 Stanford-Binet Intelligence Scale as an index of potentiality based on the assumption of a constant rate of intellectual development. The assumption has proven to be faulty. Nevertheless, the concept of the IQ has a firm hold in psychological and educational practice and in the minds of laymen. *According to a popular misconception, the IQ is an index of innate intellectual potential and represents a fixed property of the organism... This view is neither theoretically defensible nor supported by empirical data* — A. Anastasi (1976).

intelligence test a series of tests, either group or individual, for assessing general mental ability or scholastic aptitude. *Cp.* **capacity test.** See also **intelligence** (def. 2); **intelligence quotient.**

intensifier (in ten′sə fī″ər) *n.* an adverbial of degree which emphasizes the meaning of a word, as *completely* in *completely exhausted.*

intension (in ten′shən) *n.* the connotation of a word or phrase. *Ct.* **extension** (def. 1).

intensity (in ten′si tē) 1. *n.* the amount of energy measured in a given unit of time, volume, area, etc. *The intensity of the sound is 40 decibels (dB).* See also **amplitude** (def. 1). 2. *n.* the strength of a behavior, attitude, or emotion. *He spoke with great intensity. The intensity of feeling in the crowd was unbelievable. adj.* **intense; intensive.**

intensive reading a reading program in which students read one or very few selections, with emphasis upon a thorough study of many aspects of the selection(s). *Intensive reading sharpens one's critical reading abilities. Ct.* **extensive reading.**

intent (in tent′) 1. *n.* a goal to be sought, as *one's learning intent.* 2. *n.* the purpose that a writer or speaker wishes to achieve; intention; as *an intent to persuade.* 3. *n.* meaning. *This is my intent: to act swiftly.* 4. *n.* a plan or act, as *evil intent.* 5. *adj.* with steady attention to, as *intent concentration. n.* **intention.**

intentional fallacy a term in literary criticism introduced by W.K. Wimsatt, Jr., and M.C. Beardsley to describe the error of judging a literary work primarily by the author's stated purpose. *Cp.* **pathetic fallacy; affective fallacy.**

intentionality in ten″shə nal′i tē) *n.* (J. Piaget) a quality of adaptive behavior in infancy that is purposeful, goal-oriented, and indicative of the beginnings of sensorimotor intelligence.

inter- a prefix indicating *between, among*; as **interact.**

interaction (in″tər ak′shən) 1. *n.* mutual influence or reciprocal effect, as *an interaction between people and their environment.* 2. *n.* in statistical analysis, the influence of two factors or variables, taken jointly, that is distinct from their individual effects. *adj.* **interactive.** *v.* **interact.**

inter- a prefix indicating *between, among;* as **interact.**

interaction (in″tər ak′shən) 1. *n.* mutual influence or reciprocal effect, as *an interaction between people and their environment.* 2. *n.* in statistical analysis, the influence of two factors or variables, taken jointly, that is distinct from their individual effects. *adj.* **interactive.** *v.* **interact.**

interactive processing a theoretical position that reading involves both the processing of text and the use of experiences and expectancies the reader brings to the text, both sources of information interacting and modifying each other in reading comprehension. *In interactive processing, comprehension is generated by the reader under the stimulus control of the print. Cp.* **bottom-up processing; top-down processing.**

intercorrelation (in″tər kôr″ə lā′shən) *n.* a set of correlations representing the results of correlating several tests with each other, usually expressed in a table of intercorrelations. *v.* **intercorrelate.**

interdental (in″tər den′t^{ə}l) *n.* a consonant speech sound articulated between the upper and lower teeth, as /th/ in *this.*

interest (in′tər ist, -trist)
Interest is elusive in its meaning in various contexts and has many connotations, mostly non-technical. Generally, interest reflects the notion that it has something to do with the motivational system of the individual.
1. *n.* the tendency to selectively attend to something because of curiosity, con-

cern, etc., as *show an interest in language.* 2. *n.* that which arrouses such a tendency. *Lou's interest is horses.* 3. *n.* a specific, goal-directed motivational state. *The opportunity to ask questions of the author aroused the children's interest.* 4. *n.* a motivational element needed for learning, as a satisfying activity: *I wonder which approach would stimulate the greatest interest in the class?* 5. *n.* benefit; advantage. *That is not to my interest.* 6. *v.* to excite attention or curiosity, as *interest one in drama.* 7. *v.* to involve. *May I interest you in joining the book club?*

interest/difficulty level the average age level of appeal of a given piece of reading material in relation to its ease of reading. *Note:* In the selection of reading materials for poor readers, an effort is often made to find materials that tend to appeal to the student's age group and/or expressed interests, and yet are easy to read. There are a number of printed lists of such books.

interest inventory 1. a checklist informally built for exploring such things as reading preferences, work and play interests, radio and TV habits, etc. 2. a formal questionnaire designed to explore the strength and direction of interests of an individual.

interface (in′tər fās″) 1. *n.* any common boundary or surface between ideas or things. *The interface between linguistics and psychology forms the basis for the study of psycholinguistics.* 2. *v.* to form or function as a common boundary. *How do your ideas interface with mine?*

interference (in″tər fēr′əns) 1. *n.* hindrance; obstruction. *False cognates may create interference in language learning.* 2. *n.* a conflict in motives, desires, etc. *Pat's many interests were more of an interference than a help in choosing a career.* 3. *n.* the inhibiting effect of previous learning upon new learning. 4. in bilingualism, any influence of a first language on a second one. 5. *n.* meddling, as *interference in other people's affairs.* *v.* **interfere.**

interiorization (in tēr″ē ə ri zā′shən) *n.* (J. Piaget) the process, or product, of the mental representation of actions, *v.* **interiorize.**

interjection (in″tər jek′shən) *n.* a word or phrase expressing sudden or strong emotion, as *Phew* in *Phew! I made it!*

interlibrary loan a loan of material by one library to another for a specified period at the request of a patron.

interlinear (in″tər lin′ē ər) 1. *adj.* placed between lines of print or writing, as *interlinear corrections.* 2. *adj.* having alternate lines in a different language or version, as *an interlinear translation.*

interlude (in′tər lo͞od″) 1. *n.* an interval of time, space, etc. *The interruption was a welcome interlude.* 2. *n.* a form of early English drama, farcical or moralistic in tone, written in the late 15th and 16th centuries. 3. *n.* a short and often witty play performed between acts of another drama or as part of the entertainment at a feast. 4. *n.* a musical composition played between the parts of a religious service, drama, opera, etc.

intermediate school 1. in the United States, except for Hawaii, a school that bridges the upper elementary and lower junior high school grades, usually grades 6, 7, and 8. 2. in Hawaii, a school of grades 7-9. *Cp.* **middle school.**

internal auditory meatus a small opening in the skull through which the auditory nerve and artery pass from the inner ear to the brain.

internal consistency 1. the extent to which the items of a test are homogeneous, as those in a spelling test. 2. a comparison of scores on two equivalent halves of a test. See **split-half reliability coefficient.**

internalize (in tûr′nə līz″) 1. *v.* to make external values and ideas of a culture part of oneself through learning and socialization. *Children who have developed a social conscience have internalized the mores of the society in which they live.* 2. *v.* (J. Piaget) to represent actions mentally; interiorize. See **interiorization.**

internal reconstruction a method of reconstructing the structure and rules of a language as it existed in some earlier period of its history, by studying that language's present patterns, irregularities, and free variants.

internal rhyme a rhyme that occurs within a line of verse; as *dreary* and *weary* in *Once upon a midnight dreary, while I pondered, weak and weary* — E. A. Poe.

internal speech See **implicit speech.**

international language 1. a language used worldwide by speakers of different languages, as English. 2. a worldwide symbolic system, as mathematical or musical notation. 3. an artificial language, as Esperanto. See also **artificial language; lingua franca.**

International Phonetic Alphabet (IPA) a set of graphic symbols originally devised by phoneticians in the 1880's and periodically revised, which enables human speech sounds to be described and labeled in an unamibiguous manner. See table on the back flyleaf and end paper of this dictionary. *Cp.* **phonemic alphabet**.

International Standard Book Number (ISBN) an internationally agreed upon standard number that uniquely identifies a monograph.

International Standard Serials Number (ISSN) an internationally agreed upon standard number that uniquely identifies a serial publication.

interoceptor (in″tər ō sep′tər) *n.* a sense organ or sensory nerve terminal within the body that receives stimulation from the viscera, as *a stomach interoceptor. Cp.* **exteroceptor; proprioceptor.**

interpolate (in tûr′pə lāt″) 1. *v.* to alter something, as words in a text, or make insertions, as words into a text, as *an interpolated remark.* 2. *v.* to estimate or insert values which fall between known points on a graph or between numbers of a series. *One may have to interpolate in norms tables for a person with a CA of 10-2. Ct.* **extrapolate** (def. 2). *n.* **interpolation.**

interpretation (in tûr″pri tā′shən) 1. *n.* the process of inferring beyond the literal meaning of a communication; inferred meaning; 'reading between the lines.' *Interpretation is the thinking side of comprehension* — M. Tinker and C. McCullough (1968). 2. *n.* the analysis of the meaning of a communication. *Interpretation depends upon an analysis of both the surface structure and deep structure of the grammatical component of sentences as well as some semantic analysis which mediates between conceptual representation and the linguistic form that the representation takes* — D. Schwartz, J. Sparkman, and J. Deese. 3. *n.* an explanation. *This is my interpretation of what happened.* 4. *n.* a performance, usually artistic, of a play, musical number, etc., to which the performer gives distinctive meaning. *Laurence Olivier gave an outstanding interpretation of Henry V.* 5. *n.* a translation from another language. *n.* **interpreter.** *adj.* **interpretative; interpretive; interpretable.** *v.* **interpret.**

interpretation, consecutive See **consecutive interpretation.**

interpretation, simultaneous See **simultaneous interpretation.**

interrogation point (Brit.) See **question mark.**

interrogative mood See **indicative mood.**

interrogative word a word that marks a clause or sentence as a question, as one of the English *wh* words: *who, what, where, when, why.*

intersensory integration See **cross-modal integration.**

interval (in′tər vəl) See **class interval.**

intervening variable the inferred, hypothetical variable(s) involved in the relationship between an independent and a dependent variable, as between causes and results. *Fatigue is an intervening variable between the number of hours of continous reading and the ability to maintain clearly focused fixations on the page.* See also **independent variable; dependent variable.**

intervention program any one of several projects, usually with government funding, intended to give low socioeconomic children added cognitive stimulation. See **Project Head Start; Project Follow Through.**

intimate speech *or* **style** the informal style of discourse between persons who are closely related by family or by social level in which meaning is shared without the use of elaborate linguistic forms. *In intimate speech, sentences and phrases may be reduced to a word or part of a word.*

intonation (in″tō nā′s̮hən, -tə-) 1. *n.* the melody of a spoken language; the rise and fall in pitch of the speaking voice. *The frantic intonation of voices clearly meant danger. Note:* In nontonal languages, as English, intonation refers to changes in pitch primarily across words and is used to signal the meaning of phrases and sentences, as in distinguishing between a command 'Go now!' and a question 'Go now?' (See also **suprasegmental phoneme**.) In tonal languages, intonation refers to changes in pitch within words which signal their meaning and/or function. 2. *n.* the act of varying the pitch in speaking and singing. *v.* **intone.**

intra-, intro- a prefix indicating *within, inside;* as **intraocular, introspection.**

intransitive verb a verb that does not take an object, as *sit, lie*, etc., and, in English, is not used to form the passive voice. *Ct.* **transitive verb.**

intraocular muscles the three muscles inside the eyeball which serve to change the size of the pupil and to adjust the shape of the lens. *Ct.* **extraocular muscles.**

intrinsic (in trin′sik, -zik) 1. *adj.* coming from within; essential; inherent; as *intrinsic motivation.* 2. *adj.* having to do with something, especially muscles and nerves; located within the part of the body that it affects. *Intrinsic muscles in the eyeball control the iris in admitting light. Ct.* **extrinsic.**

intrinsic method a teaching-learning approach in which goals and rewards come from student self-direction and satisfaction rather than from the teacher. *Ct.* **extrinsic method.**

intrinsic motivation 1. behavior directed toward satisfaction by engaging in the behavior itself. 2. the self-control of such behavior, as in continuing to read books for enjoyment. *Ct.* **extrinsic motivation.**

intrinsic phonics any phonics approach that is made an integral part of the program of reading instruction. *Ct.* **extrinsic phonics.**

introduction (in″trə duk′s̮hən) *n.* a front section of a book containing a formal statement of the subject and a discussion of the author's treatment of the subject. *Cp.* **preface.**

introspection (in″trə spek′shən) *n.* literally, a looking into one's self; specifically, a way of reviewing one's thoughts, sensations, and experiences. *Introspection has a long history in psychology as one way of developing insight into mental processes. adj.* **introspective.**

introspective-retrospective report *the study of the reading process that encourages students to describe what went on in their minds between the printed page and their verbal response to it* — R. Strang, cited by A. Melnik.

introversion (in″trə vûr′zhən, -shən, in′trə vûr″-) *n.* the process of turning inward; specifically, a normal type of behavior focused on the self rather than on social interaction; a tendency to be absorbed with one's own thoughts and feelings. *Ant.* **extraversion.** *adj., n.* **introvert.**

intrusion (in tro͞o′zhən) *n.* a sound often mistakenly inserted in an utterance solely for ease of pronunciation, as the /ə/ in *athlete* /ath ə lēt/. *adj.* **intrusive.**

intuition (in″too ish′ən, -tyoo-) 1. *n.* the process, or result, of perception or cognition that is immediate and direct rather than subjected to reflective thought, as *mystical intuition.* 2. *n.* (J. Piaget) a characteristic of preoperational thought in which percepts are internalized directly as representational images rather than transformed and manipulated in logical thought. *adj.* **intuitive.**

intuitive correspondence (J. Piaget) a relationship that is wholly learned, recalled, and used as a percept: *Bananas and oranges have different shapes. Ct.* **operational correspondence.**

invariant (in vār′ē ənt) 1. *adj.* referring to a constant, unchanging state or function under changing conditions, as *invariant good humor.* 2. *n.* such a constant state or function. *n.* **invariance.**

invention (in ven′shən) 1. *n.* the power to express oneself creatively in one or more aspects of writing or other arts, as *the stylistic invention of Ken Kesey, the surrealistic invention of Salvador Dali.* 2. *n.* an example of such power. 3. *n.* the choice of ideas appropriate for one's speech, its audience, and the occasion. *v.* **invent.** *adj.* **inventive.**

invention-discovery *n.* (J. Piaget) the construction of a mental scheme or operation in ideational thought to achieve a goal, as form a hypothesis vs. finding or discovering something that exists in the external world, such as the idea that 2 plus 2 equals 4.

inventory (in′vən tōr″ē, -tôr″ē) *n.* a questionnaire for assessing behaviors, interests, personality characteristics, etc. *Note:* Special types of inventories, as *interest inventory*, are given under the describing term.

inversion (in vûr′zhən, -shən) 1. *n.* the reversal of normal sentence order, usually by placing the verb before the noun. 2. *n.* the reversal in speech of phonemes or syllables that are next to each other, as *aws* for *saw* or *slapback* for *backslap. Inversions are the spoken equivalent of reversals in spelling or writing.* 3. *n.* the rotation of a letter 180 degrees, as in reading *d* for *p. Note:* In education, the more general term *reversal* covers all types of inversions and rotations. See **reversal.** *v.* **invert.**

inverted commas (*Brit.*) See **quotation marks.**

IPA International Phonetic Alphabet.

IPI individually prescribed instruction.

ipsilateral (ip″si lat′ər əl, -sə-) *adj.* referring to the same side of the body, especially when a motor or sensory disorder occurs on the same side of the body as the source of the nerve damage causing the disorder. *Ct.* **contralateral.**

IQ intelligence quotient.

IRI informal reading inventory.

iris (ī ris) *n.* the circular, colored, muscular membrane in the eyeball with the pupil at its center. *Note:* The iris can expand or contract, thus changing the size of the pupil to regulate the amount of light entering the inner eye for comfortable and effective vision. Pigments in the iris determine eye color. See illustration under **eye.** *n.* **iritis.** *adj.* **irinic; iritic.**

irony (ī′rə nē, ī′ər) 1. *n.* a figure of speech in which the literal meaning of the words is the opposite of their intended meaning. See also **sarcasm; satire.** 2. *n.* a literary technique for implying, through plot or character, that the actual situation is quite different from that presented. See **dramatic irony.** 3. *n.* an incongruity or discrepancy between an anticipated and realized outcome. *Now that their attempt had failed, they could laugh at the irony of their situation. adj.* **ironic.**

irregularity (i reg″yə lar′i tē) *n.* in linguistics, an exception to a grammatical form or rule. *Cp.* **grammaticality.** *adj.* **irregular.**

irregular verb a verb whose inflectional forms indicate past and perfect forms with other than the *-ed* ending, as *go*, with forms *go/went/gone. Ct.* **regular verb.**

ISBN International Standard Book Number.

-ism a suffix indicating *action, practice*, as **criticism;** *state, condition*, as **mongolism;** *usage, characteristic*, as **sentimentalism;** *doctrine, theory*, as **realism.**

iso- a prefix indicating *equal*; as **isomorph.**

isolate (ī′sə lāt″, is′ə-) 1. *v.* to identify in or derive from a class, as *isolate a statistical factor.* 2. *v.* in psychoanalysis, to separate emotion from its referent or one idea from the other. 3. *n.* a socially isolated person, as one scoring low on a sociogram. See illustration under **sociogram.**

isolation (ī″sə lāshən, is″ə-) 1. *n.* separation from others of the same kind, as *sounds in isolation, social isolation, isolation for contagious diseases.* 2. *n.* the psychoanalytic concept of the separation of ideas, or of the separation of emotion from its referent. See also **isolate** (def. 2). 3. *n.* the psychoanalytic concept of the refusal to think or act following trauma.

isomorphic (ī″sə môrf′ik) *adj.* something identical to something else in form or structure. *A writing system with completely consistent letter-sound correspondences is isomorphic.*

isomorphism (ī″sə môr′fiz əm) *n.* in linguistics, a one-to-one correspondence: a. between words and/or word meanings between two languages. b. between written and spoken words. c. between linguistic elements and structures in two periods of a language's history. *adj.* **isomorphic.**

ISSN International Standard Serials Number

-ist a suffix indicating *one who practices in a special field*; as **optometrist.**

i/t/a *or* **i.t.a.** See **initial teaching alphabet; Augmented Roman Alphabet.**

italic (i tal′ik, ī tal′-) 1. *adj.* having to do with a light version of a typeface design with strokes slanted to the right, often used for emphasis. *This sentence is set in italic type. Ct.* **boldface; roman.** 2. **italics,** italic type. *v.* **italicize.**

item analysis an examination of the consistency of any test item with the standard measured by the whole set of test items.

item, test See **test item.**

-itis a suffix indicating *inflammation*; as **laryngitis.**

J

DEVELOPMENT OF MAJUSCULE						
NORTH SEMITIC	GREEK	ETR.	LATIN	MODERN		
				GOTHIC	ITALIC	ROMAN
SEE LETTER I				𝔍	*J*	J

DEVELOPMENT OF MINUSCULE					
ROMAN CURSIVE	ROMAN UNCIAL	CAROL. MIN.	MODERN		
			GOTHIC	ITALIC	ROMAN
SEE I	j	SEE I	𝔧	*j*	j

The tenth letter of the English alphabet developed as a variant form of I in Medieval Latin, and, except for the preference for the J as an initial letter, the two were used interchangeably, both serving to represent the vowel (i) and the consonant (y). Later, through specialization, it came to be distinguished as a separate sign, acquiring its present phonetic value under the influence of French.

Jack tales stories of the Appalachian mountain people in which the hero, Jack, through his quick wit overcomes all opponents and all difficulties. *Note:* These stories are American variations of folk tales brought from the British Isles by early settlers.

Jacotot method a way of teaching reading that began with the student's memorizing an entire book by hearing it read; to memorizing or reading sentences; to recognizing the words in the sentence; and then to learning the letters and their sounds within words. *Note:* The name derived from the French mathematician and teacher, Jean Joseph Jacotot (1770-1840), who advocated a 'universal' method in education. In American adaptations, the sentence, and eventually the word, became the starting point. *On teaching to read according to the method of Jacotot* — American Journal of Education (1834). *Cp.* **analytic approach** *or* **method; story method.**

Jaeger rating an estimate of near point visual acuity using words and phrases printed in different sizes of type as targets.

jargon (jär′gən, -gon) *n.* cant (def. 1). *'Media center,' 'student stations,' and 'open vertical grouping' are educational jargon for 'library,' 'desks,' and 'a group of children of different ages.'* *Cp.* **argot** (def. 2); **slang** (def. 2).

jingle (jing′gəl) 1. *n.* verse or doggerel with repetitious sounds such as those that result from metal objects striking together. *Most nursery rhymes are jingles.* 2. *n.* such verse, with music.

joint author See **co-author.**

joint distribution a simultaneous tabulation of two or more sets of scores for each of a large number of persons, indicating for each possible combination of scores, the number of persons having that pattern. See **scatter diagram**.

Joplin plan an organizational plan for reading instruction begun in Joplin, Missouri, and most popular in the early 1960's, in which all students in a school building receive reading instruction at the same period, the students, regardless of grade placement, reporting to a class whose members are essentially at the same reading level.

journal (jûr′n^{ə}l) 1. *n.* a diary of events in chronological order, as *Lewis' and Clark's* Journals. 2. *n.* a periodical published by a learned society, association, institution, etc. 3. *n.* a record, usually daily, as *a legislative journal.* 4. *n.* a newspaper, especially a daily one.

journalese (jûr″n^{ə}lēz′, -n^{ə}lēs′) *n.* writing of a style used in newspapers. *Note:* The term is often used in an unfavorable sense to refer to the careless, unpolished, trite style of some newspaper and magazine writers.

journalism (jûr′nəliz″əm) 1. *n.* the professional field of reporting news, including investigating, writing, editing, photographing, and broadcasting. 2. *n.* the course of study that prepares one for such a field. *n.* **journalist.**

judgment (juj′mənt) 1. *n.* the ability to make critical decisions wisely. *He showed good judgment in handling the student's complaint.* 2. *n.* an opinion. *Terry has a judgment on every subject.* 3. *n.* a ruling or decision. *Judgment was passed after the court resumed.*

juncture (jungk′chər) *n.* pauses of varying lengths in speech production which contribute to the meaning of words, phrases, and sentences; transition. *Note:* Three types of juncture - close juncture, open juncture, and terminal juncture - are recognized by phoneticians: *Close juncture* is the normal transition of one speech sound to the next in a syllable or word. *Open juncture* is the slight pause that occurs between one speech sound and the next, often distinguishing word boundaries, as *a name/an aim.* See also **terminal juncture.**

junior high school See **secondary school.** See also **middle school; intermediate school.**

junior novel *or* **book** a book written for teen-agers. See **literature for adolescents.**

junior school (*Brit.*) a school for children aged 7-11.

juvenile book a book written for children and/or adolescents. See also **children's literature; literature for adolescents.**

juvenile delinquent a child or adolescent whose behavior violates the law or a moral code. *n.* **juvenile delinquency.**

K

DEVELOPMENT OF MAJUSCULE								
NORTH SEMITIC	GREEK		ETR.	LATIN		MODERN		
						GOTHIC	ITALIC	ROMAN
↓	ᚿ	K	⅄	⅄	K	𝕶	*K*	K

DEVELOPMENT OF MINUSCULE					
ROMAN CURSIVE	ROMAN UNCIAL	CAROL. MIN.	MODERN		
			GOTHIC	ITALIC	ROMAN
—	K	—	𝔨	*k*	k

The eleventh letter of the English alphabet corresponds to North Semitic *kaph* and Greek *kappa*. The Romans, adopting the alphabet from the Etruscans, at first had three symbols (C, K, and Q) for the *k*-sound. K fell into disuse. It did not appear in English until after the Norman conquest, when, under Norman-French influence, it came into use in place of C to distinguish the pronunciation of words of native origin: such words as *cyng* became *king; cene, keen; cyn, kin; cnif, knife;* and *cnotta, knot.* Under other influences, often through loan words, the symbol entered into more general use.

k coefficient of alienation.

kana (kä′nä, -nə) *pl.* **-na, -nas.** 1. a system of syllabic writing used for Japanese, that has two sets of 46 characters each plus diacritics, one set being used for foreign words and the other for native words. 2. *n.* an orthographic character in this writing system. *Cp.* **hiragana; katakana; kanji.** See also **syllabary.**

kanji (kän′jē) *pl.* **-ji, -jis.** 1. *n.* a set of ideographic characters derived from Chinese characters and used in Japanese writing for many content words. 2. *n.* an ideographic character in this writing system. *Cp.* **ideograph** (def. 2) *Ct.* **hiragana; katakana; kana.**

katakana *or* **kata-kana** kä″tə kä′nə) *pl.* **-ana, -nas.** 1. *n.* the Japanese syllabic characters, square or angular in appearance, traditionally used for learned words, official documents, and proper names, now reserved for foreign words. 2. *n.* a character of this written set; as *mi* in Japanese *mi-ru-ku* 'cow's milk' for *milk. Cp.* **hiragana; kanji.** See also **syllabary.**

keratometer See **ophthalmometer.**

kernel sentence 1. in early transformational-generative grammar, a simple declarative sentence which can be transformed into more complex sentences by transformation rules. 2. an unmodified subject and predicate, as *man jogged* in *The man jogged slowly.*

key (kē) *n.* a style of speech or manner of discourse. *'Ladies and gentlemen, you may begin' is in a formal key while 'Go on and start' is in a casual key. Cp.* **register** (def. 1).

key vocabulary the words that have immediacy for a child and presumably are therefore easy for the child to learn. *As the pattern of any physical movement is from the body outward, so is the flow of the key vocabulary from the mind outward, from the inside out* — S. Ashton-Warner (1963).

key-word method a phonic technique used by F. Laubach and others which matches the letters of the alphabet with pictures that represent the initial sound of each.

kilohertz (kHz) (kil′ə hûrtz″) *n.* a frequency unit of 1,000 cycles per second (cps).

kindergarten (kin′dər gär″t^{ə}n, - d^{ə}n) 1. *n.* in the United States, a school or class, usually for five-year-olds. *Kindergartens are often half-day programs in public schools, with varied emphases upon the physical, socio-emotional, and intellectual aspects of child development.* 2. *n.* in the United Kingdom, an infant school for five- to seven-year-olds. 3. *n.* in Australia, usually the first year of infant school. 4. *n.* in Germany, a preschool similar to the U.S. nursery school.

kine- a combining form indicating

moving, movement; as **kinesics.**

kinescope (kin′i skōp″) *n.* the motion picture record of a television program.

kinesics (ki nē′siks, kī-) (*with sing. v.)* 1. *n.* the nonverbal signals used in spoken communication. *Kinesics includes facial expressions, eye-contact, use of hands, body postures, and head movements.* 2.*n.* the study of such nonverbal signals.

kinesthesis (kin″is thē′sis) *n.* the perception of body movement, position, and weight arising from sense receptors in muscles, tendons, joints, and the inner ear. *While vision and other externally stimulated senses may also provide information about body movement, kinesthesis usually refers to cues arising within the body. Cp.* **tactile** (def. 1). See also **Fernald (-Keller) approach** *or* **method (VAKT); kinesthetic approach** *or* **method.** *adj.* **kinesthetic.**

kinesthetic approach *or* **method.** 1. any method in which learning takes place through the sense of movement, as in the learning of handwriting by the blind. 2. a method in which learning takes place through a combination of senses including the kinesthetic, as visual-auditory-kinesthetic (VAK) or visual -auditory -kinesthetic -tactile (VAKT). 3. a method in which the student traces a word to be learned with one or two fingers while at the same time studying the word visually and saying the parts aloud; tracing method; Fernald, or Fernald-Keller, approach or method. *Note:* Some teachers advocate writing the material to be read or spelled instead of tracing it.

kinesthetic feedback information from muscles, joints, and tendons which helps one repeat a movement or movements, as in articulating words, or from the semicircular canals which help one maintain one's balance.

kinesthetic modality the use of the kinesthetic senses in acquiring sensory information. *Cp.* **auditory modality; visual modality.**

kinetic reversal See **reversal.**

knowledge (nol′ij) 1. *n.* a state of general familiarity with facts, principles, ideas, etc.; learning; erudition. *Albert Schweitzer was a man of great knowledge.* 2. *n.* such a state in a special field. 3. *n.* all that the peoples of the world have learned, as revealed in the records of civilization. 4. *n.* clear and certain comprehension of a fact or truth, as *the believable knowledge of the witness.* 5. *n.* practical experience, as *a knowledge of human nature.* 6. *n.* awareness. *Did you have knowledge that she was planning to leave? v.* **know.** *adj.* **knowledgeable.**

Ku kurtosis.

Kuder-Richardson formula any one of several formulas for determining test reliability by analysis of the internal consistency of responses to the test items of a single test form.

kurtosis (Ku) (kûr tō′sis) *n.* the relative flatness (platykurtosis) or pointedness (leptokurtosis) around the mode of a frequency curve as compared to the roundedness (mesokurtosis) of the normal frequency curve. *Note:* The term 'kurtosis' and its variants refer to the closeness to which scores cluster around the mean.

kymograph (kī′mə graf″, -gräf″) *n.* a rotating drum on which one or more markers trace a path to record variations in incoming signals. *Smoked drum kymographs were one of the earliest means of directly recording reading eye-movements by markers attached to one anesthetized eyeball.*

L

DEVELOPMENT OF MAJUSCULE								
NORTH SEMITIC	GREEK		ETR.	LATIN		MODERN		
						GOTHIC	ITALIC	ROMAN
ℓ	1	Λ	˩	⅃	L	𝔏	*L*	L

DEVELOPMENT OF MINUSCULE					
ROMAN CURSIVE	ROMAN UNCIAL	CAROL. MIN.	MODERN		
			GOTHIC	ITALIC	ROMAN
l	L	l	l	*l*	l

The twelfth letter of the English alphabet derives from North Semitic *lamed,* with its shape exhibiting consistent development. It assumed its present form as a right angle (L) in Classical Latin. The minuscule (l) is a cursive variant of the capital.

labial (lā′bē əl) 1. *n.* a speech sound made with the aid of the lips, as /b/, /p/, /m/. See also **bilabial** (def. 1); **labiodental**. 2. *adj.* having to do with the lips. *n.* **labialization.** *v.* **labialize.**

labiodental (lā″bē ō den′t^{ə}l) *n.* a consonant speech sound made when the lower lip and the upper teeth constrict the air flow, as /f/ or /v/.

laboratory experience a learning situation in a specially equipped room designed to teach students in a particular subject, as chemistry, statistics, or a foreign language. See also **language laboratory**. *Note:* In the natural and behavioral sciences, demonstration and/or experiment is emphasized; in foreign languages, demonstration, drill, and practice. In art or music, the laboratory experience is called a studio experience.

laboratory research research that takes place under the highly controlled experimental, but artificial, conditions of the laboratory. *Note:* Laboratory research is usually conducted to test hypotheses and/or theories. Usually the independent variables are clearly defined, measurement is precise, and unwanted influences excluded so that relatively sound inferences may be drawn from the study.

labyrinth (lab′ə rinth) *n.* the interconnected cavities and canals that make up the internal or inner ear; collectively, the cochlea, the semicircular canals, and the vestibule.

LAD language acquisition device.

-lalia a combining form indicating *speech defect*; as **echolalia.**

lallation *or* **lalling** (la lā′shən; la′ling) 1. *n.* a stage in language acquisition in which distinct vowel sounds are first produced, occurring after the babbling stage at about six months of age. 2. *n.* a speech defect with poor articulation of /l/ and /r/ because of faulty tongue movements.

laminating (lam′ə nā′ting) the preservation of materials with a protective coating of transparent plastic, using heat or pressure either by hand or by machine. *n.* **lamination.** *v.* **laminate.**

laminator (lam′ə nā″tər) *n.* a machine for laminating.

lampoon (lam po͞on′) 1. *n.* a sharp, often bitter satire, written to ridicule a person, his character, or his appearance. 2. *v.* to write such a satirical piece.

language (lang′gwij)

The problem in defining language is that language itself must be the medium of its own description. As a result, defining language is both a difficult and controversial effort, and a definition of this basic human activity is conditioned by the theoretical or subjective views of the definer. The following definitions are some of the principal historical and current views of language.

1. *n.* in descriptive linguistics, *a system*

of arbitrary oral symbols by means of which a social group interacts — W. Lehmann (1976). 2. *n.* in transformational-generative grammar, *a set of all the sentences a grammar generates* — D. T. Langendoen (1969). 3. *n.* the speech, vocabulary, and grammatical system shared by people of the same nation, region, community, or cultural tradition, as *Swedish, Basque, Cajun, or Brooklynese language.* 4. *n.* oral communication through speech with arbitrary, accepted symbols and meanings. 5. *n.* a system of symbols used in communication; language code: *in a broad sense . . . a system in terms of which something can be presented by one user and understood by another . . . a system of communication* — L. Bloomfield (1933). *Note:* This definition by a noted linguist includes all forms of language, human and non-human, technical and common. A second definition, by an equally noted linguist, limits the meaning of language to human language: *Language is a purely human and non-instinctive method of communicating ideas, emotions and desires by means of a system of voluntarily produced symbols* — Sapir (1921). It may be said with regard to this restriction that the purely 'human' nature of language has become a source of controversy. Although language is normally based on an arbitrary linking of semantic content, or meaning, with syntactic patterns of speech or writing, it may also be based on the linkage to visual or tactile symbols, as letters or braille dots, or to manual symbols, as those of the American Sign Language. The non-instinctive nature of language has also become a source of controversy, as it is believed by some that there is a basic part of language structure and function that is shared by all languages which is either innate, or which reflects innate language-learning strategies, among people. Also, it is now believed by others that some language structures, as sentences, are stored in the brain as wholes. 6. *n.* linguistics; specifically, the theoretical study of the nature of language. 7. *n.* any particular system of communication: a. by special symbols, as *the language of mathematics, music, Braille,* etc.; b. by gesture or body movement, as *sign language*; c. by style or writing, as *formal language*; d. by manner of speech, as *critical language.* 8. *n.* abusive language, swear words; oaths. *Watch your language*! 9. *n.* animal language, as *the language of the whales. Note:* Special types of language, as *figurative language*, are given under the describing term.

language acquisition the process of learning either a native or foreign language; language learning.

language acquisition device (LAD) in language acquisition theory, the developmental cognitive characteristics which enables a child to use the language environment to become a productive language user. *Children make use of the information of...underlying structure very early in the acquisition of language. From the first moment of speech, children have the ability to communicate grammatical relationships in a manner understandable to adults. We can overlook what an astonishing fact this is, but it means that the most abstract part of language is the first to appear in development* — D. McNeill (1970).

language across the curriculum a movement in England since the mid-1960s: a. to encourage students to construct their own understanding of knowledge through the verbal manipulation of information and the processes they use to obtain information; b. to assist teachers to consider the developmental nature of language as well as the demands of language used in schools and in specific school subjects, especially in writing.

language arts 1. the school curriculum areas particularly concerned with the development and improvement of the verbal communication processes of reading, writing, speaking, listening, and spelling. 2. communication arts in which language is the common denominator.

language arts approach any way of teaching which emphasizes an integration of several aspects of verbal communication rather than a focus on one component.

language center the area(s) of the brain, singly or collectively, which are intimately involved in the reception, understanding, and production of language; particularly, Brodmann's areas 22, 39, 40, 41, and 44. See illustration under **Brodmann's areas.**

language competence See **competence** (def. 2).

language development 1. See **language acquisition**. 2. changes in the features of a language during its historical development because of contact with other languages, technological advancements, etc., as the growth of technical terms in English after the Industrial Revolution.

language experience approach 1. an approach to learning to read in which the student's or group's own words or oral compositions are written down and used as materials of instruction for reading, writing and spelling, speaking, and listening. *The child's [oral] language and experience are used as the bridge to reading and writing* — J. Moss (1975). See also **experience approach** *or* **method**. 2. a curriculum program which emphasizes the interrelationship of various types of language experience.

language function See **function** (def. 2).

language laboratory a room designed for the audiolingual method of teaching modern foreign languages through tape recordings available in carrels or listening stations.

language learning See **language acquisition.**

language maintenance a bilingual education program for developing and maintaining language skills and literacy in the native language of the students.

language pattern the systematic arrangement of elements of a language based on their regularities and predictable qualities, as the way morphemes are grouped into words in English, or the way pitch indicates meaning in Chinese.

language performance See **performance** (def. 5).

language universal a property of languages shared by all existing or possible languages.

language variation 1. the systematic varieties of language use determined by regional, social, or situational influences. *'I ain't got' is a language variation of 'I do not have'. Cp.* **dialect; register** (def. 1); **sociolect; idiolect.** 3. the systematic varieties of a given language, historically considered. 4. the evolution of one language into several languages. *French, Italian, and Spanish are language variations of Latin.*

langue (lä ɴg) *n.* in de Saussure's (1916) description of living languages, the abstract system of grammatical rules and vocabulary of a language that is passed on from one generation to the next; language or linguistic competence. *Cp.* **parole.**

LAP learning activity package.

lap book a book read to a child while sitting on a parent's lap, thus giving the child its first experiences with books.

lapsed reader one who has learned to read but no longer does so. *Some people have developed the habit of reading books. And some have not. Among the latter, many have learned to read, but do not. Perhaps they should be called 'lapsed readers'* — R. Staiger (1979). *Cp.* **non-reader** (def. 4); **aliteracy.** *Ct.* **reading habit** (def. 1).

laryng (o)- a combining form indicating *larynx*; as **laryngoscope.**

laryngitis (lar″ən jī′tis) *n.* an inflammation of the larynx with symptons such as a sore throat, horseness, noisy breathing, a cough, or loss of voice.

laryngoscope (lə rin͡g′go skōp″) *n.* an instrument of hollow tubes, mirrors and miniature lights, used for inspecting the larynx when inserted through the mouth and throat.

larynx (lar′in͡gks) *n.* the voice box; specifically, a structure of cartilage and muscle at the top of the windpipe which contains the vocal folds and is the major organ for voice production; Adam's apple. See illustration under **speech organs.**

late bloomer one who reaches, or is predicted to reach, full potential at some point after the normal age level of development. *Cp.* **maturational lag.**

lateral (lat′ər əl) 1. *adj.* away from the middle, midline, or center. 2. *adj.* having to do with a side. 3. *n.* a consonant speech sound made when the air flow is pushed along one or both sides of the tongue, as /l/.

lateral dominance See **cerebral dominance** (def. 1).

lateral imbalance lateral heterophoria or heterotropia; specifically, an oculomotor imbalance or deviation in which one of the eyes turns in or out. *Ct.* **vertical imbalance.**

laterality (lat″ə ral′i tē) 1. *n.* cerebral dominance (def. 1). See also **crossed dominance** (def. 1); **dominant hemisphere.** 2. *n.* the awareness of the left and right sides of one's body, plus the ability to name them correctly and to project consistently the concept of left and right to the environment.

lateral lisp the substitution of an /l/-like sound for normal sibilant consonant sounds because excessive air escapes around one or both sides of the tongue, rather than over the narrowed tip.

Latin alphabet 1. the writing system used by the ancient Romans, adopted from the Greek alphabet, and the source of the English and other modern Western European alphabets; Roman alphabet. 2. the modern Western European alphabet(s).

Latin grammar school in the United States, a secondary school transplanted from England, teaching boys Latin and some Greek, that was the main kind of secondary education in New England from colonial settlement until after the American Revolution. *Note:* In theory, boys were only admitted if they already knew how to read. In practice, reading often had to be taught there.

Latin square a factorial design having as many experimental trials as there are experimental conditions.

Laura Ingalls Wilder Award an award given 'to an author or illustrator whose books published in the United States have over a period of years made a substantial and lasting contribution to literature for children.' *Note:* The award, established by the Association for Library Service to Children of the American Library Association, is given once every five years.

law (lô) *n.* a stated principle or rule of thought, action, feeling, etc., that expresses a stable, predictable relationship, as *the law of effect.*

law of effect a generalization about the modification of stimulus-response connections in learning proposed by E. L. Thorndike: satisfying responses strengthen connections, while annoying responses weaken them. *Note:* Although the law of effect does not have the force of an explanatory principle, the concept of effect in learning has received much attention, especially in reinforcement theory.

lax (laks) 1. *adj.* referring to a distinctive feature in the analysis of speech sounds in which the sound is of relatively short duration and lacks clearly defined resonance, as /a/ in *cat. Ct.* **tense** (def. 3). 2. *adj.* having relatively little muscle tension in the tongue and vocal tract in making speech sounds.

layout (lā'out") 1. *n.* the act or plan of arranging material in an appropriate design for publication, as *a newspaper layout.* 2. *v.* to so arrange.

lazy eye the nonfixating or deviating eye in strabismus, or the weaker or wandering eye in a phoria. *Vision tends to be or is suppressed in a lazy eye to avoid double vision.*

LC Library of Congress (classification).

lead[1] (lēd) 1. *n.* the first paragraph of a news story or article in which the content is summarized. *The lead usually contains basic information about the who, what, when, where, why, and how of the story.* 2. *n.* the principal character(s) in a play. 3. *v.* to have a principal part in, as in a play. 4. *v.* to hold a superior position, as *lead in scholarship.* 5. *v.* to influence, as *lead one to believe.* 6. *n.* a guide to follow, as a map, sign, clue, etc. *The police followed a new lead.*

lead[2] (led) *n.* in metal typography, a thin, narrow metal strip used to add space between lines of print. *v.* **lead.**

leading (led'in͡g) *n.* the use of a lead to make wider spaces between lines of print. *Leading is often used to make the material more readable.*

leading question a question that is phrased to produce a desired answer. *Leading questions are a feature of the Socratic method. Cp.* **open-ended question.**

leaf (lēf) *pl.* **leaves.** *n.* a sheet of paper forming two pages of a book, magazine, etc. *Cp.* **page** (defs. 1, 2).

learn (lûrn) 1. *v.* to change behavior as by memorizing, acquiring knowledge, etc. 2. *v.* to respond in a different way than formerly to a stimulus situation because of practice and/or self-study, experience, instruction, etc.

learner (lûr'nər) *n.* one who learns.

learner analysis an examination of how well an instructional program or product fits the characteristics of a target population of students. *Interest and maturity level are among the characteristics important in the learner analysis of children's readers.*

learner assessment the design, placement, and administration of mastery tests of those skills, concepts, and attitudes needed to attain given objectives.

learning (lûr'nin͡g) 1. *n.* the process, or result, of change in behavior through practice, instruction, or experience, rather than through maturation. 2. *n.* the sum of knowledge acquired by an individual; scholarship; as *a person of great learning. Note:* Special types of learning, as *associative learning*, are given under the describing term.

learning activity package (LAP) a complete kit for learning independently, including objectives, directions, subject matter, materials, and test items.

learning center 1. See **media center.** 2. a location within a classroom with listening, viewing, art, game, and other instructional materials that have clearly defined objectives stated for the learner, specific directions for reaching the objectives, provisions for different ability levels, and self-checking evaluations; learning station. See also **stations approach.**

learning contract an extended assignment, usually one of several, which the student agrees to complete in an instructional plan designed to encourage self-motivation and self-discipline.

learning curve a graphic representation of success in performance shown against trials needed or time spent. See illustration. *Note:* Performance is usually plotted on the ordinate and trials on time on the abscissa of the graph. *Ct.* **retention curve.**

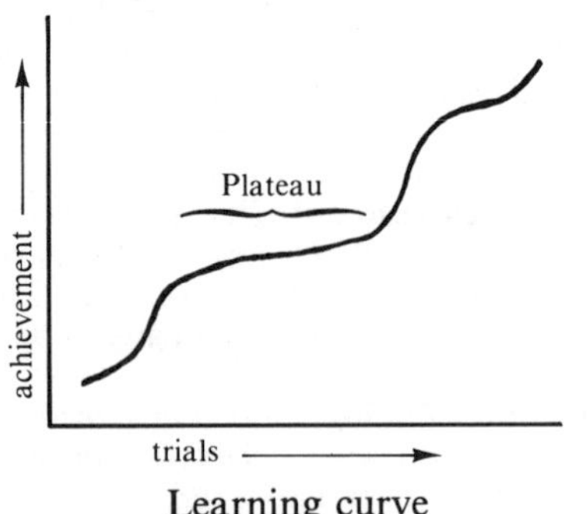

Learning curve

learning disability

The concept of learning disability, like that of dyslexia, is controversial with respect to its causes and the degree of severity required.

1. a. *a generic term that refers to a heterogeneous group of disorders manifested by significant difficulties in the acquisition and use of listening, speaking, reading, writing, or mathematical abilities. [Note:] (Such disorders are presumed to be due to central nervous system dysfunction which can result from such factors as anatomical differences, genetic factors, neuromaturational delay, neurochemical/metabolic imbalance, severe nutritional deficiency or trauma.) Even though a learning disability may occur concomitantly with other handicapping conditions (e.g., sensory impairment, mental retardation, social and emotional disturbance) or environmental influences (e.g., cultural differences, insufficient/inappropriate instruction, psychogenic factors), it is not the direct result of those conditions or influences* — National Joint Committee on Learning Disabilities (1980). b. in certification for special classes and/or funding in the United States, learning disability is defined as '. . . a disorder of one or more of the basic psychological processes involved in understanding or in using language, spoken or written, which . . . may manifest itself in imperfect ability to listen, think, speak, read, write, spell, or do mathematical calculations. Such disorders include such conditions as perceptual handicaps . . . dyslexia, and developmental aphasia. The term does not include . . . learning problems which are primarily the result of visual, hearing, or motor disturbance, or of environmental disadvantage' — HEW Standard Terminology (1975). *Note:* Students so classified need to have a specified discrepancy between expected and

actual achievement in one or more aspects of language usage, particularly in reading, or mathematical usage. 2. an indecisive term for any learning problem of any sort arising from any causes(s). *Note:* When used by persons of different disciplines and/or theoretical positions, the term 'learning disability' may take on a whole range of connotations with differing, and often conflicting, assumptions by the specialist about treatment as well as by the teacher, family, and student. As a result, educators and the public suffer from the same lack of precision in the use of this term as in the use of the term dyslexia. See also **dyslexia.**

learning hierarchy the ordering of skills, habits, etc., from simple learning tasks to progressively more complex ones. *Note:* The assumption here is that the learning of more complex tasks depends upon the prior learning of and appropriate ordering of simpler subordinate tasks.

learning laboratory an area in a school or college with programmed and other materials for self-directed study, frequently with personnel to offer instruction in learning and study skills.

learning machine See **teaching machine.**

learning module an organized group of activities and materials designed to help a learner reach a certain objective. *The study skills program was organized into six learning modules.*

learning rate the speed at which new learning occurs, often plotted as a learning curve on a graph.

learning resource any material or person that can contribute to a student's learning, including print and non-print materials, software and hardware, the advice of experts, etc.

learning station 1. See **learning center** (def. 2). 2. Any of the several locations within a media center.

learning style personality and mental factors that determine how a person goes about learning. *Superior students are frequently those whose learning styles match the instructional style of the school.* See also **cognitive style.**

learning task analysis the identification of the skills and subskills involved in a learning activity, including the criteria for judging achievement of specified levels of knowledge and/or performance.

learning to learn the acquisition of skills and attitudes for their transfer value in making future learning more efficient, as in the development of good study habits that can be generalized to new learning situations. See also **study skills.**

least effort, principle of See **principle of least effort.**

left-eyedness (left″ɪd′nis) *n.* the consistent or frequent choice of the left eye for sighting tasks which need only one eye. See **dominant eye.**

legasthenia (le″gəs thē′nē ə) *n.* dyslexia; literally, 'reading weakness.' *Note:* Legasthenie, a term widely used in Germany, suffers from the same confusion in meaning as does dyslexia.

legend (lej′ənd) 1. *n.* a traditional, historical tale of a people, handed down first by word of mouth, later in written form. *Cp.* **myth: folk tale** *or* **story; fairy tale.** 2. *n.* an explanation used with maps, charts, graphs, etc.

legibility (lej″ə bil′i tē) 1. *n.* the physical factors in print and writing, including format, which affect ease and efficiency in reading. *Optimal legibility of print is achieved... by a typographical arrangement in which the shape of letters and other symbols,* *distinctive word form, and other factors such as size of type, width of line, and leading are coordinated to permit easy, accurate, and rapid reading with understanding* — M. Tinker (1965). 2. *n.* (*An old use.*) readability. *adj.* **legible.**

leisure reading reading for personal satisfaction during unscheduled periods of one's life at any age. *Cp.* **recreational reading.**

leitmotif (līt'mō tēf") 1. *n.* in music or drama, a theme associated with a particular person, situation, or idea, as *the so-called 'fate' leitmotif in the opera Carmen.* 2. *n.* a repeated, expression, event, or idea used to unify a literary work, as 'I prefer not to' in H. Melville's *Bartleby, the Scrivener. Cp.* **motif** (def. 1).

lens (lenz) 1. *n.* a piece of glass or other transparent substance, the principal opposing surfaces of which are shaped to change light rays, usually to converge or focus them, as *an eyeglass lens.* See illustration. See also **plus**

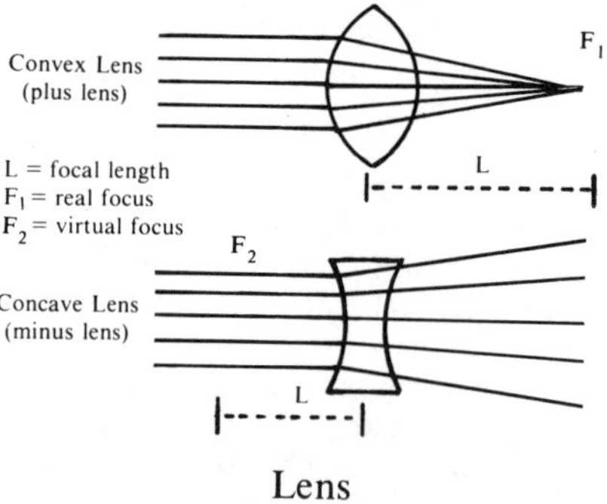

Lens

lens; minus lens. *Note:* Special types of lenses, as *convex lens,* are given under the describing term. 2. *n.* a combination of such lenses in an optical system, as *a fine camera lens.* 3. *n.* any instrument which focuses or guides some form of energy, as the grid in a TV tube or the wave guide in a radar set. 4. *n.* the transparent, crystalline lens in the eyeball by which light rays entering the eye are bent inwards to focus on or near the retina. See illustration under **eye.** *The change in the shape of the lens in accommodation allows the lens to adjust its focal length for far or near point vision.*

LEP Limited English Proficiency.

-lepsia, -lepsis, -lepsy a combining form indicating *seizure;* as **epilepsy.**

LES *or* **LESA** Limited English Speaking (Ability).

lesion (lē'zhən) *n.* an abnormal tissue change by disease or injury, usually localized and well-defined. *A lesion of the optic nerve can cause blindness.*

lesson plan a statement of objectives, procedures, and materials for a learning activity.

letter (let'ər) 1. *n.* a graphic symbol that represents a speech sound, or phoneme, belonging to a standard alphabet, as *b, a, t* in *bat*; an alphabetic character. 2. *v.* to print or write with letters. 3. *n.* a form of written communication. 4. **letters,** the alphabet. 5. **to the letter**, strict attention to detail, directions, or rules, as *He followed the directions to the letter.* 6. *v.* to write or label with letters. 7. *v.* to make a written communication. *Cp.* **character** (defs. 6-10); **grapheme.**

lettering (let'ər ing) 1. *n.* the use of letters and numbers especially to form titles, captions, and legends, or to hand-letter manuscripts and inscriptions. 2. *n.* the letters so used. *v.* **letter.**

letter method See **alphabet method** (def. 1).

letter phonics a synthetic phonics approach that emphasizes initially the identification of sounds represented by individual letters. *Ct.* **cluster phonics;**

whole word phonics.

letter phonogram a letter used as the graphic representation of a sound. *Cp.* **phonogram** (def. 2).

letter-sound correspondence See **grapheme-phoneme correspondence.**

level (lev′əl) 1. *n.* any one of several strata or planes in linguistics, as phonology, grammar, semantics, or their subdivisions. 2. *n.* a type or style of language in the study of language varieties, as standard versus nonstandard speech. 3. *n.* the loudness of sound.

level of aspiration 1. the predicted or anticipated degree of success on a particular task under specified conditions. *To be realistic in one's level of aspiration means that one is aware of how well one has done in the past or on similar activities.* 2. the degree of success acceptable to or desired by a person; ambition. *Note:* One may be quite accurate in predicting performance (def. 1) and yet not be at all satisfied with that level of success (def. 2).

level of comprehension 1. the degree of comprehension of a particular passage or set of passages, usually shown as the percent of correct responses to questions on the material. 2. the degree of comprehension ability, often shown as a grade equivalent or as a standard score such as a stanine.

level of confidence See **confidence level.**

level of performance an established, measurable degree of attainment on a learning task.

level of significance See **confidence level.** See also **statistical significance.**

lexeme (lek′sēm) *n.* the basic or dictionary form of a word, to which affixes may be added to modify meaning. *'Run' is the lexeme form of 'ran' and 'running,' but 'runner' and 're-run' are different lexemes. Cp.* **word** (defs. 1-7); **morpheme.** *adj.* **lexemic.**

-lexia a combining form indicating *inability to read* (from the Greek *speech, word*); as **bradylexia, dyslexia.**

lexical comprehension the comprehension of word meaning as contrasted to understanding its grammar or syntax.

lexical item a linguistic unit with one or more morphemes and with a specific pronunciation and meaning. The unit may be a word, word-compound, or idiom. *Note:* A linguistic item of more than one word, or an idiom, must have a meaning that is unpredictable from the meanings of its components alone. *Green house* is a noun phrase composed of two lexical items, but *greenhouse* is one lexical item whose meaning, a glass-enclosed plant-growing area, is not predictable from the meaning of its components.

lexical meaning the denotative or 'dictionary' meaning of content words. *Note:* The lexical meaning of a word is independent of the syntactical use of a word in a linguistic unit. *Ct.* **grammatical meaning; nonlinguistic meaning.**

lexicography (lek″sə kog′rə fē) *n.* dictionary-making, as writing, editing, compiling a dictionary. *n.* **lexicographer.**

lexicon (lek′sə kon″, -kən) 1. *n.* a dictionary; glossary. 2. *n.* an alphabetical list of words in a special field, as *a lexicon of reading, mathematics, etc.* 3. *n.* the total set of words or morphemes in a language.

librarian (lī brâr′ē ən) 1. *n.* a professional member of a library staff. 2. *n.* the chief administrative officer of a library.

library (lī′brer″ē, -brə rē, -brē) 1. *n.* an organized collection of books and other media administered by a staff for consultation, study, and recreational reading by users. 2. *n.* a personal or private collection of such material. 3. *n.* the space which houses such collections.

library binding See **library edition.**

library card a card issued by a library to a borrower for purposes of identification and for recording the books withdrawn on loan.

library classification system any scheme of classification used by a library to arrange the books and other materials in its collection. See **Library of Congress classification (LC); Dewey decimal classification; Universal decimal classification.**

library edition an edition prepared with a strong and durable binding for library use.

Library of Congress classification (LC) a method of classifying publications developed by the Library of Congress, using letters and numerals, which allows for unlimited expansion. *Note:* This scheme is widely used in large university and public libraries. Many books printed in the United States carry the Library of Congress classification number on the reverse side of the title page. *Cp.* **Dewey decimal classification; Universal decimal classification.**

libretto (li bret'ō) *n.* the text of an opera or other long vocal composition, as an oratorio or cantata.

Librium (lib'rē əm) *n.* a trade name for chlordiazepoxide hydrochloride, a widely used mild tranquilizer.

license, poetic See **poetic license.**

ligature (lig'ə ch̲ər, -ch̲o͝or″) 1. *n.* a stroke or bar connecting printed or written letters, as *fi, tt,* etc. 2. *n.* two letters printed or written together, as æ.

light verse short lyrical poems which may be witty, joyous, humorous, or fanciful, sometimes satiric, often sophisticated. See also **limerick; epigram; nonsense verse; *vers de société.***

limerick (lim'ər ik) *n.* a form of light verse, usually five lines with a rhyme scheme of *aabba,* with the first, second, and fifth lines having three feet, and the third and fourth lines, two feet: *There was an Old Man with a beard,/ Who said, "It is just as I feared!/ Two Owls and a Hen,/ Four Larks and a Wren/ Have all built their nests in my beard!"* — E. Lear.

limited edition an edition of a specified number of copies, seldom more than 1,500. *Note:* The plates of a limited edition are often destroyed or the type distributed. A limited edition may or may not be the first edition of a work. Commonly, individual copies of limited editions are numbered by the publisher.

Limited English Proficiency (LEP) a term used in bilingual education programs specifically to refer to a limited understanding or use of written as well as spoken English.

Limited English Speaking (Ability) (LES or LESA) a term used in bilingual education programs to refer to students who know some English but not enough to participate effectively and actively in a classroom where only English is used in instruction.

linear program in programmed learning, a series of small, planned learning steps whereby the student makes a response and checks its accuracy at the next step on the way, step by step, to a desired learning goal. *Ct.* **branching program.**

linear script a writing system, such as the English alphabet which uses non-pictorial characters to represent sound units rather than ideas or words. *Cp.* **alphabet** (def. 2); **syllabary.** *Ct.* **ideography; logography; hieroglyphics** (def. 1). See also **writing system.**

line graph a diagram to show points representing the frequency of relations or connections among data by using lines, dots, dashes, etc., to connect these points. See illustration.

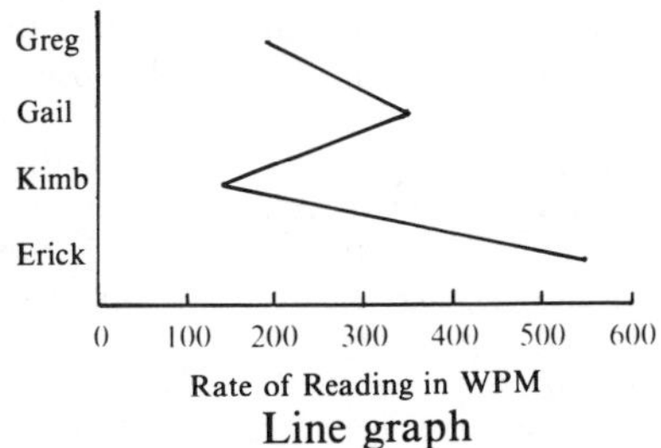

Line graph

line of sight an imaginary line connecting the point of fixation and the center of the pupil and, in normal vision, the fovea of the sighting eye.

lingo (liŋ̑′gō) 1. *n.* spoken or written language that is strange or foreign. 2. *n.* cant; jargon. 3. *n.* an individual's peculiar language or speech; idiolect.

linguadental (liŋ̑″gwə den′tᵊl) 1. *adj.* referring to the tongue and teeth. 2. *n.* a consonant speech sound made when the tongue and the teeth constrict the air flow.

lingua franca (liŋ̑′gwə fraŋ̑′kə) *pl.* **lingua francas, linguae francae** (liŋ̑′gwē fran′sē). 1. any language widely used for communication among speakers of other languages, as Latin in Europe in the Middle Ages and Swahili in Central and East Africa. 2. (*Cap.*) a simplified form of Italian used as a trade language in the eastern Mediterranean in the Middle Ages. *Note:* Lingua franca is an Italian term that literally means the 'language of the Franks.'

lingual (liŋ̑′gwəl) 1. *adj.* referring to the tongue. 2. *n.* a speech sound articulated with the aid of the tongue, especially the tip of the tongue, as /d/, /n/, /s/, or /r/. 3. *adj.* a combining term referring to the written or oral production of a language, as *bilingual speaker, trilingual road sign.*

linguist (liŋ̑′gwist) 1. *n.* one who studies the nature of language; one whose field of research is linguistics. 2. *n.* popularly, one who speaks a number of languages, or who is fluent in the use of language.

linguistically different 1. having a language or dialect that is different from a standard or from a social or educational norm, as *linguistically different learner.* 2. structural differences between languages or between dialects.

linguistic analysis the application of linguistic principles from a defined theory of language structure, function, and change to some aspect of language, as dialect variation or morphological patterning in a specific language.

linguistic approach *or* **method** 1. any approach to the teaching of reading based upon linguistic principles. 2. a beginning reading approach based upon regular sound-symbol patterns, first proposed by Neef in 1813 and more recently by L. Bloomfield in the 1930's. *Note:* The terms 'linguistic approach,' 'method,' or 'program' have been used to refer to so many different kinds of linguistic content as to be virtually meaningless: *There can be no such method as a linguistic method of teaching reading* — R. Wardhaugh (1966).

linguistic atlas an atlas in which the maps show the geographic boundaries of various linguistic features, such as phonemes, lexical items, or grammatical rules, for given dialects of a language.

linguistic awareness a linguistic postulate developed by Mattingly (1972): *an essential prerequisite to learning to read is 'the ability of a speaker-hearer to bring to bear rather deliberately the grammatical, and in particular, the phonological knowledge he does have in the course of reading.' Note:* Linguistic awareness does not need to be conscious, merely available. *Ct.* **metalinguistic awareness.** See also **cognitive clarity.**

linguistic determinism See **linguistic relativity.**

linguistic geography the study of the regional variety in types of languages and dialects to set off their similarities and differences.

linguistic reading program See **linguistic approach** *or* **method.**

linguistic relativity the theory that the language one speaks affects the way one thinks; linguistic determinism; Whorfian hypothesis.

linguistics (lin͡g gwis′tiks) *(with sing. v.)* 1. *n.* the study of the nature and structure of language and languages. 2. *n.* the study of the nature of language communication. *Note:* Linguistic study includes several areas of specialized interest, as biolinguistics, sociolinguistics, historical linguistics, etc. *adj.* **linguistic.**

linguistic variable a symbol in a grammatical or phonological rule which represents a set of elements, as features, sounds, parts of speech, etc., one of which is chosen for a specific instance of the rule's operation.

linking verb a verb that connects a subject and a complement so that the complement describes the subject; copula; as *is* in *Linda is a leader. Note:* Other common linking verbs include *become, remain, sound, look, seem,* etc.

lip (lip) *n.* one of the two outside edges of the mouth which aid articulation. See illustration under **speech organs.**

lip movement See **subvocal reading** (def. 2).

lipreading (lip′rē″din͡g) *n.* the observation of the mouth and lips during the speechreading process. *Ct.* **speechreading.**

lisping (lis′pin͡g) *n.* the faulty production of sibilant speech sounds, usually /s/ or /z/. *The loss of front teeth often causes lisping.* See also **frontal lisp; lateral lisp.** *v.* **lisp.**

listening (lis′ə nin͡g) 1. *n.* the ability to understand speech. 2. *n.* the act of understanding speech; listening comprehension; auding. 3. *n.* the act of attending to something heard, as *listening to a speaker.*

listening center a place, usually in a media center library, or classroom, where a student can use a headset to listen when convenient to recorded instructional material.

listening comprehension 1. listening (def. 2); auding. 2. the highest level of reading material which a student can understand when it is read aloud to the student. *Listening comprehension, measured by reading successively more difficult passages to a student, is useful in estimating the student's potential silent reading level.*

listening comprehension level the highest readability or grade level of material that can be comprehended well when read aloud to the student. *Note:* Better than 75 percent comprehension is often used as a standard in judging this level. The listening comprehension level is useful in investigating a possible discrepancy between reading level and listening level. See also **listening comprehension** (def. 2); **informal reading inventory (IRI).**

listening vocabulary the number of different words a person understands when heard in speech; hearing vocabulary. *A sizable listening vocabulary aids beginning reading.*

literacy (lit'ər ə sē) 1. *n.* the ability to read. *Cp.* **oracy; numeracy.** 2. *n.* the ability to read and write a language, and sometimes to perform arithmetic operations. 3. See **functional literacy.** 4. *n.* the possession of reading, writing, and sometimes arithmetic skills to a degree thought desirable by a society. 5. *n.* competency in a technical field, as *computer literacy. Ant.* **illiteracy.** *v.* **literate.**

Literacy Awards monetary prizes given through UNESCO for meritorious work in literacy and post-literacy publications; specifically, awards such as the Nadezhda K. Krupskaya Prize provided by the Soviet government and named for Lenin's widow; the International Reading Association Literacy Award sponsored by the International Reading Association since 1979; and the Noma Award provided by Shoichi Noma since 1980.

literacy fallacy the mistaken assumption that there is an invariant, one-to-one correspondence in the English language between written letters, or graphemes, and speech sounds, or phonemes. *Note:* Various phonemes, especially vowels, are symbolized or spelled in several ways in written English, as witness the /ā/ sound represented by *ay* in *day,* and *ai* in *aid.* Conversely, a grapheme, as, for example, *a,* may represent more than one sound, as in *hat, nation.* Thus the teacher who says, 'What is the sound of the letter *a*?' is making the literacy fallacy of assuming that the written language, not the spoken one, is the primary language system.

literacy gap the difference between the actual and desired level of literacy. *The literacy gap in developing countries is often very great.*

literal comprehension 1. *understanding the sense meaning of what is heard or read, presumably without making inferences* — M. D. Vernon (1978). *Note:* The implied dichotomy between literal and inferred comprehension is thought by many to be false except for the simplest, most concrete examples. 2. understanding the explicit meaning that is stated or clearly implied in a passage. *Ct.* **interpretation.**

literal meaning 1. the basic sense of a passage which can be directly understood. *Ct.* **inferred meaning.** 2. the explicit sense that is stated or clearly implied in a passage. See **literal comprehension** (def. 1). 3. See **literal translation.**

literal translation a word-for-word, non-idiomatic translation of something from one language to another. *Ct.* **free translation.**

literary analysis 1. the study of a literary work by a critic, student, or scholar. 2. a careful, detailed reading and report thereof. *Cp.* **literary criticism.**

literary appreciation 1. the study of literary works to deepen a reader's understanding of those works. 2. the awareness, perception, or evaluation of the qualities of written work.

literary criticism 1. the analysis and judgment of works of literature. *Note:* The literary critic is expected to consider both the strong and the weak points of a literary work. 2. the body of principles by which the work of writers is judged. *Note:* The principles used in judging a literary work vary from the highly personal and subjective values of the critic to relatively objective criteria. They may involve specific consideration of moral values, historical accuracy, literary form and type, etc.

literary culture 1. a culture which transmits its values, attitudes, and beliefs primarily through the written language. *Most of the peoples of Europe are members of a literary culture.* 2. a culture which values the ability to write and read more than the ability to speak effectively. *Ct.* **oral culture.**

literary form 1. the formal structure or organization of the parts of literary or other artistic works that unifies them and determines their total effect. 2. the structure used to express literary and other artistic types of content; genre; as *sonnet form, short story form.* 3. the *how* (form) rather than the *what* (content).

literary merit an overall judgment of the quality of a literary work, usually based upon several factors such as style, characterization, unity, etc. *Samuel Johnson often saw no literary merit in the recognized authors of his time.*

literate (lit′ər it) 1. *adj.* able to read and/or write a language. *A person is literate who can, with understanding, both read and write a short, single statement on his everyday life* — W.S. Gray (1956). 2. *adj.* educated. 3. *adj.* having literary background and skills, especially in reading and writing. *Shakespeare was highly literate.* 4. *adj.* clearly written or spoken, as *a literate argument. Ant.* **illiterate.** *n.* **literate.**

literati (lit″ə rä′tē, -rā′tī) *n. pl.* able persons who have scholarly interests, especially in literature and the arts.

literature (lit′ər ə chər, -cho͝or″, li′trə-) 1. *n.* writings of high quality and significance because of a successful integration of style, organization, language, theme, etc. 2. *n.* writings such as novels, plays, poems, essays, etc., taken collectively. 3. *n.* the entire body of writing of a people, language, etc., as *Russian literature.* 4. *n.* the group of works on a particular topic, as *literature of religion.* 5. *n.* the profession of a writer or author. 6. *n.* printed matter, as *street literature. Note:* Special types of literature, as *children's literature,* are given under the describing term.

literature for adolescents narratives and nonfiction which have been written especially for a teen-aged audience or which have been largely taken over by a teen-aged audience, including young adult books, transitional novels, junior novels or books, and juvenile books. *Note: The Outsiders* by S. A. Hinton was written especially for young readers; *Mrs. Mike* by Benedict and Nancy Freedman was written for an adult audience but has been kept alive by teen-aged readers. See also **young adult literature.**

litho- a combining form indicating *stone;* as **lithograph.**

lithography (li thog′rə fē) *n.* a printing process in which a flat surface is treated to absorb special inks and to print only the desired impression. *Lithography is based upon the principle that ink and water do not mix. n., v.* **lithograph.** *adj.* **lithographic.**

litotes (lī′tə tēz″, -tō-, lit′ə-, lī tō′tēz) *pl.* **-tes.** *n.* understatement; especially, the statement of something positive in a negative way: *She was not ungrateful.*

little magazine any of a number of literary journals of limited circulation which publish experimental poetry and prose and seek to extend the boundaries of literature. *Many of the works of James Joyce, T.S. Eliot, e.e. cummings, and Gertrude Stein were published in little magazines.*

living language a language which is presently used by native speakers for purposes of communication. *Ct.* **dead language.**

loan translation the literal translation of a borrowing from one language to another, as the English *counterglow* from the German *gegenschein,* literally 'against shine' or 'counter glow'; calque.

loan word a word incorporated both in form and meaning into a language from another language, often with an adaptation of the pronunciation and/or spelling of the word: in English, loan words include *amateur* (French), *patio* (Spanish), *opera* (Italian), *sabbath* (Hebrew). See also **borrowing.**

lobe (lōb) 1. *n.* a rounded projection or division, especially a division larger than a gyrus in an organ such as the lungs or the brain. *The lobes of the brain are divided by fissures.* See illustration. *Cp.* **gyrus.** 2. *n.* the soft, lower part of the auricle.

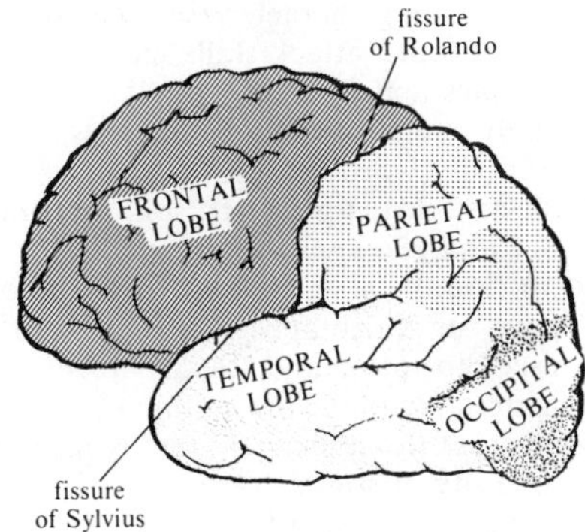

Lobes of the human brain

lobectomy (lō bek'tə mē) *n.* the surgical removal of a lobe, as of a lung or part of the brain.

lobotomy (lō bot'ə mē, lə-) 1. *n.* the cutting through or into a lobe. 2. **prefrontal lobotomy,** the surgical cutting of white nerve fibers in the brain that connect the frontal lobes and the thalamus to reduce uncontrollable psychoses or severe pain. *Note:* The operation is now little used because the development of more specific medications makes it possible to treat most such problems without radical surgery.

local color a literary movement in late 19th century America to capture in detail the life and people of a particular area. *Bret Harte and Joaquin Miller were writers of local color of the American West.*

local norm a norm determined by a local population, as a school or school district, rather than that of a broader sample.

locative case in case grammar, and in some inflected languages, the case which shows place.

locomotor ataxia loss of coordination of the voluntary muscles used in walking due to damage in the nervous system.

log (lôg, log) 1. *n.* a record of a trip of a ship or airplane. 2. *n.* a record of an activity, process, etc., as *a log of classroom observations.* 3. *v.* to make or enter records in a log.

logic (loj'ik) 1. *n.* the study of the principles of rational inference. 2. *n.* a rational way of thinking. *Use logic, not emotion, to solve your problem.* 3. *n.* good sense; sound judgment; as *a fine sense of logic.* 4. *n.* the consistency, or reason for being, found in a work of art, system, institution, etc., as *the logic of language.*

logical (loj'i kəl) 1. *adj.* observing principles of logic, as *a logical argument.*

2. *adj.* sensible. *It is logical to look before you leap.*

log (o)- a prefix indicating *word, speech;* as *logograph.*

logograph (lôg ə graf″, -gräf″, log′ə-) *n.* an orthographic symbol which represents one or more words (morphemes) of a language; logogram; as, in English, # for *number* or 2 for *two. Cp.* **ideograph; pictograph; symbol** (def. 4). *Ct.* **letter** (def. 1).

logography (lō gog′rə fē) *n.* a writing system that uses graphic symbols to represent words (morphemes) of a language; picture-writing; word-writing. *Cp.* **ideography**. *Ct.* **syllabary** (def. 1). *adj.* **logographic.**

logo-syllabic writing a writing system, such as ancient Sumerian or Egyptian, which employs both logographic and syllabic characters; hieroglyphics. *Cp.* **logography; syllabary** (def. 1).

logotype (lô′gə tīp″, log′ə-) 1. *n.* a. a nameplate. b. a company name or trademark; logo. See illustration. 2. *n.* in printing, a piece of type containing two or more combined letters.

ira

Logotype

-logy a combining form indicating *knowledge, science, discourse;* as **psychology.**

longitudinal method a way of studying behavior or development by taking repeated measures on one or more variables on the same individual or group over an extended period of time. *Ct.* **cross-section (-al) method.**

long term memory (LTM) that aspect of memory lasting over a long period of time that has great capacity and has structured, or chunked, information into patterns. *Long term memory occurs when a person can remember the gist of a story long after it has been read, and from that can work out the details. Note:* LTM is assumed to develop from continued or repeated short term memory episodes. This process may result in some telescoping or distortions of the original matter. *Ct.* **short term memory (STM).**

long vowel 1. in teaching practice, the vowel sounds in English that are also the names of the alphabet letters A, E, I, O, U, as /ā/ in *halo*, /ē/ in *demon*, /ī/ in *bind*, /ō/ in *told*, /ū/ in *unit. Note:* Technically, long vowel sounds are also represented in spelling by two or more letters, as *ai* in *aim*, *i-e* in *kite*, etc., the term more accurately referring to the diphthongs that the graphemes represent. See also **diphthong**. 2. in phonetics, the relatively long duration of time stress of a vowel sound. *Note:* Vowel length is affected by amount of stress and by regional speech habits as well as by context. *Ct.* **Short vowel**.

look-and-guess method a seriocomic paraphrase of 'look and say method'; oral reading characterized by a failure to use word attack skills, particularly phonics and structural analysis, especially when decoding is excessively difficult; word calling.

look-and-say approach *or* **method** See **analytic approach** *or* **method.**

loop (lo͞op) *n.* a circle of film, audiotape, or videotape, relatively short, used to play and replay recorded material without rewinding.

loudness (loud′nis) *n.* the perceived intensity of sound.

lower case a letter form, as *a, e, n, b, f,* that is smaller and often different in form from a capital letter; miniscule. *Cp.* **upper case.** *adj.* **lower-case**.

low vision severely reduced vision. *Low vision may reach the point of legal blindness.*

low vowel a vowel speech sound produced with the tongue near the bottom of the mouth; open vowel; as /a/. See illustration under **vowel**.

LTM long term memory.

lyric (lir′ik) 1. *n.* a short poem of personal feelings and emotions, intended to make a single impression upon the reader. 2. *adj.* description of such a poem. 3. **lyrics,** the lines or verses of a song.

M

DEVELOPMENT OF MAJUSCULE									
NORTH SEMITIC	GREEK		ETR.	LATIN		MODERN			
						GOTHIC	ITALIC	ROMAN	
﹏	Ɱ	M	Ɱ	Ɱ	M	𝔐	*M*	M	

DEVELOPMENT OF MINUSCULE					
ROMAN CURSIVE	ROMAN UNCIAL	CAROL. MIN.	MODERN		
			GOTHIC	ITALIC	ROMAN
~	m	m	𝔪	*m*	m

The thirteenth letter of the English alphabet developed from North Semitic *mem,* its form changing little through Greek *mu* (μ) to the modern capital and minuscule.

M arithmetic mean.

MA mental age.

macron (mā'kron, mak'ron) *n.* an orthographic symbol (¯) placed above a vowel letter to indicate a 'long' vowel sound, as in the pronunciation spelling (ōts) for *oats;* or, placed above a syllable in a foot or a line of verse to indicate a stressed syllable, as in *ānimal fēmurs.* See also **accent** (def. 2e).

macrostructure (mak'rō struk"chər) *n.* in text analysis, the topic and general organization of a passage. *Cp.* **microstructure.**

macula (lutea) (mak'yə lə) (lo͞o'tē ə) *n.* a small oval area in the center of the retina that includes the fovea centralis and provides the brightest and clearest central vision under well-lighted conditions. See illustration under **eye.** *adj.* **macular.**

magazine (mag"ə zēn', mag'ə zēn") *n.* a serial publication; specifically, a periodical for general reading that often contains poetry as well as fiction and nonfiction articles by various authors, photographs, and other illustrations. *Magazines frequently specialize in a particular subject, such as news, sports, a specific hobby like needlework, etc.*

magnetic board a sheet of magnet-attracting metal, coated or uncoated, for displaying materials so attracted.

magnetic tape the audiotape and videotape used in tape recorders; specifically, a tape, usually of plastic, coated with particles sensitive to magnetic polarizing impulses for recording and reproducing audio and video signals and computer data.

main clause See **independent clause.**

main effect an estimate of the contribution of a single variable or experimental treatment taken by itself.

main entry the full catalog record of an item in a library's collection, often the author entry. *Note:* The main entry card may include a tracing, or record, of all the other headings under which the item appears in the catalog and other information about the work. *Cp.* **added entry**.

main idea 1. the central thought, meaning, or gist of a passage. 2. the chief topic of a passage expressed or implied in a word or phrase. 3. *a statement in sentence form which gives the stated or implied major topic of a passage and the specific way in which the passage is limited in content or reference* — T. L. Harris. *The topic sentence of a paragraph is intended to state the main idea. Note:* There is little agreement on what a main idea is. Def. 2 is commonly accepted in the beginning phase of reading instruction. Def. 3 is a more complete statement of the denotative and connotative dimensions of the major topic.

mainstreaming (mān'strē" ming) *n.* keeping exceptional children, especially the handicapped, in the regular classroom rather than in special classes.

main topic the chief subject of a passage. *Cp.* **main idea** (def. 2).

majuscule (mə jus′kyo͞ol, maj′ə skyo͞ol″) *n.* a capital, upper-case letter.

make-believe 1. *n.* the act of pretending. *Children like to play make-believe.* 2. *n.* one who pretends; pretender. 3. *n.* the feigning of something; sham. 4. *adj.* pretended; made-up; as *a make-believe story.*

mal- a prefix indicating *bad, wrong, imperfect;* as **malformation.**

maladjustment (mal″ə just′mənt) *n.* the failure to achieve appropriate need-satisfaction and adaptation to the environment. *Ct.* **adjustment** (def. 1).

malapropism (mal′ə prop iz″əm) *n.* the misuse of words, substituting words that sound alike and producing comic results. *Note:* The term is from Mrs. Malaprop, a character in Richard Sheridan's 18th century play, The Rivals: *as headstrong as an allegory on the banks of the Nile.*

malformation (mal″fôr mā′shən) *n.* a linguistic element or structure which is irregularly formed with respect to the standard patterns of a given language, as *bited* for *bit.*

malfunction (mal fungk′shən) *n.* the failure of something to perform as expected, as *a visual malfunction.*

malingering (mə ling′gər ing) *n.* the conscious and deliberate faking of a physical or mental illness or incompetence. See also **hypochondriac.**

malleus (mal′ē əs) *pl.* **mallei** (mal′ēi) *n.* the outermost bone of the three ossicles in the middle ear, attached to the eardrum and joined with the incus. See illustration under **ear.**

malocclusion (mal″ə klo͞o′zhən) *n.* the failure of the upper and lower teeth to fit together normally so that the upper incisors overlap the lower incisors. *Malocclusion may make speech sound production difficult because the air flow is distorted.*

manic-depressive (man′ik di pres′iv) 1. *adj.* alternating, usually quite suddenly, from a state of elation and high activity to a state of profound sadness with feelings of inadequacy, low activity, and occasionally suicidal tendencies. 2. *n.* one given to such changes of mood.

manifesto (man″ə fes′tō) *n.* a public statement of beliefs, principles, or intentions, as Marx and Engel's *Communist Manifesto.*

manoptoscope (mə nop′tə skōp″) *n.* a flattened cone open at both ends, used to test for eye dominance; sighting tube. *Note:* When a target at some distance is sighted through the larger end of the manoptoscope, only one eye can fixate the target through the smaller end. Presumably the eye that fixates the target is the dominant eye.

manu- a combining form indicating *hand;* as **manual.**

manual (man′yo͞o əl) *n.* a carefully-prepared guide or handbook to a particular subject area, or activity, as a *test manual.* See also **teacher's guide** *or* **manual.**

manual alphabet an alphabet represented by the finger and hand positions used in finger spelling.

manual method a means of communicating by the hard of hearing that uses signs, gestures, and manual alphabet. *Ct.* **oralism** *or* **oral method; combined method.**

manual, teacher's See **teacher's guide** *or* **manual.**

manuscript (man′yə skript″) 1. *n.* any writing done by hand without mechanical aid such as a typewriter or printing press; especially, a handwritten book or document. 2. *n.* a finished version of a piece of writing to be submitted for publication; script (def. 3); especially, a book, article, document, or essay. 3. See **manuscript writing.**

manuscript writing a type of handwriting in which letter forms that look like ordinary type are wholly or partially unconnected within each word; printscript. See illustration. *Cp.* **print** (def. 7). *Ct.* **cursive writing.**

This is manuscript writing.

map (map) 1. *n.* a representation of geographic regions, usually on a two-dimensional surface. 2. *v.* to prepare such a representation.

mapping (map′ing) 1. *n.* the formation of one or more hypotheses or expectancies in attempting to solve a problem. 2. See **cognitive map.** 3. *v.* to survey material before careful reading to get an overview of its nature and organization.

marker (mär′kər) See **phrase-marker.**

masculine gender See **gender.**

mask (mask, mäsk) 1. *n.* a covering for all or part of the face to conceal the wearer's identity. 2. *n.* a covering for the face of an actor in Greek drama which revealed the character portrayed. 3. *v.* to put on a mask. 4. See **masque.** 5. *v.* to interfere. See also **masking.**

masking (mas′king) 1. *n.* interference with the perception of an auditory signal because of noise, as in a poor telephone connection or in audiometric testing; auditory masking. 2. *n.* interference with or elimination of any sensory process by another, as in the use of white noise to relieve pain.

masque (mask, mäsk) 1. *n.* an elaborate entertainment in 15th and 16th century Europe, especially England. *Note:* As a prelude to a celebration, as a wedding or a ball, a troop of masked and elaborately costumed dancers and actors would appear to entertain. 2. *n.* a play written for such entertainment.

mass media *or* **communication** the chief ways of communicating with large numbers of people. *Print, radio, and the cinema were for years the principal mass media, but now television, records, and tapes are also widely used.*

mass noun a noun whose referent is not countable, as *water, earth, happiness. Note:* In English, mass nouns cannot be used with the indefinite article in the singular and have no plural form. *Ct.* **count noun.**

mastery (mas′tə rē, mä′stə-) 1. *n.* demonstrable control over material or behaviors which meets or exceeds an established criterion level; proficiency. *Oral fluency is one criterion in mastery of a language.* 2. *n.* control over other people; dominance; as *military mastery by occupational forces. v.* **master.**

mastery learning the process, or result, of learning given material to an established proficiency criterion. *Mastery learning may be used to control the rate at which a student moves through materials or to determine a grade based on how much material was learned to the expected criterion.*

mastery test a test designed to measure the possession, on an all-or-none basis, of a specified level of performance. *Mastery tests are primarily useful in measuring basic skill performance.*

mastoid process the air-filled cells within the temporal bone just behind and open to the middle ear. *Infection of the mastoid process, mastoiditis, is now usually controlled by antibiotics rather than surgery.*

matched groups in an experimental design, groups which have been presumably equated on one or more variables. *Note:* Age and sex are commonly matched variables. However, when matching is done on the basis of test results, the validity of matching is questionable because of test error factors. More commonly, random assignment to groups is the preferred experimental technique.

matching test a test which requires the subject to choose, according to some criterion or criteria, items from one list which correspond to items in another list, as pictures of objects with a list of their names.

materials selection the process of choosing books and other materials for a collection, usually in accordance with predetermined policy.

mathemagenic (math″ə mə jen′ik) *adj.* referring to any covert and overt behaviors which lead to learning in an instructional situation. *Note:* According to E. Rothkopf, text questions significantly affect mathemagenic behaviors which then in turn affect how much a student learns. *n.* **mathemagenics.**

matrix (mā′triks, ma′-) *pl.* **matrices** (mā′ tri sēz″, ma′-), **matrixes.** 1. *n.* the environment in which something develops or is molded or embedded; context: as *the matrix of experience, a typeface matrix, a text matrix.* 2. *n.* a two dimensional array of numbers, symbols, or events. *A correlation matrix shows the correlation of every variable with every other variable in the set. Note:* This mathematical concept is used by extension in education, as in the use of a matrix to display variant spellings in a spelling program. 3. *n.* any array of computer components intended to perform a specific function.

matrix sampling a plan for assessing the level of performance in a group of students, in which a large pool of questions is divided into random subsets and each subset is assigned to a random fraction of the students.

maturation (mach″o͞o rā′shən, mat″ yo͞o-) 1. *n.* the total process of growing and developing from immaturity to adulthood or maturity. *Note:* Learning is influenced by and also influences maturation. 2. *n.* maturity. *adj.* **maturational.**

maturational lag late development in any aspect of an individual with no apparent organic defect; especially, the theoretical concept of a late development of areas of the brain controlling specific perceptual and motor functions. *Cp.* **late bloomer.**

mature reader a reader who possesses these qualities: *a. unique characteristics...that predispose him to reading. b. a focus, or radix, of interest...which serves as an inner drive or motivating force. c. awareness of himself as a responsible group member.... d. an ever expanding spiral of interests.... e. a high level of competence in reading, which enables him to proceed with reasonable ease and understanding in grasping and interpreting meanings, in reacting rationally to the ideas apprehended, and in applying his ideas with sound judgment and discrimination*— W.S. Gray and B. Rogers (1956).

maturity (mə to͞or″i tē, -tyo͞or′-, -cho͞or′-) 1. *n.* full development in one or more ways in an organism, as *anatomical maturity.* 2. *n.* relatively advanced development in a function or trait for a given age, as *intellectual maturity, emotional maturity. Ct.* **immaturity.** *adj.* **mature.**

maxim (mak′sim) 1. *n.* a brief, pointed statement of a general truth. 2. *n.* an expression of principle, especially as to conduct: *Never leave that till tomorrow which you can do today* — B. Franklin.

Cp. **proverb** (def. 1); **adage; aphorism.**

maze (māz) 1. *(Cap.)* a procedure for measuring reading comprehension developed by J. Guthrie in which vertically arranged choices of words are placed in the running text, thus creating a 'maze' through which the reader must find the way. *Ct.* **cloze procedure** (def. 1). 2. a complicated set of pathways used in psychological experimentation through which a subject must pass to reach a goal.

MBD minimal brain dysfuction.

McGuffey's readers one of the most popular American 19th century reading series, of which the first two readers were issued in 1836. *Note:* Famous for their moralistic selections, the first readers were texts for beginning reading instruction, unlike earlier readers which presupposed that the child had already learned to read.

Md, Mdn median.

mean (mēn) 1. *v.* to intend; signify. *How does a poem mean?* — J. Ciardi. 2. *n.* a midpoint between extremes, as *the golden mean.* 3. *n.* a measure of central tendency; specifically, the arithmetical average (M); the sum of all the values divided by the number of terms. *The mean is a basic statistic in many statistical operations and tests. Cp.* **median (Md)** (def. 1); **mode** (def. 1).

meaning (mē′niŋ)

Meaning, which is a critical concept in linguistics, is a topic of vigorous discussion and theorizing, much of it yet unresolved. A major reason for this difficulty is that semanticists must use language to describe language, the meaning of meaning thus varying with the theoretical point of view taken or with an investigator's particular interest. 1. *n.* the sense that something signifies or is intended to signify, as *the meaning of a work of art, the meaning of a word. Note:* This use of meaning, as applied to language, refers to its lexical meaning or semantic content. See **lexical meaning.** 2. *n.* the sense that is indicated by, and is dependent upon, the relations between linguistic units; grammatical meaning; as *the meaning of words in a sentence. Note:* Although the words in a sentence may have lexical meaning as well as grammatical meaning, a word out of a linguistic context has only lexical meaning. 3. *n.* the referent of a linguistic unit; referential meaning; as the object referred to by *ball* in the sentence *Tom hit the ball.* 4. *n.* the relation between a word or other linguistic unit and the situation in which it is used; contextual or situational meaning; as *the meaning of 'war' in 'Make love, not war.'* 5. *n.* See **intension** and **extension** (def. 1). 6. *n.* See **connotation** and **denotation.** 7. *adj.* expressive, as *a meaning look. Note:* Special types of meaning, as *literal meaning,* are given under the describing term. *adj.* **meaningful.**

meaning-emphasis approach a way of teaching beginning reading that emphasizes comprehending, not merely decoding, what is read.

meaning vocabulary the number of meanings a person knows for words. *Since many words have several meanings, the meaning vocabulary is usually much larger than that for known word forms.*

measure (mezh′ər) See **foot** (def. 1).

measurement (mezh′ər mənt) 1. *n.* a comparison of something with a known standard or value of an appropriate kind, as *personality measurement.* 2. *n.* the process of assigning numbers to objects to represent some property or characteristic, as 6x or nine inches. 3. *n.* the process of placing something on a qualitative scale, as gray-blue, gray-green, etc. 4. *n.* the use of tests, as *educational and psychological measurement.*

meatus (mē ā'təs) *pl.* **-tuses, -tus.** *n.* an opening or passage in the body.

mechanics of reading the basic perceptual habits, word analysis skills, word meaning development, and comprehension processes usually taught in the primary grades.

media (mē'dē ə) *n. pl.* means of communication, as books, newspapers, magazines, radio, television, motion pictures, recordings, etc. See also **medium.**

media center a place in a school in which teachers and students may find educational software and hardware and expert help in their use; learning center. *Cp.* **instructional materials center (IMC); resource center.** (def. 1).

medial (mē'dē əl) 1. *adj.* referring to the middle or center; median; specifically, toward the median plane of the body. *Ct.* **lateral** (def. 1). 2. *adj.* referring to an arithmetical mean or average, as *the medial tendency of a distribution of scores.* 3. *adj.* referring to a sound(s) or letter(s) that neither begins nor ends a syllable or word, as /t/ /a/ /m/ in *stamp* or /a/ in *cat.*

medial sound 1. any sound in the middle of a word or syllable. 2. any sound between the first and last phonemes of a word or syllable. 3. a consonant sound between two vowel sounds; intervocalic consonant.

median (Md) (mē'dē ən) 1. *n.* a measure of central tendency; specifically, the middle value or score in an ordered frequency distribution. *Cp.* **mean** (def. 3); **mode** (def. 1). 2. *adj.* referring to the middle; medial.

median plane an imaginary vertical surface or plane that divides a body into right and left halves. See also **frontal plane; sagittal plane.**

media specialist an expert in the teaching and use of media.

mediate (*adj.* mē'dē it; *v.* mē'dē āt") 1. *adj.* literally, in the middle; specifically, coming between two things, especially in a psychological process. *Perception is mediate between sensation and cognition.* 2. *v.* to connect or link. *Concepts mediate thought.* 3. *v.* to act as a referee in an argument or dispute. *n.* **mediation.**

mediation theory the theory that, in thinking, stimuli operate as signs which do not activate responses directly, but only indirectly through complex intervening, or linking, processes.

mediator (mē'dē ā"tər) 1. *n.* the connecting system between input and output in communications, as in a computer. 2. *n.* a person who acts as a neutral agent to bring about agreement between two or more parties in a dispute.

medium (mē'dē əm) *pl.* **-dia.** 1. *n.* any one of the various vehicles of communication, as books. 2. *n.* a method of communication or expression, as speech, writing, graphic art, etc.

medulla oblongata (mi dul'ə ob"lôn͡g gă'tə, -lon͡g-) *pl.* **-gatas, -gatae.** the upper extension of the spinal cord which forms the lowest portion of the brainstem just below the pons and in front of the cerebellum. See illustration under **brain.**

melodrama (mel"ə drä"mə, -dram"ə) 1. *n.* a play characterized by greatly exaggerated plot and characters, suspense often created by a villain, great emotion, and a happy ending. Ten Nights in a Barroom *is a classic melodrama.* 2. *n.* actions or events in life and literature with such characteristics, as *the melodrama of man's first flight to the moon. adj.* **melodramatic.**

memoir (mem'wär, -wôr) 1. *n.* a biography. 2. **memoirs:** a. records of people and happenings known to the writer. b. autobiographical records.

memory (mem′ə rē) 1. *n.* the reviving of past impressions and experiences, as through retention, recall, recognition, and learning. 2. *n.* a specific recollection, as *a memory of first going to school.* 3. *n.* the sum of all recollections. *The accident caused her to lose her memory.* 4. *n.* the time covered in a recollection, as *within my memory.* 5. *n.* reputation, as *a person of beloved memory.* 6. *n.* the storage capacity of a computer, indicated in bits and bytes. *v.* **memorize.**

memory image the mental reconstruction of a past experience, with the awareness that the experience is in the past and that the reconstruction may not be exact. *Cp.* **eidetic imagery.**

memory reading a method that emphasizes getting the overall meaning of a selection first by having a student memorize a selection from someone reading it before the student reads it alone. See also **Jacotot method; story method.**

memory span See **span of attention** (def. 1).

Meniere's disease a disease of the inner ear marked by loss of balance, ringing sounds in the ear, and progressive deafness.

meninges (mi nin′jēz) *n. pl.* the three membranes that cover and seal the brain and spinal cord: the tough outer layer, the dura mater; the thin middle layer, the arachnoid; and the soft inner layer, the pia mater. *adj.* **meningeal.**

meningitis (men″in jī′tis) *n.* infection and inflammation of the meninges.

mental ability 1. general abilities involved in thinking; intelligence; scholastic aptitude. 2. special abilities, as mechanical aptitude, pitch discrimination.

mental age (MA) the chronological age for which the sum of mental ability credits on an intelligence test is average. *Note:* A child is said to have a mental age of 7 if the child earns as many points on the test as the average 7-year old. Other mental ages are determined by similar comparisons. See also **intelligence quotient (IQ); basal (mental) age.**

mental defective a person with an IQ two or more standard deviations below the mean. See **mental retardation.**

mental deficiency See **mental retardation.**

mental disease See **mental disorder.**

mental disorder a severe psychological malfunction, chronic or temporary, of behavior or adjustment. *Note:* The term is preferred to **mental disease.** In standard classifications, mental disorder includes mental retardation, psychoses, neuroses, and various personality aberrations. See also **emotional disorder; neurosis; personality disorder; psychosis.**

mental health a positive, dynamic, and stable pattern of adjustment, self-acceptance, and goal achievement. *Note:* Mental health does not imply the mere absence of mental disorder. *Cp.* **mental hygiene.**

mental hygiene the science or study of mental health.

mental illness See **mental disorder.**

mental image a perceptual representation, or ideational picture, of a perceptual experience remembered or imagined.

mentally handicapped lacking in normal mental ability. *Note:* The term usually refers to persons who have mild to moderate mental retardation. *The educable mentally retarded are mentally handicapped.*

mental maturity a non-technical term for: a. the relative level of mental development for a given chronological age. *Mental maturity is one significant factor in reading readiness* — E. Betts (1946). b. an adult level of mental development. *Understanding relativity requires mental maturity.*

mental retardation significant lack of intellectual ability for a given chronological age; below normal intellectual functioning. *Note:* Mental retardation and mental deficiency have been subjected to many classifications for different purposes at different times. See the table. The EMR and TMR need special help in schooling, often with governmental aid, after their classification by certified personnel.

mental set See **set** (def. 2).

meridian (mə rid′ē ən) *n.* one of a series of imaginary lines on the eyeball used by eye specialists as reference points in the treatment of the eyes and in the prescription of eyeglasses.

merry-go-sorry *n.* a story or poem that arouses both joy and sorrow; something happy and sad all at the same time; bittersweet. Carrie's War *is a fine merry-go-sorry for ages ten and over.*

message (mes′ij) 1. *n.* any indication of meaning by a person that is perceived by another. *I get your message by your tone of voice.* 2. *n.* information intended to communicate that is contained in a symbol or a pattern of symbols. *Language exists to carry messages.* 3. *n.* a unit of one or more words in a communications system. 4. *n.* the basic theme, idea, or moral of a work, as *the humanitarian message of Ghandi.* 5. *n.* a divinely inspired communication, as *the message of the Scriptures.*

Older medical and lay usage	IQ range (Wechsler)	IQ standard deviations	World Health Organization; current medical usage	Current educational usage
	85	-1		slow
borderline			borderline	learner
	70	-2		(75-85 IQ)
moron (50-75 IQ)			mild mental retardation	
	55	-3		EMR
			moderate mental retardation	(50-75 IQ)
imbecile (25-50 IQ)	40	-4		
			severe mental retardation	TMR (25-50 IQ)
	25	-5		custodial
idiot			profound mental retardation	

Representative mental retardation classifications

meta- a prefix indicating *beyond, along with, among, after, behind;* as **metalinguistics.**

metabolism (mə tab′ə liz″əm) *n.* the total energy-consuming processes by which body cells are made and maintained, and the energy-producing processes by which proteins are broken down. See also **basal metabolic rate (BMR).** *adj.* **metabolic.** *v.* **metabolize.**

metacarpal age an age-equivalent measure of skeletal development, based upon the degree of growth in the small bones of the hand between the wrist and fingers from cartilage into hardened bones. *Cp.* **carpal age.** See also **anatomical age.**

metacognitive (met″ə kog′ni tiv) *adj.* referring to those theories and principles used in the study of thought processes.

metalanguage (met′ə laŋ̑″gwij) 1. *n.* the language used by linguists to describe natural language; *a language about language* — T. Dineen (1957). 2. *n.* a language used to describe symbol systems, as *mathematics.*

metalinguistic (met″ə liŋ̑ gwis′tik) 1. *adj.* referring to metalanguage. 2. *adj.* referring to language in relation to culture.

metalinguistic awareness the ability to reflect on and talk about language; specifically, language awareness arising when a speaker or hearer begins consciously to think about the language being used. *Metalinguistic awareness arises when a person develops language to talk about language. Ct.* **linguistic awareness.** See also **cognitive clarity.**

metalinguistics (met″ə liŋ̑ gwis′tiks) *n.* the formal study of linguistics. *Note:* Metalinguistics is the language philosophers and linguists use to talk about language. *Cp.* **metalanguage** (def. 1). See **paralinguistics.** *adj.* **metalinguistic.**

metaphor (met′a fôr″, -fər) *n.* a figure of speech in which a comparison is implied by analogy but is not stated, as *Death is slumber* — Shelley. *Note:* Metaphors in literature may be uncomplicated, as in the example given, or elaborate, as in an extended allegory. The English language commonly written and spoken is rich in metaphors because of the use of many abstract labels and expressions which imply past or present comparison with concrete objects, acts, or events. In the metaphor *the wind sings,* the implied comparison is not only between the *wind* and *singing;* the term *wind* is a metaphor for *wandering.* See also **dead metaphor.** *Cp.* **simile.**

metathesis (mə ta͟th′i sis) *pl.* **-ses** (sēz). 1. *n.* the change of the order of letters, syllables, or sounds in a word, as in *bird* from Old English *brid.* 2. *n.* change in usual word order; anastrophe.

-meter a combining form indicating *measure;* as **audiometer.**

meter *or* **metre** (mē′tər) 1. *n.* the rhythmical pattern in verse, made up of stressed and unstressed syllables. 2. *n.* any form of such a pattern, which depends on the kind and number of feet in the pattern, as iambic pentameter. See also **prosody** (def. 2). *adj.* **metrical.**

method (me͟th′əd) *n.* an instructional procedure, usually well-defined and specific, for reaching an educational objective. *Note:* Special types of method, as *kinesthetic method,* are given under the describing term. See also **approach.**

method of limits a procedure for determining just noticeable differences by a subject, either by decreasing discriminable differences until they are no longer differentiated, or by increasing non-discriminable differences until they are differentiated.

methodology (meth″ə dol′ə jē) 1. *n.* the study of the underlying principles and rules of a discipline, system, investigation, etc. 2. *n.* such a set of underlying principles and rules; especially, in education, those involved in the analysis of subjects to be taught and the methods of teaching them. *adj.* **methodological.**

metonymy (mi ton′ə mē) *n.* a figure of speech meaning 'change of name' in which the writer or speaker uses a word that is associated with or is suggested by another word. *To say he escaped the 'arm of the law' instead of 'the police' is metonomy. n.* **metonym.**

-metric a combining form indicating the process or result of measurement; as **psychometric.**

metric (me′trik) 1. *adj.* having to do with a decimal measurement system, as in measuring distance in kilometers. 2. *n.* any scale of measurement, especially an interval scale, as *a metric to express level of sociability.*

metrics (me′triks) *n. (with sing. v.)* the study of the rhythm or meter in verse; prosody. *adj.* **metrical.**

MF microfiche.

micr (o)- a combining form indicating *small;* as **microfilm.**

microfiche (MF) (mī′krə fēsh″) *n.* a microfilm about 10 x 15 cm. (4 x 6 in.) containing up to 64 pages of printed material that is too small to be read unaided. *Microfiche must be read from a machine that magnifies one page at a time. Note:* Microfiche does not include the category ultrafiche. *Cp.* **ultrafiche.**

microfilm (mī′krə film″) 1. *n.* a positive film image too small to read unaided, that is projected on a screen for reading. *Note:* Microfilm is useful in reducing pages of text, thus saving much storage space. 2. *v.* to so reduce on film.

microform reader a device which makes any microform, as microfilm, microfiche, and ultrafiche, large enough to be easily read.

microstructure (mī′krō struk″chər) *n.* in text analysis, the details of a passage. *Cp.* **macrostructure.**

microteaching (mī″krō tēching) *n.* a teacher education technique which uses short, specific episodes of teaching, sometimes videotaped, for analysis and instruction.

midbrain (mid′brān″) *n.* the uppermost part of the brain stem. See illustration under **brain.**

middle ear that portion of the ear which lies between the external and inner ear, extending from the eardrum to the windows of the inner ear, side to side, and from the Eustachian tube to the mastoid process, front to back. *The major activity of the middle ear is the transmission across the ossicles of vibrations from the eardrum to the oval window.* See illustration under **ear.**

Middle English English spoken from approximately 1100 to 1500 A.D., following the invasions in the 11th century of the Vikings and Normans. *Note:* Middle English was a product of regular language change, of dialect interborrowing, and of Scandinavian and French influence. It was also the period of the strengthening of the London dialect as the standard language and of the Great (English) Vowel Shift. See also **Old English**; **Modern English.**

middle school in the United States, a school that combines the upper elementary with the junior high school grades, usually grades 5 through 8. *Cp.* **intermediate school.**

midline (mid′līn″) *n.* the median plane of the body; central sagittal plane. *Awareness of the midline aids devel-*

opment of the concept of laterality.

mid vowel 1. See **central vowel.** 2. any front or back vowel sound in which the tongue is in a middle rather than a high or low position, as /e/ or /ə/. See illustration under **vowel.**

Miles peephole method a technique for directly observing eye movements in reading. *Note:* By making a small hole in the center of a text page and peering through the hole, it is possible to estimate roughly the number of fixations by the reader.

milli- a combining form indicating *thousandth;* as **millimeter.**

mime (mīm, mēm) 1. *n.* the art of acting out a character, mood, story, etc. by gesture and movement alone; pantomime. 2. *n.* one who so performs. 3. *n.* an ancient Greek and Roman farce with slapstick characters. 4. *n.* a clown or comedian. 5. *v.* to mimic. 6. *v.* to perform a role by pantomime.

mimicry (mim′ik rē) *n.* imitation of the speech, writing, or other behavior of another person or group of people. *v.* **mimic.**

mind (mīnd) 1. *n.* all the mental and psychic processes of an individual, as *sound of mind.* 2. *n.* intellect; intelligence; as *She has a good mind.* 3. *n.* sanity, as *to lose one's mind.* 4. **mind's eye**, imagination.

minimal brain dysfunction (MBD) a hypothetical construct used to explain the course of a learning disability, based on soft neurological signs rather than on clear evidence of brain damage. *Cp.* **brain damage** *or* **injury**.

minimal contrast a contrast between two similar linguistic units with only one point of difference. See also **minimal pair.**

minimal pair two linguistic items, usually words, whose meaning distinction is created by a single contrast of elements, as by the one phonemic contrast of /p/ and /b/ in the words *rip* and *rib.* See also **minimal contrast.**

minimum competency survey *or* **testing** in the United States, a testing movement designed to measure the lowest level of performance acceptable for a high school diploma in specified aspects of the language arts and mathematics. *Note:* The particular skills and the level of acceptable performance vary from state to state.

minuscule *or* **miniscule** (min′ə skyo͞ol″; mi nus′kyo͞ol) 1. *n.* a non-capital, lower-case letter. *Ct.* **capital letter.** 2. *adj.* in writing, using only such letters.

minus lens a concave lens used to make parallel light rays diverge. See illustration under **lens.** *Ant.* **plus lens.**

miracle play 1. a medieval play, usually about the lives and deeds of Christian saints and martyrs, often presented in cycles by the craft guilds. *Cp.* **morality play.** 2. See **mystery play.**

mirror image 1. the representation of an image with reversed right-left direction as if seen in a mirror. See also **mirror writing.** 2. the reversal of right and left direction in reading; directional confusion. See also **mirror reading; reversal.**

mirror method 1. a technique for observing eye movements in which an observer, sitting next to the reader and holding a small mirror at an angle near the text being read, can roughly estimate the number of fixations by the reader. 2. the use of a large mirror in speech therapy so that the student can easily observe the articulation of sounds and words by self and therapist. 3. a diagnostic technique involving the reading of text held up to a mirror so that the image is reversed.

mirror reading 1. reading text held up to a mirror so that word images are reversed. *Note:* Early investigators of reading disability, as S.T. Orton and M. Monroe, reported that some disabled readers could read the reverse mirror images more easily than images in normal print orientation. 2. See **reversal.**

mirror writing 1. intentional backward writing that looks like normal writing in a mirror. *The diaries of Leonardo da Vinci were kept in mirror writing, possibly to make it difficult for his apprentices to snoop.* 2. the unintentional reversal of letters or numbers, or whole words, in writing, either upside down and/or backwards. *Some mirror writing is normal in young children but becomes a source of concern if it persists.*

mis- a prefix indicating *wrong;* as **miscue.**

miscue (mis kyo͞o′) *n.* an oral reading response that differs from the expected response to the written text. *Note:* Miscues are an interaction between the reader's grammatical system, experience, and the printed page just as are accurate reading responses. For this reason, K. Goodman and his associates believe miscues reflect the strengths and weaknesses of the reading strategy of the reader. Thus an analysis of the miscues of individuals may provide information for planning reading instruction.

mise en scene (mē zăɴ sen′) (*French.*) 1. the stage setting of play, including scenery and stage properties. 2. the environment or surroundings of any event.

misnomer (mis nō′mər) 1. *n.* a name or label mistakenly given to a person, place, or thing, as to confuse the meaning of *ophthalmologist* with that of *optometrist.* 2. *n.* the error so made.

misplaced modifier See **dangling modifier** *or* **participle.**

mispronunciation (mis″prə nun″sē ā′shən) *n.* an incorrect pronunciation; specifically, in the oral reading of text, the incorrect oral reproduction of a word. *Note:* Mispronunciations are one of several types of errors commonly recorded in testing oral reading. Variations in pronunciation due to dialect, foreign accent, or speech problems are ordinarily not considered mispronunciations. See also **insertion** (def. 1); **omission; substitution** (def. 2). *v.* **mispronounce.**

misread (mis rēd′) 1. *v.* to fail to identify one or more parts of a communication correctly, as *misread a signal or letter, misread 'was' as 'saw.'* 2. *v.* to fail to comprehend the intended meaning of a communication, as *misread a set of directions, misread a person's actions.*

mixed cerebral dominance the apparent failure to establish consistent cerebral hemispheric superiority; mixed laterality. *Mixed cerebral dominance is one theory of language and speech disorders.* See **cerebral dominance** (def. 1).

mixed hearing loss reduced auditory acuity because of combined conduction and nerve hearing losses.

mixed laterality the performance of some acts with the right side of the body and others with the left, or alternating between sides. See **dominant hemisphere; cerebral dominance** (def. 1).

mixed metaphor a metaphor which makes an inappropriate comparison, as *iron out the bottlenecks.*

mixed method See **eclectic approach** *or* **method.**

mixed ocular dominance alternating eye dominance. See also **dominant eye.**

mnem- a combining form indicating *memory; as* **mnemonic.**

mnemonic (nē mon′ik, ni-) 1. *adj.* having to do with memory, especially with strategies to improve memorizing or with the improvement of memory. *VAKT is not only an acronym; it is a mnemonic aid: Visual Auditory-Kinesthetic-Tactile* 2. **mnemonics** (*with sing. v.*), devices and techniques to improve memory.

mock-up *n.* a model of a device or process used for demonstration, practice, or teaching, as *a human anatomy mockup.*

modal (mōd′ᵊl) 1. See **modal auxiliary verb.** 2. See **mode.**

modal auxiliary verb an auxiliary verb that expresses a variety of meanings, as *can, will, shall, may, must: I can go. They will go. Shall I stay? May she come? He must leave.*

modality (mō dal′i tē) 1. *n.* any of the sensory systems of receiving, processing, and responding to sensation. *This student appears to learn better through the visual modality than through the auditory.* 2. *n.* the manner of expressing an attitude in speaking and writing, as in the use of a modal auxiliary verb: *You will come?* 3. *n.* the classification of logical propositions into categories, as they assert or deny the possibility or necessity of their own content; mode. 4. *n.* in medicine, the use of a therapeutic agent, as *the modality of physical massage.*

mode (mōd) 1. *n.* a measure of central tendency; specifically, the most common score or value in a distribution. *Note:* It is possible to have more than one mode in a distribution. *Cp.* **mean** (def. 3) **median (Md)** (def. 1). 2. *n.* a way of doing or making something; method. *SQ3R is one type of study mode.* 3. *n.* frequently occurring or dominating custom, fashion, or behavior, as *a current mode of speech.* 4. *n.* modality (def. 3). See also **mood**[2]. *adj.* **modal.**

model (mod′ᵊl) 1. *n.* a standard or example for imitation or comparison. *The teacher was a good reading model because she read frequently and with pleasure.* 2. *adj.* serving, or worthy of serving, as an example, as *a model reading program.* 3. *n.* a structure or design intended to show how something is formed, or how it functions, by analyzing the relationships of its various parts to each other and to the whole. *A reading model is a theoretical representation of reading processes.* 4. *n.* a concrete representation, usually small, of something, as *a boat model.* 5. *v.* to display by wearing, as *model clothes.* 6. *v.* to form, as *model sculpture.*

modeling (mod′ᵊling) 1. *n.* the act of serving as an example of a behavior. *Modeling, as in oral reading by the teacher to the class, may improve the oral reading of the students.* 2. *n.* the imitation of another's behavior, especially as used in behavior modification. 3. *n.* the production of three-dimensional form, as in clay. 4. *n.* the shading of a two-dimensional drawing to produce a three-dimensional effect. 5. *n.* the work of a person who models.

mode of discourse the medium, either oral or written, in which language occurs. See also **discourse; register** (defs. 1, 8).

Modern English 1. English spoken since 1500 A.D. *Note:* Modern English has been influenced by the vernacular replacing Latin in scholastic and formal writing, and by the borrowing of vocabulary from many classical and nonclassical sources, largely due to increased scientific inquiry and global exploration during and following the Renaissance. See also **Old English; Middle English.** 2. in common use, a recent period of English, as that since the turn of the century or since World

War II.

modern literature See **contemporary literature** *or* **fiction** (def. 1).

modified alphabet an alphabetic writing system in which existing graphemes have been altered and/or to which graphemes have been added to make the number of graphemes correspond to the number of phonemes of the oral language. See also **phoneme-grapheme correspondence; spelling reform; Augmented Roman Alphabet.**

modifier (mod′ə fī″ər) *n.* a word, phrase, or clause that limits or qualifies the meaning of another word, phrase, or clause; qualifier; as *four galloping* in *four galloping horses.*

modulation (moj″ə lā′s̲h̲ən, mod″yə-) 1. *n.* change in the quality and volume of the voice in speech. 2. *n.* change in the stress or pitch of speech to show meaning, as *there* in *Are you there?;* voice inflection. 3. *n.* in acoustics, the varying of one or more features of a sound wave to match that of another. *adj.* **modulate.**

molar (mō′lər) 1. *adj.* referring to a whole, or gestalt, that is relatively large and unified, as the act of walking. 2. *adj.* referring to such a unit of behavior, as mind, that is a psychological, not a physiological, construct. *Ct.* **molecular.**

molecular (mō lek′yə lər, mə-) 1. *adj.* referring to parts or details that are small and discrete, as *molecular behavior, molecular physics.* 2. *adj.* referring to isolated glandular or neuromuscular units of behavior. *Ct.* **molar.**

monaural (mon ôr′əl) 1. *adj.* referring to one ear; specifically, the reception of sound by only one ear. 2. *adj.* referring to the use of a single sound reproducing system, as *a monaural record.*

mongolism (mong̑′gə liz″əm, mon′-) See **Down's syndrome.**

mongoloid (mong̑′gə loid″, mon′-) *n.* a person who has Down's syndrome.

mon (o)- a prefix indicating *one, single;* as **monosyllable.**

monocular (mə nok′yə lər) 1. *adj.* referring to one eye. *Ct.* **binocular.** 2. *n.* an optical device adapted to or requiring use of one eye, as the single eyepiece of a microscope.

monocular regression a regression involving one eye. See **regression** (def. 1).

monocular suppression available but non-functional vision in one eye. See **visual suppression.**

monocular vision seeing with one eye only; the vision of each eye considered separately. *Ant.* **binocular vision.**

monograph (mon′ə graf″, -gräf″) 1. *n.* a detailed, well-documented study in one or more volumes of a limited subject or of a limited aspect of a general subject, issued, or planned to be issued, as a unit rather than as a serial, as Buswell's *Fundamental Reading Habits* (1922). 2. *n.* in literary usage, any writing that is not a serial.

monologue *or* **monolog** (mon′ə lôg″, -log″) 1. *n.* a speech, usually lengthy, made by one person in a play. *Cp.* **soliloquy.** 2. *n.* lengthy speech by one person in conversation that discourages speech in others.

monophthong (mon′əf t̲h̲ông″, -t̲h̲ong″) *n.* a single vowel sound produced with the speech organs in a fixed position, as /a/ in *bat. Ct.* **diphthong.**

monosyllable (mon′ə sil″ə bəl) *n.* a linguistic unit of only one syllable. *adj.* **monosyllabic.**

Montessori method a systematized process of early childhood education developed by Maria Montessori (1870-1952) in Italy that emphasizes especially the use of the sensory pathways of vision, hearing, and kinesthesis in learning, with specially designed materials, individualized instruction, and the practical life activities of taking care of one's self and managing one's own environment. *Note:* In recent years a number of modifications have been made to adapt the method to other curricular approaches.

monthly (munth'lē) *n.* a serial publication issued once a month with the possible exception of certain designated months, usually during the summer.

mood[1] (mo͞od) 1. *n.* the emotional state of mind expressed by an author or artist toward his work, as *the somber mood of Poe, the vigorous mood of Picasso.* 2. *n.* the emotional atmosphere produced by an author's conscious use of language forms and devices, as *the poem's light-hearted mood, the tense mood of the chase in Melville's* Moby Dick. See also **tone** (def. 9). 3. *n.* the emotional atmosphere produced by an artistic work, as *the stern mood of Michelangelo's Moses.* 4. *n.* the emotional state of a person or group. *Terry's mood swung from fear to hope as the rescuers arrived. adj.* **moody.**

mood[2] (mo͞od) 1. *n.* a meaning signalled by a grammatical verb form that expresses the subject's attitude or intent. 2. *n.* any of several forms of syllogistic reasoning. Also called *mode,* as in **modality** (def. 3).

Moon type a writing system for the blind made up of embossed characters which require less finger sensitivity than Braille. See **Braille** *or* **braille.**

morality play a medieval allegorical play in which virtues and vices are characters and the theme is the struggle for man's soul between the forces for good and evil. *Note:* This kind of drama was developed in the Middle Ages, especially from the 14th to 16th centuries. See also **miracle play; mystery play.**

moron (mōr'on, môr'-) 1. *n.* See **educable mentally retarded (EMR).** See also **mental retardation.** 2. *n.* a foolish or careless person who fails to use reasonable judgment or common sense. *adj.* **moronic.**

morph (môrf) *n.* a phonological or orthographic representation of a morpheme. *Cp.* **morpheme.**

morpheme (môr'fēm) *n.* a meaningful linguistic unit which cannot be divided into smaller meaningful elements. *Note:* A morpheme may serve as a word, *cat,* or as a component of a word, as *-s* in *cats.* See **free morpheme; bound morpheme.** *adj.* **morphemic.**

morphemic analysis 1. See **morphology.** 2. the study of morphemics, the relations of morphemes to each other, and to morphs.

morphemics (môr fē'miks) (*with sing. v.*) 1. *n.* the structure, functions, and relations of morphemes occurring in language or in languages. 2. *n.* the study of such characteristics.

morphology (môr fol'ə jē) 1. *n.* the patterns of word-formation in a language, including derivation, inflection, and compounding. 2. *n.* the study of such patterns. *adj.* **morphological.**

morphophoneme (môr″fə fō'nēm, môr″-fō-) *n.* a minimum unit of grammar, composed of a set of phonemes which differ phonetically, but behave similarly, or whose differences are neutralized in certain grammatical or morphological contexts; as, in English, the morphophoneme {-D}, which occurs within the past tense morpheme {-ed}, but pronounced /t/, /d/ and əd/ in *stopped, snored, batted. Note:* In phonetic transcription, the past tense /-əd/ is shown as /-id/. *Cp.* **morpheme; phoneme.** See also **morphophonology.** *n.* **morphophonemics.**

morphophonemics (môr″fō fə nē'miks, -fō nē'-) *n.* (*with sing. v.*) the study of the relationships between morphemes and the phonemes which represent them. See **morphophoneme.**

morphophonology (môr″fə fō nol′ə jē, -fō-) *n.* the study of the relations of morphemes, morphophonemes, and phonemes in a language or languages. See **morphophoneme.**

mother tongue See **native language** (def. 1).

motif (mō tēf′) 1. *n.* the intentional repetition of a word, phrase, event, or idea as a unifying theme, often a dominant feature of a literary or musical work; motive. *'Nevermore' is a motif in Poe's 'The Raven.' Cp.* **leitmotif.** 2. *n.* a recurring element in a design, as *a water-lily motif.*

motion picture 1. any sequence of pictures which, when projected rapidly, give the illusion of movement; specifcally, film designed for such rapid projection. 2. the stories, events, etc. so projected. 3. **motion pictures**, the art and/or industry of producing such pictures.

motion picture projector a device for showing enlarged motion pictures on a screen. *Note:* Motion picture projectors in most educational settings take 16 mm., 8 mm., or super 8 mm. film.

motivate (mō′tə vāt″) *v.* to give an incentive to action; especially, to provide inspiration or incentive to others to perform some task, as in teaching-learning situations. *An enthusiastic introduction to a new unit helps to motivate students. Cp.* **motivation** *(Note).*

motivation (mō″tə vā′shən) 1. *n.* the forces within an organism that arouse and direct behavior, as internal sensory stimulation, ego needs, etc. 2. *n.* the process by which such forces arouse and direct behavior in one direction rather than another. *Pat's motivation led to reading science fiction at every opportunity. Cp.* **drive.** 3. *n.* activity by one person that produces need-goal behavior in another. *Teachers need to be skillful in motivation. Note:* The fundamental psychophysiological meaning of motivation is given in defs. 1 and 2 in which motivation is considered an internal state, not one imposed from without. The meaning of definition 3 is the popular extension of this concept in teaching practice, not always with the happiest results. *Cp.* **motivate.** *adj.* **motivational.**

motive (mō′tiv) 1. *n.* a conscious reason for behavior, as *a friendly motive.* 2. *n.* an unconscious reason for behavior. 3. *n.* a desired goal, as *a motive to learn Spanish.* 4. See **motivation** (def. 2). 5. See **motif** (def. 1). 6. *adj.* having to do with causing motion or action, as *motive power.*

motokinesthetic method speech therapy that involves touching and/or moving the speech articulators to help the subject learn what muscles are involved in producing a given speech sound.

motor aphasia expressive aphasia, as in Broca's aphasia.

motor area the area of the cerebral cortex most involved with voluntary movements; Brodmann's areas 4 and 6. See illustration under **Brodmann's areas.**

motor development the growth, or state of growth, of muscles, nerves, and glands that produces voluntary control of movement.

motor skill acquired muscle control. See **fine motor coordination; gross motor coordination.**

MS multiple sclerosis.

multi (i)- a combining form indicating *many;* as **multilingual.**

multi-basal approach the use of more than one basal reading series for different groups of children in a classroom or school system.

multiethnic text textbooks and other teaching materials designed to reflect the interests, vocabulary, and experiences of students from various cultural or ethnic backgrounds, and peopled with characters of differing nationalities and races.

multi-level approach the use of kits of reading materials of different levels of difficulty in teaching reading so as to meet individual differences in reading competence.

multilingualism (mul″ti lin͡g′gwəl iz″əm) *n.* the ability to speak, with some degree of proficiency, two or more languages in addition to one's native tongue. *n. adj.* **multilingual.**

multimedia (mul″ti mē′dē ə) *n. pl. (with sing. v.)* the combining of several media into a single effort, as in the use of slides, film, sound effects, etc., in a travelogue.

multiple causation (theory) the assumption that reading (and learning) disabilities arise typically from a combination of interacting factors or causes. *Note:* This is not a theory in the technical sense but an observation based upon many cases. The popularization of this notion in the 1930's served to counteract the then common assumption of a single cause of reading disabilities and led to interdisciplinary studies of reading disability.

multiple-choice item a test which requires the subject to choose the correct answer from several alternatives.

multiple correlation a coefficient expressing the statistical relationship between a criterion variable and a composite of two or more independent variables.

multiple meaning See **polysemy.**

multiple regression analysis the statistical process of comparing actual values or scores with predicted ones when a regression line is based on more than one variable.

multiple sclerosis (MS) a disease with widespread demyelination of the central nervous system, leading to incoordination, vision and speech problems, and paralysis. *Multiple sclerosis usually starts in young adulthood, with later periods of remission and relapse.*

multiplication of classes (J. Piaget) the coordination of classes in the form of a matrix, as the intersection of the rows *yellow* and *flower* which defines the category *yellow flowers.*

multiply handicapped a person with more than one physical, mental, or social disability which hinders schooling, employment, or social acceptance. *The multiply handicapped often have great difficulty obtaining proper help because their additional handicaps exclude them from the established programs for singly handicapped persons.*

multi-sensory approach an instructional approach which uses a combination of several senses, as visual, auditory, kinesthetic, or tactile. *The Fernald (-Keller) method is well-known multisensory approach.*

multisyllable (mul″tə sil′ə bəl) *n.* a word or utterance with more than one syllable. *adj.* **multisyllabic.**

multivariate analysis a complex form of statistical analysis involving more than two variables, as in factor analysis. *Ct.* **bivariate analysis.**

muscular dystrophy (MD) any of the genetic diseases which produce weakness and eventual wasting away of muscles without affecting the nerves.

muscular imbalance the inability of the eye muscles to coordinate the two eyes smoothly and easily for normal binocular vision.

Muse (myo͞oz) 1. *n.* one of the nine

daughters of Zeus who presided over the arts. 2. *n.* *(sometimes l.c.)* a source of inspiration, especially to a poet, as *Byron's muse.*

mute (myo͞ot) 1. *adj.* not speaking; silent. *He remained mute.* 2. *adj.* not capable of speech; dumb. See also **mutism.** 3. *adj.* referring to a letter that does not represent a sound in a word, as the *e* in *fate.* See **silent letter.** 4. *n.* a person unable to speak. 5. *v.* to soften or muffle a sound.

mutism (myo͞o′ tiz əm) 1. *n.* lack of speech from either congenital or early developmental causes. 2. *n.* inability to speak because of emotional conflicts.

myelin (mī ə lin) *n.* the white sheath of fatty insulation around the axons of some nerve fibers. *The developmental process of myelinization aids in controlling the transmission of nerve impulses along the axons. n.* **myelinization.**

myopia (mī ō′pē ə) *n.* nearsightedness; specifically, a visual condition in which the focus of light rays tends to fall in front of the retina so that vision tends to be blurred, a condition particularly noticeable in distance vision. See illustration under **emmetropia.** *n.* **myope.** *adj.* **myopic.**

mystery play a medieval religious play about the Scriptures. *Note:* The mystery plays later left the church and were performed by the trade guilds. Such a performance was often called a *miracle play. Cp.* **morality play.**

mystery story a narrative in which the chief element is usually a crime around which the plot is built. *Note:* Detective stories, Gothic novels, and spy stories are examples of mystery stories.

myth (mitℎ) *n.* an anonymous, usually primitive, story designed to explain the mysteries of life and nature with bigger than life characters. *Note:* Every country and culture has its own myths, the most famous of which in Western culture are the Greek, Roman, and Norse. B. Bettelheim characterizes myths as stories appealing 'simultaneously to our conscious and unconscious mind' through stories that are 'unique,' 'awe-inspiring,' and 'miraculous;' are tragic in their ending; and are pessimistic in tone. By contrast, fairy tales are told in an 'ordinary,' 'casual' way with an optimistic tone and a happy ending. *Cp.* **folk tale** *or* **story; fairy tale; legend** (def. 1). *adj.* **mythic; mythical.**

N

DEVELOPMENT OF MAJUSCULE								
NORTH SEMITIC	GREEK		ETR.	LATIN		MODERN		
						GOTHIC	ITALIC	ROMAN
		N			N	𝔑	*N*	N

DEVELOPMENT OF MINUSCULE					
ROMAN CURSIVE	ROMAN UNCIAL	CAROL. MIN.	MODERN		
			GOTHIC	ITALIC	ROMAN
	N	n	n	*n*	n

The fourteenth letter of the English alphabet developed from North Semitic *nun,* has preserved its original form, with little change, through Greek *nu* (ν). It has usually followed M, and during most of its history, paralleling that letter, it has retained its similarity to it.

n the number of observations, subjects, or events in a subgroup of a total population, as *n's of 5 boys and 8 girls in the study. Ct.* **N.**

N the number of observations, subjects, or events in a total population, as *an N of 13 students in the study. Ct.* **n.**

narration (na rā′shən) 1. *n.* one of the four traditional forms of composition in speech or writing. *Cp.* **argumentation** (def. 2); **description** (def. 1); **exposition** (def. 1). 2. *n.* the giving of an account or the telling of a story. 3. *n.* the art of telling or narrating. *v.* **narrate.**

narrative (nar′ə tiv) 1. *n.* a form of writing in which a person tells a story, actual or fictional, in prose or verse. 2. *adj.* referring to such writing.

narrative poem a poem which tells a story, often at some length, as in the epic. *Cp.* **epic** (defs. 1, 2); **ballad.**

narrow diphthong a diphthong in which there is little back-front movement of the tongue during production, as in the English /ow/ in *cow. Ct.* **wide diphthong.**

nasal (nā′zəl) 1. *adj.* referring to the nose or to the nasal cavities. See illustration under **speech organs.** 2. *n.* a speech sound made when all or most of the air flow passes through the nose so that the nasal cavity acts as a resonator. *Note:* In English, it is usual for nasals to be voiced consonants with no air escaping through the mouth, as /m/, /n/. In French, on the other hand, both consonants and vowels are formed sometimes with air passing out both the nose and the mouth. The term nasal also refers to a distinctive phonological feature used to distinguish one phoneme from another: that some or all of the air flow passes out through the nose and that the nasal cavity serves as a resonator of the sound. *Ct.* **oral** (def. 3). *n.* **nasality.**

nasal septum the partition of bone and cartilage which separates the two nasal cavities from each other.

nasoscope (nā′zə skōp″) *n.* an instrument of hollow tubes, lenses, and miniature lights, used to inspect the nasal cavities.

National Book Award See **American Book Awards, The (TABA).**

national language a language which has been selected and accepted as the official, major language in a country for historical or political reasons, as Mandarin Chinese for a long period of time in China. See also **official language.**

native language 1. one's first language; the first language one learns to speak and understand; mother tongue. 2. the primary or oldest language still spoken in a community, district, or country.

nativistic theory a theory of language acquisition that children inherit a predisposition for using or recognizing certain grammatical patterns; innate theory. See also **language acquisition device (LAD).**

natural class in phonology, a class of

systematic phonemes whose distinctive features form an important part of many or most languages, especially with respect to language acquisition and the phonological universals of language and language change.

naturalism (nach′ər ə liz″əm, nach′rə-) *n.* writing that indicates a great interest in nature. *Note:* Naturalism was a literary movement of the late 19th and early 20th centuries in Europe and America that turned to nature to explain man's motivation. The movement paralleled, especially in the novel, developments in science by Darwin and others. *Cp.* **realism** (defs. 1, 3).

natural language a language, as English or French, used as a native tongue by members of a speech community. *Ct.* **artificial language.**

natural method See **activity approach** *or* **method.**

n.d. no date.

near point an accepted distance of about 35-45 cm. (14-18 in.) for measuring visual acuity and functioning, as at a comfortable reading distance. *Ct.* **far point.**

near-point acuity keenness of vision at normal reading distances.

near point of accommodation the nearest distance at which an object is in focus *Ct.* **far point of accommodation.**

near point of convergence the nearest point at which the eyes can turn inward while maintaining single binocular vision on a target. *Ct.* **far point of convergence.**

near point of fusion the nearest distance at which an object can still be fixated with single binocular vision before fusion is broken, a point usually further away than the near point of convergence.

nearsightedness (nēr sī″tid′ nis) See **myopia.**

need (nēd) 1. *n.* a lack of something, or that which is lacking; specifically, an unsatisfied motive that leads to goal-directed activity, as *the personal, social, and physiological needs of the individual.* 2. See **drive.** 3. See **felt need.** 4. *n.* the want of something, either necessary or simply desired, as *one's economic needs, a need to be fashionably dressed.* 5. *n.* a physiological lack in body tissue. *Dehydration creates a need for water.*

needs assessment in education, a broad-based study of educational objectives and conditions in a particular situation as they interrelate; an attempt to relate goals to existing strengths, weaknesses, and feasible changes. *Note:* A needs assessment may examine the goals, assets, limitations, etc., of a particular school system and may lead to specific recommendations for improvement.

negation (ni gā′shən) 1. *n.* a statement or predicate denying something. 2. *n.* the language devices used to express the concept of negation. See **negative** (def. 1). *v.* **negate.**

negative (neg′ə tiv) 1. *adj.* expressing denial. *Note:* English negative morphemes include *un-, in-, not, never,* and *-less.* 2. *adj.* bad; unpleasant; undesirable; as *a negative connotation.*

negative diagnosis See **diagnosis** (def. 3).

negative transfer the reduction of the effectiveness of some behavior or learning because of earlier behaviors or of prior learning efforts. *Ct.* **positive transfer.** *Cp.* **proactive inhibition.** See also **transfer** (def. 1).

negative utopia an inhumane, totalitarian society, the opposite of the ideal society described in utopian literature; anti-utopia. *George Orwell's novels* 1984 *and* Animal Farm *describe negative utopias. Ct.* **Utopia** *or* **utopia.**

negativism (neg′ə ti viz″əm) *n.* a willful

pattern of obstructive behavior. *Note:* Examples of negativism may range from chronic stubbornness in a normal person to bizarre patterns in catatonic schizophrenia. Negativism is normal and very common in late infancy.

neo- a combining form indicating *new;* as **neologism.**

neoclassicism (nē″ō klas′i siz″əm) *n.* a revival of the principles of classicism in Europe during the 17th and 18th centuries. See **classicism.** *adj.* **neoclassic.**

neologism (nē ol′ə jiz″əm) 1. *n.* the formation of a new word or saying. 2. *n.* a newly formed word; coined word; as *Vaseline* from German *wasser* (water) and Greek *elaion* (oil).

nerve (nûrv) 1. *n.* a bundle of neurons, usually in a sheath, that carry impulses to or from the central nervous system and other parts of the body. 2. *adj.* having to do with such neurons, as *nerve tissue.*

nerve deafness a hearing loss caused by damage to, or a defect of, the cochlea or the auditory nerve; sensorineural loss. *Ct.* **conduction deafness.**

nerve fiber 1. the axon of a nerve cell. 2. a nerve (def. 1).

-neur (o)- a combining form indicating *nerve, tendon, sinew:* as **neurology, psychoneurosis.**

neural (no͝or′əl, nyo͝or′-) *adj.* having to do with neurons or their functioning, as *neural maturation, neural excitation.*

neurological impairment (NI) damage to the central or peripheral nervous system for which there are hard neurological signs.

Neurological Impress Remedial Technique a method designed to improve fluency in reading. *Note:* The teacher sits slightly behind the student and orally reads the text while one of them points out the part of the text being read. The student attempts to read along as quickly and accurately as possible. In beginning sessions, the teacher reads louder and slightly faster than the student. Later, the teacher decreases in volume and speed so that the student will be in the lead.

neurologist (no͞o rol′ə jist, nyo͞o-) *n.* a medical doctor whose specialty is the nervous system and its disorders.

neurology (no͞o rol′ə jē, nyo͞o-) *n.* that branch of medicine having to do with the study of the structure, function and abnormalities of the nervous system. *adj.* **neurological.**

neuromuscular (no͝or″ə mus′kyə lər nyo͝or″-) *adj.* having to do with nerves and muscles, especially with their relationship to each other, as *neuromuscular disorders.*

neuron *or* **neurone** (no͝or′on, nyo͝or′- *n.* a conducting cell of the nervous system; nerve cell. *Neurons are composed of dendrites, cell bodies, and axons.*

neurophysiology (no͝or″ə fiz″ē ol′ə jē nyo͝or″-) *n.* the study of the normal development and functioning of nerve tissue and of the nervous system. *adj* **neurophysiological.**

neuropsychiatry (no͝or′ō sī kī′ə trē nyo͝or″-) *n.* a special field of medicine that combines neurology and psychiatry. *A neuropsychiatrist studies both organic and functional disorders of the nervous system.*

neuropsychology (no͝or″ō sī kol′ə jē nyo͝or″-) *n.* a special field of clinical psychology concerned with the relation of neurology to behavior. *A neuropsychologist studies disorders of the brain by observing behavior or psychological tests.*

neurosis (no͞o rō′sis, nyo͞o-) *pl.* **neuroses** *n.* a functional emotional disorder with generalized anxiety of which the patient is aware; psychoneurosis. *Note:* Most neurotic behaviors are phobias, com pulsions, obsessions, or hysterical reactions. *Cp.* **psychosis.** *adj.* **neurotic.**

neuter gender a grammatical gender found in many languages; in English, the pronouns *it, itself, its.*

neutralization (no͞o″trə li zā′s̮hən, nyo͞o″) *n.* a situation in which two sounds, normally different in the language, end up being pronounced the same in certain words, thereby cancelling, or neutralizing, their normal phonemic difference, or opposition, as the same pronunciation of /t/ and /d/ in *ladder/latter.*

neutral vowel an unstressed vowel speech sound produced with the tongue in the mid-central position and made with little force to the air flow; schwa (def. 1). *The neutral vowel is the most common English vowel sound. Cp.* **central vowel.**

Newbery Medal Award an annual award which honors the author of the most distinguished children's book of the year. *Note:* The award is sponsored by the Association for Library Service to Children of the American Library Association. It is named after John Newbery, a British publisher in 18th-century England, the first person to realize the importance of publishing books for children.

New England Primer the most famous and popular of all colonial imprints, with a continuous publishing history from before 1690 to the early 19th century: a textbook designed for reading instruction, which included the alphabet, syllabarium, words up to six syllables, alphabet verses, Lord's Prayer, Creed, John Roger's poem, and a catechism. *Note:* It was not the 'first book' used for reading instruction in the colonies; John Eliot's *Indian Primer* was. Nor was it the most widely used schoolbook from 1700 to 1850; after about 1790, Webster's American Spelling Book was more widely sold.

New England Psalter The Book of Psalms, published in colonial New England and used for reading and spelling instruction. *Note:* The "Bay Psalm Book", as it was known, is the oldest extant book printed in colonial America, dated 1640. In 1651, hymns were added, and the work was known as the *New England Psalm Book. The New England Psalter... Being an Introduction for the training up Children in the Reading of the Holy Scriptures* was published in Boston from 1757 on. It contained no specific reading instructional material, but added the Proverbs, the Sermon on the Mount, and the Creed. The *New England Psalter, improved by the Addition of a variety of Lessons in Spelling...,* a Philadelphia publication of 1760, included a few pages of reading instructional material prefatory to the Psalms. Up to the 1750s, the conventional texts for reading instruction were still the hornbook, primer, psalter, and New Testament.

new realism the breakdown of taboos in children's literature with the introduction of such subjects as drugs, violence, sex, homosexuality, death, suicide, severe emotional disturbances, and alcoholism.

newspaper (no͞oz′pā″pər, nyo͞oz′-) *n.* a periodical issued at regular frequent intervals, usually daily or weekly, which reports on and discusses events and topics of current interest, and contains advertising.

newsprint (no͞oz′print″, nyo͞oz′-) *n.* the large sized, poor quality paper which is used in the printing of newspapers and is often used for instructional purposes in the classroom, as for drawing, recording experience stories, etc.

NI neurological impairment.

night vision See **scotopic vision.**

node (nōd) 1. *n.* a knotlike mass of tissue; knob or swelling. *Nodes in the body may be normal or abnormal.* 2. *n.* a junction. *There are many nodes in a computer.* 3. *n.* the point where the branches divide in a tree diagram of the structure of a sentence. See illustration under **tree diagram**. 4. *n.* a point, line, or region in a wave form where there is little or no vibration. 5. *n.* a complicated and difficult matter, as a complex plot in a novel or play; nodus.

noise (noiz) 1. *n.* any sound, especially when unpleasantly loud or harsh. 2. *n.* a complex, inharmonious sound pattern without a specific pitch. 3. *n.* any distortion in the transmission of a communications signal which interferes with the ease or clarity of its reception, as static on a radio, a misprint in a text, snow on the TV.

nom de plume (nom″də plo͞om′; *Fr.* nôɴ də plʏm′) *pl.* ***noms de plume*** (nomz′ də ploom′; *Fr.* nôɴ də plʏm′) See **pen name.**

nomenclature (nō′mən klā″chər, nō men′klə-) *n.* a set or system of terms used in a particular field, as *the nomenclature of statistics.*

nominal (nom′ə n^əl) 1. *n.* a word or expression that functions as a noun. 2. *adj.* referring to a noun; substantive. See also **noun.**

nominal aphasia See **anomia.**

nominalization (nom″ə nᵊl ī zā′shən) 1. *n.* the process, or result, of forming a noun from another part of speech by adding an affix, as adding *-ation* to *nominalize* to form *nominalization.* 2. *n.* the process, or result, of using a noun phrase in place of a subordinate clause or verbal construction, as *Frightened people show great strength* for *People show great strength when they are frightened.*

nominative case the case form in some inflected languages, such as Latin, which indicates a noun is the subject of a sentence or a predicate noun. *Cp.* **subject** (def. 3); **predicate nominative.**

-nomy a combining form indicating *systematized knowledge of, or laws governing, a certain field;* as **taxonomy.**

nonbook materials materials such as films, tapes, recordings other than conventional printed books. *The library's collection of nonbook materials is growing rapidly.*

nonce word (nons′wûrd″) *n.* a word created for a particular situation or event, as *mileconsuming* in *the wagon beginning to fall into its slow and mileconsuming clatter* — W. Faulkner.

non-conservation (non″kon sər vā′shən) *n.* (J. Piaget) the failure in logical thinking ability to keep an invariant property of something in mind under changing perceptual conditions. *Ant.* **conservation.**

non-count noun See **mass noun.**

nondirective therapy See **client-centered therapy.**

non-discursive (non″di skûr′siv) *adj.* clear in purpose, tight in organization, and free of digressions, as *non-discursive writing or speaking. Ct.* **discursive.**

nonfiction (non fik′shən) *n.* prose designed primarily to explain, argue, or describe rather than to entertain; specifically, a type of prose literature other than fiction but includig biography and autobiography. *Note:* Nonfiction is often written for specific purposes, as in articles, diaries, journals, editorials, essays, and textbooks. Although its emphasis tends to be factual, fictional elements are often found in the more personal forms of nonfiction. *Ct.* **fiction.**

nongraded class *or* **school** a class or school in which students progress at individual rates according to their level of achievement. *Syn.* **ungraded class** *or* **school.**

non-language *or* **nonverbal test** a test which requires a response to pictures and/or objects rather than to words. *Some of the tests on the Wechsler Intelligence Scales are nonverbal tests.*

nonlinguistic meaning meaning expressed by posture, body movement, or voice tone; paralinguistic meaning. See **paralinguistics.** *Ct.* **lexical meaning.**

nonoral method a way of teaching beginning silent reading by attempting to suppress oral responses while reading. *Note:* this method, sponsored by McDade in Chicago in the 1930's and 1940's, was shown by G. Buswell's eye-voice span research (1945) not to be superior to conventional methods of teaching beginning reading.

non-parametric statistics statistical methods appropriate for the analysis of data that are not assumed to be normal in distribution, as in the use of Chi-square.

nonphonetic word in teaching practice, a word whose pronunciation may not be accurately predicted from its spelling. *Note:* In linguistic terms, no word is 'nonphonetic' in the sense of not being pronounceable. See also **phonetic word.**

non-print materials educational media other than print, as film, tapes, etc.

nonreader (non rē′ dər) 1. *n.* a person who is unable to read even after extensive instruction; one who fails to learn to read. 2. *n.* a case of severe reading disability. *The nonreaders are the extreme cases of disability* — A. Gates (1947). 3. *n.* an illiterate. 4. *n.* one who knows how to read but who chooses not to read.

nonrestrictive clause a dependent clause that modifies or adds descriptive detail to a noun without limiting or specifying its meaning, as *who likes baseball* in *Charlie, who likes baseball, is a good runner. Note:* In English, a nonrestrictive clause is usually set off by commas. *Cp.* **relative clause.** *Ct.* **restrictive clause.**

nonsense (non′sens) 1. *n.* that which has no sense or makes no sense. *This report is nonsense.* 2. *n.* foolish, absurd, or frivolous language or behavior, as *stop that nonsense.* 3. *adj.* meaningless, as *nonsense syllables.*

nonsense syllable a pronounceable combination of graphic characters, usually trigrams, which do not make a word in the language in which it is used for experiments and testing, as *kak, vor, mek. Note:* Nonsense syllables are sometimes used in reading to test phonics knowledge, or in spelling to test for desired patterns while avoiding known words.

nonsense verse a form of light verse, strong on rhythm, light on logic or meaning, often with coined words, as in *Lewis Carroll's* Jabberwocky: *'Twas brillig, and the slithy toves/Did gyre and gimble in the wabe.'*

nonsense word a linguistic form with a permissable phonological or orthographic structure but without meaning in a language. See **nonsense verse.**

nonstandard (non′stan′dərd) *adj.* referring to any language form or language variety that is considered unacceptable according to a prescriptive grammar or social convention. See also **prescriptive grammar.**

nonstandard American English any variety of American English which differs from that of most textbooks, governmental and media publications, and from the regionally standard varieties of American English which are spoken by members of groups with social, economic, and political power. See also **nonstandard dialect.**

nonstandard dialect 1. a social or regionally limited variety of a standard dialect. *Cockney is an English nonstandard dialect. Note:* Non-standard dialect is recognized more often in literature than in grammars and dictionaries. *Dialects . . . are not degenerate versions of a standard dialect; they are not an accumulation of mistakes; they are neither deficient forms nor imperfect copies of the standard dialects. Non-standard dialects are as highly structured, logical, systematic, and adequate for communication as standard dialects* — K. Hess (1974). 2. a language variety spoken by members of a less powerful or prestigious social group than that using standard dialect. 3. Black English. See also **sociolect.**

nonverbal (non vûr′bəl) 1. *adj.* not verbal, as *nonverbal noises.* 2. *adj.* with little or no use of language, as *nonverbal communication. 3. adj.* without skill in language use, as *a nonverbal home environment.*

nonverbal communication the unspoken signals of body language that accompany speech. See also **paralanguage** (def. 1); **kinesics** (def. 1).

nonverbal IQ the IQ score for nonlanguage based tasks, as on the Wechsler Intelligence Scales. *Ct.* **verbal IQ.**

nonverbal test See **non-language** *or* **nonverbal test.**

noodlehead story a kind of story in folk literature in which a foolish figure does absurd things, often the right thing at the wrong time; numbskull story; as *Lazy Jack, Hans in Luck.*

norm (nôrm) 1. *n.* normal or average performance. *The swimming was up to the norm.* 2. **norms,** a range of scores or values that represent an average or a central tendency in a distribution, as *a table of norms.* 3. *n.* a standard; model; pattern; as *a speech norm, a social norm.*

normal (nôr′məl) 1. *adj.* close to the average, as *normal reading speed.* 2. *adj.* within the normal range, as *a normal pulse.* 3. *adj.* sane, as *normal adjustment.* 4. *adj.* referring to a distribution. See **normal frequency distribution.** 5. *adj.* perpendicular. *The slanting light rays deviated from their normal course as they entered the water.*

normal (frequency) curve a graphic representation of the normal frequency distribution. See illustration.

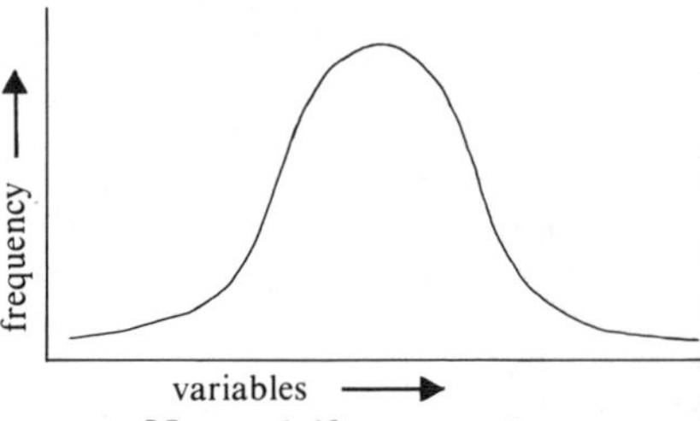

Normal (frequency) curve

normal frequency distribution the theoretical probability distribution of an infinite, continuous series of values represented by a bell-shaped, normal curve in which the conditions for mean, median, and mode are the same. *A normal frequency distribution is probable when there are a large number of factors, each contributing a small amount to the variation in scores.*

normal hearing the perception of sound within usual expectations of clarity and loudness; specifically, in audiometric testing, a hearing loss no greater than 25 dB in the 500 Hz - 8 kHz range, according to commonly accepted standards.

normal school a school which arose in Europe and the United States in the 19th century for training primary or elementary teachers, usually in a two-year curriculum.

normal vision See **emmetropia.**

normative (nôr′mə tiv) 1. *adj.* referring to norms as standards or values. *'Ain't' is a normative usage in some cultural groups.* 2. *adj.* tending to set up a norm, especially by rules, as *normative grammar.*

norming population the group of subjects who have served as the population to establish test norms or levels of performance by various subgroups.

norm-referenced measurement the assessment of performance in relation to that of the norming group used in the standardization of the test. *Ct.* **criterion-referenced measurement.**

notation (nō tā′s̱hən) 1. *n.* the process, or result, of representing speech sounds by graphic symbols. *Note:* Types of notation include *alphabetic writing,* consisting of letters; *analphabetic notation,* as shorthand; and *phonetic transcription,* a system using both letters and diacritics. 2. *n.* any system of specialized symbols, as those used in phonetics or in music. *adj.* **notational.**

notemaking (nōt′mā″king) *n.* the act of writing down reactions, queries, references, etc., in the course of one's reading or listening. *Cp.* **notetaking.**

notetaking (nōt′tā″king) *n.* the study skill of outlining and/or summarizing the important ideas of a lecture, book, or other source of information to aid in the organization and retention of ideas.

noun (noun) *n.* a part of speech which often names or denotes persons, places, things, qualities, or acts, and which may function as a subject or object. *Note:* Special types of nouns, as *abstract nouns,* are given under the describing word. See also **nominal** (def. 1); **nominalization.**

noun adjunct an optional noun in that it is not part of the subject or predicate of a sentence, as a noun that functions as an adjective, as *reading* in *reading matter. Note:* A word may sometimes be both adjective and noun, and therefore phrases may be ambiguous, as *lady killer, criminal lawyer, gingerbread man.*

noun marker a part of speech, as an article or adjective, which identifies or accompanies a noun in a phrase, clause, etc., as *the* in *the man* or *fresh* in *She likes fresh strawberries.*

noun phrase (NP) in transformational-generative grammar, a construction headed by a noun plus all modifiers and articles associated with that noun, as *The tall man* in *The tall man was a suspect.* See **head.** *Ct.* **verb phrase** (def. 2).

novel (nov′əl) 1. *n.* a fictional prose narrative, usually long, which allows the author to provide fuller character and plot development than in the short story. 2. *n.* the class of such narratives. 3. *adj.* suggestive of something new or different, as *a novel beginning.*

novelization (nov″ə lī zā′s̱hən) *n.* a novel based on a screenplay of a motion picture. *Joseph Krumgold's* And Now Miguel *is a novelization.*

novella (nō vel′ə) 1. *n.* a fictional prose narrative, midway in length between a short story and a novel; tale; as Norman McLean's *A River Runs Through It.* 2. *n.* a short novel.

NP noun phrase.

nth 1. the last number in an infinite series; as *2, 4, 6. . . nth.* 2. **nth degree, nth power,** a. a high degree or power. b. the utmost degree or extent.

nuance (no͞o′ äns, nyo͞o′-, no͞o äns′, nyo͞o-; *Fr.* ny äns′) *n.* a subtle difference in meaning or shade of meaning.

nucleus (no͞o′klē əs, nyo͞o′-) *pl.* - **clei** (-kle ī″), **cleuses.** *n.* the high point, or peak, in the resonance, volume, or energy of a syllable. See illustration under **spectogram.**

null hypothesis a formal statement that no differences exist between variables or samples. *Note:* Rather than the positive assertion that differences will be found, the null hypothesis is usually used in experimentation. The reason for this is that the finding of any significant difference permits the rejection of the null hypothesis, but the finding of a significant difference does not necessarily allow the acceptance of the truth of the positive statement.

number (num′bər) *n.* the inflection of nouns, pronouns, determiners, and verbs to show singular, dual, or plural forms. *Note:* English has two forms of number, *singular* and *plural.* Singular subjects usually take singular verbs; plural subjects usually take plural verbs.

numeracy (no͞o′mər ə sē) *n.* (*especially Brit.*) fluency in mathematical operations. *Cp.* **literacy** (def. 1); **oracy.**

nursery rhyme verse for very young children, as: *Hey, diddle, diddle! / The cat and the fiddle, / The cow jumped over the moon; / The little dog laughed / To see such sport, / And the dish ran away with the spoon.*

nutshell *(Brit.)* (nut′s͜hel″) See **potted book.**

nystagmus (ni stag′məs) 1. *n.* any rapidly repetitive, involuntary back and forth movement of the eye. *Ct.* **saccade.** 2. *n.* an extremely rapid tremor of the eyeball which allows retinal cells to be freshly stimulated; physiological nystagmus.

O

DEVELOPMENT OF MAJUSCULE								
NORTH SEMITIC	GREEK		ETR.	LATIN		MODERN		
						GOTHIC	ITALIC	ROMAN
O	O	O	O	O	O	O	*O*	O

DEVELOPMENT OF MINUSCULE					
ROMAN CURSIVE	ROMAN UNCIAL	CAROL. MIN.	MODERN		
			GOTHIC	ITALIC	ROMAN
o	o	o	o	*o*	o

The fifteenth letter of the English alphabet descended from the Greek vowel *omicron* (o). In form, however, the letter was adopted in Greek from the North Semitic consonant *ayin*, North Semitic having no vowel symbols. Since its appearance in Greek, this sign has changed little throughout its history.

oak tag See **tagboard.**

ob- a prefix indicating *to, toward, directed toward* (in a negative way); as **obstruent.**

object (ob′jikt, -jekt) 1. *n.* the person or thing that receives or is affected by the action of a transitive verb in a sentence, either directly or indirectly, or is the word which a preposition relates to some other unit in a sentence. See also **direct object; indirect object.** 2. *n.* in psychology, anything, animate or inanimate, of which a person is aware, has an attitude toward, or responds to. *Note:* In this sense, object may refer to persons, things, attitudes, astract ideas, etc. 3. *n.* See **objective** (defs. 1, 2).

object complement the second of two elements in a complement, as *president* in *They elected him president, white* in *Bill painted the fence white,* or *to stop* in *They ordered Phyllis to stop.* See **complement.**

objective (əb jek′tiv) 1. *n.* a goal; something to direct one's efforts toward, as involving parents in a home-reading program. 2. *n.* a target toward which instruction is specifically directed; instructional objective. *Note:* An objective in this sense, while somewhat general and broad, is usually more specific than an educational goal. See also **behavioral objective.** 3. *adj.* referring to something that can be known through the senses, the existence of which is verifiable by non-subjective or scientific methods. *Television is an objective phenomenon.* 4. *adj.* having to do with communication that is free of bias, emotion, and intentional distortion. *The researcher reported his findings in an objective way.* 5. *n.* in English, the case form of a pronoun which is the object of a transitive verb or of a preposition, as *me* in *He hit me.* See also **objective case.** 6. *adj.* referring to such a grammatical case form.

objective case 1. the case of a noun or pronoun which is the direct object of a transitive verb or is in construction with a prepositional phrase. See also **object** (def. 1); **direct object; indirect object.** 2. in case grammar, the noun which is affected by the action, as *window* in *He broke the window* and in *The window was broken.*

objective refraction measurement of the refractive power of the eyes independent of the patient's self-reports. *Ct.* **subjective refraction.**

objective test a test having a high degree of objectivity.

objectivity (ob″jek tiv′i tē) *n.* in testing, *the extent of agreement found when qualified persons score the performance, whether they are dealing with the behavior directly or are dealing with a written record* — L. Cronbach (1970).

object language the language being described in a linguistic framework. *Note:* Elements of the object language are commonly enclosed in quotation marks in linguistic analysis, as in *'contain' is a verb.*

object method in teaching, the use of objects and other materials as a basis for presenting concepts. *Note:* Although traditionally associated with the name of Pestalozzi (1746-1826), the Swiss educator whose principles were familiar to American educators in the 1820's, the 'object method' as a pedagogical technique was not popularized in the U.S. until the 1860's. This method *probably influenced such innovations in reading as the introduction of the word method, the appearance of many pictures in primary readers, and the inclusion of material dealing with objects and experiences familiar to children* — N. B. Smith (1965).

object permanence (J. Piaget) the understanding that an object exists separate from and independent of the self.

oblique (ə blēk′) 1. *adj.* at an angle neither parallel nor perpendicular, as of a line or plane. *Ct.* **orthogonal** (def. 1). 2. *adj.* indirect, as *an oblique allusion.*

oblique case a case other than the nominative or vocative.

obscenity (əb sen′i tē, -sē′ni-) 1. *n.* indecency. 2. *n.* any expression which is offensive to others; indecent or lewd remark. 3. *n.* an indecent state or condition, leading to sexual arousal or lust.

observation (ob″zûr vā′shən) 1. *n.* the act of noticing, as *casual observations of how people dress.* 2. *n.* an intentional examination, study, or search, as *the observation of language patterns by linguists.* 3. *n.* a test score or other bit of data thus gathered; finding; as *a frequency distribution of all observations made in testing.* 4. *n.* a comment or opinion, as *a humorous observation. v.***observe.** *adj.***observant.**

observed response in miscue analysis, the actual oral reading of a text to which it may or may not conform.

obsession (əb sesh′ən) 1. *n.* a compulsive idea that dominates behavior, usually from anxiety or fear. *Note:* Examples of obsessions may range from mild intermittent ones to severe chronic ones. 2. *n.* such an idea or state. *adj.* **obsessive; obsessional.**

obsessive-compulsive (əb ses′iv kəm pul′siv) 1. *adj.* irrational and repetitious; specifically a syndrome of anxiety associated with neurotic behavior. 2. *n.* a person with such symptoms.

obstruent (ob′stroo̅ ənt) *n.* any speech sound produced with some constriction or stoppage of the air flow. *Ct.* **resonant.**

occipital lobe (ok sip′i tᵊl) that portion of the cerebral hemisphere which is continuous with the parietal and temporal lobes and lies furthest back in the skull. See illustration under **lobe.**

occluder (ə klo̅o̅′ dər) *n.* an object placed in front of an eye to block vision or break fusion, as *an occluder in visual testing.*

occlusion (ə klo̅o̅′zhən) 1. *n.* the closure, blockage, or shutting-off of something, as a clot in an artery, a vocal stop, a blinking of the eyelids. 2. *n.* the blocking or dimming of vision by placing something in front of the eye(s). 3. *n.* the contact between the upper and lower teeth.

occult story See **supernatural story.**

occupational therapy a form of medical or psychiatric therapy which uses work or hobby activities, usually in a group setting, as a means of redeveloping physical and/or mental skills.

octavo (ok tā′vō, -tä′-) *n.* a book printed on sheets folded to make eight leaves or 16 pages, approximately 15.5 x 23 cm. (6 x 9 in.) See also **book size** *or* **format.**

ocul (o)- a combining form indicating *eye;* as **oculomotor.**

ocular (ok′yə lər) 1. *adj.* having to do with or resembling the eye(s), as *an ocular shape.* 2. *adj.* having to do with what is perceived by the eye; visual; as *an ocular image.*

ocular dominance the superiority of one eye over the other without apparent differences in acuity or functioning of the two eyes. See also **dominant eye.**

ocular mobility *or* **motility** the ease, coordination, and accuracy of eye movements as in following a target, shifting fixations, or making saccades in reading.

ocular muscles the eye muscles inside and outside the eyeball. See **intraocular muscles; extraocular muscles.**

ocular pursuit See **pursuit eye movements.** *Ct.* **saccadic eye movements.**

oculist (ok′yə list) *n.* See **ophthalmologist.** *Note:* While the term oculist is sometimes loosely used to refer to an optometrist, this represents a fundamental misconception. Both oculists and ophthalmologists are medical doctors; optometrists are not.

oculomotor (ok″yə lō mō′tər) 1. *adj.* having to do with the movement of the eyes. 2. *adj. (Cap.)* referring to the 3rd cranial nerve.

oculomotor imbalance binocular imbalance; strabismus.

oculus dexter (O.D.) the right eye.

oculus sinister (O.S.) the left eye.

oculus uterque (O.U.) both eyes.

O.D. 1. oculus dexter; right eye. 2. Doctor of Optometry.

ode (ōd) *n.* an elaborate, formal, and dignified lyrical poem; originally, a Greek verse intended to be sung.

off-glide (ôf′glīd″, of′-) *n.* the movement of the articulators, often the production of a speech sound, to a neutral or another speech sound position; after-glide; final glide. *Note:* This term refers to the movement of the speech organs, while glide, alone, refers to a class of speech sounds. *Ct.* **on-glide.**

official language a language approved by a government, often to resolve conflicting problems of multilingualism, used especially for the conduct of governmental affairs, business, and schooling. *Hindi and English are the official languages of India.* See also **national language.**

offprint (ôf′print″, of′-) 1. *n.* the separate printing of a part of a larger publication. 2. *v.* to so print.

offset (ôf′ set″, of′-) 1. *n.* a lithographic process in which an inked impression is transferred to a rubber-covered roller which makes the print. *Very high speed printing is possible in offset because of the use of rollers rather than flat printing plates.* 2. *n.* the image thus printed. *adj.* **offset.**

ogham script (og′əm, ô′gəm) an alphabetic writing system used among Celts around the 5th century in the British Isles, with characters made of lines and notches carved into the edges of stones or blocks of wood. Also spelled *ogam; ogum. Cp.* **rune** (def.1).

ogive (ō′jīv, ō jīv′) *n.* an S-shaped, mathematical curve. *A cumulative frequency curve is an ogive. adj.* **ogival.**

-oid a combining form indicating *resembling; as* **choroid.**

Old English English spoken from approximately 500 A.D. to 1000 A.D. *Note:* Following the invasion of England by the Angles and Saxons, Celtic was replaced by a variant of Western Germanic as the Britons' language. West Saxon emerged as the standard official and literary language of this period. See also **Middle English; Modern English.**

omission (ō mish′ən) *n.* the leaving out of one or more words in the oral reading of text; one of several types of oral reading errors commonly recorded in testing oral reading. See also **insertion** (def. 1); **mispronunciation; substitution** (def. 2). *v.* **omit.**

omni- a combining form indicating *all;* as **omniscient.**

omnibus book (om′nə bus″) a one-volume collection of reprinted works either by a single author or by several authors whose works are related in form or theme.

one-to-one correspondence 1. any relationship in which every member of one set is matched exactly to one different member of a second set. 2. in graphemics, the representation of each phoneme of oral language by one and only one unique grapheme, and vice versa, as the use of *s* to represent only one speech sound, /s/, and the sound /s/ represented only by *s. Note:* One-to-one correspondence is the chief goal of spelling reform in English.

on-glide (ôn′glid″, on′-) *n.* the movement of the articulators, just before the production of a speech sound, from a neutral or prior speech sound position; initial glide; fore-glide. *Note:* This term refers to the movement of the speech organs, while *glide,* alone, refers to a class of speech sounds. *Ct.* **off-glide.**

onomatopoeia (on″ə mat″ə pē′ə) 1. *n.* the use of words the sound of which suggests their meaning, as *buzz* and *purr.* 2. *n.* a poetic device to produce this effect: *To the tintinnabulation that so musically dwells/From the bells, bells, bells, bells,/Bells, bells, bells* — E. A. Poe. *adj.* **onomatopoetic.**

onset (on′set″, ôn′-) *n.* that part of a syllable preceding the syllable peak, or nucleus; normally, the consonants preceding the vowel of a syllable, as *str* in *strip.* See illustration under **spectrogram.**

onto- a combining form indicating *being;* as **ontogeny.**

ontogeny *or* **ontogenesis** (on toj′ə nē; on″tə jen′i sis) 1. *n.* the origin and development of an individual. 2. *n.* the development of a specific behavior pattern in a lifetime, as *the ontogeny of a person's speech habits. Ct.* **phylogeny** *or* **phylogenesis.** *adj.* **ontogenetic.**

o.p. out of print.

opaque projector a device which projects nontransparent text and graphics onto a screen by a mirror and lenses.

open access See **open stacks.**

open class in early language acquisition, words which occur in more than one position in a sentence, as *Daddy* and *truck* in *allgone Daddy, allgone truck, Daddy home.* See also **pivot class.**

open classroom 1. a classroom area, often large and flexibly arranged, which may be divided into several centers differing in purpose, size, and content for instruction. 2. any decentralized classroom arrangement. 3. *a style of teaching involving flexibility of space, student choice of activity, richness of learning materials, integration of curriculum areas, and more individual or small-group than large-group instruction* — R. Horwitz.

open-class word a word with a full lexical meaning; content word; as *book, house, television. Ct.* **function word.**

open-ended question a type of question that is used to explore a person's understanding of what is read or heard, and that is intended to produce a free response rather than a directed one. *'What does the ending of this story suggest to you?' is an open-ended question. Cp.* **leading question.**

open enrollment in the United States, a policy whereby a community or junior college will admit any high school graduate or any person who is more than 18 years old and seems capable of profiting from instruction. Also called *open door admissions policy.*

open juncture See **juncture** (def. 1. *Note*).

open school 1. a school, usually at the elementary level, which seeks to create 'psychological openness' in learning, often through such means as a student-centered curriculum, individualized learning and progress, and flexible grouping. *Note:* There are many varieties of open schools... *that have the common element of replacing planned curriculum sequences with child-centered and, to a large extent, child-initiated learning activities.... Much of the present interest has been generated by a desire to emulate the British informal infant and junior schools* — A. Harris and E. Sipay (1975). 2. a school in which classrooms are flexible in size and shape, presumably to create an 'environmental openness' to accommodate the instructional needs of students and teachers; open space school. *Note:* The physical characteristics of classrooms do not necessarily insure 'psychological openness' for learning.

open space school See **open school** (def. 2).

open stacks library book shelves to which users have direct access. *Open stacks make it easier for a reader to examine all the works of a particular author. Ct.* **closed stacks.**

open syllable a syllable ending in a vowel sound rather than a consonant sound, as /bā/ and /bē/ in *baby. Ct.* **closed syllable.**

open vowel a vowel which is made with relatively open lips and jaw and with the tongue away from the palate; as /a/ in *hat* or /o/ in *hot. Syn.* **low vowel.** *Cp.* **lax** (def. 1). *Ct.* **closed vowel** (def. 2).

operant conditioning a type of instrumental conditioning. *Note:* This is a term used by B. F. Skinner in which repeated conditioned responses at a satisfactory rate are required. *Ct.* **classical conditioning.** *Cp.* **instrumental conditioning.**

operant learning See **operant conditioning.**

operational correspondence (J. Piaget) a relationship that is learned, recalled, and used as a concept: *Oranges and grapefruit are circular in shape. Ct.* **intuitive correspondence.**

operational definition the act, or result, of defining a term by showing how it functions or is considered to function, as in defining reading as what a reading test measures.

operations (op″ə rā′shənz) *n. pl.* (J. Piaget) internalized actions or thought processes that are reversible and involve some conservation and invariances. *Note:* For Piaget, no operation exists alone, but is related to a system of operations or to a total logical structure. See also **preoperational thought; concrete operations; formal operations; infralogical operations.** *adj.* **operational.**

operativity (op″ər ə tiv′i tē) *n.* (J. Piaget) the active, generalizable, and structuring aspect of intelligence. *Operativity implies the ability to mentally construct, transform, incorporate, and logically manipulate ideas. Ct.* **figurative knowledge.**

ophthalm (i) (o)- a combining form indicating *eye;* as *ophthalmic, ophthalmologist.*

ophthalmic (of thal′mik, op-) *adj.* having to do with the eye; ocular.

ophthalmograph (of″thal′mə graf″, -gräf″, op″-) *n.* an eye-movement camera which photographs corneal reflections.

ophthalmologist (of″thal mol′ə jist, -thəl-, -the-, op″-) *n.* a person with a Doctor of Medicine degree (M.D.) and advanced specialization in the diseases and disorders of the eye; specifically, in their diagnosis, medication, surgery, and correction, including the prescription of glasses; oculist. *Cp.* **optometrist.**

ophthalmology (of″thal mol′ə jē, -thəl-, -thə-, op″-) *n.* the branch of medicine having to do with the structures, functions, and diseases of the eye. *Cp.* **optometry.**

ophthalmometer (of″thal mom′i tər, -thəl-, thə-, op″-) *n.* an instrument for measuring the curvature of the front of the cornea; keratometer.

ophthalmoscope (of thal′mə skōp″, op-) *n.* an instrument with adjustable lenses that is used by the eye specialist to inspect closely much of the interior of the eyeball.

-opia a suffix indicating *visual defect;* as **hyperopia.**

opposition (op″ə zish′ən) 1. *n.* a relationship that is logically contradictory. *Your proposition is in opposition to mine.* 2. *n.* a phonological difference that permits discrimination of sound, as /k/ and /p/. 3. *n.* a grammatical difference that permits discrimination of tense, number, etc., as present vs. past. 4. *n.* a semantic difference that represents a paired contrast in meaning, as *big-small, male-female, husband-wife.* 5. *n.* resistance by force or ideas. *Old habits foster opposition to change. adj.* **opposite.** *v.* **oppose.**

opti-, opto- a combining form indicating *eye, vision;* as **optic, optometry.**

optical image See **image** (def. 3).

optic chiasma (op′tik kī as′mə) *pl.* **mas, -mata** (-mə tə). the point at which the optic nerves from each eye come together, and the nasal fibers from each eye cross over to the opposite side while the temporal fibers remain on the same side.

optic disk See **blind spot** (def. 1).

optician (op tish′ən) *n.* a person who makes and sells eyeglasses and other optical instruments. *Note:* The term *dispensing optician* is sometimes used to distinguish a person who generally fits eyeglasses to the wearer, from the *prescription optician* who grinds and puts together eye lenses according to the eye specialist's prescription. In British usage, an *ophthalmic optician* means an optometrist.

optic nerve the second cranial nerve. See illustration under **eye.** *The optic nerve carries information from the retina through the optic chiasma to the visual sensory cortex, Brodmann's area 17.*

optometric training See **visual training.**

optometrist (op tom′i trist) *n.* a person with a Doctor of Optometry degree (O.D.) who is licensed to practice optometry. *Cp.* **ophthalmologist.**

optometry (op tom′i trē) *n.* the professional field of the eye specialist whose practice includes examining the eye for refractive and other defects, prescribing lenses, and conducting visual training or orthoptic programs. *Cp.* **ophthalmology.** *adj.* **optometric.**

oracy (ōr′ə sē, ôr-) *n. (especially Brit.)* fluency in speaking and listening. *Cp.* **literacy** (def. 1); **numeracy.**

oral (ōr′əl, ôr′-) 1. *adj.* referring to spoken utterances or to speaking, as *oral literature, oral reading, oral examination.* 2. *adj.* referring to the mouth or oral cavity. See illustration under **speech organs.** 3. *n.* a speech sound made when all the air flow passes through the mouth and none through the nose. *Note* (def. 3): The term oral also refers to a distinctive feature used to distinguish one phoneme from another: that most or all of the air flow passes out through the mouth which serves as the resonator of the sound. 4. *adj.* in psychoanalytic theory, referring to the first stage of psychosexual development and its accompanying behaviors and results. 5. *adj.* something done through the mouth, as *the oral taking of medicine. adj.* **orally.**

oral culture 1. a culture in which its values, attitudes, and beliefs are transmitted through oral language or languages. *Most North American Indians traditionally belong to oral cultures.* 2. a culture which values the ability to speak effectively more than the ability to read and write. *Ct.* **literary culture.**

oralism *or* **oral method** *n.* the philosophy and methods of deaf education that stress lip reading and verbal communication rather than signing or finger spelling. *Ct.* **manual method; combined method.**

oral reading the process of reading aloud to communicate to another or to an audience. *Oral reading is a social process* — E. Dale, in Gray (1940). *Oral reading is a much more difficult process than silent reading* — A. Gates (1947).

oral reading test an individually administered test or inventory for assessing oral reading performance or competence. *Note:* One type of standardized oral reading test has passages of increasing difficulty which the student reads aloud. The passages are scored for errors such as substitutions, mispronunciations, omissions, etc. The student's fluency, articulation, and attitude toward the reading task may also be noted by the examiner. Representative oral reading tests are those by W.S. Gray, A. Gates, D. Durrell, and J. Gilmore. *Cp.* **informal reading inventory (IRI).** A second type of inventory developed by Goodman and Burke is designed to explore in depth the nature of the miscues in language processing when the student reads and retells a rather difficult passage calculated to produce 25 or more miscues. The scoring of the inventory provides information concerning the strategies used by the readers in integrating grapheme-phoneme correspondences, syntax, and meaning. See also **miscue.**

oral vocabulary See **speaking vocabulary.**

Orbis Pictus any of various editions and translations of the *Orbis Sensualium Pictus*, the first significant schoolbook with pictures, by Johann Amos Comenius, first published in 1658. *Note:* The *Orbis Pictus* aimed to present to children the nomenclature for 'all the chief things that are in the world.' The numbered pictures were identified by numbered words, in parallel columns of Latin and English. An immediate success, its popularity declined in the 18th century. It has often, but erroneously, been cited as the first book to advocate the word method of teaching reading.

order (ôr′dər) 1. *n.* a systematic arrangement or classification as by sequence, rank, or quality: *alphabetical order, order of command, pecking order.* 2. *n.* the state of being so arranged or classified. 3. *v.* to arrange in sequence, as *order books by their library number.* 4. *n.* a predictable method of procedure, as *syllogistic order of reasoning.* 5. *v.* to arrange or classify objects according to perceived relationships, as *order the pieces of a puzzle.* 6. *n.* such an arrangement or classification. 7. *n.* a grammatical sequence or rule, as *word order.* 8. *n.* the raising of a number or amount by itself. *Second order means that a number is squared.* 9. *n.* a social class, as *the lower orders.*

ordinate (ôr′dᵊnāt″, -dᵊnit) 1. *n.* the vertical axis of a graph or chart; upright line; y axis. 2. *n.* the distance from a point in a two-dimensional graph along a line which is at right angles to the horizontal axis. *Cp.* **abscissa.**

organic (ôr gan′ik) 1. *adj.* referring to a body organ or to living tissue, as the eye, nervous system, etc. 2. *adj.* referring to or coming from a living organism, as *organic fertilizer.* 3. *adj.* caused by a known or suspected change in body structure rather than function. *A brain lesion may be an organic cause of reading disability.* 4. *adj.* organized; systematic; as *an organic outline.* 5. *adj.* like the development of living organisms, as *an organic view of reading.*

organic disorder a disturbance in function or behavior with an organic basis. *Loss of speech is sometimes an organic disorder which reflects damage to the speech areas of the brain. Ct.* **functional disorder.**

organicity (ôr″gə nis′i tē) 1. *n.* the condition of being organic. 2. *n.* a disorder of the central nervous system; brain damage.

organismic (ôr″gə niz′mik) 1. *adj.* having to do with an organism, as *organismic hormones. Cp.* **psychosomatic.** 2. *adj.* holistic in point of view, as an *organismic hypothesis.*

organismic age the average of all measures of a person's development, as of mental age, carpal age, social age, etc.

organ of Corti the sense, or end, organ of hearing; specifically, the basilar membrane, with the hair cells resting on it, in the cochlea. *Note:* When the basilar membrane vibrates from the pulsing of the fluid in the inner ear in response to sound vibrations, the hair cells trigger impulses in the acoustic nerve that are perceived in the brain as sound.

organs of speech See **speech organs.**

orientation (ōr″ē en tā′s̲h̲ən, ôr″-) 1. *n.* physical alignment with respect to some point or frame of reference. 2. *n.* the process or ability to determine where one is in relation to time, space, goals, and other aspects of reality; rationality; sanity. 3. *n.* an enduring tendency or inclination toward a particular direction. See also **predisposition** (def. 1). 4. *n.* a change in position as a result of external pressure. 5. *n.* preparation or state of preparation for learning; readiness. 6. *n.* the process or activities involved in introducing or adjusting one to a new school or other new environment.

origin (ôr′i jin, or′-) 1. *n.* source, beginning, or start. *The origin of language is lost in time.* 2. *n.* birth, parentage, or ancestry, as *of Swedish origin.* 3. *n.* the place of attachment of a muscle to the more fixed parts of the skeleton. *Cp.* **insertion** (def. 3). 4. *n.* the beginning of a cranial or spinal nerve. 5. *n.* the reference point for a mathematical or statistical operation; especially, the point where the axes of a graph intersect.

original source See **primary source.**

ortho- a combining form indicating *straight, correct;* as **orthography.**

orthoepy *or* **orthöepy** (ôr t̲h̲ō′ ə pē, ôr′ t̲h̲ō ep″ē) 1. *n.* the study of pronunciation. 2. *n.* accepted or customary pronunciation.

orthogenic (ôr″t̲h̲ə jen′ik) 1. *adj.* steady

in development or evolution in one direction. 2. *adj.* leading to normal development; corrective; specifically, referring to any educational, psychological, or medical treatment that seeks to restore normal functioning. *Students with severe handicaps need orthogenic education.*

orthogonal (ôr t͟hog′ə nᵊl) 1. *adj.* right-angled; perpendicular. *The abscissa and ordinate axes are orthogonal. Cp.* **oblique.** 2. *adj.* referring to an experimental research design with several statistically independent variables.

orthographic (ôr″t͟hə graf′ik) 1. *adj.* referring to orthography or to spelling. 2. *adj.* spelled correctly.

orthographic transcription 1. the representation of language by a standard spelling system or orthography. 2. the recording of language by the use of a system of letters. *Cp.* **transcription** (defs. 1, 2). 3. a writing system; orthography (def. 3).

orthography (ôr t͟hog′rə fē) 1. *n.* the study of the nature and use of symbols in a writing system. *Cp.* **graphemics**. 2. *n.* correct or standardized spelling according to established usage. *Ct.* **cacography** (def. 2). 3. *n.* a writing system; generally, one in which the speech sounds of a language are represented by alphabetic characters; orthographic transcription.

orthopedically handicapped a person crippled by disabilities of the bones, joints, and associated muscles caused by congenital defects, disease, or accident. *Orthopedically handicapped students in a school need provisions for wheelchair movement or facilities for braces and restrainers of various sorts. Note:* Some groups, as the World Health Organization, do not recognize physical disabilities which were caused by damage to the central nervous system as orthopedic handicaps. But in most settings, such as schools, the term orthopedically handicapped is applied to any person with impairment of the spine or extremities, including cerebral palsy.

orthophoria (ôr t͟hō fō′rē ə) *n.* the absense of heterophoria; specifically, the normal balance of the external eye muscles so that the lines of sight are parallel.

orthopsychiatry (ôr″t͟hō si kī′ ə trē, -sī-) *n.* that branch of medicine that deals with the identification, treatment, and prevention of mental disorder, especially in children and adolescents. *n.* **orthopsychiatrist.** *adj.* **orthopsychiatric.**

orthoptics (ôr t͟hop′tiks) *n.* (*usually sing.*) the improvement of various visual conditions, such as binocular vision and visual perception, through specialized vision training programs; visual training; optometric training. *adj.* **orthoptic.**

O.S. oculus sinister: left eye.

oscill- a combining form indicating *movement back and forth; as* **oscilloscope.**

oscillograph (ə sil′ə graf″, -gräf″) *n.* an instrument for making a permanent record of electrical current variation. *Sound oscillograph records, or oscillograms, are useful in the study and training of speech for showing visually the tonal complexity and amplitude variation of an oral utterance.*

oscilloscope (ə sil′ə skōp″) *n.* an instrument which has the same function as an oscillograph but which makes only a temporary image on a cathode ray tube.

-osis a suffix indicating *state, condition* (in pathology); as **neurosis.**

ossicle (os′i kəl) *n.* any small bone; especially, one of the three small bones in the middle ear: the malleus, the incus, or the stapes.

ostensive definition to define something by pointing to or demonstrating it.

OT occupational therapy.

otitis media (ō tī′tis mē′ dē ə) an inflammation of the middle ear. *Note:* The inflammation and the fluid it causes temporarily reduce hearing acuity or even harm the ossicles. Chronic otitis media may also be one source of reading disability since the most common ages for otitis media are the same as the critical ages for making phonemic discriminations and for learning how to process spoken language.

oto- a combining form indicating the ear; as **otology.**

otolaryngology (ō″tō lar″ing gol′ə jē) *n.* that branch of medicine which specializes in the study and treatment of the ear, nose, and throat. *An otolaryngologist is a doctor who treats ears, noses, and throats as a specialty area of training and interest. n.* **otolaryngologist.**

otology (ō tol′ə jē) *n.* that branch of medicine which specializes in the study and treatment of disease of the ear. *Cp.* **audiology.** *n.* **otologist.**

otosclerosis (ō″tə skli rō′sis) *n.* a growth of spongy, new bone in the middle ear that prevents its moving parts, particularly the stapes and the oval window, from responding to sound vibrations, thus causing progressive deafness.

O.U. oculus uterque: both eyes.

outcome (out′kum″) *n.* a result or consequence; especially, the result of learning and/or experience. *Concepts are a type of learning outcome.*

outer ear See **external ear.**

outline (out′līn″) 1. *n.* a graphic line, often without shading, which shows the shape of a figure or object. 2. *n.* a short verbal sketch which reveals through its organization the pattern of ideas of something read or of a draft prepared for speaking or writing. 3. *n.* a summary or synopsis, as *an outline of the plot of a Shakespearean play.* 4. *v.* to prepare an outline.

outlining (out′lī′ning) *n.* the process of making an outline.

out of print (o.p.) unavailable from the publisher because the supply of printed material is exhausted.

output (out′pŏŏt″) 1. *n.* something that is produced; response; yield; as *research output, learning output.* 2. *n.* the act of so producing. 3. *v.* to produce or respond in a communications system. *The computer can output data at 6000 characters per second.* 4. *n.* information produced within a specified period of time, as at the rate given in def. 3. 5. *n.* information that can be transmitted or transferred in a computer, either within or without. 6. *adj.* referring to a communications device for giving out information, as *a computer output terminal for a typewriter. Ct.* **input.**

outside-in theories See **bottom-up processing.**

outtake (out′tāk″) 1. *n.* something removed from a manuscript or motion picture film during production. *There were many outtakes in the preparation of this dictionary.* 2. *n.* a computer term for data retrieved from storage.

oval window the opening from the middle ear into the inner ear which is nearly filled by the base of the stapes; fenestra ovalis. *Note:* The flexible membrane surrounding the base allows vibrations of the ossicles to be converted to fluid pulses in the inner ear. *Cp.* **round window.**

overachievement (ō″vər ə c̱hēv′mənt) *n.* achievement above that expected; specifically, achievement above one's performance on tests of ability. *Ct.* **underachievement.**

overcompensation (ō′vər kom″pən sā′ s̱hən) 1. *n.* trying too hard to make up for feelings of guilt, inferiority, or incompetence. *Note:* A pattern of overcompensation may be harmful, or it may result in turning a negative trait into a positive one. 2. *n.* inappropriately, a mild form of compensation.

overcorrection (ō″vər kə rek′s̱hən) See **hypercorrection.**

overfocused (ō″vər fō′kust) *adj.* tending to attend to certain stimuli to the exclusion of others. *Ct.* **underfocused.**

overgeneralization (ō′vər jen″ər ə li zā′s̱hən) 1. *n.* the process, or result, of making an inference that is not justified by the data on which it is based. *Ct.* **generalization.** 2. *n.* in language acquisition, the inappropriate extension of a phonological or grammatical rule to a word or phrase to which the rule does not apply, as *goed* for *went, foots* for *feet.*

overhead projector a device used to enlarge and show images from transparent material. *Note:* The image is placed on a flat surface over a light source so that the image is reflected from an angled mirror above the light source onto a screen.

overt (ō vûrt′, ō′ vûrt) *adj.* viewable; observable. *Lip movements are an overt indication of slow silent reading.* *Ant.* **covert.**

overtone (ō′vər tōn″) 1. *n.* an additional meaning that may be inferred; connotation. *The phrase 'earn your bread and butter' may have an overtone of having to prove oneself.* 2. *n.* that part of a sound that is higher in frequency than its lowest, or fundamental, tone. *Most sounds have one or more overtones.*

overview (ō′vər vyo͞o″) *n.* an introduction to a survey of some subject, text, etc. *Abstracts in journal articles provide an overview for the reader.*

oxymoron (ok″si mōr′on, -môr′-) *pl.* **-ra.** *n.* a figure of speech in which contrasting or contradictory words are brought together for emphasis: *cruel kindness; living death.* See also **antithesis.**

P

DEVELOPMENT OF MAJUSCULE								
NORTH SEMITIC	GREEK		ETR.	LATIN		MODERN		
						GOTHIC	ITALIC	ROMAN
7	7	Π	7	Γ	P	𝔓	*P*	P

DEVELOPMENT OF MINUSCULE					
ROMAN CURSIVE	ROMAN UNCIAL	CAROL. MIN.	MODERN		
			GOTHIC	ITALIC	ROMAN
p	p	p	𝔭	*p*	p

The sixteenth letter of the English alphabet developed from the North Semitic letter *pe,* which means "mouth," but even in its earliest extant form, the shape of the letter has no obvious connection with this meaning. Its further history can be traced through Greek *pi* (π), Etruscan, and Latin, but except in the case of the last, its present form bears little if any resemblance to its earlier forms. The minuscule (p) is derived from the capital by lengthening the descender.

p 1. probability. 2. that part of a sample that has a specific characteristic. *Ct.* **q.** 3. percentile. 4. the percent getting an item right.

pacer (pā′sər) *n.* any instrument which controls the rate of reading; reading accelerator. *Pacers control one's rate through the uses of light beams, opaque shutters, rapidly changed slides, etc.*

pacing (pā′siŋ) 1. *n.* using a pacer to control rate of reading, usually over some extended text selection. 2. *n.* the learning rate(s) for which a teaching machine or computer-assisted instruction program is designed. 3. *n.* allowing one to set one's own schedule in an individualized reading program. 4. *n.* the adjustment of instructional materials in teaching to individual differences.

page (pāj) 1. *n.* one side of a leaf. *Cp.* **leaf.** 2. *n.* the entire leaf. See **pagination.** 3. *v.* to turn pages. *Rusty paged through the book rapidly.*

page proof a trial printed impression made after type is made up into pages. *Cp.* **galley proof.**

pagination (paj″ə nā′shən) *n.* a system of ordering the pages of a book or manuscript by numbers or other characters on both sides of each leaf. *v.* **paginate.**

paired associates method an experimental procedure for presenting material to be learned and remembered in pairs. *Note:* In the paired associates method, one item of a pair, as the stimulus *car,* is presented, the subject attempting to learn or to remember the other item of the pair, as the response *vehicle.*

palatal (pal′ə t^{ə}l) *n.* a consonant speech sound made when the tongue stops or constricts the air flow by nearing or touching the hard palate, as /j/, /l/, /sh/.

palate (pal′it) 1. *n.* the roof of the mouth; specifically, the structure that separates the mouth from the nasal cavities, made up of the bony hard palate and the flexible soft palate. See illustration under **speech organs.** 2. *n.* a refined sense of taste, either literally, as *a dish to please the palate* or figuratively, as *a discriminating palate for modern literature.*

paleography (pā″lē og′rə fē, pal″ē-) 1. *n.* any ancient writing system. 2. *n.* the study of the development and decipherment of ancient writing systems, including their origin and dates. See also **epigraphy; philology.** *adj.* **paleographic.**

palindrome (pal′in drōm) *n.* a word, phrase, or number with the same sequence of letters or numbers whether read from right to left or from left to right, as *Anna; Madam, I'm Adam, 1771. Cp.* **anagram.**

palsy (pôl′zē) 1. *n.* partial paralysis with weakened muscle control and tremor; paresis. *Cerebral palsy is the most common type seen in schools.*

2. *n.* paralysis.

pamphlet (pam′flit) 1. *n.* an unbound publication of a few leaves stitched or stapled together in paper covers. 2. *n.* a short, unbound essay or treatise, usually controversial in tone, on a topic of contemporary interest, as *a political pamphlet.*

panegyric (pan″i jir′ik, -jī′rik) 1. *n.* a formal statement in praise of someone either living or dead. 2. *n.* overpraise, as *an advertising panegyric.*

pantomime (pan′tə mīm″) 1. *n.* a stylized form of nonverbal communication using gestures and movement of the face, hands, and other parts of the body. *Marcel Marceau has popularized the ancient art form of pantomime.* 2. *n.* a form of entertainment in which performers use gestures instead of dialogue. 3. *n.* (*Brit.*) a theatrical spectacle chiefly for children during the Christmas season. 4. *v.* to express or represent by pantomime.

paper (pā′pər) 1. *n.* the material that books, newspapers, magazines, etc., are commonly printed on. 2. *n.* a piece of such material. 3. *n.* something written formally for school or other particular purpose, as *a term paper, a paper on definitions of reading.* 4. *n.* a newspaper. 5. *adj.* made of paper, as *paper money.* 6. *adj.* referring to events that happen in written communications only, as *a paper war.* 7. *adj.* referring to events that do not really happen, as *paper profits.*

paperback (pā′pər bak″) *n.* a book in paper covers, often a less expensive edition of a clothbound book. *adj.* **paperbacked.**

paper hole test any of several tests of eyedness. *Note:* The subject is asked to sight a distant target through a small opening in a sheet of paper. The dominant eye is determined by noting which eye is used to see the target.

paperless book a book from a computer databank that is read, or is to be read, on an electronic viewing screen.

para- a combining form indicating *with, alongside;* as **paranatal, parathyroid.**

parable (par′ə bəl) 1. *n.* a story, rather short, intended to teach a moral lesson; allegorical tale; as *the parable of the Good Samaritan.* 2. *n.* the making of a point indirectly by comparison or analogy. *n.* **parabolist.**

paracentral vision vision in which the image falls just next to or around the macular area; retinal stimulation between the central and peripheral areas; perimacular vision.

paradigm (par′ə dim, -dīm″) 1. *n.* a pattern; example. *Physics is a paradigm for psychological research.* 2. *n.* in grammar, a set of all the inflected forms of a word that can be declined, as *reader, reader's, readers, readers',* or conjugated, as *read, reads, reading.*

paradigmatic par″ə dig mat′ik) *adj.* referring to the set of linguistic units that may occupy the same place in a phrase or sentence, as '*Susan reads: /widely/, /as quickly as possible/, /detective stories. /* ' *Cp.* **syntagmatic.**

paradox (par′ə doks″) 1. *n.* an apparently contradictory statement that suggests a truth: *Life is but a dream.* 2. *n.* a self-contradictory, illogical statement. *Include me out* — S. Goldwyn. 3. *n.* a person, thing, or situation of a contradictory nature, as *the paradox of unethical conduct in public office. adj.* **paradoxical.**

paragrammatism (par′ə gram′ ə tiz ᵊm) *n.* an aphasia without the usual patterns of syntax and/or grammar.

paragraph¹ (par′ə graf″, -gräf″) 1. *n.* one or more sentences developed around a single topic, grouped together, and usually with an indented first line. 2. *v.* to so write. 3. *n.* a presumably logical cluster of sentences.

4. *n.* an arbitrary section set off in print, as in a newspaper.

paragraph² *n.* a character, ¶, indicating the beginning of a new paragraph; or, in proofreading, the need for a new paragraph.

paragraph meaning the content or significance of a paragraph. *Paragraph meaning may include vocabulary, main idea, details, etc.*

paragraph structure the way that a paragraph is constructed or organized, or a description thereof.

paralanguage (par′ə lan̂g′gwij) 1. *n.* voice quality features, as a whine or quaver, that accompany speech. 2. *n.* the range of intonation patterns characteristic of a speaker; tone of voice. 3. *n.* the intonation patterns of a language, as stress, pitch, and juncture in speech. 4. *n.* in print, stylistic features, as boldface or italics. *n.* **paralinguistics.**

paralexia (par″ə lek′sē ə) *n.* a reading difficulty marked by the transposition and substitution of letters, syllables, and words so that the exact text is not reproduced.

paralinguistics (par″ə lin̂g gwis′tiks) *n.* the study of language-associated human behavior, as voice pitch, loudness, or duration, and body movements.

parallax (par′ə laks″) 1. *n.* the apparent shifting or displacement of an observed object because of a difference in two points of view, as the separate images perceived by each eye in binocular vision or by a change in the observer's position. See **binocular parallax.** 2. *n.* the illusion of observed movement. See **phi phenomenon.**

parallel form See **comparable form.**

parallelism (par′ə lel″iz əm) *n.* the phrasing of language so as to balance ideas of equal importance; parallel construction: *Now if a thousand perfect men were to appear it would not amaze me,/Now if a thousand beautiful forms of women appear'd it would not astonish me* — W. Whitman. *Note:* Parallelism may apply to phrases, sentences, and paragraphs, or to longer passages or whole selections.

parallel repetition the repetition of the same words or phrases, especially in or between the stanzas of a poem, as the identical refrain in some popular ballads. *Ct.* **incremental repetition.**

paralysis (pə ral′i sis) *pl.* **-ses.** 1. *n.* the loss of voluntary motor function and sensation because of injury to or disease of the nerve supply. 2. *n.* palsy; paresis. 3. *n.* the loss of any function or competence, as *paralysis of one's will to live. adj.* **paralytic.** *v.* **paralyze.**

parameter (pə ram′i tər) 1. *n.* a variable represented by an arbitrary constant in a mathematical formula. *Each specific value of the particular shape of a mathematical curve is determined by its parameter.* 2. *n.* a fixed criterion, limit, or standard used in making judgments. *Teachers need to work within the parameters of the curriculum guide.* 3. *n.* any statistical value derived from a set of scores, as a mean, believed or designed to estimate a property of a population. *A parameter is to a population what a statistic is to a sample* — Lyman. 4. *n.* any technique in psychoanalytic therapy other than interpretation, as reassurance. *adj.* **parametric.**

parametric statistics See **statistics.** (def. 1).

paranatal (par″ə nāt′ᵊl) *adj.* related to or occurring during the birth process. *Cp.* **perinatal.**

paranoia (par″ə noi′ə) *n.* psychosis involving systematic delusions, usually of persecutions and/or grandeur, often in an otherwise apparently normal person. *adj.* **paranoid.**

paraphrase (par′ə frāz″) *n.* the act, or result, of stating something in a different linguistic form in a language without altering the meaning. *'We saw the sun come up'* is a paraphrase of *'We were up at daybreak.'* *v.* **paraphase.**

paraplegia (par″ə plē′jē ə, -jə) *n.* paralysis of the lower half of the body. *Ct.* **hemiplegia.**

paraprofessional (par″ə prə fesh′ə nᵊl) 1. *n.* a person trained to assist a professional; aide. *A teaching paraprofessional is not a certified teacher.* 2. *adj.* referring to paraprofessionals or to their work.

parasympathetic nervous system that portion of the autonomic nervous system that serves to conserve the body and tends to balance the sympathetic nervous system. *The parasympathetic nervous system slows the heart rate, constricts the pupil, empties the bladder, etc.*

parathyroid glands the small endocrine glands located on the back surface of the thyroid glands in the lower neck area. *The parathyroid glands secrete hormones that control the metabolism of calcium and phosphorous.*

parenthesis (pə ren′thi sis) *pl.* **parentheses.** 1. *n.* a phrase, as 'John Brown, *a friend of mine,* won the sweepstakes,' set off by punctuation marks or orthographic symbols. *Cp.* **appositive.** 2. *n.* one or a pair of curved orthographic symbols ( ) used to enclose a word, number, or phrase not central to the sentence in which it occurs. See also **bracket** (def. 1). *adj.* **parenthetical.**

paresis (pə rē′sis, par′i sis) *n.* incomplete paralysis. See **palsy** (def. 1). *adj.* **paretic.**

pariah group an outcast social group that, having different standards, may influence persons against the primary or main social group.

parietal lobe that portion of the cerebral hemisphere which lies between the frontal and occipital lobes and above the back end of the temporal lobe. See illustration under **lobe.**

parody (par′ə dē) 1. *n.* a work, often humorous, which imitates by burlesque or satire another work, usually serious in nature. *Parody attempts to hold up to ridicule the subject matter and/or the style of the original work.* 2. *n.* this class of writing. *Parody is to literature what caricature is to art.* 3. *v.* to imitate the work of another by satirizing it. *The Harvard Lampoon's parody of Tolkien's trilogy is called* Bored of the Rings.

parole (pᴀ rōl′) *n.* in de Saussure's (1916) description of living language, what an individual speaker of a language actually says and writes; language or linguistic performance. *Cp.* **langue.**

paroxysm (par′ək siz″əm) 1. *n.* a sudden, strong outburst of action and/or emotion. *His continued frustration led to a paroxysm of anger.* 2. *n.* a severe attack or sudden increase in the violence of a disease.

parsing (pär′ sing, pär′ zing) *n.* the process of analyzing sentences by grammatical labels as subject, predicate, object, etc. *v.* **parse.**

partial correlation the relationship between two variables when the influence of other variables on the relationship is controlled. *An observed relationship between rate of reading and reading comprehension might differ if vocabulary power is controlled by partial correlation.*

partially sighted See **visual impairment.** (def. 2).

participipial phrase a group of words containing a participle, as *the running water.*

participle (pär′ti sip″əl, sə pəl) *n.* a verbal form used as an adjective or to make a compound verb form, as *reading* in *He is a reading man* or *She is reading.* See **present participle; past participle; participial phrase.**

particle (pär′ti kəl) *n.* a small word that has functional or relational use, as *on, or, by,* etc., rather than a lexical use, and is usually uninflectable.

part of speech any of the grammatical form classes into which words have traditionally been categorized, chiefly by inflections or syntactic function, as, in English, *noun, pronoun, verb, adjective, adverb, preposition, conjunction,* and *interjection.*

pasigraphy (pə sig′rə fē) 1. *n.* a writing system consisting of signs which are interpretable to speakers of any language, and represent ideas rather than sound sequences, such as the Arabic numerals 1, 2, 3, etc. 2. *n.* an artificial international written language. *Cp.* **ideography** (def. 1)**; artificial language; international language.** *adj.* **pasigraphic.**

passage (pas′ij) *n.* a portion or selection of text, usually greater than a sentence; paragraph, verse, etc.; as *a passage from the Scriptures.*

passive vocabulary the number of different words understood in listening and reading. *Ant.* **active vocabulary.**

passive voice See **voice** (def. 7).

pastoral (pas′tər əl, pä′stər-) 1. *adj.* dealing with shepherds and/or country or rural life. 2. *n.* a poem dealing with shepherds and rural or rustic life. 3. *n.* an idealized picture of country life. See also **idyll** (def. 1). 4. *adj. putting the complex into the simple* — W. Empson. *Note:* This is a modern literary criticism term applied to such works as Lewis Carroll's *Alice in Wonderland* or to George Orwell's *Animal Farm.*

past participle a verb form that indicates past meaning, as *stolen* in *The watch was stolen,* and can be used as an adjective, as *the stolen watch.*

past perfect aspect (tense) an aspect of English verbs that indicates an action or state that both occurred and was completed before the utterance, marked by the auxiliary verb *had* plus a past participle, as *She had laughed*; pluperfect tense. *Cp.* **present perfect aspect (tense).**

past progressive aspect (tense) a verb aspect in English that indicates an action or state going on at some time in the past: *Charlotte was weaving her web. Cp.* **imperfect tense.**

past tense a verb tense form that indicates past or completed action: preterit; as *fished* in *We fished last week.*

patellar reflex the sudden extension of the leg when the tendon attached to the front of the kneecap is given a sharp blow; knee jerk.

path-, patho- a combining form indicating *suffering, disease;* as **pathos, pathogenic.**

path analysis a form of multiple regression analysis intended to identify the variability of an outcome attributable to a specific factor.

pathetic fallacy the act of giving nature or inanimate objects human characteristics and feelings; especially, emotional descriptions of nature by poets: *See the mountains kiss high Heaven* — P.B. Shelley, *Cp.* **intentional fallacy; affective fallacy.**

pathogenic (path″ə jen′ik) *adj.* causing, or capable of causing, disease *Polio virus is pathogenic. n.* **pathogen.**

pathology (pə thol′ə jē) 1. *n.* the study

of disease, especially of abnormal body processes. 2. *n.* a branch of medicine which studies the origin and progress of diseases, especially the structural and functional changes in diseased organs and tissues. 3. *n.* any deviation from a normal, efficient condition, living or non-living, as *the pathology of reading failure, the pathology of a nuclear reactor breakdown. adj.* **pathological.** *n.* **pathologist.**

pathos (pā'thos) *n.* the quality in literature and other arts which calls forth pity or sorrow in the reader or viewer.

patois (pat'wä; *Fr.* PA*t* WA'), *pl.* (pat'wāz; *Fr.* PA TWA'). 1. *n.* a regional or social variety of a language often spoken in rural areas. See also **dialect; regional dialect; sociolect.** 2. *n.* an ungrammatical mixture of two or more languages. *Note* (def. 2): Patois comes from a French word meaning 'clumsy speech.' 3. *n.* jargon.

pattern (pat'ərn) 1. *n.* in linguistics, a set of predictable and describable relations between elements of language, as phonology, word order, or affixation. 2. *v.* to so identify such relations. 3. *v.* to arrange in a pattern.

pattern analysis 1. a cluster analysis of test items to determine whether items clustered on the basis of theory or heuristic judgments belong together. 2. a profile analysis of test scores to determine patterns of profiles which have different degrees of effectiveness in predicting the independent criterion.

patterning (pat'ərn ing) *n.* a method of providing proprioceptive and kinesthetic stimuli to the brain, using specific sequential motor activities.

pause (pôz) 1. *n.* in speech and oral reading, a slight interruption of the voice, as in phrasing, to emphasize meaning or to stress a grammatical relationship. See also **juncture.** 2. *v.* to make such an interruption of the voice.

Pavlovian conditioning See **classical conditioning.**

P.B. words a collection of monosyllabic words presented with equal stress and used to evaluate speech discrimination during audiometric testing. *P.B. means 'phonetically balanced' since the speech sounds used in the words approximate their distribution in normal speech.*

P.D. 1. prism diopter. 2. interpupillary distance.

PE, P.E. probable error.

Pearsonian correlation See **product-moment correlation.**

ped- a combining form indicating *child*; as **pediatrics.**

pedagese (ped'ə gēz) *n.* the speech or writing of educationists marked by complex syntax, circumlocution, and polysyllabic and obscure words. *If spoken or written correctly, pedagese is perfectly incomprehensible.*

pedagogy of reading the study of the teaching of reading; specifically, an examination of the materials, methods, and problems involved in learning to read and in improving existing reading abilities. *Note:* The pedagogy of reading includes such diverse fields as the history and status of reading, comparative reading, teacher education in reading, literary appreciation, the reading curriculum, and developmental, corrective, and remedial reading.

pediatrics (pē"dē a'triks, ped"ē-) *n.* (*with sing. v.*) that branch of medicine which deals with the health and illnesses of children. *adj.* **pediatric.** *n.* **pediatrician.**

peephole method See **Miles peephole method.**

peer group 1. a group in which a child, adolescent, or young adult is a social equal. *Children's reading preferences are often strongly influenced by their peer group.* 2. any group of persons that is on an equal social or professional, and often age, basis.

pegboard (peg'bōrd″, -bôrd″) *n.* a board with holes into which pegs are fitted for the display of teaching materials, student products, etc.

pejorative (pi jôr'ə tiv, -jor'-, pej'ə rā″-, pē'jə-) *adj.* having a bad connotation. *Poetaster is a pejorative term for one who writes poetry of poor quality. n.* **pejorative; pejoration.**

penmanship (pen'mən ship″) 1. *n.* The art of handwriting. 2. *n.* a person's style of handwriting. *Ted's penmanship is poor.*

pen name an assumed name used by an author. *Mark Twain was Samuel Langhorne Clemens' pen name.*

penny dreadful (*Brit.*) 1. a novel of violence or crime which sold in late Victorian England for a British penny. See also **dime novel.** 2. any story of this sensational nature.

pentameter (pen tam'i tər) *n.* a line of poetry with five feet.

percentile (p) (pər sen'tīl, -til) 1. *n.* a value on a scale of 100 showing the percent of a distribution that is equal to or below it. *A score in the 75th percentile is equal to or better than 75 percent of the scores. Cp.* **centile.** 2. *adj.* referring to such a point, as *percentile rank.*

percept (pûr'sept) 1. *n.* the object of perception. 2. *n.* the mental result of an act of perception. *Note* (def. 2): Some psychologists reject the notion of 'percept' on the grounds that perception is a process limited to the act of information processing of sensory stimuli. See **perception.**

perception (pər sep'shən) 1. *n.* the extraction of information from sensory stimulation. *Note:* Perception is an active and selective process and so may be influenced by a person's attitude and by prior experience. In all forms of communication, perception is the crucial link between incoming stimuli and a response that is meaningful. *Cp.* **cognition.** 2. *n.* the result of perceptual processing; comprehension; understanding. *Yes, I have a good perception of the situation.* 3. *n.* the direct, intuitive recognition of truth, beauty, value, etc., especially in moral or artistic judgments; insight. *His perceptions of poetry were always brilliant. Note:* Special types of percepton, as *auditory perception,* are given under the describing terms. *v.* **perceive;** *adj.* **perceptual.**

perceptual analysis the differentiation of a perceptual field into separable component parts, as in identifying correct letter order in a spelling word.

perceptual constancy the tendency for perceived properties of things to remain the same under changing conditions. *Note:* The size of a chair is perceived as constant regardless of the angle from which it is viewed. Properties such as size and shape are perceived as constant under perspective transformations.

perceptual decentration See **decentration.**

perceptually handicapped a person or group with faulty functioning in one or more aspects of perception: sensory, integrative, expressive, or social.

perceptual-motor learning learning characterized by change in overt motor responses that are activated and guided primarily by nonverbal rather than by verbal stimuli, as handwriting, typewriting, etc. *Note:* In perceptual-motor learning, someone may or may not give information about the task, but it is mainly learned by matching motor output with perceptual input.

perfect aspect (tense) See **present perfect aspect (tense).**

performance (pər fôr′məns) 1. *n.* task-directed activity, as *test performance.* 2. *n.* the result of such activity, as *a superior performance.* 3. *n.* entertainment, often dramatic or musical, as *a performance of* The Mikado. 4. *n.* the act or manner of providing entertainment, as *a splendid singing performance.* 5. *n.* in transformational-generative grammar, *the actual use of language in concrete situations* — N. Chomsky (1970). *Note:* The language used in speech may not reflect the speaker's knowledge of, or competence in, language because of speech errors, distortion of the speech signal, or emotional states. Recently, however, linguists are coming to recognize the value of information from actual speech, including slips of the tongue, to adequately describe both competence and performance of a native speaker of a language. *Cp.* **competence** (def. 2).

performance objective See **behavioral objective.**

performance standard an absolute or relative criterion level for judging the attainment of specified objectives. *Many reading programs with behavioral objectives use a performance standard of 80-85 per cent.*

performance test 1. a test composed of tasks that call for nonverbal responses, as *the object assembly test in the Wechsler Intelligence Scales.* 2. any test that calls for responses that are an actual work sample of the activity being measured, as in taking dictation by shorthand, typing business letters, etc.

perimacular vision vision involving the central area of the retina, including and surrounding the macula; paracentral vision.

perinatal (per″ə nāt′əl) *adj.* occurring at or near birth. *Cp.* **paranatal.**

period (pēr′ē əd) 1. *n.* a punctuation mark (.) used at the end of a declarative sentence, abbreviation, as Dr., or outline heading. 2. *n.* the full pause following the production of a sentence. 3. *n.* an utterance; a sentence. 4. *n.* a division of a school day.

periodical (pēr′ē od′i kəl) *n.* a type of serial, as a magazine or journal. See **serial** (def. 2).

periodical index 1. an index to one or more volumes of a single periodical contained within an issue of the periodical, or issued separately. 2. an index to a group of different periodicals issued at regular intervals and usually cumulative. Education Index *is a helpful periodical index for teachers.*

peripheral (pə rif′ər əl) 1. *adj.* having to do with the boundary, outside surface, or edge, as *peripheral vision.* 2. *adj.* having to do with the superficial rather than the essential aspects of something, as *peripheral knowledge.* 3. *adj.* away from the center, especially of the body; external; as *peripheral organs.* 4. *adj.* referring to nerves and nerve ends furthest from the brain and spinal cord. 5. *adj.* separate in place or function from the main computer but connected to it, as *a peripheral tape unit.* 6. *n.* the computer equipment thus separated. *n.* **periphery.**

peripheral field the outer visual field of the retina surrounding the macula and/or perimacular area. *The influence of visual cues in the . . . peripheral* *field is not a random one. Words are not likely to be pulled in from the peripheral field unless they fit in some ways with the semantic and syntactic cues the reader is processing and the predictions he is making* — K. Goodman (1975).

peripheral vision vision by the stimulation of the peripheral field of the retina, largely in shades of gray and most effective in low light conditions; indirect vision. *Word forms indistinctly seen in peripheral vision begin the perceptual process much in advance of direct vision* — M. Tinker (1965). *Ct.* **foveal vision** (def. 1).

periphrastic (per′ ə fras′tik) *adj.* referring to the use of an auxiliary word to indicate a grammatical function or relation rather than the use of an inflected form, as *her mother did know* for *her mother knew.*

perseveration (pər sev″ər ā′shən) 1. *n.* the tendency to repeat behavior(s) no longer useful or appropriate, or to fail to adapt to changing tasks and/or circumstances. 2. *n.* a compulsive repetition of such behavior, as the constant beating of the breast by a psychotic patient. 3. *n.* stuttering that continues because of failure to break away from a prior mental set. 4. *n.* the continuing of speech habits beyond normal developmental expectancy, as *the perseveration of baby talk in adolescence. Note:* Do not confuse *perseveration* with *perseverance. v.* **perseverate.**

person (pûr′sən) *n.* in English, the classification of pronouns according to the person speaking, or *first person* (*I, me*), the person spoken to, or *second person* (*you*), and the person or thing spoken about, or third person (*he, she, it, they*).

persona (pər sō′nə) *pl.* **personae** (-nē), **-nas.** 1. *n.* the role, literally 'mask,' assumed by a person in various situations, as *the persona of the president, Jim's persona in psychotherapy.* 2. *n.* a narrator introduced in a story, as Marlow in J. Conrad's *Lord Jim.* 3. **personae**, the cast of characters in a piece of fiction or in a play.

personality (pûr″sə nal′i tē) 1. *n.* the sum of all those characteristics that make one a unique person. 2. *n.* the pattern of a person's behavior as a whole. 3. *n.* a person's character as revealed to others. 4. *n.* a famous, infamous, or prominent person. 5. *n.* a distinctive property or characteristic of a thing. *This old farm house has a lot of personality.*

personality disorder a psychiatric term for any long-standing maladjustment that is not a psychosis, usually without feelings of anxiety, fear, or depression; character disorder. *Note:* A personality disorder is differentiated from a neurosis in that the latter is characterized by anxiety; a personality disorder is not. *Cp.* **mental disorder; emotional disorder.**

personality inventory a self-report questionnaire or checklist of personality characteristics, or a questionnaire about personality functioning.

personal pronoun a pronoun referring to one or more persons, as *I, he, she, it, we, they, me, us, my, mine.*

personification (pər son″ə fə kā′shən) 1. *n.* a metaphorical figure of speech in which animals, ideas, things, etc. are represented as having human qualities: *Come away, come away, Death,/And in sad cypress let me be laid* — Shakespeare. 2. *n.* that which a person, real or imaginary, represents. *She is the personification of good taste. Mars is the personification of war. v.* **personify.**

perspective (pər spek′tiv) 1. *n.* the representation of three-dimensional space on a two-dimensional surface so that angles retain their three-dimensional relations with respect to the position of the viewer; linear perspective; as *the perspective in a painting.* 2. *n.* a comprehensive, balanced view of the relationships of parts to the whole, as *a sound perspective of the situation.* 3. *n.* a scenic view: *What a lovely perspective!* 4. **temporal perspective,** a more balanced view of events, people, etc., that comes with time. 5. **in perspective,** in proper balance. *A good teacher must keep many demands in perspective.*

persuasion (pər swā′zhən) *n.* the intent to influence the reader or hearer to believe or do as the author or speaker suggests. *adj.* **persuasive.** *v.* **persuade.**

peruse (pə ro͞oz′) 1. *v.* to read carefully and critically; study. *It took two hours to peruse the report.* 2. *v.* to look over leisurely and casually; *He perused the newspaper while waiting for his air flight to leave. Note:* Context determines which of the meanings of *peruse* is intended.

petit mal (pə tē′ mal′; *Fr.* pə tē mᴀl′) an epileptic seizure with a sudden, very brief loss of consciousness with little visible movement. *The apparent signs of petit mal may be no more than a brief loss of visual fusion and an interruption in the continuity of experience. Cp.* **grand mal.** See also **epilepsy.**

petroglyph (pe′trə glif″) 1. *n.* a carving or inscription on a rock. 2. *n.* a primitive pictograph or set of pictographs cut into rock; petrograph. *adj.* **petroglyphic.**

petrogram (pe′trə gram″) See **petroglyph.**

petrograph (pe′trə graf″) See **petroglyph.** *n.* **petrography.** *adj.* **petrographic.**

phantasy (fan′tə sē, -zē) See **fantasy.**

pharyng (o)- a combining form indicating *the throat or pharynx;* as **pharyngeal, pharyngitis.**

pharynx (far′ingks) 1. *n.* that part of the throat which forms a chamber below the nasal cavity, behind the tongue and above the larynx and the esophagus, that is a flexible cavity for resonating speech sounds and for aiding swallowing. See illustration under **speech organs.** 2. *n.* the throat. *adj.* **pharyngeal.**

-phasia a combining form indicating *disordered speech;* as **dysphasia.**

phatic communion a term coined by B. Malinowski for stereotyped expressions spoken for social rather than informational purposes, as *'Have a nice day,' 'uh-huh,' 'You don't say?'*

phenobarbital (fē″nō bär′bi tal″, -tôl″, -nə-) *n.* a medical drug used as a sedative and as an anti-convulsant.

phi coefficient (ϕ) a measure of association between two variables, each of which is divided into two categories.

philology (fi lol′ə jē) *n.* the study of language through historical written records to understand more fully the interaction of people, language, and the historical-cultural setting, and to clarify texts and word origins. *Cp.* **linguistics; etymology.** *n.* **philologist.** *adj.* **philological.**

phi phenomenon perception of motion when one stationary light is flashed and followed by a flash from a second light stationed at a distance from the first, the two flashes giving the appearance of movement from the position of the first flash to that of the second when properly timed and spaced.

phobia (fō′bē ə) 1. *n.* an abnormal, irrational fear. 2. *n.* such a fear used as the final base in a compound word, as *claustrophobia.*

Phoenician alphabet one of the first alphabets, developed by Phoenicians and other Semites around 1000 B.C., from which Greek, Roman, and other western alphabets were derived.

phon (o) a combining form indicating *sound, voice;* as **phonic, phonovisual.**

phonation (fō nā'shən) *n.* the use of vocal fold vibrations by the air flow in making voiced speech sounds; voice production. *Cp.* **voicing** (def. 1).

phone (fōn) *n.* the smallest sound unit that is identifiable in spoken language and for which phonetic transcription is used, as in the *International Phonetic Alphabet.*

phoneme (fō'nēm) *n.* a minimal linguistic unit in spoken language whose replacement can result in a meaning difference, as */p/*, */b/* in *pin, bin. Note:* The application of this definition to a particular language is a linguistic problem, since phonemes must be determined by the nature and extent of their distribution in the language, their etymology, and their reality for speakers of the language. *Cp.* **allophone; phone.** *adj.* **phonemic.**

phoneme-grapheme correspondence the relationship between a phoneme and its graphemic representation(s), as /s/, spelled *s* in *sit, c* in *city, ss* in *grass. Note:* Technically, phoneme-grapheme correspondence refers to sound-to-letter correspondence, not vice versa. *Ct.* **grapheme-phoneme correspondence.**

phonemic alphabet 1. See **phonemic transcription.** 2. a writing system with a predominant one-to-one correspondence of phonemes with graphemes, and in which other correspondences are predictable by simple rules, as Turkish or Finnish alphabets.

phonemic analysis linguistic research designed to identify the number and distribution of speech sounds for a given language. See **phoneme.**

phonemic contrast an identifiable contrast between speech sounds which may occur in words with similar shapes but different meanings in the same context, as the difference between /t/ and /d/ in *lit* and *lid.*

phonemics (fə nē'miks, fō') (*with sing. v.) 1. n.* the pattern of relations between phonemes and between phonemes and their allophones. See **phoneme; allophone.** 2. *n.* the study of such relations. *Cp.* **phonology** (def. 1).

phonemic transcription 1. a notation system used by linguistics for recording speech in which a unique graphic symbol is provided for each phoneme of a language being studied; phonemic notation. *Note:* In phonemic transcription, discrete phonetic elements are not recorded as with a phonetic alphabet such as IPA. Rather, the major distinguishing speech sounds, or phonemes, are recorded. *Cp.* **phonetic transcription** (def. 1) 2. a text or string of words written in such a system.

phonetic (fə net'ik, fō-) 1. *adj.* referring to the nature, production, and transcription of speech sounds. 2. *adj.* corresponding to pronunciation. See **phonetic transcription** 3. *adj.* agreeing with pronunciation. See **phonetic spelling** (def. 1). 4. *adj.* referring to the description of non-distinctive elements of a language. *Vowel length in English is phonetic but not phonemic.* 5. *n.* in Chinese orthography, an element of a Chinese character which indicates sound.

phonetic alphabet 1. an alphabet containing a distinctive graphic character for each distinguishable speech sound, or phone, of a language, as the *International Phonetic Alphabet.* See **International Phonetic Alphabet (IPA).** *Note:* Phonetic alphabets are used by phoneticians and other linguists to record speech sounds on the basis of their articulatory features. Because different languages have different articulatory features, a phonetic alphabet with a uniform symbol for each human speech source makes it possible to record language differences uniformly. 2. a writing system developed for a language in which each speech sound is represented by its own distinctive letter or other graphic symbol. See **one-to-one correspondence** (def. 2). *Note:* Such alphabets are more properly called *phonemic alphabets* since a writing system that had symbols to record every distinguishable sound would be unwieldy and inefficient. See **phoneme.** *Cp.* **phonemic alphabet** (def. 2).

phonetic analysis 1. in teaching practice, a misnomer for phonic analysis. 2. in linguistics, the classifying and recording of individual speech sounds, or phones.

phonetician (fō″ni tish′ən) *n.* a specialist in the study and classification of speech sounds, including their transcription.

phonetic method 1. See **phonic method.** 2. a reading method in which the letters of a modified or augmented alphabet, as the Initial Teaching Alphabet or UNIFON, represent sounds. 3. an approach to the improvement of articulation by teaching the use and control of speech mechanisms.

phonetic notation See **phonetic transcription.**

phonetics (fə net′iks, fō) *(with sing. v.)* 1. *n.* the scientific study of speech sounds; specifically, their physical structure, production, transmission, and reception, as well as their transcription, analysis, and classification. *Note:* Phonetics is a general science that is not limited to any particular language. The International Phonetic Alphabet (IPA) is generally used by all phoneticians for language transcription. *Ct.* **phonics** (def. 1). 2. *n.* the application of this science to aid in distinguishing meanings among words. *Ct.* **phonemics.** 3. *n.* the system of speech sounds in any specific language.

phonetic spelling 1. the respelling of entry words in a dictionary or glossary according to a pronunciation key that shows the sounds represented by letters, as *read (rēd); read (red).* 2. incorrect spelling of a word as though it were phonically regular, as *det* for *debt.* 3. See **phonetic transcription.** See also **International Phonetic Alphabet (IPA).**

phonetic structure the sound patterns of a given language.

phonetic transcription 1. a system of graphic symbols for representing speech sounds or pronunciation; phonetic notation. See also **International Phonetic Alphabet (IPA.)** 2. the result of such representation.

phonetic word a misnomer for a phonically regular word whose pronunciation may be accurately predicted from its spelling. *Note:* 'Hit' is a phonically regular word, but 'colonel' and 'choir' are not.

phonetic writing See **phonetic alphabet; phonetic transcription.**

phonic analysis in teaching practice, the identification of words by their sounds. *Note:* The process of phonic analysis involves the association of speech sounds with letters and the blending of these sounds into syllables and words. See also **phonics; analytic phonics; synthetic phonics.**

phonic cue evidence in a spelling pattern in a word of the speech sound or sounds represented by a letter or group of letters. *Cp.* **phonic generalization; word family** (def. 1).

phonic generalization a statement or rule which indicates under which condition(s) a letter or group of letters represents a particular sound or sounds:

A silent e at the end of a syllable or word usually indicates that the preceding vowel sound is long, as the a *in* 'fate.'

phonic method a way of teaching reading in which the sounds represented by letters and letter combinations are emphasized in learning to identify words; sometimes called *phonetic method.*

phonics (fon′iks, fō niks) *(with sing. v.)* 1. *n.* an approach to the teaching of reading and spelling that stresses symbol-sound relationships, especially in beginning reading instruction. 2. *n.* instructional activities designed to teach reading and/or spelling through an emphasis upon the relationship of speech sounds to the letters and letter combinations that represent them. 3. *adj.* referring to such an approach or activities . . . *let any instructional activity (teaching strategy or independent practice) that emphasizes symbol-sound correspondence or rules (explicit or implicit) be called a phonics activity* — P. D. Pearson. *Note:* Special types of phonics, as *analytic phonics,* are given under the describing term. *Ct.* **phonetics** (def. 1).

phonogram (fō′nə gram″) 1. *n.* a graphic symbol, such as one in a phonetic alphabet, which can represent a sound, phoneme, or word. *Cp.* **character** (defs. 6-10); **letter** (def. 1); **graph** (def. 2); **grapheme.** 2. *n.* in some reading programs, a graphic sequence comprised of a vowel grapheme and an ending consonant grapheme, as the spelling *-ed* in *red, bed, fed.*

phonograph (fō′nə graf″, - gräf″) *n.* a machine which reproduces and amplifies sounds from records, usually discs, made for its use.

phonological feature See **distinctive feature** (def. 2).

phonological perception auditory perception applied to speech sounds, as in listening.

phonological rule 1. a concise account of some aspect of the sound patterns and processes of language or a language. 2. in transformational-generative phonology, a rule governing a particular phonological feature of a construction, including elements which precede and/or follow it, or are part of the same element. *Note:* A phonological rule may also delete, add, or exchange segments.

phonological system the pattern of phonological elements and rules that is either constructed or hypothesized to account for speech.

phonology (fō nol′ə jē, fə-) 1. *n.* the study of speech sounds and their functions in a language or languages. 2. *n.* the relation of the surface structure of a sentence to its actual physical representation. See also **generative phonology.**

phonotactics (fō″nō tak′tiks) *n. pl.* 1. the permissible arrangements of speech sounds in forming morphemes and words of a language or languages. 2. the study of such arrangements. *adj.* **phonotactic.**

phonovisual method a synthetic phonics program that uses a pictured key word for each sound.

phoria (fôr′ē ə) *n.* the tendency for the line of sight of the eyes to deviate when fusion is broken; heterophoria. *Ct.* **tropia.**

photo- a combining form indicating *light*; as **photophobia.**

photochemical (fō″tō kem′i kəl) *adj.* having to do with a chemical reaction produced or stimulated by light. *Visual images are formed by photochemical changes in the retina.*

photograph (fō′tə graf″, -gräf″) 1. *n.*

a camera image that may be printed on some kind of opaque sensitive material. 2. *v.* to take such a picture. *n.* **photography.** *adj.* **photographic.**

photo-offset (fō″tō ôf′set″, -of′-) *n.* an offset process in which photography is used to form the impression to be reproduced.

photophobia (fō″tə fō′bē ə) *n.* extreme sensitivity to light even at reasonably low light levels.

photopic vision (fō top′ik, -tō′ pik) daylight vison; vision under conditions of bright light; specifically, vision which relies mostly on the cones in the center of the retina for sharp color vision and for accurate visual discrimination. *Ct.* **scotopic vision.**

photostat (fō′tə stat″) *n.* a copy of the contents of a page, document, etc., reproduced on sensitized paper by a special camera.

phrase (frāz) 1. *n.* a grammatical construction without a subject and a predicate. a. in traditional grammar, such a group of two or more words. b. in transformational-generative grammar, a noun or verb construction consisting of either one word or two or more words. See **noun phrase; verb phrase.** *Ct.* **clause.** 2. *n.* one or more spoken words set off from the rest of an utterance by pauses. *A phrase represents a meaningful unit that is perceived by the speaker and that may help the listener understand the intended meaning* 3. *v.* to so group words to express meaning. 4. *n.* a saying or expression, as *a familiar phrase.* 5. *v.* to use words in a particular way, as *phrase ideas clearly in writing.* See also **phrasing.**

phrase-marker (frāz″mär′kər) 1. *n.* a syntactic description of the structure of a sentence, by a label in brackets or a tree diagram of its parts. 2. *n.* a preposition that marks a prepositional phrase.

phrase method a 'look-and-say' approach in which pupils first learn phrases rather than words in isolation.

phrase reading reading in which a meaning unit larger than a single word but less than a sentence is used in recognition.

phrase structure the arrangement of words and phrases into larger units up to the level of the sentence.

phrase structure grammar grammar concerned with identifying constituents of grammatical constructions and how they are related.

phrase structure rule in transformational-generative grammar, an instruction for rewriting a phrase structure. *For example, S ⟶ NP + VP is a phrase structure rule that indicates that S(entence) is 'rewritten' as a N(oun) P(hrase) and a V(erb) P(hrase).* See also **co-occurrence.**

phrasing (frā′ziŋ) 1. *n.* the way in which words are grouped in speaking or writing. *Note:* Phrasing may refer to the choice of words as well as to their manner of grouping pattern. 2. *n.* reading in thought units. 3. *n.* using slashes or extra spaces to mark thought units in material to be read, as *The man walked / into the room.* See also **phrase.**

phyl (o)- a combining form indicating *race, tribe, clan;* as **phylogenesis.**

phylogeny *or* **phylogenesis** (fī loj′ə nē; fī″lə jen′i sis) 1. *n.* the evolutionary development of an organism or a species; racial history. 2. *n.* the history or development of something, as *the phylogeny of a word. Cp.* **ontogeny** *or* **ontogenesis.** *adj.* **phylogenetic.**

physical abstraction (J. Piaget) the extraction of information directly from objects themselves, as color, weight, etc. *Ct.* **reflective abstraction.**

physical therapy (PT) physiotherapy.

physiogenic (fiz″ē ō jen′ik) *adj.* having to do with conditions arising from within the organism; organic. *Ct.* **functional** (def. 2); **psychogenic.**

physiology (fiz″ē ol′ə jē) 1. *n.* the study of life processes in living organisms or in their parts. 2. *n.* the life processes thus involved. *adj.* **physiological.**

physiology of reading 1. broadly, the study of physiological factors which affect or are affected by the reading process. 2. specifically, the application of medical, neurological, anatomical, and physiological concepts and techniques to an examination of organic functions and dysfunctions involved in the act of reading. *Note:* The physiology of reading usually includes the specific fields of vision, speech, and hearing, and sometimes severe reading difficulties, learning disabilities, and the exceptional child.

physiotherapy (PT) (fiz″ē ō ther′ə pē) *n.* medically directed treatment which uses natural and physical forces rather than drugs or surgery; physical therapy. *Water, heat, light, massage, and special exercises are used in physiotherapy to provide comfort and healing treatment to ill persons. n.* **physiotherapist.**

pica (pī′kə) 1. *n.* a unit of measurement in printing that is slightly more than 4 mm. (1/6 in.) 2. *n.* a rather large type size, popular for typewriters. *Ct.* **elite.**

picaresque (pik″ə resk′) 1. *adj.* referring to an episodic novel originating in Spain, with a rascal hero whose escapades are told in realistic and often humorous detail, as Cervantes' *Don Quixote.* 2. *adj.* referring to any fiction dealing with rogues or adventurers.

pickin' up corn disjointed oral reading by letters and syllables, just as chickens peck at corn, kernel by kernel.

pictogram (pik′tə gram″) 1. *n.* See **pictograph.** 2. *n.* any pictorial representation of numerical information.

pictograph (pik′tə graf″, -gräf″) 1. *n.* a picture representing a word, or idea, as the pointing hand used to direct the reader to the index of a book. 2. *n.* one character in a pictographic writing system. *adj.* **pictographic.**

pictography (pik tog′rə fē) 1. *n.* a graphic system in which pictures are drawn to directly represent objects, events, and ideas, as ☼ for *sun. Ct.* **ideography** (def. 1). 2. *n.* the use of such a system; picture-writing. See **logo-syllabic writing; hieroglyphics.**

pictorial writing 1. a writing system in which words or concepts are represented by pictographs; pictography; picture writing. 2. any representation of ideas or words by pictures. *Cp.* **rebus.** See also **writing system.**

picture (pik′chər) *n.* a graphic illustration, including photographs, drawings, paintings, and their reproductions.

picture book a book in which the illustrations are as important as the text or written story. *Note:* Picture books are 'read' by very young children as well as those in primary grades. They are also usually the first books that parents show and read to their children.

picture clue information from a picture or other nonverbal illustration that helps the reader understand the meaning of the text or identify a word in that text.

picture dictionary a dictionary of words in alphabetical order, with corresponding pictures designed to introduce children to the concept of a dictionary and aid word identification.

pidgin (pij'ən) 1. *n.* a non-native language developed when speakers of different languages are placed in close social contact, as traders in the western Pacific. *Note:* If pidgin becomes a native language, it is said to have become creolized. *Cp.* **creole** (def. 1); **lingua franca.** 2. *adj.* referring to such a language, as *pidgin English.*

pinna (pin'ə) *pl.* **-nae** (ē), **-nas.** *n.* the auricle, the most visible part of the outer ear.

piracy *or* **pirating** *n.* the publication of a work without the permission of its copyright owner. *Note:* Such an edition is known as a *pirated edition.*

pitch (pich) 1. *n.* the rise and fall of the voice, or intonation pattern, in an utterance which helps a listener understand the intended meaning of the speaker. 2. *n.* the perception of the tonal level of sound ranging from high to low depending on the frequency of sound waves. 3. *n.* standard tonal frequency with which tonal levels of sound may be compared. *The pitch of middle C is 264 Hz. Pat sings off pitch.*

pitch discrimination the ability to detect small differences in the tonal level of sounds. *Pitch discrimination is very important in tonal languages such as Chinese, but much less so in other languages.*

pituitary gland an endocrine gland located at the base of the brain which secretes hormones that aid in the growth, development, and reproduction of the individual.

pivot class in early language acquisition, a small number of frequently used words which occur in a fixed position in a sentence. See also **open class.** *Note:* Young children use pivot words as anchors to build sentences upon, as *allgone* in *allgone milk, allgone truck, allgone Daddy.*

placebo (plə sē'bō) *n.* a medication, often in the form of a pill, or a procedure that is given to patients which makes them feel better because they are getting treatment, but which actually has no active medical or therapeutic value. *A placebo is often used as a control in research studies to conceal the active medicine from both the patient and the physician. Note:* Placebo comes from the Latin 'I shall be pleasing.'

placement test a test used to assign persons to different levels of instruction, as *a college English placement test.*

plagiarism (plā'jə riz"əm, -jē ə riz"-) *n.* the presentation of another's writing ideas as one's own; stealing another's work. *n.* **plagiarist.** *v.* **plagiarize.**

plan (plan) 1. *n.* a purposeful scheme for action that is thought about in advance to reach a specified goal, as *a plan for vacation reading.* 2. *v.* to make such a plan. 3. *n.* a graphic representation of spatial relations, as in a map, sketch, diagram, blueprint, etc. 4. *n.* a psychological construct to explain goal-oriented behavior in animals, as in learning to run a maze.

plateau (pla tō') *n.* a period of little or no apparent change in performance which, however, may represent periods of consolidation of subordinate types of learning *The relatively long, flat parts of a learning curve are plateaus.* See illustration under **learning curve.**

play therapy a structured therapeutic technique in which a therapist encourages a child to act out, usually with puppets, dolls, or other toys, familial and other conflicts to release tensions or to provide insight into the nature of psychological problems. *Cp.* **family therapy; psychodrama; role-**

playing (def. 3); **sociodrama.**

-plegia, -plegy a combining form indicating *paralysis*; as **paraplegia.**

PLORE an acronym for Predict, Locate, Organize, Remember, Evaluate—a sequential approach to study, each step of which can be taught directly by classroom teachers.

plosive (plō′siv) *n.* any speech sound made by stopping the air flow and then suddenly releasing it through the mouth, as /p/ in *put.* See also **stop** (def. 2).

plot (plot) 1. *n.* the structure of the action of a story. *Note:* In conventional stories, written or acted, plot has three main parts: rising action, climax, and falling action (resolution or denouement.) See also **action** (def. 2), **climax** (def. 1). 2. *v.* to so structure the action of a story. 3. *n.* a pattern of related episodes: *the arrangement of the incidents* — Aristotle. 4. *n.* a secret plan, usually evil or unlawful. 5. *v.* to make such a plan, as *plot to assassinate.* 6. *v.* to plan or lay out something, as *plot a graph, plot a course on a map.* 7. *v.* to make a frequency table or scatter diagram of scores. 8. *n.* a scatter diagram.

plot structure See **plot** (def. 1).

pluperfect aspect (tense) See **past perfect aspect (tense).**

plural (plŏŏr′əl) *n.* in English, a grammatical category of number referring to more than one, as *boys* and *girls* in *The boys and girls played baseball.* See **number.** *Ct.* **singular.**

plurilingualism (plŏŏr″ə liŋ′gwəl izm) See **multilingualism.**

plurisyllable (plŏŏr″ē sil′ə bəl) *n.* a word with more than one syllable; polysyllabic word. *adj.* **plurisyllabic.**

plus lens a convex lens used to make parallel light rays converge, thus magnifying objects. See illustration under **lens.** *Ant.* **minus lens.**

pneumoencephalogram (nŏŏ″mō en sef′ə lə gram″, nyŏŏ″-) *n.* an X-ray of the head taken after the fluid in spaces of the brain and spinal cord has been drained and replaced with a gas. *A pneumoencephalogram shows the shape and location of the ventricles in the brain.*

pocket chart a holder for flash cards or other educational material.

poem (pō′əm) 1. *n.* a composition in which word images are selected and expressed in metrical form to create imaginative impressions of power and beauty in the listener or reader. 2. *n.* such a composition not in metrical form, as *a prose poem.* 3. *n.* something suggestive of the qualities of a poem. *The dance was as beautiful as a poem.* See also **poetry; verse** (def. 2).

poet (pō′it) 1. *n.* a composer of poetry. 2. *n.* a highly imaginative and creative person with remarkable powers of poetic expression, as *a Dante, a Goethe, or a Walt Whitman.*

poetic (pō et′ik) 1. *adj.* having to do with poets or poetry, as *poetic license.* 2. *adj.* expressed in verse. *The ode is a poetic form.* 3. *adj.* having the qualities of a poet, as *poetic imagination. adj.* **poetical.**

poetic justice 1. the view often found in fiction and drama that, ideally, the good are rewarded and the evil punished. 2. an instance in which a person or character gets, in an unsympathetic and often ironic manner, what is deserved.

poetic license the liberty taken by poets and other writers to depart from convention or logic to attain a desired end by adjustments in rhyme, meter, etc.

poetics (pō et′iks) *(with sing. v.)* 1. *n.* the study of the principles and rules for the composition of poetry or other aesthetic forms. 2. *n.* an example of such a study. 3. *n.* poetic expressions or feelings.

poetic writing a term employed by J. Britton and others (1975) to describe the use of prose or poetry as an art form; specifically, one in which the sounds of the writer's language, the writer's feelings, and the writer's ideas are patterned in a way that is pleasing to the writer and that likewise may be shared and enjoyed by the reader. *Cp.* **creative writing.** See also **expressive writing; transactional writing.**

poetry (pō′i trē) 1. *n.* the selection and expression of word images in metrical form to create imaginative impressions in the listener or reader. 2. *n.* literature in metrical form; verse. *Note:* While all poetry is verse, such verse as doggerel is not poetry. 3. *n.* the art of writing poems. 4. *n.* something that has poetic qualities, as *prose poetry, the poetry of ballet.* See also **poem.**

point (point) 1. *n.* a reason or purpose, usually valid, for an argument or action. *What is the point you are making?* 2. an idea presented for consideration. *The point is that we must act now.* 3. *n.* a diacritical mark. 4. *n.* a unit of measurement in printing, .34mm. (about 1/72 in.), used for determining type height, as *10-point type*, and amount of spacing.

point-biserial correlation a correlation between two variables, only one of which is assumed to be continuous and normal in distribution, the other having only two conditions, as a correlation between grade point average and male or female sex. *Cp.* **biserial correlation; tetrachoric correlation.**

pointing test a test of eyedness. *Note:* The subject is asked to point to a distant object with one arm fully extended and both eyes open. The dominant eye is determined by noting which eye is in line with the finger and the target.

point of regard the point in the visual field to which attention is directed.

point of view the way in which an author reveals characters, events, and ideas in telling a story. *Note:* With an omniscient or 'all-knowing' point of view, an author sees all, hears all, knows all. A limited point of view, by contrast, may be that of one person who knows only what he sees, hears, and feels, or what others tell him. Although this term is usually restricted to fiction, it may be used to differentiate points of view in nonfiction, as in the personal essay, the judicial editorial, or the encyclopedia article in terms of their relative subjectivity or objectivity.

Pollyanna theme a narrative with the same characteristics of the heroine Pollyanna who sees only the best in every person or situation, no matter how deplorable.

poly- a prefix indicating *many*; as **polysyllabic.**

polygenesis (pol″ē jen′i sis) 1. *n.* a theory that a myth with origins in several cultures is derived from the fact that all persons have the same needs and desires. 2. *n.* a theory that the world's languages have different origins as opposed to a common one.

polyglot (pol′ē glot″) 1. *adj.* knowing several languages; multilingual. 2. *adj.* having, made up of, or in several languages, as *a polyglot edition.* 3. *n.* a mixture or confusion of languages. 4. *n.* a multilingual person. 5. *n.* a book, notably the Bible, printed in many languages.

polygraph (pol′ē graf″, -gräf″) *n.* an instrument for recording several kinds of data at once; especially, for recording physiological reactions, as blood pressure, heart rate, breathing patterns, galvanic skin response, etc. *A lie detector is a polygraph used to assess stress.*

polyphony (pə lif′ə nē) *n.* the representation of more than one speech sound by the same grapheme, as *o* in *son, roll,* and *cod. Cp.* **heterography** (def. 1); **one-to-one correspondence** (def. 2). *n.* **polyphone.** *adj.* **polyphonic.**

polysemantic (pol″ē si man′tik) *adj.* having more than one related meaning.

polysemy (pol′ē sē″mē) *n.* a term applied to words that have more than one related meaning; multiple meaning. *Note:* The term is used only to refer to the variant meanings of one base word or dictionary entry; it does not apply to all meanings of homonyms such as *mood*[1] (feeling) and *mood*[2] (verb form).

polysyllabic (pol″ē si lab′ik) *adj.* containing more than one syllable, as *a polysyllabic word. n.* **polysyllable.**

pons (ponz) *pl.* **pontes** (pon′tēz). 1. *n.* the uppermost portion of the brainstem connecting the cerebellum and the cerebrum, as *the pons cerebelli, pons Varolii.* See illustration under **brain.** 2. *n.* any bridge of tissue connecting two parts of an organ. *adj.* **pontine.**

pop culture the art, fashions, music, etc., of a period of contemporary mass culture, as blue jeans, rock and roll, Andy Warhol's oversize painting of a can of tomato soup.

population (pop″yə lā′shən) 1. *n.* in statistical analysis, the entire group of persons, objects, etc., finite or infinite, to which a study refers; universe. *Populations are what samples are drawn from.* 2. *n.* all the persons, objects, etc., found in a given area at a particular time; geographical population.

pornography (pôr nog′rə fē) *n.* obscene literature or graphic art having little or no aesthetic merit or redeeming social value. *adj.* **pornographic.**

portapak (pōr′tə pak″, pôr′-) *n.* a portable videotape recorder/player.

portmanteau word (pōrt man′tō, pôrt-; port″man tō′) a word made by putting together parts of other words, as *motor* and *hotel* to make *motel. Cp.* **fusion** (def. 6); **syncretism** (def. 3).

positive degree the base form of an an adjective, as *old,* or adverb, as *rapidly,* in contrast to the comparative and superlative degrees. *Cp.* **comparative degree; superlative degree.**

positive diagnosis a finding which indicates that the diagnosis was correct. *An audiometric test gave a positive diagnosis of a hearing difficulty. Ct. negative diagnosis* under **diagnosis** (def. 3).

positive transfer the improvement of the effectiveness of some behavior or learning because of earlier behaviors or of prior learning efforts. *Ct.* **negative transfer.** See also **transfer** (def. 1).

possessive (pə zes′iv) 1. *adj.* showing possession, ownership, or origin. 2. *n.* a noun or pronoun form indicating ownership or possession, as *cat's* in *cat's claws, his* in *his shoes,* and *hunger's* in *hunger's pain. Note:* In English, the apostrophe (') is commonly used to indicate the possessive. 3. See **possessive case.** *Cp.* **genitive.**

possessive case a case form which shows possession, origin, etc.

post- a prefix indicating *after* (in time or position); as **posttest.**

post alveloar behind the gum ridge: referring to any speech sound made with the tongue near or touching the back of the alveolar ridge.

poster (pō′stər) *n.* a large picture, illustration, or placard exhibited in a public place to announce or advertise something.

posterior (po stēr′ē ər, pō-) 1. *adj.*

toward the back. *The visual centers of the brain are in the posterior part of the head. Ant.* **anterior** (def. 1). See also **dorsal.** 2. *adj.* coming after in time. *Conclusions are usually posterior to hypotheses.* 3. *adj.* referring to the tail end of the body; caudal.

posterior chamber the space inside the eyeball behind the lens, from the lens to the retina, filled with vitreous humor. See illustration under **eye.** *Cp.* **anterior chamber.**

posttest (*n.* pōst′test″; *v.* pōst test′) 1. *n.* the assessment of learning at the end of an experiment, a learning task, or an instructional period. 2. *v.* to so assess. *Cp.* **pretest** (def. 1).

postulate (*n.* pos′c̣hə lit, -lāt″; *v.* pos′c̣hə lāt″) 1. *n.* a proposition or principle assumed to be true, even without direct evidence, in an argument or reasoning process; premise; axiom. *Postulates often have heuristic value in theory development.* 2. *v.* to take something for granted; accept something as true without proof.

potboiler (pot′boi″lər) *n.* (*Informal.*) a work without literary or artistic merit, produced for money. *Many noted authors have written potboilers for economic reasons.*

potential (pə ten′s̱həl) 1. *adj.* possible as opposed to actual, as *the potential need for reading specialists.* 2. *adj.* capable of being or becoming, as *a potential area of crime.* 3. *n.* unexerted ability; undeveloped intellectual capability. *Few students ever reach their full potential. n.* **potentiality.**

pothook (pot′ho͝ok″) (*Brit.*) 1. *n.* (*An old use.*) a curved or hooked stroke (J) made in writing; an element practiced in beginning handwriting instruction, usually in the phrase *pothooks and hangers: She's scrawling pothooks and hangers on a dirty piece of paper* (1887). See also **hanger.** 2. *n.* a written scrawl, as that used by many noted writers.

pourquoi story (po͝or kwä′) a folk tale that explains the *why* (*pourquoi,* from the French) of certain customs, physical events, or animal behavior, as *Why the Bear Is Stumpy-Tailed.*

power (pou′ər) 1. *n.* the ability to function effectively, as *the power of belief.* 2. *n.* a specific capacity or skill; often *pl.,* as *one's powers of concentration.* 3. *n.* authority; control. *The power of the teacher to enforce school rules comes directly from the School Board.* 4. *v.* to exercise authority, control, or strength, as *power oneself through the crowd.* 5. *n.* the amount of magnification of a lens or optical system; refractive power; focal power. *Optical power is usually expressed in diopters.* 6. *n.* the product of a number times itself one or more times, or an exponent of a number which indicates how many times the number is to be multiplied by itself, as the superscript ^{3} of 10^3.

power test a test with items usually ranging from easy to very difficult, and with time limits generous enough to permit all items to be attempted. *Ct.* **speed test.**

practice (prak′tis) 1. *n.* an act that is the specified response(s) to a given stimulus situation; specifically, an act that is repeated one or several times, presumably to improve or fixate it, as *spelling practice. Note:* Practice is considered an essential element in many kinds of learned behaviors. 2. *v.* to so act or repeat an act. 3. *v.* to rehearse or drill, as *band practice.* 4. *n.* an habitual or usual act, as *one's practice to have ham and eggs for breakfast.* 5. *n.* a professional occupation, as *medical practice.*

practice effect change due to practice; specifically, in test performance, any change desirable or otherwise, as *the practice effect of taking a test.*

practicum (prak'tə kəm) *n.* the supervised practice of professional skills, often in an academic training program, and usually conducted in a clinic or in the field.

pragmatic (prag mat'ik) *adj.* practical in point of view, application, outcome, etc., as *a pragmatic approach. n.* **pragmatism.**

pragmatics (prag mat'iks) (*with sing. v.)* 1. *n.* the study of meanings as they are influenced by social or cultural context or by the use of language for particular intentions. *Ct.* **semantics** (def. 3). 2. *n.* the study of the relation of signs to their interpreters and/or the study of the *origin, uses and effects of signs within the behavior in which they occur* — C. Morris. See **semiotics; sign** (defs. 1-3). 3. *n.* the analysis of meaning in natural language use, as opposed to that in formal logical systems.

pre- a prefix indicating *before* (in time or position); as **prenatal.**

prebound (prē'bound) 1. *adj.* prelibrary-bound. 2. *n.* a new book bound in library binding before or at the time of original sale. See **library edition.**

précis (prā sē', prā'sē) *n.* a concise written summary of the essential ideas in something read. *Students wrote a short précis to show their understanding of the novel.*

pre-determiner *n.* a word or group of words in a noun phrase occurring before an article or other determiner, as *all* in *all my children.*

predicate (*n., adj.* pred'ə kit; *v.* pred'ə kāt") 1. *n.* the part of a sentence which expresses something about the subject; verb phrase; as *is difficult* in *The book is difficult. Ct.* **subject** (def. 3). 2. *adj.* belonging to the predicate, as *a predicate adjective.* 3. *n.* that part of a proposition which asserts something about the subject or about an argument. See **proposition** (defs. 3, 4). 4. *v.* to imply or to assert something. *The ability to read predicates language and intellectual competence.* 5. *v.* to be a basis for.

predicate adjective an adjective or adjectival phrase which modifies a noun in the complement of a predicate, as a *good teacher* in *She is a good teacher.*

predicate nominative a noun or noun phrase used as a complement of a linking verb; predicate noun; as *a painting* in *Her gift to John was a painting.*

predicate noun See **predicate nominative.**

predication (pred"ə kā'shən) 1. *n.* the act of asserting, as *the predication of a proposition.* 2. *n.* something so asserted. 3. *n.* the relation expressed by a predicate to a subject in a sentence, as that between *rang* and *the telephone* in *The telephone rang.*

predicative sentence a sentence that identifies something by name or class: *John is a Catholic. Ct.* **existential sentence.**

predictability (pri dikt"ə bil'i tē) *n.* the quality of a written work which enables the reader to foretell how it will develop and end. *adj.* **predictable.**

prediction (pri dik'shən) *n.* the act, or result, of making a forecast or prophecy; specifically, in scientific method, a statement of what is expected from observation or experiment. *v.* **predict.** *adj.* **predictive.** *n.* **predictor.**

prediction strategy a person's use of knowledge about language and the context in which it occurs to anticipate what is coming in writing or speech. *If, at the end of a line, one reads 'Thanks-,' one's prediction strategy might be to* *expect the word 'Thanksgiving.'*

predictive validity the capability of a test to foretell future performance. See also **validity** (def. 3).

predisposition (prē dis″pə zis͟h′ən, prē″dis-) 1. *n.* a tendency to act in a predictable way; inclination; as *a predisposition to laugh at any joke.* 2. *n.* a more than usual tendency to contract disease(s), sometimes because of genetic factors. *v.* **predispose.**

preface (pref′is) *n.* a preliminary statement, often made by the author in a publication, giving its purpose, organization, and scope, acknowledging assistance, etc. *Cp.* **introduction.**

prefix (prə̄′fiks) *n.* an affix which precedes the root or stem of a word, as *re-* in *reprint.*

prejudice (prej′ə dis) 1. *n.* an attitude expressed as a preconceived opinion either favorable or unfavorable; bias. 2. *n.* a strong, unfavorable attitude, especially toward other racial groups, 3. *v.* to express a biased attitude.

preliterate (prē lit′ər it) 1. *adj.* referring to a culture not having or leaving a written record. 2. *adj.* referring to a child, usually before entering school or in kindergarten, who has not yet learned to read.

premature (prē″mə to͝or′, -tyo͝or′, -c͟ho͝or′, prē′mə c͟ho͝or″) 1. *adj.* coming too soon; occurring or done before the proper time; as *premature diagnosis.* 2. *adj.* born before the normal period of gestation.

premise (prem′is) 1. *n.* an assumption; a proposition that supports or leads to a conclusion. *A premise of Aristotle's philosophy is: 'Man is a rational animal.'* 2. *v.* to make or state such an assumption.

prenatal (prē nāt′ᵊl) *adj.* before birth or before giving birth.

preoperational thought (J. Piaget) representational rather than logical thought in mental development, usually from about 2-7 years, that is characterized by egocentrism, centration, syncretism, absence of reversibility, and lack of concern with proof or logical justification.

preposition (prep′ə zis͟h′ən) *n.* a class of function words that are followed by nouns, creating a prepositional phrase, as *in, at, by, with* in *in the house, at the game, by the river, with a grin.*

prepositional phrase a preposition plus the noun phrase that follows it, as *over the river.* See also **preposition.**

preprimer (prē prim′ər) *n.* in a basal reading series, a booklet or booklets in which stories to be read by students are first introduced.

prereading (prē rē′diŋ) 1. *n.* reading something silently before oral reading to determine the type of expression, pacing, and voice projection needed for oral interpretation. 2. *adj.* having to do with activities before learning to read or before the act of reading, as *prereading skills, a prereading introduction to an author.*

pre-reading activities 1. activities designed to develop needed attitudes and skills before formal instruction in reading. *These activities may range from learning to recognize their own names in print to listening to the teacher read a story or poem* — M. Monroe and B. Rogers (1964). 2. activities engaged in before the reading act, as the student looking over study questions, the teacher giving the background of a story, etc.

presbyopia (prez″bē ō′pē ə, pres″-) *n.* the loss of accommodation power as the crystalline lens of the eye becomes less elastic with age. *A person with presbyopia needs either eyeglasses or longer arms to read a book. n.* **presbyope.** *adj.* **presbyopic.**

preschool (*adj.* prē′skool′; *n.* prē′skool″)

1. *adj.* having to do with educational programs for children between infancy and entrance to grade 1 or to kindergarten, but usually for three- or four-year-olds. 2. *n.* a school or class for preschool children.

prescriptive grammar 1. an approach to language which attempts to establish rules for correct usage. 2. a grammar based on such an approach, often called traditional grammar. *Ct.* **descriptive grammar** (def. 1).

prescriptive linguistics See **prescriptive grammar.**

prescriptive teaching See **diagnostic-prescriptive instruction.**

present participle a verb form that indicates ongoing action, as *sleeping* in *She was sleeping,* and can be used as an adjectival, as *sleeping* in *the sleeping baby. Note:* The present participle is identical in form with a gerund, as *Sleeping* in *Sleeping on the job can get you fired.* See also **gerund.**

present perfect aspect (tense) a verb aspect in English that indicates an action or state that was begun and completed before the utterance, or is still going on at the time of the utterance. *Note:* It is marked by the auxiliary verb *have* plus a past participle, as *have* and *eaten* in *I have already eaten.*

present progressive aspect (tense) a verb aspect in English that indicates an action or state going on at the time of the utterance, as *We are going now,* or will happen in the future, as *We are leaving tomorrow.*

present tense a verb form that shows an action or state which occurs at the time of the utterance, as *speaks* in *She speaks well.*

preservice education education, either undergraduate or graduate, in preparation for employment.

prestige dialect a social or regional variety of a language spoken by a privileged and socially-esteemed class. *Parisian French and Received Pronunciation (the King's or Queen's English) are prestige dialects, respectively, in France and in England.*

prestige effect an effect of reading noted by Waples; specifically, one which makes one feel better about oneself by reducing feelings of inferiority. *Prestige effects are served by sentimental fiction... with characters expressly drawn to encourage the readers to identify themselves with characters they would like to resemble.* —D. Waples and others (1940). *Cp.* **effects of reading.**

prestige language a language spoken by members of groups who enjoy a certain degree of esteem, power, and social prominence, as French in Haiti.

prestige newspaper a newspaper generally thought to be of very high quality. The New York Times *and* The Christian Science Monitor, *among others, are prestige newspapers.*

presupposition (prē″sup ə zish′ən) *n.* a notion or concept assumed or supposed by an individual in advance of communication with another. *Authors make a presupposition of knowledge on the part of the readers. v.* **presuppose.**

preterit *or* **preterite** (pret′ər it) *n.* a verb tense form indicating past or completed action; past tense.

pretest (*n.* prē′test; *v.* prē test′) 1. *n.* a test given before instruction or experiment; specifically: a. a test comparable to a posttest to be administered later. b. a test designed to help interpret instruction or experimental behavior, as a test of ability. 2. *n.* a practice test. 3. *v.* to give such a test.

preview (prē′vyo͞o″) 1. *n.* a survey to

get an overview of something that will be read or viewed later in a different way, as *a preview of a text.* 2. *v.* to make such a survey, as *preview a film.*

primary accent 1. the vowel or syllable in a word, phrase, or metrical foot, with the strongest and loudest emphasis; primary stress. 2. an orthographic symbol placed above a vowel grapheme (ʹ), adjacent to a syllable (ʼ), or above a syllable in a line of verse (¯), to indicate that the marked vowel or syllable has the strongest emphasis in contrast to some other vowel or syllable. *In pronunciations given in this dictionary, the diacritical mark (ʹ) is used to show primary accent or stress. Ct.* **secondary accent.** See also **stress** (def. 7); **diacritic** *or* **diacritic (-al) mark.**

primary reading disability *or* **retardation** developmental dyslexia. *Note:* According to R. Rabinovitch, primary reading retardation reflects a disturbance in neurological organization without evidence of brain injury. *Cp.* **secondary reading disability** *or* **retardation.**

primary school *(Brit.)* a school for children aged 5-11. *Note:* Primary school children are often separately housed by age in an infant school and in a junior school.

primary source an original record, document, etc., of an authoritative nature consulted in preparing a later work on some subject. *Boswell's letters and journals are primary sources for his biographers. Ct.* **secondary source.**

primary stuttering nonfluent speech which young children use without awareness. Ct. **secondary stuttering.**

primary typewriter a machine for typing large manuscript lettering, often used by teachers in preparing seatwork for beginning readers, or for typing children's own stories in the experience approach.

prime (prīm) 1. *n.* in text copy, any mark placed above and to the right of a letter to indicate a letter different from the unmarked version, as in *a′, a*[1]*, a.″* 2. *n.* a mark placed above and to the right of a number to indicate a quantity being measured, as *the prime 6′ to represent feet, minutes of angle, or minutes of time.*

primer (prim′ər) 1. *n.* a beginning book for the teaching of reading; specifically, the first comprehensive textbook in a basal reading series, usually preceded by a readiness book and one or more preprimers. 2. *n.* an easy-to-read, introductory book on any subject. 3. *n. (Brit.)* from the 14th century, a devotional handbook for laypersons, offering the fundamental prayers of Christianity: *this Primer or boke of praiers in Englyshe* (1546). 4. *n.* a small book for introducing children to reading and to Christianity as in def. 3, but with reading instructional material added in the form of the alphabet, lists of syllables, and words: *The Indian Primer; or, the way of training up of our Indian Youth... in the Knowledge of the Scriptures and in an ability to Reade* — Eliot (1669).

principal parts the set of inflected forms of a grammatical class, as *sing, sang, sung.*

principle (prin′sə pəl) 1. *n.* a basic law; axiom; as *principles of geometry.* 2. *n.* a generalization about natural phenomena that is usually not as well-verified as a law, as *the principle of feedback.* 3. *n.* an accepted rule of action or conduct. 4. *n.* a sense of responsibility for one's right conduct, as *act on principle.*

principle of least effort the notion that all organisms tend to choose the easiest path to the goal.

print (print) 1. *n.* a way of communicating by books, newspapers, magazines, etc.; a printed publication. *Print is a channel of communication* — D. Waples and others (1940). 2. *n.* the process of reproducing impressions by transferring them from an inked surface to another surface, as paper, cloth, plastic, etc.; printing. 3. *n.* the impressions so produced. 4. *v.* to so reproduce impressions or cause them to be reproduced; publish. 5. See **manuscript** (def. 1). 6. See **manuscript writing.** 7. *v.* to write using manuscript forms. 8. *n.* a positive photographic image. 9. *v.* to make such a finished photographic image. 10. *v.* to publish. 11. **in print,** published or available from a publisher. 12. **out of print,** no longer available from a publisher. 13. **printout,** a record made by a computer. *adj.* **printed.**

printing (prin′ting) 1. See **print** (def. 2). 2. See **manuscript writing.**

print-script See **manuscript writing.**

prism (priz′əm) *n.* a transparent, solid body, with two or more plane surfaces that are not parallel, which reflects, bends, or disperses light rays passing through it. *Prisms in eyeglasses are used to bend light to help a deviating eye receive visual stimuli in the foveal area. adj.* **prismatic.**

prism diopter (P.D.) a unit of measurement of the turning power of a prism; specifically, the angle that would cover a target one centimeter at a distance of one meter from the prism. *Prism diopters are used for measuring the deviation of the lines of sight in heterophoria, heterotropia, and convergence* — F. Jobe (1976). *Cp.* **diopter.**

private school See **independent school.**

proactive inhibition in learning a series of numbers, names, etc., the interfering effect of the learning of the earlier part of the series with learning the latter part of the series. *Ct.* **retroactive inhibition.**

probability (prob″ə bil′i tē) 1. *n.* a likely event or occurrence. 2. *n.* the likelihood (p) that a particular event will occur. *If the results of an experiment have a probability of* $p<.01$*, such results have a probability of happening less than once in a hundred similar instances. adj.* **probable.**

probable error (PE, P.E.) an estimate, now seldom used, of the typical size of errors of measurement. *The probable error is 0.6745 times the standard error. Cp.* **standard error (SE, S.E.).**

problem novel *or* **play** a novel or play in which the action is focused on difficult choices, as in Steinbeck's *Grapes of Wrath,* Ibsen's *An Enemy of the People.*

problem-solving 1. *n.* the process of selecting appropriate behaviors for reaching desired goals. *Trial-and-error is the least organized form of problem-solving.* 2. *adj.* referring to such a process.

process (pros′es; *esp. Brit.* prō′ses) 1. *n.* a systematic series of actions toward some end, as *the process of diagnosis.* 2. *n.* a specific, continuous action, operation, or change, as *the reading process, growth processes.* 3. *n.* the act of advancing or proceeding, as *a disease process.* 4. *n.* something projecting outward or from within the body, as *the mastoid process.* 5. *v.* to use a process, as *process a case study, process a court summons.* 6. *adj.* having to do with photomechanical or photoengraving methods, as *process printing.*

processing (pros′es″ing̑) 1. *n.* the course of active change in some specific way, especially in psychological activity, as *the processing of text.* See **bottom-up processing; interactive processing; top-down processing.** 2. *n.* the mechanical or electronic handling of data; information processing.

process objective an educational goal that is stated in terms of how it is to be reached.

product (prod′əkt, -ukt) 1. *n.* an outcome; end result. *Good listening habits are the product of learning to pay attention to what is said.* 2. *n.* the result of multiplication. *Four is the product of two times two.*

productive language speaking and writing.

product-moment coefficient (r) the coefficient obtained by product-moment, or Pearsonian, correlation. See **product-moment correlation.**

product-moment correlation a correlation expressed by the coefficient r between two or more variables. *Note:* A positive r, as r = .63, means that two variables change in the same direction; i.e., when one variable increases in value, so does the correlated one. A negative r, as r = -.46, means that the variables change in opposite directions. *Cp.* **rank-order correlation.**

proficiency (prə fish′ən sē) *n.* skill; ability; expertness. *adj.* **proficient.**

proficiency test a test of performance in a skilled task, as playing a musical instrument.

profile (prō′fīl) 1. *n.* an outline of an object, especially the side view of the human head. 2. *n.* a graph of test scores in comparable units. 3. *n.* a short biographical article. 4. *v.* to draw or write a profile.

prognosis (prog nō′sis) *pl.* **ses** (sēz). *n.* a prediction; forecast; specifically, the predicted course and result of a disease. *adj.* **prognostic.** *v.* **prognosticate.**

program *or (Brit.)* **programme** (prō′gram, -grəm) 1. *n.* any plan to be followed; specifically, planned educational subject matter or experience, as *a reading program, an educational program.* 2. *n.* a performance or production, as *a TV program.* 3. *n.* a description chiefly of the characters and action of such a performance or production. 4. *v.* to form or schedule a program. 5. *n.* a plan prepared for computer use. 6. *v.* to prepare a program for a computer.

programmed instruction *or* **learning** instruction or learning in which a skill or subject matter is broken up into very small parts to which the learner responds, step by step, and gets an immediate check on the accuracy of each response. See also **linear program; branching program.**

programmed reading programmed instruction in reading.

programmer (prō′gram ər) *n.* one who prepares computer programs.

programming (prō′gram ing̑) 1. *n.* the preparation of material to be learned into a series of very small steps through which the learner moves, usually in a sequence from easy to difficult and/or simple to complex. 2. *n.* the preparation of computer data-processing operations. Also **programing.**

progress chart a chart for recording student accomplishment and used primarily as a self-motivational device, as in showing the number of books read, new words learned, etc.

progressive aspect (tense) a verb aspect in English that indicates an ongoing action or state, either present, past, or future, as *hope* in *I hope to see you.*

project (*n.* proj′ ekt; *v.* prə jekt′) 1. *n.* a specific scholarly task, as *a research project.* 2. *n.* an extended school assignment, as *a book collection project.* 3. *n.* something considered or planned, as *a summer project.* 4. *v.* to consider or plan something. 5. *v.* to speak or act clearly and forcefully enough to communicate to an audience.

Project Follow Through a federal educational project in the United States designed to provide educational stimulation of children in grades 1, 2, and 3.

Project Head Start a federal educational program in the United States designed to stimulate the intellectual, physical, and socioemotional development primarily of low-income pupils of ages 4, 5, and 6, and thus to improve their later performance in school.

projection (prə jek′s͟hən) 1. *n.* the act or result of showing an enlarged image on a screen, wall, etc. 2. *n.* blaming one's faults on others. 3. *n.* a defense mechanism to protect one's unrecognized feelings of hostility and inadequacy by accusing others of such feelings. 4. *n.* a scheme or plan, especially for the future.

projective technique *or* **test** the use of an unstructured stimulus or task to assess perceptual functioning and personality characteristics as revealed in a person's responses. *The use of the Rorschach and word association tests involves projective techniques.*

project method a teaching-learning plan in which students work on extended scholarly tasks related to their interests, the usual school subjects being related to these tasks. *The project method often involves the formal steps of problem-solving.*

projector (prə jek′tər) *n.* a device for showing enlarged images, especially of motion pictures, transparencies, or slides.

prologue *or* **prolog** (prō′lôg, -log) 1. *n.* an introduction or preface to a literary work, usually a play. 2. *n.* any introductory event. 3. *v.* to introduce with a prologue. *Ct.* **epilogue** *or* **epilog.**

pronation (prō nā′s͟hən) 1. *n.* the placing of the body face downward. 2. *n.* the turning of the hand downward, as in handwriting. *v.* **pronate.**

pronominalization (prō nom″ə nəl ī zā′s͟hən, -i zā′s͟hən) 1. *n.* the process, or result, of using a pronoun in the place of another part of speech or syntactic structure, as using *she* and *her* to represent *Diane* in *Diane said she would not sell her home.* 2. *n.* in transformational-generative grammar, a syntactic rule which transforms one of two equivalent or identical phrases into a pronoun.

pronoun (prō′noun″) *n.* a part of speech used as a substitute for a noun or noun phrase. *Note:* In English, personal pronouns have subjective *(I/we),* objective *(me/us),* first possessive *(my/our),* and second possessive *(mine/ours)* forms.

pronounceability (prə nouns″ə bil′i tē) *n.* ease (or difficulty) of pronunciation. *English words with silent letters, as in Worcester, sometimes create problems in pronounceability.*

pronunciation (prə nun″sē ā′s͟hən) 1. *n.* the act of speaking, including the articulation and intonation of speech sounds. 2. *n.* an accepted way of uttering words, syllables, etc. *The pronunciation 'ə dult'' is generally preferred to 'ad′ult.'* 3. *n.* the way in which the sounds of a language are ordinarily made, as *the pronunciation of German.* 4. *n.* the phonetic transcription of phonemes or graphemes such as that shown in a dictionary, as the pronunciation *rēd′ing* for *reading.* *v.* **pronounce.**

pronunciation key the set of graphic symbols used to represent accurately the speech sounds of a language, as *a dictionary pronunciation key.* See table on the front end paper of this dictionary.

pronunciation symbol 1. a graphic symbol representing a particular speech sound. See also **graph** (def. 2); **letter** (def. 1). 2. See **pronunciation key.**

proofread (pro͞of′rēd″) 1. *v.* to compare a manuscript copy, or printer's proof, against the original manuscript to locate printing errors. 2. *v.* to read over any written or printed material to correct errors of spelling, grammar, logic, content, etc. See also **proofreading marks.** *n.* **proofreading.**

proofreading marks the graphic symbols used to indicate changes needed in a manuscript text or a printer's proof. See the table on page 382.

propaedeutic (prō″pi do͞o′tik, -dyo͞o′-) 1. *adj.* having to do with basic or introductory instruction, as *a propaedeutic overview.* 2. *n.* learning of an elementary or introductory nature.

propaganda (prop″ə gan′da) 1. *n.* an extreme form of persuasion intended to influence the reader or listener strongly, though sometimes subtly, usually by one-sided rather than objective arguments, as *wartime propaganda. Cp.* **indoctrinate** (def. 1). 2. *n.* speaking or writing which attempts to persuade listeners or readers to accept a particular point of view, either 'good' or 'bad' depending on the speaker's or writer's intent, as *advertising propaganda to sell mouthwash. Cp.* **bias** (def. 1). 3. *n.* information spread by supporters of a cause or an organization, as *political propaganda.*

propaganda analysis a type of content analysis designed to reveal the sources and techniques of propaganda as well as its purposes.

propaganda techniques any one of several ways of using propaganda, as by overgeneralization, guilt by association, etc.

proper noun a noun which names a particular person, place, or thing as a referent, as *Mrs. Olson, New York, Mona Lisa. Ct.* **common noun.**

prophylaxis (prō″ fə lak′sis, prof″ə-) 1. *n.* the prevention of disease, as by treatment. 2. *n.* any action or treatment intended to prevent the occurrence of any specified problem. *Patent medicines are often sold as a prophylaxis. adj.* **prophylactic.** *n.* **prophylactic.**

proposition (prop″ə zish′ən) 1. *n.* a statement offered as true or for testing for truth, as *the proposition to be debated.* 2. *n.* a plan offered for action. *The proposition to raise taxes was loudly booed.* 3. *n.* a thought unit expressed in an independent or dependent clause: *I breathe hard/when I run.* 4. *n.* a thought unit containing a relation, or attribute, and an argument. *adj.* **propositional.**

propositional operations See **formal operations.**

proposition density a term used by W. Kintsch to describe the proportion of different propositions (def. 4) in a text in relation to text length. *Cp.* **concept load** *or* **density** (def. 1); **vocabulary burden** *or* **load** (def. 1).

proprioceptor (prō″prē ə sep′tər) *n.* a sense organ or sensory nerve terminal within the labyrinth of the inner ear, and in muscles, tendons, and joints, which receives stimulation by changes in tonus or movement. *Proprioceptors give information about balance and the position of the body. Cp.* **exteroceptor; interoceptor.**

prose (prōz) 1. *n.* written or spoken language that is not verse. 2. *adj.* referring to non-metrical language, as *fluent prose style.* 3. *n.* ordinary, dull language, as *marketplace prose.* 4.

adj. referring to dull language; prosaic. *adj.* **prosaic.**

prosodic feature (prə sod′ik) any characteristic involving more than one division of a speech utterance, as stress, pitch, juncture, etc. See also **intonation** (def. 1).

prosodic sign (prə sod′ik) a graphic mark which denotes a metric feature in poetry or a stress or intonation feature of speech. See also **accent** (def. 2d); **prosodic feature; diacritic** *or* **diacritic (-al) mark.**

prosody (pros′ə dē) 1. *n.* the stress and intonation patterns of spoken language. 2. *n.* the study of the form and metrical structure of verse.

protagonist (prō tag′ə nist) *n.* the central figure (hero or heroine) in a drama or narrative. *King Lear is the protagonist in Shakespeare's play of that name. Ct.* **antagonist.**

protocol (prō′tə kôl″, -kol″, kōl″) *n.* an original, unmodified record of events, experiments, speech, etc., made at the time of occurrence or immediately afterwards, as *the protocol of a projective test.*

prototype (prō′tə tīp″) 1. *n.* the original form, pattern, or model from which other ones are taken. The Iliad *and* The Odyssey *are prototypes of epic poetry. Cp.* **archetype** (def. 1). 2. *n.* someone or something taken as an example of its kind. *The model T Ford is a prototype of the mass-produced automobile.*

proverb (prov′ərb) 1. *n.* a brief saying which effectively states a commonly-held truth. 2. *n.* a profound saying, as in the Bible: *A wise man will hear and will increase learning; and a man of understanding shall attain unto wise counsels* — Book of Proverbs. *Cp.* **maxim; aphorism; adage.** *adj.* **proverbial.**

proxemics (prok sē′miks) *n. (with sing. v.) the study of the way in which the participants in social interaction adjust their posture and relative distance from one another according to the degree of intimacy that obtains between them, their sex, the social roles they are performing, and so on* — J. Lyons (1977). *adj.* **proxemic.**

proximal (prok′sə məl) *adj.* towards the center of the body or towards the point of origin or attachment, as of an organ or bone. *The inner ear is the proximal part of the ear. Ant.* **distal.**

Psalter (sâl′tər) *n.* the Book of Psalms. See also **New England Psalter.**

pseudo- a prefix indicating *false, superficially resembling;* as **pseudonym.**

pseudonym (so͞od′ᵊnim) See **pen name.**

psychiatric social worker a social worker with the special training and skills needed to deal with emotionally disturbed persons as well as with those having less serious emotional and/or social problems.

psychiatry (si kī′ə trē, sī-) *n.* that branch of medicine that specializes in the study and treatment of mental disorders. *adj.* **psychiatric.** *n.* **psychiatrist.**

psycho- a combining form indicating *mind;* as **psychogenic.**

psychoactive drug a drug that stimulates, depresses, or distorts behavioral processes, especially cognitive and affective ones. *Tranquilizers are psychoactive drugs.*

psychoanalysis (sī″kō ə nal′i sis) 1. *n.* a theoretical concept of the relation between unconscious and conscious processes. 2. *n.* a method or school of psychotherapy developed by Sigmund Freud and designed to bring unconscious material to a conscious level so it can be understood and managed by the patient. 3. *n.* any of several modifications of Freud's method in which the analysis of dreams and free association is prominent. *Note:* A practitioner of psychoanalysis may be either a psychiatrist or a clinical psychologist, each of whom must have undergone psychoanalysis before practicing it. *n.* **psychoanalyst.** *adj.* **psychoanalytic.**

psychodrama (sī″kō drä′mə, -dram′ə) *n.* a group therapy technique in which subjects act out, through assigned but impromptu roles, their problems and conflicts in order to release tensions, to gain insight into themselves and others, and to learn desirable social behavior. *Cp.* **play therapy; sociodrama; role-playing** (def. 3).

psycho-educational clinic a clinic that supplements the work of schools, using skilled personnel to provide a psychological approach in the study and treatment of difficult behavior and learning problems.

psychogenic (sī″kō jen′ik) 1. *adj.* psychological in origin and development. *Attitudes are psychogenic.* 2. *adj.* caused by mental or emotional problems; psychosomatic; as *a psychogenic headache.* *n.* **psychogenesis; psychogenetics.**

psycholinguistics (sī″kō liŋ gwis′tiks) *n.* (*with sing. v.*) the interdisciplinary field of psychology and linguistics in which language behavior is examined. *Psycholinguistics includes such areas of inquiry as language acquisition, conversational analysis, and the sequencing of themes and topics in discourse, adj.* **psycholinguistic.**

psychological block See **emotional block.**

psychological clinic a clinic designed to prevent, diagnose, treat, or research emotional, behavioral, or learning disorders.

psychological evaluation an overall assessment of the emotional, behavioral, and learning functions of an individual, usually based upon interviews, observations, and psychological tests.

psychological novel 1. a type of novel in which the motivation of the characters — the why of their actions — is of central importance and is revealed by what they say and do. *Henry James is considered the father of the modern psychological novel.* 2. an example of such a novel, as Judith Guest's *Ordinary People.*

psychologist (sī kol′ə jist) *n.* a professional worker in psychology.

psychology (sī kol′ə jē) *n.* the science or study of emotions, behavior, and learning in humans or animals.

psychology of reading the study of the reading process; specifically, the application of psychological and linguistic concepts and techniques to an examination of the reading act and its outcomes.

psychometric (sī″kō me′trik) *adj.* referring to the study, practice, or research in psychological measurement; specifically, the development, administration, and interpretation of psychological tests, as *psychometric data. n.* **psychometrics; psychometry.**

psychometrician *or* **psychometrist** (sī kom″i trish′ ən, sī kom′ə trist) *n.* a professional worker in psychological testing and research.

psychomotor domain the psychological field of physical activity. *Ct.* **affective domain; cognitive domain.**

psychomotor test a test of motor performance, as a tapping test.

psychoneurosis (sī″kō noo rō′sis, -nyoo-) See **neurosis.**

psychopathic (sī″kə path′ik) 1. *adj.* referring to a person who is extremely antisocial, lacking in feelings of guilt or remorse, and largely unaffected by punishment. 2. *adj.* referring to any major mental disorder other than a psychosis, especially one not specifically identified. *n.* **psychopath; psychopathy.**

psychopathology (sī″kō pə thol′ə jē) *n.* the science or study of severe mental disorders; a branch of psychology or medicine that deals with the causes of mental illness. See also **psychopathic.**

psycho-phonemic method a way of teaching reading in which sound-letter correspondences and syllables are taught by comparing similar syllabic patterns.

psycho-phonetic method a term sometimes used to refer to a phonic method based upon research rather than upon a purely logical rationale characteristic of early formal phonic methods. *The order in which the elements are introduced has been modified in the light of detailed studies of their frequency, differences in form that facilitate or interfere with recognition, similarities in meaning, etc.* — W. S. Gray (1956). See **phonic method.**

psychosis (sī kō′sis) *n. pl.* **psychoses.** *n.* any major and disabled mental disorder, organic or functional, marked by disorganization of the personality and loss of contact with reality; insanity; madness. *Note:* The symptoms of psychosis are often delusions, illusions, hallucinations, or extreme withdrawal. *Cp.* **neurosis.** *adj.* **psychotic.** *n.* **psychotic.**

psychosomatic (sī″kō sō mat′ik, -sə-) *adj.* referring to a physical disorder or disease presumably brought about by cognitive and/or affective factors in the absence of any apparent organic cause. *A stomach ache just before a school test may be psychosomatic.*

psychotherapy (sī″kō ther′ə pē) *n.* the treatment of behavior disorders; specifically, treatment of a subject by one professionally trained in psychology or psychiatry. *Note:* Although psychotherapy is chiefly the domain of clinical psychologists and psychiatrists, others such as psychiatric nurses, counselors, and psychiatric social workers may also be involved. *n.* **psychotherapist;** *adj.* **psychotherapeutic.**

PT physiotherapy; physical therapy.

ptosis (tō′sis) *n.* a drooping of the eyelids.

puberty (pyo͞o′bər tē) *n.* the developmental level at which secondary sex characteristics emerge, and sexual reproduction is possible as individuals enter adolescence.

publication (pub″lə kā′shən) *n.* something printed for the purpose of public information or for sale to the public.

public language an early term for 'retricted code' used by British sociologist B. Bernstein.

public library a library or group of libraries receiving support from public funds and providing free services to all residents of a specified area. *Note:* In some cases, certain public libraries charge for special services.

public school 1. a school in the United States which is supported by tax dollars and controlled by public officials. 2. *(Brit.)* a select private school, as Eton.

publisher (pub′li shər) 1. *n.* an individual or company that issues books, periodicals, and other media for sale. 2. *n.* the business head of a newspaper organization, frequently the owner. *v.* **publish.**

pulp (pulp) *n.* a magazine or book printed on cheap, rough paper, usually with stories of a sensational or lurid type that are written according to a routine, predictable formula. *Cp.* **slick.**

pun (pun) 1. *n.* the use of a word or phrase to suggest more than one meaning, often humorous. 2. *n.* a play on words, as in 'the kitten caboodle.' 3. *v.* to say or write such a play on words.

punctuation (pun͡gk″c̮hōō ā′s̮hən) 1. *n.* the use of standard marks other than letters in writing and printing to clarify the meaning of text. 2. *n.* a mark which is part of such a system; punctuation mark. *v.* **punctuate.**

punctuation mark one of the set of graphic marks used in writing phrases and sentences to clarify the meaning of sentences and to give speech characteristics to written material. *Note:* In English, and other writing systems based on the Latin alphabet, punctuation marks include those indicating a *pause,* such as the comma (,), semicolon (;), colon (:), dash (—) and period (.); a *sentence-type,* such as question mark (?) and exclamation mark (!); a *quotation,* by quotation marks ("... " and '... '); an *incidental or parenthetical notion,* by brackets ([ ], ( ), < >); a word *compound,* by a hyphen (-); or the *absence of sounds,* by apostrophe ('), *or of words,* by a dot series (...) or dash (—). *Cp.* **diacritic** *or* **diacritic (-al) mark.**

pupil (pyōō′pəl) 1. *n.* a school learner, usually young. *At higher grade levels, pupils usually are called students.* 2. *n.* a person who studies, often individually, with a special teacher or tutor, as *a music pupil.* 3. *n.* the round opening in the center of the iris which lets light into the eye.

pupillary reflex the automatic opening or closing of the pupil in response to the amount of light falling on the eye. *The contraction of the pupil to protect the eye from excessive brightness and its expansion to provide maximum stimulation in dim light constitute the pupillary reflex.*

puppetry (pup′i trē) *n.* the art of creating figures to interpret characters, stories, etc. *Note:* Puppets range from stick figures, paper-bag puppets, and hand puppets to more sophisticated marionettes, manipulated from above by strings attached to various parts of the puppet. *n.* **puppet.**

pure tone audiometer an instrument which sounds tones of selected frequencies at certain volume levels to determine the hearing level, or threshold, for such tones. See also **audiometer.**

purple curriculum a humorous term for the overuse of duplicating masters in schools; ditto delirium; busy work. *The purple curriculum is also sometimes called the 'purple flood,' 'purple panacea,' 'purple plague,' or 'purple tide.'*

purpose for reading 1. the reason a person reads. 2. the goal(s) which a reader seeks to attain in each reading experience. 3. the goal(s) set by the teacher or text for a reading task or experience. *Note:* Purpose for reading is a major determinant of speed of reading and of comprehension strategies.

purposive (pûr′pə siv) *n.* a grammatical construction that expresses intent, as *I plan to go.*

pursuit eye movements the smooth tracking of a moving target by the eyes; ocular pursuit; as in watching a car speed by. *Ct.* **saccade.**

Pygmalion effect the hypothetical notion that teachers give more encouragement to students for whom they have high expectations.

Q

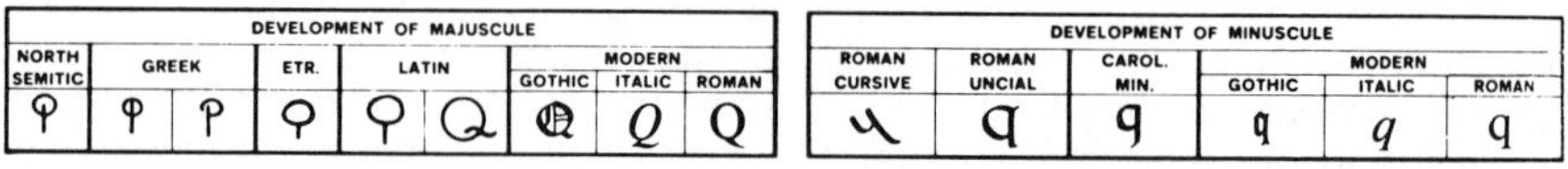

DEVELOPMENT OF MAJUSCULE								
NORTH SEMITIC	GREEK		ETR.	LATIN		MODERN		
						GOTHIC	ITALIC	ROMAN
Ϙ	Ϙ	Ϙ	Ϙ	Ϙ	Q	Q	*Q*	Q

DEVELOPMENT OF MINUSCULE					
ROMAN CURSIVE	ROMAN UNCIAL	CAROL. MIN.	MODERN		
			GOTHIC	ITALIC	ROMAN
q	q	q	q	*q*	q

The seventeenth letter of the English alphabet developed in its present form from Latin. Its equivalent in Greek was *koppa* (Ϙ), which became obsolete except as a numeral, and in North Semitic it was *qoph*, which represented a guttural *k*-like sound. When adopted from the Etruscans, the Latin alphabet contained three symbols for the *k*-sound (Q, C, K), and the use of Q was limited to the sound (k) when it was labialized and followed in spelling by U, a practice generally maintained today.

In Old English the Q does not appear, its labialized sound being written CW or, later, KW.

q that part of a sample that does not have some specified characteristic. *Cp.* **p** (def. 2).

Q 1. quartile. 2. question. 3. quarto.

qualifier (kwol′ə fī″ər) 1. See **modifier.** 2. *n.* a function word used before an adjective to show the degree of the adjective, as *rather* in *This is rather disappointing.* 3. *n.* an intensifier.

qualitative (kwol′i tā″tiv) *adj.* having to do with essential or characteristic quality or qualities. *The consultant made a qualitative judgment of the reading program.*

quantitative (kwon′ti tā″tiv) *adj.* having to do with measuring and describing numerically. *A standardized reading test gives a quantitative description of achievement.*

quarterly (kwôr′tər lē) 1. *adj.* occurring every three months. 2. *n.* a publication issued four times a year.

quartile (Q) (kwôr′tīl, -til) *n.* one of the three points that divide a distribution into four equal parts of 25 per cent each. *Note:* Q_1 is the lowest of these points, Q_2 the median, and Q_3 the highest.

quarto (kwôr′tō) *n.* a book measuring approximately 24 x 31 cm. (9½ x 12) in.) printed on sheets folded to make 4 leaves or 8 pages. See also **book size** *or* **format.**

quasi-experimental design a research design that does not meet the criteria of external or internal validity: external validity in the sense that the design considerably limits the generalizability of any findings; internal validity in the sense that the design does not control all but a single variable. *Note:* Most educational research, because of the complexities of the learning-teaching situation, is quasi-experimental in design.

quatrain (kwo′trān) 1. *n.* a stanza or poem of four lines. 2. *n.* a poem of four verses.

question (kwes′chən, kwesh′-) 1. *n.* the act of requesting information, confirmation, or action. 2. *v.* to make such a request. 3. *n.* a. a sentence whose function is to ask for something. b. a sentence having the grammatical form of a question though actually a command; whimperative; as *Would you take your seat?* 4. *adj.* referring to a question, as *a question mark.*

question mark 1. a punctuation mark (?) used in English at the end of a sentence to indicate that the sentence is a question, as in *Is he working?.* 2. (*Brit.*) interrogation point.

questionnaire (kwes″chə nâr′) *n.* a self-report instrument for assessing typical behavior or gaining useful information through questions, as *a linguistic questionnaire, a reading questionnaire.*

quotation (kwō tā′shən) *n.* words or a

passage used by one speaker or writer but attributed to someone else, as *a quotation from Shakespeare.*

quotation marks punctuation marks ("..." or '...') used to enclose a directly quoted passage, as *Bill said, "I'll stay",* or to indicate a word or phrase which is not part of the writer's vocabulary or of appropriate vocabulary for the written context, as *The play was a 'howling' success.* See also **punctuation mark.**

quote (kwōt) 1. *n.* a quotation. 2. *v.* to say or write the words of another and attribute them to that person.

R

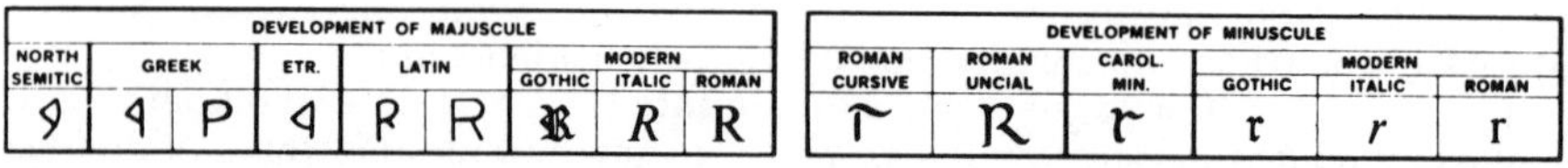

DEVELOPMENT OF MAJUSCULE								
NORTH SEMITIC	GREEK			ETR.	LATIN		MODERN		
						GOTHIC	ITALIC	ROMAN
𐤓	ᑫ	P	ᑫ	Ρ	R	𝕽	*R*	R

DEVELOPMENT OF MINUSCULE					
ROMAN CURSIVE	ROMAN UNCIAL	CAROL. MIN.	MODERN		
			GOTHIC	ITALIC	ROMAN
⌈	R	r	𝔯	*r*	r

The eighteenth letter of the English alphabet developed from North Semitic. The Greek *rho* (ρ, P) is a later version of the same symbol. Its form in Latin (R) derives from a variant used in a local Greek script which added the short stroke at the right.

r product-moment, or Pearsonian, correlation coefficient.

R 1. response, as *S -R theory*. *Ct.* **S.** 2. (*italicized*) multiple correlation coefficient. 3. one of the three R's, as *reading*.

racism (rā′siz əm) 1. *n.* the idea that certain races are superior to others because of the belief that race determines human abilities. 2. *n.* strong negative feelings toward a race or races other than one's own. 3. *n.* racially determined actions, policies, institutions, etc.; racial discrimination. *adj.* **racist.**

radical (rad′i kəl) 1. *n.* in some logographic writing systems, the part of a graphic character which assigns the word represented to a particular semantic or lexical class. *In Chinese, about 220 radicals form the basic semantic classes to which all characters can be assigned.* 2. *n.* in some logographic writing systems, the component of a graphic character considered to be the basic or first stroke, and the one by which the character is classified in a dictionary or other work. *In some Japanese writing primers, kanji are classified by their radicals.* See also **logography**.

radio (rā′dē ō″) 1. *n.* the medium of wireless, non-pictorial communication: its message and its broadcasting apparatus. 2. *adj.* referring to this medium. 3. *v.* to send a message by radio.

random access the ability to retrieve a specific memory without having to go through the entire store of memories in some fixed order. *Some students and advanced computers have random access, but others do not.*

random error the variability in a distribution that occurs by chance. *Random errors may raise or lower scores.*

randomize (ran′də mīz″) *v.* to assign subjects, objects, events, etc., in a completely chance manner to experimental treatments.

random sample an experimental sample drawn by chance from a population. *A random sample helps eliminate systematic bias and strengthens inferences to the population from which the sample was drawn.*

random sampling the act of drawing a random sample, as by using a table of random numbers.

range (rānj) *n.* the difference between the highest and lowest scores or values in a distribution.

range of accommodation the distance between the nearest and the farthest points at which clear vision can be achieved.

rank order the placement of scores or values according to increasing or decreasing size, as 1,2,3,4,5; large, medium, and small apples.

rank-order correlation a statistical procedure which yields a coefficient expressing the relationship in terms of rank only between two sets of rankings. *Cp.* **product-moment correlation.**

rapid reading See **speed reading.**

rapport (ra pōr′, -pôr′) *n.* a comfortable, harmonious personal relationship; especially, such a relationship between teacher and students or tester and subject.

rare book a book that is old, scarce, or has other distinguishing features, as a first or limited edition, special illustrations or binding, etc., which make it sought after and valuable.

rate of comprehension See **speed of comprehension.**

rate of reading how fast a person reads, usually silently; reading speed. *Note:* Rate of reading has been of great interest to students of reading and to the public since schools in the United States began to stress silent reading in the second decade of the 20th century. A formula for expressing the average number of words read per minute was quickly devised, and students were tested for reading speed regardless of comprehension. Later, separate comprehension scores were given as some arbitrary percent of correct responses to content questions on the text; and still later, rate adjustments were introduced in relation to comprehension. Rate of reading scores are so affected by other variables, as purpose for reading, the nature of the content, format, etc., that comparative studies are difficult. Furthermore, since rate of reading scores are average scores, they mask normal and desirable variations in reading speed. See also **speed of comprehension.**

rating scale an instrument, sometimes in graphic form, for recording estimates of the functioning of selected aspects of behavior, as personality traits.

ratiocination (rash″ē os″ə nā′shən) *n.* the process, or product, of logical reasoning.

rationalization (rash″ə nᵊl i zā′shən) *n.* a defense mechanism, or its result, in which excuses and other forms of self-deception are used to avoid reality.

rauding (rô′ding) *n.* a term introduced by R. Carver (1977) to refer to the receptive communication skills of reading with comprehension and listening with comprehension (auding).

raw score the number of points earned by a student on a test, sometimes modified by a correction for guessing or by conversion to a percentage of the possible score. *Ct.* **derived score.**

r-controlled vowel sound the modified sound of a vowel immediately preceding /r/ in the same syllable, as in *care, never, sir, or, curse,* etc.

re- a prefix indicating *back, again;* as **recall, reread.**

reaction time the interval between the stimulus event and the subject's response.

read (*v., n.* rēd; *adj., v.* [past tense] red)

The definitions of *read* are more numerous and tend to be more discrete than those of *reading.* Many are drawn from a long literary heritage and are a catalog of subtle meaning distinctions, often metaphorical extensions of more basic definitions, made by writers and speakers. The chief but not exclusive referent of most definitions of *read* is silent reading.

1. *v.* to seek to understand, without reading aloud, the intended meaning of a graphic communication; read silently. 2. *v.* to say aloud the words one sees in reading; read orally. 3. *v.* to engage in an unspecified reading activity. *He likes to read all evening.* 4. *v.* to get the literal or stated meaning from something read. *Cp.* **literal meaning; literal comprehension.** 5. *v.* to

find an unstated meaning in something read, as *read between the lines. Cp.* **interpretation; inferred meaning.** 6. *v.* to quickly look over or scan, as *read the newspaper headlines.* 7. *v.* to react critically to something read. *Cp.* **critical evaluation; critical reading.** 8. *v.* to react creatively to something read. *Cp.* **creative reading.** 9. *v. (Chiefly Brit.)* to study, usually at a university, a subject matter field, as *read law.* 10. *v.* to acquire knowledge about some topic by reading; learn; as *read about dinosaurs.* 11. *v.* to comprehend the fuller significance of something that is read. *Can you read Melville's message behind the story of Moby Dick?* 12. *adj.* having acquired breadth of knowledge through reading, as *well-read.* 13. *v.* to empathize with characters in imaginative literature. *As the young girl read* Little Women, *she wept with Jo at Beth's bedside.* 14. *v.* to identify the mood, setting, and events of a story or play. 15. *v.* to accept without hesitation or criticism the author's conditions at the outset of a story or play: engage in *that willing suspension of disbelief* — S. Coleridge. 16. *v.* to give meaning to non-graphic or non-verbal signs, as *read the signs of spring, read a person's mood or character.* 17. *v.* to discover or explain, as *read the meaning of a riddle.* 18. *v.* to predict or foresee. *Carmen could read her fate in the cards.* 19. *v.* to understand another graphic or verbal language when reading it, as *read German, read music, read finger spelling.* 20. *v.* to indicate or show, as *the scale reads 19 kilos.* 21. *v.* to have a certain wording, as *Test A reads 'percept' but text B reads 'precept.'* 22. *v.* to give directions about, as *read 'x' for 'y'.* 23. *v.* to examine reading material for mechanical errors, or to check the conformity of a copy with its original; proofread. 24. *v.* to edit. *He read the manuscript to consider changes in its substance and form.* 25. *v.* to scan or transfer data in the internal operation of a computer or between computers. *One computer read corrections to another. Note:* READ is an acronym for Real-time Electronic Access and Display. 26. *n.* the matter read, as *a splendid read* — B. Behan; *a fast read.* 27. **read in,** to supply information to a computer. 28. **read into,** to infer a meaning in something read. 29. **read oneself to sleep,** put oneself to sleep by reading. 30. **read out,** a. to get information from a computer. b. to force a person to leave a group, usually a political one. c. to scold severely. 32. **read you loud and clear,** a. to hear. b. to understand the intent of an oral message. See also **reading; reader; reading comprehension.**

readability (rē″də bil′i tē) 1. *n.* ease of understanding or comprehension because of style of writing. *Note:* Many variables in text may contribute to readability, such as format, typography, content, literary form and style, vocabulary difficulty, sentence complexity, idea or proposition density, cohesiveness, etc. Many variables within the reader also contribute, such as motivation, abilities, and interests. Text and reader variables interact in determining the readability of any given piece of reading material for any given individual reader. *Cp.* **comprehensibility.** 2. *n.* an objective estimate or prediction of reading comprehension of material, usually in terms of reading grade level, based upon selected and quantified variables in text, especially some index of vocabulary difficulty and of sentence difficulty. See **readability formula.** *Note:* In teaching practice, def. 2 may sometimes be accepted as accurately predicting level of readability without regard to the other variables noted in def. 1, although it is wiser to combine subjective judgments of those variables with objective estimates in the prediction of readable writing. Similarly, in writing practice, changes in vocabulary and sentence difficulty may sometimes be considered sufficient in producing correspondingly more readable material. More cautious writers, however, realize that the variables in def. 1 must also be considered in the production of readable writing. 3. *n.* ease of reading because of the interest value or pleasantness of writing, as *the readability of a good mystery story.* 4. *n.* (*An old use.*) legibility of handwriting or typography. *adj.* **readable.**

readability formula any of a number of objective methods of estimating or predicting the difficulty level of reading materials, determined by analyzing samples of the materials and usually expressed by means of a reading grade level. *Note:* Readability formulas have been based on vocabulary difficulty, syntactic difficulty, and a number of related factors singly and in combination, usually in terms of a multiple regression equation. Word length or familiarity and average sentence length in words tend to be the most significant and/or convenient predictors of the reading difficulty of materials as measured by readability formulas. Estimates of formula validity have usually been based upon relationships with three types of criteria: a. reading comprehension scores. b. reading speed and/or efficiency. c. acceptability determined either by judgments by readers or experts, or by reader perseverance. See **Dale-Chall readability formula; Flesch readability formula; Fry readability graph (scale); Spache readability formula.** *Cp.* **cloze procedure** (def. 1).

reader (rē′dər) 1. *n.* a book used for instruction in reading, as *McGuffey's Readers. Graded readers represent different levels of difficulty.* 2. *n.* one who reads. *There are four kinds of readers. The first is like the hour-glass; and their reading being as the sand, it runs in and runs out, and leaves not a vestige behind. A second is like the sponge, which imbibes everything, and returns it in nearly the same state, only a little dirtier. A third is like a jelly-bag, allowing all that is pure to press away, and retaining only the refuse and dregs. And the fourth is like the slaves in the diamond mines of Golconda, who, casting aside all that is worthless, retain only pure gems* — Coleridge. 3. *n.* a person who reads to an audience; elocutionist. 4. *n.* a person employed to read for some special purpose, as a judge of manuscripts, a teaching assistant who grades papers and examinations, etc.

Reader's Guide to Periodical Literature an index to a group of general interest periodicals issued periodically, and cumulatively, published by H. W. Wilson Company.

readership (rē′dər s̮hip″) 1. *n.* those who read a publication. 2. *n.* the particular audience for which a publication is intended. 3. *n.* the habit of regular reading, as in *the promotion of readership.*

reader's theater a simply staged performance of literature, as a story, play, poetry, etc., read aloud by one or more persons.

readiness (red′ē nis) *n.* preparedness to cope with a learning task. *Note:* Readiness for learning of any type and at any level is determined by a complex pattern of intellectual, motivational, maturational, and experiential factors in the individual which may vary from time to time and from situation to situation. Readiness is a holistic concept, not one specific trait such as mental age, as is sometimes assumed. See also **reading readiness**.

readiness test a test designed to determine whether the individual possesses or fails to possess the skills and abilities required for a new activity.

reading (rē′ding)

As J. Carroll has noted, many definitions of reading are value-laden, hypothetical statements of what reading ought to be, not neutral statements of what reading is in the strictly definitive sense. Therefore, in perusing these varied definitions, *caveat lector* — let the reader beware.

The several parts of definition 1 reflect the views of reading specialists with particular reference to the silent reading process. Many of their concepts of the nature of the reading process represent specific theoretical points of view; others are eclectic. The effect of certain points of view on reading instruction has been aptly described by R. Strang: *If we think of reading primarily as a visual task, we will be concerned with the correction of visual defects and the provision of legible reading material. If we think of reading as word recognition, we will drill on the basic sight vocabulary and word recognition skills. If we think of reading as merely reproducing, we will direct the student's attention to the literal meaning of it. If we think of reading as a thinking process, we shall be concerned with the reader's skill in making interpretations and generalizations, in drawing inferences and conclusions. If we think of reading as contributing to personality development and effecting desirable personality changes, we will provide our students with reading materials that meet their needs or have some application to their lives* (1961). G. Spache has noted that reading is a developmental task: *Reading changes from what is primarily considered word recognition, through development of sight and meaning vocabulary and several methods of word attack, through different types and degrees of comprehension, to a mature act involving most of the higher mental processes* (1977).

Definitions 1a-1f are grouped according to the particular aspect(s) emphasized in the reading process. 1. *n.* the use of psychomotor, cognitive, and affective processes to suit the reader's purpose(s) in an effort to comprehend a graphic communication. a. *n.* a one-stage process of perceiving the graphic symbols of language accurately by associating their symbols with their sounds in speech. [*Reading*] *is distinguishing the separate letters both by the eye and by the ear, in order that, when you later hear them spoken or see them written, you will not be confused by their position* — Plato. *Before 1900 . . . it was assumed that reading was primarily a perceptual act and that other steps required for achieving certain other purposes of reading were not essential* — A. Otis (1916), cited by W. S. Gray (1956). *Reading involves nothing more than the correlation of a sound image with its corresponding visual image* — L. Bloomfield (1938). *Teach the child what each letter stands for and he can read* — R. Flesch (1955). b. *n.* a two-stage process involving . . . *the perception and comprehension of written messages in a manner paralleling that of the corresponding spoken messages* — J. Carroll (1964). c. *n.* an interaction process between the psycho-experiential background of the reader and the lexical and grammatical information carried by graphic symbols in deciphering an author's message. *Reading is the reconstruction of the events behind the symbols* — A. Korzybski (1941). *Reading . . . [is] an interaction between the reader and written language, through which the reader attempts to reconstruct a message from the writer* — K. Goodman (1968). *Reading . . . [is] an interaction by which meaning encoded in visual stimuli by an author becomes meaning in the mind of the reader. The interaction always involves three facets: 1) material to be read; 2) knowledge possessed by the reader; and 3) physiological and intellectual activities* — W. Gephart et al. (1970). d. *n.* the application of thinking or reasoning skills, as observation, prediction, verification, etc., in analyzing an author's meaning. *Reading is reasoning* — E. L. Thorndike (1922). *To whatever extent it is true that reading is learning, it is true that reading is thinking* — M. J. Adler (1940). *Reading [is] the central thought process by means of which meaning is 'put into' the symbols appearing on the printed page* — W. S. Gray (1940). *Reading is a sampling, selecting, predicting, comparing and confirming activity in which the reader selects a sample of useful graphic cues based on what he sees and what he expects to see* — K. Goodman (1975). e. *n.* a process of socialization whereby the vicarious experiences of reading may affect the reader's understanding of his environment. *Reading [is] a social process relating the reader to his environment and conditioning that relation* — D. Waples and others (1940). f. *n.* a complex, multi-dimensional process that involves several interacting levels of purposeful behavior as the reader seeks to determine the meaning of the author's writing. *Good reading includes an understanding not only of the literal or sense meaning of a passage but also the meanings implied by the author's mood, his tone, his intent, and by his attitude toward his subject, his reader, and himself* — I. A. Richards (1935, 1938), paraphrased by Gray (1940). *Reading is a highly complex activity including various important aspects, such as recognizing symbols quickly and accurately, apprehending clearly and with discrimination the meanings implied by the author, reacting to and using the ideas secured through reading in harmony with the reader's purposes, and integrating them into definite thought and action patterns* — W. S. Gray (1940). *Reading involves the recognition of printed or written symbols which serve as stimuli for the recall of meanings built up through past experience, and the construction of new meanings through manipulation of concepts already possessed by the reader. The resulting meanings are organized into thought processes according to the purposes adopted by the reader. Such an organization leads to modified thought and/or behavior, or else leads to new behavior which takes its place, either in personal or in social development* — M. Tinker and C. McCullough (1968). 2. *n.* the process of saying aloud what one is reading with comprehension: oral reading. *Reading consists: first, in gaining the thoughts of an author from written or printed language; second, in giving oral expression to these thoughts, in the language of the author so that the same thoughts are conveyed to the hearer* — G. Farnham (1905). 3. *n.* the act of orally interpreting something read, as *in giving a dramatic reading.* 4. *n.* the process of making discriminative responses. *In the broadest sense, reading is the process of interpreting sense stimuli and of adapting one's behavior with regard to them* — P. Spencer, cited by W. S. Gray and B. Rogers (1956). 5. *n.* any examination and interpretation of symbolic data, as *the reading of test results, a thermometer reading.* 6. *n.* any material that is read, as *the reading assigned in the course.* 7. *n.* a particular version or form of material to be read, as *a modern reading of the Bible.* 8. *n.* the breadth of knowledge acquired through reading. *Bacon was a man of wide reading.* 9. **readings,** a collection of writings of a particular type or of a particular field, as *readings in literature. Note:* Readings are often used as supplementary text materials. See also **read; reader; reading comprehension; literal meaning; interpretation; critical reading; creative reading.**

reading ability skill in processing text accurately and rapidly, in interpreting it, and in using it.

reading accelerator See **pacer.**

reading acquisition the early stages in the process of developing fluency in the basic skills in reading. *Ct.* **reading to learn.**

reading age an outmoded type of age equivalent score based upon the age in the test standardization population at which the average person earns a given reading score.

reading autobiography an account of a person's own experiences in first learning to read and in growing up with reading. *John's reading autobiography was of great help to his teacher in understanding his reading problems.*

reading backwardness See **backwardness in reading.**

reading between the lines an idiomatic expression referring to the understanding of more than the literal meaning of a communication; interpretation.

reading by fits and starts a seriocomic term describing the manner in which some oral readers speed up on familiar words and slow down for unfamiliar words with a resulting lack of comprehension.

reading center (-tre) a place, usually in a school, where students may get help to improve their reading. *Cp.* **reading clinic.**

reading circle a common physical arrangement for formal reading instruction. *Note:* A reading circle may be either a 180 degree arrangement with each student equidistant from the teacher, or a 360 degree arrangement.

reading clinic a clinic for persons with reading problems. *Note:* With the widespread development of reading clinics in the past 30 years, the term has lost much of its early, highly specialized clinical connotation.

reading clinician a person who works in a reading clinic; specifically, a teacher with specialized training in reading and reading difficulties who diagnoses and treats the more severe reading disability cases.

reading comprehension 1. understanding what is read. 2. one or more of several levels of a presumed hierarchy of reading comprehension processes: *a.* getting the literal meaning; see **literal comprehension.** *b.* getting the interpretive or suggested meaning in reading; see **interpretation** (defs. 1, 2). *c.* evaluating what is read in a critical way; see **critical reading.** *d.* reacting to what is read in a creative, intuitive way; see **creative reading.** 3. the linguistic process of reconstructing the intended message of a text by translating its lexical and grammatical information into meaning units that can be integrated with the reader's knowledge and cognitive structures. *Comprehension involves the recovery and interpretation of the abstract deep structural* *relations underlying sentences.* — J. Bransford and M. Johnson; *Comprehension is a process of integrating new sentences with antecedent information in extrasentential structures* — P. Thorndyke. 4. the result of reading comprehension processes. See also **comprehension.**

reading consultant a reading specialist who works with the teachers and administrators of a school system to carry out a reading program. See also **reading coordinator; reading supervisor.**

reading coordinator a reading specialist whose chief function is to help make the complex reading programs of large school systems work smoothly together. See also **reading consultant; reading supervisor.**

reading corner a special place in a classroom where students may read quietly. See also **book corner** *or* **nook.**

reading deficiency the lack of one or more specific skills, as those of structural analysis, which keep the individual from reading effectively. See also **reading disability.**

reading difficulty level 1. a judgment, estimate, or prediction of the degree to which reading material will be difficult to understand, usually expressed as a grade level; comprehensibility; readability. 2. the estimated grade level or other index value resulting from the application of a readability formula, cloze procedure, or a traditional comprehension test.

reading disability 1. an inability to read, often severe, in spite of intensive reading instruction. 2. reading performance below expectancy. 3. reading performance one or more years below one's mental ability. 4. any reading difficulty. *Note:* There is no clear present consensus about the precise nature of reading disability. Persons with a psychological background tend to think of reading disability as a deviation from normal behavior and to seek to measure and correct a wide range of possible contributing causes. Persons who are medically oriented tend to lean toward neurological hypotheses and labels and toward the use of the techniques and therapies of clinical medicine. See also **dyslexia; learning disability.**

reading disorder See **reading disability.**

reading distance the viewing distance when reading. *Note:* In near-point reading, ordinary-sized material should be held from 36 to 46 cm. (12-18 in.) from the eyes for clear, comfortable vision — M. Tinker (1965).

reading efficiency the ability to achieve one's reading purpose without waste of time or effort; reading competence.

reading expectancy a level of reading performance that a given student should be able to reach. *Note:* Reading expectancy predictions may be based on many factors, as age, grade, IQ, or listening comprehension, or on a formula that uses and weighs several such factors.

reading flexibility the adjustment of one's reading speed to one's purpose, to one's knowledge and background, and to the nature of the material being read.

reading for details reading to note the specific parts of a passage, including the sequence of these parts. *Reading for details is a common objective in reading instruction. Note:* A good reader is skilled in selecting details relevant to the main idea and in generating implied main ideas from detailed information: *Reading for details requires not only a grasp of the main ideas but also a putting together of the smaller ideas to bring about a better rounded and more nearly accu-*

rate understanding — E. Betts (1946).

reading game a game for improving one or more specific skills in reading.

reading grade level See **reading level.**

reading growth a measure of the difference in periodic samplings of a person's reading ability, usually shown by test scores, as in vocabulary, paragraph meaning, etc. *Note:* Reading growth preferably should reflect additional factors, as books read, changed attitude toward reading, etc., to give a more accurate picture of such growth.

reading guidance help provided, usually by a teacher or librarian, to aid students in selecting what to read.

reading habit 1. the use of reading as a regular activity. *Mary's reading habit is well-established.* 2. a repetitive act in reading, as in continuing to read the same kind of material (as horse stories) or in persisting in a particular way of reading (as omitting words).

reading in content areas *or* **fields** See **content area** or **field.**

reading index a formula developed by M. Monroe and B. Backus (1937) to compare a student's reading performance with arithmetic performance, intelligence, and chronological age. *Note:* The index assumes that reading age should equal chronological age. A reading index of 1.0 means that the student is reading at the level expected. A reading index of less than 1.0 represents a reading difficulty, while one greater than 1.0 represents greater than expected reading performance.

reading interests those topics and content fields about which a person not only shows a desire to read but does read, reflecting... *an active disposition toward some specific goal* — J. W. Getzels (1966). *Cp.* **reading preferences; reading tastes.**

reading inventory a checklist or questionnaire for assessing reading interests, habits, books read, etc.

reading kit a boxed set of commercial materials for reading instruction.

reading laboratory a specialized facility with materials and programs for the teaching of developmental and/or remedial reading and study skills. *Note:* The term is often a euphemism for remedial reading clinic.

reading ladder 1. a progression from the easiest reading materials to the most difficult and most mature. *Note:* The American Council on Education publishes a reading list, Reading Ladders for Human Relations, based on this concept, the various sections of each major theme being school level: primary, intermediate, junior, senior, mature. 2. a step-by-step upward progression from easy-to-read or mediocre books at the bottom of a figurative ladder, each rung of which lists increasingly more difficult works, until at the top one finds classics and other mature works of literary merit.

reading level an estimate of the reading skills of a student, usually expressed as a grade level; reading grade level. *Reading level often means instructional reading level.*

reading list a collection of titles, usually prepared by an instructor, of books or other reading materials appropriate to the course, unit, or topic under study. *The teacher suggested a reading list of short stories and novels on the theme of the new unit, 'Personal Courage.'*

reading locator test an initial placement test; usually, a short test used to identify a student's instructional level.

reading maturity a high level of reading development in which the individual reads expertly, widely, profitably, and responsibly. *Maturity in reading as one aspect of total development is distinguished by the attainment of those interests, attitudes, and skills which enable young people and adults to participate eagerly, independently, and effectively in all the reading activities essential to a full, rich, and productive life. . . . In the satisfaction of interests and needs through reading, a mature reader will continue to grow in capacity to interpret broadly and deeply* — W. S. Gray and B. R. Rogers (1956).

reading method 1. any of several relatively specific procedures or steps for teaching one or more aspects of reading. *Note:* The term properly denotes an overall approach to teaching reading, as the 'synthetic' or 'alphabetic' method. Each method embodies, explicitly or implicitly, some theory of how children learn and of the relationship between the written and spoken language. 2. sometimes, a specific reading program which translates a general approach into specific instructional materials, as i/t/a. *Cp.* **approach; program** (def. 1); **reading program.** Special types of reading method, as *alphabet method,* are given under the describing term.

reading pacer See **pacer.**

reading placement test a test used to assign students to reading levels or groups.

reading preferences the kinds of material a person reads when offered a choice. *Note:* Reading preferences may or may not coincide with reading interests. If a reader is given the study task of reading one of two books that are equally distasteful, the preference for one does not indicate a reading interest. *Cp.* **reading interests; reading tastes.**

reading process an operation or change which takes place in the act of reading. *The reading process has given rise to the construction of many models of reading.* See **reading.**

reading profile a graph of several scores of reading performance of the same person or of different aspects of reading.

reading program 1. a plan for reading development. *A reading program should be all-inclusive, incorporating diverse plans, media, and approaches for the provision of a wide range of individual differences in the entire student body of a school or school system* — A. Melnik. See **basal reading program** *or* **series.** 2. any specific reading plan — developmental, corrective, or remedial.

reading, rate of See **rate of reading.**

reading readiness 1. the readiness to profit from beginning reading instruction: *the teachable moment for reading — E. Dechant (1970).* 2. the readiness to profit from reading instruction beyond the beginning reading level. *Note:* According to N. B. Smith (1965), the concept of reading readiness was not widely accepted in American public schools until about 1925-1935. The concept was first limited to def. 1, then extended to def. 2. The concept itself has grown in depth and complexity, though not necessarily in clarity. See also **readiness.**

reading readiness test a test for predicting a student's performance upon entering a formal reading instruction program, usually in first grade.

reading retardation 1. reading performance significantly below one's grade placement level. 2. reading performance significantly below one's intellectual or reading potential level, regardless of grade placement; reading disability. *Note:* There is considerable confusion about the referent of this term — grade placement level or capacity for learning — as well as about the amount of retardation needed to justify applying this term to a particular student. The use of def. 1 as a major criterion for assigning students to remedial reading classes has filled many such classes and clinics with students who profit little from intensive reading instruction while ignoring more able students who could profit greatly from such instruction. For this reason, and since retardation commonly means 'below grade level,' the term 'reading disability' as used in def. 2 appears to be preferable in identifying reading problems that are remediable.

reading scheme *(Brit.)* See **basal reading program** *or* **series.**

reading school 1. a school in Europe and colonial America for the earliest formal instruction in the alphabet, in beginning reading, and in religious matters, for which the first instructional material was the hornbook. *By that time I had a little passed my sixth year, I had left my reading-school* — Barnard (1766). See **dame school.** *Cp.* **writing school.** *Note:* The separation of reading and writing schools, chiefly in the 17th century, was a fairly widespread but by no means universal practice in Europe and colonial America. 2. in the late 18th century, an occasional term for elementary school.

reading span See **span of recognition.**

reading specialist 1. a teacher usually with advanced training in the special skills needed to diagnose and correct reading difficulties, as well as in developmental reading, who works directly, but not necessarily exclusively, with students. *Note:* Such teachers also may have administrative functions in schools. See also **reading consultant; reading coordinator; reading supervisor.** 2. See **resource teacher.** 3. loosely, any teacher with some advanced training in the teaching of reading.

reading, speed of See **rate of reading.**

reading standards a statement of reading objectives, and the levels to which they should be attained by individuals, schools, departments, etc., issued by a governmental or professional agency.

reading supervisor a reading specialist whose chief functions are coordinating the reading program in a school system; reading coordinator. See also **reading consultant.**

reading survey the assessment of the reading achievement of individuals, schools, school systems, etc. *Observation, interviews, and inventories may be used as well as tests in a reading survey.*

reading tastes 1. one's personal inclination to enjoy certain kinds of reading materials, irrespective of their quality. 2. the aesthetic and critically discerning judgments reflected in the choice of materials for reading; especially, the recognition of materials of high literary merit. *Note:* Reading tastes are acquired reactions that are personal and relative, and are changeable while in the process of development. They grow out of experiences in reading. For some, reading tastes may remain at the relatively low levels found in most comic books and pulp magazines. However, when reading teachers speak of developing tastes in reading, the reference is usually to the higher level functions noted in def. 2 and involve the development of explicit standards of critical evaluation. *Cp.* **critical evaluation.**

reading teacher 1. a teacher, usually a classroom teacher, with special skills in the teaching of developmental reading. 2. a teacher with training in the special skills needed to teach corrective and remedial reading in or outside of the classroom. See also **reading specialist** (def. 1). 3. loosely, any teacher whose work includes the teaching of reading.

reading test any test for assessing silent or oral reading performance, as vocabulary meaning, word identification, comprehension, rate of reading comprehension, etc.

reading to learn the use of reading skills to acquire knowledge, broaden understandings, and develop appreciations. *Ct.* **reading acquisition.**

reading versatility See **reading flexibility.**

reading vocabulary the number of different words recognized and understood in silent reading. *Mature readers have large reading vocabularies.*

real focus the point at which convergent rays intersect. See illustration under **lens.** *Ct.* **virtual focus.**

realia (rē ā'lē ə, rā ä'lē ə) *n.* actual objects or specimens, in contrast to abstractions or models.

real image an optical image that is formed by converging light rays, as one that can be shown on a screen. *Ct.* **virtual image.** See also **real focus.**

realism (rē'ə liz"əm) 1. *n.* a practical, receptive attitude toward life as it actually is, marked by sensitivity and concern for concrete things rather than abstract ideas. *Note:* In literature, realism is a quality of writing which attempts to show life as it is rather than to interpret it philosophically. In art, realism is an emphasis upon actual rather than abstract representation. In educational philosophy, realism is training for the real world rather than education in the liberal arts. 2. *n.* the philosophic view that objects exist independently of the perceiver. 3. *n.* a 19th century literary movement in reaction to romanticism. 4. *n.* (J. Piaget) the tendency of the young child at the preoperational level of thinking to make no distinction in an egocentric way between the self and the external world. *Cp.* **egocentrism.** *adj.* **realistic.**

realistic fiction a story that attempts to portray characters and events as they are in real life. *Ct.* **fantasy.**

real time 1. the actual time it takes to complete a process; net, rather than gross time. *Computer billing is for the real time the computer was involved, not for how long the operator sat at the console.* 2. the actual time over which an event occurs when the perception or recording of the event occurs at nearly the same time. *Spoken sentences are physical events in real time.* *adj.* **real-time.**

reasoning (rē'zə ning) *n.* the process of logical thinking; ratiocination. *v.* **reason.**

rebus (rē'bəs) *n.* the use of a picture or symbol that suggests a word or a syllable: U R the 2 my .

recall (*n.* ri kôl', rē'kôl"; *v.* ri kôl') 1. *n.* the process of bringing back from memory a representation of prior learning or experience by images or words, sometimes exact, as *recall of Lincoln's* Gettysburg Address. *See also* **memory** (def. 1). 2. *v.* to so bring back from memory.

recall item a test item that requires the formulation of a response from memory, as 'The author of *Oliver Twist is* ______________ .' *Ct.* **recognition item.**

receiver (ri sē'vər) *n.* a communication device or system that changes electric waves or other signals into visible or audible form, as *a TV receiver.*

receptive aphasia difficulty in perceiving and comprehending spoken or written language, as in Wernicke's aphasia.

receptive language reading and listening. *Ct.* **expressive language** (def. 3).

receptive processes the action of the sense organs or cognitive systems which are responsive to incoming stimuli. *Seeing and hearing are the primary receptive processes in reading.*

receptor (ri sep′tər) *n.* a sense organ or sensory nerve terminal which responds to stimuli. *Note:* Receptors may be described by location, as exteroceptor, interocepter, and proprioceptor; by the type of sensitivity to stimulation, as visual, touch, etc.; or by the physical aspects of the stimulus, as light, mechanical, chemical, or temperature.

receptor system a neurosensory system in an organism, as that used to receive stimuli for seeing, hearing, etc.

reciprocal pronoun a pronoun expressing a mutual relationship. *Note:* In English, *each other* and *one another* are reciprocal pronouns.

recitation (res″i tā′s͟hən) 1. *n.* the act of repeating something, as a list of dates. 2. *n.* an oral statement in the classroom of something learned or memorized. 3. *n.* a period of classroom instruction. 4. *n.* an oral presentation of something from memory in a formal or public situation. *We will listen to a recitation of* The Night Before Christmas. *v.* **recite.**

recode (rē kōd′, ri-) 1. *v.* to change information from one code into another, as *recode writing into oral speech. Note:* No necessary assumption about meaning is made in this process: *The reader recodes the coded graphic input as phonological or oral output* — K. Goodman (1967). See also **decode; encode** (def. 1). 2. *v.* to identify, relate, and then combine, or chunk two or more symbols, as *recode 3 and 9 into 39*, presumably in long term memory. *n.* **recoding.**

recognition (rek″əg nis͟h′ən) 1. *n.* the act of identifying a new stimulus object or event as the same as something previously experienced, as *word recognition, the recognition of a friend.* See also **memory** (def. 1). 2. *n.* the state of being so identified. 3. *n.* the perception of truth or validity, as *the recognition of a fact.* 4. *n.* merit, as *recognition for outstanding service. v.* **recognize.**

recognition item a test item that requires identification of the correct choice, as 'The author of *Oliver Twist* was (1) Dickens (2) Scott (3) Thackeray (4) Austen.' *Ct.* **recall item.**

recognition span See **span of recognition.**

recognition vocabulary the number of different words known without the necessity of word analysis; words understood quickly and easily; sight vocabulary.

recollection (rek″ə lek′s͟hən) *n.* the conscious recall of past experience(s).

reconstruction (rē″kən struk′s͟hən) 1. *n.* a method of inferring the common ancestry of a group of related languages by analyzing their shared history or by reviewing changes that have occurred in their development. 2. *n.* the modification in comprehension that may result from continued reading or in retelling. *v.* **reconstruct;** *adj.* **reconstructive.**

recording (ri kôr′diŋ) *n.* the act, or result, of putting music, songs, dialogue, etc., on a record or a tape, as *a tape recording.*

recreational reading reading for pleasure, rather than study. *Cp.* **leisure reading.**

recto (rek′tō) 1. *n.* the right-hand page of an open book. 2. *n.* the front outside cover of a book. 3. *n.* the front side of a single manuscript leaf; the side intended to be read first. *Ct.* **verso.**

recursiveness (ri kûr′siv nəs) *n.* a characteristic of all languages that enables the grammar of a language to produce an infinite number of sentences; specifically, in transformational-generative grammar, the grammatical property that enables a sentence to be expanded indefinitely by repeatedly applying the same rule, as *This is the boy who stole the dog that bit the woman who....* *Cp.* **embedding.**

reductionistic (ri duk″s͟hə nis′tik) *adj.* referring to the process of reducing complex data or phenomena to simple terms. *The claim is reductionistic that reading comprehension is merely understanding word meanings and the main ideas.*

redundancy (ri dun′dən sē) 1. *n.* the occurrence of essentially the same information in more than one form, often built into a message to provide greater assurance that the message will be understood. 2. *n.* a needless and possibly distracting repetition of words or linguistic forms, as *hurriedly raced.* 3. *n. the property which enables a reader with experience and knowledge about the written code to know that only certain patterns of letters are possible out of all possible combinations* — R. Hodges and H. Rudorf (1972). *adj.* **redundant.**

reduplication (rē″do͞o plə kā′s͟hən) *n.* the creation of compound-like words whose parts rhyme or contain repeated sounds, as *fuddy-duddy, ding-dong, super-duper.* *Cp.* **neologism.**

reference (ref′ər əns) 1. *n.* an incidental mention; allusion. *In the diary, passing reference was made to several famous people.* 2. *n.* a source, or direction to a source, of information, as *an encyclopedia reference.* 3. *v.* to give sources in a book or article. 4. *n.* what a linguistic symbol represents. See **referent** *or* **referend** (def. 1). 5. *n.* language represented by graphemes in a writing system. *Note:* The reference of graphemes is generally to phonemes in alphabetic writing systems, but to morphemes, or words, in logographic ones.

reference book a book designed to be consulted for specific items of information, as a yearbook, atlas, dictionary. The Statesman's Yearbook *is a reference book that provides current information about the governments of many countries.*

reference materials a collection of books and other media useful for supplying information, kept together for easy access, and usually not allowed to circulate; reference collection.

referent *or* **referend** (ref′ər ənt; ref′ə rend) 1. *n.* what a word or symbol refers to either concretely or in the abstract. *The referent of 'dog' in 'Lynne's dog' is concrete, but the referent of 'comprehension' in 'reading comprehension' is abstract.* 2. *n.* that to which an indefinite or relative marker as *which* or *that* refers: *In 'This is the house that Jack built,' 'house' is the referent of 'that.'* 3. *n.* the word or symbol indicating meaning. *'Word recognition' is my referent for what you call 'word identification.'* *v.* **refer.**

referential (ref″ə ren′s͟həl) 1. *adj.* being or containing a reference. 2. *adj.* used or capable of being used for reference, as *the referential use of study notes for review.*

reflection (ri flek′s͟hən) 1. *n.* the process, or result, of seriously thinking over one's experiences, especially those valued. *Emerson and Carlyle spent a pleasant visit in unspoken reflection.* 2. See **introspection.** 3. *n.* a sign. *Hunger is a reflection of poverty.* 4. *n.* the suggestion of reproach. *This is* *no reflection upon your good intentions.* 5. *n.* the reversal of an algebraic sign in a set of data for clearer interpretation. 6. *n.* the turning back, as light from a mirror, or its result. *adj.* **reflective.**

reflective abstraction (J. Piaget) the reworking of the constructions at lower stages of development into the structure of higher stages. *Ct.* **physical abstraction.**

reflex (rē′fleks) 1. *n.* an automatic motor response to stimulation, as *the patellar reflex.* 2. *adj.* responsive; in reaction to; as *a reflex answer.* 3. *adj.* having to do with being reflected or bent back, as *light in a reflex camera.* 4. **reflexes,** the ability to respond to a situation. *Dan's reflexes enabled him to dodge the ball. adj.* **reflexive.**

reflexive pronoun a pronoun object that refers back to the subject, as *himself* in *Paul cut himself.*

refraction (ri frak′shən) 1. *n.* the change in direction of an energy wave as it goes obliquely from one transmission medium to another of different density. *Note:* Light passing through the air will bend if it strikes a glass lens obliquely, but not if it strikes the lens at a right angle. 2. *n.* the power of the eyes to bend light rays to achieve a clear image; refractive power of the eyes. 3. *n.* the identification of refractive errors of the eyes in prescribing corrective lenses. 4. **atmospheric refraction,** the bending of light rays from changes in atmospheric density or temperature that cause the apparent displacement of stars in the sky and create mirages on the earth's surface. *adj.* **refractive.**

refrain (ri frān′) 1. *n.* a verse or phrase repeated at intervals in a poem or song, usually at the end of a stanza; chorus. *In Tennyson's* The Owl, *the refrain is: Alone and warming his five wits/ The white owl in the belfry sits.'* 2. *v.* to keep oneself from saying or doing something.

Regina Medal an award made by the Catholic Library Association for a 'continued distinguished contribution to children's literature.'

regional dialect a variety of a language which contains shared features, used by most individuals in a regionally defined area, as Pennsylvania Dutch.

regionalism *or* **Regionalism** (rē′jə nᵊliz″əm) 1. *n.* the faithful representation in literature or painting of the important characteristics of a geographical area, as in the work of the American writers Willa Cather and William Faulkner and in that of the Dutch painter Vermeer. 2. *n.* an example of such representation. *Cp.* **local color.**

register (rej′i stər) 1. *n.* the language variety determined by social circumstances. *Note:* Most persons have a repertoire of registers. While an employee chatting with other workers might say, "The boss's latest memo makes no sense at all," he would likely use a more respectful register in speaking to his employer, as "Sir, I'm having a bit of difficulty understanding your memo." 2. *n.* the tonal range of a voice or musical instrument. *She spoke in a low register.* 3. *v.* to show feeling, as *express joy.* 4. *v.* to make an impression upon. *His angry words registered deeply.* 5. *n.* the exact adjustment of printing type or color to the page. 6. *v.* to make such an adjustment. 7. *n.* the memory storage unit of a computer; sometimes, the hardware for storing some specific type or category of data. *The newer electronic calculators have several addressable registers into which the user may put information to be saved.* 8. **reading register,** the special terminology used to teach reading; the terms needed to develop metalinguistic awareness.

register switching the change from one language variety to another to fit perceived changes in social situations. See also **register** (def. 1).

regression (ri gresh'ən) 1. *n.* movement backwards; specifically, a backward eye movement in reading continuous text. *Regressions may be binocular or monocular.* See illustration under **eye-movement pattern.** 2. *n.* See **regression toward the mean.** 3. *n.* the return to an earlier developmental state or condition, as *regression to childhood behavior under stress. adj.* **regressive.** *v.* **regress.**

regression analysis a statistical procedure for the analysis of variables as predictors, and for determining the degree of relationship between an independent and a dependent variable. *An attempt to predict grade point averages from membership in one of the three categories of work habits (needs help, average, good) might involve regression analysis.*

regression coefficient 1. the coefficient of any independent variable in a regression formula. 2. the constant in a mathematical equation giving the slope of a regression line that shows the relationship between the variables being measured.

regression equation a mathematical formula which expresses the most probable value of one variable when the other variable is known.

regression toward the mean the shift toward the mean on repeated or correlated measures, as of predicted scores. *The apparent lack of improvement in very competent students is sometimes merely a regression toward the mean.*

regular verb a verb that is conjugated according to a regular pattern of conjugation, as, in English, the formation of the past tense by the addition of *-ed* to the present tense. See also **paradigm** (def. 2).

regulation (reg″yə lā'shən) See **self-regulation.**

reify (rē'ə fī″) *v.* to treat abstract ideas as concrete objects or events. *Idols reify gods. n.* **reification.**

reinforcement (rē″in fōrs'mənt, -fôrs'-) 1. *n.* the strengthening of something; especially, strengthening by increased response strength and/or frequency. 2. *n.* the conditioning process of increasing the probability of a response by rewarding the desired behavior, as *verbal reinforcement for good schoolwork.* 3. *n.* the facilitation of a neural impulse by the simultaneous arousal of another neural impulse. 4. *n.* that which so strengthens; reinforcer. 5. *n.* simple repetition or repeated practice. *In some classrooms, simply doing worksheets is called reinforcement.* 6. *n.* in programmed materials and computer learning programs, feedback about the correct or incorrect responses; knowledge of results. *v.* **reinforce.** *n.* **reinforcer.**

reinforcement schedule a time plan, either regular or intermittent, for rewarding behavior. *Note:* Many schedule variations have been developed for specific purposes. A schedule for operant conditioning depends upon the response behavior and is intermittent. The schedule may be of two kinds: *ratio reinforcement,* based on number of responses, or *interval reinforcement,* based on some time interval.

rejection (ri jek'shən) 1. *n.* the refusal to accept a person, psychologically and/or physically, as *parental rejection, social rejection.* 2. *n.* the feeling(s) attached by the subject to an act of rejection. 3. *n.* removal from a category because of a lack of fit or appropriateness, as *rejection of faulty computer input data.* 4. *n.* the refusal of a body part to accept a graft or transplant. *n., v.* **reject.**

relational thought a form of thinking that proceeds by analogy and indirection rather than by strict logical expectations. *Poetry is relational thought. Cp.* **conjunctive thought; disjunctive thought.**

relationship of ideas the way in which thoughts are put together or patterned. *The identification of such relationships of ideas as cause/effect, sequence, and whole/part is essential for adequate comprehension.* See these terms for definitions.

relative clause a dependent clause that modifies a noun or pronoun and is introduced by a relative pronoun or adverb, as *who ate the whole pizza* in *The boy who ate the whole pizza. Cp.* **restrictive clause.** *Ct.* **non-restrictive clause.**

relative pronoun a pronoun that refers to an antecedent, as *whom* in *the man whom you were talking to. Note:* Other relative pronouns include *who, that, which, whose.*

relevant (rel'ə vənt) *adj.* pertinent; suitable; as *relevant comments. n.* **relevance; relevancy.**

reliability (ri lī''ə bil'i tē) *n.* consistency in measurements and tests; specifically, a correlation coefficient describing the extent to which two applications of the same measuring procedure would rank persons in the same way.

reliability coefficient a correlation coefficient of test consistency. *Reliability coefficients may be run between scores on two test forms, between scores on repeated test administrations, or between scores on the two halves of a test.* See also **coefficient of correlation.**

reluctant reader a euphemism for one who does not like to read. *Note:* A reluctant reader may not have the ability or skills to read; or may have the skills but, for a variety of reasons, not choose to read.

remediable (ri mē'dē ə bəl) *adj.* capable of being cured or corrected.

remedial (ri mē'dē əl) *adj.* corrective or reeducative, as *remedial spelling, remedial reading.*

remedial centre *(Brit.)* a reading clinic.

remedial reading 1. any specialized reading instruction adjusted to the needs of a student who does not perform satisfactorily with regular reading instruction. 2. intensive, specialized reading instruction for students reading considerably below expectancy. *Note:* Remedial reading is usually highly individualized reading instruction that is conducted outside the classroom in a special class, school, or clinic by a teacher trained in the use of clinical methods in reading. Eligibility for some remedial reading programs may be determined by legal definition or by specific age/grade requirements. Reading achievement two or more years below expectancy is a frequent eligibility requirement. 3. reading instruction which is more specialized than corrective reading in the classroom but not as specialized as that in definition 2. 4. developmental reading instruction set at a different pace and designed for an individual student or a selected group. ... *The principles of remedial and of initial instruction are the same .... Remedial reading ... is in some degree present in all reading programs* — P. Witty and D. Kopel (1939).

remedial reading class 1. a course designed to improve the reading of disabled readers. 2. the students in such a class. 3. a teacher education class in remedial reading.

remedial reading program 1. the

curriculum and operation of a program designed to provide intensive remediation in reading, usually by a teacher with advanced training and in a setting that allows flexible adjustment of materials and methods to individual differences. 2. any set curriculum or material for the remediation of reading skill deficits, usually commercially prepared, into which the student is fitted.

remedial teaching See **remediation.**

remediation (ri mē″dē ā′shən) 1. *n.* teaching which includes diagnosis of a student's reading ability, and corrective, remedial, or clinical approaches to improve that ability. *After three weeks of remediation, the student's reading improved.* 2. *n.* the process of correcting a deficiency.

remember (ri mem′bər) 1. *v.* to recall consciously in memory; recollect. *Try to remember what you said.* 2. *v.* to actively hold something in memory, as *remember these dates.* 3. *v.* to reward; show appreciation. *Mr. James remembered the library in his will.*

remission (ri mish′ən) 1. *n.* generally, reduced effort, intensity, or amount; specifically, the lessening of disease symptoms. *In many forms of cancer, a period of remission is common just before the terminal stages.* 2. *n.* the forgiveness of obligations, payments, etc. *There was a remission of all fines for books returned to the library during the month of May.* 3. **spontaneous remission,** the disappearance of symptoms without specific treatment.

repeated measures design an experimental design in which the same experimental group of subjects is exposed to more than one treatment; dependent sample design. *Ct.* **independent groups design.**

repertoire of registers See **register** (def. 1. *Note.*).

repetition (rep″i tish′ən) 1. *n.* the repeated use of sounds, words, or ideas for effect or emphasis, as *alliterative repetition.* 2. *n.* the intentional going over and over material for the purpose of learning it; drill; rehearsal; practice. 3. *n.* in oral reading, saying one or more words over again. *Note:* Repetitions often serve as place-markers for collecting one's thoughts. *Cp.* **hesitation** *(Note.).*

replication (rep″lə kā′shən) 1. *n.* a copy; duplicate: as *Ditto replication.* 2. *n.* the repetition of an experiment, often in different settings, to compare and verify findings. *Note:* The replication of experiments in educational research is often highly desirable because of the likelihood of uncontrolled variables. The replication may be carried out at either the same or different time periods. *v.* **replicate.**

representational level the relative degree of concreteness or abstractness of an idea or image. *Direct experience with a book is at a different representational level than a discussion of the concept of 'book.'*

representative sample an experimental sample which reflects to a high degree the composition of the population from which it is drawn. *Ct.* **stratified sample.**

repression (ri presh′ən) 1. *n.* unaware and uncontrolled blocking of a thought or desire from consciousness, as *repression of feelings of guilt. Ct.* **suppression** (def. 2). 2. *n.* control by exerting physical or social pressure. *The tyranny of the minority is a form of repression. v.* **repress.** *adj.* **repressive.**

reprint (*n.* rē′print″; *v.* rē print′) 1. *n.* something printed again, either as originally printed or as a new edition or impression, sometimes of inferior quality. *Paperbacks are often reprints* *of hardbound books.* 2. *v.* to so print again. 3. See **offprint** (def. 1).

reread (rē rēd′) 1. *v.* to read something again for a specific, and often different, purpose, *as read for detailed understanding after skimming.* 2. *v.* to read orally after silent reading. *n.* **rereading.**

research (ri sûrch′, rē′ sûrch) 1. *n.* a systematic inquiry into a subject or problem in order to discover, verify, or revise relevant facts and/or principles having to do with the subject or problem; especially, scientific or empirical investigation. *Note:* Many research methods are used to explore the complexities of education. Some methods of research are: historical; descriptive, as surveys, questionnaires, interviews, oberservations, etc.; longitudinal, as studies of the growth of individuals; and clinical, as case studies. 2. *n.* a particular system-systematic inquiry, as *research in the use of dictionaries.* 3. *v.* to investigate; look into; as *research an available apartment.* 4. *v.* to conduct research. *There is much in language to research.*

residual (ri zij′o͞o əl) 1. *adj.* left over; remaining. *After the head injury, John had little residual vision.* 2. *n.* what is left over; specifically: a. the difference between a predicted and an observed value. b. the variance remaining in a correlation matrix after the variance of each factor has been removed.

residual gain a statistic for measuring individual differences in improvement through training of subjects who have been statistically equated on the basis of pre-training measurement.

residual hearing any usable hearing possessed by a person with a hearing impairment.

resolution (rez″ə lo͞o′shən) 1. *n.* the events following the climax in a narrative or play which lead to solving the problem or resolving the conflict; falling action; denouement. 2. *n.* something determined or being determined, as *a resolution to act.* 3. *n.* firmness of purpose, as *a resolution to succeed.* 4. *n.* a formal statement made by a group, as *a legislative resolution. v.* **resolve.**

resonance (rez′ə nəns) 1. *n.* the vibration of air in a cavity, such as the mouth, nose, and throat, in the production of sound. 2. *n.* the quality of speech caused by such vibrations. *Resonance makes speech sounds fuller and richer.*

resonant (rez′ə nənt) *n.* a speech sound, as a vowel, which can be produced and held a long time. *Ct.* **obstruent.**

resonator (rez′ə nā″tər) 1. *n.* any of several vocal cavities which make speech sounds fuller and richer. See **resonance** (def. 1). 2. *n.* any cavity which makes sound fuller and richer by acoustic wave reflection, as in a loudspeaker. *v.* **resonate.** *n.* **resonation.**

resource center 1. a site in a school or library in which teaching materials are housed, often on a single subject. *Cp.* **instructional materials center (IMC); media center.** 2. *(Brit.)* **resource centre,** a resource unit.

resource teacher a teacher with specialized skills for assisting other teachers in their instructional problems, as *a reading resource teacher.*

resource unit 1. a collection of materials on a single topic from which a teacher can draw in developing a teaching unit, as family life, understanding other cultures, etc. 2. *(Brit.)* a resource centre.

respelling (rē′spel ing) 1. *n.* a repeated or different spelling of a word. 2. *n.* the spelling of words in a new, usually phonemic, system, as in the Augmented Roman Alphabet. 3. *n.* a new spelling system, usually phonemic and simpler. See **phonemic alphabet** (def. 2).

respite effect an effect of reading noted by Waples; specifically, relief from tension. *Respite effects are served by all sorts of writing — comic strips, joke columns, human-interest stories, and other diverting items, which come between the reader and his worries* — D. Waples and others (1940). *Cp.* **effects of reading.**

response (R) (ri spons′) 1. *n.* a written or spoken answer to a question, as *a test response.* 2. *n.* an overt or covert reaction to stimulation, as *a glandular response, a muscular response. Note:* Responses are measureable, either by direct inspection or through some electro-chemical or mechanical means. 3. *n.* the class of reactions to which def. 2 refers. *Ct.* **stimulus.** *v.* **respond.** *adj.* **responsive.**

response generalization the tendency of a learned response to a stimulus to make that stimulus more likely to call forth similar responses. *Cp.* **stimulus generalization.**

restricted code a term coined by the British sociologist B. Bernstein to describe largely ritualistic and predictable speech patterns. See also **public language.** *Note:* A restricted code relies upon manner of expression to imply complex meanings rather than upon the use of complex syntactic patterns. *Ct.* **elaborated code.**

restrictive clause a dependent clause that modifies a noun and limits or specifies its meaning, as *who had a camera* in *The man who had a camera took our picture. Note:* In English, a restrictive clause is not set off by commas. *Cp.* **relative clause.** *Ct.* **nonrestrictive clause.**

retardation, reading See **reading retardation.**

retarded reader a person who is disabled or backward in reading. See **reading disability; reading retardation; backwardness in reading.**

retarded speech delayed development in speech, especially in articulation.

retelling (rē tel′ing) 1. *n.* in discourse analysis, a measure of comprehension. 2. *n.* in miscue analysis, the process in which the reader, having orally read a story, describes what has happened in the story. *Note:* The purpose of including retelling in miscue analysis is to gain insight into the reader's ability to interact with, interpret, and draw conclusions from the text. *v.* **retell.**

retention (ri ten′shən) 1. *n.* the act or power of remembering; memory. *Superior retention is not the sole province of the slow reader.* 2. *n.* the persistence of changed performance in learning. *The class showed good retention on the test of new spelling words.* See also **memory** (def. 1). *adj.* **retentive.** *v.* **retain.**

retention curve a graphic representation of success in performance shown against time since last learning practice. See illustration. *Note:* Performance in remembering is usually plotted on the ordinate and time on the abscissa of the graph. *Ct.* **learning curve.**

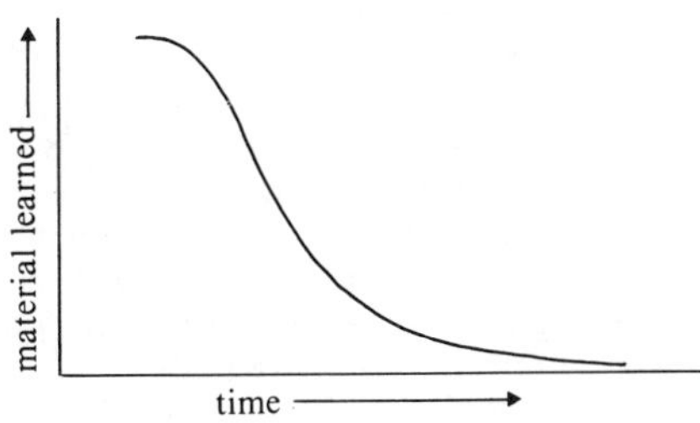

Retention (forgetting) curve

retention test a delayed assessment of

learning to discover its relatively long-term effects.

retest (rē'test) 1. *n.* a second application of the same test. 2. *n.* a second assessment of performance, usually with an alternate test form or with a different test.

reticular (ri tik'yə lər) *adj.* like a net in appearance or function, as *the reticular formation in the brain stem.*

retina (ret'ᵊnə, ret'nə) *n.* the sense organ for sight; specifically, an extension of the optic nerve inside the eyeball in a thin layer of cells sensitive to light and color that extends around the back and sides of the inner eye and receives stimulation from light refracted by the lens. See illustration under **eye.** *adj.* **retinal.**

retinal image the representation of the visual field formed on the retina by the refractive system of the eye.

retinal rivalry the irregular alternation of retinal impressions when each of the two eyes looks at sharply differing patterns or colors and cannot readily fuse the separate images; binocular rivalry. *Ant.* **binocular fusion.**

retinoscope (ret'ᵊnə skōp") *n.* an instrument for determining the refractive power of the eye; skiascope. *By determining refractive error of the eye with a retinoscope, eye specialists can prescribe proper corrective lenses.*

retro- a prefix indicating *backward;* as **retrospective.**

retroactive inhibition the interfering effect of later learning upon previously learned material, especially in remembering similar material. *Retroactive inhibition is a strong influence in forgetting. Ct.* **proactive inhibition.**

retroflex (re'trə fleks") *n.* a speech sound made with the tip of the tongue turned up and back toward the hard palate, as in some pronunciations of /r/ as in *bird.*

return sweep the long eye-movement, or saccade, from the end of one line of print to the start of the next. *Return sweeps go right-to-left and down a line when reading English, but they go up to the top of a column and a line to the left when reading Chinese.* See illustration under **eye-movement pattern.**

reversal (ri vûr'səl) *n.* a turnabout in direction, or rotation; specifically, the misreading or miswriting of letters, numbers, or words by the rotation of a symbol, as *d* for *p* in *pot,* or by an error in the direction of word attack, as *bat* for *tab. Note:* Changes of rotation are called *static reversals;* changes in direction of attack are called *kinetic reversals.*

reversibility (ri vûr"sə bil'i tē) *n.* (J. Piaget) the principle that for every operation there is an inverse or counter operation to cancel it. *Reversibility is shown in the process of addition vs. subtraction, argument vs. counter-argument, etc.*

reversible (ri vûr'sə bəl) *adj.* referring to forms, or to sequences of letters or words, that can be meaningfully perceived in more than one direction, as *a reversible figure, the reversible word 'eye.'* See also **palindrome.**

review (ri vyōō') 1. *v.* to study again for better understanding and/or retention, as *review a lesson.* 2. *n.* the act of studying again. 3. *n.* a critical report, as *a book review, a drama review.* 4. *v.* to so report. 5. *v.* to make a survey of something, as *review the research on reading readiness.* 6. *n.* the report of a survey. 7. *v.* to look back upon, as *review one's experiences in reading.*

review copy a sample publication, sometimes in galleys, sent to selected persons for inspection and comment, usually before, on, or shortly after the publication's general release. *Note:* Review copies may be sent directly to such persons or indirectly through magazines and journals that print reviews of publications. Reputable publishers seek critical reactions to review copies.

revised edition a new edition of a publication in which changes of a substantial nature have usually been made in content and/or scope.

rewrite rule See **phrase structure rule.**

rheme (rēm) *n.* in linguistics, an entire expression (sentence); *the expression which contains the information [that a] speaker wishes to communicate* — J. Lyons (1977). *Ct.* **theme** (def. 3).

rhetoric (ret'ər ik) 1. *n.* the study of the theory and principles of effective communication. 2. *n.* the art or science of using language in prose or verse. 3. *n.* the effective use of language in oratory to influence or persuade an audience, as *Churchill's command of rhetoric.* 4. exaggerated language; bombast. *The speech was nothing but rhetoric.* 5. *n.* a textbook on rhetoric. *adj.* **rhetorical.**

Rh factor any one of a group of inherited substances in the blood which produce substances that attack other blood cells, often causing severe reactions; rhesus factor, first discovered in rhesus monkeys.

rhyme *or* **rime** (rīm) 1. *n.* identical or very similar recurring final sounds in words within, or more often, at the ends of lines of verse: *Here Skugg lies snug/As a bug in a rug* — B. Franklin. 2. *n.* verse or recurring words that represent such sounds. 3. *v.* to write words or lines of verse with such recurring sounds, as *seek a rhyme for 'lyric.'*

rhyme scheme the pattern of rhyme in verse, usually coded a, b, etc., as in that for a limerick: *aabba.*

rhythm (rith'əm) 1. *n.* the pattern of recurring strong and weak syllabic stress in speech. 2. *n.* a recurring emphasis in the flow of spoken or written speech; beat; cadence; as *the rhythm of iambic pentameter.* 3. *n.* metrical form. *The rhythm of the sonnet was Shakespearean.* 4. *n.* the planned recurrence of a motif, as a symbol or theme, in literature or in other art forms. *adj.* **rhythmic; rhythmical.**

right-eyedness *n.* the consistent or frequent choice of the right eye for sighting tasks which need only one eye. See **dominant eye.**

rigidity (ri jid'ə tē) 1. *n.* stiffness; taut muscles; strong and continued muscle contractions; inflexibility. 2. *n.* difficulty or inability to make a new response even when conditions would call for such a change; discomfort in changing one's behaviors or attitudes; narrowmindedness. *Cp.* **perseveration.**

Rinne test a hearing test in which tuning forks are used to detect the difference between an air conduction hearing loss and a bone conduction hearing loss by placing the tuning forks alternately against the mastoid bone and near the ear canal. *Note:* Hearing the tuning forks longer by bone conduction indicates conductive hearing loss. Hearing them longer by air conduction indicates normal hearing or nerve loss.

rising diphthong a diphthong in which the final vowel is dominant, as in the /yōō/ in *few. Ct.* **falling diphthong.**

Ritalin (rit'ə lin) *n.* a trade name for methylphenidate hydrochloride, an amphetamine used in some forms of hyperactivity in children to increase the ability to focus attention and to maintain concentration.

rites of passage those experiences, often required by one's culture, which represent the move from one period in life to another, as from boyhood to manhood, from unmarried woman to married woman.

robust (rō bust′, rō′bust) *adj.* referring to a stable statistical procedure. *A robust test such as the t test is not necessarily invalidated by sample distributions that vary from an assumed normal distribution. n.* **robustness.**

rods (rodz) *n. pl.* light-sensitive, but only slightly color-sensitive cells in the retina which are needed especially for peripheral vision and for seeing in dim light. *Vision by rods is mostly in shades of gray. Cp.* **cones.**

role (rōl) 1. *n.* the function a person has in a group, as *the role of student, doctor, musician, etc.* 2. *n.* the expected behavior of a person in a group, as proper social behavior. *Cp.* **status** (def. 1). 3. *n.* a part to be played by an actor, actress, or singer, as *the role of Hamlet, Carmen, etc.* 4. *n.* the purpose or function of something, as *the role of the newspaper.*

role-playing 1. *n.* acting, as in a play. 2. *n.* imitating someone or something. 3. *n.* a therapeutic technique of improvising before an audience the role of another person, particularly one important to the role-player, to gain insight into the self, the person played, or the situation depicted. *Cp.* **play therapy; psychodrama; sociodrama.**

roman (rō′ mən) *adj.* referring to the common upright styles of printing type, as that in which this definition is printed. *Ct.* **italic.**

Roman alphabet See **Latin alphabet.**

romance (*n.* rō mans′, rō′mans; *adj.* rō′mans) 1. *n.* a highly imaginative novel or other narrative, often in an imaginary or historical setting, that tells of great deeds, pageantry, courtly love, etc. 2. *n.* the life, times, and spirit of such stories. 3. *n.* a medieval story, often in verse, which describes such life and times. 4. *n.* a love story. 5. *adj. (Cap.)* referring to a language derived from Latin, as Spanish and French. *adj.* (defs. 1-4) **romantic.**

romanization (rō″mə ni zā′shən) *n.* the rewriting of the graphic symbols of a writing system, such as the Chinese form, pinyin, in Roman or Latin alphabetic letters. See also **transliteration** (def. 1). *v.* **romanize.**

romanticism (rō man′ti siz″əm) 1. *n. (Usually cap.)* a literary and artistic movement in the late 18th and early 19th centuries which expressed individual human feelings and values freely. *Note:* Romanticism was a reaction, as in the poetry of Burns, Wordsworth, and Shelley, to the immediately preceding neoclassic emphasis upon form over content. The concept of romanticism is extremely complex, different authorities extending its meaning in subtle and diverse ways. 2. *n.* romantic spirit.

root (ro͞ot, ro͝ot) 1. *n.* a morpheme which forms a base to which derivational affixes may be added to form stems, and to which inflectional affixes can be added to form words. *Note:* A root may be independent or free, as in *fish*, or may be dependent or bound, as *-ceive* in *receive*. *Cp.* **stem** (def. 1); **base word.** 2. *n.* in historical linguistics, a morpheme or word from which other words have been formed, as the Indo-European root *bhard* from which comes the English *beard.*

root creation See **neologism** (def. 1).

rotation (rō tā′shən) 1. *n.* continuous movement around an axis or pivotal point. 2. *n.* one such complete turn. 3. *n.* a recurring series, as *the rotation of the days of the week.* 4. *n.* any one step forward within a recurring series, as *a rotation in volleyball.* 5. *n.* a static reversal in reading or writing, as *p* for *d.* 6. *n.* the shifting of factor axes and their hyperplanes after factor extraction.

rote learning the acquisition of information or behaviors by repetitive drill rather than by understanding. *The chief value of rote learning is in producing automatic psychomotor responses.*

rote memory the process of exact recall of what was learned, often with little or no understanding. *An idiot savant has great powers of rote memory.*

round-robin reading the practice of calling on students to read orally one after the other, suggesting the image of a nest of baby birds wherein the one that gets fed next is the one holding its head highest and making the most noise.

round vowel a vowel speech sound produced with rounded lips, as /o͞o/ in *food.*

round window an opening, from the middle ear into the inner ear, that is covered by a membrane which, when flexed, allows the fluid in the inner ear to pulse back and forth in response to the vibrations of the footplate of the stapes in the oval window; fenestra rotunda. *Cp.* **oval window.**

rubric (ro͞o'brik) 1. *n.* a title, heading, etc., in a manuscript or book printed to be distinguishable from the rest of the text, as a heading written or underlined in red. 2. *n.* a classification; category. *The rubric 'alphabet' does not include 'numbers.'*

rule (ro͞ol) 1. *n.* a guiding principle of behavior. 2. *n.* a generalized grammatical statement of conventional usage, as *the rule of subject-predicate agreement.* 3. *n.* a prescription for correct or preferred language use, as in prescriptive grammar. 4. *n.* in transformational-generative grammar, a phrase structure rule or rewrite rule. 5. *n.* a thin line used in printing to separate or decorate text.

rune (ro͞on) 1. *n.* a letter in the runic alphabet, used by northern Germanic peoples, especially the Scandinavians and Anglo-Saxons. See illustration under **futhork** *or* **futhark.** 2. *n.* a poem, riddle, or incantation written in runic characters. 3. *n.* any occult character or incantation. *adj.* **runic.**

running head a word, phrase, etc., at the top of each page of printed material, as a book title or chapter title; running title. *Cp.* **guide words.**

running title a running head, containing a publication title, chapter, section, etc.

running words 1. an uninterrupted series of words in a text. *Note:* Running words is a term used in describing the development or application of some readability formulas, informal reading inventories, cloze procedure, etc.: *The average student should miss no more than one of 20 running words.* 2. in linguistic analysis, tokens, or a count of all words in a piece of writing as opposed to different words, or types. See **type-token ratio (TTR).**

run-on sentence two independent clauses run together without any punctuation or conjunction to separate them, as *I walked in the door she was sitting by the fire.* See also **comma fault** *or* **splice.**

S

DEVELOPMENT OF MAJUSCULE								
NORTH SEMITIC	GREEK		ETR.	LATIN		MODERN		
						GOTHIC	ITALIC	ROMAN
W	ʃ	Σ	ϟ	ϟ	S	𝔖	*S*	S

DEVELOPMENT OF MINUSCULE					
ROMAN CURSIVE	ROMAN UNCIAL	CAROL. MIN.	MODERN		
			GOTHIC	ITALIC	ROMAN
ʃ	S	s	𝔰	*s*	s

The nineteenth letter of the English alphabet developed from North Semitic, where its form was similar to that of the modern W. Descending through Greek *sigma* (ς), which itself exhibited some variety of use (ς, σ), it acquired its present form in Latin.

s *or* **s factor** See **specific factor.**

S 1. stimulus, as *S-R theory. Ct.* **R.** 2. an experimental subject. 3. in transformational-generative grammar, a sentence.

saccade (sa käd′) *n.* the quick, jumping movements of the eye as it shifts fixation from place to place, usually without awareness of the viewer.

saccadic eye movements the saccades used in searching a visual field, as in moving along a line of print in reading. *Note:* If you look over the top of a page across from someone reading, you will see the quick saccadic eye movements that alternate with the longer fixations during which print is actually viewed. The eye is essentially blind during saccadic eye movements. See illustration under **eye-movement pattern.**

saga (sä′gə) 1. *n.* a medieval story of Icelandic and Scandinavian origin, passed on orally to succeeding generations. *Cp.* **epic** (def. 1). 2. *n.* a narrative of heroic deeds and events, usually of a person or family. 3. *n.* a modern story of a family, as *John Galsworthy's* The Forsyte Saga.

sagittal (saj′i tᵊl) 1. *adj.* having to do with the seam joining the top halves of the skull, as *the sagittal suture.* 2. *adj.* shaped like an arrow or arrowhead.

sagittal plane any imaginary surface or plane which passes vertically through the body at or parallel to the median plane. See also **frontal plane; median plane.**

sample (sam′pəl, säm′-) 1. *n.* a part that represents a whole, as *the three most typical samples from the penmanship class.* 2. *n.* in experimentation, that part of a population which is selected for observation. *Note:* Special types of sample, as *stratified sample,* are given under the describing term. 3. **sampling,** the act of getting an experimental sample. 4. *v.* to examine or test something by considering only a part of a larger whole. *The effective reader knows when to sample and when to read material in detail.*

sampling error any difference between a sample and the population from which it is drawn that makes the sample inaccurate.

sandhi (san′dē, sän′-) 1. *n.* a morphophonemic change, as *gimme* for *give me.* 2. *n.* a phonological modification occurring especially at a word boundary.

sanserif *or* **sans serif** (sanz″ser′if) *n.* a typeface without serifs, as commonly found in manuscript typefaces. *Cp.* **serif.**

sarcasm (sär′kaz əm) 1. *n.* a harsh form of irony, intended to taunt or hurt someone. 2. *n.* a harsh or cutting remark. See also **satire; irony** (def. 1). *adj.* **sarcastic.**

satellite center a branch of a central resource center, offering a sampling of the same kinds of services and materials but in a location closer to users in its area.

satellite program a branch adult basic education program located away from the primary learning center, offering similar but usually more limited services.

satire (sat'ī°r) 1. *n.* the use of ridicule or scorn, often in a humorous or witty way, to expose vices and follies. 2. *n.* a literary example of such ridicule or scorn. *Jonathan Swift's* A Modest Proposal *is one of the great satires in English literature.* 3. *n.* the class of such writings. *Cp.* **irony** (def. 1). **lampoon; sarcasm.** See also **burlesque** (defs. 1-3); **caricature; parody; travesty** (def. 1). *adj.* **satirical.**

saw (sô) *n.* a familiar saying or maxim: *A rolling stone gathers no moss.*

saying (sā'ing) *n.* a proverb or adage. See **saw.**

S-B Stanford-Binet Intelligence Scale.

scale (skāl) 1. *n.* any device, or representation thereof, for measuring quantity in a series of ordered units, as *a metric scale, a map scale, an economic scale.* 2. *n.* a standard of measurement. *Efficiency is the scale by which you will be judged.* 3. *n.* a graded series of tasks or tests for measuring performance, as *The Gesell Developmental Schedules.* 4. *v.* to make or place on a scale.

scan (skan) 1. *v.* to examine or read something quickly, but selectively, for a particular purpose; skim; as *scan an article for the general idea, scan a directory for a telephone number.* 2. *v.* to examine or read something carefully; look at closely. *Please scan this drawing for flaws. He proceeded to scan the text for clues to the murderer.* 3. *n.* the act or result of making a detailed survey, as *a brain scan.* 4. *v.* to analyze the metrical structure of verse. 5. *v.* to follow, in verse, the rules of meter. *The poem scans well.* 6. *v.* to make a visual, electronic, or mechanical search of computer data, as *scan the computer printout. n.* **scanner.** *n.* **scanning.**

scanning (skan'ing) See **scan.**

scansion (skan'shən) *n.* a way of analyzing verse to note the poem's rhythmic effects and rhyme scheme; scanning.

scapegoating (skāp'gō"ting) *n.* shifting guilt or blame to another person or group; displaced aggression. *n.* **scapegoat.**

scatter (skat'ər) 1. *v.* to spread out; disperse. *The students scattered in all directions. A convex lens scatters light.* 2. *n.* the degree of spread, or dispersion, of test scores; variance. 3. *adj.* referring to such a spread, as *a scatter diagram.* 4. *n.* the spread, or variability, of item difficulty in a test.

scatter diagram a graphic distribution of two sets of scores that shows their relationship to each other; scattergram. See illustration.

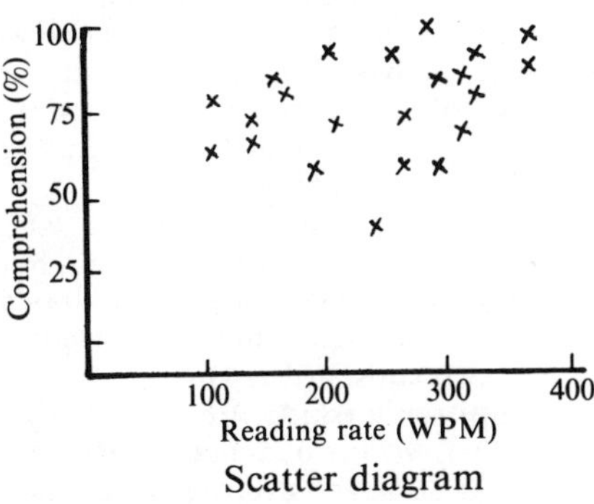

Scatter diagram

scattergram See **scatter diagram.**

scenario (si nâr'ē ō", -när'-) 1. *n.* a brief outline of the plot of a play, indicating the chief characters and their actions. 2. *n.* a detailed film or TV script. 3. *n.* a projected series of events. *What is the scenario for today?*

scene (sēn) 1. *n.* a division of an act in a play, with continuous action in the same setting. 2. *n.* the setting of a play or narrative where the action will take place. *In* Our Town, *the opening scene is a street in Grover's Corners, New Hampshire, on May 7, 1901.* 3. *n.* an episode in a dramatic work or narrative, as *the coronation scene in Moussorgsky's* Boris Goudonoff. 4. *n.* a film or TV script sequence, as *a closeup scene.*

schema (skē′mə) *pl.* **-mata** (-mə tə). 1. *n.* a generalized description, plan, or structure, as *a schema of the reading process.* 2. *n.* a conceptual system for understanding something. *Grace's mathematical schema helped her understand statistics.* 3. *n.* (J. Piaget) an image representing reality that is held in thought, but not transformed through thought.

schematic (skē mat′ik) 1. *n.* a diagram or plan; schema (def. 1); as a flow chart in a science textbook. 2. *adj.* referring to such a diagram or plan.

scheme (skēm) *n.* (J. Piaget) in operational activities, that which can be repeated and generalized in an action.

schizo- a combining form indicating *split;* as **schizophrenia.**

schizoid (skit′soid, skiz′oid) 1. *adj.* schizophrenic. 2. *adj.* similar to, but not, schizophrenia. 3. *adj.* withdrawn from social interaction; introspective. See also **autism** (def. 1).

schizophrenia (skit″sə frē′nē ə, -frēn′yə, skiz″ə-) *n.* any of a number of severe mental disorders involving dissociation from reality, characterized by delusions, hallucinations, misinterpretations, withdrawal, or bizarre reactions in the intellectual, emotional, and behavioral domains. See also **dissociation** (def. 1). *adj.* **schizophrenic.**

scholastic aptitude See **academic** *or* **scholastic ability.** See also **intelligence** (def. 2).

school (sko͞ol) 1. *n.* one of several types and levels of institutions for teaching and learning, as the British infant school, the German gymnasium, the French école nationale, or the American vocational school. 2. *n.* the process of teaching and learning, as *books are useful in school.* 3. See **schooling** (def. 2). 4. *n.* persons engaged in teaching and learning. *The school was very quiet.* 5. *v.* to teach. 6. *n.* persons identified with a particular set of ideas or point of view, as the *Prague School* in linguistics. 7. *adj.* having to do with school or schools.

schooling (sko͞o liŋ) 1. *n.* teaching and learning in a school. 2. *n.* learning from experience out of school. *The chef's schooling was in the kitchen.*

school psychologist 1. a certified psychologist who helps a school or school system to appraise, understand, and deal with difficult behavior and learning problems. 2. *(Brit.)* educational psychologist.

school without walls a high school, often with very informal and nontraditional instructional and housing arrangements, that offers alternative programs for disadvantaged and/or disaffected students. See also **storefront school; street academy.** *Note:* By comparison, a university without walls offers an individualized higher education program for adults who have not begun or completed traditional degree programs at this level.

schwa (shwä) 1. *n.* in English, the mid-central vowel in unaccented or unstressed syllables; neutral vowel; as the first vowel sound in *about* /əbout/. 2. *n.* the graphic symbol (ə) used to represent such a short, unstressed, mid-central vowel.

Schwabach test a hearing test which uses tuning forks to compare the bone conduction hearing level or threshold of the subject with that of an examiner with normal hearing. *Note:* The tuning fork is alternately held against the mastoid bone of the subject and examiner. By counting how many seconds longer the examiner can hear a tone, the hearing loss may be detected.

science fiction an imaginary story based upon current or projected scientific and technological developments, as Jules Verne's *20,000 Leagues Under the Sea* or Ray Bradbury's *Fahrenheit 451. Note:* While the time frame of science fiction is usually unlimited and may be set in the present, future, or past, the term *science fantasy* is sometimes used to refer to science fiction set in future time.

scintillating scotoma an irregular black spot with ragged, brightly-colored edges in one or both eyes, which may move across the visual field or vary in size, and usually occurs before a migraine headache.

sclera (sclĕr'ə) *n.* the tough, white, opaque, outer layer of the eyeball that covers the entire eye to give it strength and shape, except for the area covered by the transparent cornea.

-scope a combining form indicating *instrument for viewing or detecting;* as **laryngoscope.**

scope and sequence a curriculum plan, usually in chart form, in which instructional objectives, skills, etc., are arranged according to the levels at which they are taught. *adj.* **scope-and-sequence.**

-scopy a suffix indicating *observation*; as **telescopy.**

score (skōr, skôr) 1. *n.* the credits or points earned on a test, as *a score of 25. Note:* Special types of score, as *converted score,* are given under the describing term. 2. *n.* an item of credit on a test, as *miss only three scores.* 3. *v.* to make a given score, as *score the highest.* 4. *v.* to assess the credits or points earned, as *score the test.* 5. *v.* to keep track of credits or points earned. *Will you score the tennis match?* 6. *v.* to gain or achieve. *The play scored a great success.* 7. *v.* to criticize severely. *The reviewer scored the novel unmercifully.*

scoto- a combining form indicating *darkness*; as **scotopic**.

scotoma (skō tō'mə) *pl.* **-mas, -mata**. *n.* a spot of reduced or absent retinal sensitivity; a blind spot other than the optic disk. *Note:* Scotomas may have many causes and may vary or be fixed in time and place. See also **scintillating scotoma.**

scotopic vision (skə top'ik, skō-) night vision; specifically, vision under conditions of dim light which relies mostly on the rods around the edge of the retina and is thus not very sensitive to color. *Ct.* **photopic vision.**

screening (skrē'niṅg) 1. *n.* the process of selection of persons, test items, etc. 2. *n.* a rough sorting out of persons before final selection. 3. *n.* a presentation of a motion picture, as for early review.

scribble (skrib'əl) 1. *v.* to write carelessly, without attention to the shape or legibility of the letters, accuracy of the spelling, or grammatical correctness. 2. *v.* to produce meaningless written marks. 3. *n.* careless written marks or writing; scribbling.

script (skript) 1. *n.* the letters or characters used in handwriting. 2. *n.* cursive handwriting. *Ct.* **manuscript** (def. 1). 3. *n.* the text of a manuscript. 4. *n.* a written or printed text used to guide the speech and actions of performers, as in a play, motion picture, radio or TV show, etc. 5. *v.* to write the text of a play, television show, etc. *He scripted five of the shows for a new television series.* 6. *v.* to transform a novel or a play into a television script. 7. *n.* a typeface which looks like handwriting. 8. *n.* See **schema** (def. 1). *n.* **scripter.**

script writing a style of handwriting with cursive characters; cursive script.

SD standard deviation.

SE standard error.

seatwork (sēt′wûrk″) *n.* study by a student in a classroom.

secondary stress 1. the vowel or syllable in a word, phrase, or metrical foot with the second strongest and loudest emphasis; secondary stress. 2. an orthographic symbol placed above a vowel grapheme (′) or (″), adjacent to a syllable (ˌ), or above a syllable in a line of verse (˘), to indicate that the marked vowel or syllable has greater stress than some other vowel or syllable in the same word, phrase or metrical foot, except for that with primary stress, as in *còn sérv va tion*, or ˌ*con sér va tion. In pronunciations in this dictionary, the diacritical mark (″) is used to show secondary accent or stress. Note:* A very weakly stressed syllable is not marked for stress, even if it occurs in a two-syllable word, as the *-thy* in *wealthy. Ct.* **primary accent.** See also **stress** (def. 8); **diacritic** *or* **diacritic (-al) mark.**

secondary reading disability *or* **retardation** a reading disability resulting from such factors as emotional disturbance, environmental deprivation, poor vision, etc., rather than a basic language difficulty or brain damage. *Cp.* **primary reading disability** *or* **retardation.**

secondary school in the United States, a school or schools between the elementary school and college; high school; specifically, either grades 9-12, or the junior high school, usually grades 7-9, and/or senior high school, usually grades 10-12.

secondary source any source other than a primary source consulted in preparing a work on some subject. *Any text that cites Huey's* The Psychology and Pedagogy of Reading *is a secondary source. Ct.* **primary source.**

secondary stuttering a lack of fluency of which the speaker is aware; stuttering. *Ct.* **primary stuttering.**

second language the next language learned in addition to one's native tongue.

second language acquisition the process of acquiring, informally or formally, a language different from one's native tongue.

second person referring to the person(s) being spoken to, as, in English, the pronoun *you. Ct.* **first person; third person.** See also **person.**

see-and-say approach *or* **method** See **analytic approach** *or* **method.**

segment (*n.* seg′mənt; *v.* seg ment′) 1. *n.* a discrete, or separate, chunk of speech or text, as a phoneme, word, sentence, etc. 2. *v.* to form such a chunk. *adj.* **segmental.** *v.* **segment.**

segmental phoneme any of the individual speech sounds used in a language. *In English the segmental phonemes are the consonants and vowels. Cp.* **supra-segmental phoneme.**

segmentation (seg″mən tā′shən) *n.* the process, or result, of dividing into appropriate parts; specifically, the recognition of phonemes, morphemes, and syntactic word order, whether in graphic or spoken form. *Segmentation is a skill that is critical for reading development.*

segregation (seg″rə gā′shən) *n.* the provision, often by law but more usually by custom, of separate facilities and opportunities for different races and/or groups. *Ant.* **desegregation.** [See also **integration** (def. 3)].

seizure (sē′zhər) *n.* the sudden onset

of a disease, especially an epileptic attack; convulsion.

selection (si lekt′ shən) 1. *n.* a passage chosen to be read, often orally: *I will now read a selection from Carl Sandburg.* 2. **selections,** a group of passages chosen as readings on some topic, period, etc., as *selections of Third World literature.*

selection aid any reference or bibliographic tool used to make decisions about adding material to a library or personal collection, as book reviews, trade bibliographies, etc.

self-concept (self″kon′sept) *n.* how one thinks and feels about oneself; self-appraisal. See also **ego** (def. 1).

self-contained classroom a classroom in which the same teacher teaches all or nearly all subjects.

self-correction See **correction strategy.**

self-regulation (self″reg″yə la′shən) *n.* (J. Piaget) a sub-principle of equilibration which refers to the active tendency to keep things in balance biologically and through cognitive operations; autoregulation.

self-report (self″rē port′, -pôrt′) *n.* any information supplied by oneself, as on a questionnaire, checklist, etc.

self-selection (self″ se lek′shən) *n.* the educational principle of allowing the student to choose materials for reading and viewing. *Self-selection is a basic principle of individualized reading.*

semantic aphasia 1. receptive aphasia marked by difficulty in understanding the full meaning of words and sentences, as in Wernicke's aphasia. 2. expressive aphasia marked by difficulty in recalling and using previously known names and other symbols.

semantic count a record of how often different meanings for words appear in a representative sample of reading material. *A semantic count shows the multiple meanings of many word forms.*

semantic cue evidence from the general sense or meaning of a written or spoken communication that aids in the identification of an unknown word. *Cp.* **syntactic cue.**

semantic differential a technique for rating selected stimuli on 7-point scales of adjectival opposites, as hard-soft, fair-unfair, etc., developed by C. Osgood and others for research into perception, meaning, and attitudes.

semantic factor the sense or meaning dimension in material to be comprehended, as the measure of the number of hard words that is commonly used in readability formulas. *Cp.* **syntactic factor.**

semantic pair a pair of words related in meaning: synonyms such as *find/locate*, contrasting items such as *give/take*, and antonyms such as *up/down.* See **synonym** (def. 1); **antonym; opposition** (def. 4).

semantics (si man′tiks) *(with sing. v.)* 1. *n.* the study of meaning; especially, the study of the relations between referents and names, and between concepts and names. 2. *n.* the formal study of the meaning of meaning; especially, the study of the relation of signs to verbal referents or to objects. See also **sign** (defs. 1, 2); **signification** (def. 1); **semiotics.** 3. *n.* the study of meaning in artificial language systems, rather than in natural language; pure semantics. *Ct.* **pragmatics** (def. 1). 4. *n.* See **generative semantics.** *adj.* **semantic.**

semantic triangle a model of language communication developed by C.K. Ogden and I.A. Richards; semiotic triangle. See illustration. *Note:* The illustration shows the relationships among that referred to (C), the symbol used to refer (A), and the idea or sense made to the speaker or listener (B). The solid lines AB and BC are basic signifying relations; the broken line AC shows that the sign-referent relation is derived and not basic. See also **signification** (def. 1); **referent** *or* **referend** (def. 1).

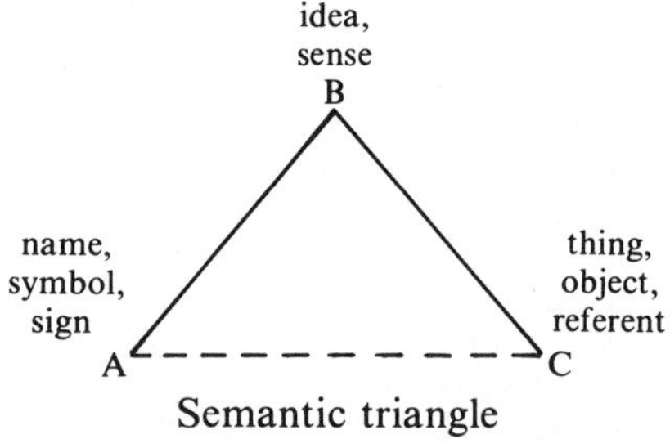

Semantic triangle

semi- a prefix indicating *half, partly;* as **semicircular, semilingual.**

semicircular canals the three fluid-filled tubes in the labyrinth of the inner ear that serve as the sense organs for balance. See illustration under **ear.**

semicolon (sem′i kō″lən) *n.* a punctuation mark (;) sometimes used to separate independent clauses, especially those which already contain commas or are structurally complex, as *I like tea; nevertheless, I don't drink it. Cp.* **colon** (def. 1); **comma** (def. 1); **period** (def. 1).

seminar (sem′ə när″) 1. *n.* an advanced course for a select group of students, usually for the study of a specialized topic. 2. *n.* the topic, and/or students, of such a course. 3. *n.* a special meeting or series of meetings to exchange information, often new developments, as *a seminar on recent brain research.*

semiotic function See **symbolic function.**

semiotics (sē″mē ot′iks, sē″mī-, sem″ē-, sem″ī-) *(with sing. v.) n.* the analysis and theory of signalling systems and signs; the study of signs and their relations, consisting of three subbranches: pragmatics, semantics, and syntactics. See these terms. See also **sign** (defs. 1-3). *adj.* **semiotic.**

semivowel (sem′ē vou″əl) 1. *n.* a speech sound with features of both a consonant and a vowel; specifically, a consonantal resonant; glide (def. 3); as /w/ in wash, /m/ in spasm, /y/ in yes. 2. *n.* a sound that can serve as either a vowel or consonant, /y/ or /w/. 3. *n.* a letter representing any of these sounds. *adj.* **semivowel; semivocalic.**

senior high school See **secondary school.**

sensation (sen sā′shən) 1. *n.* the process of receiving sensory stimuli, as in seeing, hearing, etc. 2. *n.* the perception of, or the ability to perceive; sensory feeling; as *the sensation of pain, an organ of sensation.* 3. *n.* a generalized feeling. *Scrooge finally experienced the sensation of good will toward all.* 4. *n.* excitement; thrill. *The first flight to the moon created a worldwide sensation.* 5. **phantom sensation,** a feeling which still seems to come from amputated parts of the body. *adj.* **sensational.**

sensationalism (sen sā′ shə nəliz″ əm) *n.* an appeal to the wildly dramatic aspects of a story, situation, topic, etc., to gain attention.

sense (sens) 1. *n.* literal or cognitive meaning: denotation. *What is the sense of the dictionary definition of 'meaning'?* 2. *n.* semantic meaning; connotation. *The sense of 'old' depends on one's age. Cp.* **meaning** (defs. 1, 2). 3. *n.* agreement or understanding between two or more, as *the sense of the meeting.* 4. *n.* any of the means, as sight, hearing, smell, etc., by which one perceives stimuli outside or within the body. 5. See **sense organ**. 6. *v.* to perceive by the senses. 7. *n.* See **sense modality**. 8. *n.* a general awareness, as *a sense of cold.* 9. *n.* a particular awareness, as of a moral value, danger, appreciation, etc. 10. *n.* the capacity to enjoy, as *a sense of humor.* 11. *n.* good judgment. *Lou's comment makes sense.*

sense meaning See **literal meaning.**

sense modality any of the pathways by which particular stimuli are received: sight, hearing, touch, taste, smell. *Kinesthetic methods actually call upon more than one sense modality.*

sense organ any of the receptor organs and related structures which receive stimulation and convert it into sensation. *The eye, ear, nose, and taste buds are sense organs.*

sensitivity training 1. the study of group processes and organization. 2. a directed, interactive group process by which individuals explore personal problems and interpersonal relations. *Note:* Def. 1 is the earlier meaning of the term; def. 2 the more recent.

sensorimotor (sen″sə rē mō′tər) 1. *adj.* having to do with both the sensory and the motor aspects of behavior. 2. *adj.* indicating a nerve with both afferent and efferent fibers.

sensorimotor stage (J. Piaget) the developmental period from birth to approximately two years during which intellectual development relies primarily upon sensory input and motor activities prior to the attainment of symbolic functioning and representational thought.

sensorineural deafness deafness caused by disease or damage to the inner ear and/or the auditory nerve. *Ct.* **conduction deafness.**

sensory (sen′sə rē) 1. *adj.* having to do with sensations or with one of the senses, as *sensory projection areas of the cortex.* 2. *adj.* indicating an afferent nerve.

sensory aphasia receptive aphasia marked by difficulty in producing and understanding speech, as in Wernicke's aphasia.

sensuality (sen″shōō al′i tē) *n.* preoccupation with satisfying the senses or physical appetites. *Cp.* **sexuality** (def. 2). *adj.* **sensual.**

sentence (S) (sen′tᵊns)

Most speakers of a language appear to know what a sentence is, but grammarians and linguists have difficulty agreeing upon its definition. There is, however, considerable current agreement that the notion of a sentence as a complete thought is unsatisfactory.

1. *n. an expression of thought or feeling by means of a word or words used in such form and manner as to convey the meaning intended* — G. Curme (1931). *Note:* While a subject and predicate are often considered essential parts of a sentence, either one may be omitted if the immediate or situational context, and/or the speaker's intonation, conveys the intended meaning. 2. *n.* operationally, a grammatical unit of one or more words, with little necessary syntactic relation to surrounding grammatical units, often punctuated in speech by pauses and marked by recognizable intonation patterns, and typically expressing an independent statement, question, command, etc. 3. *n.* the largest linguistic unit, composed of at least one subject and its predicate, that is not part of a larger comparable linguistic form, and which can be studied by linguistic analysis, as in transformational-generative grammar. 4. *n.* in tagmemics, a linguistic unit inter-

mediate between a clause and a paragraph.

sentence-combining a teaching technique developed by F. O'Hare to improve writing skills in which complex sentence chunks and paragraphs are built from basic sentences by means of syntactic manipulation. *Sentence-combining is essentially a rewriting skill* — F. O'Hare (1973).

sentence factor See **syntactic factor.**

sentence method an extension of the word and phrase methods of teaching reading in which students first learn whole sentences. *The sentence first being presented as a whole, the words are discovered, and after that the letters composing the word* — G. Farnham, cited by E. Huey (1908).

sentence modifier a word, phrase, or clause which qualifies or limits the meaning of an entire sentence, as *Fortunately* in *Fortunately, the horse won the race.*

sentence pattern any of a number of basic sentence types in a language. *Note:* The number and description of the various kinds of sentence patterns of a given language are dependent on the grammatical theory that is used. *In traditional grammar*, sentence patterns are described in terms of function, as statement, question, exclamation, command. *In structural grammar,* sentence patterns are described in terms of a noun, kind of verb, and the number and kind of elements following the verb. *In transformational-generative,* the nature of the verb and the kinds of transformations a sentence may undergo determine its pattern.

sentence transformation in a transformational grammar, the rearrangements, deletions, and copyings of elements in a phrase structure grammar that are part of the process of generating a sentence.

sentimental (sen″tə men′tᵊl) 1. *adj.* appealing to one's feelings or emotions, as love, pity, etc., as *a sentimental play.* 2. *adj.* given to overemotional responses, as *sentimental weeping at love scenes in motion pictures. n.* **sentimentalism; sentimentality.**

sentimentalism (sen″tə men′tᵊ liz″əm) 1. *n.* the tendency in literature to emphasize the goodness of human nature rather than its sinfulness, as in Laurence Sterne's *A Sentimental Journey.* 2. *n.* the tendency to engage overmuch in emotion; bathos (def. 2); as *sickly sentimentalism. n.* **sentimentality.** *adj.* **sentimental.**

septum (sep′təm) *pl.* **-ta**. *n.* a dividing wall or membrane. *The nasal septum divides the nasal cavities.*

sequel (sē′kwəl) 1. *n.* a story, complete in itself, that is a continuation of an earlier story, as in novels, motion pictures, and television shows. Little Men *is one of the sequels to* Little Women. 2. *n.* an event or happening which is a follow-up or consequence of another event. *The Allied landing at Normandy in World War II was a sequel to months of careful planning.*

sequence (sē′kwəns) 1. *n.* the order in which something is learned or taught. 2. *n.* See **sequential relationship.** *adj.* **sequential.**

sequential analysis the analysis of incoming sample data to determine when there is sufficient information to accept or reject an experimental hypothesis. *Cp.* **trend analysis.**

sequential constraint in phonology, a restriction on what phonemes or phonological features may occur next to one another in a sequence of phonemes, morphemes, or words. *Cp.*

phonotactics. See also **sequential redundancy.**

sequential order placement in a systematic pattern according to time or rank. *In spelling, letters must be perceived and written in the correct sequential order.*

sequential redundancy 1. in generative phonology, the restrictions placed on permitted phonological sequences in given contexts; as, for example, if an initial consonant cluster begins with /s/ in English, as in *spring,* the next consonant must be voiceless, as /p/, /t/, /k/. 2. any completely predictable sequence in any aspect of language, as *u* after *q* in most English spellings.

sequential relationship an association, stated or implied in a communication, of successive order among ideas and/or events.

serial (sēr′ē əl) 1. *n.* a story or play presented in parts in writing, TV, radio, or motion pictures. *Many of Charles Dickens' novels were first published as serials in periodicals.* 2. *n.* any periodical planned and issued as an indefinite series of numbered, consecutive parts, as periodicals, newspapers, journals, etc. 3. *adj.* referring to a series. *Give the serial order of the alphabet from A to Z. v.* **serialize.**

serial order placement in a systematic pattern that has a specified sequence for learning and remembering. *Language, to be understood, must be spoken, written, and read in its proper serial order.*

seriation (ser″i ā′s̱hən) 1. *n.* the sequential ordering and processing of input signals, as words in sentences. *Note:* It is unlikely that seriation of letters occurs when reading a known word. 2. *n.* (J. Piaget) the ability to logically order a set of objects. *Seriation is a major feature of concrete operations.*

series (sēr′ēz) 1. *n.* an ordered set of objects, events, ideas, etc., that has direction and sequence, as *a series of numbered blocks, a series of false hypotheses.* 2. *n.* a set of related publications: a. a set of textbooks usually ordered in difficulty, as *a reading series.* b. a set of publications with some common connection (author, topic, form, publication), as *the Rivers of America series.*

series story 1. one of a group of books with a common element written by the same author. *Note:* Many series books for children have the same improbable characters and predictable plots and endings, as in the Nancy Drew series. Others, as Laura Ingalls Wilder's stories of pioneer life or C. S. Lewis' stories of the land of Narnia, have literary merit. 2. one of a collection of informational books, usually with the same format but on different subjects.

serif (ser′if) *n.* a short finishing stroke found at the end of lines on a typeface, as at the top and bottom of capital I. *Cp.* **sanserif** *or* **sans serif; bar.**

serotonin (ser″ə tō′nin) *n.* a substance naturally found in the brain, intestines, and blood platelets which induces muscle contractions and constriction of the blood vessels.

service word 1. a word that appears many more times than others in ordinary reading material; high-frequency word; as *in, of, the. Basic word lists are mostly if not entirely made up of service words.* 2. See **function word.**

servomechanism (sûr′vō mek″ə niz″əm, sûr″vō mek′-) *n.* a control system which uses feedback to modify the operation of the machine or process which it is monitoring, as the process which controls the size of the pupil according to how much light is entering the eye.

SES socioeconomic status.

set (set) 1. *n.* any coherent group of items, as *a set of cardinal numbers, an alphabetic set, a set of books.* 2. *n.* a tendency to selectively attend to and respond to certain stimuli rather than to others. *Note:* Set in this sense usually refers to a temporary state but one which may recur from time to time. It may also, however, refer to a practiced mental set such as that needed in proofreading. 3. *adj.* in an habitual, stereotyped manner, as *a set speech.* 4. See **setting** (def. 3). 5. *v.* to place; adjust; arrange; as *set type, set the pacer at 325 WPM.*

set reading *(Brit.)* materials assigned to be read for a course or examination.

setting (set′iŋ) 1. *n.* the physical and psychological background against which the action in a story takes place, as in a play or narrative. 2. *n.* the time and place in which a narrative occurs. 3. *n.* the scenery and stage effects for a drama, motion picture, etc.; set. 4. *n.* context.

sexism (sek′siz əm) *n.* discrimination against another sex, especially women and women's rights, roles, etc. *Many studies of sexism in children's reading materials have been made. adj.* **sexist.**

sex role the lifestyle and attitudes that identify the expected behavior of a male or female individual.

sexuality (sek″sho͞o al′i tē) 1. *n.* the psychological, cultural, and physical characteristics that distinguish male from female. 2. *n.* a preoccupation with sex. 3. *n.* participation in, or readiness for, sexual activity.

shades of meaning slight differences in meaning; nuances. *In silent reading, a shift in context may indicate a new shade of meaning; in oral reading, shades of meaning are often shown by intonation, gesture, etc.*

shape constancy the tendency to perceive the shape of an object as the same regardless of angle of view. *Cp.* **size constancy.** See also **perceptual constancy.**

shelf list a record on cards of library holdings, filed by call number, in the order in which material will be found on the shelves.

shibboleth (shib′ə lit͟h, -let͟h′) 1. *n.* a distinctive or peculiar use of some aspect of speech that identifies a social group. 2. *n.* in popular usage, a slogan, catchword, or common saying, as, in the 1920's, *the shibboleth 'You're the cat's pajamas.'*

shift of meaning the change in meaning of words or passages because of a change in context. 'Touchstone: *For my part, I had rather bear with you than bear you.'* — As You Like It (Shakespeare).

short answer test 1. an essay examination with responses sharply restricted in length. 2. any brief response test, including those with completion and selective response items.

shortening (s͟hôr′tᵊniŋ, s͟hôrt′niŋ) *n.* an abbreviation or short form: a. in historical linguistics, a process by which distinctively long vowels or consonants become distinctively short. b. in phonetics, any reduction in the time duration of a linguistic segment. c. in grammar, the omission of a segment from a word. *Cp.* **syncope** (def. 1).

shorthand (s͟hôrt′hand″) *n.* a system of rapid handwriting that uses, instead of the standard letters, other symbols to represent sounds, syllables, words, or phrases; stenography.

short story a brief fictional prose narrative, designed to create a unified impression quickly and forcefully, as in the Biblical story of David and Goliath, Poe's *The Telltale Heart,* Hemingway's *The Snows of Kilimanjaro. Note:* The modern short story often uses unresolved situations instead of the more familiar narrative pattern of resolution of the action. *Cp.* **novel** (defs. 1, 2); **tale** (def. 2).

short term memory (STM) that aspect of memory that lasts only briefly, has rapid input and output, is very limited in capacity, and depends directly on stimulation for its form, as memory developed after one has attended to a stimulus array but before one has mastered all the details. *In current models of reading behavior, STM enables the reader to keep parts of the reading material in mind until enough material has been processed to make sense. Ct.* **long term memory (LTM).**

short vowel 1. in teaching practice, the sound qualities of /a/, /e/, /i/, /o/, and /u/ heard in *bat, bet, bit, bob,* and *tub.* See also **schwa.** 2. in phonetics, the relatively short duration of a vowel sound. *Note* (def. 2): Vowel length is affected by the amount of stress and by regional speech habits as well as by context. *Ct.* **long vowel.** See also **checked** (def. 2).

sib (sib) 1. *n.* any relative; especially, a blood relative. 2. *n.* one of two or more children of either parent; sibling. *Note:* Sib sometimes refers to one of two or more children, other than a twin, of both parents only.

sibilant (sib′ə lənt) 1. *n.* a fricative consonant sound made with a hiss, as /s̱h/ in *shut.* 2. *adj.* having a hissing sound.

sibling (sib′lin͡g) 1. *n.* a sib (def. 2). 2. *adj.* referring to a brother or sister.

sibling rivalry competition between sibs, as in the attempts of a brother or sister to displace each other in parental affection. *In our family we refer to this phenomenon by the more felicitous phrase coined by novelist Peter DeVries —'sibling revelry'—* W. and M. Morris.

sight (sīt) *n.* the sense that responds to light. See also **vision** (def. 1); **blindness.**

sight conservation special care taken to provide those who have limited sight with large, easy-to-read materials and other appropriate eye hygiene services, sometimes including special class placement.

sighted (sī′ted) *adj.* having useful vision.

sighting eye the eye usually chosen for monocular sighting tasks; dominant eye (def. 2).

sighting tube See **manoptoscope.**

sight method See **word method.**

sight-read (sīt′rēd) *v.* to read a text or play music without having seen it before. *An oral reading test measures one's ability to sight-read.*

sight vocabulary See **recognition vocabulary.**

sight word 1. a word that is immediately recognized as a whole and does not require word analysis for identification. See also **recognition vocabulary**. 2. a word taught as a whole word. *Note:* A word may be taught as a sight word if it is not phonically regular or is important to learn before the student has the skills to decode it.

sight word list one of several lists of frequently occurring words which students are expected to learn to recognize automatically as whole units in the early stages of reading instruction, as *and, have, of.*

sigma (sig′mə) 1. *n.* standard deviation (σ). 2. *n.* the sum of (Σ).

sign (sīn) 1. *n.* anything used to represent something else, as a grapheme, phoneme, word, Arabic number, etc. 2. *n.* the phonic or graphic representation of a word with a meaning referent;

linguistic sign. *Cp.* **symbol** (def. 4). 3. *n.* a language system in which gestures are used to communicate; sign language. 4. *v.* to communicate by signs or sign language. 5. *adj.* having to do with such communication. 6. *n.* something which represents or signifies something beyond itself; symptom; as a blush of embarrassment. 7. *n.* a meaningful conventional gesture. 8. *n.* in conditioning, a conditioned stimulus. 9. *n.* the positive or negative value of a mathematical expression, as +6, -x. See also **signal** (defs. 1-4); **signification** (def. 1).

signal (sig′nᵊl) 1. *n.* a sign which occurs in immediate association with that which is signified, as *a stop sign. Cp.* **symbol** (defs. 1, 2). 2. *n.* a message encoded by a transmitter and sent over a channel, as *a TV signal.* 3. *v.* to communicate by signal. 4. *adj.* serving as a signal, as *a signal tower.* 5. *adj.* outstanding, as *a signal honor.*

signature (sig′nə ch̲ər) 1. *n.* a printed sheet folded to form one section of a book, magazine, etc. 2. *n.* a mark identifying the proper position of a series of sections of a publication. 3. *n.* an individual's personally written name or its authorized copy.

signboard (sīn′bōrd″, -bôrd″) *n.* a board which has on it a message, direction, warning, etc.

significance (sig nif′ə kəns) 1. *n.* meaning. *What is the significance of your remark?* 2. *n.* importance; value; worth; as *the significance of motivation in learning.* 3. See **signification.** 4. See **statistical significance.** *adj.* **significant.**

significant difference any between-sample difference, as between means, test-retest performance, etc., which is unlikely to have arisen by chance.

significate (sig″nif′ə kāt, -kət) 1. *v.* to stand for or represent. 2. *v.* to suggest; symbolize. *adj.* **significative.**

signification (sig″nə fə kā′sh̲ən) 1. *n.* the relation between a linguistic symbol and the concept or concrete object to which it refers. See also **appelation** (def. 3); **semantics** (def. 2); **signifier; semantic triangle.** 2. *n.* the intended meaning or sense. 3. *n.* the implying or revealing of meaning.

signifier (sig′nə fī″ər) *n.* the verbal or graphic symbol used to indicate or label a referent, either concrete or abstract. See also **referent** *or* **referend** (defs. 2, 3); **sign** (def. 2).

signify (sig′nə fī″) *v.* to stand for; serve as a sign or representation of something. *The sign signifies the object of signification. adj.* **signified.**

sign language See **sign** (def. 3).

sign reading the interpretation of graphic signs. *Note:* The term usually refers to the recognition of simple signs and directions, such as stop-and-go signs, road signs, etc., rather than to alphabetic letters.

silent letter in common usage, a letter which is used in the spelling of a word but which seemingly represents no sound in that word, as *h* in *ghost. Note:* Originally some silent letters in English represented sounds, which for various reasons, have dropped out, as *k* in *knife* and *e* in *name.* The term is based on a long, widely held belief that speech sounds should be spelled with individual alphabet letters; hence any extra letters in a word that seem to serve no useful function are silent letters. See also **e, final.**

silent reading reading without saying aloud what is read. *In silent reading one reads to oneself, not others. Note:* While the intent of silent reading is not to vocalize, some subvocal activity has been shown to take place. Beginning with the second decade of the 20th century, the emphasis upon the teaching of silent reading soon replaced that upon oral reading. Silent reading is now the most common form of reading emphasized in the teaching of reading.

silent reading test a group test in which the student responds to items typically designed to measure word meaning and passage comprehension in several content fields, and sometimes work-study skills and speed of comprehension.

silent speech See **subvocal speech.**

simile (sim′ə lē) 1. *n.* a comparison of two things that are unlike, usually using the words *like* or *as: O my love is like a red, red rose* — R. Burns. 2. *n.* such a figure of speech. *Cp.* **metaphor**.

simple predicate a predicate consisting of a single verb phrase, as *was singing* in *He was singing. Ct.* **compound predicate.**

simple sentence a sentence with but one subject and one verb, as *The man bit the dog.*

simple subject a noun, singly or in a noun phrase, or a pronoun that is the subject of a sentence, as *dog* in *The dog bit the man.*

simplified vocabulary the substitution of easy to understand words for hard to understand words or concepts. *Adapted classics have a simplified vocabulary.*

simultaneous interpretation the rendition, in a continuous, parallel utterance in another language, of a speaker's message. *Note:* The interpreter(s), usually professional(s), may work with a microphone in speaking to an audience equipped with earphones. Whispering the interpretation into one's ear is also common. *Cp.* **consecutive interpretation.**

simulation (sim″yə lā′shən) 1. *n.* the act of pretending. 2. *n.* the creation of a realistic learning situation by duplicating as closely as possible an actual situation. *v.* **simulate.**

simultaneous vision See **binocular vision.**

singular (sing′gyə lər) *n.* a grammatical category of number, referring to one or an uncountable mass, as *boy* in *The boy fished by himself,* or *sand* in *The sand was warm underfoot.* See **number.** *Ct.* **plural.**

sinister (sin′i stər) *adj.* threatening or intending evil, harm, or trouble. *Shakespeare's Richard III is a sinister figure. Note:* Literally, sinister means 'on the left hand or side,' the direction from which the Romans believed unfavorable omens came. *Cp.* **gauche.** *Ct.* **dexterity** (def. 1).

sinistrad writing writing which proceeds from right to left, as Hebrew. *Cp.* **boustrophedon.**

sinistral (sin′i strəl) 1. *adj.* having to do with the left side; moving from the right to the left. *Arabic is a sinistral language written and read from right to left.* 2. *n.* a person who consistently chooses to use the left side, left hand, etc. See also **sinister**. *Ant.* **dextral.**

sinus (sī′nəs) *n.* a cavity or channel in body bone or tissue, as *nasal sinus.*

sitcom (sit′kom″) *n.* a comedy, as in a television series, in which the characters act out a humorous plot, often with hilarious results. *Note: Sitcom* comes from the first syllables of *sit*uation and *com*edy.

size constancy the tendency to perceive the size of an object as the same regardless of angle of view and/or distance. *Cp.* **shape constancy.** See also **perceptual constancy.**

sk skewness.

skewness (sk) (skyoo′nis) *n.* the extent to which the long tail of a frequency distribution moves to the right or left of the center of a normal frequency curve. *adj.* **skewed.**

skiascope (skī′ə skōp) See **retinoscope.**

skill (skil) 1. *n.* an acquired ability to perform well; proficiency. *Note:* The term skill often refers primarily to motor acts, especially to finely-coordinated, complex ones that are the result of perceptual-motor learning, as handwriting, golf, or pottery. However, skill is also used to refer to acts that are primarily intellectual, as *comprehension skills, thinking skills.* See also **basic skills.** Special types of skill, as *study skills,* are given under the describing term. 2. *n.* a craft or activity requiring a high degree of competence, as *the skill of making fine jewelry. adj.* **skilled.**

skim (skim) *v.* See **scan** (def. 1). *Note:* Skim shares only the first of two primary meanings of scan: to read rapidly and selectively, but purposefully, rather than to read carefully. *n.* **skimming.**

slang (slang͡) 1. *n.* informal speech composed of newly-coined, rapidly changing terms and expressions. *Slang enjoys short-lived popularity.* 2. *n.* speech used by social or professional peer groups for in-group communication; jargon; cant. *Adolescents dig slang.*

slanting (slan′ting͡) *n.* the use of words, usually intentionally, to present a particular point of view or to influence a special audience. *adj.* **slanted.** *v.* **slant.**

slapstick (slap′stik″) *n.* broad comedy with much noisy and good-natured physical action; pratfalls. *The comedies of Mack Sennett are classic slapstick motion pictures. Note:* The word comes from the laths used long ago by such performers as clowns to make loud but harmless slapping noises.

slash (slash) See **virgule.**

SLD specific language disability.

slick (slik) *n. (Informal.)* a glossy, mass-produced magazine with superficial stories and articles. *Cp.* **pulp.**

slide (slīd) *n.* a positive transparency on glass or film, made to be projected on a screen or used in a viewer.

slide projector a device used to project slides or transparencies, commonly in 5.1 x 5.1 cm. (2 x 2 in.) frames, onto a screen.

slide viewer a device, often hand-held, for viewing a single lighted slide directly rather than by projection.

slope (slōp) 1. *n.* an inclination or slant, especially upward or downward. *The slope of a learning curve provides information about the rate or success of responding.* 2. *n.* the amount of deviation from the vertical or the horizontal, as the *slope of a coordinate.* 3. *v.* to form at a slant, as *the learning curve sloped upward.*

slot (slot) *n.* a position in a string of grammatical functions into which a word, phrase, or clause may fit to form a larger phrase or clause. *The type of word which fits into the slot in 'The ___ is new,' is a noun.* See **tagmeme.**

slow learner a person whose intellectual functioning is between one and two standard deviations below the mean, usually between 70 and 80 IQ: a borderline, dull-normal, or backward person. *Slow learners are usually placed in regular classes, but if their social and emotional skills are very limited, they may be placed in classes for the educable mentally retarded.* See also **mental retardation.**

slurring (slûr′ing͡) *n.* the act of speaking indistinctly by running sounds together, as in hurried, careless, or mumbling speech. *v.* **slur.**

small capitals upper-case letter forms reduced in size to those of lower-case letters.

smoothing (smo͞o'thing) *n.* in a frequency curve or in a trend line, constructing a curve to fit the major trend of the data without distorting it.

smooth muscle any of the muscles which line the digestive tract and blood vessels, and which are involved in the vegetative function of the organism. *The smooth muscles are controlled by the autonomic nervous system. Cp.* **striate muscle.**

Snellen test *or* **rating** a test or rating of visual acuity, with one eye occluded, made by using a Snellen chart with letters of different standardized sizes and shapes to determine the smallest size of letter a patient can read from a standard distance, usually for far point testing at six meters (20 ft.), under presumably standard light conditions. *Note:* The *Snellen ratio* is the distance of testing divided by the distance at which the smallest size of letter read by the patient can normally be read: 20/20 vision is normal vision, while 20/60 vision means that the patient could only read at 6 meters (20 feet) letters which people with normal vision could read at 18 meters (60 feet).

social adjustment 1. the ability to achieve mutually satisfying relationships with others. 2. the process of personal, social, and environmental change by which this takes place. *Ct.* **social maladjustment.**

social class a group of persons of similar socioeconomic, educational, and cultural level or status, as *the professional class, working class,* etc. *Note:* The terms upper, middle, and lower class, while frequently used, are oversimplifications of the varieties of social class and are often used interchangeably with socioeconomic status.

social climate the sum of all social factors which cause an individual to feel accepted or rejected; psychological climate.

social dialect See **sociolect.**

social issue story a narrative, usually a novel, with a focus on a major problem of society. *Note:* S.E. Hinton's *That Was Then, This Is Now* is a story about teen-agers and drug abuse.

socialization (sō"shə li zā'shən) *n.* the processes and results of learning to adapt to the culture to which one belongs; enculturation. *Schools are institutions for socialization.*

social maladjustment 1. chronic inability to achieve mutually satisfying relationships with others. 2. the process of personal, social, and environmental change by which this takes place. *Ct.* **social adjustment.**

social mobility 1. change from one social class to another, as from lower to middle class. 2. change from one social group to another without change in status, as from one job to an equivalent job.

social transmission the process of passing on the values and norms of a culture, as from one generation to another.

social worker a person with special training and skills to deal with the interacting needs of individuals, families, and communities. *Note:* A school social worker is often a part of a diagnostic team that helps the school system understand and deal with the personal-social needs of students, especially of those suffering neglect or abuse in the home that requires legal action.

sociodrama (sō"sē ō drä'mə, -dram'ə, so'shē-) *n.* plays, skits, and role-playing that are used to teach socially desirable behavior, one's own roles in society, and empathy with the behavior and roles of others. *Cp.* **play therapy;**

psychodrama; role playing (def. 3).

socioeconomic status a person's position or standing in a society because of such factors as social class, level of education, income, and type of job.

sociogram (sō'sē ə gram", sō'sħē-) *n.* a diagram, chart, or paradigm that shows how individuals interact or would choose to interact within a group. See illustration. *Note:* A sociogram is usually based on self-report in response to such a question as *Who are your three best friends in this classroom?*

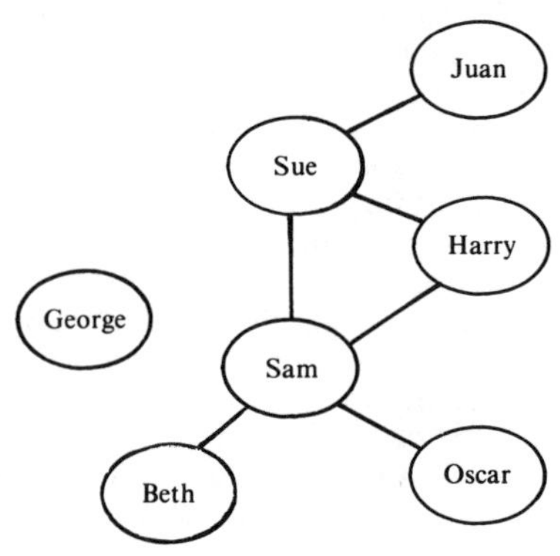

Sociogram

sociolect (sō'sē ə lekt", sō'sħē-) *n.* a variety of speech used primarily by members of a given social group. *Cp.* **dialect.**

sociolinguistics (sō"sē ō liŋ gwis'tiks, sō"sħē-) *n. (with sing. v.)* the study of the relationships between linguistic behavior and other aspects of social behavior. *Note:* Sociolinguists examine such relationships as those between an individual's speech and that of others in a speech community; the effects of travel and media on language; and effects of political, social, and economical power structures on the perception of language differences. *n.* **sociolinguist.** *adj.* **sociolinguistic.**

sociology (sō"sē ol'ə jē, sō"sħē-) *n.* the scientific study of human society; particularly, the study of group relationships and societal institutions. *n.* **sociologist.**

sociology of reading 1. the study of the effects of reading upon a reader's habits and attitudes; the interaction between people and print. 2. the study of the characteristics of the print media; content analysis. 3. the study of organizations and their effects on reading acquisition and use.

sociometric (sō"sē ə me'trik, sō"sħə-) 1. *adj.* having to do with measuring social relationships in a group. 2. *adj.* having to do with J. L. Moreno's technique for measuring and showing in a sociogram the expressed likes and dislikes of group members toward one another. *n.* **sociometrics.** *n.* **sociometry.**

Socratic method the art of asking leading questions to stimulate rational thinking and lead to philosophic truths.

sodium amytal amylobarbitone sodium, a central nervous system sedative and hypnotic sometimes used to disinhibit and to produce a relaxed state. *Sodium amytal is used in the Wada test.*

softback *or* **softbound** *or* **soft cover** See **paperback.**

soft consonant a voiceless consonant; one produced without vibration of the vocal cords, as /f/ in *face* and /h/ in *house.*

soft neurological sign a finding on neurological examination that is thought to reveal neurological immaturity rather than damage. *Poor fine motor control, hyperactive behavior, mild speech impairment, laterality inconsistencies, and distractibility are all considered soft* *neurological signs. Ct.* **hard neurological sign.**

soft palate the soft, muscular, and movable back part of the roof of the mouth; velum. *The soft palate closes off the nose during swallowing and during the production of most English speech sounds.*

software (sôft′wâr″, soft′-) *n.* the materials used in the equipment or hardware of a computer and/or educational system. *Ct.* **hardware.**

soliloquy (sə lil′ə kwē) *n.* a speech by a character in a play, given while or as if alone; literally, talking to oneself; as *a soliloquy of Hamlet. Cp.* **monologue** *or* **monolog** (def. 1).

soma (t) (to)- a combining form indicating *body*; as **psychosomatic.**

somatic (sō mat′ik, sə-) 1. *adj.* having to do with the body rather than the mind; physical. *Cp.* **psychosomatic.** See also **organismic** (def. 1). 2. *adj.* having to do with body cells except germ cells. 3. *adj.* having to do with the wall or framework of the body. *Ct.* **viscera** (def. 1). 4. *adj.* having to do with the trunk of the body.

somesthesia *or* **somaesthesia** (sō″mes thē′zhə, -zhē ə, -zē ə) 1. *n.* the sense which provides information about body conditions through kinesthetic, proprioceptive, and cutaneous feedback. 2. *n.* the body sensations so felt, as those of position, pressure, movement, and temperature.

sonant (sō′nənt) *n.* a voiced consonant speech sound, as /v/. *Ant.* **surd.**

sonic (son′ik) 1. *adj.* having to do with sound, especially sounds within the audible range. *Note:* Sounds of a frequency too low to be heard are called *infrasonic;* those of too high a frequency, *ultrasonic.* 2. *adj.* having to do with a speed approximating that of the speed of sound. *Note:* Speed less than sound is called *subsonic;* speed faster than sound, *supersonic;* and speed five or more times faster than sound, *hypersonic.* 3. **sonic boom,** the loud explosive noise that slaps both people and windows with the shock waves of the supersonic aircraft that caused it.

sonnet (son′it) *n.* a poetic form or poem of 14 lines, usually in iambic pentameter and rhyming according to a formal scheme, which expresses a thought or feeling in a complete and unified way. *Note:* The *Italian* or *Petrarchan sonnet* has two divisions: the first eight lines called the octave and the last six lines called the sestet. The *English* or *Shakespearean sonnet* has four divisions: three sets of four lines, or quatrains, and a final set of two lines, or couplet.

sonority (sə nôr′ i tē, -nor′-) *n.* a full, rich sound; resonance; especially, the resonant quality of a speech sound. *Vowels have more sonority than consonants. adj.* **sonorous.**

sound (sound) 1. *n.* energy that is transmitted as pressure waves or vibrations through an elastic medium as air or water. *Too loud sound may injure hearing.* 2. *n.* the sensation of hearing; specifically, the sensory response to vibration in the inner ear that is transmitted to the brain by the auditory nerve. 3. *n.* a discretely perceived hearing sensation. *The sound of the clock woke him.* 4. See **phone; phoneme.** 5. *n.* a distinctive feature of a speech sound. 6. *n.* in teaching practice, how a letter is pronounced, as *the sound of 'b.'* 7. *v.* to speak; articulate; pronounce. *Sound the word.* 8. *n.* noise. *The sounds outside disturbed the class.* 9. *v.* to make noise. *The truck sounded its horn.* 10. *n.* the meaning or implication of something. *I* *don't like the sound of that.* 11. *n.* recorded audio material, as on film or tape. 12. *adj.* comprehensive; complete; as *sound scholarship.*

sounding (out) *n.* the application of phonics skills in reproducing the sound(s) represented by a letter or group of letters in a word.

sound *or* **speech spectrograph** an electronic instrument for analyzing short intervals of speech to show their component sound wave frequencies and intensities. *Note:* The graphic form of the analysis, a spectrogram, can be read by an expert and can be used to recreate speech electronically by a speech synthesizer. Computers are often used to analyze sound spectrographs and to store spectrograms. See illustration under **spectrogram.**

sound-symbol correspondence See **phoneme-grapheme correspondence.**

sound symbolism the use of sound for certain literary effects, as in onomatopoeia and synaesthesia.

sound wave the representation in graphic form of vibrations which show changes in pressure as they move through air or some other elastic medium. *Sound waves provide the data for sound spectrograph analysis.*

source (sōrs, sôrs) *n.* any communication medium, as a book, person, electronic device, etc., that supplies information.

source credibility whether or not a person or document giving information may be believed. *Source credibility is a constant problem in news reporting.*

space perception perception of the dimensional characteristics of the surface layout, as distance, size, position of objects, etc.

Spache readability formula a method developed by G. Spache and originally published in 1953 for estimating the difficulty of primary level reading materials, based upon average sentence length in words and number of words (in a sample of 100) not on the Stone revision of an earlier list of easy words by Dale. *Note:* The formula has undergone several revisions since 1953, chiefly in the list of words used. *Cp.* **Dale-Chall readability formula; Flesch readability formula; Fry readability graph (scale).**

span of apprehension See **span of attention** (def. 1).

span of attention 1. the number of items an individual can correctly reproduce after a single short exposure, either visually or orally; memory span. *Cp.* **span of recognition.** 2. the length of time that an individual can concentrate on one thing or activity; interest span.

span of perception See **span of attention** (def. 1).

span of recognition in the continuous reading of a passage, the average number of words taken in per eye fixation. *Cp.* **span of attention** (def. 1).

spasm (spaz′əm) 1. *n.* a sudden, involuntary muscular contraction, often intense. *A charley horse is a spasm of the leg muscles.* See also **clonic; tonic** (def. 1). 2. *n.* a sudden narrowing of a body passage or opening, as of a blood vessel or the colon. *Hiccups are caused by spasms of the diaphragm.* 3. *n.* a sudden, intense, but usually temporary burst of activity or emotion, as *a spasm of reading, a spasm of anger. adj.* **spasmodic.**

spastic (spas′tik) 1. *n.* a person with cerebral palsy whose movements are stiff and awkward. 2. *adj.* having to do with spasms; hypertonic; having stiff muscles and increased muscle reflexes; as *spastic paralysis. Ant.* (def. 2) **flaccid** (def. 2).

spasticity (spas tis′i tē) 1. *n.* a state of

abnormal muscle tonus from any of many causes; hypertonicity; as disease of or injury to the brain. 2. *n.* one of the major syndromes of cerebral palsy, with stiff, awkward movements, as in the head, arm(s), and/or leg(s). *Cerebral palsy spasticity may affect one or more areas.*

spatial orientation 1. awareness of one's position and movement in space, primarily from visual and kinesthetic clues. *Directionality depends on spatial orientation.* 2. turning toward or away from external stimulation, as in turning the head to listen.

speaking (spē′kiñg) 1. *n.* the act of communicating through speech. 2. *n.* the giving of a public address or lecture. 3. *n.* productive oral/aural language. *v.* **speak.**

speaking vocabulary the number of different words ordinarily used by a person for meaningful oral communication; oral vocabulary.

Spearman-Brown formula a formula showing the relationship between test length and test reliability. *Note:* It is commonly used to estimate the reliability of a whole test from the correlation between the two halves of the test, the split-half reliability.

special edition a limited edition of a publication printed with greater than usual care and expense. *Special editions typically have a superior quality of paper, typography, and binding, with illustrations by featured artists.*

special education schooling for those who are very different in one or more ways in intellectual, physical, social, or emotional development from that of the usual student. *Special education includes a variety of adjustments in content, method, and rate of learning to meet the needs of atypical students.* See also **exceptional child; mainstreaming; mental retardation.**

specific developmental dyslexia a reading difficulty assumed to be due to maturational delay or genetic defects in neurological structure without evidence of brain damage; developmental dyslexia.

specific factor (s) a factor hypothesized by C. Spearman (1904) to be specific to a given intellectual activity.

specific language disability (SLD) 1. a developmental difficulty reflected in all aspects of expressive and receptive language, often in persons of normal or better mental ability and arithmetic skills. 2. a particular language problem, as dyslexia, thought to be the result of some form of central nervous system dysfunction, and not a result of emotional or intellectual factors, or of insufficient or inappropriate education.

specific learning disability a developmental learning disability rather than one due to demonstrable brain damage.

specific reading disability See **developmental dyslexia.**

spectrogram (spek′trə gram″) *n.* the graphic form of a spectrograph, as a picture or a computer printout which shows energy sources and levels, usually of light or sound; spectrum. See illustration. See also **sound** *or* **speech spectrograph.**

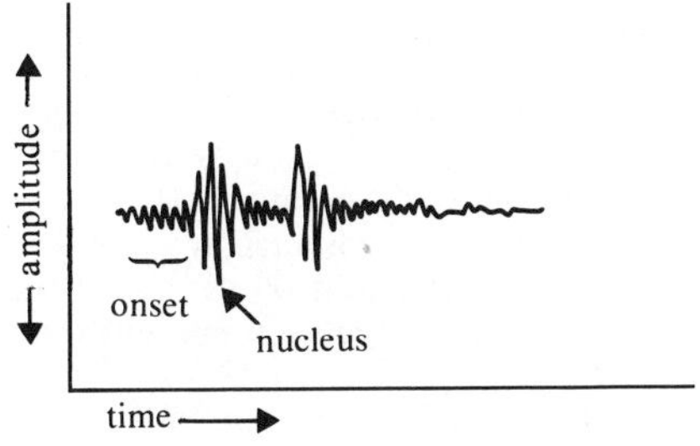

Spectrogram for the word "stop"

spectrum (spek'trəm) See **spectrogram.**

speech (spēch) 1. *n.* oral communication. 2. *n.* the act of speaking. 3. *n.* something spoken; utterance 4. *n.* an utterance for a particular purpose, as *a graduation speech.* 5. *n.* a single utterance by an actor. 6. *n.* the dialect or language of a particular region or social group, as *Pennsylvania Dutch speech.* 7. *n.* the way in which someone speaks, as *careless speech.* 8. *n.* the study of the theory and practice of oral communication.

speech act *n.* an utterance.

speech and language therapy a current term for the study and correction of speech, language, and voice disorders by a speech and language therapist. *Syn* **speech correction; speech pathology; speech therapy**.

speech community all those who communicate by a common language or variety of a language. *Note:* The term speech community is often used to identify some subgroup that shares a common dialect or argot not used by the majority of the population, as the Cajuns in Louisiana or the Basques in France and Spain. Persons may be members of more than one speech community, thus enhancing communication between such groups.

speech correction See **speech and language therapy.** *n.* **speech correctionist.**

speech defect See **speech disorder.**

speech discrimination in speech audiometry, the assessment of the ability to distinguish different sounds, words, sentences, etc., presented at a constant level, usually about 40 dB above the threshold for speech. *Cp.* **speech reception.**

speech disorder any deviation of speech that seriously interferes with normal oral communication or that causes adjustment problems for the speaker; speech impediment; deviant speech. *Note:* Since speech disorders are defined in relation to the existing speech community, a particular form of speech deviation may be considered a disorder in one community but normal in another.

speech event any of the several units of linguistic interaction; specifically, participants, mode of discourse, shared language codes, context, linguistic form and style, topic, and comments. See also **ethnography of communication.**

speech frequencies that portion of the sound frequency spectrum which includes most speech sounds, usually from 125 to 8000 Hz.

speech organs the body structures used to produce speech sounds: the articulators, the larynx, the resonators, and the lungs. See illustration.

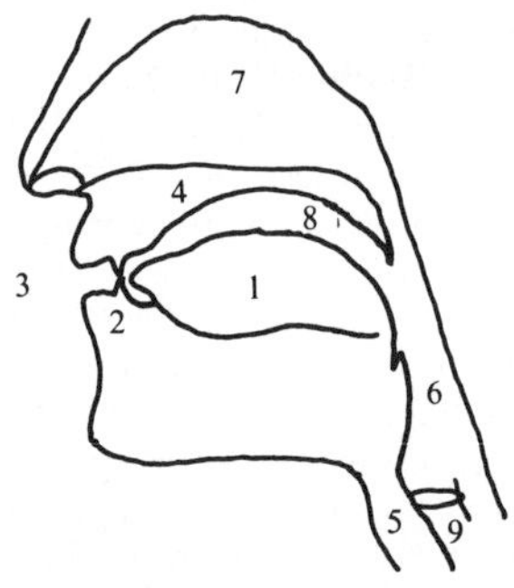

Articulators: tongue (1); lips (2); teeth (3); palate (4); larynx (5); resonators: pharynx (6); nasal cavity (7); oral cavity (8); trachea (9).

Speech organs

speech pathology See **speech and language therapy.** *n.* **speech pathologist.**

speechreading (spēch' rē" ding) *n.* the process of getting a speaker's intended meaning, without hearing the voice, by watching the speaker's lips, facial expressions, and gestures. *Speechreading, used often by the hard of hearing, is not synonymous with lipreading. Ct.* **lipreading.**

speech reception in speech audiometry, the assessment of the threshold level at which two-syllable words can be repeated correctly at least half of the time. *Cp.* **speech discrimination.** See also **spondee words.**

speech reception threshold (SRT) See **speech reception.**

speech re-education *or* **rehabilitation** speech and language therapy for restoring a lost speech function.

speech therapy See **speech and language therapy.** *n.* **speech therapist.**

speedboats, sailboats, and rafts one of several types of references to the practice of having three ability-based reading groups, implying very little social or psychological difference between placement in the high or middle groups, but attaching considerable stigma to placement in the low group.

speed of comprehension the rapidity with which one understands what is read, usually in silent reading. *Note:* Speed of comprehension is usually measured in relation to the number of passages successfully understood, and the speed score is not converted to a words per minute score.

speed of reading See **rate of reading.**

speed reading instruction focused on increasing rate of comprehension, often with the aid of such mechanical devices as pacers, tachistoscopes, etc. *Note:* Too often such instruction aims merely at one high rate of reading without considering either comprehension to an adequate degree or the desirability of developing flexibility of reading rate with speeds adjusted to the reader's purpose, the level of difficulty of the subject matter, and the reader's knowledge and background. *Syn.* **accelerated reading** (*Brit.*); **advanced reading** (*Brit.*); **rapid reading.**

speed test a test with time limits so short that a substantial number of persons cannot attempt all items. *Ct.* **power test.**

spelldown (spell'doun″) 1. *n.* a game or contest in which a student who misspells a word is eliminated; spelling bee. See **spelling-school.** 2. *v.* to eliminate a competitor in a spelling contest, by spelling a word correctly, when the competitor has failed. *To have "spelled down" the master is next thing to having whipped the biggest bully* — Eggleston (1871).

speller (spel'ər) 1. *n.* one who names or writes the letters of a word in their proper sequence. 2. *n.* in the United States, a spelling textbook. See also **spelling book** (def. 1).

spelling (spel'ing) 1. *n.* the process of representing language by means of a writing system, or orthography. 2. *n.* orthography (def. 3). 3. *n.* the study of writing words according to their correct letters or graphemes; orthography (def. 2). 4. *n.* the way a word is spelled on a particular occasion, whether correct or incorrect. 5. *n.* reciting the letters composing a word, in their correct sequence, as in *b-i-d,* bid. *v.* **spell.**

spelling bee See **spelldown** (def. 1).

spelling book 1. a textbook with exercises for learning to write words in standard orthography; a speller (def. 2). 2. an early type of children's textbook designed primarily for reading instruction, and secondarily for spelling instruction. *Note:* Spelling books traditionally included the alphabet, syllabarium, and then 'tables' (lists of words, organized into words of an increasing number of syllables) interspersed with 'lessons' (reading matter mainly based on words in the preceding lessons).

spelling demon a common word that is particularly difficult or tricky to spell correctly, as *accommodation.*

spelling method 1. any of several approaches to teaching students to spell. 2. a way of teaching reading. See also **alphabet method** (def. 1).

spelling pronunciation the oral production of a word on the basis of its standard spelling rather than its standard pronunciation in speech, as /komp trō'lər/ for *comptroller* rather than /kən trō'lər/. *Note:* Spelling pronunciations occur when sounds are attributed to each letter of a written word regardless of whether the letter(s) represent(s) a speech sound. Some spelling pronunciations have become acceptable in spoken language, as /of'tən/ for *often*, /fōr'hed/ for *forehead.*

spelling reform an individual or organized effort to simplify an orthography, generally one based on a correspondence of phonemes and graphemes so that spelling conforms to pronunciation, and vice-versa. See also **phoneme-grapheme correspondence; one-to-one correspondence** (def. 2); **orthography** (def. 3).

spelling-school *n.* a spelling competition which was popular in the U.S. in the 19th century, held outside normal school hours, and in which both children and adults competed. *What a dress party is to Fifth Avenue, a spelling-school is to Hoopole County* — Eggleston (1871).

spelling-sound correspondence See **grapheme-phoneme correspondence.**

Spencerian script a handwriting style named after an early nineteenth century American handwriting expert, Platt Rogers Spencer, that uses rounded ornate letters slanting to the right.

sphygm (o)- a combining form indicating *pulse;* as **sphygmomanometer.**

sphygmomanometer (sfig″mō mə nom′i tər) *n.* an instrument for measuring blood pressure.

spike (spīk) *n.* the sharp up and down tracing representing a sudden electrical discharge as on an electroencephalogram. *An epileptic seizure produces a characteristic pattern of EEG spikes.*

spine (spīn) *n.* the part of a book cover that holds it together, hiding the sewn or bound edges of the signatures.

spiral curriculum a curriculum designed to present important concepts, skills, topics, etc., for study at successive levels of student maturity. Also called **concentric method** *or* **curriculum (Brit.).**

spirant (spī′rənt) See **fricative.**

spit-and-cough method a comic phrase describing oral reading characterized by a reader's excessive dependence upon the use of phonics, usually to the extent of a disjointed sounding out of each letter. *Note:* The use of this term implies that the reader possesses an inadequate sight vocabulary and gains little meaning from reading. *Syn.* **grunt-and-groan method.**

split-half reliability coefficient a test reliability coefficient obtained by correlating scores on one-half of a test, as even-numbered items, with scores on the other half of the test, as odd-numbered items, and applying a correction formula such as the Spearman-Brown formula.

split infinitive the *to* before an infinitive verb form separated from its verb by an adverb or adverbial phrase, as *carefully* in *to carefully consider. Note:* Although some grammarians consider this construction incorrect, it appears frequently in the language of respected speakers and writers.

spoken language 1. language used in speaking as distinct from writing. 2. that style of language that is written as if spoken, as in conversation. *Ct.* **written language.**

spondee (spon′dē) *n.* a metrical foot of two stressed syllables. *Note:* The spondee is rare in English verse. It is sometimes found as a part of a line of verse: *Hére Ī ám, ăn óld mán ĭn ă drý mónth*—T.S. Eliot.

spondee words words of two equally stressed syllables, as *goodbye, sunshine,* etc., used in testing speech reception.

spoonerism (spo͞o′nə riz″əm) *n.* the accidental transposition of initial sounds or syllables of two words, usually with humorous results, as *weans and bieners* for *beans and wieners. Note:* The word comes from Dr. W.A. Spooner, a warden of New College at Oxford, who is said to have made many such transpositions, as *Is this pie occupewed?*

sports (spōrts, spôrts) 1. *n.* the class of fiction, biography, and information books on sports of all kinds. 2. *adj.* referring to such material.

SQ3R (study method) a series of steps to be used in reading a textbook for study purposes: Survey the assignment to note the points emphasized; pose a Question initially on the first section, later on successive sections; Read to answer the question; Recite the answer to the question; and, after several questions and answers, Review the material read. *Note:* This study method was first introduced by F. Robinson in 1946, but it has since been adopted and adapted by many other writers and programs.

squib (skwib) 1. *n.* a short spoken or written saying, usually witty or sarcastic. 2. *v.* to so speak or write.

squint (skwint) 1. *n.* See **heterotropia.** 2. *v.* to look with the eyes partly closed, as to protect them from bright sunlight or to concentrate on sighting a gun, etc.

SRT speech reception threshold. See **speech reception.**

SSR See **uninterrupted sustained silent reading.**

stacks (staks) *n. pl.* 1. rows of shelves to hold books and other library materials. 2. the area containing such shelves. See also **closed stacks; open stacks.**

stage (stāj) 1. *n.* a single phrase and qualitatively distinct period in a process or series. 2. *n.* (J. Piaget) one of four developmental periods postulated by Piaget, each characterized by certain types of mental activities or operations: a. *sensorimotor*, birth-2 years; b. *preoperational*, 2-7 years; c. *concrete operations*, 7-11 years; d. *formal operations*, 12-15 years. *Note:* (def. 2): These stages are sequential because each is necessary for the formation of the following one. The ages given for each stage are approximate. 3. *n.* a platform or area for performing plays, music, etc. 4. *v.* to present a performance in such a place. 5. **the stage**, the theatrical profession.

stammering (stam′ər iŋ̂) See **stuttering** (def. 1).

standard (stan′dərd) See **criterion.**

standard American English 1. that variety of American English in which most educational texts, government, and media publications are written in the United States. 2. English as it is spoken and written by those groups which have social, economic, and political power in the United States. *Note:* Standard American English is a relative concept, varying widely in pronunciation and in idiomatic use but maintaining a fairly uniform grammatical structure. See also **prestige dialect.**

standard deviation (SD) a measure of the variability of a distribution; specifically, the square root of the mean of the squares of the deviations of all scores of a test or set. *Standard scores are based upon the standard deviation.*

standard dialect See **standard language** (def. 1).

standard error (SE, S.E.) an estimate of the typical size of errors of measurement. *Note:* On the average, the scores of individuals will depart from the score that would be obtained with a highly accurate test by more than one SE in one-third of the cases.

standard error of estimate an estimate of variability of predictions made from a regression line of one variable to another; specifically, the standard deviation of the differences of actual values from those predicted by a regression line. *The standard error of estimate allows the development of a confidence band about a predicted score.*

standard error of mean a statistic used to indicate the variation of means to be expected in successive samples.

standard error of measurement an estimate of the standard deviation of obtained scores for a given value of the true score.

standardized test 1. a test with specified tasks and procedures so that comparable measurements may be made by testers working in different geographical areas. 2. a test for which norms on a reference group, ordinarily drawn from many schools or communities, are provided.

standard language 1. a culturally dominant language in a country or region; language of well-educated people; standard dialect. *Note:* Standard language is usually the language specifically recognized in grammars and dictionaries for use in education, government, and business. 2. a variety of language favored by the well-educated in socially important situations. 3. the established dialect or style of any language variety.

standard score a derived score used to *express the individual's distance from the mean in terms of the standard deviation of the distribution* — A. Anastasi (1976). *Stanines and z-scores are standard scores.*

Stanford-Binet Intelligence Scale (S-B) an individual test of general mental ability, published as a revision of the Binet-Simon scales by L. Terman and others in 1916, with later revisions in 1937 and 1960, and renormed in 1972. *Cp.* **Wechsler Intelligence Scales.**

stanine (stā′nīn) *n.* a normalized standard score representing an interval in a nine-point scale, with a mean of 5 and a standard deviation of 2.

stanza (stan′zə) *n.* a division of a poem or song into groups of lines with an identifiable pattern of meter and often rhyme. *Note:* Some poems have a single stanza, as in many of Emily Dickinson's poems.

stapes (stā′pēz) *pl.* **stapes, stapedes** (stə pē′dēz). *n.* the innermost of the three bones, or ossicles, in the middle ear, fitting into the oval window of the cochlea and joining with the incus. *The stapes is shaped like a stirrup, whence its name.* See illustration under **ear.** *adj.* **stapedial.**

statement (stāt′mənt) *n.* a sentence pattern used to declare or assert something rather than to question or command: *Susan enjoys reading.*

static reversal See **reversal.**

stations approach a classroom or laboratory in which a number of stations or centers are set up, each with its own directions, materials, and tasks to be used by the student who moves from station to station either at his own choosing and at his own pace, or as a result of the teacher's diagnosis.

statistic (stə tis′tik) 1. *n.* a score or value based upon one or more samples that represents a parameter of a population, as a mean, a standard deviation, etc. 2. *n.* any single score or value in a set which has been derived as the end product of the quantitative analysis of other variables. See also **statistics.**

statistical significance a statistical expression of the probability that an experimental finding did not happen by chance. See also **confidence level.**

statistics (stə tis′tiks) 1. *n.* (*with sing. v.*) the science of collecting and mathematically analyzing data so that the random effects of chance may be estimated or controlled in seeking to establish significant facts and relationships. 2. *n.* (*with pl. verb*) data thus collected, as *statistics on high school dropouts.*

status (stā′təs, stat′əs) 1. *n.* the social position or standing of a person, especially one valued and honored, as *the high status of the priest. Cp.* **role** (def. 2). 2. *adj.* referring to the social recognition given to a language, dialect, or speech usage, or to its speaker, as *the status salutation 'Your Excellency.'*

stem (stem) 1. *n.* a root or base word plus its derivational affixes which together form the unit to which inflectional morphemes may be affixed: the root *black* plus the derivational affix *-en* form the stem *blacken,* to which an inflectional morpheme as *-ed* may be added to form the word's inflected form, *blackened. Cp.* **root** (def. 1); **base word.** 2. See **brainstem.** **3.** *n.* the heavy, usually vertical, line of a typeface.

stencil (sten′səl) 1. *n.* a specifically prepared sheet through which typed, written, or drawn impressions may be transferred by ink or paint to paper or other surfaces, as *a ditto stencil.* 2. *v.* to so transfer impressions.

stenography (stə nog′rə fē) *n.* the process, or product, of writing shorthand. *n.* **stenographer.** *adj.* **stenographic.**

stereo- a combining form indicating *firm, solid,* or *three dimensional*; as **stereotype, stereopsis.**

stereognosis (ster″ē og nō′sis, stēr″-) *n.* the ability to identify objects by touch; haptic perception. *Ant.* **astereognosis.**

stereograph (ster′ē ə graf″, -gräf″, stēr′-) *n.* a visual target made of two photographs or drawings side by side which, when seen through a stereoscope, may appear as a single three-dimensional image. *Note:* The three-dimensional effect is achieved by a camera with two lenses spaced approximately the distance between human eyes. Also **steregram.** See **stereoscope.**

stereopsis (ster″ē op′sis, stēr″-) See **stereoscopic vision** *or* **stereopsis.**

stereoscope (ster′ē ə skōp″, stēr′-) *n.* an instrument which allows each eye to see only one of the pair of pictures on a stereograph so that, normally, stereopsis occurs and a single picture is seen as three-dimensional. *Clinical specialists use stereoscopes for testing and training vision, but many people are more used to seeing stereoscopes as small wooden frames with lenses for* *viewing double postcards at antique sales.* See **stereograph.**

stereoscopic vision *or* **stereopsis** the perception of depth or of an apparent three-dimensional effect primarily because of binocular parallax which slightly displaces the corresponding retinal images of an object. See also **depth perception** (def. 2).

stereotype (ster′ē ə tīp″, stēr′-) 1. *n.* a commonly held view, often simplified and rigid, especially of the characteristics of groups, beliefs, and institutions. 2. *n.* a cast or mold used in printing to make identical copies, a meaning from which def. 1 is derived. 3. *v.* to hold such a view or make such copies. *n.* **stereotyping.**

stereotyped (ster′ē ə tīpt″, stēr′-) 1. *adj.* unoriginal; biased; conventional in form, as *a stereotyped utterance, a stereotyped character.* 2. *adj.* cast or molded to make identical copies.

stimulant (stim′yə lənt) 1. *n.* something that increases nervous and/or physical activity; an energizer. *Coffee and tea are common stimulants. Ct.* **depressant** (def. 1). 2. *adj.* raising one's spirits. *Good news is a stimulant.*

stimulation (stim″yə lā′shən) 1. *n.* the excitation of a receptor by various forms of energy, as light, temperature, pressure, etc. *Note:* Stimulation is sometimes limited to the application of energy to the receptor. 2. *n.* the total stimulus-response process. 3. *n.* the arousal to action or effort, as *the stimulation of competition. v.* **stimulate.**

stimulus (S) (stim′yə ləs) *pl.* **-li (-lī)** 1. *n.* anything that arouses sensory activity leading to a response. *Note:* This general meaning is derived from a long history of conflict between physical and mental interpretations of the term. Stimuli, which may be internal or external, may also be primarily physical, as in hunger contractions in the stomach, or psychological, as in a verbal signal. 2. *n.* the class of reactions to which def. 1 refers. 3. *n.* an incentive. *The good news was a stimulus for a celebration. Ct.* **response.**

stimulus generalization the extension of a response to a stimulus to other stimuli that previously did not call forth such a response. *A dog trained to salivate to a tone of 1500 cps. will also salivate by stimulus generalization to a tone of 1600 cps. Cp.* **response generalization.**

STM short term memory.

stochastic (stə kas′tik) *adj.* referring to chance effects; random. *To assume a stochastic model of the world is to believe that fate's fickle finger operates on the best laid plans of men, mice and molecules: to assume otherwise is to be naive* — G. S. Bartush.

stock response a reaction to literature that is conventional, stereotyped, or superficial: *The plot is weak. The characters are wooden.*

stop (stop) 1. *n.* in voice production, any complete stoppage and sudden release of the air flow, usually, but not always, referring to a stoppage anywhere in the vocal tract, as a plosive, a glottal stop, a click, etc. 2. *n.* a consonant speech sound made by stopping the air flow and then suddenly releasing it through the mouth. *The English stops are /p/, /b/, /t/, /d/, /k/, /g/. Ct.* **continuant.** 3. *adj.* referring to such a speech sound. *Syn.* **plosive.**

storefront school an alternative school that provides educational opportunities such as after-school tutoring for disadvantaged adults and high school students in informal housing arrangements, as in a store. See also **street academy.** *Note:* Storefront schools began in urban slums, but have currently spread into less economically disadvantaged areas.

story (stōr′ē, stôr′ē) 1. *n.* a prose or poetry narrative, real or imagined;

tale. 2. *n.* an imaginative tale shorter than a novel but with plot, characters, and setting, as *a short story.* 3. *n.* the plot of a novel, poem, etc. 4. *n.* a branch of literature, as *song and story.* 5. *n.* something narrated, as *tell me a story.* 6. *n.* a lie.

storyboard (stōr'ē bōrd", stôr'ē bôrd") 1. *n.* the telling of a story by a bas relief carving on wood. *Note:* The storyboard is a popular way of preserving stories in the islands of the South Pacific, especially Palau. 2. *n.* a panel on which sketches show the scene and plan of action for the production of a motion picture, TV show, etc.

story grammar in text analysis, a grammar designed to specify relations among episodes in a story and to formulate rules for generating other stories.

story method an extension of the sentence method of teaching reading introduced toward the end of the 19th century, in which students first learn a whole story before attending to its parts.

storytelling (stōr'ē tel"ing̃, stôr'-) *n.* the art of telling a story orally rather than reading it aloud.

strabismus (strə biz'məs) *n.* heterotropia; squint. *Ct.* **heterophoria.**

strategy (strat'i jē) *n.* a systematic plan for achieving a specific goal or result. *Effective study skills give students strategies for mastering study tasks.*

stratificational grammar a system of linguistic analysis based on the work of S. M. Lamb (1966) which is developed from the premise that language has two fundamental components—meaning and sound—and that between these two components are several interrelated levels or strata, including phonemic, morphemic, and lexemic strata.

stratified sample a sample which is selected from a population that has been divided into categories. *A stratified sample contains members from each category in approximately the same proportion that the category bears to the entire population. Ct.* **representative sample.**

Strauss syndrome a group of behavior patterns, essentially hyperactive, in persons with learning difficulties. *Note:* This syndrome, which includes symptoms of distractability, perseveration, and hyperactivity, was first described by A. Strauss in studying brain-damaged persons. The term has since been used to describe any hyperactive child, with possibly unfortunate implications.

streaming (strē'ming̃) *n. (Brit.)* ability grouping within classes.

stream of consciousness 1. a term coined by William James to describe the random, but continuous flow of thoughts, feelings, memories, etc. through a person's mind at a given moment or interval; free association. 2. a narrative technique used in such novels as Sterne's *Tristram Shandy* and Joyce's *Ulysses.*

street academy an alternative, or storefront, urban school that provides academic programs often taught by volunteers, and work programs for high school dropouts. See also **storefront school.**

street literature the inexpensive pamphlets and broadsides sold on the streets after the development of printing and well into the 19th century. *Note:* Street literature could be bought for half a penny in England, and reflected the tastes, concerns, and prejudices of the common people. Its varied content included love songs, religious tracts, news, political dialogues, playbills, etc. See **broadside.**

streph (o)- a combining form indicating *turn, twist;* as **strephosymbolia.**

strephosymbolia (stref'ə sim bō'lē ə)

n. dyslexia. *Note:* The term strephosymbolia means 'twisted symbols.' It was coined by S. T. Orton (1937) to refer to the reversals and transpositions which he believed to be prime evidence of reading disability.

stress (stres) 1. *n.* emphasis; importance; significance; urgency; concern. *Much stress was placed on accuracy.* 2. *n.* a physiological response to a disturbance in the balanced functioning of body processes: *The nonspecific response of the body to any demands upon it* — H. Selye. 3. *n.* the psychological tension associated with physiological stress. 4. *n.* the emphasis from increased force of breath that makes a syllable, word, or group of words stand out; accent. *Note:* Stress, often considered as sentence stress and as word stress, is a major marker of meaning in speech. Sentence stress changes meaning, as *Í did not say that* vs. *I did not say thát.* Word stress may likewise change meaning, as *óbject* vs. *objéct,* or may simply mark pronunciation emphasis within a word. In the latter sense, three or four levels of stress are recognized: a. *primary stress,* /ʹ/, is the heaviest accent; b. *secondary stress,* /^/, is less heavy but still emphatic; c. *tertiary stress,* /\/, has little emphasis , but the vowel sound is still distinct; d. *weak or minimal stress,* or *unstressed,* /ˇ/, or not marked, are terms used to indicate the least force, as for a neutral vowel or schwa. *Élěvàtŏr ôpěràtór demonstrates all four levels of stress.* See also **suprasegmental phoneme.** 5. *v.* to accent one's speech; to emphasize parts of an utterance; to pronounce strongly. 6. *v.* to emphasize. *Stress the application part of your research* 7. **primary stress,** a. the part(s) of a word to be given greatest emphasis in pronunciation. b. the mark used to show this, often by a bold-face apostrophe (ʹ). 8. **secondary stress,** a. the part(s) of a word to be emphasized in pronunciation, but less so than in primary stress. b. the mark used to show this, often by single (′) or double (″) apostrophe.

stressed syllable 1. a syllable having the greatest stress in the word or phrase in which it is located. *Note:* In English, a stressed syllable may occur in any portion of a word, as *decent* /dē′ sənt/ versus *descent* /di sent′/. 2. any syllable which has any degree of stress. *Note:* In English, a word or phrase may have several differentially stressed syllables, usually either primary or secondary. See also **stress** (defs. 4, 7, 8).

stress mark See **accent** (def. 2).

striate muscle the heart and skeletal muscles which pump the blood and move body parts. *The striate muscles are controlled by the central nervous system. Cp.* **smooth muscle.**

strident (strīd′ənt) *adj.* having a harsh quality. *A strident voice is often shrill, loud, and unpleasant to the ears.*

string (string) *n.* a linear sequence of grammatical units, as article + adjective + noun + auxiliary verb + verb + noun. See also **terminal string.**

stroke (strōk) 1. *n.* a single mark made by a writing tool. 2. *n.* a mark which is a component of a letter or character; as the strokes *(l) and (o)* used to form *b.* 3. (*Brit.*) See **virgule** (def. 1). 4. *v.* to make such a mark. 5. *v.* to make the horizontal line of a *t.*

strong verb in English, a verb that forms its perfect aspect (tense) by means of a vowel change, as from *sink* to *(have) sunk, begin* to *(have) begun. Ct.* **weak verb.**

structural analysis a word identification technique for breaking a word into its pronunciation units. *Note.* Structural analysis elements commonly taught are the identification of roots affixes, compounds, hyphenated forms, inflected and derived endings, contractions, and, in some systems, syllabication. *Cp.* **morphology.**

structural equation a mathematical formula which includes a stochastic, or random component, and which serves as a model to explain complex relationships, as in economics or psychology.

structural grammar 1. a descriptive model of the grammar of speech; descriptive linguistics; structural linguistics. 2. an approach to the study of language which analyzes its sounds, word formation, and syntactic structure.

structural linguistics 1. the study of language in terms of its form and the distribution of elements within its parts, as the form and distribution of phonemes and morphemes in English. *Cp.* **descriptive linguistics** (def. 1). 2. the study of language at a particular point in time; synchronic linguistics.

structure (struk′chər) 1. *n.* the way in which parts are organized into a stable, related whole, as *body structure, mental structure, social structure.* 2. *n.* the patterns and relations of a language independent of linguistic analysis, as in the language user's brain. 3. *n.* the principles underlying such patterns and relations. 4. *v.* to create or impose organization. *Structure your essay more tightly. adj.* **structural.**

structured overview a form of cognitive organizer in which important concepts of a topic or unit of study, as reflected in its vocabulary, are identified and made into a visual pattern that may be used to anticipate, revise, and confirm relationships among the concepts. *A structured overview . . . actually serves as an advance organizer, a process organizer, and as a post organizer in content area reading* — Earle.

structure word See **function word.**

student (sto͞od′ənt, styo͞od′-) 1. *n.* a person who attends school. 2. *n.* any person who investigates carefully, observes fully, or studies seriously; one motivated by learning; scholar.

study (stud′ē) 1. *n.* attentive, thoughtful examination of a subject, activity, problem, etc., with a view to gaining knowledge or skill; *systematic and purposeful activities in the thoughtful use of books* — E. Betts (1946). 2. *n.* a field of knowledge, as *the study of law.* 3. *n.* a scholarly publication reporting the results of a detailed examination of a particular field of knowledge. 4. *n.* a literary composition done as an exercise, as *a study in characterization.* 5. *n.* a state of abstraction or absorption. *He was in such a deep study that he did not hear the call to dinner.* 6. **studies,** personal effort to gain knowledge, as *pursue one's studies.* 7. *v.* to apply oneself in gaining knowledge, as *study Chinese.* 8. *v.* to think through carefully, as *study the implications of a story. adj.* **studious.**

study guide 1. a set of suggestions designed to lead the student through a reading assignment by directing attention to the key ideas in a passage and suggesting the application of skills needed to read a passage successfully. 2. any one of several types of specific sets of suggestions for a particular study emphasis, as to comprehend at the literal, interpretative, or applied levels (H. Herber 1978), to emphasize a pattern of ideas, or to identify key concepts, or chunks, in a passage.

study habits a person's usual ways of applying study skills, effective or otherwise.

study-habits inventory a checklist or questionnaire on methods and conditions of study.

study skills a general term for those techniques and strategies which help a person read or listen for specific purposes with the intent to remember. *Note:* Although reading specialists may differ in terms of the specific skills to be included, study skills commonly include following directions; locating, selecting, organizing, and retaining information; interpreting typographic and graphic aids; and reading flexibility.

study strategy *or* **technique** a systematic process for the intensive study of a selection for retention and recall. *SQ3R is a study strategy.*

study-type reading See **study** (def. 1); **study skills.**

stuttering (stut′ər in͡g) *n.* spasmodic, involuntary, blocked speech marked by hesitation and by sound prolongations and/or repetitions. *Severe stuttering is often accompanied by bodily tension, as facial grimaces, clenched hands, rigid posture, etc.* See also **clonic block; tonic block; primary stuttering; secondary stuttering.** *n.* **stutterer.** *v.* **stutter.**

style (stīl)

Style, as applied to writing and speaking, is an elusive and subtle concept. In the broadest sense it refers to the characteristic way in which a person conceives and expresses ideas through language. Great writers and speakers develop fresh ideas and ways of thinking about them which they express in unique ways. Thus when such classics are 'simplified' or translated, style is distorted: neither the ideas nor the way they were expressed are truly represented.

1. *n.* the characteristics of a work which reflect its author's distinctive way of writing. *Style is to the work of a writer what personality is to an individual.* 2. *n.* an author's use of language, its effects, and its appropriateness to the author's intent and theme. *Style is the dress of thought* — Lord Chesterfield. 3. *n.* the identifying aspects of a piece of writing or some other kind of performance. 4. *n.* the manner in which something is said or done, in contrast to its message. 5. *n.* the particular identifying characteristics of something, as *writing style, acting style, baroque style.* 6. *n.* the particular way in which a person uses language in a given social environment; idiolect. *In Shaw's* Pygmalion, *Eliza was forced to adopt a new style of speaking.* 7. *n.* a set of rules for preparing published material, as the University of Chicago Press *Manual of Style.* 8. *n.* a way of living, dressing, etc., as *living in style; one's life style.*

style of discourse language use as determined by the roles taken or assumed by speaker and listener, or by writer and reader. *Style of discourse may range from the casual to the formal.* See also **stylistic variation; register** (def. 1).

stylistics (stī lis′tiks) *(with sing. v.)* 1. *n.* in linguistics, the study of the grammatical, phonological, and practical aspects of style in language. 2. *n.* the study or practice of the art of using linguistic devices to make communication more precise, connotative, or personal. *adj.* **stylistic.**

stylistic variation 1. differences in choice of words and/or syntax to convey much the same idea or information. *'I request the honor of your presence' and 'I sure do hope you can come' are examples of stylistic variation.* See **register** (def. 1). 2. differences in structure between various literary forms.

sub- a prefix indicating *under, beneath in position,* or *forming a part of the whole*; as **subskill.**

subculture (sub′kul″chər) *n.* a distinctive group within a larger cultural group. *A subculture may accept or reject the values of the larger group.*

subhead *or* **subheading** 1. *n.* a division of a larger topic or heading. 2. *n.* in a library catalog, a division of a major subject entry.

subject (sub′jikt) 1. *n.* a topic of discussion, thinking, observation, etc., as *the subject of the argument.* 2. *n.* an area of learning and study; discipline, as *the subject of history.* 3. *n.* the main topic of a sentence or proposition; that to which a predicate refers; as *day* in *The day was hot.* 4. a person or animal that is observed, experimented on, created, etc., as *the subject of the experiment.* 5. *n.* in philosophy: a. mind, as distinguished from that which is thought about. b. an essential substance which possesses qualities and attributes, as *the subject of excellence.*

subject catalog a library catalog alphabetically arranged by subject. *The subject catalog enables users to identify library material on a particular topic, as books on semantics.*

subject entry a bibliographic description of a work found under any given subject heading or classification number. *Cp.* **author entry; title entry.**

subject index an indexed guide to information sources arranged by subject. The Reader's Guide to Periodical Literature *is in part a subject index.*

subjective (səb jek′tiv) 1. *adj.* having to do with the ideas and thought processes of a person rather than with the objects of thought. *Thinking is a subjective act. Ct.* **objective** (def. 3). 2. *adj.* personal; individual; idiosyncratic; unverifiable. *Introspection is a subjective experience.* 3. *adj.* referring to the use of self-reports of subjects. See **subjective refraction.** 4. *adj.* imaginary, as *subjective fears.* 5. *adj.* referring to internal sensation. *A pain in the neck may be subjective as well as metaphorical.* 6. *adj.* referring to the subject of a sentence; nominative. *English pronouns take the subjective, objective, or possessive case.*

subjective refraction refraction of the eyes which uses self-reports of the patient.

subject matter 1. broadly, a content area or field of study and the learning associated with such a discipline. 2. a specific topic in the curriculum or in the course of study.

subjunctive mood a verb form that expresses an attitude of conditional fact, contrary to fact, etc., rather than expressing a fact, in a way that *represents the action or state as a conception of the mind rather than as a reality* — J. Curme (1931).

sublimation (sub″lə mā′s̲h̲ən) *n.* the diversion of the energy of a basic drive, as sex, from its immediate goal to a higher social, moral, or aesthetic one. *v.* **sublimate.**

subliminal (sub lim′ə nᵊl, -lī′mə-) *adj.* referring to stimuli below the threshold of awareness. *Note:* Subliminal stimuli may be too weak to be consciously perceived, but may be strong enough to influence behavior. *Ct.* **supraliminal.**

subordinate clause See **dependent clause.**

subordinate conjunction a conjunction that introduces or begins a dependent clause, as *If* in *If it rains, we'll stay home.*

subordination (səb ôr″də nā′s̲h̲ən) *n.* the relationship between an independent and dependent clause, indicated by the use of a subordinate conjunction to introduce the dependent clause, as *Because* in *Because of a nail, the shoe hurt. v.* **subordinate.** *n.* **subordination.**

subscript (sub′skript) *n.* a graphic symbol placed below a letter or number, as the cedilla (,) in façade.

subscription book a book made available by a publisher to readers at a lowered cost, usually through book clubs or agents.

subskill (sub′skil″) *n.* a skill which is part of a more complex skill or body of skills. *Some reading tests attempt to identify reading subskills.*

substantive (sub′stən tiv) 1. *n.* a noun or pronoun, or a noun phrase, that functions as a noun; nominal. 2. *adj.* referring to a noun.

substitution (sub″sti to͞o′shən, -tyo͞o′-) 1. See **consonant substitution.** 2. *n.* the replacing of one or more words in the oral reading of text with an incorrect word or words; one of several types of oral reading errors commonly recorded in testing oral reading. *Note* (def. 2): Substitutions often make contextual sense to the reader but bear little or no phonic resemblance to the word or words they replace. See also **insertion** (def. 1); **mispronunciation; omission.** 3. *n.* an adjustment mechanism, conscious or subconscious, wherein an unacceptable or unattainable behavior or goal is replaced with a behavior or goal that is acceptable or attainable.

subtest (sub′test″) *n.* a division or section of a longer test, usually containing items on a similar topic or type of problem. *'Vocabulary meaning' is often a subtest on a silent reading test.*

subvocal (sub vō′kəl) *adj.* referring to words and ideas thought but not spoken aloud.

subvocalization (sub″vō kə li zā′shən) *n.* the movements of the lips, tongue, and larynx during silent reading. *Excessive subvocalization hinders fluent silent reading. Ct.* **implicit speech.**

subvocal reading 1. reading to oneself so quietly that others can only hear a murmur; covert oral reading. 2. observable movements of the speech muscles, directly or on an electromyogram, during silent reading. *Note:* Def. 1 refers to voluntary speech activity, as in rehearsing a part in a play privately. Def. 2 refers to an involuntary part of processing language that is present in all readers.

subvocal speech movements of the speech articulators without producing speech sounds.

suffix (*n.* suf′iks) *n.* a morpheme attached to the end of a base word, as *en* added to *ox* to form *oxen.*

sulcus (sul′kəs) *pl.* **sulci.** *n.* a groove or furrow, especially between two convolutions or folds of the brain. *Cp.* **fissure.**

summary (sum′ə rē) *n.* a brief statement which contains the essential ideas of a longer passage or selection.

summation (sə mā′shən) 1. *n.* a numerical total (Σ) of a series or group of things. 2. *n.* any cumulative effect or joint action, as the effect of several rapid light stimulations being perceived as one. 3. *n.* a summary; a bringing together of all the relevant information; as *the summation of a speech.*

summative evaluation the final determination of the degree to which the goals and objectives of a process of change have been met, as to learn how far students have progressed toward the objectives of an instructional program.

super- a prefix indicating *above, beyond, to a high degree;* as **supernatural.** *Cp.* **supra-.**

superego (so͞o″pər ē′gō, -eg′ō) *n.* in Freudian theory, the largely unconscious part of the psyche which represents the internalization of cultural standards and those processes that advance civilization. *The superego is* *presumed to exercise self-censorship and the repression of primitive and instinctual drives that are derived first from parental standards, then from those of society. Ct.* **id; ego** (def. 2).

superfix (so͞o'pər fix″) *n.* the stress pattern of a word or phrase, as *ob' ject* (noun)/*ob ject'* (verb). See **suprasegmental phoneme.**

superior (sə pēr'ē ər, so͞o-) 1. *adj.* higher in place, as *the superior rung on a ladder.* 2. *adj.* referring to the upper half of the body. See also **cephalic** (def. 2). 3. *adj.* higher in status or degree, as *a superior job.* 4. *adj.* higher in importance or value, as *superior self-confidence, a superior product.* 5. *adj.* above average, as *superior intelligence.* 6. *adj.* greater in quantity, as *a superior number.* 7. *adj.* more important, better, etc., as *a superior attitude.* 8. *adj.* not affected by, as *superior to bribery.* 9. *n.* a person higher in rank or worth than another. *Ant.* (defs. 1-4, 9) **inferior** (defs. 1-5). 10. *n.* a superscript as the 2 in x^2. *Ct.* **inferior** (def. 6). *n.* **superiority.**

superlative degree the form of an adjective or adverb that shows the most or least in quality, quantity, or intensity, as the adjectival forms *oldest* or *least old,* or the adverbial forms *most rapidly* or *least rapidly. Cp.* **positive degree; comparative degree.**

supernatural story 1. a narrative about situations and events that cannot be explained by known natural causes. 2. a narrative about ghosts and other unworldly beings. 3. a secret, magic, or mysterious narrative.

superordinate unit any item in a linguistic class or category under which subordinate units may be placed. *Sentences are superordinate units composed of subordinate word units.*

superscript (so͞o'pər skript″) *n.* a symbol placed higher than the x-height of letters or numbers, as *2* in x^2 or the footnote symbol (*) in *book**. *Ct.* **subscript.**

supplement (sup'lə mənt) *n.* a part added to a book, sometimes as a separate volume, to add to, update, or correct information, usually at greater length than in an addendum. *Cp.* **addendum.**

supplemental *or* **supplementary material** seatwork exercises, as for reading practice. *The silent reading movement brought in its train a host of supplemental materials other than readers* — N. B. Smith (1965).

supplementary reader a reader used to reinforce or extend the skills and abilities developed in a basic reader.

supplementary reading 1. reading material of a different type than that used in basic reading instruction, as trade books to broaden the experience of students. 2. See **supplemental** *or* **supplementary material.**

suppletion (sə plē'shən) *n.* in morphology, the replacement of an expected word form with a word completely different in structure, as *went* as the past tense of *go*, and *better* as the comparative form of *good. adj.* **suppletive.**

supportive therapy See **(ego) supportive therapy.**

suppression (sə presh'ən) 1. *n.* the intentional stopping or inhibition of an activity, as *the suppression of the news, the suppression of a need to make puns.* 2. *n.* the intentional blocking of a thought or desire from conscious thought, as *the suppression of all thoughts of home. Ct.* **repression** (def. 1). See **visual suppression.** *v.* **suppress.** *adj.* **suppressive.**

supra- a prefix indicating *above* (particulary in location or position); as

suprasegmental. *Cp.* **super-.**

supraliminal (so͞o″prə lim′ə nəl) *adj.* referring to stimuli above the threshold of awareness. *Ct.* **subliminal.**

suprasegmental (so͞o″prə seg men′təl) *n.* a phonological feature which carries over more than one speech sound, as the syllable stress that distinguishes /*af′ fekt*/ (*n.*) from /*a fect′*/ (*v.*).

suprasegmental phoneme a prosodic feature, as pitch, stress, or juncture which occurs simultaneously with a sequence of segmental phonemes and which influences meaning.

surd (sûrd) *n.* a voiceless speech sound, as /f/. *Ant.* **sonant.**

surface structure 1. in transformational-generative grammar, the relationship among elements of a spoken or written sentence that results from the sequencing of those elements. *Ct.* **deep structure.** *Note:* Two sentences may have the same deep structure but different surface structures, as *Bill broke the window* and *The window was broken by Bill.* 2. what is actually said or written.

surrealism (sə rē′ə liz″əm) *n.* a 20th century movement in art and literature, especially in France, portraying the random nature of association in the unconscious, such as that revealed in dreams.

surrogate (sûr′ə gāt″, -git, sur′-) 1. *n.* a substitute. 2. *adj.* acting as a substitute. *H. Harlow used surrogate mothers in studying early social-emotional behavior in rhesus monkeys.* 3. *n.* unconscious parental substitution. *The teacher is often the unwitting surrogate of the affection or anger that a child feels for a parent.* 4. *n.* a deputy; one who is officially appointed to act for another.

survey (*n.* sûr′vā, sər′vā; *v.* sər vā′) 1. *n.* the overview of a field to determine its status and the trends and issues surrounding it. 2. *n.* a sampling of individual responses to a question, topic, etc., as *a survey of television use.* 3. *n.* an overall examination of performance, as *a reading survey.* 4. *v.* to make a comprehensive overview, as *survey a textbook.*

survey book a nonfiction or informational book designed *to give an overall view of a substantial topic and to furnish a representative sampling of facts, principles, or issues* — C. Huck (1976).

survey test a test, usually a group test, designed to sample knowledge or proficiency, usually broadly, in a given area. *Ct.* **diagnostic test.**

survival reading skills See **functional literacy.**

survival story a narrative, real or imagined, which describes the courageous spirit of characters who overcome the problems of frontier life, war, dangerous adventure, etc.

suspense (sə spens′) *n.* the sustained interest in a narrative or drama created by delaying the resolution of the conflict.

sustained silent reading (SSR) See **uninterrupted sustained silent reading (USSR).**

sweep check test a rapid procedure for identifying possible hearing loss in which a few selected frequencies, often 1, 2 and 4 kHz, are presented at a set intensity, usually 20 dB in schools, with those individuals who fail to hear these tones being selected for further audiometric testing.

syllabarium (sil ə ber′ē əm) *pl.* **-ia** (ē ə). *n.* a list of nonsense syllables, organized alphabetically, that followed the alphabet in the hornbook, primer, and spelling book: as *ab eb ib ob ub* / *ba be bi bo bu*/ etc.

syllabary (sil′ə ber″ē) 1. *n.* a writing system in which orthographic symbols represent syllables, as Japanese kana or the Cherokee orthography created by Sequoyah. 2. *n.* a list of syllables, or of the characters representing syllables, in a given language. 3. *n.* a writing system, such as ancient Sumerian, in which orthographic symbols represent either a syllable, as /ba/ or /dal/, or a syllable sequence, as /bala/. *Cp.* **alphabet; logography.** See also **syllable.**

syllabic (si lab′ik) 1. *adj.* referring to syllables. 2. *adj.* in linguistics, referring to any sound which serves as the nucleus of a syllable. *Note:* In English, syllabic is normally applied to vowels although sometimes applicable to liquids and nasals. *Cp.* **nucleus; syllable.**

syllabication *or* **syllabification** (si lab″ ə kā′shən; si lab″ə fi kā′shən) *n.* the division of words into syllables. *v.* **syllabicate; syllabify**.

syllabic consonant a consonant sound that, in the absence of a vowel sound, has sufficient energy or sonority to function as a syllable, as /m/ in *prism. Cp.* **semivowel** (def. 1).

syllabic verse verse in which one pays attention to the number of syllables in a line, as in haiku, rather than to stressed and unstressed syllables.

syllabic writing system See **syllabary** (def. 1).

syllable (sil′ə bəl) 1. *n.* a phonological segment of speech with a vowel or vowel-like sound as its nucleus. 2. *n.* in a writing system, the set of graphemes that represents such a speech segment. *Note* (def. 2): In English, there is not always a one-to-one correspondence between spoken and written syllables because of printers' practices in syllabicating written language. For example, *happen* in speech contains the two syllables /hap′/ and /ən/, /hap′ən/, but in print they would be syllabicated *hap-pen.*

syllable (syllabic) nucleus the single sound of greatest loudness and resonance in a syllable. *The /i/ in 'pit' is the syllable nucleus.*

syllabus (sil′ə bəs) *pl.* **-buses, -bi** (-bī′). *n.* an outline for a college course, usually including a schedule of topics, assignments, and examinations, plus a reading list.

syllogism (sil′ə jiz″əm) 1. *n.* a type of formal argument in logic to test the truth of a conclusion when given two statements assumed to be true; deductive reasoning: *All A is B; all B is C; therefore, all A is C. Note:* The conclusion of a syllogism may be untrue even though the argument appears to have correct form and face validity. 2. *n.* a misleading argument in which the apparent logic of a syllogistic presentation is used to deceive. *adj.* **syllogistic.**

Sylvian fissure See **fissure of Sylvius.**

sym-, syn- a prefix meaning *with, together;* as **sympathy, synthesis.**

symbol (sim′bəl) 1. *n.* anything that represents something else, often by indirect association or by the convention of an emblem, token, word, etc., as *the cross as a symbol, a ring as a symbol of authority, a symbol of pride, the printed symbols on this page.* See also **concept** (def. 4. *Note*). 2. *n.* anything recognized as a sign. *She saw the broken lock as a symbol of danger.* 3. *n.* an idea or mental image. *Einstein used abstract symbols in his thinking.* 4. *n.* any arbitrary, conventional written or printed mark intended to communicate. *Letters, numerals, and ideographs, as ÷, >, and ~ are symbols in common use.* 5. *n.* the disguised form of unconscious thoughts, feelings, and experiences, often appearing in dreams.

Psychoanalysts interpret the symbols of their patients' dreams to help the patients resolve their conflicts. adj. **symbolic.**

symbolic function (J. Piaget) the ability to represent something not presently perceived by symbols or signs, as language, gesture, drawings, mental imagery, etc.; semiotic function.

symbolic representation See **cognitive representation.**

symbolism (sim′bə liz″əm) 1. *n.* the use of one thing to suggest something else; specifically, the use of symbols to represent abstract ideas in concrete ways. *Myths and fairy tales are classics of symbolism* 2. *n.* the implied meaning of a literary or artistic work, as *the symbolism of* Yeats' *'Leda and the Swan.'* 3. *n. (Cap.)* the writing style and themes of the European Symbolists of the later 19th century. 4. *n.* the psychoanalytic theory that symbols are used to bring into consciousness material from the unconscious. *v.* **symbolize.** *n.* **symbolization.**

sympathetic nervous system that portion of the autonomic nervous system that serves to prepare the body for crises and acts in oppostion to the parasympathetic nervous system. *The sympathetic nervous system increases the heart rate, dilates the pupil, decreases blood supply to the viscera, etc.*

symptom (simp′təm) 1. *n.* a sign or indication of something. *Her red eyes were a symptom of her grief.* 2. *n.* a sign or evidence of disease or mental disorder, as *symptoms of diabetes, symptoms of paranoia.* See also **syndrome** (def. 1). *adj.* **symptomatic.**

synaeresis *or* **syneresis** (si ner′i sis) *n.* the contraction of two syllables into one, as /dī′mənd/ rather than /dī′ə mand/ for *diamond,* or two vowels into one, as in a diphthong.

synapse (sin′aps, si naps′) *n.* the point at which a nerve impulse is transferred from one neuron to another, usually from the axon of the first to a dendrite or the cell body of the next; synaptic junction. *adj.* **synaptic.**

synchronic (sin kron′ik) *adj.* referring to the study of a language as it presently exists or would have existed at one point in time, as *synchronic linguistics. Ct.* **diachronic.**

syncope (siŋ′kə pē, -pē″; sin-) 1. *n.* the omission or loss of a sound segment or group of sound segments from the middle of a word; as the loss of /w/ in *coxswain,* now pronounced /kok′sən/. 2. *n.* the omission of a syllable from a poetic foot, often balanced by extending an adjacent syllable. 3. *n.* a brief loss of consciousness; faint. *adj.* **syncopic.**

syncretism (siŋ′kri tiz″əm, sin′-) 1. *n.* any attempt to reconcile inconsistent or conflicting ideas, as *religious syncretism.* 2. *n.* any uncritical merger of inconsistent or conflicting ideas. 3. *n.* in the historical development of language, the merging of different inflectional suffixes into one form. 4. *n.* (J. Piaget) the linking in a complex configuration of unrelated ideas into some total impression without details or logical organization. See also **egocentric logic.** *v.* **syncretize.** *adj.* **syncretic.**

syndrome (sin′drōm, sin′drə mē″) 1. *n.* a group of symptoms of a disease or disorder. *Such symptoms as sweating, rapid and shallow breathing, noticeable beating of the heart, loss of color, and a sense of panic indicate an anxiety syndrome.* 2. *n.* a group of behaviors, events, or things, that happen together and form a pattern. *The words in this dictionary represent a syndrome of meanings.*

synecdoche (si nek′də kē) *n.* a specific metaphor in which a part represents the whole, or the whole represents a part, as *all hands on deck. Note:* An effective synecdoche occurs when an important element of the whole is selected to represent it, as the winged foot for the Greek god Hermes, messenger of the gods, or 'Scrooge' for a miser.

syneresis See **synaeresis.**

synergic (si nûr'jik) *adj.* referring to cooperative working together to produce or improve an effect, as *synergic muscles, synergic drugs. n.* **synergy; synergism.** *adj.* **synergetic; synergistic.**

synesthesia *or* **synaesthesia** (sin″is thē'zhə, -zhē ə, -zē ə) 1. *n.* a type of psychological association in some persons in which stimulation in one sensory mode produces images in another mode, as in hearing sounds in color. 2. *n.* a description of one sensation in terms of another: *the furry warmth/And purring sound of fires was in his voice* — E. Sitwell.

synonym (sin'ə nim) 1. *n.* one of two or more words in a language that have highly similar meanings, as sadness, grief, sorrow, etc. *Exact synonyms in the English language are rare. Ct.* **antonym.** 2. *n.* a word used in a figurative sense, as the *deep* for *water,* a *heel* for a *person,* etc.; metonym. *adj.* **synonymous.**

synopsis (si nop'sis) *n.* a brief summary, as a *synopsis of a play.*

syntactic (al) (sin tak'tik; -ti kəl) *adj.* referring to the grammatical relations and functions of sentence components. See **syntax.**

syntactic cue evidence from a knowledge of the rules and patterns of language that aids in the identification of an unknown word from the way it is used. *Cp.* **semantic cue.**

syntactic factor the language complexity dimension in material to be comprehended, as the measure of sentence length, commonly used in readability formulas. *Cp.* **semantic factor.**

syntactics (sin tak'tiks) *(with sing. v.) n.* the study of the arrangement and relations between symbols in syntactic sequences.

syntagmatic (sin″tag ma'tik) *adj.* referring to a linear relationship between elements in a phrase or clause, as in *Go* and *away* in the sentence *Go away. Cp.* **paradigmatic.**

syntax (sin'taks) 1. *n.* the study of the structure of grammatical sentences in a language. 2. *n.* the pattern or structure of word order in sentences, clauses, and phrases.

synthesis (sin'thi sis) *pl.* **-ses** (sēz). 1. *n.* the process, or result, of forming a whole, either concrete or abstract, from the logical relation of its parts. *Deductive thinking requires synthesis. Ant.* **analysis** (def. 1). 2. *n.* the process, or result, of the formation of utterances, as *speech synthesis.* 3. *n.* speech production, as in *speech synthesis* (by machine). 4. *n.* the generation or prediction by rule of various transformations of sentences. *v.* **synthesize.**

synthetic (sin thet'ik) 1. *adj.* putting, or having been put, together, as *synthetic phonics.* 2. *adj.* artificial, as *synthetic flowers.*

synthetic approach *or* **method** a way of teaching beginning reading by starting with word parts or elements, as letters, sounds, or syllables, and later combining them into words. *The beginning emphasis in a synthetic method is learning the sound-symbol correspondence* — M. Dallman (1974). *Ct.* **analytic approach** *or* **method.**

synthetic phonics a part-to-whole phonics approach to reading instruction in which the student learns the sounds represented by letters and letter combinations, blends these sounds together to pronounce words, and is taught the phonic generalizations that apply in learning symbol-sound correspondences; inductive phonics. *Ct.* **analytic phonics; whole word phonics.**

system (sis′təm) 1. *n.* an ordered arrangement of ideas, elements, etc., that form a unified whole, as *a theoretical system.* 2. *n.* such an arrangement in a specific area, as *a linguistic system.* 3. *n.* a set of functionally related items, as *a railroad system, a computer system.* 4. *n.* a classification scheme, as *the Dewey decimal system.* 5. *n.* a set of related languages, as *the Indo-European system of languages.* 6. *n.* a relationship of members of a paradigmatic class, as *the gender system in grammar. adj.* **systematic.**

systematic desensitization a behavior therapy technique, developed chiefly by J. Wolpe, that uses deep muscle relaxation and controlled anxiety-inducing stimuli to treat neurotic response patterns. *Note:* Subjects are first exposed to imagined situations that produce little anxiety. Stronger imagined anxiety-provoking situations are gradually introduced until the neurotic response pattern is dissipated. *Cp.* **implosive therapy.**

systematic error repeated bias or distortion, especially in the collection and/or analysis of data; constant error.

systems analysis the identification of the dimensions and component parts of an instructional or institutional system, including the interaction of the component parts.

systems approach a procedure for planning analysis and development to reach a specified objective. *Note:* A systems approach involves such steps as stating the objective in behavioral terms; designing, selecting, and integrating possible approaches; and evaluating the effectiveness of the planned steps, or system, in reaching the objective.

systolic pressure the highest blood pressure level in the arteries, occurring just after the chambers of the heart contract to pump the blood through the body. *Ct.* **diastolic pressure.**

T

DEVELOPMENT OF MAJUSCULE								
NORTH SEMITIC	GREEK		ETR.	LATIN		MODERN		
						GOTHIC	ITALIC	ROMAN
+	X	T	ፐ	T	T	𝔗	*T*	T

DEVELOPMENT OF MINUSCULE					
ROMAN CURSIVE	ROMAN UNCIAL	CAROL. MIN.	MODERN		
			GOTHIC	ITALIC	ROMAN
ፐ	T	ፒ	t	*t*	t

The twentieth letter of the English alphabet developed from North Semitic *taw*. The symbol has changed but little in its long history, and its minuscule (t) is only a slight variant of the capital.

TABA See **American Book Awards, The.**

table (tā′bəl) *n.* a systematic listing of data in rows and columns, as *a table of names. adj.* **tabular.**

table of contents a list, with page numbers, of the principal parts of a book, as chapters of a book, titles of magazine articles, etc., that appears near the front of a publication.

taboo (tə bo͞o′, ta-) 1. *adj.* socially improper and unacceptable in genteel use; referring especially to language to be avoided or replaced by euphemisms; as *taboo words.* 2. *adj.* set apart and forbidden for general use, as *a taboo temple.* 3. *n.* something so set apart and forbidden.

tach (y)- a combining form indicating speedy, swift; as **tachistoscope, tachylogia.**

tachistoscope (tə kis′tə skōp″) *n.* any mechanical device for the controlled and usually very brief exposure of visual materials, as pictures, letters, numbers, words, phrases, and sentences. *Note:* Tachistoscopes are used in research in perception and learning with individuals and groups. They are also used for testing and for teaching speed of, or perception in, reading in order to increase reading speeds. *adj.* **tachistoscopic.**

tachylalia (tak″ə lā′lē ə) *n.* talking too rapidly, usually due to nervousness.

tachylexia (tak″ə lek′sē ə) *n.* a variant of dyslexia marked by extreme rapidity in reading not due to habit, low intelligence, or familiarity with the subject of the text. *Ct.* **bradylexia.**

tachyphemia (tak″ə fē′mē ə) See **tachylalia.**

tactile (tak′til, -tīl) 1. *adj.* having to do with the sense of touch; tactual, as *tactile agnosia.* 2. *adj.* capable of being felt; providing information to the sense of touch; tangible. *Braille is tactile writing.*

tactile approach any of the various teaching methods which involve touching the material to be learned, often making use of sandpaper letters on a field of felt or similar materials of high textual contrast. *The 'T' in VAKT represents 'tactile.'*

tactual (tak′cho͞o əl) *adj.* having to do with the sense of touch or with sensations derived from touching; tactile.

tagboard (tag′bōrd″, -bôrd″) *n.* a strong cardboard especially useful in making charts in the primary grades; oak tag.

tagmeme (tag′mēm) *n.* the basic unit in tagmemics. *Note:* The tagmeme is both a grammatical function or slot and the class of items that fill the slot. In the sentence *Vera is a fantastic dancer, Vera* is a tagmeme denoting actor-as-subject.

tagmemics (tag mē′miks) *(with sing. v.) n.* a linguistic theory developed by Kenneth Pike in the 1940's, which views language as a patterned part of general cultural behavior, and composed of sound, morpheme, and functional levels.

tag question a short phrase in the form of a question that is added to a statement, often for confirmation, as *isn't it* in *It is time to go, isn't it?*

tale (tāl) 1. *n.* a relatively short and detailed story of a real or imagined event. 2. *n.* a literary example of such a story, as *tales from* The Arabian Nights. See also (defs. 1, 2) **folk tale** *or* **story; tall tale**. 3. *n.* a falsehood; fib. *That's an unlikely tale!* 4. *n.* a rumor or piece of gossip, often malicious.

talent (tal'ənt) 1. *n.* a high degree of ability or aptitude. *Da Vinci was a man of talent.* 2. *n.* a special ability or aptitude, as *mathematical talent, muical talent. adj.* **talented.**

talking book written material recorded on tape or records for persons with limited sight.

talking page an audio-visual teaching aid consisting of a large page with instructions and exercises on one side and magnetic tape for recording audio material on the other, the page fitting onto a device which permits random access to the taped materials.

talking typewriter a typewriter, in a computer-assisted instructional program, which can 'tell' a student when a response is wrong. See also **autotelic system.**

tall tale a story about impossible or exaggerated happenings related in a realistic, matter-of-fact, and often humorous way. *Paul Bunyan, John Henry, and Mike Fink are heroes of American tall tales.*

tambour (tam'bo͝or) *n.* an instrument for mechanically converting changes in air or liquid pressure to traces on a recording chart by responsive movements of a membrane stretched across the air or liquid container.

tangible (tan'jə bəl) *adj.* capable of being identified by touch alone, as Braille.

tape (tāp) See **magnetic tape.**

tape recorder an electrical device which uses magnetic tape, or audiotape, to record voice, music, etc., and then play it back. *Note:* In reading diagnosis the tape recorder is especially valuable, as in recording the responses to an oral reading test; and in instruction, as in recording a student's reading which can then be replayed and studied with the subject.

target language 1. a language which someone or some group seeks to learn. 2. the language into which a text is translated.

task analysis a systematic study of the components of a skill or other activity for determining a sequence for learning.

task orientation one's attitude toward a task or toward work in general as distinguished from one's human relations orientation. *Note:* Persons with high achievement motivation usually have a strong task orientation.

tautology (tô tol'ə jē) *n.* redundancy or unnecessary repetition in speech or writing, as *widow woman. adj.* **tautologic; tautological.** *v.* **tautologize.**

taxonomy (tak son'ə mē) *n.* classification, as *a taxonomy of reading comprehension. Note:* T. Barrett has proposed a taxonomy of the cognitive and affective domains of reading comprehension based upon the taxonomies of B. Bloom and others (*Cognitive Domain,* 1956) and D. Krathwohl and others (*Affective Domain,* 1964): *recognition, recall, reorganization, inferential comprehension, evaluation, appreciation.*

teach tēch) *v.* to instruct; educate; tutor; as *teach reading, teach the illiterate.*

teacher center a place where professional and instructional materials are gathered together for teacher use.

teacher expectation the mental set through which teachers filter their perceptions of individual student performance, as in the Pygmalion effect.

teacher librarian a teacher with special training in library science who manages a school library and educates students in the pleasures, use, and care of library materials; school library supervisor.

teacher's guide *or* **manual** a handbook on the use of specific teaching materials, as books in a reading series. *Note:* Teacher's manuals for basal reading materials are often comprehensive and detailed. They may include the rationale of the reading series; detailed lesson plans; supplementary readings and other activities; complete vocabulary lists; and professional references.

teaching (tē'ching) 1. *n.* what teachers do in the instruction of students. 2. *n.* something taught, as a skill, maxim, doctrine.

teaching aide a person, usually without teaching credentials, who assists a teacher or other educational staff member in instructional and/or clerical tasks; teaching paraprofessional.

Teaching English as a Second Language (TESL) 1. a set of philosophies and approaches for teaching English to those for whom another language is their first. 2. a department in a college or university devoted to research and teaching within the framework of such philosophies and approaches.

teaching machine a device which presents a prearranged program of instruction, one small part at a time and at the pace of the learner's responses; learning machine.

team teaching an instructional technique in which several teachers plan and carry out an integrated teaching approach.

technical school a school which offers courses in the applied sciences and arts that bridge the gap between the skilled trades and the professions, as that of the medical technician, computer programmer, dietician, interior decorator, etc. See also **vocational school.**

technical word 1. a word form with a specialized meaning in one or more content fields or professions, as *class, assimilation, code.* 2. a meaning of a common word form specific to a content field, as the technical meaning of *mean* in statistics. *Ct.* **common word.**

technique (tek nēk') 1. *n.* the proficiencies needed for a given skilled performance, as *scanning technique.* 2. *n.* the systematic method used to handle a complex task, as *the technique of scientific method, the technique of teaching.*

technology (tek nol'ə jē) 1. *n.* the systematic use of technical knowledge for practical purposes, as *educational technology.* 2. *n.* the branch of knowledge dealing with applied science, industrial arts, engineering, etc. 3. *n.* the provision of the material things of life by a social group, as *the technology of Mayan civilization.*

teeth (tēth) *n. pl.* the hard structures attached in rows to each jaw which aid articulation. See illustration under **speech organs.**

tel (e)- a combining form indicating *distant;* as **telecommunication.**

telecommunication (s) (tel'ə kə myōō″nə kā'shən, -z) *n.* any electronic communication of sounds, images, or other signals, as by telephone, satellite transmission of computer signals, radiotelegraphy, etc.

telegraphic speech 1. a stage in language development in which all but the essential words of an utterance are omitted, as *Mommy give cookie* for *Mommy, give me one of those cookies.* 2. a communication technique, which uses simple constructions and omits nonessential words, as captioned television news.

teleplay (tel′ə plā″) *n.* a filmed production made especially for TV showing.

telescoping (tel′i skōp″inġ) 1. *n.* shortening a word or phrase by omitting parts of it, either by error or by custom, as in writing *letr* for *letter* or saying *ham 'n eggs* for *ham and eggs.* 2. *n.* blending or forming a word by omitting one or more parts when combining two words, as *botel* from *boat* and *hotel*; portmanteau word. 3. *n.* writing using letters but omitting most vowels; speedwriting.

television (TV) (tel′ə vizh″ən) 1. *n.* the broadcasting of audiovisual images via radiowaves to receivers that project the images on a picture tube for viewing. 2. *n.* a set for receiving television broadcasts. 3. *n.* the television industry. *v.* **televise.**

telewriting (tel′ə rī″tinġ) *n.* a device, sometimes used in telelectures, which transmits and makes visible sketches, designs, handwriting, etc., over telephone lines.

telly (tel′ē) *(Brit.)* 1. *n.* television. 2. *n.* a television set.

template (tem′plit) *n.* a thin, flat sheet with cutouts, used to guide tracing or drawing, as in the formation of letters, geometrical forms, etc.

tempo (tem′pō) 1. *n.* the characteristic rate, rhythm, or pattern of activity. *The tempo of shorthand is fast. They liked a waltz tempo. The tempo of life is complex.* 2. *n.* the rate of articulation of speech sounds, especially syllables. *In English, the tempo of unstressed syllables speeds up rather than remaining relatively constant as in French.* 3. *n.* the speed indicated for playing a musical piece, as *largo* (slowly), or *presto* (very fast), etc.

temporal (tem′pər əl, tem′prəl) 1. *adj.* having to do with the side of the head, as *the temporal bone, the temporal lobe,* etc. 2. *adj.* referring to either the passage of time or a particular interval of time, as *a temporal period.* 3. *adj.* having to do with this present life; worldly; as *temporal pleasures.* 4. *adj.* lay, clerical, or civil rather than of the church, as *temporal power, temporal law.*

temporal lobe that portion of the cerebral hemisphere which lies below and is separated from the parietal and frontal lobes by the fissure of Sylvius, and which is continuous with the occipital and parietal lobes at its back end. See illustration under **lobe.**

tense (tens) 1. *n.* the inflection on a verb with reference to the time of the utterance. *Note:* In English, there are two tenses: *past* and *non-past. Future* is expressed by the use of *will. Cp.* **aspect.** See also **mood**[2] (def. 1). *Note:* Special types of tense, as *present tense,* are given under the corresponding term. 2. *adj.* having considerable muscle tension in the tongue and vocal tract walls when making speech sounds, as /ē/ in *eat,* /t/ in *tense.* 3. *adj.* referring to a distinctive feature in the analysis of speech sounds in which the sound is prolonged and has clearly defined resonance, as /ē/ in *feet,* /o͞o/ in *cool. Ct.* **lax** (def. 1).

tension (ten′shən) 1. *n.* the act of stretching or straining, as by contracting muscles. 2. *n.* the state of being stretched or strained and made taut. 3. *n.* emotional or psychological stress, especially in situations of possible threat or danger. *Student tension rose rapidly before the final examination.*

4. *n.* a strained relationship; uneasiness or hostility between individuals and/or groups. *adj.* **tensional.**

terminal juncture an intonation pattern used to connect one phrase or clause with another, or terminate a phrase or clause, to help show the speaker's meaning. *Note:* Three types of terminal juncture are commonly recognized: *sustained juncture,* in which the intonation level remains much the same; *rising juncture,* in which the intonation level moves upwards, as in a question; and *falling juncture,* in which the intonation level moves downward, as at the end of a declarative statement. See also **juncture.**

terminal objective a statement of an expected behavioral outcome of a specified learning experience.

terminal sound the ending sound(s) of a word; usually, the sound represented by the final consonant, digraph, or blend, but in some cases the last vowel sound and its following construction, as /ope/ in *rope,* or /asm/ in *chasm.*

terminal string in transformational-generative grammar, the product of a series of phrase structure rewrite rules, as the terminal string *Nom*(inal) + *Vt* (verb transitive) + *Det*(erminer) + *Nom*(inal), which could become the sentence *Mary caught the spider,* to which transformational rules may be applied. See also **phrase structure; phrase structure rule.**

terminology (tûr″mə nol′ə jē) 1. *n.* the technical words and expressions used in a special field, as medicine, mathematics, psychology, etc. 2. *n.* the science of developing a system of terms for a special field, subject, etc.; nomenclature.

TESL Teaching English as a Second Language.

TESOL Teaching of English to Speakers of Other Languages.

test (test) 1. *n.* a set of systematic tasks or questions to which responses may be quantified and performance interpreted, as *an oral reading test.* 2. *n.* a measurement, as *a hearing test, a statistical test.* 3. *n.* a criterion to determine the truth or accuracy of something, as *a test of lying, a test of good judgment.* 4. *n.* procedures for determining whether a hypothesis is tenable, as *a test of the null hypothesis.* 5. *v.* to put to a trial. *The class tested the teacher.* 6. *v.* to undergo a trial. *The teacher was tested by the class.* *Note:* Special types of tests, as *alternate response test,* are given under the describing term. *adj.* **testable.** *n.* **testing.**

test anxiety feelings of insecurity and fear that sometimes arise before and during the taking of a test.

test battery 1. a group of selected tests used together to study a given aspect of behavior, as *a clinical battery of reading tests.* 2. a group of tests standardized on the same population.

test item a single statement, question, or problem to be responded to on a test, as *a multiple-choice test item.*

test manual a guide or handbook to test administration, scoring, and interpretation.

test-retest reliability coefficient a reliability coefficient obtained by correlating the scores on two suitably separated administrations of the same test.

testwise (test′wīz″) *adj.* used to the ways of test-taking and, presumably, profiting from such experience.

tetr (a)- a combining form indicating *four;* as **tetrameter.**

tetrachloric correlation a correlation between two variables, both of which are assumed to be continuous and normal in distribution, but both of which have been divided into only two classes, as a correlation between tall/short and fair/dark persons. *Cp.* **biserial correlation; point-biserial correlation.**

tetrameter (te tram′i tər) *n.* a line of verse with four metrical feet.

text (tekst) 1. *n.* that part of a page or book which is the written or printed matter, in contrast to illustrations; words. *For some students, looking at the pictures is more informative than is trying to decipher the text.* 2. *n.* the main part of a composition, other than title, footnotes, etc. 3. *n.* a textbook. 4. *n.* the topic or theme of a discourse, as *a text of a lecture.* 5. the original spoken or written words or wording, in contrast to translations, abridgments, quotation errors, etc. 6. *n.* the exact sequence of words in an utterance. *Accurate text is necessary for linguistic analysis.* 7. the entirety of a linguistic communication, as a conversation and its situational context. 8. *n.* a passage from the Bible. 9. **text hand,** handwriting which uses large, bold lettering. *adj.* **textual.**

textbook (tekst′bo͝ok″) 1. *n.* a book on a specific subject matter used as a teaching-learning guide, especially in schools and colleges. 2. *adj.* handled in approved textbook style, as *a textbook method of teaching.*

text signal any typographical device, as italics or boldface, special symbols or headings, or special format arrangements used to call the reader's attention to desired aspects of written material.

text (structure) analysis the analysis of the structural characteristics of text, as coherence, hierarchical organization, propositional density, etc., as they relate to comprehensibility.

textual constraint See **contextual constraint.**

thalamus (t͟hal′ə məs) *pl.* **mi** (-mī″). *n.* a mass of gray matter located at the base of each cerebral hemisphere. *The thalamus relays afferent impulses from several sensory organs to the cerebral cortext. adj.* **thalamic.**

theater (-tre) (t͟hē′ə tər, t͟hēə′-) 1. *n.* a building or part of a building, as an auditorium or an outdoor area, for presenting plays, motion pictures, or other entertainment. 2. *n.* the audience at such a performance. *The theater roared.* 3. *n.* a large room or lecture hall with seats in tiers for laboratory demonstrations, etc., as *the medical school theater.* 4. **the theater,** drama. 5. *n.* dramatic works, as *the theater of Molière.* 6. *n.* the quality of dramatic performance, as *an evening of splendid theater.*

theater of the absurd an avant-garde type of drama in which the usual conventions of plot, characterization, and theme are distorted, often to stress the isolation of man in an irrational world, as in Samuel Beckett's *Waiting for Godot. Cp.* **black comedy** *or* **humor.**

theme (t͟hēm) 1. *n.* a major idea, proposition, or topic broad enough to cover the entire scope of a literary or other work of art. *Note:* A theme may be stated or unstated, but clues to it may be found in those ideas which are given special prominence, or which tend to recur again and again. 2. *n.* a short school composition; informal essay. 3. *n.* in linguistics, the topic of an expression (sentence), as *John* in *John talked on the telephone. Ct.* **rheme.**

theme approach a method of organizing classroom instruction and materials around themes such as Differences Between Generations, Profiles in Courage, etc., in units in such subjects as English or social studies.

theorem (thē'ə rəm, thēr'əm) 1. *n.* a statement which is proven true or which easily could be so proven; proposition (def. 1). 2. *n.* a rule or formula in logic or mathematics stated in symbolic form.

theory (thē'ə rē, thēr'ē) 1. *n.* a system of ideas, often stated as a principle, to explain or to lead to new understandings, as *a scientific theory.* 2. *n.* that aspect of a particular science or art concerned with general principles rather than specific techniques. *Instructional theory should allow a teacher to modify any particular teaching technique without losing sight of the critical features of the technique.* 3. *n.* such a body of principles, as *number theory.* 4. *n.* abstract reasoning, as contrasted to common sense. *Dale was great on theory but never could fix a leaky faucet.* *v.* **theorize.** *adj.* **theoretical.**

therapeutic (ther″ə pyōō'tik) 1. *adj.* having to do with the treatment and cure of disease or disorders. *Physiotherapists make therapeutic use of massage, heat, water, etc.* 2. *adj.* having to do with the remediation or correction of any problem. *Bibliotherapy is designed to have therapeutic value.* 3. **therapeutics,** *(with sing. v.)* the branch of medicine which deals with the science of healing.

therapy (ther'ə pē) 1. *n.* the treatment of disease or disorders. 2. *n.* psychotherapy, as *in therapy.* 3. *n.* the treatment of social maladjustment. 4. *n.* an activity, hobby, sport, etc. that provides relief from tension or overwork. *Reading a good book is good therapy for many people. Note:* Special types of therapy, as *group therapy,* are given under the describing term.

thesaurus (thi sôr'əs) *pl.* **-sauri** (sôr'ī). 1. *n.* a dictionary of synonyms and antonyms, often grouped by broad topics. 2. *n.* a dictionary or reference book in a special field, as art, music, etc. 3. *n.* an index system for classifying and retrieving information, books, etc.

thesis (thē'sis) *pl.* **-ses** (sēz). 1. *n.* a formal piece of writing, sometimes required for a bachelor's degree and commonly required for a master's degree. *Cp.* **dissertation** (def. 2). 2. *n.* the basic argument advanced by a speaker or writer who then attempts to prove it. 3. *n.* a subject or major argument of a speech or composition, as *the thesis of an essay.*

theta rhythm *or* **wave** a brain wave pattern of slow frequency, 4 to 7 cps. *Theta waves are normal in young children, but indicate abnormality in adults.* See **electroencephalogram (EEG).**

thinking (thiñg'kiñg) 1. *n.* the process(es), or product(s), of cognition; ideational thought. See **cognition.** See also **conjunctive thought; disjunctive thought; relational thought.** 2. *n.* any use of symbols and/or percepts in cognition. *Much thinking involves perceptual data.* 3. *n.* ideational problem solving, as *John Dewey's concept of thinking.* 4. *n.* meditation or reflection upon an idea or problem. *After thinking, I decided not to go.* 5. *adj.* rational. *Man is a thinking animal.* 6. *adj.* thoughtful. *Thinking people detect false propaganda.* *v.* **think.**

third person referring to the person(s) or thing(s) spoken of, as, in English, the third person singular pronouns *he, she, it,* and the plural *they.* *Ct.* **first person** (def. 1); **second person.** See also **person.**

Third World literature 1. writings from the developing countries of the world, especially those in Africa and Asia. 2. literature of minority groups.

Thorazine (thōr'ə zēn″, thôr'-) *n.* a

trade name for chlorpromazine hydrochloride, a tranquilizer used to reduce motor activity.

thought (t̲hôt) 1. *n.* thinking (defs. 1-4). 2. *n.* any part of thinking activity, as *collect one's thoughts.* 3. *n.* intention, often half-hearted. *We had some thought of going.* 4. *n.* anticipation. *It was my thought you might be here.* 5. *n.* consideration, as *speak without thought of others.* 6. *n.* judgment; opinion; as *the thought of the majority.* 7. *n.* the thinking characteristic of a given place, class, or time, as *Greek thought.*

threshold (t̲hres̲h̲'ōld, t̲hres̲h̲'hōld) *n.* the minimum stimulation necessary to produce awareness or a response; the minimum change necessary for recognition of a difference, either absolute or differential.

throat (t̲hrōt) *n.* the passage leading from the mouth through the pharynx to the stomach and lungs. *adj.* **throaty.**

thrombosis (t̲hrom bō'sis) *n.* a clot formed by the blood that blocks circulation. *Cp.* **embolism.**

thumb index a series of labeled notches cut into the fore-edge of a book to indicate divisions or sections, as *the thumb index of a dictionary.*

thyroid gland an endocrine gland on the sides of the trachea that produces hormones which help regulate metabolic rate. *Iodine is necessary for the proper functioning of the thyroid gland, for without enough iodine, goiters develop.* See also **cretinism.**

tic (tik) *n.* a brief, localized spasm, often repetitive; twitch. *Tics of the face, eyes, or head are common and are often a nervous habit.*

tilde (til'də) 1. *n.* the diacritic mark (~) placed above an *n* in some orthographies to indicate a palatalized sound, as *ñ* in *cañon.* 2. *n.* the same mark placed above a vowel in phonetic transcription to indicate that the vowel is nasalized. See also **nasal** (def. 2); **palatal.**

timbre (tim'bər; *Fr.* taɴ'ʙʀᵊ) 1. *n.* the characteristic quality or tonal color of a sound given to its resonant overtones, as *the nasal timbre of a vowel sound, the timbre of Pavarotti's voice.* 2. *n.* the perception of such a quality, especially in distinguishing differences in sounds of the same frequency, as *the difference in the timbre of middle C on a piano and on a French horn.*

time-compressed speech See **compressed speech.**

timed reading practice any time-controlled reading experience for increasing reading speed or efficiency.

time-limit test See **speed test.**

time line a graphic outline of data, the chronology of facts, events, etc., as *a historical time line.*

tinnitus (ti nī'təs) *n.* a ringing or buzzing sensation of sound in the ear, without external stimuli, which may have many physiological causes. *Tinnitus is one of the main symptoms of Ménière's disease.*

title (tīt'ᵊl) *n.* the distinguishing name of any complete bibliographic unit of printed, audio-visual, or microfilm material.

title entry a bibliographic description of a work located in a file according to the first word of its title, excluding articles. *Cp.* **author entry; subject entry.**

title page a page near the beginning of a book which gives the title of the book and ordinarily the name(s) of the author(s), the publisher(s), and sometimes the place and date of publication.

TMR trainable mentally retarded.

T.O., t.o. traditional orthography.

token (tō'kən) 1. *n.* a sign or symbol. *Grades are academic tokens of accom-*

plishment, as are the cap and gown. 2. *n.* a specific observed instance of language use, as a spoken or written word, a speech sound, a mathematical symbol, etc. *In the proposition A is to B, as B is to C, the B's represent two tokens of the same type. Cp.* **type** (def. 2); **type-token ratio (TTR).** 3. *n.* the number of running words in a passage as contrasted to the number of different words (types).

token system the overt reinforcing of actions, particularly in a behavior modification program. *Tokens are given as rewards in direct proportion to work completed or time on task.*

-tomy a suffix indicating *cutting* (in surgery); as **tracheotomy.**

tone (tōn) 1. *n.* any sound of well-defined pitch, quality, and duration. 2. *n.* the quality or character of such a sound. 3. *n.* the effect produced by a regularly repeating sound wave. *Ct.* **noise** (def. 2). 4. *n.* a vocal or musical sound. *Her voice had a soft, mellow tone. The piano tone was rich and full.* 5. *n.* an expressive way of using the voice. *His joyful tone showed all was well with mother and child.* 6. *n.* the inflections which mark the speech of a person or region; accent. 7. *n.* the syllabic stress in a word. 8. *n.* the pitch or pitch changes in a word which distinguish it from similar words in tonal languages, as Thai. 9. *n.* a particular style of writing or speaking, as *the crisp tone of Hemingway's dialogue.* See also **mood**[1] (def. 2). *Note* (def. 9): In literary analysis, there is some difference of opinion about the distinction between *tone* and *mood.* The terms are sometimes used synonymously, but some authorities use *tone* to apply to the author's attitude that is reflected in the style of the written word, reserving *mood* to refer to the effect created by the author's use of various literary devices. 10. *n.* the characteristic style of a period, as *the tone of the Gay Nineties.* 11. *n.* elegance of style, as *the aristocratic tone of Henry James.* 12. *n.* a tint or shade of color, as *a gray tone.* 13. *n.* the total effect, often harmonious, of color and color values, as *the soft tone of a Raphael painting.* 14. *n.* the normal state of body tension in muscles and organs, in which body functions are healthy and responsive to stimulation. 15. *n.* a healthy mental condition. 16. **tone down,** to soften or deemphasize, as *tone down your language. adj.* **tonal.**

tone deafness difficulty or lack of tonal discrimination. *A person with tone deafness can neither sing on key nor, what is worse, tell when singing is off key.*

tongue (tuŋ͡g) 1. *n.* the movable muscular organ at the base of the mouth which is the primary articulator for speech as well as being useful in chewing and swallowing. See illustration under **speech organs.** 2. *n.* the power to speak. *The child has lost his tongue.* 3. *n.* a language or dialect of a group, region, or nation. 4. *n.* a way of speaking, as *a persuasive tongue.* 5. *n.* any foreign language. 6. **hold one's tongue,** to be silent; refrain from talking. 7. **on the tip of one's tongue,** being unable to recall something known. 8. **tongue-in-cheek,** mockingly, often with humorous exaggeration. 9. **tongue-lash,** to scold severely; read out. 10. **tongue twister,** an utterance which is difficult to say, as *She sells sea shells.* 11. **speak with forked tongue,** to lie. 12. **have a sharp tongue,** to be sarcastic.

tongue-tied (tuŋ͡g'tīd") 1. *adj.* having unusually limited tongue movement because of a short lingual frenum. See **frenulum.** 2. *adj.* being too shy to speak.

tonic (ton′ik) 1. *adj.* referring to continued tension in a muscle without producing movement, as *a tonic spasm. Ct.* **clonic.** 2. *adj.* involving tone or pitch differences in words. *Note:* Some non-tonic languages, as English, use tone as a suprasegmental phoneme, but other languages, as Thai, are tonic because they use differences in tone to distinguish words otherwise phonetically identical. 3. *adj.* referring to tone or accent in speech, especially to the primary accent in a word.

tonic block in stuttering, the prolonging of speech sounds and hesitations. *Ct.* **clonic block.**

tonicity (tō nis′i tē) 1. *n.* the normal, healthy condition of body tissues and muscle tension; tonus. 2. *n.* any strong, healthy condition.

tonus (tō′nəs) *n.* the normal slight contraction of muscles that aids the body's posture against the pull of gravity and aids in the return of blood to the central cavity; muscle tone; tonicity (def. 1).

tool subject a subject made up of skills and abilities useful in studying other subjects; tool. *Reading and other language arts are tool subjects.*

top-down processing a theoretical view of reading as a process of using one's experiences and expectations in order to react to text and build comprehension. *In top-down processing, comprehension is seen as reader-driven, rather than text-driven. Ct.* **bottom-up processing; interactive processing.**

topic (top′ik) *n.* the general category or class of ideas, often stated in a word or phrase, to which the ideas of the passage as a whole belong; thesis (def. 3).

topical (top′i kəl) 1. *adj.* having to do with a specific and limited place; local; as a *topical reference to a date.* 2. *adj.* something which is organized by topic or subject matter. *The subject matter catalog in a library is topical.* 3. *adj.* having to do with current or local matters, as *topical news.*

topical allusion a reference to something in a writer's or speaker's contemporary world.

topic sentence a sentence intended to express the main idea in a paragraph or passage.

topological (top″ə loj′i kəl) *adj.* referring to a geometric concept involving the study of invariant relationships that exist irrespective of changes in size. *Note:* K. Lewin proposed a topological model for the study of psychological activity such as that involved in needs-goal behavior. Such a relationship remains unchanged in spite of changes in the number, size, complexity, etc., of needs and goals. *n.* **topology.**

toponomy (tə pon′ə mē) *n.* the study of place names.

total communication an approach to deaf education which encourages the use of any or all procedures, as sign, oral, finger spelling, etc., for communicating.

trace (trās) 1. *v.* to copy, as by drawing, imitating, etc. 2. *v.* to follow something, as *trace the clues in a mystery.* 3. *n.* evidence of the prior existence of something. *Novels often contain traces of the author's life.* 4. *n.* a very small amount of something, as *a trace element, a trace of humor.* 5. *n. engram.* 6. *n.* a fine line, as *an electroencephalographic trace.*

trachea (trā′kē ə; *Brit.* trə kē′ə) *pl.* **-cheae** (-kē ē″) (*Brit.* trə kē′ē) *n.* a tube forming an airway between the larynx and the lungs; windpipe. See illustration under **speech organs**.

tracheotomy (trā″kē ot′ə mē) *n.* the cutting of an opening into the trachea through the neck below the larynx, usually to allow or improve breathing.

tracing (trā′siṅg) 1. *n.* the act of making a copy or repeating the surface outline of something. *Tracing the word to be learned is a critical element in the VAKT method.* 2. *n.* a traced copy. 3. See **trace** (def. 6). 4. *n.* the listing on a catalog card of all the other entries made for that particular item. 5. *adj.* for use in copying, as *tracing paper.*

tract (trakt) 1. *n.* a long pathway; specifically, a bundle of nerves starting and ending at the same place and with the same function, as *the optic tract.* 2. *n.* a number of organs involved in sequential functions, as *the speech tract.* 3. *n.* a religious or political leaflet. *Self-appointed censors often prefer to replace textbooks with tracts representing one point of view.*

trade book a book published for sale to the general public. *Ct.* **textbook** (def. 1).

traditional grammar See **prescriptive grammar.**

traditional orthography (T.O., t.o.) 1. the standard writing system of a language. 2. in English, the use of the conventional alphabet letters to spell words, as contrasted to words spelled with a modified alphabet such as the Initial Teaching Alphabet (i/t/a).

tragedy (traj′i dē) 1. *n.* a play, or the dramatic form it represents, in which the leading character suffers intense conflicts and an unhappy fate, often because of some weakness. King Lear *is one of Shakespeare's great tragedies.* 2. *n.* any such story. 3. *n.* any literary work, prose or verse, that has a somber or serious theme and leads to an unfortunate conclusion, as Arthur Miller's *Death of a Salesman.* 4. *n.* a dreadful or fatal happening; disaster.

tragic flaw the flaw or defect of the tragic hero or heroine which eventually causes his or her downfall. *Ambition is the tragic flaw of Shakespeare's* Macbeth.

tragicomedy (traj″i kom′i dē) 1. *n.* a play or other literary work which contains elements of both tragedy and comedy. 2. *n.* a play which progresses as a tragedy but, because of the turn of events, ends as a comedy, as Shakespeare's *The Merchant of Venice.*

trainable mentally retarded (TMR) referring to a person with moderate to severe mental retardation; specifically, one with an IQ between three and five standard deviations below the mean, usually between 25 and 50 IQ. *The trainable mentally retarded are not usually able to maintain themselves but they can be taught self-care, oral communication, and social adjustment skills so that they may function in a sheltered environment.* See also **mental retardation.**

training (trā′niṅg) 1. *n.* all of the instructional procedures and circumstances used to induce learning. *Note:* This respectable psychological meaning is often viewed with suspicion by educators because of the presumed implication of narrowly-focused, authoritarian, rote drill as distinguished from the broader concept of education. *Cp.* **education** (def. 2). 2. **in training**, the state of being trained. *v.* **train.** *adj.* **trainable.**

trait (trāt) 1. *n.* any characteristic tendency toward a behavior determined by an enduring motivation and/or habit, as one that can be measured by a personality test. 2. *n.* an inherited characteristic. 3. *n.* in statistics, a term sometimes used to refer to a variable.

trans- a prefix indicating *across, over;* as **transposition.**

transactional theory a view of reading in which the focus is on the relationship between the reader and the text during the act of reading. *'Transaction' designates... an ongoing process in which the elements or factors are... aspects of a total situation, each conditioned by and conditioning the other* — L. Rosenblatt (1978).

transactional writing a term used by J. Britton and others (1975) to describe *language to get things done: to inform people..., to advise or persuade or instruct people. Cp.* **exposition** (def. 1). See also **expressive writing; poetic writing.**

transcription (tran skrip'shən) 1. *n.* in linguistics, the act of making a written copy of spoken language using phonetic or phonemic symbols, or standard orthography. 2. *n.* the written copy so produced. 3. an electronic reproduction on magnetic tape. *v.* **transcribe.**

transductive reasoning (J. Piaget) irreversible reasoning characteristic of preoperational thought. *Irreversible reasoning is neither deductive nor inductive, is full of undetected contradictions, and relies on analogy.*

transfer (*n.* trans'fər; *v.* trans fûr'; trans'fər) 1. *n.* in general, the carryover process, or effect, of one response or set of responses upon another, as *the transfer of reading skills to writing skills. Note:* The carryover may be positive, negative, or zero. Special types of transfer, as *negative transfer*, are given under the describing term. 2. *v.* to so transfer. 3. *n.* the process, or effect, of the carryover of grammatical forms from language to language, often in an interfering way. 4. *n.* the change of speech symbols into another medium of expression, as writing. 5. *n.* a metaphor. 6. *n.* a design to be carried over onto another surface, as by a printing press, a decal, etc. 7. *n.* one who changes from school to school. 8. *v.* to so change. *adj.* **transferable.**

transfer of training *or* **learning** the doctrine that training or learning can be carried over into stimulus situations that the learner recognizes as similar to one(s) previously learned. *Note:* This concept has a long history in educational theory and practice. E. L. Thorndike proposed that such transfer involved the recognition of identical elements. C. H. Judd, on the other hand, proposed that such transfer takes place through a process of generalization. Both positions profoundly influenced instructional practice. See also **transfer** (def. 1).

transformation (trans″fər mā'shən) 1. *n.* the process, or result, of any comprehensive change or alteration of something, as *the transformation of the classroom into a reading laboratory.* 2. *n.* in transformational grammar, the process, or result, of change from one linguistic construction to another according to syntactic rules, as *the transformation of the declarative structure 'It is ten o'clock.' to the interrogative 'Is it ten o'clock?* 3. *n.* the process that converts a deep structure to a surface structure. 4. *n.* a change in form without a change in value or basic content, as *a transformation in perspective.* 5. *n.* a change in the nature or form of symbols according to the formal rules of logic or mathematics, as *symbolic logic and transformations.* 6. *n.* a conscious expression of a disguised feeling that is usually opposite to one's repressed feelings. 7. *n.* a change in a mathematical expression without altering the values represented: 2 + 3 is the same as 3 + 2. *v.* **transform.** *adj.* **transformational.**

transformational-generative grammar

a linguistic theory that contains a set of rules for producing, or generating, all possible grammatical sentences in a language with the purpose of revealing the grammatical completeness that a native speaker intuitively exercises. *Note:* Transformational-generative grammar, based on the work of N. Chomsky (1957), is an attempt to discover the universal characteristics of language. Transformational-generative grammar now includes phrase structure, transformational, morphophonemic, and semantic components. See also **sentence transformation; transformation** (def. 2).

transformational-generative linguistics See **transformational-generative grammar.**

transformation rule in transformational-generative grammar, a set of instructions for converting one grammatical pattern to another, stated as a general proposition. See **transformation** (def. 2).

transition (tran zish′ən, -sish′-) See **juncture**.

transitive verb a verb that takes a direct object and may form the passive voice, as *took* in *The burglar took the money* and *was taken* in *The money was taken by the burglar. Ct.* **intransitive verb.**

transitivity (tran″si tiv′i tē) *n.* (J. Piaget) the understanding that when A has a relationship to B which B also has to C, A has the same relationship to C.

translation (trans lā′shən, tranz-) 1. *n.* the process of converting the meaning of phrases, sentences, etc., from one language to another. *Note:* Translation usually refers to the written form of language, but may be oral. See also **simultaneous interpretation; consecutive interpretation.** 2. *n.* the completed material in the translated form. *Note:* Translation, whether free or literal, is seldom if ever successful in capturing the meaning and spirit of the original. *Reading poetry in translation is like kissing a girl through a veil*—an old Jewish proverb. See **free translation; literal translation.** *v.* **translate.**

transliteration (trans lit″ə rā′shən) 1. *n.* the representation of orthographic symbols of one writing system by those of another writing system. 2. *n.* a written message or text resulting from such a change. *Cp.* **romanization.** *v.* **transliterate.**

transmission (trans mish′ən, tranz-) 1. *n.* the sending of something from one place or person to another; transfer; as *the transmission of knowledge, the transmission of TV signals, the transmission of social attitudes.* 2. *n.* something sent, as *a radio transmission.* 3. *n.* the passing of a disease from one to others, as from one child to classmates. 4. *n.* the passing of a trait or characteristic through heredity. 5. *n.* the firing of neurons in sequence along a nerve pathway. *v.* **transmit.** *n.* **transmitter.**

transmitter (trans mit′ər, tranz-) *n.* any means for encoding a message to be sent through a communication channel, as *a radio transmitter. Note:* In conversation, the vocal apparatus and gesture act as a transmitter.

transparency (trans pâr′ən sē, -par′-) *n.* a picture, text, design, etc., on a glass or light-admitting surface to be viewed by light shining through from behind.

transposition (trans″pə zish′ən) 1. *n.* a change in sequence of two or more language units, as in reading *the brown little dog* for *the little brown dog,* writing *desrcibe* for *describe,* or sounding *spaghetti* as though it were spelled *pshgetti.* 2. *n.* the movement of an algebraic term from one side of an equation to the other with the appropriate change of sign. 3. *n.* the change from one musical key to another. *v.* **transpose.**

transverse plane any plane which passes horizontally through the body and is parallel to both a frontal plane and a sagittal plane; horizontal plane.

trauma (trou′mə, trô′-) *pl.* **-mata** (mə tə), **-mas.** 1. *n.* a body injury or wound that is externally caused, as *surgical trauma.* 2. *n.* a severe psychological shock, as *emotional trauma.* 3. *n.* the condition resulting from injury or shock. *The auto wreck left each rider in trauma. adj.* **traumatic.**

travesty (trav′i stē) 1. *n.* an extreme form of burlesque (def. 1), in which a grand style is usually used to treat a simple subject, or sometimes a vulgar style is used to treat a grandiose subject. Don Quixote *is a travesty on the medieval romance.* 2. *n.* an extremely poor imitation of another work.

treatise (trē′tis) *n.* a formal and systematic statement in writing of the principles of a subject, generally longer and more detailed than an essay but shorter than a book, as *a treatise on how to write a book.*

treatment (trēt′mənt) 1. *n.* instruction given to an individual, based on needs determined by diagnosis. 2. *n.* any form of medical or therapeutic aid by self or professionals, as *psychiatric treatment.* 3. *n.* the manner expressed toward something. *Voltaire's treatment of the clergy in* Tartuffe *is satiric.* 4. *n.* the independent variable in an experiment. 5. *n.* the systematic handling of data to determine statistical relationships.

tree diagram 1. in phrase structure grammar, a graphic illustration of the grammatical relationship between morphemes in a sentence; phrase marker. See illustration. 2. a graphic illustration of the historical relationship among related languages, such as the Latin origin of the family of Romance languages.

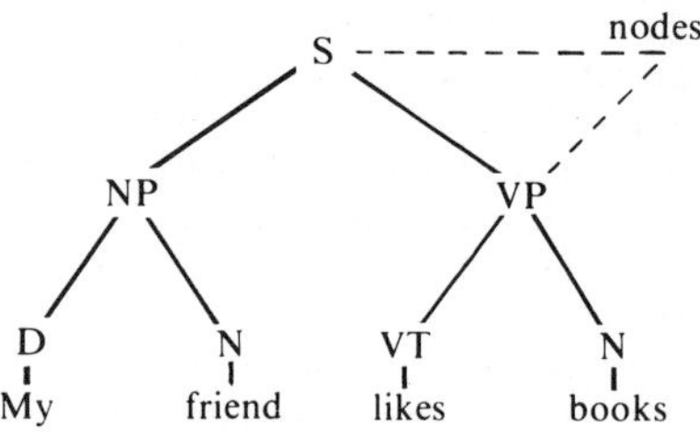

Tree diagram

tremor (trem′ər, trē′mər) 1. *n.* uncontrolled shaking, trembling, or spasms, especially from disease, as in cerebral palsy. 2. *n.* any vibration, as *an earthquake tremor.* 3. *n.* a quavering sound or effect, as *a voice tremor.*

trend analysis the observation and evaluation of changes in some variable over some period of time to determine long-term variations rather than short-term ones. *Cp.* **sequential analysis.**

trial (trī′əl, trīl) 1. *n.* a single opportunity for response; especially, one of a series of such opportunities. *It took Lee three trials to identify the word correctly.* 2. *n.* a completed response pattern in an experiment or test. 3. *adj.* used as a sample, as *a trial test item. v.* **try.**

trial and error learning a pattern of learning efforts in problem situations that is unsystematic and apparently unplanned. *Note:* This term, which was first used by E.L. Thorndike to describe animal behavior, is felt by many psychologists and educators to be less appropriate in describing goal-oriented human behavior than is 'approximation and correction.'

trigram (trī'gram) See **trigraph.**

trigraph (trī'graf, -gräf) *n.* a sequence of three letters representing a single speech sound or phoneme, as *sch* for /sh/ in *schmaltz,* or *eau* for /ō/ in *beau. Cp.* **digraph** (def. 1).

trill (tril) 1. *n.* any rapid alternation of two tones, usually close together; warble; shake; as *a trill in music.* 2. *n.* a rapid vibration or repetition of the same speech sound or musical note. *Speech trills require rapid fluttering of the tip of the tongue or of the uvula.* 3. *v.* to make such a speech sound. *Roll your r's to trill.*

trochee (trō'kē) *n.* a metrical foot of two syllables, the first accented, the second unaccented: *Dóublĕ, dóublĕ, tóil ănd tróublĕ* — **Macbeth (Shakespeare).** *adj.* **trochaic.**

trope (trōp) *n.* a rhetorical or literary technique of using words in other than their literal sense; figure of speech.

-tropia a combining form indicating *turn* (in vision); as **esotropia, exotropia.**

tropia (trō'pē ə) 1. *n.* heterotropia. 2. *n.* strabismus; squint.

true-false item an objective test item with two response options only: *T* or *F.*

true score a hypothetical score, never obtained, free of measurement error. *True score is a theoretical reference point for estimating measurement error. Cp.* **standard error.**

T score a normalized standard score with a mean of 50 and a standard deviation of 10.

t test the ratio of a statistic to its standard error. *The t test is often used to determine the significance of the difference between two means.*

TTR type-token ratio.

tuning fork a two-pronged, tempered steel instrument which gives off a consistent, fixed tone when struck. *Note:* The tuning fork is used as a standard for music tuning and as a tool for testing differences between air and bone conduction hearing.

tunnel vision the reduction or loss of peripheral vision so that the sight is constricted as if looking through a long tube or tunnel. *There are many causes of tunnel vision, including hysteria.*

tutor (to͞o'tər, tyo͞o'-) 1. *v.* to instruct on an individual basis, often privately, 2. *n.* a person who so instructs. *n.* **tutoring.**

TV television.

twelvemo (twelv'mō) See **duodecimo.**

tympanic cavity the middle ear or tympanum; specifically, the air-filled space between the eardrum and the exterior surface of the inner ear, opening into the mastoid processes at the back and connecting to the upper throat by way of the Eustachian tube.

tympanic membrane the eardrum; specifically, a thin membrane which transmits variations in air pressure from the outer ear to the middle ear as mechanical vibrations. See illustration under **ear.**

tympanometry (tim″pə nom'i trē) *n.* in audiometry, the evaluation of the effectiveness of tone transmission across the tympanic membrane under various pressure conditions. *Note:* This test is a part of acoustic impedance audiometry from which a graph of the test results, called a *tympanogram,* may be made.

tympanum (tim'pə nəm) *n.* the middle ear or tympanic cavity. *Note:* The tympanum does not refer to the tympanic membrane, the cover of the drum, but to the tympanic cavity, the drum itself.

type (tīp) 1. *n.* in linguistics, the class or category to which an observed linguistic unit (token) belongs, as a sentence, grammatical class, phoneme, etc. 2. *n.* one such representative token used as a model of a class or category. 3. *n.* a block, usually of metal, with a typeface for printing. 4. *n.* a collection of such type. 5. *n.* typeface of the same style, as *italic type.* 6. *n.* characters printed or typewritten, not handwritten.

type I error rejection of the null hypothesis when it should be accepted. See **alpha risk.**

type II error acceptance of the null hypothesis when it should be rejected. See **beta risk.**

typeface (tīp′fās″) 1. *n.* the surface of type which is inked to make an impression; face. 2. *n.* type of the same design.

types of literature a classification of literature which includes novels, short stories, dramas, poetry, essays, biography, and sometimes journals and letters.

type style the particular design which distinguishes one set of typefaces from another. *Type style or design varies in size, heaviness of line, spacing, etc.*

type-token ratio (TTR) the number of times a particular linguistic item (token) occurs in a text in relation to the linguistic class (type) to which it belongs, as of all the nouns in this dictionary, or the number of times the noun *linguist* occurs.

typographical error a mistake in typesetting, typewriting, etc.

typography (tī pog′rə fē) 1. *n.* the process of setting something in type, arranging, and printing it. 2. *n.* the makeup or appearance of something printed. *adj.* **typographic; typographical.**

typology (tī pol′ə jē) *n.* a system of classifying all languages into broad classes based on phonological or grammatical criteria. *adj.* **typological.**

U

DEVELOPMENT OF MAJUSCULE								
NORTH SEMITIC	GREEK		ETR.	LATIN		MODERN		
						GOTHIC	ITALIC	ROMAN
Y	ᛋ	Y	Y	V	V	𝔘	*U*	U

DEVELOPMENT OF MINUSCULE					
ROMAN CURSIVE	ROMAN UNCIAL	CAROL. MIN.	MODERN		
			GOTHIC	ITALIC	ROMAN
u	u	u	u	*u*	u

The twenty-first letter of the English alphabet developed as a transformation of North Semitic *waw* into Greek *upsilon* (υ). (See also **F** and **W**.) In Etruscan, the *u*-sound was signified by V, and Classical Latin monumental writing later used the V for both U and V. U and V were used interchangeably for both sounds in the early Middle Ages, with V appearing in the monumental writing and U in the manuscripts. Their separation did not crystallize until after the Middle Ages.

ultra- a prefix indicating *extreme, beyond the ordinary;* as **ultrasonic.**

ultrafiche (ul′trə fēsh″) *n.* a microfiche in which the images are reduced more than 90 times their original size. *Note:* Ultrafiche is not included in the category *microfiche. Cp.* **microfiche.**

ultrasonic (ul″trə son′ik) 1. *adj.* having to do with sound frequencies above human hearing, usually about 20 kHz and above. 2. **ultrasonics** (*with sing. v.*) a. the study of high frequency sounds. b. the technology of using very high frequency sounds, as for medical diagnosis or surgery, or for industrial use in cleaning, cutting, etc.

umlaut (o͝om′lout) 1. *n.* a change of a vowel sound occurring as the result of assimilating some feature of a following vowel or semivowel sound, as the ö in German *Töpfer* ('potter') from *Topf* ('pot'). See also **assimilation** (def. 5). 2. *n.* a vowel which has undergone such a change. 3. *n.* the orthographic mark (¨) placed directly above a vowel in German and some other languages to indicate this pronunciation; diaeresis.

un- a prefix indicating *not, opposed to;* as **unabridged.**

unabridged dictionary the most comprehensive edition of a given dictionary. *Webster's* Third New International Dictionary *is an unabridged dictionary. Ct.* **abridged dictionary**.

unabridged edition the original, unshortened form of a book or other written material. *Ct.* **abridged edition.**

unaccented syllable 1. See **unstressed syllable.** 2. a syllable which is without a strong beat in a literary rhythmical pattern composed of strong and weak beats.

uncertainty (un sûr′t^{ə}n tē) 1. *n.* a state or instance of not being quite sure; doubt. *The spelling -ough sometimes causes uncertainty in pronouncing such words as* through, though, trough. 2. *n.* something which cannot be predicted. *Yes, Virginia, there are uncertainties in this life.* 3. See **entropy** (def. 2).

uncial (un′shē əl, -shəl) 1. *n.* a style of handwriting characterized by rounded capitals, and found especially in Greek and Latin manuscripts of the 4th to 8th centuries A.D. See illustration. 2. *n.* a letter produced in this style. 3. *n.* a Medieval capital letter. 4. *adj.* referring to such letter or style of writing. *Cp.* **cursive writing.**

ROMAN UNCIAL

Uncial

unconscious motivation a motivating force or drive which is apparent to others but not to the subject.

underachievement (un″dər ə chēv′mənt) *n.* achievement below that expected; specifically, achievement below one's performance on tests of ability. *n.* **underachiever.** *v.* **underachieve.** *Ct.* **overachievement.**

underfocused (un″dər fō′kust) *adj.* tending to be distracted by stimuli irrelevant to a task. *Ct.* **overfocused.**

underlining (un′dər lī″niñg) *n.* the process, or result, of marking below a line of text those words or passages one wishes to emphasize, remember, etc., especially as a study aid.

underlying structure See **deep structure.**

understand (un″dər stand′) 1. *v.* to engage in or have understanding. See **understanding.** 2. *n.* to learn or hear. *Do I understand you are leaving?* 3. *n.* to believe. *What am I given to understand?* 4. *n.* to interpret in a particular way. *Understand exactly what I say.* 5. *n.* to complete a thought. *Help me understand this sentence.*

understanding (un″dər stan′diñg) 1. *n.* the process, or result, of acquiring meaning; comprehension; as *understanding of the printed page.* 2. *n.* intelligence; mind; especially, superior power of abstract thought. *The study of philosophy requires understanding.* 3. *n.* particular knowledge or skill, as *understanding of literary criticism.* 4. *n.* mutual agreement, as *arrive at an understanding.* 5. *n.* compassion; tolerance; empathy; as *an attitude of understanding.* 6. *adj.* having compassion or empathy, as *an understanding parent.*

understatement (un″dər stāt′mənt) 1. *n.* the representation of something as less than it actually is. 2. *n.* a form of irony or humor. *v.* **understate.**

ungraded class *or* **school** See **nongraded class** *or* **school.**

ungrammatical (un″grə mat′i kəl) *adj.* speech or writing that is incorrect according to criteria of prescriptive grammar or the usage of competent speakers and writers, as *we was right.*

uni- a prefix indicating *one, single;* as **unilateral.**

UNIFON *n.* a modified alphabet containing 40 orthographic symbols, developed by J. Malone (1962) as a medium for teaching children to read. *Cp.* **i/t/a, i.t.a.**

unilateral (yōō″nə lat′ər əl) 1. *adj.* having to do with one side of the body, as *a unilateral stroke.* 2. *adj.* having to do with only one of many sides or parties, as *a unilateral discussion or agreement.* 3. *adj.* referring to a genetic trait on either the mother's or father's side but not on both sides. *Baldness is a unilateral trait. Ct.* **bilateral.**

uninterrupted sustained silent reading (USSR) a period of time during the school day when children in a class or in the entire school read books of their own choosing. *Note:* In some schools, everyone — students, teachers, principal, secretaries, custodians, etc. — stops to read, usually for 30 minutes.

union catalog a catalog that lists the holdings of several libraries and shows where they may be found. *The union catalog is usually a cooperative effort and is of particular value to scholars.*

unique (yōō nēk′) 1. *adj.* non-universal; singular; idiosyncratic. *Ct.* **universal** (def. 2). 2. *n.* The quality of being singular; specifically, the singular characteristic of a concept advanced by D. Feldman which proposes that the goal in cognitive development is an individual who possesses certain non-universal, or unique, traits as well as universal traits.

unit (yo͞o′nit) 1. *n.* a part of a course or subject that is taught as a whole, as *a short story unit in English literature.* 2. *n.* a basic part of the structure of linguistic knowledge. *Phonology and grammar are units of language.*

unit approach *or* **plan** a teaching approach in which materials from one subject, such as English, or from several subject areas are related to a central theme.

unity (yo͞o′ni tē) 1. *n.* oneness. 2. *n.* the harmony among the parts of a work in literature or the arts that reflects an organic whole and produces a single, major effect on the reader. *Note:* Literary unity may be the result of a single unifying element, as plot, character, mood, etc., or some combination of these. 3. *n.* the parts of something combined to make a whole. 4. *n.* complete agreement among persons, as *unity of feeling.*

universal (yo͞o″nə vûr′səl) 1. *adj.* referring to any area, sphere, or category of things, ideas, etc., as *the universal nature of randomness.* 2. *adj.* characteristic of all. *Laughter is a universal human trait.* 3. *n.* a characteristic of all languages. *The convention of assigning arbitrary meaning to symbols is a language universal.* 4. *n.* something which exists everywhere. *Oxygen is a universal of air.* 5. *n.* a proposition in logic that applies to all members of a class: *All squares have four equal sides.*

Universal decimal classification a library classification scheme, international in scope, which is an expansion of the Dewey decimal classification. See also **Library of Congress classification (LC).**

universal grammar a grammar which attempts to discover, explain, or describe linguistic structures that are common to all languages.

universe (yo͞o′nə vûrs″) 1. *n.* everything known, as *the universe of ideas, the galactic universe.* 2. *n.* everything in a particular area, sphere, or category; specifically, the experimental population which is sampled in statistical analysis. 3. **universe of discourse,** all that is referred to in a discussion. *adj.* **universal.**

unread (un red′) *adj.* illiterate (def. 4): *the illiterate or unread person usually participates only in a very narrow and limited subculture in our society* — L. Rosenblatt (1978).

unstable (un stā′bəl) 1. *adj.* not firm; unsteady; as *an unstable political situation.* 2. *adj.* emotionally changeable; labile. *Adolescent attachments are often unstable.* 3. *adj.* tending toward abnormal behavior, as *an unstable personality.*

unstressed syllable in polysyllabic words, the syllable(s) with least stress or emphasis. *Note:* In dictionaries, unstressed syllables do not have accent or stress markers.

upper case a letter form, as A, B, C, that is usually larger than and different from a lower-case letter; capital letters; majuscule. *Cp.* **lower case.** *adj.* **upper-case.**

usage (yo͞o′sij, -zij) 1. *n.* the way in which language or dialect is actually used by members of a speech community. 2. *n.* the sum of all idiolects within a language or language variety.

usage label a word or phrase in a dictionary entry which describes the appropriateness of that entry for specific contexts, as *informal, British,* etc.

USSR See **uninterrupted sustained silent reading.**

Utopia *or* **utopia** (yo͞o tō′pē ə) *n.* a place, or state, of ideal social and/or political organization, real or imagined. *Note:* The term, meaning *nowhere,* comes from Sir Thomas More's 16th century novel of that name which describes an imaginary island with such characteristics. *Ct.* **negative utopia.** *adj.* **utopian.**

utterance (ut′ər əns) *n.* an actual production of a meaningful sequence of words; speech act. *v.* **utter.**

uvula (yo͞o′vyə lə) *pl.* **-las, -lae** (lē). *n.* any fleshy projection of an organ or body tissue; specifically, the small mass of tissue hanging down from the rear of the soft palate. *The uvula is an articulator in producing a few speech sounds, as the German uvular r, which is trilled. adj.* **uvular.**

V

DEVELOPMENT OF MAJUSCULE							
NORTH SEMITIC	GREEK	ETR.	LATIN		MODERN GOTHIC	MODERN ITALIC	MODERN ROMAN
SEE LETTER U		V	V	V	𝔙	*V*	V

DEVELOPMENT OF MINUSCULE					
ROMAN CURSIVE	ROMAN UNCIAL	CAROL. MIN.	MODERN GOTHIC	MODERN ITALIC	MODERN ROMAN
SEE U	Y	—	𝔳	*v*	v

The twenty-second letter of the English alphabet originated in Etruscan, where it signified the *u*-sound. The use of V for the *v*-sound dates from the end of the Middle Ages. (See also **U**.)

VAKT See **Fernald (-Keller) approach** *or* **method (VAKT).**

validation (val″i dā′shən) 1. *n.* the process of attempting to assess the degree of test validity. *The validation of the Stanford-Binet Intelligence Scale took many years.* 2. *n.* the process of attempting to get objective evidence, as of a logical proposition.

validity (və lid′i tē) 1. *n.* a truthful or factual condition. *Your report has validity.* 2. *n.* a logical argument. *Read to determine if there is validity to the author's thesis.* 3. *n.* the characteristic of a test that determines that the test measures what it is supposed to measure and/or that it can predict performance on other measures. *Note:* Special types of validity, as *content validity,* are given under the describing term. *adj.* **valid.**

validity coefficient any correlation between a test and its criterion. *A validity coefficient was run between scores on a teacher education test and teacher ratings.*

value (val′yo͞o) 1. *n.* the relative worth, merit, or usefulness of something, as *the value of reading to school success. Attitudes reflect values.* 2. *n.* something thought to be worthy for its own sake, as *the value of beauty, truth, etc.* 3. *v.* to show or express the worth of something. 4. *n.* in phonetics, the phonetic equivalent of a letter or grapheme, as /e/ in *bet.* 5. *n.* a quantity given to a mathematical symbol or expression. *The* y *has a value of* 3.

value judgment 1. a moral or ethical decision. *A determination to avoid wrongdoing represents a value judgment.* 2. a personal opinion that cannot be objectively verified: *Beauty is in the eye of the beholder.*

values of reading the particular worth or merits of the act of reading or its outcomes, as control of purpose and speed, portability, vicarious experience, access to the best in human thinking and writing, etc.

value word a word which conveys an abstract or aesthetic meaning rather than practical information. *Truth, goodness, and beauty are value words.* See also **abstract word** (def. 2); **abstract noun.**

vanity press a publishing house that offers to print, at a cost, the efforts of would-be writers whose writings would otherwise not be likely to see the light of day.

variability (vâr″ē ə bil′i tē) 1. *n.* changeableness, as *reading rate variability.* 2. *n.* the dispersion, spread, or scatter of scores or values in a distribution, usually about the mean. *The standard deviation is a unit of variability.*

variable (vâr′ē ə bəl) 1. *n.* any quantity that is subject to change, as *dependent and independent variables. Note:* Special types of variable, as *dependent variable,* are given under the describing term. 2. *n.* anything that is subject to quantitative change, as behavioral responses, temperature, etc. 3. *adj.* changeable, as *a variable wind.* 4. *adj.* fickle, as *a variable temper.*

variance (vâr′ē əns) 1. *n.* a measure of variability; specifically, the square of the standard deviation (σ^2). 2. **at variance,** being in dispute or containing a discrepancy. *Lynnette's story was at variance with the known facts.*

variance, analysis of See **analysis of variance.**

variant (vâr′ē ənt) 1. *n.* a subset of a linguistic class which shares features but also differs in some way from other members of the class. *Dialects are variants of a language.* 2. *n.* an alternate pronunciation of a word which is less common in usage.

variation (vâr″ē ā′s̱hən) 1. *n.* that which is different. 2. *n.* change, or the process of change; especially, change from the normal or typical. 3. *n.* the spread or dispersion of scores in a distribution, as *variation from the mean.* 4. *n.* deviation from the structure or characteristics of the parents or from the group to which the individual belongs. 5. *n.* a modified theme or pattern, especially in music.

vector (vek′tər) 1. *n.* a graphic representation of a score of a variable, as a line whose length and direction represent, respectively, the size of the score and its relation to other variables. 2. *n.* a unidimensional set of numbers, as *validity coefficient vectors. Ct.* **matrix** (def. 2).

velar (vē′lər) 1. *adj.* having to do with the velum. 2. *n.* a consonant speech sound made when the air flow is stopped or deflected as the back of the tongue approaches or touches the soft palate, as the sounds /k/ in *cool* or /n͡g/ in *sing.* 3. *adj.* having to do with a speech sound so made. *Syn.* **guttural** (def. 3).

velum (vē′ləm) *pl.* **-la** (-lə). *n.* the soft palate.

ventral (ven′trəl) 1. *adj.* having to do with the belly or abdomen; anterior. 2. *adj.* in front of the backbone or towards the front of the body. *Ant.* **dorsal.**

ventricle (ven′tri kəl) *n.* a small, normal cavity in the body, as in the brain or heart.

verb (vûrb) *n.* a word expressing an action or state that forms the main element in a predicate, may be inflected for tense, aspect, voice, and mood, and shows agreement with subject and/or object. *Note:* Special types of verbs, as *transitive verb,* are given under the describing word.

verbal (vûr′bəl) 1. *adj.* having to do with words, as *verbal fluency.* 2. *adj.* oral, as *a loud verbal argument.* 3. *adj.* clever in using a large vocabulary, as *a most verbal young man.* 4. *n.* a word in verb form used like a noun, adjective, or adverb, as *reading* in *reading is fun.* See also **gerund; infinitive; participle.**

verbal ability the ability to understand and/or use language.

verbal fluency 1. ease in the use of language in speaking and writing. 2. speed in making word associations.

verbal IQ the IQ score for language-based tasks, as on the Wechsler Intelligence Scales. *Ct.* **nonverbal IQ.**

verbalization (vûr″bə li zā′s̱hən) 1. *n.* expressing oneself in words; making an utterance. 2. *n.* the converting of a part of speech into a verb by a grammatical process, as the verbalization of *black* to *blacken. v.* **verbalize.**

verbal reasoning logical thinking using words, as contrasted with the use of other forms of symbolic expression. *Verbal reasoning ability is often tested separately from mathematical reasoning ability.*

verbal scale *or* test 1. the language-based portion of an intelligence test, as on the Wechsler Intelligence Scales. 2. any scale or test for which the understanding and/or use of language is necessary.

verbal thought thinking in words. *Note:* L. S. Vygotsky (1962) describes verbal thought as *a complex, dynamic entity* [in which] *the relation of thought and word within it* [is] *as a movement through a series of planes... from the motive which engenders a thought to the shaping of the thought, first in inner speech, then in meanings of words, and finally in words.*

verbatim (vər bā′tim) 1. *adv.* in the same words. *Charlie repeated the story verbatim.* 2. *adj.* reproduced word-for-word, as *a verbatim typescript.*

verbiage (vûr′bē ij) *n.* an overuse or excessive use of words in speaking or writing; verbal foliage.

verb marker See **auxiliary verb.**

verb phrase (VP) 1. in traditional grammar, a group of words whose head word is a verb, as *must be going* in *I must be going.* 2. in transformational-generative grammar, the complete predicate, as *washed their ears* in *The boys washed their ears. Ct.* **noun phrase (NP).**

veridical (və rid′i kəl) *adj.* real; not illusory; corresponding to fact. *Veridical observations are verifiable by others.*

verification (ver″ə fə kā′shən) 1. *n.* the act, or result, of confirming the truth or accuracy of something, using established rules, facts, or logic, as *the verification of test scores.* 2. *n.* the evidence needed to confirm the truth or accuracy of something. *The shoe that was found provided the necessary verification of her disappearance.* 3. *n.* the research process used to confirm the accuracy of something, as *the verification of sources. v.* **verify.**

verisimilitude (ver″i si mil′i to͞od,″ -tyo͞od″) *n.* the appearance of or resemblance to truth, as *the verisimilitude of some of Poe's writings.*

vernacular (vər nak′yə lər) 1. *n.* the current spoken language of a speech community. 2. *n.* the native spoken language of a speech community. 3. *n.* the special way words are used by a class or profession, as *legal vernacular.* 4. *adj.* having to do with such meanings.

versatility, reading See **reading flexibility.**

vers de societe (ver′di sō″sē i tā′; vəʀ də sô syā tā′) (*French.*) a form of humorous light verse, or an example thereof, which usually deals with fashions and social relationships with grace and sophistication: *Out upon it, I have loved/Three whole days together!/And am like to love three more/If it prove fair weather* — J. Suckling.

verse (vûrs) 1. *n.* one line of a poem. 2. *n.* a metrical composition. 3. *n.* poetry without imaginative and conceptual power. See **poetry** (def. 2). 4. *n.* one sentence or a part of a long sentence in a chapter of the Bible. 5. *adj.* referring to verse, as *a verse form.* 6. *v.* to compose in verse. *v.* **versify.** *n.* **versification.**

version (vûr′zhən, -shən) 1. *n.* translation, as *an English version of* Don Quixote. 2. *n.* any of several variations on a story, play, etc., sometimes in different media, as *the film version of Peter Pan.* 3. *n.* a personal account of something. *How does your version of the robbery compare with mine?*

vers libre (ver lē′bʀᵊ) (*French.*) See **free verse.**

verso (vûr′sō) 1. *n.* the left-hand page of an open book. 2. *n.* the back outside cover of a book. 3. *n.* the reverse side of a single manuscript leaf; the side intended to be read second. *Ct.* **recto.**

vertical imbalance vertical hyperphoria, hypertropia, hypophoria, or hypotropia; specifically, the tendency of one eye to turn, or the obvious turning of one eye, up or down when one of the two eyes does not fixate at the same point.

vertigo (vûr′tə gō″) *n.* the sensation of dizziness. *Vertigo may be sought after by children and adolescents as they spin themselves around, but it is usually caused by disease of the inner ear.*

vestibule (ves′tə byo͞ol″) *n.* the cavity of the inner ear between the cochlea and the semicircular canals.

vicarious experience indirect, imagined participation in events in the experience of others. *Reading is a prime source of vicarious experience. Ct.* **direct experience.**

video (vid′ē ō″) 1. *n.* the visual part of television. *Ct.* **audio** (def. 1). 2. *n.* television as communication. 3. *adj.* having to do with television, especially its visual part.

videodisc (vid′ē ō disk″) *n.* a thin, flat disc similar to a small phonograph record on which are recorded video and/or audio signals for television.

videotape (vid′ē ō tāp″) *n.* a magnetic tape for television on which visual and auditory signals are recorded.

videotape recorder a machine for recording images and sound on videotape for televised playback.

viewdata (vyo͞o′dā″tə, -dat″ə, dä″tə) *n. (pl. but often sing. in use)* any form of computer data that may be retrieved and viewed upon an electronic screen.

virgule (vûr′gyo͞ol) 1. *n.* an orthographic symbol (/) used to separate alternatives such as *and/or,* parts of a date such as 6/03/52, a fraction such as ½, or to represent *per,* as in *6 miles/hour;* slash; *(Brit.)* stroke. 2. *n.* one of a pair of such marks used to enclose a phonemic transcription, as /kik/ for *kick.*

virtual focus the point from which divergent rays appear to originate. See illustration under **lens**. *Ct.* **real focus.**

virtual image an optical image formed by the interception of diverging light rays, as the uninverted image seen in the direct examination of the eye through an ophthalmoscope. *Note:* The virtual image is an optical representation that cannot be shown on a screen since it consists of the backward extension of diverging rays to an imaginary point of focus. *Ct.* **real image.** See also **virtual focus.**

vis (i) (u)- a combining form indicating *look, see;* as **visible, visual.**

visceral (vis′ər əl) 1. *adj.* having to do with any of the internal organs of the body, especially those of the abdomen. *Ct.* **somatic** (def. 3). 2. *adj.* felt deep inside the body; emotional and earthy in motivation and appeal. *Much modern fiction is visceral. n.* **viscera.**

visible speech 1. the use of symbols to indicate the proper placement of the speech organs to produce specific sounds in teaching the deaf to speak. 2. the use of both speech and sign in communication. See **combined method.** 3. the electronic conversion of audible speech into visual patterns which may be read. See **oscillograph.**

vision (vizh′ən) 1. *n.* the act or power of seeing; sight; visual acuity. *Note:* Special types of vision, as *binocular vision,* are given under the describing term. 2. *n.* something seen. *She was a vision of beauty.* 3. *n.* something not seen, but imagined and pictured; hallucination. *The vision of Hamlet's father appeared to several men.* 4. *n.* having the imaginative intelligence, or foresight, to anticipate the future consequences of present behaviors and trends. *He is a man of vision.*

vision screening See **visual screening test.**

visual (vizh'ōō əl) 1. *adj.* having to do with the use of the eyes or with sight, as *a visual method, a visual interpretation.* 2. *adj.* referring to information gained by sight, as *visual impressions.* 3. *adj.* capable of being seen; seeable; visible; as *a visual alphabet.* 4. *adj.* optical, as *a visual illusion.* 5. *adj.* referring to projected or displayed representations such as pictures, models, charts, etc., used for educational purposes, as *visual aids.* 6. **visuals,** the pictured portion rather than the sound portion of audiovisual aids, as of films or TV.

visual acuity the sharpness of seeing which is the result of the clarity of the image falling on the retina, the sensitivity of the retina and the nervous system, and the keenness of perception. *Note:* In visual acuity testing by a Snellen chart or its clinical equivalent, with both eyes open and no corrective lenses, the symbols require little interpretation. Such a test is considered primarily one of checking refractive power and the ability to resolve fine details accurately. *Cp.* **refraction** (defs. 2, 3).

visual alternation 1. the theory that sensory impulses from each eye are very rapidly and alternately suppressed and received in cortical perceptual processing. 2. the alternating suppression of one and then the other eye when strabismus or some other condition prevents fusion of the two images; alternating vision. *Alternation is one form of visual suppression.*

visual analysis See **visual discrimination.**

visual array an arrangement of items for viewing, usually in a row or column, often presented tachistoscopically.

visual closure the process, or ability, to fill in missing parts of a visual stimulus; especially, the process of supplying a letter missing from a word or a word missing from a sentence. See also **closure** (def. 1).

visual coordination the smooth working together of both eyes; binocular coordination.

visual cue a distinctive sight feature that triggers a response; especially, a distinctive shape that aids identification of a letter, letter group, or word. See also **configuration clue; cue** (def. 3); **visual perception.**

visual discrimination 1. the process of perceiving similarities and differences in stimuli by sight. 2. the ability to engage in such a process. *Note:* An educational aspect of this processing ability is that of acquiring sensitivity to the distinctive features of common printed material, as letters, words, and phrases. This may lead to more rapid and accurate processing of those stimuli in the future. If such features as the difference between *m* and *w* or *then* and *than* are not learned, errors of letter or word identification will tend to persist and block reading progress.

visual dominance ocular dominance. See also **dominant eye.**

visual fatigue eyestrain; tiredness presumably due to excessive and/or improper use of the eyes. *Note:* Visual fatigue is an inexact descriptive term, not a diagnostic one. It may refer to many symptoms of tiredness associated with the eyes, as in the neck, back, etc. Early experiments of visual fatigue while reading conducted by W. Dearborn and others at the turn of the century suggest that the external eye muscles are remarkably resistant to fatigue in adults with normal vision. However, M. Vernon states that *the eye of the child is much more liable to fatigue and strain than that of the adult* (1978).

visual field the entire area visible to an eye without shifting fixation. *Note:* When the eye is looking straight ahead, the range of this field is normally about 65° upward from the center of the eye, 95° outward, 75° downward, and 60° inward. Noses and eyebrows limit the visual field. *Binocular visual field* refers to the total area seen when both eyes are looking at one spot.

visual fusion See **fusion** (def. 2).

visual image See **image** (def. 3).

visual impairment 1. the loss of acuity of the visual field because of a physical or physiological defect, as in tunnel vision. 2. visual acuity of 20/200 - 20/70 in the better eye after correction; partially sighted. *Note:* Visual impairment usually can be improved by magnifying aids.

visualization (vizh″o͞o ə lī zā′shən, -li-) *n.* the process, or result, of mentally picturing objects or events that are normally experienced directly. See also **imagery** (def. 2). *v.* **visualize; visualizing.**

visual literacy the ability to interpret and communicate visual symbols in media other than print.

visually handicapped 1. having serious loss of useful sight. 2. See **visual impairment** (def. 2).

visual maturity the full growth and development of the structures and functions of the eyes.

visual memory the retention, recall, and/or recognition of things seen. *In reading, visual memory is helpful in learning letter forms and their sequence in words.*

visual memory span the number of items, usually in the correct order, that one can recall immediately after seeing them, as in a briefly exposed number series.

visual modality the use of the sense of vision in acquiring information. *Cp.* **auditory modality; kinesthetic modality.**

visual-motor coordination the guiding and interacting relationship of vision to body movement, as in handwriting, drawing, playing a musical instrument, etc.

visual-motor method a modified kinesthetic method of learning words by emphasizing seeing and writing them without tracing. *Cp.* **Fernald (-Keller) approach** *or* **method (VAKT).**

visual-motor skills skills requiring a specified degree of visual-motor coordination, usually tested by having a person copy a design.

visual perception the extraction of information about things, places, and events in the visible world; the process of seeing such characteristics of things as shape, color, size, distance, etc., and identifying them meaningfully. *For sighted persons, the accurate visual perception of letters, words, phrases, and other units of meaning is needed to learn to read.* See also **word perception.**

visual processing the activity of receiving, examining, weighing, understanding, ordering, and remembering visible stimuli, especially the characters in reading, and considering their meanings. *Note:* The nature and operation of visual processing is under intensive study in recent research in reading comprehension. *Cp.* **auditory processing.**

visual pursuit See **pursuit eye movements.**

visual screening test any of a group of tests used to get a quick sampling of visual skills, usually to identify those who need a more careful examination by an eye specialist; vision screening. *Note:* In a comprehensive diagnosis of disabled readers, a visual screening test is often used for visual acuity, phorias, stereopsis, and sometimes color perception.

visual skills those skills which enable the visual functions to operate in a normal, efficient way.

visual span 1. See **span of attention** (def. 1). 2. all that can be perceived in any instant in the visual field.

visual suppression failure to use, or the inhibition of, vision of one eye to avoid double vision or visual confusion. *Note:* Visual suppression may involve cortical inhibition of all or part of the neural information coming from the retina of one eye due to a lack of binocular fixation, or to hysteria. *Cp.* **visual alternation** (def. 2). See also **amblyopia.**

visual tracking 1. See **pursuit eye movements.** 2. the process or ability to follow the line(s) of print.

visual training See **orthoptics.**

visuomotor (vizh'o͞o ō mō″tər) *adj.* visual-motor, as in *visuomotor method.*

vitreous chamber the large space in the eyeball between the lens and the retina, which is filled with vitreous humor; posterior chamber. See illustration under **eye.**

vitreous humor the clear, jellied matter which fills the posterior chamber of the eyeball. *Cp.* **aqueous humor.**

vocabulary (vō kab'yə ler″ē) 1. *n.* a list of words, as in a dictionary or glossary; lexicon. 2. *n.* those words known or used by a person or group. *Shakespeare's vocabulary was immense.* 3. *n.* all the words of a language. 4. *n.* nonverbal forms of expression, as the vocabulary of the painter, the dancer, etc. 5. *n. (Cap.)* a subtest of several intelligence and reading tests. *Note:* Special types of vocabulary, as *meaning vocabulary,* are given under the describing term.

vocabulary burden *or* **load** 1. the degree to which the number of difficult words, their rate of introduction, and the comprehensibility of the words affects readability. 2. the frequency of hard words, as determined by specific criteria, used as a variable in readability formulas. *Cp.* **concept load** *or* **density** (def. 2); **proposition density.**

vocabulary control the practice of limiting the number of new words introduced in successive pages or lessons in basal reading texts. *Note:* The strict vocabulary control of mid-20th century basal readers, based principally on assumptions about the number of repetitions needed to learn a word, has been relaxed greatly as motivational factors in the pupil and in story content have received greater attention.

vocabulary development 1. the growth of a person's stock of known words and meanings. *Wide reading aids vocabulary development.* 2. the teaching-learning principles and practices which lead to such growth, as comparing and classifying word meanings, using context, analyzing word roots and affixes, etc.

vocabulary diversity 1. the extent to which different words are used in writing or speaking; lexical variety. 2. in linguistic analysis, the ratio of different words or types, in a written or spoken message, to the total number of words, or tokens. See **type-token ratio (TTR).**

vocabulary test any test of word knowledge, oral or silent.

vocal (vō'kəl) 1. *adj.* with an unblocked airflow between the vocal cords and the lips, as in the movement of air during vowel production. 2. *adj.* referring to any aspect of speech production or speech, as *vocal organs, vocal tract,* etc. 3. *adj.* outspoken.

vocal cords See **vocal folds.**

vocal folds 1. either of the two sets of vocal ligaments and muscles with their covering mucous membranes which project medially into the larynx. 2. usually, the lower pair of these structures which, when pulled together during expiration, release puffs of air which produce voice; true vocal folds; vocal bands.

vocalic (vō kal′ik) 1. *adj.* having to do with vowels or their sounds. 2. *adj.* having to do with speech sounds functioning as vowels, as do some consonants. See **semivowel** (def. 1).

vocalization (vō″kəl ī zā′shən) 1. *n.* voice production; utterance; phonation. 2. *n.* subvocalization. 3. *n.* causing the vocal folds to vibrate during speech; voicing. 4. *n.* articulating a consonant as a vowel sound. 5. *n.* supplying vowel indicators in writing systems that do not use vowels. 6. *n.* singing, especially singing syllables to practice or warm up for a performance. *v.* **vocalize.**

vocal tract collectively, the entire set of speech organs which together produce speech sounds: the lungs, larynx, resonators, and articulators.

vocational school a school which offers courses in one or more skilled trades or occupations, as that of the carpenter, electrician, mason, etc. *Note:* The vocational school and the technical school are both occupational, or vocational, in their orientation. The distinction between the two is also blurred by the fact that some schools are *vocational-technical schools.* See also **technical school.**

vocative case the case form in inflected languages that indicates the person or personified object being directly addressed. *Note:* In English, this denotation is shown by voice inflection and/or punctuation, as *George, what are you doing?*

vocoid (vō′koid) *n.* a phonetic term for vowel. *Note:* This little used term is sometimes used to distinguish vowel sounds, vocoids, from letters representing the sounds and from vowel speech sounds used in a specific language.

voice (vois) 1. *n.* any sound produced by the vocal tract of a vertebrate, or a sound similar to it. 2. *n.* the speech sounds, or their range, produced by the larynx and modified by the resonators. 3. *n.* the ability to produce such sounds, as *have enough voice to speak, lose one's voice.* 4. *v.* to make such sounds; talk; speak. 5. **give voice,** to express aloud, as *give voice to one's sorrow.* 6. *n.* the distinctive features of a person's speech and speech patterns. *It's Sylvia: I would know her voice anywhere.* 7. *n.* in English grammar, a syntactic pattern which indicates the verb-subject relationship. *Note* (def. 7): The principal English voices are active and passive voices. In the *active voice,* the subject of the verb carries out some action, as in the pattern *He hit the ball.* In the *passive voice,* the subject of the verb is the receiver of some action or state indicated by the verb, as in the pattern *He was hit by the ball.* 8. *n.* in some languages, as in Latin, the inflection of verb forms to show verb/subject relationships.

voiced (voist) 1. *adj.* referring to any speech sound which requires vibrations of the vocal cords: */v/ is voiced while /f/ is voiceless even though the articulators are in the same position for both sounds. Ct.* **voiceless** (def. 1). 2. *adj.* having a specific kind of voice, as *shrill-voiced.* 3. *adj.* expressed vocally, as a *voiced opinion.*

voice disorder a difficulty in one or more aspects of voicing or resonation which is serious enough to interfere with ease of communication. *A severely gutteral, strident, or hoarse voice may represent a voice disorder. Note:* This term does not cover articulatory or fluency problems, for which the more general term 'speech disorder' is used.

voiceless (vois′lis) 1. *adj.* referring to any speech sound which does not require vibrations of the vocal cords, as /f/, /p/, /th/. *Ct.* **voiced** (def. 1). 2. *adj.* without voice; mute; dumb. *He was voiceless from birth.* 3. *adj.* silent; without words. *Julie was startled voiceless.*

voiceprint (vois′print″) *n.* a spectrogram of a person's voice. *Presumably, each person has a unique voiceprint.*

voicing (voi′sing) 1. *n.* the conversion of the energy of the moving air flow in speech into acoustic energy in the larynx; phonation. 2. *n.* the vibration of the vocal cords during speech. *Voicing is a characteristic of vowel sounds.* See also **vocalization.**

volume (vol′yo͞om, -yəm) 1. *n.* the loudness of a sound perceived and judged by the intensity of the sound. 2. *n.* a book, considered as a unit. *May I see that volume by Mark Twain?* 3. *n.* one of a set, or series, of related book units. *May I see the last volume of the* Lord of the Rings *series?* 4. *n.* a limited, consecutive series of periodical, newspaper, etc., issues, usually numbered year by year, as *Volume 15, Number 12; Volume 16, Number 1.*

vowel (vou′əl) 1. *n.* a voiced speech sound made without friction or stoppage of the air flow as it passes through the vocal tract. *Note:* Vowels may also be classified by the way in which they are formed, as by specifying the position of the tongue (1), the elevation of the tongue (2), and the position of the lips (3). Such distinctions are given under the describing term. See illustration. 2. *n.* the most prominent sound in a syllable, as /e/ in *Ted. This contrast in loudness and resonance distinguishes vowels from consonants phonetically.* 3. *n.* a letter representing any such sounds. *Note:* Special types of vowels, such as *long vowel,* are given under the describing term.

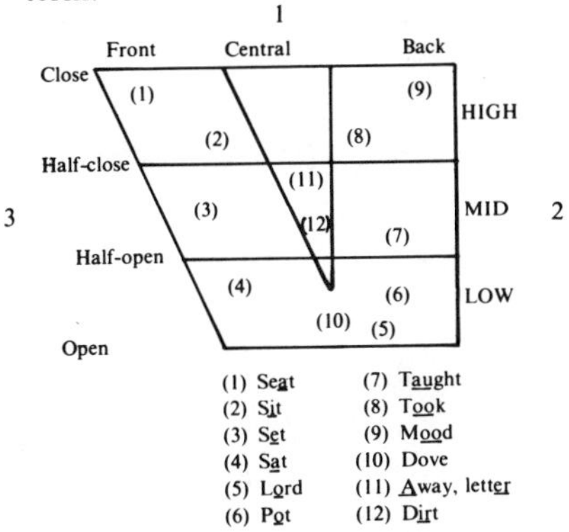

Vowel formation

vowel cluster in teaching practice, a sequence of two or more vowel sounds in a word, as in *aorta,* or a sequence of two or more vowel letters, as *oa* in *boat.*

vowel controller the letters *r, l,* and, in some phonic systems, *w,* when the sounds they represent modify an immediately preceding vowel sound in the same syllable, as in *fir, fall, saw,* See also **r-controlled vowel sound.**

vowel digraph a spelling pattern in which two or more adjoining letters represent a single vowel sound, as *eigh* for /ā/ in *sleigh, ea* for /e/ in *bread,* or *aw* for /ô/ in *saw. Ct.* **diphthong.**

vowel letter an alphabet letter used singly or with other such letters to represent a vowel sound, as *e* in b*e*d, b*ea*d. *Ct.* **consonant letter.** See also **vowel** (def. 3).

vowel, long See **long vowel.**

vowel, short See **short vowel.**

VP verb phrase.

vulgar (vul′gər) 1. *adj.* without good taste or breeding; unrefined; crude; as *a vulgar remark.* 2. *adj.* obscene. 3. *adj.* current; popular; as *a vulgar hit.* 4. *adj.* in the vernacular, or in low social status, as in *vulgar speech.*

W

DEVELOPMENT OF MAJUSCULE						
NORTH SEMITIC	GREEK	ETR.	LATIN	MODERN		
				GOTHIC	ITALIC	ROMAN
SEE LETTERS F AND U				𝔚	*W*	W

DEVELOPMENT OF MINUSCULE					
ROMAN CURSIVE	ROMAN UNCIAL	CAROL. MIN.	MODERN		
			GOTHIC	ITALIC	ROMAN
—	ꝡ	—	𝔴	*w*	w

The twenty-third letter of the English alphabet, called "double-u," created about the 11th century A.D. by the Norman scribes to represent the English sound for which they had no need in their own language, and to distinguish two U's from a U and a V. (See also **U** and **V**.) The *w*-sound was represented in North Semitic by *waw,* which in the Greek alphabet became *digamma* (ϝ) and *upsilon* (υ). (See **F**.) The Anglo-Saxons used a special character *(ƿ, wyn)* for the *w*-sound, but rather than use a foreign letter in their alphabet, the Norman French preferred to double one of their own characters.

Wada test a test for determining cerebral dominance for language functions. *Note:* Sodium amytal is injected directly into the carotid artery on one side of the neck. This produces a partial paralysis in the cerebral hemisphere on the opposite side of the brain and, if the hemisphere controls language, temporary aphasia. The test is used prior to brain surgery intended to control epileptic seizures to inform the surgeon whether the side of the cerebrum for the proposed operation subserves a language function.

WAIS See **Wechsler Intelligence Scales.**

walking beam a beam approximately 5 x 10 cm. (2 x 4 in.) placed slightly above ground level for developing balance and postural skills. *Note:* The sometimes presumed effect of such exercise upon laterality, or hemispheric dominance, is unclear.

watch tick test a crude test of hearing in which a loud ticking watch is held at varying distances from the subject's head and compared with the distance at which the tester, with known good hearing, can hear it.

wave length 1. the distance, measured in the direction of the movement of a wave, between two successive points in the corresponding phases of a series of waves in a uniform medium, as the distance between two crests of a sound wave moving through air next to each other. *Wave length is inversely proportional to its frequency.* 2. **on the same wave length**, having mutual understanding or empathy.

weak verb in English, a regular verb which forms the past tense and the past participle with *-ed,* as in *walked, hummed, rated. Ct.* **strong verb.**

Weber test a hearing test to determine the nature of a hearing loss in one ear, in which a vibrating tuning fork is placed on the middle of the skull. *Note:* If the subject hears the tone in the poorer ear, it is a conductive hearing loss; if in the better ear, it is a sensorineural hearing loss.

Wechsler Intelligence Scales any of several general, individual, mental ability tests developed by D. Wechsler, which give separate verbal and nonverbal IQ's as well as a total IQ. *Note:* The three scales in current use are the Wechsler Preschool and Primary Scale of Intelligence (WPPSI), the Wechsler Intelligence Scale for Children-Revised (WISC-R), and the Wechsler Adult Intelligence Scale (WAIS). See also **Stanford-Binet Intelligence Scale (S-B).**

weekly (wēk′lē) *n.* a newspaper or periodical issued once a week.

weight (wāt) 1. *n.* how heavy something is, as *a 10 kilogram weight.* 2. *n.* a burden, as *the weight of constant worry.* 3. *n.* importance. *His opinion had great weight.* 4. *n.* in statistics: a. the numerical coefficient by which a score or value is multiplied to give it a desired relative importance. b. the relative contribution made to the variance of a test. 5. *v.* to give statistical weight to a variable.

weighting (wā'tiṅg) *n.* the determination and/or assignment of weights to scores to produce a desired total score or to improve the predictive ability of an equation.

Wernicke's aphasia a type of aphasia, largely receptive, identified by the German neurologist, Wernicke. See **Wernicke's area.**

Wernicke's area the area of the cerebral cortex which is most involved in the reception and interpretation of language, corresponding to Brodmann's areas 22, 39, and 40. See illustration under **Brodmann's areas.** *Cp.* **Broca's area.**

western *or* **Western** (wes'tərn) *n.* a work of fiction which features the setting of the American West and those who lived there in yesteryears, particularly the cowboys, as Zane Grey's *Riders of the Purple Sage.*

whimperative (hwim″per'ə tiv, wim″-) *n. a command stated in a question form with a "wh-" word* — R. P. McDermott (1977): *Why don't you close the door?*

whisper (hwis'pər, wis'pər) 1. *n.* speech produced without voicing and with little carrying power; a hushed voice. 2. *v.* to speak in this way. 3. *n.* any quiet, rustling sound, as *the gentle whisper of the tea kettle.* 4. **stage whisper,** a loud whisper, meant to be heard.

whisper test a crude hearing test in which the subject turns away and the examiner whispers words or digits which the subject tries to repeat.

white matter that part of the central nervous system made up mostly of nerve axons, and which appears lighter in color because of the myelinization of the extended nerve fibers. *The white matter underlies and connects the gray matter of the brain and forms long strings of peripheral nerves.*

white noise a sound made up of irregular sound waves containing all the audible frequencies at about equal intensities and which sounds much like a continuous flow of water. *White noise is often used for masking during audiometric examination.*

whole/part relationship an association, stated or implied in a communication, between a general idea and one or more specific ideas included in the general idea.

whole word method See **word method.**

whole word phonics an analytic phonic approach to reading instruction in which the sounds represented by certain letters and groups of letters within whole words are compared and contrasted to those in other whole words, avoiding the separate sounding of word parts. *Cp.* **analytic phonics.** *Ct.* **synthetic phonics.**

Whorfian hypothesis the view advanced by B. L. Whorf (1897-1941), which states in its strongest form that the structure of a language determines modes of thought and cultural patterns and thereby influences social structures.

wide diphthong a diphthong in which there is considerable back-front tongue movement during production, as in the /yo͞o/ sound of *few.* *Ct.* **narrow diphthong.**

wide reading the reading pattern of a person who reads on a great variety of subjects, types, and/or themes.

windpipe (wind'pīp") See **trachea.**

WISC-R See **Wechsler Intelligence Scales.**

wit (wit) 1. *n.* a keen perception, cleverly and amusingly expressed, of connections among ideas, things, etc., that are often incongruous. See also **humor** (def. 1). 2. *n.* something so perceived. 3. *n.* one with such perception. *Oscar Wilde was a famous wit.* 4. **wits,** a. ingenuity, as *live by one's wits.* b. the power of reasoning, as *lose one's wits.* 5. **have (keep) one's wits,** to remain alert. *adj.* **witty.** *n.* **witticism.**

word (wûrd)

A word is a key meaning unit in reading, as in listening, speaking, and writing. It is not, however, the only unit with which the reader must deal. *It should constantly be remembered that words are functional, and that their main function is to help express a total meaning which always requires or implies their association together with other words* — E. Huey (1908). Although people generally know what a word is in actual use and can identify a word in the speech of others, its precise definition is less certain, and, like language, is subject to the theoretical or subjective views of the definer.

1. *n. a morpheme or group of morphemes that is regarded as a pronounceable and meaningful unit* — R. Wardhaugh (1966). 2. *n. segments of language recorded as independent entities in dictionaries* — W. Lehmann (1976). 3. *n. any linguistic form considered to be independent in distribution and meaning* — W. H. Francis (1958). 4. *n.* in speech, a phoneme or series of phonemes that conveys meaning and consists of at least one free morpheme, as the main entry of a dictionary. 5. *n.* in writing, *a sequence of letters with a white space on either side* — F. Smith (1975). 6. *n.* in word identification, *a complex of features, a composite representation of five classes of information: graphic, phonological, orthographic, semantic, and syntactic.... Full recognition of a word depends upon the extraction of all these kinds of information* — E. Gibson and H. Levin (1975). 7. *n.* the smallest lexical unit of meaning in speech and writing; more technically, a morpheme or unit of morphemes that can be used in syntactic constructions: *...a minimum free form (morpheme)* — L. Bloomfield (1933). *Note:* Single morphemes may be combined in compounds, as *black* and *bird* to form the word *blackbird.* Some types of words, as *are, the, very, of,* etc., are usually dependent upon their relation to other words for meaning except in such references as the *'the'* in *Watch the parade.* See also **free form.** 8. **words,** a. speech that is insincere and of little significance; prattling. b. the lyrics of a song. c. angry, quarrelsome speech. *The rivals exchanged heated words.* 9. *n.* a short talk or conversation, as *May I have a word with you?* 10. *n.* an expression, as *words of praise.* 11. *n.* a promise, as *I give you my word.* 12. *n.* news; information. *What word do you bring?* 13. *n.* a verbal signal, as a password. 14. *n.* an order; command. *His word was law.* 15. *n.* (*Cap*) The Bible; also, *The Word.* 16. *v.* to put into words. 17. **in a word,** in summary; in short. *In a word, there is no more time left.* 18. **in so many words,** literally. *He explained in so many words what was to be done.* 19. **by word of mouth,** speaking. *Note:* Special types of words, as *compound word,* are given under the describing term.

word analysis 1. *usually, the analysis of words into their constituent letters*

— M. Vernon (1978). 2. phonic and structural analysis. 3. *sight vocabulary, phonics, structural analysis, context clues, and dictionary skills* — W. S. Gray (1960). 4. *all methods of word attack* — E. Dechant (1973). *Cp.* **word attack; word identification.**

word association test a projective test in which a person is asked to respond to a series of stimulus words by saying the first word that each stimulus word suggests; free association test. *Note:* The various forms of such tests are limited chiefly to clinical use. See also **projective technique** *or* **test.**

word attack in common usage, word analysis or word identification. *Note:* Word attack is frequently limited to the act of 'sounding it out.'

word bank 1. a file of words mastered or being studied by a student. 2. originally, *a student's sight word vocabulary* — E. Betts (1957).

word blindness 1. alexia. 2. dyslexia. *Note:* T. Hepworth (1971) makes this observation: *The dyslexic child can see words, but for him some words and letter shapes do not have perceptual constancy — that is, they are perceived differently in different phrases or sentences and in different positions.*

word boundary in linguistics, any limit that defines the extent of a word by phonological, morphological, or syntactic constraints or rules. See also **sandhi** (def. 2).

word-by-word reading 1. a halting, labored type of oral reading with a very slow rate of word recognition, poor phrasing and comprehension, and sometimes mispronunciations; word calling. *The child just bumps along from word to word without any notion of what he is reading* — I. H. Anderson and W. J. Dearborn (1952). 2. very slow silent reading, often with lip and head movements suggestive of a narrow span of recognition.

word calling 1. See **word-by-word reading** (def. 1). 2. proficiency in the mechanics of oral reading with little or no attention to meaning, often the result of an overemphasis on word analysis, oral reading, and drill on isolated words. *Note:* Problems of word calling are often ignored under the assumption that because a reader can pronounce the individual words, comprehension also takes place. *Cp.* **barking at print.**

word card 1. a card on which a student writes a word he has learned, often with its definition, and can keep for study and review. 2. a card used or prepared by a teacher to show words to students.

word class in linguistics, a set of words with similar grammatical functions, as noun, verb, etc. *Cp.* **part of speech.**

word configuration See **configuration clue.**

word deafness See **auditory aphasia.**

word discrimination the process of noting differences in words; especially in their visual outlines or overall shapes. *Note:* Teachers often use the term to refer to noting similarities as well as differences. See also **auditory discrimination; discrimination** (def. 1); **visual discrimination; word identification; word perception; word recognition.**

word entry See **entry** (def. 1).

word family 1. a group of words sharing a common phonic element, as /īt/ spelled *ite* in *bite, kite, despite.* 2. a group of words sharing the same root or base, as *-phon-* in *phonemic, phonation, telephone*, or *jump* in *jumps, jumped, jumping.*

word fluency See **verbal fluency.**

word form the form of a word performing a particular grammatical function, as the past tense form of a verb.

word formation 1. the production of new words in a language by invention, onomatopoeia, borrowing, etc.; specifically, the production of new words in a language by morphological processes, as by using derivational affixes, as in *happiness,* or by compounding, as in *cupcake.* 2. the regular morphological rules of a language. *Cp.* **morphology.**

word frequency count *or* **list** a list showing how often words appear in a representative sampling of reading material, as the Thorndike-Lorge *Teacher's Word Book of 30,000 Words* which sampled newspapers, books, and magazines of general interest.

word game See **reading game.**

word history an explanation of the origin and development of the meaning or meanings of a word. The Oxford English Dictionary *gives word histories of terms in the order of their appearance in the English language.* *Cp.* **etymology.**

word identification the process of determining the pronunciation and some degree of meaning of an unknown word. *Note:* Word identification skills commonly taught are phonic analysis, structural analysis, context clues, configuration clues, dictionary skills, and sometimes picture clues. Some reading authorities, as M. Tinker (1965), make a sharp distinction between the identification of an unknown word and the recognition of a word previously met. *Cp.* **word recognition** (def. 2). See also **word perception; word analysis.**

wordless book a picture book that has no text, as Brinton Turkles' *Deep in the Forest* for younger children or John Goodall's *The Story of an English Village* for older students.

word meaning the concept or concepts associated with a spoken or written word: *...in word meaning ...thought and speech unite into verbal thought* — L. S. Vygotsky (1962).

word method 1. a way of teaching reading in which a substantial number of words are learned as whole units for reading before word analysis is started; a *'words-to-reading'* system — M. Mathews (1966). *The word method, beginning with the* Orbus Pictus *of Comenius, 1657,... was very little used in America until 1870.... The pictures of the* Orbus Pictus *were intended to suggest the names printed below, without using any tedious spelling* — E. Huey (1908). *This is a modern system, known since the close of the eighteenth century, but put into widespread practice about 1900... . In the 1830's and 1840's, it was called the new method, later the word method, and later still the look-and-say method... The method is that of starting children in reading by having them memorize words without analyzing them into letters and sounds* — M. Matthews (1966). 2. a way of teaching reading which begins with whole words but either immediately subjects the words to word analysis or introduces a parallel phonics program; a *'words-to-letters'* system — M. Mathews (1966). 3. any analytic approach or method for teaching reading; sight method. *If the word method is not accompanied by the analysis of words into their elements, it should not be classified as an analytic method* — W. S. Gray (1956). *Note:* The historical differences in meaning attached to 'word method' still exist.

The strong trend to combine analytic and synthetic approaches early in an eclectic approach makes the term of questionable value. *Ct.* **alphabet method** (def. 1); **synthetic approach** *or* **method.**

word order the sequence(s) of words in a clause or phrase that signals grammatical relations in a sentence. *Note:* In languages with few inflections, as English, word order is often crucial to meaning, as *The boy hit the ball* versus *The ball hit the boy.*

word origins See **etymology.**

word perception 1. the visual and/or auditory identification of a word, including some degree of meaning. 2. the understanding of the appropriate meaning of a word following its identification or recognition. *The perception of words... depends upon the meanings that are present in the identification and recognition of the words* — M. Tinker (1965). See also **word identification; word recognition.**

word processing the use of typewriters with electronic storage, display, correction/revision, and reproduction features in communication.

word processor a person or machine that does word processing.

word recognition 1. the process of determining the pronunciation and some degree of meaning of any word in written or printed form. See also **word perception.** 2. the quick and easy identification of the form, pronunciation, and appropriate meaning of a word previously met in print or writing. *Cp.* **word identification.**

word recognition test 1. a test of ability to identify words already learned. 2. a test of ability to identify words not learned before, by applying word identification techniques. *Note:* A word recognition test may be informal or formal. An informal test may be merely a list of words to be identified. Formal tests may also include phonics, structural analysis, dictionary, and context items.

words per minute (WPM) rate of reading or speaking in terms of words. *For ease of computation, most speed reading estimates are expressed as words per minute even though ideas are not evenly spread over the words of any text. Cp.* **characters per minute (CPM).**

word square letters arranged in a square space to form words when read either horizontally or vertically; acrostic.

word study 1. vocabulary building exercises. 2. practice in word attack, as in phonics, structural analysis, etc. 3. spelling practice.

word superiority effect *the superior ease of recognizing a target letter embedded in a word* — E. Gibson and H. Levin (1975).

word wheel a cardboard or stiff paper device with two concentric circles fastened together, each of which has on it a series of word elements which, when combined with each other, make up words for practice in vocabulary building and word analysis.

work (wûrk) *n.* a product of active effort; production; especially, a literary or artistic production, as *the works of Thomas Mann, the works of Rodin.*

workbook (wûrk′bo͝ok″) 1. *n.* a book, usually expendable and paperbound, with practice lessons on one or more skills or concepts. 2. *n.* a supplementary exercise book for skill development in a basal reading series. *Note:* In most basal reading programs there is a workbook for each basal reader.

work-limit test See **power test.**

work-pad *n.* a type of seatwork material containing student directions, cutouts, and outline pictures for strengthening silent reading skills. *The work-*

pad was developed largely by N. B. Smith in the 1920's and was a forerunner of the modern reading workbook.

worksheet (wûrk'shēt″) 1. *n.* an exercise sheet containing student directions and space for student response. 2. *n.* any sheet for recording work done, ideas, plans, etc.

workshop (wûrk'shop″) *n.* a seminar or special course for productive activity, either on a common topic or on topics of interest to individuals in the group. *Note:* Historically, the workshop in education arose as an alternative to formal courses because of teachers' concerns with practical teaching problems.

work-study skills See **study skills.**

work-type reading See **study** (def. 1); **study skills.**

WPM words per minute.

WPPSI See **Wechsler Intelligence Scales.**

writing (rī'ting) 1. *n.* the act of recording language graphically, as by letters, logograms, and other symbols. 2. *n.* the result of such graphic recording. 3. *n.* a person's distinctive style of such graphic recording; handwriting. *Note:* Special types of writing, as *cursive writing,* are given under the describing term. 4. *n.* a meaningful set of ideas so expressed. 5. *n.* literary form, as *the writing of Stephen Crane.* 6. *n.* the work of an author.

writing approach to reading a way of introducing children to reading by first using materials prepared by themselves and later materials prepared by others. See also **experience approach** *or* **method.**

writing school from the late 16th century, schools to which grammar school boys were sent at specific times each day to learn writing and arithmetic. *Note:* In American colonies, the most famous grammar schools were the three Writing Schools of Boston which survived until the end of the 18th century. They gave instruction to girls as private students when the boys were not there. *Cp.* **reading school.**

writing system 1. a standardized set of graphic symbols used to represent the speech sounds, syllables, morphemes, or words of a given language. 2. an alphabet. 3. any system of readable symbols, including alphabets, shorthand systems, etc. *Note:* The historical development of writing systems (def. 1) is believed to have evolved from *pictorial writing,* using pictograms (up to 3500 B.C.); to *logography,* using logograms, as in Egyptian hieroglyphics (3000 B.C.), and Chinese characters (1500 B.C.); to *logo-syllabic writing,* as in the Sumerian and Hittite cuneiform (2500 B.C.); to *syllabic writing,* using syllabograms, as in Japanese kana; and culminating in *alphabetic* writing, using letters, as in Phonecian (1000 B.C.), Greek (800 B.C.), Arabic and Gothic (400 A.D.), and Cyrillic (900 A.D.), writing systems.

writing vocabulary the number of different words ordinarily used in writing. *The writing vocabulary is usually but not always smaller than the reading, speaking, and listening vocabularies.*

written language 1. the representation of language by graphic characters. 2. the grammatical style used in writing, especially formal writing, as business letters, resumés, reports, essays, etc.

DEVELOPMENT OF MAJUSCULE								
NORTH SEMITIC	GREEK		ETR.	LATIN		MODERN		
						GOTHIC	ITALIC	ROMAN
—	—	X	—	—	X	𝔛	*X*	X

DEVELOPMENT OF MINUSCULE					
ROMAN CURSIVE	ROMAN UNCIAL	CAROL. MIN.	MODERN		
			GOTHIC	ITALIC	ROMAN
x	x	x		*x*	x

The twenty-fourth letter of the English alphabet originated in form with a variant of North Semitic *taw,* where it signified the *t*-sound. It was adopted by Classical Greek for the *KH*-sound (as in Scottish *loch)* and in some local scripts for the *ks*-sound. In the latter representation it passed from Latin into English and has been maintained, despite its redundancy, for the letter-combination KS.

X 1. raw score. 2. a signature mark made by persons who cannot write their names. 3. a mark for an error or a mistake, as in correcting a test.

$\bar{X}$ arithmetic mean.

Xerox (zēr′oks) 1. *n.* the trademark of a patented process for copying text, illustrations, etc. 2. *v. (l.c.)* to reproduce by, or as by, Xerox. *n.* **xerography.**

x-height the distance, not including ascenders and descenders, between the top and bottom of a lower-case letter, as *read.*

Y

DEVELOPMENT OF MAJUSCULE								
NORTH SEMITIC	GREEK		ETR.	LATIN		MODERN		
						GOTHIC	ITALIC	ROMAN
SEE LETTER U					Y	𝔜	*Y*	Y

DEVELOPMENT OF MINUSCULE					
ROMAN CURSIVE	ROMAN UNCIAL	CAROL. MIN.	MODERN		
			GOTHIC	ITALIC	ROMAN
y	y	—	𝔶	*y*	y

The twenty-fifth letter of the English alphabet, as a consonant, developed from North Semitic *yodh,* whence it was adopted into Greek as a vowel (*iota*) and became English I. (See **I.**) The Y-form goes back to Greek Y, a variant of North Semitic *waw.* (See **U, V, W.**) After the conquest of Greece by the Romans in the 1st century B.C., it was used in Latin for transliterating the Greek Y-sound (as in French *pure,* German *über*) in such words as *zephyros.*

yearbook (yēr′bo͝ok″) *n.* a book published annually with information about the previous year, as *an encylclopedia yearbook.*

young adult literature 1. books selected by young adults, ages 13 to 18, for their reading whether published specifically for them or published for the general adult public. 2. See also **literature for adolescents.**

Z

DEVELOPMENT OF MAJUSCULE								
NORTH SEMITIC	GREEK		ETR.	LATIN		MODERN		
						GOTHIC	ITALIC	ROMAN
I	I	Z	I	—	Z	Z	*Z*	Z

DEVELOPMENT OF MINUSCULE					
ROMAN CURSIVE	ROMAN UNCIAL	CAROL. MIN.	MODERN		
			GOTHIC	ITALIC	ROMAN
z	Z	—	ʒ	*z*	z

The twenty-sixth and last letter of the English alphabet developed from the seventh letter of the North Semitic alphabet, *zayin*. Adopted into Greek as *zeta* (ζ), it passed on to the Etruscans. The Romans dropped it because there is no *z*-sound in Latin, giving its seventh position to the new letter G. The letter Z does not reappear in Latin until after the conquest of Greece by the Romans in the 1st century B.C., when it was adopted to transliterate the Greek *z*-sound in words like *zeugma* and *zephyros*. Placed at the end of the alphabet together with Greek-derived Y, it passed to all West-European alphabets in this position.

z-score See **standard score.**

Appendix A

Word meaning equivalents for selected dictionary entries in French, Spanish, German, Danish, and Swedish.

ENGLISH	FRENCH	SPANISH	GERMAN	DANISH	SWEDISH
ability	capacité	habilidad	Fähigkeit	evne; færdighed	färdighet
accent	accent	acento	Akzent; Betonung	betoning	betoning; brytning (i tal)
accommodation	accommodation	acomodación	Akkomodation	akkommodation	anpassning
alexia	alexie	alexia	Alexie	aleksi	oförmåga att läsa
analytic approach *or* method	approche *ou* méthode analytique (*ou* globale)	enfoque *o* método analítico; método global de análisis estructural	Ganzheitsverfahren *oder* analytische Methode	analytisk angrebsmåde *eller* metode	analytisk metod
applied reading	lecture appliquée	lectura aplicada	Anwendung der Lesefähigkeit	anvendt læsning	tillämpad läsning
appreciation	appréciation	apreciación; aprecio	Verständnis; Würdigung	værdsættelse; forståelse	uppskattning
aptitude	aptitude	aptitud	Leistung; Begabung; Eignung	egnethed*	fallenhet; anlag
assimilation	assimilation	asimilación	Assimilation	assimilation	sammansmältning; likdaning
association	association	asociación	Assoziation	association	förknippning; förening

ENGLISH	FRENCH	SPANISH	GERMAN	DANISH	SWEDISH
auding	écoute	audición	Hören; Aufnehmen und Verstehen gesprochener Sprache	aktiv og konstruktiv opfattelse af sproget gennem øret	lyssnande
auditory discrimination	discrimination auditive	discriminación auditiva	auditive Unterscheidung	auditiv skelnen	auditiv åtskillnad
backwardness in reading	retard en lecture	torpeza lectora; atraso lecto	Zurückgebliebenheit im Lesen *oder* in der Leselernentwicklung	læsesvaghed	lässvaghet
basal reading program *or* series	programme standardisé de lecture	método *o* programa básico de lectura; programa de lectura básica	Leselehrgang; Leselernprogramm; Fibel	begynder-læsebog *eller* -system	grundläggande läsprogram *eller* läseboksserie
behavioral objective	objectif de comportement	objetivo de comportamiento; objetivo conductual	Verhaltensziel	adfærdsmæssigt mål	mål för beteende
bilingual	bilingue	bilingüe	zweisprachig	tosproget	tvåspråkig
blend	fusion (de) sons *ou* de syllabes	grupo consonántico; combinación consonántica; enlace	Lautverschmelzung	sammenglidning af lyd	sammanljuda
block	blocage	impedimento	Block; Sperre; Hemmung; Stockung	blokering	hinder
capacity	capacité	capacidad	Leistungsvermögen	formåen; kapacitet	förmåga
cerebral dominance	dominance cérébrale	dominio cerebral	Hemisphärendominanz	hemisfæredominans	hjärndominans

ENGLISH	FRENCH	SPANISH	GERMAN	DANISH	SWEDISH
classification	classement	clasificación	Klassifikation	klassificering	klassifikation
cloze procedure	technique de closure	técnica de canevá*	Lückenverfahren	cloze procedure	användning av lucktest
cluster	complexe	grupo; grupo consonántico; agrupación	Gruppierung	gruppe	knippe
code	code	código	Kode	kode	regelsystem
cognition	acte *ou* procédé de la connaissance	cognición; conocimiento; sentido; entendimiento; inteligencia	Kognition	kognition	kunskapsprocess
cognitive style	style cognitif	estilo cognitivo *o* cognoscitivo	kognitiver Stil	kognitiv stil	kunskapsinriktning
communication	communication	comunicación	Kommunikation	kommunikation	överföring
compensation	compensation	compensación	Ausgleich; Kompensation	kompensation	ersättning
comprehension	compréhension	comprensión	Verständnis	forståelse	förståelse
concept	concept	concepto	Begriff; Konzept	begreb	begrepp
constraint	contrainte	restricción; traba; constreñimiento	Einschränkung	begrænsning	hinder
context	contexte	contexto	Zusammenhang; Kontext	sammenhæng; kontekst	sammanhang

ENGLISH	FRENCH	SPANISH	GERMAN	DANISH	SWEDISH
context(ual) clue	indication d'après le contexte	indicio *o* clave contextual	kontextueller Hinweis	fremgår af sammenhængen	ledtråd grundad på sammanhanget
correlation	correlation	correlación	Zusammenhang; Korrelation	korrelation	samband
creative reading	lecture spontanée *ou* creative	lectura creadora	schöpferisches Lesen	kreativ læsning	läsning som leder till fortsatt aktivitet
critical evaluation	evaluation critique	evaluacion	kritische Bewertung *oder* Beurteilung	kritisk evaluering	kritisk utvärdering
critical reading	lecture critique	lectura crítica	kritisches Lesen	kritisk læsning	kritisk läsning
cue	indice; signe; repère	pista (lectora)**	Hinweis	stikord	signal; ledtråd
culturally deprived *or* disadvantaged	défavorisé cul-turellement	culturalmente mar-ginado *o* desven-tajado	kulturell benachteiligt	kulturelt under-stimuleret *eller* underpriviligeret	kulturellt undernärd *eller* missgynnad
culturally different	différent cul-turellement	culturalmente diverso	kulturell verschieden	kulturelt anderledes	kulturellt annorlunda
culture	culture	cultura	Kultur	kultur	kultur
decode	décoder	descifrar; descodi-ficar	dekodieren; entschlüsseln	afkode	avläsa
deep structure	structure profonde	estructura profunda *o* subyacente	Tiefenstruktur	dybdestruktur	djupstruktur

**Term coined by Adela Artola Stewart

ENGLISH	FRENCH	SPANISH	GERMAN	DANISH	SWEDISH
developmental dyslexia	dyslexie progressive	dislexia de desarrollo	Entwicklungs-legasthenie	udviklingsbetinget dysleksi	fortsatta lässvårigheter
developmental reading	lecture progressive; post apprentissage; avancement en lecture	lectura de ampliación; lectura progresiva	Entwicklung (und Förderung) des Lesens	udviklingsbetinget læsning	fortsatt läsning
deviate	dévier	desviar	abweichen	afvige	avvika
deviation	déviation; écart	desvío; desviación	Abweichung	afvigelse	avvikelse
directed reading activity	activité de lecture dirigée	(actividad de) lectura dirigida	angeleitete Leseaktivität	styret læseaktivitet	styrd läsövning
disabled reader	handicapé en lecture	lector inhabilitado *o* incapacitado	Person mit Lesestörungen	person med læsevanskeligheder*	svag läsare
disadvantaged	défavorisé	desventajado	benachteiligt	ufordelagtigt stillet*	missgynnad
discrimination	discrimination	discriminación; distinción	Unterscheidung	skelnen	särskillnad
distribution	distribution	distribución	Verteilung	fordeling	fördelning
dyslexia	dyslexie	dislexia	Legasthenie	dysleksi; ordblindhed	dålig läsning
eclectic approach *or* method	approche *ou* methode eclectique	enfoque *o* método eclectico	eklektische(s) Verfahren *oder* Methode; Mischverfahren	eklektisk angrebsmåde *eller* metode	kombinerad metod
encode	encoder	(en)codificar	verschlüsseln; enkodieren	omsætte til kode	tolka

*Term coined by Mogens Jansen

ENGLISH	FRENCH	SPANISH	GERMAN	DANISH	SWEDISH
enrichment	enrichissement	enriquecimiento	Anreicherung	berigelse	berikande
evaluation	évaluation	evaluación	Bewertung; Einschätzung; Evaluation	evaluering	utvärdering
exceptional child	enfant exceptionnel (surdoué ou handicapé)	niño fuera de la media de promedio normal (superdotado o incapacitado)	aussergewöhnliches Kind, das im Lernen von der Norm abweicht (begabt oder behindert)	barn, der afviger fra normen (positivt eller negativt)	barn avvikande från det normala
fixation	fixation	fijación óptica	Fixation(spunkt); Haltepunkt	fiksering	fixering
frustration reading level	niveau de frustration en lecture	nivel de frustración en la lectura	Lesestufe, die Leser überfordert und zu Frustrationen führt	læseniveau hvor læseren blokerer	läsfärdighetsnivå över ens förmåga
functional literacy	capacité fonctionnelle de lire; instruction fonctionnelle	alfabetismo funcional	Beherrschung der Schriftsprache	funktionel læsning og skrivning	läsfärdighet som motsvarar individens och samhällets behov
gifted	doué	(super)dotado; precoz	(besonders) begabt	højt begavet	begåvad
grammar	grammaire	gramática	Grammatik	grammatik	grammatik
grapheme	graphème	grafema	Schriftzeichen; Graphem	grafem	betydelseavskiljande bokstavstyp
guided reading	lecture orientée *ou* dirigée	lectura dirigida *o* guiada	Lesen mit Anleitung und Hilfe (des Lehrers)	læsning under vejledning	handledd läsning

ENGLISH	FRENCH	SPANISH	GERMAN	DANISH	SWEDISH
higher-order structure	structure d'ordre supérieur	estructura de nivel superior	Struktur höherer Ordnung	strukturer af højere orden	avancerad struktur (i skriftspråket)
hygiene of reading	prophylaxie de la lecture	higiene de la lectura	Lesehygiene	læsemiljø; ydre betingelser for læsning	läshygien
illiterate	analphabète; illettré	analfabeto	Analphabet	analfabet	oförmàgan att läsa
image	image	imagen	Bild; Wahrnehmungsbild	forestillingsbillede	bild
implication	implication	implicación	Implikation; Folgerung	implikation	implikation
impression	impression	impresión	Eindruck	indtryk	intryck
individualization	individualisation	individualización	Individualisierung	individualisering	individualisering
individualized reading	lecture individualisée	lectura individualizada *o* personalizada	individualisiertes Lesen	individualiseret læsning	individualiserad läsundervisning
inferred meaning	sens déduit	sentido inferido	abgeleitete *oder* erschlossene Bedeutung	betydning man har ræsonneret sig til	förståelse genom slutledning
inflection	inflexion	inflexion	Flexion	bøjning	böjning (av ord)
initial blend	fusion initiale (de sons *ou* de syllabes)	enlace inicial	Konsonantengruppe am Anfang eines Wortes	sammenglidning af konsonanter i forlyd	inledande sammanljudning

ENGLISH	FRENCH	SPANISH	GERMAN	DANISH	SWEDISH
interpretation	interprétation	interpretación	Deutung; Interpretation	fortolking	tolkning
kinesthetic approach *or* method	approche *ou* méthode kinésique	enfoque *o* método kinético	kinästhetische(s) Verfahren *oder* Methode	kinæstetisk angrebsmade *eller* metode	kinestetisk metod
language	langue; langage	habla; lenguaje; lengua; idioma	Sprache	sprog	språk
language experience approach	approche fondée sur l'expérience langagière	método de enseñanza de la lectura a base de experiencia	Leselernverfahren, das auf Spracherfahrung basiert	LEA oversættes måske bedst med LTG, et svensk system *L*äsning på *T*alens *G*rund	arbetssätt baserat på elevens språkliga förutsättningar
lateral dominance	latéralité	dominio lateral	Seitigkeit; Körperdominanz	sidedominans	sidodominans
learning disability	trouble d'apprentissage	incapacitación de aprendizaje; ineptitud para el aprendizaje	Lernstörung	indlæringsvanskeligheder	inlärningssvårigheter
lexeme	lexème	lexema	Lexem	ord i visuel fremtrædelsesform*	i sig betydelsebärande del av ett språks ordförråd
linguistic approach *or* method	approche *ou* méthode linguistique	enfoque *o* método de lectura con base lingüística	linguistische(s) Verfahren *oder* Methode	lingvistisk angrebsmåde *eller* metode	lingvistisk metod
listening comprehension	compréhension auditive *ou* orale	comprensión auditiva *o* aural	Hörverständnis	lytte-forståelse	förståelse vid lyssnande

*Term coined by Mogens Jansen

ENGLISH	FRENCH	SPANISH	GERMAN	DANISH	SWEDISH
listening vocabulary	vocabulaire de compréhension auditive	vocabulario pasivo *o* auditivo	Hörwortschatz	lytte-ordforråd	ordförråd som förstås vid lyssnande
literacy	degré d'instruction	alfabetismo	Beherrschung der Schriftsprache	det at kunne læse og skrive på et i forhold til sam fundet funktionelt niveau	läs- och skrivfärdighet
literal meaning	sens littéral	sentido literal	wörtliche *oder* eigentliche Bedeutung	bogstavelig betydning	ordagrann mening
long vowel	voyelle longue	vocal larga	Langvokal	lang vokal	lång vokal
main idea	idée principale	idea central *o* principal	Hauptidee	hovedidé	huvudtanke
mastery test	test de compétence	prueba *o* test de comprobación	Test zur Überprüfung eines festgelegten Lernkriteriums	test, der dokumenterer beherskelse af et emne, et stofområde eller en færdighed	prov för undersökning om vederbörande behärskar den undersökta färdigheten
meaning	sens; signification	sentido; significado	Bedeutung	betydning	mening; innebörd
miscue	fausse piste; mauvaise réponse	despiste (lector)**	Verlesung; Lesefehler	læsefejl; fejltydning	feluppfattning
morphophoneme	morphophonème	morfofonema	Morphophonem	morfofonem	betydelsebärande ljud
nonreader	alexique	analfabeto	Analphabet; leseunfähig; Nichtleser	ikke-læser	en som inte läser

**Term coined by Adela Artola Stewart

ENGLISH	FRENCH	SPANISH	GERMAN	DANISH	SWEDISH
nonstandard American English	américain non-courant	inglés norte-americano fuera de la norma lingüística	nichtstandard-gemässes amerikanisches Englisch	ikke-standard amerikansk engelsk	avvikelse från normal amerikansk engelska
objective	objectif	objetivo	Ziel	mål	mål; syfte
open school	école ouverte	escuela activa (sin curriculo estructurado)	Schule mit offenen Curricula	åben-plan skole	öppen skola
perception	perception	percepción	Wahrnehmung	perception	uppfattning
perceptual constancy	constance de perception	constancia perceptiva	Wahrnehmungs-konstanz	perceptuel konstans	uppfattningskonstans
phoneme	phonème	fonema	Phonem	fonem	betydelseskiljande ljudtyp
phonetic analysis	analyse phonétique	análisis fonético	phonetische Analyse	fonetisk analyse	ljudanalys
phonetic method	méthode phonétique *ou* synthétique	método fonético	phonetische Methode	fonetisk metode	ljudmetod
phonetic word	mot phonétique	palabra pronunciada fonéticamente	phonetisches Wort	fonetisk ord	ljudenligt ord
phonics	phonétique	fonetismo;** silabeo; solfeo	Phonetik; phonische Methode des Lesenlernens	hvad der har med lyd at gøre (i forbindelse med læsning)	användning av ljudmetod
polysemantic	polysémantique	polisemántico	vieldeutig	mangetydig	med många betydelser

**Term coined by Adela Artola Stewart

ENGLISH	FRENCH	SPANISH	GERMAN	DANISH	SWEDISH
print	(en) caractères d'imprimerie	material impreso	Druck	tryk	tryck
propaganda	propagande	propaganda	Propaganda	propaganda	propaganda
psycholinguistics	psycholinguistique	psicolingüística	Psycholinguistik	psyko-lingvistik	språkpsykologi
purpose for reading	but de la lecture	propósito para *o* de la lectura	Leseziel; Lesezweck	formål med læsning	avsikten med läsningen
rate of reading	rapidité de lecture	velocidad lectora	Lesegeschwindigkeit; Leserate	læsehastighed	läshastighet
read	lire	leer	lesen	læse	läsa
readability	lisibilité	legibilidad	Lesbarkeit	læselighed	läsbarhet
reading	lecture	lectura	Lesen	læsning	läsning
reading comprehension	compréhension en lecture	comprensión lectora *o* de la lectura	Leseverständnis	læseforståelse	läsförståelse
reading deficiency	deficience en lecture	deficiencia lectora	Leseschwäche	læsevanskeligheder	lässvårighet; läsproblem
reading disability	trouble de lecture	inhabilidad lectora; incapacitación lectora	Lesestörung	manglende læsefærdighed	läs- och skrivsvårighet
reading flexibility	flexibilité en lecture	soltura lectora	Leseflüssigkeit; flexibles Lesen	læsefleksibilitet	flexibilitet vid läsningen
reading readiness	aptitude à l'apprentissage de la lecture	apresto para la lectura; predisposicion lectora; maduraz para empezar la lectura	Lesereife	læse-parathed	läsmognad

ENGLISH	FRENCH	SPANISH	GERMAN	DANISH	SWEDISH
reading retardation	retard en lecture	retraso lector; atraso en la lectura	Leseretardierung; Leseverzögerung	læseretardering	lässvaghet; läshämning
recode	recoder	recodificar	rekodieren	omkode	omtolka
remedial reading	lecture corrective	lectura de nivelación, de corrección *o* de mejoramiento	Förderunterricht im Lesen	specialundervisning i læsning	särskild lästräning
remediation	enseignement correctif	corrección; nivelación; reparación	Förderung; Therapie	specialundervisning (i læsning)	stödundervisning
review	révision	repaso	Rückblick; Wiederholung	anmeldelse	översikt
scholastic aptitude	aptitude scolaire	aptitud escolar	schulische Begabung *oder* Eignung	skolebegavelse	skolbegåvning ("läshuvud")
semantics	sémantique	semántica	Semantik	semantik	betydelselära; semantik
sentence	phrase	frase; oración; enunciado	Satz	sætning	mening; sats
short vowel	voyelle brève	vocal breve	Kurzvokal	kort vokal	kort vokal
sign	signe	signo	Zeichen	symptom; tegn	tecken
silent letter	lettre muette	letra muda	nicht hörbarer Laut *oder* Buchstabe	stumt bogstav	tyst bokstav
sound	son	sonido	Laut	lyd	ljud
standard American English	américain courant	norma lingüística del inglés norteamericano; dialecto estándar	standardgemässes amerikanisches Englisch	standard amerikansk engelsk	normal amerikansk engelska

ENGLISH	FRENCH	SPANISH	GERMAN	DANISH	SWEDISH
standard dialect	dialecte courant	norma lingüistíca; dialecto modelo *o* estándar	Standarddialekt	standard-dialekt	standarddialekt; allmänt accepterad dialekt
stress	accent	acento; énfasis	Betonung; Akzent	tryk	tryck; betoning; accent
study skills	méthodes d'étude	destrezas *o* prácticas de estudio	Arbeitstechniken	studiefærdigheder	studiefärdigheter
style	style	estilo	Stil	stil	stil
surface structure	structure de surface	estructura superficial	Oberflächenstruktur	overfladestruktur	ytstruktur
symbol	symbole	símbolo	Symbol; Zeichen	symbol	symbol; tecken; sinnebild
synthetic approach *or* method	approche *ou* méthode synthétique	enfoque *o* método sintético	synthetische(s) Verfahren *oder* Methode	syntetisk ansgrebsmåde *eller* metode	syntetisk metod
synthetic phonics	phonétique synthétique	fonetismo sintético; **silabeo	synthetisches Verfahren, in dem die einzelnen Laute zu einem Wort verschmolzen werden	syntese af lyd	metod för sammanljudning
tone	ton	tono	Ton; Klang; Lautmelodie	tone; tonefald	ton
visual discrimination	discrimination visuelle	discriminación visual	visuelle Unterscheidung	visuel skelnen	särskillnad med hjälp av synen

**Term coined by Adela Artola Stewart

ENGLISH	FRENCH	SPANISH	GERMAN	DANISH	SWEDISH
visual memory	mémoire visuelle	memoria visual	visuelles Gedächtnis	visuel hukommelse	synminne
visual perception	perception visuelle	percepción visual	visuelle Wahrnehmung	visuel perception	visuell uppfattning
vocabulary development	développement du vocabulaire	desarrollo del vocabulario	Wortschatzerweiterung	udvikling af ordforråd	utveckling av ordförrådet
word	mot	palabra; voz; vocablo; signo	Wort	ord	ord
word analysis	analyse des mots	análisis morfológico	Wortanalyse	ord-analyse	ordanalys
word attack	identification des mots; déchiffrage	destrezas de descifre	Technik(en) der Wortentschlüsselung	angrebsteknik	helordsläsning
word blindness	agnosie visuelle du mot	ceguera de las palabras	Wortblindheit	ordblindhed	ordblindhet
word identification	identification *ou* reconnaissance des mots	idenficación *o* visualización de la palabra	Wortidentifikation	ord-identifikation	identifiering av ord
word method	approche fondée sur le mot	método global	ganzheitliche Methode	ordbilledmetode; ordmetode	ordmetod
word perception	perception des mots	percepción de la palabra	Wortverständnis	ordopfattelse	uppfattning av ord
word recognition	reconnaissance des mots	reconocimiento de la palabra	Worterkennen	ordgenkendelse	igenkännande av ord

Appendix B
Bibliography

A representative sampling of older standard references and of newer books is given below for the fields of reading and linguistics. With the exception of the *Reading Research Quarterly*, which was reviewed in its entirety, the journals listed were reviewed in part and principally for the 1970s by volunteer citation gatherers. In addition to the specialized dictionaries noted, standard dictionaries were regularly consulted, as well as textbook glossaries, lexicons supplied by state departments of education, and word lists submitted by other interested persons.

Books on Reading and Supporting Fields

Abrams, J. Personal communication to the editors, 1980.

Adler, Mortimer J. *How to Read a Book*. Simon and Schuster, 1940.

Allen, Roach Van. *Language Experiences in Communication*. Houghton Mifflin, 1976.

Anastasi, Anne. *Psychological Testing* (4th ed.). Macmillan, 1976.

Anderson, Irving H., and Dearborn, Walter F. *The Psychology of Teaching Reading*. Ronald Press, 1952.

Ashton-Warner, Sylvia. *Teacher*. Bantam Books, 1963.

Austin, Mary, and Morrison, Coleman. *The First R*. Macmillan, 1963.

Betts, Emmett. *Foundations of Reading Instruction*. American Book, 1946.

Bond, Guy L., and Tinker, Miles A. *Reading Difficulties: Their Diagnosis and Correction* (3rd ed.). Appleton-Century-Crofts, 1973.

Burmeister, Lou E. *Reading Strategies for Secondary School Teachers*. Addison-Wesley, 1974.

Burns, Paul C., and Roe, Betty. *Teaching Reading in Today's Elementary Schools*. Rand McNally, 1976.

Bush, C.L., and Huebner, M.H. *Strategies for Reading in the Elementary School*. Macmillan, 1970.

Carroll, John B., and Chall, Jeanne. *Toward a Literate Society*. McGraw-Hill, 1975.

Chall, Jeanne. *Learning to Read: The Great Debate*. McGraw-Hill, 1967.

Chicago, University of. *Clinical Studies in Reading* I (1949), II (1953), III (1968).

Cronbach, Lee J. *Essentials of Psychological Testing* (3rd ed.). Harper and Row, 1970.

Dallman, Martha, and others. *The Teaching of Reading* (4th ed.). Holt, Rinehart and Winston, 1974.

Davis, Fred (Ed.). *The Literature of Research in Reading with Emphasis on Models*. Rutgers University, 1971.

Dechant, Emerald V. *Improving the Teaching of Reading* (2nd ed.). Prentice-Hall, 1970.

Dechant, Emerald V. *Reading Improvement in the Secondary School.* Prentice-Hall, 1973.
de Hirsch, Katrina, and others. *Predicting Reading Failure.* Harper and Row, 1966.
Downing, John, and others. *Comparative Reading.* Macmillan, 1973.
Durkin, Dolores. *Teaching Young Children to Read* (2nd ed.). Allyn and Bacon, 1976.
Edfelt, A.W. *Silent Speech and Silent Reading.* University of Chicago Press, 1960.
Farr, Roger (Ed.). *Measurement and Evaluation of Reading.* Harcourt, Brace and World, 1970.
Fernald, Grace. *Remedial Techniques in Basic School Subjects.* McGraw-Hill, 1943.
Gans, Roma. *Guiding Children's Reading through Experiences.* Teachers College, Columbia University, 1941.
Gates, Arthur I. *The Improvement of Reading* (3rd ed.). Macmillan, 1947.
Gibson, E., and Levin, H. *The Psychology of Reading.* MIT Press, 1975.
Gray, William S. *On Their Own in Reading* (Rev. ed.). Scott, Foresman, 1960.
Gray, William S., (Ed.). *Reading in General Education.* American Council on Education, 1940.
Gray, William S. *Teaching of Reading and Writing.* Unesco, 1956.
Hammill, Donald D., and Bartel, Nettie R. *Teaching Children with Learning and Behavior Problems.* Allyn and Bacon, 1975.
Harris, Albert J., and Sipay, Edward R. *How to Increase Reading Ability.* (6th ed.). David McKay, 1975.
Harris, Larry H., and Smith, Carl B. *Reading Instruction.* (2nd ed.). Holt, Rinehart and Winston, 1976.
Harris, Theodore L. "Reading," *Encyclopedia of Educational Research.* Macmillan, 1970.
Harrison, M. Lucile. *Reading Readiness* (Rev. and enlarged). Houghton Mifflin, 1939.
Hepworth, T.S. *Dyslexia: The Problem of Reading Retardation.* St. Martin's Press, 1971.
Herber, Harold L. *Teaching Reading in Content Areas* (2nd ed.). Prentice-Hall, 1978.
Hertzler, Joyce O. *A Sociology of Language.* Random House, 1965.
Horn, Ernest. *Methods of Instruction in the Social Studies.* Scribner's, 1937.
Horn, Ernest. *Teaching Spelling.* American Educational Research Association, 1954.
Huck, Charlotte S. *Children's Literature in the Elementary School* (3rd ed.). Holt, Rinehart and Winston, 1976.
Huey, Edmund Burke. *The Psychology and Pedagogy of Reading.* Macmillan, 1908.
Johnson, Doris J., and Myklebust, Helen R. *Learning Disabilities: Educational Principles and Practices.* Grune and Stratton, 1964.
Karlin, Robert. *Teaching Reading in High School: Improving Reading in Content Areas* (3rd ed.). Bobbs-Merrill, 1977.
Kephart, Newell C. *The Slow Learner in the Classroom.* Charles E. Merrill, 1960.

Kirk, Samuel. *Teaching Reading to Slow-Learning Children.* Houghton Mifflin, 1940.

Lee, Dorris M., and Allen, R.V. *Learning to Read through Experience* (2nd ed.). Appleton-Century-Crofts, 1963.

Lerner, Janet. *Children with Learning Disabilities* (2nd ed.). Houghton Mifflin, 1976.

Levin, Harry, and Williams, Joanna P. (Eds.). *Basic Studies in Reading.* Basic Books, 1970.

Mathews, Mitford M. *Teaching to Read: Historically Considered.* University of Chicago Press, 1966.

McKee, Paul. *Reading.* Houghton Mifflin, 1966.

Melnik, Amelia, and Merritt, John (Eds.). *Reading: Today and Tomorrow.* University of London Press/ Open University Press/ General Learning Press, 1972.

Melnik, Amelia, and Merritt, John (Eds.). *The Reading Curriculum.* University of London Press/ Open University Press/ General Learning Press, 1972.

Money, John (Ed.). *Reading Disability.* Johns Hopkins Press, 1962.

Monroe, Marion. *Children Who Cannot Read.* University of Chicago Press, 1932.

Monroe, Marion, and others. *Remedial Reading.* Houghton Mifflin, 1937.

Monroe, Marion, and Rogers, Bernice. *Foundations for Reading.* Scott, Foresman, 1964.

National Society for the Study of Education. Relevant yearbooks on *Reading,* 1921.

Orton, S.T. *Reading, Writing, and Speech Problems in Children.* W.W. Norton, 1937.

Otto, Wayne, and Chester, Robert D. *Objective-Based Reading.* Addison-Wesley, 1976.

Reid, Jessie F. (compiler). *Reading: Problems and Practices.* Ward Lock, 1972.

Robeck, Mildred C., and Wilson, John A.R. *Psychology of Reading: Foundations of Instruction.* John Wiley and Sons, 1974.

Robinson, Helen M. *Why Pupils Fail in Reading.* University of Chicago Press, 1969.

Robinson, Helen M. "Reading Instruction: Research," *Encyclopedia of Education.* Macmillan, 1971.

Rosenblatt, Louise M. *The Reader, the Text, and the Poem.* Southern Illinois University Press, 1978.

Ross, Alan O. *Psychological Aspects of Learning Disabilities and Reading Disorders.* McGraw-Hill, 1976.

Roswell, Florence G., and Natchez, Gladys. *Reading Disability: A Human Approach to Learning* (2nd ed.). Basic Books, 1971.

Ruddell, Robert, and Singer, Harry (Eds.). *Theoretical Models and Processes of Reading* (2nd ed.). International Reading Association, 1976.

Russell, David H. *Children Learn to Read* (Rev. ed.). Ginn, 1961.

Shepherd, David L. *Comprehensive High School Reading Methods.* Charles E. Merrill, 1973.

Smith, Nila B. *American Reading Instruction.* Silver Burdett, 1934.

Smith, Nila B. *American Reading Instruction* (Rev. ed.). International Reading Association, 1965.

Spache, George, and Spache, Evelyn. *Reading in the Elementary School* (4th ed.). Allyn and Bacon, 1977.
Staiger, Ralph C. *Roads to Reading*. Unesco, 1979.
Stauffer, Russell G. *Directing Reading Maturity as a Cognitive Process*. Harper and Row, 1969.
Stauffer, Russell G. *Teaching Reading as a Thinking Process*. Harper and Row, 1969.
Strang, Ruth. *Diagnostic Teaching of Reading*. McGraw-Hill, 1969.
Strang, R., McCullough, C.M., and Traxler, A.E. *The Improvement of Reading* (3rd ed.). McGraw-Hill, 1961.
Tinker, Miles A. *Bases for Effective Reading*. University of Minnesota Press, 1965.
Tinker, Miles A., and McCullough, C. *Teaching Elementary Reading* (3rd ed.). Appleton-Century-Crofts, 1968.
U.S. Department of Health, Education and Welfare, Education Division. *A Handbook of Standard Terminology and a Guide for Recording and Reporting Information about Educational Technology*. U.S. Government Printing Office, 1975.
Veatch, Jeannette. *Individualizing Your Reading Program*. G.P. Putnam's Sons, 1959.
Vernon, M.D. *Backwardness in Reading*. Cambridge University Press, 1960.
Vernon, M.D. *Experimental Study of Reading*. Cambridge University Press, 1931.
Vernon, M.D. Unpublished correspondence with dictionary editors, 1978.
Waples, Douglas, and others. *What Reading Does to People*. University of Chicago Press, 1940.
Wilson, Robert M. *Diagnostic and Remedial Reading for Classroom and Clinic* (3rd ed.). Charles E. Merrill, 1967.
Witty, Paul, and Kopel, David. *Reading and the Educative Process*. Ginn, 1939.
Zintz, Miles V. *Corrective Reading* (3rd ed.). William C. Brown Company, 1977.
Zintz, Miles V. *The Reading Process* (2nd ed.). William C. Brown Company, 1975.

Books on Linguistics

Bloomfield, Leonard. *Language*. Holt, 1933.
Chomsky, Noam. *Aspects of the Theory of Syntax*. MIT Press, 1970.
Chomsky, Noam. *Syntactic Structures*. Mouton and Co., 1957.
Fries, Charles C. *Linguistics and Reading*. Holt, Rinehart and Winston, 1964.
Goodman, Kenneth S., (Ed.). *The Psycholinguistic Nature of the Reading Process*. Wayne State University Press, 1973.
Goodman, Kenneth S., and Fleming, James T., (Eds.). *Psycholinguistics and the Teaching of Reading*. International Reading Association, 1969.
Gunderson, Doris V., (Compiler). *Reading and Language: An Interdisciplinary Approach*. Center for Applied Linguistics, 1970.
Hanna, Paul R., Hodges, R.E., and Hanna, J.S. *Spelling: Structure and Strategies*. Houghton Mifflin, 1971.

Hodges, Richard E., and Rudorf, E. Hugh. *Language and Learning to Read.* Houghton Mifflin, 1972.

Kavanaugh, James, and Mattingly, I.G. *Language by Eye and Ear.* MIT Press, 1972.

Langacker, Ronald W. *Fundamentals of Linguistic Analysis.* Harcourt Brace Jovanovich, 1972.

Lefevre, Carl A. *Linguistics and the Teaching of Reading.* McGraw-Hill, 1964.

Lyons, John. *Semantics* (Vols. 1 & 2). Cambridge University Press, 1979.

Ogden, C.K., and Richards, I.A. *The Meaning of Meaning.* (10th ed.). Harcourt Brace Jovanovich, 1952.

Sapir, Edward. *Language.* Harcourt, Brace and World, 1921.

Saussure, Ferdinand de. *A Course in General Linguistics.* Philosophical Library, 1916.

Schane, Sanford A. *Generative Phonology.* Prentice-Hall, 1973.

Smith, E.B., Goodman, K.S., and Meredith, R. *Language and Thinking in School.* Holt, Rinehart and Winston, 1976.

Smith, Frank. *Comprehension and Learning.* Holt, Rinehart and Winston, 1975.

Smith, Frank. *Understanding Reading.* Holt, Rinehart, and Winston, 1977.

Vygotsky, Lev S. *Thought and Language.* MIT Press, 1962.

Wardhaugh, Ronald. *Reading: A Linguistic Perspective.* Harcourt Brace Jovanovich, 1966.

Journals

American Educational Research Journal
British Journal of Educational Psychology
Elementary School Journal
Harvard Educational Review
Journal of Developmental Reading
Journal of Educational Psychology
Journal of Educational Research
Journal of Experimental Child Psychology
Journal of Learning Disabilities
Journal of Reading
Journal of Reading Behavior
Journal of Verbal Learning and Verbal Behavior
Language Arts Journal
Phi Delta Kappan
Reading Improvement
Reading Research Quarterly
Reading Teacher
Research in the Teaching of English
Review of Educational Research
Visible Language

Specialized Dictionaries and Handbooks

Bush, Clifford C., and Andrews, Robert C. *Dictionary of Reading and Learning Disabilities.* Educational and Psychological Associates Press, 1973.

Dorlund's Illustrated Medical Dictionary (25th ed.). W.B. Saunders, 1974.

English, Horace B., and English, Ava C. *A Comprehensive Dictionary of Psychological and Psychoanalytical Terms.* David McKay, 1974.

Fairchild, Henry P. *Dictionary of Sociology and Related Sciences.* Littlefield, Adams, 1970.

Good, Carter V. (Ed.). *Dictionary of Education* (3rd ed.). McGraw-Hill, 1973.

Hartmann, R.R.K., and Stork, F.C. *Dictionary of Language and Linguistics.* Applied Science Publishers, London, 1972.

Holman, Hugh C. *A Handbook to Literature* (3rd ed.). Bobbs-Merrill, 1977.

Hoult, Thomas. *Dictionary of Modern Sociology.* Littlefield, Adams, 1969.

Nicolosi, Lucille, and others. *Terminology of Communication Disorders.* Williams and Wilkins, 1978.

Page, G.T., and Thomas, J.B. *International Dictionary of Education.* Kogan Page/Nichols, 1977.

Schubert, Delwyn G. *A Dictionary of Terms and Concepts in Reading* (2nd ed.). Charles C. Thomas, 1969.

Shaw, Harry. *Dictionary of Literary Terms.* McGraw-Hill, 1972.

Stedman's Medical Dictionary (23rd ed.). Williams and Wilkins, 1976.

Wolman, B.J. (Compiler and Ed.). *Dictionary of Behavioral Science.* Van Nostrand, Reinhold, 1973.

Proofreading

In preparing a manuscript for the typesetter or in checking the proofs of typeset material, one should use the conventional system of proofreader's marks. Shown below are the marks that are most commonly used. They should be legibly written in the margin and the place of the desired correction should be clearly marked in the text. If there are several marks that pertain to the same line, the marks are separated by a vertical or diagonal line.

Marginal Mark	*Explanation*	*How indicated in the Copy*
1. Marks of Instruction		
℘	Delete, take out	He sent the copy.
stet.	Let it stand	He sent the copy.
sp.	Spell out	He sent (10) copies.
tr.	Transpose	He the sent copy.
¶	Paragraph	read. He sent the copy.
no ¶	No paragraph—run in	read. He sent the copy.
(sent/?)	Query to the author	He the copy.
2. Marks Regarding Type Style		
ital.	Set in *italic*	He sent the copy.
s.c.	Set in SMALL CAPITALS	He sent the copy.
caps.	Set in CAPITALS	he sent the copy.
c.+s.c.	Set in CAPITALS AND SMALL CAPITALS	he sent the copy.
b.f. or bf.	Set in **boldface**	He sent the copy.
rom.	Change from *italic* to roman	He sent the *copy*.
l.c.	Set in lower case	He Sent the Copy.
u.+l.c. or c.+l.c.	Set in Upper and Lower Case	he sent the copy.
3. Marks Regarding Defects in the Type		
⊗	Broken letters	He sent the copy.
w.f.	Wrong font	He sent the copy.
9	Turn inverted letters	He sent the copy.
//	Straighten marked lines	He sent the copy. He sent the copy.
=	Out of alignment—straighten	He sent the copy.
⊥	Push down space	He sent the copy.
4. Marks Regarding Spacing		
⁀	Close up	He s ent the copy.
℘	Delete and close up	He seent the copy.
#	Insert space	He sent thecopy.
eq. #	Equalize the spacing	He sent the copy.
□	Indent one em	□He sent the copy.
□□	Indent two ems	□□He sent the copy.
□□□	Indent three ems	□□□He sent the copy.
[	Move left as indicated	[He sent the copy.
]	Move right as indicated	He sent the copy.]
⌐¬	Raise as indicated	He sent the copy.
∟⌋	Lower as indicated	He sent the copy.
ld.>	Insert lead between lines	
5. Marks of Punctuation		
⊙	Period	He sent the copy
,/	Comma	He sent the copy
;/	Semicolon	He sent the copy
:/	Colon	He sent the copy thus
=/	Hyphen	He was copyediting.
✓	Apostrophe	It is the authors copy.
❛❛ ❜❜	Open and close quotes	He said: Send the copy.
!/	Exclamation	Send the copy
?/	Question mark	Did he send the copy
1/N or en	One-en dash	Copy, 17, 34, 227–8
1/M or em	One-em dash	We went—with copy.
( )	Open and close parens	It the copy was sent.
[ ]	Open and close brackets	He send sic the copy.
⌃	Inferior figure	H_2O
⌄	Superior figure	xy^2

THE INTERNATIONAL PHONETIC ALPHABET

(Revised to 1951)

		Bi-labial	Labio-dental	Dental and Alveolar	Retro-flex	Palato-alveolar	Alveolo-palatal	Palatal	Velar	Uvular	Pharyn-gal	Glottal
CONSONANTS	Plosive	p b		t d	ʈ ɖ			c ɟ	k g	q ɢ		ʔ
	Nasal	m	ɱ	n	ɳ			ɲ	ŋ	ɴ		
	Lateral Fricative			ɬ ɮ								
	Lateral Non-fricative			l	ɭ			ʎ				
	Rolled			r						ʀ		
	Flapped			ɾ	ɽ					ʀ		
	Fricative	ɸ β	f v	θ ð s z ɹ	ʂ ʐ	ʃ ʒ	ɕ ʑ	ç ʝ	x ɣ	χ ʁ	ħ ʕ	h ɦ
	Frictionless Continuants and Semi-vowels	w ɥ	ʋ	ɹ				j (ɥ)	(w)	ʁ		

		Bi-labial	Front	Central	Back
VOWELS	Close	(y ʉ u)	i y	ɨ ʉ	ɯ u
	Half-close	(ø o)	e ø		ɤ o
				ə	
	Half-open	(œ ɔ)	ɛ œ		ʌ ɔ
			æ	ɐ	
	Open	(ɒ)		a	ɑ ɒ

(Secondary articulations are shown by symbols in brackets.)